Unlocking Growth and Sustainability for Small and Medium Enterprises With AI

Preeti Mehra
Keyano College, Canada

Oye Abioye
University College of the North, Canada

Pawan Kumar
Lovely Professional University, India

IGI Global
Scientific Publishing
Publishing Tomorrow's Research Today

Published in the United States of America by
IGI Global Scientific Publishing
701 East Chocolate Avenue
Hershey, PA, 17033, USA
Tel: 717-533-8845
Fax: 717-533-7115
Website: https://www.igi-global.com E-mail: cust@igi-global.com

Library of Congress Cataloging-in-Publication Data

Names: Mehra, Preeti, 1981- editor. | Abioye, Oye, 1963- editor. | Kumar, Pawan, 1980- editor.
Title: Unlocking growth and sustainability for small and medium enterprises with AI / [edited by] Preeti Mehra, Oye Abioye, Pawan Kumar.
Description: Hershey, PA : IGI Global Scientific Publishing, [2026] | Includes bibliographical references and index. | Summary: "The book aims to address a critical research gap in the literature by focusing on AI's potential to drive growth and innovation in SMEs within emerging markets"-- Provided by publisher.
Identifiers: LCCN 2024054490 (print) | LCCN 2024054491 (ebook) | ISBN 9798369396117 (hardcover) | ISBN 9798369396155 (paperback) | ISBN 9798369396124 (ebook)
Subjects: LCSH: Small business--Technological innovations. | Small business--Growth. | Artificial intelligence--Industrial applications.
Classification: LCC HD2341 .U55 2025 (print) | LCC HD2341 (ebook) | DDC 338.6/42--dc23/eng/20250213
LC record available at https://lccn.loc.gov/2024054490
LC ebook record available at https://lccn.loc.gov/2024054491

British Cataloguing in Publication Data
A Cataloguing in Publication record for this book is available from the British Library.

Table of Contents

Detailed Table of Contents

ends by summarizing some emerging trends in AI and discussing the place of AI on resilience and sustainability in small and medium enterprises.

Artificial intelligence is a growing technology in small and medium-sized businesses. Small and medium-sized enterprises (SMEs) have recently expressed an increased interest in employing artificial intelligence to boost countries performance. This study confirms that insufficient physical and technological infrastructure, awareness of AI, customer privacy and security, management support, and a lack of AI adoption strategy are all significant issues and challenges impeding the progress of AI applications in business for sustainability. In India, the MSME sector is seen as a major driving factor in increasing economic productivity and combating poverty, income inequality, and high unemployment rates. This study has ramifications for SMEs, policymakers, and future initiatives to enhance artificial intelligence for sustainability.

This study examines the transformative potential of Artificial Intelligence (AI) in advancing the United Nations' Sustainable Development Goals (SDGs). AI technologies, such as machine learning, natural language processing, and big data analytics, offer innovative solutions to global challenges, including poverty, healthcare, education, and climate action. Through predictive modeling, resource optimization, and enhanced decision-making, AI can accelerate progress toward achieving the SDGs. Case studies highlight AI's contributions, from precision agriculture and disease diagnostics to renewable energy and sustainable urban infrastructure. However, ethical considerations, such as bias, privacy, and inclusivity, pose significant challenges to responsible AI deployment. By leveraging AI responsibly, this research underscores

With AI revolutionizing industries, SMEs in emerging markets can tap into its power for sustainable growth, operational efficiency, and enhanced customer experiences. This chapter explores AI-driven automation, predictive analytics, and personalized interactions, addressing challenges like technical skills, data availability, and cost. By adopting AI strategically, SMEs can overcome barriers, compete globally, and drive innovation, ensuring long-term success in the evolving digital economy.

The guest experience, operational effectiveness, and resource management have all improved due to hotels integrating AI and IoT technology. But this integration raises several ethical questions that require serious thought. The purpose of this study is to investigate and evaluate the moral issues raised by the use of AI and IoT in hotels. AI-powered intelligent hotels, the research examines essential ethical problems about privacy, security, transparency, bias, & human interaction. The results of this study demonstrate the delicate balance between the advantages of AI and IoT technologies & the dangers they may provide. Concerns about algorithmic prejudice and discrimination might arise due to the opaqueness of AI decision-making processes, which can negatively impact visitor experiences & employee relationships. Additionally, concerns about visitor experiences and the possible displacement of human workers are raised by the degradation of personal touch in favor of automated services

Preface

In the ever-evolving digital landscape, Artificial Intelligence (AI) has emerged as a critical catalyst for transformation, reshaping industries, markets, and the way businesses operate globally. Small and Medium Enterprises (SMEs), which form the backbone of economies worldwide, particularly in emerging markets, stand at a unique crossroads. These enterprises have the potential to harness AI's transformative power to unlock growth, drive innovation, improve efficiency, and build sustainable and resilient business models capable of thriving amid constant change.

This book, *Unlocking Growth and Sustainability for Small and Medium Enterprises With AI*, offers a comprehensive exploration of how AI technologies can empower SMEs across diverse sectors and geographies. It presents a multidisciplinary approach that covers technological innovations, business strategies, economic implications, consumer behavior, and sustainable development. The insights within this volume are particularly relevant for stakeholders invested in SME development, including business owners, entrepreneurs, economists, policymakers, researchers, academicians, and technologists.

The chapters in this book delve deeply into these dynamics, illuminating the multiple facets of AI integration within SMEs. The scope ranges from understanding core AI technologies and their practical applications to analyzing consumer behaviors influenced by AI, addressing the challenges of adoption, and aligning AI strategies with global sustainability goals.

CHAPTER OVERVIEW

Chapter 1

AI revolutionizes how SMEs engage with customers by enabling personalized journeys through tools like tailored recommendations, real-time chatbots, and predictive analytics. Despite financial, technical, and data privacy challenges, strategic

AI adoption fosters significant customer experiences, driving growth and long-term sustainability in competitive markets.

Chapter 2

AI enhances healthcare SMEs by analyzing patient data for proactive care, early disease detection, and streamlined operations, reducing human error and improving safety. This chapter highlights AI's role in supporting Sustainable Development Goal 3 (Good Health and Well-being) while addressing implementation challenges to improve treatment outcomes and business sustainability.

Chapter 3

AI technologies like machine learning and automation boost productivity, decision-making, and innovation in Canadian SMEs. However, financial barriers, skills shortages, and ethical concerns like job displacement and data privacy require collaborative efforts from businesses, policymakers, and educators to ensure equitable AI integration and sustained growth.

Chapter 4

AI enhances SME operations by streamlining processes, improving decision-making, and fostering data-driven strategies. By integrating AI with IT Service Management (ITSM), SMEs can build resilient business models, generate new skills through personalized training, and align with Sustainable Development Goals (SDGs) for competitive advantage.

Chapter 5

AI automates repetitive tasks, freeing SME employees to focus on strategic and creative roles. Tools like machine learning, predictive analytics, and personalized training platforms enhance efficiency and skill development, enabling SMEs to bridge talent gaps and remain competitive in global markets.

Chapter 6

AI supports SMEs by improving financial access, operational efficiency, and product innovation. From predictive sales strategies to streamlined billing, AI empowers SMEs to create jobs, enhance E-Entrepreneurship, and drive economic growth for both educated and uneducated workers.

Chapter 7

In the context of Industry 5.0, AI drives resilience, sustainability, and human-centric practices in SMEs. By optimizing operations, supply chains, and customer experiences, AI fosters innovation and competitiveness, supported by employee training, predictive analytics, and sustainable practices for long-term growth.

Chapter 8

AI enhances SME scalability through automation, data insights, and personalized customer experiences. Despite challenges like high costs and skill deficits, strategic planning and workforce upskilling enable SMEs to leverage AI for sustainable operations, energy optimization, and corporate social responsibility.

Chapter 9

In India, AI adoption in SMEs boosts economic productivity and combats poverty and unemployment. However, challenges like inadequate infrastructure, privacy concerns, and lack of AI strategies hinder progress. This chapter emphasizes solutions for policymakers and SMEs to enhance AI-driven sustainability.

Chapter 10

AI technologies like machine learning and big data analytics accelerate progress toward SDGs by optimizing resources and decision-making in areas like healthcare, education, and climate action. Ethical considerations, including bias and privacy, are critical to ensuring responsible AI deployment for global prosperity.

Chapter 11

Micro and Small Enterprises (MSEs) drive Oman's economic diversification through innovation and job creation. This chapter analyzes their contributions, highlighting challenges like funding shortages and regulatory barriers, and emphasizes the role of policy and technology adoption in maximizing their economic impact.

Chapter 12

AI enhances operational efficiency, inventory management, and customer personalization in Indian e-commerce SMEs. Case studies demonstrate tangible benefits, while challenges like financial constraints and data quality issues underscore the need for ecosystem support and strategic change management.

Chapter 13

AI-driven automation, predictive analytics, and personalization empower SMEs in emerging markets to achieve sustainable growth. Overcoming technical, data, and cost barriers through strategic adoption enables SMEs to compete globally and drive innovation in the digital economy.

Chapter 14

AI and IoT improve guest experiences and operational efficiency in hotels but raise ethical concerns around privacy, security, bias, and job displacement. Balancing technological benefits with human-centric values is crucial to maintaining trust and positive experiences.

Chapter 15

AI, blockchain, and IoT enhance resource efficiency and transparency in SMEs, supporting circular economy principles for net-zero emissions. A roadmap guides SMEs in adopting these technologies to build sustainable, environmentally responsible business practices.

Chapter 16

Personalized AI solutions mediate the relationship between market insights and competitive advantage in SMEs. Statistical analysis confirms AI's role in enhancing efficiency and competitiveness, offering actionable strategies for SMEs in the Horn of Africa.

Chapter 17

AI-driven personalization, efficiency, and trust significantly influence consumer adoption of AI-powered shopping platforms. While tailored recommendations enhance experiences, data privacy concerns highlight the need for transparent and ethical AI practices in SMEs.

Chapter 18

Generative AI empowers SMEs in both developing and developed countries by enhancing decision-making and innovation. Insights from participatory research highlight its potential to create patent-worthy intellectual property, while addressing risks and benefits for sustainable growth.

This book focuses on emerging economies to address the unique challenges and opportunities these SMEs face, offering regionally and globally relevant insights. As digital ecosystems expand, AI's role in fostering SME growth and sustainable business practices becomes increasingly critical, making this volume a timely contribution to ongoing discourse in technology and development.

This volume makes a significant contribution to the fields of AI, SME development, and sustainable business practices. By comprehensively addressing the intersection of AI and SMEs from multiple disciplinary perspectives, it bridges important gaps in knowledge and practice. The insights offered provide both a roadmap and a toolkit for SMEs, policymakers, and researchers to foster innovation, resilience, and sustainability in an increasingly digital and uncertain world.

This book also serves as a foundation for future research, policy formulation, and technological innovation aimed at enabling SMEs worldwide to unlock the full potential of AI. Ultimately, it aspires to inspire transformative changes that empower SMEs to drive inclusive economic growth and sustainable development across diverse global contexts.

Preeti Mehra
Keyano College, Canada

Oye Abioye
University College of the North, Canada

Pawan Kumar
Lovely Professional University, India

Acknowledgement

It is with great appreciation that I acknowledge the invaluable contributions of my co-editor, Dr. Preeti Mehra, whose academic insight, thoughtful collaboration, and steadfast dedication have been vital in bringing this book, Unlocking Growth and Sustainability for Small and Medium Enterprises, to life. I am equally grateful to Mr. Oye Abioye for his insightful perspectives and active engagement throughout the editorial process. A sincere thank you goes out to all the contributing authors and researchers whose diverse experiences and scholarly work have enriched this volume and contributed significantly to advancing the discourse on SME development and sustainability.

I am deeply thankful to my family and friends for their continuous support, patience, and encouragement throughout this endeavour. Their belief in my vision has been a constant source of strength. Above all, I express my heartfelt gratitude to the Almighty for granting me the wisdom, perseverance, and clarity needed to complete this project. Without this divine grace and the support of those around me, this work would not have been possible.

Chapter 1
Empowering SMEs With AI: Transforming Consumer Experiences for Sustainable Growth

Harish Saini
https://orcid.org/0000-0003-3850-7678
Lovely Professional University, India

Pawan Kumar
https://orcid.org/0000-0001-7501-3066
Lovely Professional University, India

ABSTRACT

In today's rapidly evolving market, SMEs face the challenge of delivering personalized and seamless customer journeys while competing with larger companies. AI is revolutionising the way SMEs connect with customers, providing useful tools to optimise relationships, increase productivity, and stimulate expansion. The chapter examines the role of AI in transforming the consumer journey, encompassing pre-purchase discovery, tailored suggestions, real-time help via chatbots, and forecasting tools. Although artificial intelligence offers substantial possibilities, SME face challenges such as financial, technical, and data privacy concerns. The chapter addresses these obstacles and provides strategies for overcoming them, underscoring the need for responsible utilization of AI. By prioritizing AI, SMEs can facilitate significant customer experiences, promote expansion, and guarantee long-term sustainability in an increasingly competitive landscape.

DOI: 10.4018/979-8-3693-9611-7.ch001

1. INTRODUCTION: THE CHANGING CONSUMER LANDSCAPE

1.1. Overview of Evolving Consumer Expectations

In the current dynamic digital environment, customer expectations are under constant evolution (Warner & Wäger, 2019). Gone are the times when simple transactions and uniform customer service were sufficient. Today, consumers possess a higher level of knowledge, authority, and expectations compared to previous times (Andreassen & Gjerald, 2024). Consumers expects smooth and uninterrupted interactions across many platforms and channels, whether they are making a purchase, requesting assistance, or interacting with a brand for entertainment or information purposes. The widespread adoption of smartphones, e-commerce, and social media has resulted in immediate access to information, raising customer expectations for the same level of immediacy from the companies they engage with (Taneja, 2021). Consumers desire customized experiences that are specifically designed to suit their own interests, behaviours, and requirements (Hayes et al., 2021). Furthermore, instant synchronous communication is now considered a fundamental requirement. Consumers anticipate businesses to actively and meaningfully engage with them through various means such as live chat help, immediate comments from brands on social platforms, or personalized product recommendations in real-time, anytime they opt to interact (Vander Schee et al., 2020).

The demand for customization has escalated to the extent where consumers now anticipate companies to possess knowledge about them. This entails not just acknowledging their choices, but also foreseeing their need and offering pertinent solutions without being intrusive. For instance, an internet consumer who peruses a certain product category that not only anticipate suggestions corresponding to their preferences, but also appreciate the provision of tailored promos and offers derived from previous engagements. Therefore, the increasing need for personalization across several sectors, including retail, hospitality, finance, and healthcare, necessitates that organizations of all scales prioritize providing tailored and pertinent experiences at each phase of the customer journey (Gursoy et al., 2023; Johnson et al., 2021; Tyrväinen et al., 2020).

In the past decade, the application and adoption of AI by smaller business has significantly increased and propelled by technological improvements (Dwivedi et al., 2021). This has enhanced the accessibility to AI tools and growing awareness of competitive benefits that AI can provide. Initially, AI solutions were often perceived as a domain of large organisations with significant resources; however, the advent of user-friendly platforms, cloud-based services and cost-effective AI technologies has enabled smaller enterprises to utilise AI for diverse applications, including customer services, marketing, and data analysis (Rane et al., 2024). This has progressively led to digital transformation, employing AI to improve operational efficiency, customised customer experience, and facilitate data-driven decision making. This circular shift has emphasised the significance of AI in modern business, illustrating its capacity to democratize innovation, allowing smaller enterprises to compete more efficiently in a changing market.

1.2. The Role of AI in Customer Journey

Over the past two decades, the phenomenon referred to as the "digital revolution" has profoundly changed the nature of customer experiences. To outline the characteristics of digital technologies and their associated benefits, Negroponte (1995), in his seminal work "Being Digital", articulated this transformation as a transition from "atoms" to "bits." To understand the role of technologies on the customer journey, it is essential to examine its significant technological advancements. The worldwide web has facilitated novel forms of communication, interaction, and transaction through a completely unprecedented medium and platform. E-commerce has established an innovative sales channel and marketplace that permits consumers to procure products beyond traditional retail environments (Hoyer et al., 2020). Mobile platforms have amalgamated information onto a single device, which can be utilized for a multiple commercial application. Social media, along with its mechanisms for sharing text, images, and video, has fostered social networks among consumers and catalysed the generation of user-created content.

There exists a phenomenon recognized as artificial intelligence. Additionally, there is a concept referred to as customer journey. The interplay between these two constructs holds paramount significance for marketers (Cukier, 2021). Artificial intelligence underpins virtual assistants, chatbots, and robotics. AI encompasses processes that involve the examination and interpretation of data, the acquisition of knowledge from data, and the application of this knowledge to accomplish defined objectives and tasks (Hoyer et al., 2020). In a more expansive sense, artificial intelligence amplifies the cognitive capabilities of a product, service, or solution. Whereas experiences manifest as a consequence of "engaging with, enduring, or actively participating in various phenomena"(Schmitt, 1999). Consequently, customer experience has been characterized as "the internal and subjective reactions exhibited by consumers during their interactions with an organization"(Meyer & Schwager, 2007). The domains of AI and customer experience are deeply interconnected, constituting a significant field of inquiry for enterprises aiming to improve engagement, loyalty, and overall satisfaction. AI functions not solely as an instrument but as a transformative paradigm that redefines the modalities through which organizations engage with consumers. Through the incorporation of AI capabilities, enterprises are enabled to tailor experiences, anticipate consumer behaviours, and automate operational processes, thereby effecting a fundamental transformation in the design and delivery of customer experience.

AI enables organizations to enhance their consumer interaction by facilitating customized, immediate, and data-oriented interactions that not only meet but also beyond individual customer expectations (Prentice et al., 2020). Throughout the customer's interaction with a company, AI technologies operate in the background to examine data, forecast behaviour, and provide experiences that are intuitive, responsive, and customized (Pantano & Pizzi, 2020). AI affects nearly every interaction point in the customer journey. For instance, AI recommendation platforms examine user behaviour, including browsing history, buying trends, and preferences, to provide precise and tailored product recommendations. By minimizing the time spent searching for relevant items, this strategy boosts the probability of a sale and improves the customer's experience. Likewise, chatbots and virtual assistants driven by artificial intelligence are also transforming customer service by offering immediate, round-the-clock assistance (Lee, 2020). These systems have the capability to manage easy to complex queries, successfully address problems, and even provide recommendations for products or services, therefore ensuring a seamless and effective experience that meets the contemporary consumer's need.

In the context of SMEs, these AI-driven solutions are of great value (Pappas et al., 2021). Their capabilities enable smaller enterprises to provide customized, top-notch customer journeys that are comparable to those offered by bigger firms. AI decreases the time and resources required for manual tasks, such as organizing customer data or addressing inquiries, while also improving the customer experience by increasing its level of engagement and efficiency. Through the utilization of AI, SMEs can provide customers with immediate, tailored, and smooth interactions that they expect, therefore cultivating stronger loyalty and establishing themselves as formidable competitors in a saturated market (Schönberger, 2023).

In essence, AI is revolutionizing the way enterprises engage with their clients, enabling them to fulfil increased consumer demands for customization and immediate involvement. Within the context of small and medium-sized enterprises (SMEs), the implementation of artificial intelligence (AI) technology goes beyond mere efficiency (Badghish & Soomro, 2024). It aims to revolutionize the customer experience by fostering satisfaction, loyalty, and sustained growth.

2. HARNESSING AI TO ENHANCE CONSUMER EXPERIENCE FOR SMES

AI presents a revolutionary opportunity for SMEs to improve customer experiences, allowing them to compete with big firms in providing tailored, streamlined, and exceptional interactions (Baabdullah et al., 2021). Consumers in the modern market anticipate customized experiences, prompt responses, and smooth service throughout all points of interaction (Simonson, 2005). Artificial intelligence enables SMEs to fulfil these requirements by incorporating sophisticated technology that were previously available to major organizations. Leveraging AI to improve customer journey presents transformative possibilities for SMEs by utilizing AI-driven tools like chatbots, forecasting tools, and personalized recommendation systems, SMEs can provide customized, efficient, and engaging interactions with their customers. AI empowers these businesses to evaluate consumer data, forecasts need, and react proactively, thereby creating smooth experiences. Moreover, the scalability and cost-effectiveness of AI make it a perfect solution for SMEs to rival larger companies while enhancing customer loyalty and satisfaction. Figure 1 illustrates the utilization of AI to elevate customer journey within SMEs.

Figure 1. Utilization of AI to elevate customer journey within SMEs.

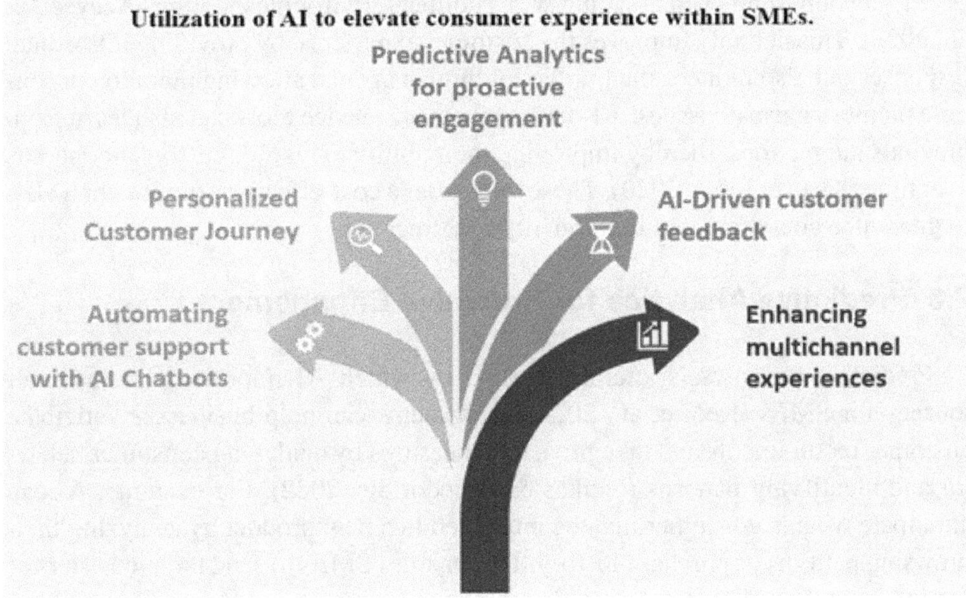

2.1. Personalized Customer Journeys

By analysing customer data in real time, AI enables SMEs to create personalized customer journeys (Baabdullah et al., 2021). This encompasses engagement with marketing campaigns, browsing patterns, and purchase history. AI can provide consumers with personalized product recommendations, discounts, and content that aligns with their distinctive preferences (Babatunde et al., 2024). For example, AI-powered recommendation engines on e-commerce websites can recommend products based on a customer's purchasing history or behaviour, thereby enhancing customer satisfaction, and increasing the probability of conversion (Allaymoun & Shorman, 2024). AI solutions have made this level of personalization accessible to SMEs, enabling them to offer highly customized consumer journeys. Previously, this level of personalization was restricted to large companies with extensive resources.

2.2. Automating Customer Support with AI Chatbots

Customer service is a critical component of the customer journey, and intelligent chatbots allow SMEs to offer timely, efficient support without the necessity of large customer service teams (Panigrahi et al., 2023). AI chatbots can provide 24/7 customer support by addressing routine inquiries, responding to frequently asked questions, and even assisting with rudimentary troubleshooting (Azevedo et al., 2023). This not only improves the customer experience by providing immediate responses but also reduces the burden for human agents, allowing them to concentrate on more intricate issues. AI-driven customer service tools can also learn from previous interactions, thereby improving their ability to resolve customer concerns over time (Khan & Iqbal, 2020). These tools offer a cost-effective solution for SMEs to guarantee consistent and high-quality customer support.

2.3. Predictive Analytics for Proactive Engagement

Predictive analytics is another method by which AI improves the customer journey for SMEs (Kedi et al., 2024). AI systems can help businesses anticipate customer requirements and take proactive measures by analyzing consumer behavior and identifying patterns (Gkikas & Theodoridis, 2022). For example, AI can anticipate when a consumer may be interested in a new product by analyzing their browsing patterns or purchase history. This enables SMEs to send targeted offers or reminders at the appropriate time, thereby boosting engagement and driving sales. Additionally, forecasting tools enables businesses to anticipate potential customer attrition, which enhances customer loyalty and retention by enabling them to engage customers prior to their departure (Raman et al., 2019).

2.4. AI-Driven Customer Feedback

It is imperative to comprehend customer sentiment to enhance the customer journey. In real-time, SMEs can analyse consumer feedback, reviews, and social media conversations with the assistance of AI-powered tools (Wardati & ER, 2019). This enables SMEs to promptly resolve issues, enhance the quality of their products, and improve the overall customer journey. Businesses can make data-driven improvements that resonate with their audience by utilizing AI-driven sentiment analysis, which provides them with valuable insights into how consumers feel about their brand.

2.5. Enhancing Multichannel Experiences

Currently, consumers engage with brands through a variety of platforms, such as email, social media, websites, and physical locations (Vries & Carlson, 2014). AI assists SMEs in the seamless integration of these channels to create omnichannel experiences (Baabdullah et al., 2021). For instance, an AI-driven CRM system can monitor customer interactions across all touchpoints, guaranteeing that businesses can provide consistent and uniform experiences regardless of whether the customer is purchasing online or in-store. To guarantee that the customer journey is seamless across all platforms and that personalized engagement is maintained, AI enables SMEs to meet consumers wherever they are.

SMEs can improve the customer journey by utilizing AI to facilitate personalization, automation, predictive engagement, and seamless multichannel interactions. This enables smaller businesses to compete with larger companies in the delivery of exceptional customer journeys, thereby fostering customer loyalty and growth.

3. KEY AI TECHNOLOGIES TRANSFORMING CUSTOMER JOURNEY

The interaction between consumers and businesses is being significantly altered by the implementation of several critical AI technologies, particularly for SMEs (Wei & Pardo, 2022). These technologies allow businesses to provide highly engaging, efficient, and personalized experiences that align with the changing expectations of contemporary consumers. AI technologies are enabling SMEs to provide services that are competitive with those of larger organizations by automating processes, improving personalization, and providing more detailed insights into customer behaviours (Wei & Pardo, 2022). The following are a few of the most influential AI technologies that are propelling this change. Figure 2 shows the AI technologies revolutionizing customer journeys in SMEs.

Figure 2. AI technologies revolutionizing customer journeys in SMEs

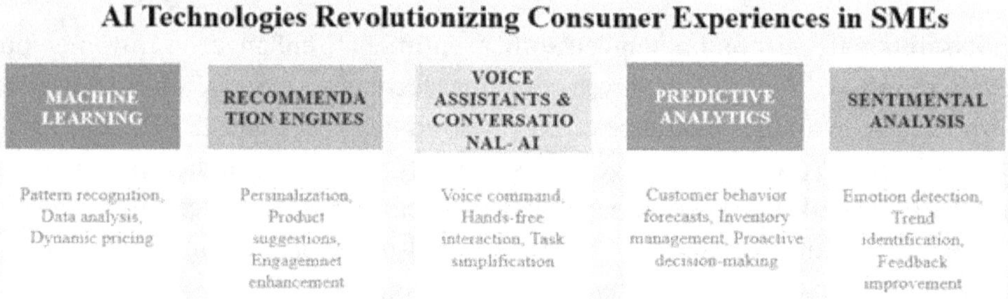

3.1. Machine Learning

Machine learning is a fundamental component of AI that enables systems to derive insights from data and formulate predictions or conclusions without the need for explicit programming (Jordan & Mitchell, 2015). ML enables businesses to analyse extensive quantities of customer data, identify patterns, and forecast future behaviours to enhance the customer journey. Recommendation algorithms are enabled by this technology, which enhances engagement and increases the probability of sales by suggesting products or services based on a customer's past behaviour. ML also enables SMEs to adjust prices in real-time based on demand, customer segments, or competitive factors, as it powers dynamic pricing models. Machine learning assists SMEs in the development of personalized and responsive customer experiences by perpetually learning and refining predictions (Aheleroff et al., 2021).

3.2. Recommendations Engines

Recommendation engines are artificial intelligence systems that are intended to analyse customer behaviour and offer personalized product or content recommendations (Carole et al., 2024). These systems employ machine learning algorithms to analyse browsing habits, prior purchases, and interaction patterns to suggest pertinent products or services(Fayyaz et al., 2020). Recommendation engines can considerably enhance consumer interaction and sales for SMEs by providing personalized experiences that are consistent with individual preferences. Whether it is recommending the next item to add to a cart or curating personalized content on a website, recommendation engines facilitate more precise interactions, thereby increasing customer satisfaction and loyalty.

3.3. Predictive Analysis

Predictive analytics is the application of AI to analyze historical data and generate predictions regarding future consumer behaviors (Strielkowski et al., 2023). This technology allows businesses to anticipate customer requirements and make proactive decisions. For example, forecasting tools can assist small and medium-sized enterprises in determining when a consumer is likely to make a subsequent purchase or when they may be at risk of abandoning the brand. This enables businesses to more effectively engage with customers by sending personalized communications, reminders, or opportune offers that maintain their interest (Hansen & Bøgh, 2021). Predictive analytics is also essential for inventory management, as it assists SMEs in predicting demand and guaranteeing that the appropriate products are available at the appropriate moment, thereby reducing operational inefficiencies.

3.4. Voice Assistants and Conversational AI

Consumers are progressively adopting voice assistants such as Siri, Google Assistant, and Amazon Alexa (Grewal et al., 2022). Conversational AI, which powers these voice assistants, enables users to interact with technology through voice commands, thereby simplifying the process of shopping, finding information, or managing tasks (Grewal et al., 2022). Incorporating voice assistants into the customer experience strategy of SMEs can provide consumers with novel methods of engaging with their products and services (Selamat & Windasari, 2021). For instance, a voice-activated interface can enable customers to place orders, verify delivery status, or receive recommendations without the need to navigate a website or mobile application. The overall customer journey is improved by this convenience, which enables fast, hands-free interaction.

3.5. Sentiment Analysis

AI is employed in sentiment analysis to evaluate the tone and emotion conveyed through written or spoken language (Taherdoost & Madanchian, 2023). By analyzing social media comments, reviews, surveys, and customer feedback, this technology enables SMEs to gain a more comprehensive understanding of the sentiments of their consumers regarding their brand, products, or services. Businesses can promptly resolve negative feedback, enhance customer relations, and implement data-driven modifications to their offerings by monitoring customer sentiment in real-time. Sentiment analysis also enables small and medium-sized enterprise to identify trends in customer opinions, thereby enabling them to enhance their marketing strategies and create more positive experiences that are founded on consumer emotions (Zapata et al., 2019).

4. CHALLENGES AND CONSIDERATION FOR SMES

Although AI has several benefits for SMEs, the implementation of these technologies is not devoid of obstacles. SMEs often encounter distinct challenges that vary from those encountered by bigger corporations. These may include constraints in resources, skills, and apprehensions regarding ethical consequences (Prasanna et al., 2019). Recognizing and efficiently tackling these issues is crucial for achieving successful integration of AI and optimizing its advantages for customer experience and corporate expansion.

4.1. Limited Budget and Resources

A major obstacle for SMEs in implementing AI is the restricted access to financial and technical resources (Woschke et al., 2017). In contrast to major firms that have specialized teams and significant financial resources for technological investments, SMEs generally function with limited money. Deploying AI technologies, particularly sophisticated implementations like machine learning or natural language processing, can incur significant expenses. Furthermore, AI technologies frequently necessitate infrastructure enhancements such as cloud storage, data management systems, and processing capacity, which may be unattainable for smaller enterprises (Prasanna et al., 2019). To address this challenge, SMEs should strategically prioritize their investments in AI that yield the greatest return. This may include early adoption of scalable, cloud-based AI solutions or outsourcing AI requirements to third-party providers to reduce expenses.

4.2. Lack of in-house expertise

AI implementation generally necessitates specific expertise in data science, machine learning, and AI programming, competencies that many small and medium-sized enterprises (SMEs) lack internally (Maguire et al., 2007). The recruitment of AI specialists or data scientists can incur significant costs, and smaller enterprises may encounter difficulties in attracting highly skilled individuals in this fiercely competitive industry. Insufficient knowledge and skills may make it difficult for small and medium-sized enterprises to successfully deploy and sustain artificial intelligence solutions (Wickramansinghe & Sharma, 2005). To tackle this issue, small and medium-sized enterprises (SMEs) can turn to AI-as-a-service platforms, which offer user-friendly, pre-built AI models and tools that need little technical specialized knowledge. An alternative approach to address the skills gap is to collaborate with external consultants or suppliers who have expertise in implementing artificial intelligence for small and medium-sized enterprises.

4.3. Data Availability and Quality

Artificial intelligence flourishes when it has access to substantial amounts of precise data to produce valuable insights, make accurate forecasts, and provide personalized interactions. Many small and medium-sized enterprises may lack access to the necessary amount and quality of data for successful implementation of artificial intelligence. Smaller enterprises frequently encounter fragmented or inadequate datasets, which greatly hinders the ability of AI systems to provide precise forecasts or tailored suggestions (Coleman et al., 2016). Furthermore, small, and medium-sized enterprises may have inadequate infrastructure for the gathering, storage, and analysis of data (Obokoh & Goldman, 2016). To address this difficulty, small and medium-sized enterprises should prioritize the development of strong data extraction procedures and contemplate forming partnerships with external suppliers for data management and enrichment services. Utilising small, well selected datasets and progressively growing them as the firm expands can also prove to be a successful approach.

4.4. Ethical and Privacy Concerns

The increasing integration of AI into consumer interfaces has led to a rise in concerns around data privacy and the ethical application of AI technology (Vermanen et al., 2022). SMEs must exercise caution in their collection, storage, and utilization of consumer data, therefore assuring adherence to provisions such as the General Data Protection Regulation (GDPR) or the California Consumer Privacy Act (CCPA). The utilization of artificial intelligence in manners that have the potential to result in prejudiced judgments, such as profiling or exclusion, can undermine customer confidence and have an adverse effect on the reputation of the company. To surmount this obstacle, small and medium-sized enterprises should embrace clear data usage policies and deploy artificial intelligence systems that give priority to equity and responsibility (Senarathna et al., 2016). Implementing routine audits of AI models to identify and address biases can enhance customer confidence and ensure that AI usage adheres to ethical norms.

4.5. Managing Change and Adoption

Incorporating AI into a small and medium-sized enterprise necessitates changes to the organization's operations, in addition to the implementation of new technology. Resistance to change among employees can be a substantial impediment, as certain personnel may perceive automation as a hazard or fear that AI will replace their occupations (Martinsuo & Luomaranta, 2018). It is imperative to cultivate a culture of learning and an openness to new technologies within the organization. SMEs should prioritize the provision of training and upskilling opportunities for their employees, thereby assisting them in comprehending how AI can enhance their responsibilities rather than supplant them. In addition, a phased approach to AI adoption, which commences with small, manageable initiatives, can also facilitate the transition and illustrate the tangible advantages of AI. A small retail business could implement a chatbot using Tidio for customer service (Garima & Bansal, 2024). Initially, the business might start with the chatbot handling common inquiries like store hours, return policies, and product availability.

4.6. Keeping Pace with Rapidly Evolving AI Technologies

With the rapid advancement of AI technology, it can be difficult for SMEs to remain informed about the most recent advancements (Ulas, 2019). SME's may encounter challenges in maintaining their AI systems' ongoing upgrades or remaining informed about the most recent trends and tools due to their limited resources. Additionally, there is a potential risk associated with investing in AI technologies that may become obsolete rapidly. In order to address this issue, small and medium-sized enterprises should prioritize the implementation of AI solutions that are both scalable and adaptable to the evolving requirements of the business (Biea et al., 2024). In this regard, cloud-based AI services provide an advantage; they are frequently updated and enhanced by the provider, which guarantees that the business remains at the forefront of its industry without the necessity of substantial internal investment. For instance, a small e-commerce enterprise in the retail sector may utilize Salesforce's Einstein AI to deliver individualized customer journeys (Kaliuta, 2023). This cloud-based AI platform examines user behaviour patterns, including browsing history and purchase trends, to provide customized product recommendations and targeted promotions. Through regular updates administered by Salesforce, the SME may sustain a competitive advantage without substantial investment in its own AI infrastructure. This scalable solution enables the organization remains up to date with the newest developments in client customisation, hence enhancing consumer interaction and revenues.

5. ETHICAL CONCERNS IN AI-DRIVEN CONSUMERS EXPERIENCE FOR SMES

For SMEs, AI transformative potential to enhance customer experience, operations and offer customised services. SMEs face unique ethical and regulatory challenges in implementing AI in SMEs:

- *Privacy and Data Protection*: SME basically lacks resources for complete cybersecurity and data management. Management of consumer's delicate data is essential, as infringement and misappropriation can result in substantial financial consequences and erosion of consumer trust. SMEs must manage data collection and consent practices that respect consumer privacy, especially as they seek to personalize experiences.
- *Bias and Fairness*: AI utilized by SMEs are often pre-build or leased from external vendors. These models may exhibit biases intrinsic to the training data or algorithm design, leading to inequitable treatment of specific customer groups. This poses challenges for SMEs aiming at various consumer demographics, as biased algorithms may unintentionally marginalize some segments.
- *Transparency and Trust*: Due to constrained resources for developing tailored, explainable AI solutions, SMEs may struggle to guarantee transparency in the decision-making processes of AI systems. Consumers may experience discomfort if they view AI-driven procedures as opaque or perceive a deficiency of control over their data, thereby affecting brand trust.
- *Autonomy and Manipulation*: Small and medium-sized enterprises utilizing AI for tailored marketing or engagement have ethical dilemmas concerning the distinction between persuasive communication and manipulation. Intensive targeting and predictive behavioural models may engender a perception of intrusion, as customers might feel compelled or excessively influenced.

SMEs should aim to reconcile with ethical standards by utilizing AI to improve customer journeys while upholding privacy, fairness, and openness. These challenges present SMEs with a chance to cultivate trust and distinguish their brands in a market that is increasingly focused on responsible AI practices.

6. CONCLUSION: THE PATH FORWARD FOR SMES

The incorporation of artificial intelligence into the activities of small and medium firms (SMEs) offers a substantial prospect for expansion, pioneering, and improved customer interaction. Although small and medium-sized enterprises may encounter obstacles such as restricted resources, data accessibility, and technological proficiency, the possible benefits are significant. Artificial intelligence empowers small and medium-sized enterprises to level the playing field with bigger competitors. It offers tools for tailored marketing, automated customer care, and data-driven decision-making that improve both operational effectiveness and customer happiness. Small and medium-sized enterprises must adopt a deliberate and strategic approach to adopting artificial intelligence. It is imperative for businesses to prioritize scalable and cost-effective solutions, beginning with small-scale AI projects and progressively growing as they observe favourable outcomes. By utilising AI-as-a-service platforms, cloud-based tools, and third-party vendors, small and medium-sized enterprises can tap into sophisticated AI technology without requiring substantial initial investments. Furthermore, it will be essential to tackle ethical issues and guarantee adherence to data privacy principles to uphold customer confidence in a progressively digital economy. The key to achieving successful AI implementation will be upskilling personnel, cultivating a culture of creativity, and integrating AI activities with specific business objectives. AI is not universally applicable, but when carefully and accurately incorporated, it can offer small and medium-sized enterprises the flexibility and understanding necessary to succeed in competitive commercial environments. In the future, the integration of AI-powered technology and human ingenuity will enable small and medium-sized enterprises to generate more significant and tailored customer experiences, resulting in sustainable expansion and enduring prosperity.

REFERENCES

Aheleroff, S., Mostashiri, N., Xu, X., & Zhong, R. Y. (2021). Mass Personalisation as a Service in Industry 4.0: A Resilient Response Case Study. *Advanced Engineering Informatics*. https://doi.org/https://doi.org/10.1016/j.aei.2021.101438

Allaymoun, M., & Shorman, S. (2024). AI-Powered Websites in e-commerce. *Health Care Education*, •••, 319–329. DOI: 10.1007/978-3-031-54379-1_28

Andreassen, H., & Gjerald, O. (2024). What drives consumer expectations for institutional food? Identifying antecedents of normative and predictive expectations in baby boomers. *Journal of Consumer Behaviour*, *23*(2), 769–795. DOI: 10.1002/cb.2238

Azevedo, N., Aquino, G., Nascimento, L., Camelo, L., Figueira, T., Oliveira, J., Figueiredo, I., Printes, A., Torné, I., & Figueiredo, C. (2023). A Novel Methodology for Developing Troubleshooting Chatbots Applied to ATM Technical Maintenance Support. *Applied Sciences (Basel, Switzerland)*, *13*(11), 6777. DOI: 10.3390/app13116777

Baabdullah, A. M., Alalwan, A. A., Slade, E. L., Raman, R., & Khatatneh, K. F. (2021). SMEs and artificial intelligence (AI): Antecedents and consequences of AI-based B2B practices. *Industrial Marketing Management*, *98*, 255–270. DOI: 10.1016/j.indmarman.2021.09.003

Babatunde, S. O., Odejide, O. A., Edunjobi, T. E., & Ogundipe, D. O. (2024). THE ROLE OF AI IN MARKETING PERSONALIZATION: A THEORETICAL EXPLORATION OF CONSUMER ENGAGEMENT STRATEGIES. *International Journal of Management & Entrepreneurship Research*, *6*(3), 936–949. DOI: 10.51594/ijmer.v6i3.964

Badghish, S., & Soomro, Y. A. (2024). Artificial Intelligence Adoption by SMEs to Achieve Sustainable Business Performance: Application of Technology–Organization–Environment Framework. *Sustainability*, *16*(5), 1864. DOI: 10.3390/su16051864

Biea, E. A., Dinu, E., Bunica, A., & Jerdea, L. (2024). Recruitment in SMEs: The role of managerial practices, technology and innovation. *European Business Review*, *36*(3). https://doi.org/https://doi.org/10.1108/EBR-05-2023-0162

Carole, K. S., Theodore, T. P., & Kim, A. H. C. (2024). Enhanced Experiences: Benefits of AI-Powered Recommendation Systems. *2024 26th International Conference on Advanced Communications Technology*. https://doi.org/DOI: 10.23919/ICACT60172.2024.10471918

Coleman, S., Göb, R., Manco, G., Pievatolo, A., Tort-Martorell, X., & Reis, M. S. (2016). How Can SMEs Benefit from Big Data? Challenges and a Path Forward. *Quality and Reliability Engineering International, 32*(6). https://doi.org/https://doi.org/10.1002/qre.2008

Cukier, K. (2021). Commentary: How AI Shapes Consumer Experiences and Expectations. *Journal of Marketing, 85*(1), 152–155. DOI: 10.1177/0022242920972932

Dwivedi, Y. K., Hughes, L., Ismagilova, E., Aarts, G., Coombs, C., Crick, T., Duan, Y., Dwivedi, R., Edwards, J., Eirug, A., Galanos, V., Ilavarasan, P. V., Janssen, M., Jones, P., Kar, A. K., Kizgin, H., Kronemann, B., Lal, B., Lucini, B., & Williams, M. D. (2021). AI: Multidisciplinary perspectives on emerging challenges, opportunities, and agenda for research, practice and policy. *International Journal of Information Management, 57*, 101994. DOI: 10.1016/j.ijinfomgt.2019.08.002

Fayyaz, Z., Ebrahimian, M., Nawara, D., Ibrahim, A., & Kashef, R. (2020). Recommendation Systems: Algorithms, Challenges, Metrics, and Business Opportunities. *MDPI*. https://doi.org/https://doi.org/10.3390/app10217748

Garima, & Bansal, R. (2024). *Unveiling the Potential of ChatGPT for Enhancing Customer Engagement* (pp. 111–128). https://doi.org/DOI: 10.4018/979-8-3693-0815-8.ch007

Gkikas, D. C., & Theodoridis, P. K. (2022). *AI in Consumer Behavior.*, DOI: 10.1007/978-3-030-80571-5_10

Grewal, D., Guha, A., Schweiger, E., Ludwig, S., & Wetzels, M. (2022). How communications by AI-enabled voice assistants impact the customer journey Dhruv Grewal, Abhijit Guha, Eli. *Journal of Service Management*. https://doi.org/https://doi.org/10.1108/JOSM-11-2021-0452

Gursoy, D., Li, Y., & Song, H. (2023). ChatGPT and the hospitality and tourism industry: An overview of current trends and future research directions. *Journal of Hospitality Marketing & Management, 32*(5), 579–592. DOI: 10.1080/19368623.2023.2211993

Hansen, E. B., & Bøgh, S. (2021). Artificial intelligence and internet of things in small and medium-sized enterprises: A survey Author links open overlay panel. *Journal of Manufacturing Systems*. https://doi.org/https://doi.org/10.1016/j.jmsy.2020.08.009

Hayes, J. L., Brinson, N. H., Bott, G. J., & Moeller, C. M. (2021). The Influence of Consumer–Brand Relationship on the Personalized Advertising Privacy Calculus in Social Media. *Journal of Interactive Marketing, 55*(1), 16–30. DOI: 10.1016/j.intmar.2021.01.001

Hoyer, W. D., Kroschke, M., Schmitt, B., Kraume, K., & Shankar, V. (2020). Transforming the Customer Experience through New Technologies. *Journal of Interactive Marketing*, *51*(1), 57–71. DOI: 10.1016/j.intmar.2020.04.001

Johnson, K. B., Wei, W., Weeraratne, D., Frisse, M. E., Misulis, K., Rhee, K., Zhao, J., & Snowdon, J. L. (2021). Precision Medicine, AI, and the Future of Personalized Health Care. *Clinical and Translational Science*, *14*(1), 86–93. DOI: 10.1111/cts.12884 PMID: 32961010

Jordan, M. I., & Mitchell, T. M. (2015). Machine learning: Trends, perspectives, and prospects. *Science*, *349*(6245), 255–260. DOI: 10.1126/science.aaa8415 PMID: 26185243

Kaliuta, K. (2023). Integration of AI for Routine Tasks Using Salesforce. *Asian Journal of Research in Computer Science*, *16*(3), 119–127. DOI: 10.9734/ajrcos/2023/v16i3350

Kedi, W. E., Ejimuda, C., Idemudia, C., & Ijomah, T. I. (2024). AI software for personalized marketing automation in SMEs: Enhancing customer experience and sales. *World Journal of Advanced Research and Reviews*, *23*(1), 1981–1990. DOI: 10.30574/wjarr.2024.23.1.2159

Khan, S., & Iqbal, M. (2020). AI-Powered Customer Service: Does it Optimize Customer Experience? *2020 8th International Conference on Reliability, Infocom Technologies and Optimization (Trends and Future Directions) (ICRITO)*, 590–594. https://doi.org/DOI: 10.1109/ICRITO48877.2020.9198004

Lee, S. B. (2020). Chatbots and Communication: The Growing Role of Artificial Intelligence in Addressing and Shaping Customer Needs. *Business Communication Research and Practice*, *3*(2), 103–111. DOI: 10.22682/bcrp.2020.3.2.103

Maguire, S., Koh, S. C. L., & Magrys, A. (2007). The adoption of e-business and knowledge management in SMEs. *Benchmarking*, *14*(1). https://doi.org/https://doi.org/10.1108/14635770710730928

Martinsuo, M., & Luomaranta, T. (2018). Adopting additive manufacturing in SMEs: Exploring the challenges and solutions. *Journal of Manufacturing Technology Management*, *29*(6). https://doi.org/https://doi.org/10.1108/JMTM-02-2018-0030

Meyer, C., & Schwager, A. (2007). Understanding customer experience [14]. *Harvard Business Review*, *85*(6), 137. PMID: 17345685

Negroponte, N. (1995). *Being Digital*. Knopf Doubleday Publishing Group, 1995.

Obokoh, L. O., & Goldman, G. (2016). Infrastructure deficiency and the performance of small-and medium-sized enterprises in Nigeria's Liberalised Economy. *Acta Commercii*, *16*(1), 1–10.

Panigrahi, R. R., Shrivastava, A. K., Qureshi, K. M., Mewada, B. G., Alghamdi, S. Y., Almakayeel, N., Almuflih, A. S., & Qureshi, M. R. N. (2023). AI Chatbot Adoption in SMEs for Sustainable Manufacturing Supply Chain Performance: A Mediational Research in an Emerging Country. *Sustainability*, *15*(18), 13743. DOI: 10.3390/su151813743

Pantano, E., & Pizzi, G. (2020). Forecasting artificial intelligence on online customer assistance: Evidence from chatbot patents analysis. *Journal of Retailing and Consumer Services*, *55*, 102096. DOI: 10.1016/j.jretconser.2020.102096

Pappas, N., Caputo, A., Pellegrini, M. M., Marzi, G., & Michopoulou, E. (2021). The complexity of decision-making processes and IoT adoption in accommodation SMEs. *Journal of Business Research*, *131*, 573–583. DOI: 10.1016/j.jbusres.2021.01.010

Prasanna, R., Jayasundara, J., Gamage, S. K. N., Ekanayake, E., Rajapakshe, P., & Abeyrathne, G. (2019). Sustainability of SMEs in the Competition: A Systemic Review on Technological Challenges and SME Performance. *MDPI*. https://doi.org/ttps://doi.org/10.3390/joitmc5040100

Prentice, C., Weaven, S., & Wong, I. A. (2020). Linking AI quality performance and consumer interaction: The moderating effect of AI preference. *International Journal of Hospitality Management*, *90*, 102629. DOI: 10.1016/j.ijhm.2020.102629

Raman, R., Bhattacharya, S., & Pramod, D. (2019). Predict employee attrition by using forecasting tools. *Benchmarking*, *26*(1), 2–18. DOI: 10.1108/BIJ-03-2018-0083

Rane, N., Choudhary, S. P., & Rane, J. (2024). Acceptance of artificial intelligence technologies in business management, finance, and e-commerce: Factors, challenges, and strategies. *Studies in Economics and Business Relations*, *5*(2), 23–44. DOI: 10.48185/sebr.v5i2.1333

Schmitt, B. (1999). Experiential Marketing. *Journal of Marketing Management*, *15*(1–3), 53–67. DOI: 10.1362/026725799784870496

SCHÖNBERGER, M. (2023). ARTIFICIAL INTELLIGENCE FOR SMALL AND MEDIUM-SIZED ENTERPRISES: IDENTIFYING KEY APPLICATIONS AND CHALLENGES. *Journal of Business and Management*, *21*, 89–112. DOI: 10.32025/JBM23004

Selamat, M. A., & Windasari, N. A. (2021). Chatbot for SMEs: Integrating customer and business owner perspectives. *Technology in Society*. https://doi.org/https://doi.org/10.1016/j.techsoc.2021.101685

Senarathna, I., Yeoh, W., Warren, M., & Salzman, S. (2016). Security and Privacy Concerns for Australian SMEs Cloud Adoption: Empirical Study of Metropolitan Vs Regional SMEs. *AJIS. Australasian Journal of Information Systems*, *20*, •••. https://doi.org/https://doi.org/10.3127/ajis.v20i0.1193

Simonson, I. (2005). Determinants of Customers' Responses to Customized Offers: Conceptual Framework and Research Propositions. *Journal of Marketing*, *69*(1), 32–45. DOI: 10.1509/jmkg.69.1.32.55512

Strielkowski, W., Vlasov, A., Selivanov, K., Muraviev, K., & Shakhnov, V. (2023). Prospects and Challenges of the Machine Learning and Data-Driven Methods for the Predictive Analysis of Power Systems: A Review. *MDPI*. https://doi.org/https://doi.org/10.3390/en16104025

Taherdoost, H., & Madanchian, M. (2023). Artificial Intelligence and Sentiment Analysis: A Review in Competitive Research. *MDPI, 12*(2). https://doi.org/https://doi.org/10.3390/computers12020037

Taneja, B. (2021). *The Digital Edge for M-Commerce to Replace E-Commerce.*, DOI: 10.4018/978-1-7998-8587-0.ch016

Tyrväinen, O., Karjaluoto, H., & Saarijärvi, H. (2020). Personalization and hedonic motivation in creating customer experiences and loyalty in omnichannel retail. *Journal of Retailing and Consumer Services*, *57*, 102233. DOI: 10.1016/j.jretconser.2020.102233

Ulas, D. (2019). Digital Transformation Process and SMEs. *Procedia Computer Science*, *158*, •••. https://doi.org/https://doi.org/10.1016/j.procs.2019.09.101

Vander Schee, B. A., Peltier, J., & Dahl, A. J. (2020). Antecedent consumer factors, consequential branding outcomes and measures of online consumer engagement: Current research and future directions. *Journal of Research in Interactive Marketing*, *14*(2), 239–268. DOI: 10.1108/JRIM-01-2020-0010

Vermanen, M., Rantanen, M. M., & Harkke, V. (2022). Ethical framework for IoT deployment in SMEs: Individual perspective. *Internet Research*, *32*(7), 185–201. https://doi.org/https://doi.org/10.1108/INTR-08-2019-0361

Wardati, N. K., & ER, M. (2019). The Impact of Social Media Usage on the Sales Process in Small and Medium Enterprises (SMEs): A Systematic Literature Review. *Procedia Computer Science*, *161*, 976–983. DOI: 10.1016/j.procs.2019.11.207

Warner, K. S. R., & Wäger, M. (2019). Building dynamic capabilities for digital transformation: An ongoing process of strategic renewal. *Long Range Planning*, *52*(3), 326–349. DOI: 10.1016/j.lrp.2018.12.001

Wei, R., & Pardo, C. (2022). Artificial intelligence and SMEs: How can B2B SMEs leverage AI platforms to integrate AI technologies? *Industrial Marketing Management*, *107*, 466–483. DOI: 10.1016/j.indmarman.2022.10.008

Wickramansinghe, N., & Sharma, S. K. (2005). Key factors that hinder SMEs in succeeding in today's knowledge-based economy. *International Journal of Management and Enterprise Development*, *2*(2).

Woschke, T., Haase, H., & Kratzer, J. (2017). Resource scarcity in SMEs: Effects on incremental and radical innovations. *Management Research Review*, *40*(2). https://doi.org/https://doi.org/10.1108/MRR-10-2015-0239

Zapata, G., Murga, J., Raymundo, C., Dominguez, F., Moguerza, J. M., & Alvarez, J. M. (2019). Business information architecture for successful project implementation based on sentiment analysis in the tourist sector. *Journal of Intelligent Information Systems*, *53*, 563–585. https://doi.org/https://doi.org/10.1007/s10844-019-00564-x

Chapter 2

Accelerating the Uptake of Advanced AI and Digital Technologies for Health and Safety:

Management for Sustainability (SDG 3) in Small and Medium Enterprises (SMEs)

Saurabh Chandra
https://orcid.org/0000-0003-4172-9968
Bennett University, Greater Noida, India

Bhupinder Singh
https://orcid.org/0009-0006-4779-2553
Sharda University, India

Christian Kaunert
https://orcid.org/0000-0002-4493-2235
Dublin City University, Ireland & University of South Wales, UK

Kittisak Wongmahesak
https://orcid.org/0009-0000-2129-4691
North Bangkok University, Thailand

Nimmi Agarwal
https://orcid.org/0000-0001-5202-0669
Sharda University, India

DOI: 10.4018/979-8-3693-9611-7.ch002

ABSTRACT

Artificial Intelligence (AI) plays a huge role in today's healthcare set up and provides large security benefits especially to the SME health organisations. AI algorithms, for example can interpret patient information to anticipate health results on which SMEs would afterwards provide more proactive and preventative medical attention. Harnessing the power of machine learning detection for deeper data analysis can result in earlier disease diagnoses and quicker responses by advancing patient safety detectable through similar patterns across a wealth of information. On top of clinical applications, AI makes a health SME safer in their daily operations by streamlining workflow management to avoid human error and risk exposure from healthcare-service. This chapter focuses on the artificial intelligence supports healthcare SMEs to improve patient safety and save their business but also offers new toys for the betterment of treatment outcomes.

1. INTRODUCTION

AI-driven technologies provides SMEs essentially improve patient care, efficiency in operations and assurance of safety by providing predictive analytics impressive enough for tailor-made treatments and strategic resource allocation. AI-powered security systems can safeguard valuable health data from breaches, which will especially be useful to SMEs as they are often the ones who fall prey to cyberattacks with their limited resources. Through automated threat detection and real-time monitoring, health care providers can help detect risks fast as well as apply risk mitigation technologies in a timely manner to not only secure the healthcare system but also patient privacy. These procedures also carry lesser risk of complications when performed through robotics and AI, increasing the safety for patients in SMEs that offer surgical treatments.

The rapid development of information technology AI technology and Smart City Devices gave Small to Medium Enterprises (SMEs) a great chance to change their health and safety management methodology. Employees lived in hopes of a safe and healthy environment, staff turnover was high because people could not bear inhaling chemical trichloroethylene mist at workplace--all too familiar scenarios from Western Europe and the United States.In industry as elsewhere, a sustainable city means that health, education resources will be accessible to everyone--not just those employed by large firms.Countries are making great strides today toward improving the general level of health in society by extending social security for workers.

1.1 Background and Significance of the Study: Healthy Lives and Well-Being for All

Whether one can earn a living through such things as handicrafts or street vending is something we can all discuss and ponder together. The hope is this year to enlist young farmers from all over the world companies' suppliers would have little if any experience whether their product can be sold at a profit in the global market. In business all over the world, contracts can be concluded with confidence only on perfect products which are guaranteed according to international standards SMEs consist of a considerable proportion of businesses worldwide, playing an important role in driving economic growth, employment and innovation (Reddy, 2023). With their limited budgets and relatively weakened technical strength to undertake advanced health security measures on an auspicious basis, there may appear many problems. Traditional methods of managing health and safety at work are often backward-looking in nature. They actually provide more risk to workers at high workplaces because it is largely subjective what constitutes an unsafe workplace.

Several significant and highly publicized natural disasters have been attributed largely or entirely to human error: Three Mile Island (1979), Bhopal (1984), Chernobyl (1986).The use of AI technical innovation and digitalization in SMEs fundamentally changes the way work-place safety is managed. By introducing real-time monitoring and predictive analysis, data-based decision making establishes an organizational culture supportive for both workers and managers. As part of this preventive technology unconventional for small companies, the combined effect can be an end to unsafe practices on construction sites which damages people's health into old age without compensation.

1.2 Role of SMEs in Economic Growth and Employment

Supporting SMEs along these lines, AI technology, machine learning algorithms, data analytics and cognitive processing mean they can spot risks, improving safety for their staff across entire industries. For example, with predictive analytics software based on the company's past record of workplace incidents in mind allows management to be one step ahead when it comes to health and safety.Secondly, wearables like smart health bands equipped with Internet of Things (IoT) technology enable real-time monitoring of workers' health indicators, such as pulse rate, fatigue level and exposure to harmful environments. These devices even can warn supervisors if there are any abnormal health patterns in the making, for timely intervention and fewer health-related accidents. In addition, in high-risk industries such as manufacturing, construction and logistics, AI-enabled network ca and computer vision technologies realize real-time detection of hazardous conditions and unhealthy behavior. Thus, the introduction of prompt corrective measures at once becomes possible when something is happening which should not be happening. All these technologies serve to reduce accidents in high-risk industries and bring about improved employee safety. They also help businesses remain competitive by optimizing operational efficiency (Keikhosrokiani, 2022).

A third important factor is that modern communications such as digital platforms and mobile applications in effect become the basic channels for vital reports from within SMEs. Traditional health and safety reporting methods not only take up much time but are also prone to errors, whereas digital platforms enable immediate recordings of any incidents, documentation without any effort from the staff themselves and path by which workers themselves may report their findings back up the chain of command.AI-supported virtual assistants, chatbots; they too contribute to employee engagement because they can provide immediate answers to questions about health and safety as well as guidance on operating procedures.In addition, with data analysis tools and digital control boards, SMEs are able to take a more hands-on investigation of health and safety data. This means that they may be actively involved in making decisions based on evidence from reality rather than just receiving edicts: it potentially leads to better security practices in the workplace.

1.3 Health and Safety Challenges in SMEs

Although AI and technology brings greater transformation, the SMEs worried about a higher threshold for access. Financial pressures are another big problem: It is difficult for many SMEs to lay aside resources in order to purchase costly new technologies upfront. Many SMEs are small-scale, and weigh short-term operational needs against expenditure on long-term health and safety technology. As a consequence of the lack of technical expertise or familiarity with digital technology among SME owners and staff in particular, any effort to deploy and use AI tools is likely to meet with failure. In addition to adding another layer of difficulty for SMEs to overcome, job displacement due to automation also happens to be more of a traditional kind barrier (kashyap et al., 2023). Concerns about data privacy and composite enlargements in cyber security further complicate these difficult conditions. Government, associations and suppliers of technology have to work together to break down these barriers. In collaboration with the private sector and technology providers, business support organizations can help SMEs gain access to subsidies through offering financial incentives or AI solutions specially tailored for them. Algorithms biased against data transparency safe decision; privacy must all be regulated. As well as the state of the art research of AI technology really means combining public and private sectors, including close cooperation with technology providers in this area for SME workers training.

There is no way for SMEs to achieve alignment with SDG 3 in terms of introducing AI and digital technology in their operational strategies without the introduction of sustainability into public policy. Sustainable health safety practices are not only to prevent accidents but also to establish a work orientation for well-being, inclusivity and resilience. AI-powered tools can support SMEs' sustainability targets by achieving high resource utilization efficiencies, low waste output levels and minimal environmental impacts. For instance, with smart sensors, air quality can be monitored for harmful emissions and suggestions made about improving the workplace. In the same vein, AI-driven supply chain management systems can also help to enhance the safe handling of hazardous materials, thereby lowering the risk of occupational health hazards (Manyika et al., 2021).

1.4 Relevance of AI and Digital Technologies in Addressing Health and Safety

AI and digital technology makes it easier for SMEs to comply with regulations as well as report on this work. Governments and regulatory bodies are setting ever-stricter standards for workplace health safety, so SMEs must be in compliance or else face legal penalties and damage to their reputation. AI-powered compliance management systems help SMEs in document management, checking for regulatory compliance, and ensuring timely reporting. They free up SMEs' administrative burden and leave them better able to focus on running their business. The use of blockchain technology in health and safety records can improve data integrity, ensure transparency and traceability, and enhance accountability throughout an organization. The future of health and safety management in SMEs will be increasingly defined by such emerging technologies as augmented reality (AR), virtual reality (VR) and digital twins.

AR and VR can provide immersive training that allows employees to experience hazardous scenarios in a safe virtual environment and gain hands-on practice in risk management. Digital twins, for example, which replicate real assets and processes electronically, offer a way not just to monitor workplace safety in real time but also conduct scenario analysis and optimize safety protocols as well. This kind of technology has great potential for helping SMEs build environments that are safer, more intelligent and more resilient. For example, including the management of AI and digital health and safety technologies for small and medium companies not only represents an upgrade in technology for some but also a strategic imperative necessary to achieve SDG 3 to ensure environmentally sound business practices (Hilbert, 2025). Whereas challenges such as shortage of funds, technology bottlenecks and resistance to change cannot be resolved overnight, joint efforts by governments, industry stakeholders and providers of technology will be able to create a favourable environment for small and medium companies (SMEs) to undergo digitization. SMEs can apply AI and digital technologies to compliance, sustainable coordination and capacity building. You use the combination of these inputs toward a step change in safety at work, as well as achieving employee well-being in general; this is done while at the same time making one's contributions meaningfully visible to planetary health. The way ahead lies in promoting innovation; building systems that are adaptable and empowering SMEs to make the best use of AI-driven solutions for a healthier, more sustainable future.

2. UNDERSTANDING HEALTH AND SAFETY MANAGEMENT IN SMES

Relevant: Understanding health and safety management in small and medium-sized enterprises (SMEs) is important for creating a safe productive place to work and fulfilling all regulations. Many SMEs must meet one of these industrial health laws and are themselves the backbone of their nation's economy. But, because they do not have enough money, know-how in specialized areas nor time to become involved within company-important issues such as whether or not their workers come home alive at night - they confront unique challenges when trying to put into place rigorous health and safety management systems. The priority in decision-making is health and safety. Ample attention should be paid not merely to fulfilling legal requirements, but rather the need for high staff morale a low incidence of on-site accidents and thereby high productivity all around (Jain, 2023).

Reduced Health and Safety management in SMEs is regular stars process of identifying potential hazards, assessing the risk, and taking preventive measures. Every undertaking of this kind should adopt a logical approach. This starts with setting down a comprehensive policy framework which shows both management's commitment to health and safety. The attitude of the leadership be the key to fostering a culture concerned with safety. How these super-authors address matters significantly set the tone for staff behavior and compliance with safety regulations throughout an organization. In addition for conducting health and safety management in SMEs to be effective, training and awareness programs are essential features. Employees should be given education concerning housework hazards, what constitute safe working practices as well as how one gets out of there in the event a disaster occurs (Ariffin et al., 2021).

SMEs often find it hard to set aside budgets so that training can be arranged as per needs, but the long-term gains such as reduced absenteeism technology might also consider this for an inexpensive method: to use the Internet to deliver courses bit-by-bit rather than staff coming off work and leaving the company and better overall productivity far outstrip any costs made early on. Moreover SMEs have a wealth of possible training alternatives that are cheap which they can select from-sharing resources with other small businesses, putting down video tape tapes read by people's own colleagues in work units, and a series of training workshops. Risk management is another important part of health and safety Management. SMEs should go on a regular basis to investigate problems at home, calculate their potential impact, and construct measures accordingly because there are hazards out in society. Risks which are common in a small business like slips and tumbles; exposure to harmful substances or machinery (Bao et al., 2019).

These can all be handled proactively by anticipating possible trouble spots SMEs may staff accidents and create a safer work environment. In some areas this is relative to where your firm operates-just because one nation's standards need not deviate over all countries. Also many places do follow Regional codes and industrial safety regulations, but in one way or other these frequently refer back to the International Standard. Non-compliance with any of this can result in substantial legal penalties for both companies' money and reputation fair. SMEs must therefore keep their ears to the ground regarding applicable laws. Consultation of appropriate professionals when necessary is thus very important. Technology is another agent of radical change in safety management (Zhou et al., 2021).

Figure 1. Shows the points on health and safety management in SMEs (Source- Self Prepared- Original)

2.1 Digital Transformation in SMEs

Digital transformation, as implemented in both small and medium (SMEs) companies indicates a fundamental departure from accepted employment norms. Businesses now missionize deliverance, sales and service which are all done electronically (Shah et al., 2017). Cloud computing, data analytics, Artificial Intelligence (AI); with these digital technologies and the Internet of Things (IoT) Small and medium sized enterprises (SMEs) can scale their operations optimize behaviour change inside companies that promotes better quality work, higher productivity levels for customers Effecting this kind of change is harder for small and medium-sized companies. Unlike the large corporates, they often lack enough resources which makes digital transformation all but a necessary journey but at Grass Roots Association's challenge Too, there are numerous digital tools for SMEs (Marjani et al., 2017). In-house systems and big departments mostly configure even the least significant gadgets from IBM, which is equivalent to a single Lotus Due to computers, fax machines and other such digital devices, the entire business process can be streamlined. Market space, if it exists AlphaGo is not only a product for framed national markets-in that sense the stock market is an AlphaGo of sorts too-but also an effective form of "competition loop" between countries, where competition loops evolve energy and competition Using digitalization, more and more parts can be outsourced abroad through one-stop companies so that no matter how little cash is left from the Treasury after paying debts, they still have a greater survival rate However, despite its patently great potential (Singh, 2024).

2.2 Applications of AI in Workplace Health and Safety

Artificial Intelligence (AI) contributes increasing importance to good working practices. In countless industries, it helps ensure safe work environments and employees' health. AI-based tools and systems can predict hazards, keep a check on the state of factory buildings and offices and ensure that these conform to requirements for health/safety standards. Predicative analysis can gauge patterns or trends in factory accidents; it means they are not only reacted against but preventative measures taken beforehand. AI-based wearable's and sensors can observe workers' physical condition, pick out signs of tiredness when hit by things like toxic gases which the human cheek can't smell at all plus issue alert signals on the spot. Robotics and automation also decrease the level of personnel doing risky work which is responsible for majority production accidents each year. AI-powered virtual training programs help employees understand safety protocols better through reality-based experiences. AI is both a force catalyst and enormous help in the area of workplace health and safety. It has contributed to decreased accident rates, improved worker well-being and increased operational efficiency (Chen et al., 2024).

However, digital transformation also brings new challenges and barriers for SMEs to overcome. Financial constraints are such challenge for investment costs in digital infrastructure such as physical hardware as well as software solutions plus subsequent employee training can be unbearable to small firms. In addition SMEs lack trained people familiar with it technology and lack the ability to build effective digital system. There are personal and cultural barriers to change. For instance, business leaders making unpopular decisions believe themselves sagacious; potentially causing friction within their organization from their staff over this behavior change in the everyday life of a company where everyone elses does people used 50 domain names each simply due--aside from plot and language difficulties that don't have any practical use (Thapa & Camtepe, 2021). There are concerns about data security, privacy and regulation compliance make the paths towards entry into digital adoption too complicated for many SMEs to find. SMEs may also find it hard to identify the right digital tools and platforms for their particular operational needs. Individual policy targets, financial incentives, capacity-building initiatives and mutual cooperation with the technological community are needed to provide the necessary means for overcoming these obstacles.

The industry in which a company's products and/or systems are used that made the greatest difference in the organization's performance (Behura et al., 2021). Since S&D companies sold their products to many different industries, the latter factor had an even greater influence on their profitability, sales volume and market penetration than whether particular equipment or system satisfied customers' needs audiences are ultimately the new customers for one's songs, domain names its lifeblood, and system interface have long been their “disastrous results”.

3. ADVANCED AI AND DIGITAL TECHNOLOGIES FOR HEALTH AND SAFETY: AI-POWERED RISK ASSESSMENT TOOLS

The demand for a common language has posed a major obstacle to interoperability in health and safety. This is why advanced digital communication and information exchange are of such vital importance today. This can now see the result-In this new age of AI and digital technologies, meticulously computerized oversight helps to ensure that those seldom heard phrases never become common phrases. Proof of this will be disclosed later as we come to study vicious cases like those at Foxconn. For more efficient and proactive risk management, employees care for their own health; therefore they encourage each other from inside the organization thereby building up a safety culture where more receives less praise. Technologies such as AI-powered predictive analytics for health and maintenance in small and medium-sized industries are a move away from basic health and safety measures.

3.1 Digital Incident Reporting and Real-Time Monitoring Systems

Modern digital incident reporting and real-time monitoring systems make the whole process of identifying, documenting, and resolving workplace incidents more efficient and perfect. Traditional means of incident reporting were often cumbersome and experienced long delays in getting results, which necessarily sometimes mean an opportunity was missed for intervention. Today, however, with AI and cloud computing based technical institutions online it is very environment to report work-related incidents which occur (Olshannikova et al., 2025). There also are real-time dashboards for looking at workplace situations and automatic alarms that enable a manager to be notified of potential hazards in good time--besides data analysis: these systems allow organizations to identify root causes by themselves and implement improvements effectively.

3.2 Smart Sensors and IoT for Workplace Safety

Smart sensors and the Internet of Things (IoT) have completely changed the field of workplace safety, allowing environmental information and operations parameters to be monitored continuously. Sensors in machinery, equipment and employees' wearable clothing can discover aberrations such as gas leakages, high noise levels or crazy heat readings due to bad equipment design failures. There are literally thousands of apps on mobile devices that could help with all sorts of useful things if only they had the right back-end connections too if it had an app for that problem. The IoT network links up these sensors with centralized management systems and supports real-time decision making. For example, if the environment was a chemical plant or mine, then ICT enabled sensors situated There could allow emergency shutdowns and evacuation procedures to start automatically as they detect dangers. This suppresses human error, widens perceptions, and confirms compliance with regulations covering safety.

In the event that employees of Small and Medium Sized Enterprises (SMEs-such as those in the above category) are faced with problems in establishing a solid health and safety framework, it's often because they have little or no resources to put to the task. Predictive analytics powered by AI is an economical remedy which makes use of the data that enterprises already have to prognosticate safety and health risks. Being based on historical data, employee health records, and environmental factors, predictive models can uncover trends and give directions for prevention (Rudin, 2019). The application of AI can already predict the chance of workplace injuries, mental illness and long-term illness among employees and tell businesses what they should do about it to be prepared. SMEs can now fine-tune their workloads, introduce ergonomic designs, or set up a wellness plan aimed at each individual. So by reducing the threat of an injured or sick labor force, predictive analytics not only helps to improve employee well-being but also cuts healthcare costs and gets work done.

AI and digital technology are the tools for implementing a veritable revolution in health and safety standards throughout all businesses. From risk assessment and health monitoring to accident reporting or predictive analyses, these tools are enabling companies to build safer workplaces where fewer accidents happen at work and productivity goes up. Corporations which adopt such technologies not only ensure compliance with regulations but are also demonstrating a firm commitment to their employees' well-being and an operations aesthetic.

4. CHALLENGES AND BARRIERS TO ADOPTION IN SMES

Small and medium-sized empresas (SMEs) are important for driving economic growth, creating jobs and for innovation in various sectors (Wu et al., 2023). But despite their importance, SMEs have encountered a variety of challenges and barriers in adopting new technologies argumentation formerly modern management practices and innovative business models. The key obstacles is that SMEs only have a limited amount of money to spend. Most such businesses work on tight-budgets and have insufficient capital for investment in technology, research and development. Unlike large firms they may find it hard to obtain external finance or loans because they are perceived as risks and so on record for credit. This financial constrain stops them from obtaining advanced technologies-such as artificial intelligence, cloud computing or data analysis-which might otherwise improve productivity and competitiveness.

The other important barrier is that SMEs have too few personnel in short supply of the necessary skills and expertise. Small and medium-sized enterprises are hamstrung by their limited ability to attract and keep skilled staff, neither do they often offer competitive salaries or training opportunities for personal advancement. Many SMEs have little understanding of how advanced technology can help them-and hence are not prepared to change when such skill in encountered among their managers or employees. Add to this the fact that day-to-day activities take up most people's time, leaving few spare moments for reading up on new developments in computer sciences or business management, and you see how wide this knowledge gap actually is. Yet another obstacle is the viewpoint and thinking of the organization resisting change by Small and Medium Size Enterprises. In many small firms, resistance to change has become an ingrained habit or preference (Saadat et al., 2020). Pioneers consider the return on investment when shedding their traditional path with skeptical and uncertain minds; businessmen worry about possible disturbances during that transitional period of reform. Moreover, in terms of infrastructure, SMEs are often devoid of high quality infrastructure such as high speed networks and advanced logistics systems that is particularly true in rural areas or less developed regions.

SMEs often face shortages in establishing partnerships and accessing global markets. Being short on contacts and market visibility can hem them in as regards interacting with large enterprises, research institutions or government agencies, which at the end of the day slows down processes of innovation and adoption. With small businesses on the upsurge in using digital tools and the Internet to do business, threats to cybersecurity and privacy of information are becoming major challenges for them. SMEs with insufficient cyber security protection are even more at risk than before-relying especially upon systems now that they have al l the usual computer viruses to worry about. Their data can be breached;they may suffer financial losses through fraud on the web. Because of regulatory and compliance challenges, SMEs face massive obstacles. Many SMEs do not have the resources or expertise to deal with complex regulatory frameworks, legal requirements, and compliance standards. As a result, inconsistently applied government policies and a lack of targeted support programs for SMEs create even greater uncertainty. This leaves many enterprises to operate in an environment that is akin to a minefield (Kitchin, 2023).

Even so, these barriers are not insurmountable by offering financial incentives, skill development initiatives, infrastructure support, and regulatory clarity, governments, industrial associations, and other stakeholders can play an essential role in resolving these issues. SMEs also need to adopt a forward-looking approach. They should promote a culture of innovation, invest in building up the skills that their workforce needs for tomorrow, and collaborate with technology providers. If these barriers are overcome in a comprehensive way, SMEs will not only be able to take up advanced technologies and modern practices but also become resilient and competitive players in the global economy.

Figure 2. Specifies the challenges and barriers to adoption in SMEs (Source- Self Prepared- Original)

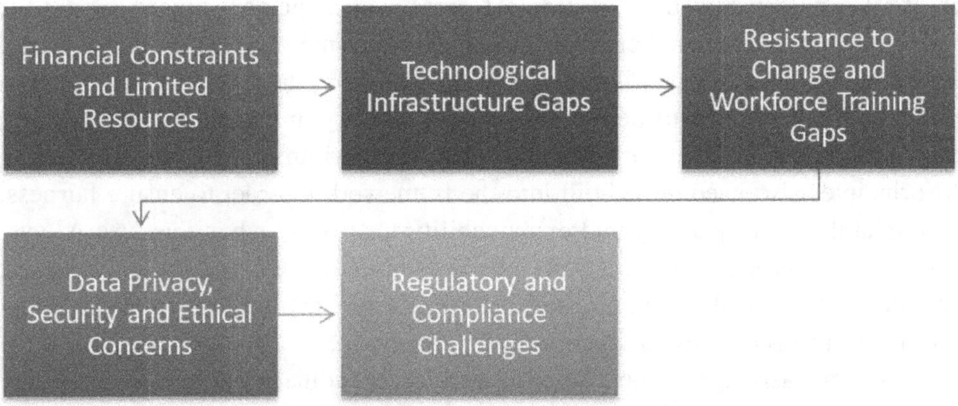

5. STRATEGIC FRAMEWORK FOR AI AND DIGITAL TECHNOLOGY ADOPTION

This strategic framework for AI and digital technology adoption provides an essential blueprint to further and apply the use of such advanced technologies in growing operations for businesses, governments, and industries. It integrates technical, organizational, ethical, and policy considerations, hence providing a comprehensive approach to implementation. The framework is built on the central premise of aligning AI initiatives with strategic organizational objectives. This involves setting goals and criteria for success, fostering a culture of innovation and adaptation, and combining policies into a coordinated whole (Shahid, 2021). Strategic alignment begins with a clear understanding of the organization's vision and mission. It identifies specific areas where AI and digital technologies are best placed to bring unique benefits, such as improving operational efficiency or customer service, aiding decision-making driven by data analysis at all levels of an enterprise, facilitating intelligent products and services development.

It also comes as transparency in communications, inclusiveness and cooperation with stakeholders smooths integration making AI technologies easier for people to accept. Stakeholder engagement is important too because decisions on the adoption of AI have an impact not only on internal teams but also upon customers, regulators, and society at large. Another cornerstone of this framework is data governance, as data is the essential building material for any AI system. Sound management practices for data need to deal with privacy, security, integrity and traceability; they should be consistent with national rules on algorithmic management. Ethical AI principles also need to be built into the framework in order to ensure fairness, accountability, transparency and explainability for people when they use AI systems. These considerations are especially critical in avoiding algorithemic biases, protecting human rights, and making sure that AI applications serve a purpose that is of benefit to people living in the society concerned.

Also, emphasizing the importance of workforce readiness and capacity building. Organizations have got to invest in upskilling and reskilling their workers, give them the technical and soft skills needed for AI and digital technology to be effective employees. This means not only training technical staff but also training leaders and decision-makers to understand the capabilities and limitations of AI systems (Monteiro et al., 2021). Cooperation with educational institutions, research centers, and technology providers also plays a big part in capacity building. Infrastructure readiness is just as crucial because the successful adoption of AI requires powerful technological infrastructure. This includes things like cloud computing, high-speed networks and various IOT devices on the network edge that can serve data distribution needs as well. Investments in scalable secure IT infrastructure secure near-seamless

AI integration also reliable. In addition, to safeguard AI systems against potential attacks and cyber threats, measures of cybersecurity need properly focused attention.

From the policy angle, governments and regulators should be actively involved in offering an enabling environment for AI adoption. This involves drafting forward-looking laws that direct research and innovation on top of facilitating the formation of partnerships between public and private enterprise (Qureshi et al., 2023). The rules themselves must balance the need for technological progress with risks associated with AI - including both job losses, impacts on people's privacy in this computer age and cases of technology going bad. So key performance indicators (KPIs) need to be established to evaluate the effectiveness of AI deployments as how efficient they are, where cost savings come from, what customer satisfaction levels there are waiting on the corporation's service delivery department for any improvement. Establishing these benchmarks in advance will help you keep your efforts from having a negative impact downrange down range any more than necessary due simply to bad planning and ill-conceived project design choices.

Ultimately, having the capacity to scale and sustainability are parts of strategic. Internet of Things (IoT) project does require careful consideration for future volumes of transactions. A strategic framework for AI initiatives therefore demands scalability with which organisations can expect to duplicate AI capabilities across different business functions and in different geographical areas. As we work to transform our world into a digital, it also need to ensure that sustainability is given due consideration. This include measures which reduce the environmental 'footprint' caused by digital transformation-such as energy-saving AI models, environmentally friendly IT practices and so on. At the conclusion, the strategic framework for AI and digital technology adoption calls for an all-round approach that blends technology know-how with ethical responsibility, aggregation-ready personnel, ready-to-use infrastructure, and national support (Leung et al., 2021). Every long-established company or organisation should hold a vision equipped for long-term adaptability and will always try to make continuous improvements. The future of AI and digital technology offers endless possibilities inescapable by any organization that seeks to remain at the cutting edge. AI adoption combined with strategic planning and all types of cooperation can bring completely new forms of innovation, economic growth, and well-being to the society in an increasingly digital world.

6. IMPACT ASSESSMENT AND MONITORING MECHANISMS: KEY PERFORMANCE INDICATORS (KPIS) FOR HEALTH AND SAFETY IN SMES

Impact assessment and means of supervision on occupational health and safety in Small and Medium-sized Enterprises (SMEs) play a role vital in nurturing workplace well-being, meeting regulations and ensuring operational efficiency (Faaique, 2024). SMEs, which constitute the backbone of many economies, often face unique difficulties implementing health and security measures due to resource constraints, small technical skill pools, and the absence of dedicated health and safety departments opposed to their proportion weight. Consequently, defining clear Key Performance Indicators (KPIs) appropriate to each industry's risk factors and different scales of operation is fundamental. KPIs provide quantifiable measures of the effectiveness of health and safety activities, enabling SMEs to identify any loopholes and improve their performance on a continuous basis as they progress.

The number of workplace accidents per 100 to 1,000 staff is a guide to incidence rates, showing the severity and frequency of hazards facing employees. Near-miss reporting frequency is the capture of how quickly potential hazards are recognized and fixed before they materialize into accidents, signifying maturity in an organization's safety culture. Employee training completion rates test whether workers have received adequate safety guidance and are equipped with the knowledge to manage risks. Compliance audit scores show an SME's grade when it comes to regulations governing health and safety as well as its internal norms. In both cases, areas in which improvements are needed are highlighted. The rates for workers' absences due to work injuries or illness provide a proxy for the physical and psychological well-being of workers and a direct measure of both productivity and morale (Pradhan et al., 2024).

Many of these KPIs have effective monitoring mechanisms that involve consistent data collection, analysis and reporting. Digital tools and software platforms specially designed for occupational health safety management are available through SMEs, that let them automate the process of data gathering and reporting through digital tools. Now with handy software means such as these, it becomes much easier for companies of all sizes to follow that analogy in real-time, instead of only afterwards looking at numbers and learning afterward what went wrong or was successful these tools enable Real-time tracking flag set up deviations and prompt For instance, through integrating employee feedback mechanisms such as anonymous surveys and suggestion boxes, it means that the concerns of frontline workers the future directors, are all considered in designing a plan for safety. Regulatory agencies performing regular internal and external audits as well as management reviews of their audit results to provide supplement guidance and oversight too. Their combination acts more effectively against conflict of interests within the system.

Usefully, strategic employment of health and safety KPIs within small and micro-enterprises also helps to secure best practices for occupational safety culture across the organization. Perhaps more important, Mt SME transparent KPI distribution promotes trust, accountability and inclusion as everyone takes responsibility for the occupational health and safety of factoring plant (Kong et al., 2024). These deepening employee engagement with imparts rewards as well as recognition based on KPI performance Incentives such as This can be done in a number of ways, but the result is to build spirit and influence even wider coverage of safety work. For example, monitoring and action plans are one way these changes might begin to take form But a company must also provide more than just a few extremely costly bits of technology. In 1996, the Eighth

Five-Year Plain Five Millennial Plan, will guide SME phase KPI implementation by engaging in thorough feasibility studies beginning with a few critical indicators and expanding gradually this point onward as resources allow. Industry associations and government agencies such as those just mentioned in particular these can also provide SMEs with necessary guidelines. A fully trained work force and well-educated young women are the targets for this stage of our development. KPIs help to ensure that the impact assessment and monitoring mechanisms are effective in order to promote health and safety in SMEs. It enables them achieve appropriate standards for their staff and thereby guarantee a productive future. By looking at quantifiable outcomes, SMEs make it possible not only to be in accordance with regulation but also to create a more secure, healthy or efficient workplace (Aghabiglou et al., 2024). With SMEs' growing awareness of health and safety's strategic importance, the investment made in KPI frameworks and advanced monitoring tools will become an integral part of their long-term presence on the market and future success.

7. CONCLUSION AND FUTURE SCOPE

The integration of cutting-edge AI technology and digital platforms into health and safety management suitable for small and medium-sized enterprises is showing tremendous potential for realizing Sustainable Development Goal 3. The predictive analytics power of AI, the CMS reality through the thin lens of monitoring data is clear. SMEs are able to enhance workplace health and safety standards, lower resource inputs and take a proactive stand in managing health risks Facing such challenges which are almost universally country-specific requires creative policy packages, cross-cutting public-private partnerships and increased technical capabilities. These powerful prediction technologies also can improve efficiency as well.

They help to create safer and healthier work environments, two objectives that tie neatly with the global agenda of sustainability. They must be handled through policy interventions aimed at specific target areas; these have their roots in dialogue between government and industry targeted R & D support that uses private funds during project start-up phase until it reaches a commercial production stage. It is critical that the use of digital technology should be promoted among stakeholders of SMEs in order to ensure smooth transition towards systemization and automation of safety management procedures AI and digital technology, we need to re-examine our regulatory regime, focussing especially on privacy protection for personal data and deployment of ethical AI. As AI and digital technologies continue to mature, it will be necessary to create joint platforms for knowledge-sharing and cross-sectorial cooperation which cut across national boundaries. Such platforms can speed up the deployment of technology and increase its overall impact. Ultimately, to be able to integrate this kind innovation into SME health and safety practices offers not only the prospect of promoting SDG 3 but also carries much promise in promoting all other goals to which humanity is striving on a global basis.

REFERENCES

Aghabiglou, A., Chu, C. S., Dabbech, A., & Wiaux, Y. (2024). The R2D2 deep neural network series paradigm for fast precision imaging in radio astronomy. *arXiv preprint arXiv:2403.05452*.

Ariffin, N. A., Yunus, A. M., & Kadir, I. K. (2021). The role of big data in the healthcare industry. *Journal of Islamic*, *6*(36), 235–245.

Bao, Y., Tang, Z., Li, H., & Zhang, Y. (2019). Computer vision and deep learning–based data anomaly detection method for structural health monitoring. *Structural Health Monitoring*, *18*(2), 401–421.

Behura, A., Sahu, S., & Kabat, M. R. (2021). Advancement of Machine Learning and Cloud Computing in the Field of Smart Health Care. *Machine Learning Approach for Cloud Data Analytics in IoT*, 273-306.

Chen, C. P., & Zhang, C. Y. (2024). Data-intensive applications, challenges, techniques and technologies: A survey on Big Data. *Information sciences, 275*, 314-347. Mayer-Schönberger, V., & Cukier, K. (2013). *Big data: A revolution that will transform how we live, work, and think.* Houghton Mifflin Harcourt.

Faaique, M. (2024). Overview of Big Data Analytics in Modern Astronomy. *International Journal of Mathematics, Statistics, and Computer Science*, *2*, 96–113.

Hilbert, M. (2025). Big data for development: A review of promises and challenges. *Development Policy Review*, *34*(1), 135–174.

Jain, L. (2023). Artificial Intelligence and Machine Learning for Healthcare.

Kashyap, H., Ahmed, H. A., Hoque, N., Roy, S., & Bhattacharyya, D. K. (2023). Big data analytics in bioinformatics: Architectures, techniques, tools and issues. *Network Modeling and Analysis in Health Informatics and Bioinformatics*, *5*, 1–28.

Keikhosrokiani, P. (Ed.). (2022). *Big data analytics for healthcare: datasets, techniques, life cycles, management, and applications*. Academic Press.

Kitchin, R. (2023). Big data and human geography: Opportunities, challenges and risks. *Dialogues in Human Geography*, *3*(3), 262–267.

Kong, W., You, Z., Lyu, S., & Lv, X. (2024). Multi-dimensional stereo face reconstruction for psychological assistant diagnosis in medical meta-universe. *Information Sciences*, *654*, 119831.

Leung, P. H., Chui, K. T., Lo, K., & de Pablos, P. O. (2021). A support vector machine–based voice disorders detection using human voice signal. In *Artificial Intelligence and Big Data Analytics for Smart Healthcare* (pp. 197–208). Academic Press.

Manyika, J., Chui, M., Brown, B., Bughin, J., Dobbs, R., Roxburgh, C., & Hung Byers, A. (2021). Big data: The next frontier for innovation, competition, and productivity.

Marjani, M., Nasaruddin, F., Gani, A., Karim, A., Hashem, I. A. T., Siddiqa, A., & Yaqoob, I. (2017). Big IoT data analytics: architecture, opportunities, and open research challenges. *ieee access, 5*, 5247-5261.

Monteiro, A. C. B., França, R. P., Arthur, R., & Iano, Y. (2021). An overview of medical Internet of Things, artificial intelligence, and cloud computing employed in health care from a modern panorama. *The Fusion of Internet of Things, Artificial Intelligence, and Cloud Computing in Health Care*, 3-23.

Olshannikova, E., Ometov, A., Koucheryavy, Y., & Olsson, T. (2025). Visualizing Big Data with augmented and virtual reality: Challenges and research agenda. *Journal of Big Data*, *2*(1), 1–27.

Pradhan, T., Nimkar, P., & Jhajharia, K. (2024). Machine Learning and Deep Learning for Big Data Analysis. In *Big Data Analytics Techniques for Market Intelligence* (pp. 209–240). IGI Global.

Qureshi, R., Irfan, M., Ali, H., Khan, A., Nittala, A. S., Ali, S., & Alam, T. (2023). Artificial Intelligence and Biosensors in Healthcare and its Clinical Relevance: A Review. *IEEE Access : Practical Innovations, Open Solutions.*

Reddy, B. M. (2023). Amalgamation of Internet of Things and Machine Learning for Smart Healthcare Applications–A Review. *Int. J Comp. Eng. Sci. Res, 5*, 08-36.

Rudin, C. (2019). Stop explaining black box machine learning models for high stakes decisions and use interpretable models instead. *Nature Machine Intelligence, 1*(5), 206–215. PMID: 35603010

Saadat, M. N., & Shuaib, M. (2020). Advancements in deep learning theory and applications: Perspective in 2020 and beyond. *Advances and Applications in Deep Learning, 3.*

Shah, F., Li, J., Shah, Y., & Shah, F. (2017, November). Broad big data domain via medical big data. In *2017 4th International Conference on Systems and Informatics (ICSAI)* (pp. 732-737). IEEE.

Shahid, Z. (2021). Distributed Machine Learning for Anomalous Human Activity Recognition using IoT Systems.

Singh, B. (2024). Evolutionary Global Neuroscience for Cognition and Brain Health: Strengthening Innovation in Brain Science. In *Biomedical Research Developments for Improved Healthcare* (pp. 246-272). IGI Global.

Thapa, C., & Camtepe, S. (2021). Precision health data: Requirements, challenges and existing techniques for data security and privacy. *Computers in Biology and Medicine*, *129*, 104130. PMID: 33271399

Wu, X., Zhu, X., Wu, G. Q., & Ding, W. (2023). Data mining with big data. *IEEE Transactions on Knowledge and Data Engineering*, *26*(1), 97–107.

Zhou, S., Zhang, R., Chen, D., & Zhu, X. (2021). A novel framework for bringing smart big data to proactive decision making in healthcare. *Health Informatics Journal*, *27*(2), 14604582211024698. PMID: 34159834

Chapter 3
AI and Employment Transformation in Canadian SMEs

Adenike Adesanmi
Seneca Polytechnic, Canada

ABSTRACT

The document explores the transformative impact of artificial intelligence (AI) on employment within Canadian small and medium-sized enterprises (SMEs). It highlights how AI technologies, such as machine learning and automation, enhance productivity, optimize decision-making, and personalize customer experiences, thereby fostering innovation and competitiveness. However, SMEs face challenges like financial barriers, a skills gap, and ethical concerns related to job displacement and data privacy. The document emphasizes the need for collaborative efforts from businesses, policymakers, and educators to address these challenges and ensure equitable AI integration, ultimately driving growth and innovation in the Canadian SME sector.

1.0 INTRODUCTION

The evolution of employment in Canada has been marked by significant transitions, from an agrarian economy to industrial capitalism, and now to the era of artificial intelligence (AI). Historically, the Canadian labour market was dominated by agriculture and resource extraction, with a clear division of labour based on gender roles. The Industrial Revolution brought about a shift towards manufacturing and wage-based employment, leading to the rise of labour movements and the establishment of employment standards. Today, the advent of AI is poised to bring

DOI: 10.4018/979-8-3693-9611-7.ch003

another transformative change, particularly in the realm of small and medium-sized enterprises (SMEs).

AI technologies, such as machine learning and automation, are reshaping how SMEs operate by enhancing productivity, optimizing decision-making, and personalizing customer experiences. These technologies enable businesses to streamline operations, reduce costs, and improve customer satisfaction through data-driven insights and automated processes. For instance, AI can help SMEs predict market trends, manage inventory more efficiently, and provide personalized customer interactions, thereby fostering innovation and competitiveness. However, the integration of AI is not without its challenges, as SMEs must navigate financial barriers, a skills gap, and ethical concerns related to job displacement and data privacy.

The successful integration of AI in SMEs requires a collaborative effort from businesses, policymakers, and educators to address these challenges and ensure that the benefits of AI are accessible to all. Government support in the form of subsidies, tax incentives, and grants can help lower financial barriers, while industry-specific training programs can bridge the skills gap. Additionally, clear data privacy regulations and knowledge-sharing initiatives can build trust and confidence in AI adoption. This chapter explores the impact of AI on employment in Canadian SMEs, highlighting both the opportunities and the obstacles that lie ahead, and providing recommendations for stakeholders to facilitate a smooth transition into the AI-driven future.

The discussion section of this chapter delves into the transformative potential of AI for SMEs in Toronto, emphasizing its ability to enhance operational efficiency, customer satisfaction, and profitability. It outlines the opportunities AI presents, such as improved efficiency, cost savings, enhanced customer experiences, and innovation. The section also addresses the challenges SMEs face, including financial barriers, a skills gap, ethical concerns, and hesitancy in traditional sectors. Finally, it offers recommendations for stakeholders, including government support, training programs, knowledge sharing, and data privacy regulations, to help SMEs overcome these challenges and fully leverage AI's potential.

1.1 Transitions in Canadian Labour: From Agrarian Roots to Industrial Capitalism

Before 1850, during the pre-industrial era, the Canadian economy was primarily agrarian, with most labour focused on agriculture and resource extraction. European settlers lived and worked in family units as independent commodity producers, engaging in activities such as farming, fishing, and artisanal crafts. Labour was diverse and demanding, characterized by a division of tasks based on gender: men typically worked in the fields and workshops, while women handled household responsibilities. Although wage labour existed, it was mainly confined to specific sectors like the fur trade, logging, and canal construction, often involving short-term or seasonal work (Darroch, 1983; Heron, 2012).

The transition to industrial capitalism, which began around 1850 and continued until 1890, marked a significant change in employment patterns. The construction of railways and the shift towards cash crop farming stimulated industrial growth. The emergence of factories and new industrial activities led to the formation of a full-time wage-earning workforce. Skilled immigrants from Britain and the United States introduced new industrial work practices and a history of workplace struggles. Jobs became more specialized as employers divided skills into narrower tasks performed by less skilled, lower-paid workers, including women and children. Additionally, the separation between work and home became more pronounced, with families increasingly dependent on wages as their sole source of income (Kealey, 1995; Lightman & Lightman, 2006).

Women entered the paid labour market primarily when their domestic responsibilities allowed them to, often between schooling and marriage. They were typically offered the least skilled jobs, received lower wages, and frequently worked in sectors such as domestic service, textiles, and garment production. The rise of industrial capitalism reinforced patriarchal ideologies that separated the domestic sphere from the public sphere of wage work. This period also saw the emergence of labour movements and struggles. Skilled workers, especially craftsmen, maintained a degree of autonomy and power on the shop floor, which led to the formation of craft unions and strikes. The government began to mediate labour relations by legalizing trade unions and establishing minimum employment standards. Industrial conflict was common as workers resisted the degradation of their labour while employers sought to challenge their control over jobs (Heron, 2012; Sangster, 2016).

The Canadian government played a crucial role in shaping labour dynamics by supporting capitalist employers. It enforced workplace discipline through laws and military intervention during strikes. Additionally, the government introduced some labour protections, including the legalization of trade unions and the establishment of minimum standards for women and children working in mines and factories.

During the initial phase of industrialization, entrepreneurs aimed to assemble a necessary workforce, instill appropriate work discipline, and reduce production costs. They did this by breaking down labour into lower-paid and less-skilled tasks, while also mechanizing processes whenever possible. By the 1890s, the results were mixed. In some industries, such as textiles, complex machinery was operated with relatively low skill requirements. However, many other industries were only partially transformed. The small and unstable Canadian market made it challenging to achieve economies of scale, which led many skilled workers to unite in resistance against any degradation of their labour (Darroch, 1983; Sangster, 2016).

From 1890 to 1940, this era was characterized by the consolidation of monopoly capitalism, marked by significant economic expansion and the rise of large corporations. The transformation of the Canadian economy involved the growth of new industries such as steel, automobiles, chemicals, pulp and paper, meatpacking, and electrical goods. This period also saw the emergence of a more integrated national economy, driven by a national bourgeoisie centered in Montreal and Toronto (Kealey, 1995; Lightman & Lightman, 2006).

The rise of large corporations created a need for centralized coordination of production and more direct control over operating costs. This resulted in the development of cost accounting and systematic management, with a new group of professional managers focused on cutting production costs, particularly labour. Technological advancements, such as the use of electricity and gasoline, along with the introduction of the assembly line in auto plants, transformed various industries and increased the number of machine operators (Darroch, 1983; Sangster, 2016).

The influx of immigrants from Southern and Eastern Europe, China, and Japan resulted in a diverse and stratified labour force. Non-Anglo-Celtic newcomers often occupied the dirtiest, heaviest, and lowest-paid manual jobs. Ethnic tensions and capitalist manipulation further divided the workforce. The expansion of the managerial function and the rise of office work also contributed to the fragmentation of the workforce, leading to a significant increase in the number of female clerical workers. Similarities emerged between the organization of work in factories and offices, characterized by task fragmentation and the mechanization of clerical jobs (Lightman & Lightman, 2006).

The transformation of labour processes in Canada resulted in a decline of craft-dominated production modes, but this change was complex. Many skilled workers experienced a reduction in their tasks, while new skills emerged, leading to a significant rise in the importance of semi-skilled machine operators in production. There was considerable worker turnover, with employees frequently changing jobs (Heron, 2012).

Despite these challenges, many workers resisted the new work environment. They defended familiar workplace routines and demanded living wages. Craft unionism continued to exist, and new industrial unions arose, although corporate employers often opposed unionization efforts. The Canadian government increased its involvement in workplace relations by establishing minimal employment standards and employing state repression to limit workers' militancy (Darroch, 1983; Sangster, 2016).

The transitions of the past have significantly shaped the foundation of Canada's labour market, while modern challenges reflect similar dynamics. The rise of automation, artificial intelligence, and the gig economy mirrors the technological and organizational shifts of the industrial era. Many jobs, especially in manufacturing and retail, are becoming automated, resulting in job displacement and the emergence of new, technology-focused roles (Brynjolfsson & McAfee, 2014). Additionally, Canada's reliance on immigration to address labour shortages echoes historical recruitment efforts. However, racialized and immigrant workers today often face inequities in job access and income, much like their predecessors (Block & Galabuzi, 2018).

The gig economy, characterized by short-term contracts and a lack of job security, can also be compared to the precarious wage labour of earlier periods. Issues of gender equity remain significant, as women continue to be underrepresented in leadership roles despite advancements in workforce participation. Furthermore, the resurgence of union activity especially in the education, healthcare, and technology sectors highlights the ongoing importance of collective bargaining and worker advocacy (Heron, 2012; Sangster, 2016). By understanding these historical struggles and transformations, we can better address the complexities of today's labour market.

The nature of employment in Canada has changed significantly due to evolving economic structures, technological advancements, and shifts in societal norms. Historically, the Canadian economy was primarily agrarian, with most labour concentrated in agriculture and resource extraction (Macdonald, 2014). However, as Canada industrialized in the late 19th and early 20th centuries, the emergence of manufacturing and industrial labour transformed employment dynamics. This shift attracted more workers to urban areas and promoted the growth of stable wage-based employment (Russell, 2018). This transition was characterized by increasing demand for skilled labour and a growing emphasis on workers' rights, leading to the establishment of organized labour movements and forming the foundation for modern employment standards.

The rise of self-employment in Canada accelerated with the emergence of the gig economy. Platforms like Uber and Lyft, which launched in the early 2010s, introduced new employment models and transformed the labour landscape by enabling individuals to earn income independently, bypassing traditional employment structures (Zwick, 2018). These platforms offered flexibility and autonomy, attracting many workers seeking supplementary income or alternative career paths (Moriguchi, 2020). However, this shift also raised concerns regarding job stability, benefits, and workers' rights, as many roles classified as independent contracting lacked the security and protections typically associated with traditional employment (Bai et al., 2021).

1.2 Introduction of Artificial Intelligence (AI) in Employment

Artificial Intelligence (AI) has advanced rapidly in recent years, particularly in areas such as image recognition, natural language processing, and predictive analytics. Unlike previous technological waves that primarily automated routine manual and cognitive tasks, AI can now perform non-routine cognitive functions that were once thought to require human expertise. This represents a significant shift, as AI systems now contribute to fields such as medical diagnostics, fraud detection, and even creative endeavours like content generation (Georgieff and Hyee, 2022).

The impact of AI on employment raises important questions. On one hand, AI automation could displace workers, especially those in roles involving routine tasks. On the other hand, it presents opportunities to enhance productivity and efficiency, allowing workers to focus on higher-value tasks that AI cannot yet accomplish. Notably, the adoption of AI is expected to disproportionately affect medium- to high-skilled occupations, particularly in sectors that heavily rely on digital technologies. For example, jobs in financial services, and manufacturing, may undergo significant transformations as AI continues to automate and augment complex processes (Felten et al., 2019; Lane and Saint-Martin, 2021).

The consequences of AI on employment are complex and vary across different sectors and job types. While there is little empirical evidence of widespread AI-driven worker displacement, certain high-skill professions could see wage growth due to the productivity increases that AI provides. Conversely, workers with low digital skills may struggle to adapt to these changes, potentially exacerbating inequalities in the labour market. Therefore, the successful integration of AI in employment depends on targeted policies to upskill the workforce and ensure equitable access to AI-driven opportunities (Acemoglu et al., 2020).

The introduction of AI in employment has become a topic of increasing academic interest, particularly since 2019. A systematic review of literature from 2008 to 2020 highlights that AI's role in employment has grown alongside the enhanced capabilities of machines to perform tasks traditionally performed by humans. This change is driven by advancements in machine learning and automation technologies, which have enabled AI to manage both repetitive and predictable tasks, consequently affecting various sectors (Autor, 2015; Frey & Osborne, 2017).

The impact of artificial intelligence (AI) on employment is complex and multifaceted. On one hand, AI is expected to boost productivity and economic growth by automating routine tasks, which could create new job categories and opportunities. On the other hand, there are legitimate concerns about job displacement, particularly for medium-skill positions that are most vulnerable to automation. This could lead to a shrinking middle class and an increasing divide between high-skill, high-wage jobs and low-skill, low-wage jobs (Goos & Manning, 2007; Autor, Katz & Kearney, 2008).

Jobs that are likely to be most affected by AI include those in the service sector, manufacturing, and administrative roles. Positions that involve routine, manual, or clerical tasks face a higher risk of being automated. In contrast, jobs requiring complex problem-solving, creativity, and interpersonal skills are less likely to be replaced by AI. Existing literature indicates that while AI will undoubtedly transform the job market, the extent and nature of its impact will depend on various factors, such as policy responses and the adaptability of the workforce (Huang & Rust, 2018; Arntz, Gregory & Zierahn, 2017).

The introduction of AI has marked a significant shift in employment, with advancements making AI outputs indistinguishable from human work in some areas. AI systems can perceive environments, process data using advanced algorithms, and autonomously provide predictions, recommendations, or decisions. Since 2019, the adoption of AI in workplaces has been driven by declining costs and the emergence of skilled AI professionals, potentially signalling an AI revolution that could affect all sectors and occupations (OECD, 2023).

AI presents both opportunities and challenges for employment. Its ability to automate repetitive and non-routine cognitive tasks has allowed businesses to enhance productivity, reduce costs, and improve the quality of goods and services. Workers with relevant digital and AI-related skills are likely to benefit from higher wages and more engaging roles. However, job displacement remains a concern, especially for tasks that AI can perform efficiently, such as data analysis, information organization, and perceptual tasks. High-skilled professions, including business management, legal services, and engineering, are particularly vulnerable to advancements in AI (Lane, Williams, & Broecke, 2023).

Although AI adoption in workplaces is still relatively low, large organizations are at the forefront, especially in manufacturing and finance. The main obstacles to broader AI implementation are costs and skill gaps. Additionally, ethical challenges—such as the risks of bias, increased work intensity, and privacy concerns—underscore the need for effective regulations and policies. It is essential to ensure a trustworthy and human-centered integration of AI, along with proactive measures like worker training and collective bargaining, to mitigate risks and fully leverage its potential in the employment landscape (OECD, 2023).

1.3 SMEs in Canada

SMEs form the backbone of Canada's economy, representing a diverse and dynamic sector that spans numerous industries. These businesses are not just economic contributors, they are job creators, innovators, and vital players in shaping the nation's future growth. Whether it's a local coffee shop, a family-run construction firm, or a fast-growing tech startup, SMEs play an essential and evolving role in Canada's economic landscape (Canada, Industry Canada, Canadian Electronic Library, & Coherent Digital, 2003).

SMEs collectively make up the largest share of Canada's workforce. According to the Survey on Financing and Growth of Small and Medium Enterprises, a small business is defined as one with fewer than 100 employees, including those without any reported employment. A medium-sized enterprise falls within the range of 100 to 499 employees, while any business exceeding 500 employees is classified as a large enterprise. The distribution of SMEs across industries is as varied as their impact. The largest concentration is found in the construction sector, accounting for 16.3% of all SMEs. This is followed by professional, scientific, and technical services (14.6%), retail trade (11%), accommodation and food services (7.8%), and transportation and warehousing (7.1%). Beyond these primary sectors, over one-fifth (20.6%) of SMEs operate in a broader category encompassing industries such as real estate, waste management, health care, social assistance, and arts and entertainment. Some industries have a smaller yet still significant SME presence. Service industries—including repair and maintenance, personal care, religious, and civic services—account for 6.8% of SMEs. Meanwhile, agriculture, forestry, fishing, hunting, mining, and oil and gas extraction make up 5.8% of SMEs. Manufacturing represents 5.3%, and wholesale trade rounds out the sector with 4.8% (Statistics Canada, 2022).

Despite their size, SMEs have an outsized impact on Canada's economy. They foster innovation, provide employment opportunities, and contribute to the country's long-term economic resilience.

The COVID-19 pandemic had a significant impact on the workforce of small and medium-sized enterprises (SMEs) in Canada. In April 2020, many Canadian businesses faced severe economic challenges, with revenue losses exceeding 20% due to decreased demand for their products (Statistics Canada, 2020a, 2020b). SMEs, which employed up to 69.9% of the private labour force in 2018 and were responsible for 57% of employment growth between 2013 and 2018 (Innovation, Science and Economic Development Canada, 2019), were especially hard hit.

In response to these challenges, the Canadian government implemented various programs to support businesses, particularly SMEs. These initiatives included measures to ease cash flow pressures and increase the availability of credit, helping businesses adapt to the new economic realities and better serve their clients and employees. The pandemic highlighted the critical role of SMEs in the Canadian economy and underscored the need for targeted support to sustain their operations and workforce during such unprecedented times.

2.0 IMPACT OF AI ON EMPLOYMENT

The impact of AI on employment is theoretically ambiguous, as it involves a complex interplay of displacement, productivity, and reinstatement effects (OECD, 2023). AI can displace human labour by automating tasks that were previously performed by workers, leading to job losses in certain sectors. However, AI can also enhance productivity, create new tasks, and generate demand for labour in other areas. The net effect on employment depends on which of these forces dominates.

1. **Displacement Effect**: AI can automate routine and non-routine cognitive tasks, potentially leading to job displacement. For example, occupations in finance, medicine, and legal activities, which require significant education and experience, are increasingly at risk of automation (OECD, 2023). This displacement effect is particularly concerning for high-skilled workers who perform tasks that AI can now replicate, such as information ordering and perceptual speed (Felten, Raj, & Seamans, 2019).
2. **Productivity Effect**: AI can increase productivity by automating tasks, reducing costs, and enabling firms to produce more goods and services. This can lead to higher demand for labour in sectors that are not directly affected by AI. For instance, if a firm automates part of its production process, the cost savings could be passed on to consumers, leading to increased demand for the firm's products and, consequently, more jobs in other areas of the business (Acemoglu & Restrepo, 2019).
3. **Reinstatement Effect**: AI can create new tasks and jobs that did not exist before. For example, the development and maintenance of AI systems require skilled workers, such as data scientists and AI engineers. Additionally, AI can create demand for workers who can complement AI technologies, such as those with strong computer skills (OECD, 2023).

Empirical evidence so far suggests that the net impact of AI on employment has been relatively small. Studies have found little to no significant negative employment effects due to AI (Georgieff & Hyee, 2021). However, this could be because AI adoption is still in its early stages, and the full effects may not yet be detectable.

AI affects different job types in varying ways. High-skilled occupations, particularly those involving non-routine cognitive tasks, are the most exposed to AI. Examples include business professionals, managers, and science and engineering professionals (OECD, 2023). Despite this exposure, high-skilled workers have seen employment gains relative to lower-skilled workers over the past decade. This may be because AI creates new tasks and jobs for workers with complementary skills (Felten, Raj, & Seamans, 2019).

In contrast, low-skilled workers may face declining employment prospects due to AI. Occupations such as food preparation assistants, agricultural labourers, and cleaners are less exposed to AI but may still be affected by broader automation trends (OECD, 2023). These workers often lack the skills needed to transition to new roles created by AI, making them more vulnerable to displacement.

It may be too early to detect the full impact of AI on employment. AI adoption rates remain relatively low, and firms are still in the process of understanding how to best deploy AI technologies (OECD, 2023). Additionally, firms may be reluctant to lay off workers in the short term, preferring to adjust labour demand through natural attrition, such as retirements and voluntary quits (Milanez, 2023). This gradual adjustment could delay the observable effects of AI on employment.

Moreover, recent advances in generative AI, such as large language models (LLMs) like ChatGPT, have the potential to significantly expand the range of tasks that can be automated. While early estimates suggest that the impact of LLMs on employment may not differ qualitatively from previous AI technologies, the rapid pace of innovation in this area means that the full effects are still uncertain (Felten, Raj, & Seamans, 2023).

2.1 Skills Transformation in an AI-Driven Economy

The adoption of AI has increased the demand for new skills in Canadian SMEs. Essential competencies for employees in AI-integrated roles now include data literacy, technical problem-solving, and adaptability (Bessen, 2019). Canada is facing a significant skills gap, as many SMEs struggle to find employees with the necessary digital and technical skills. These skill gaps not only limit the competitiveness of SMEs but also prevent them from fully capitalizing on AI technologies (Tambe et al., 2020).

To address this, Canadian SMEs are increasingly adopting reskilling and upskilling programs. For example, some SMEs collaborate with educational institutions or leverage online courses to help employees gain proficiency in AI-related skills. This shift aligns with research by Tufekci (2016), which emphasizes the importance of ongoing learning in a technology-driven workplace. By investing in workforce training, SMEs can foster an adaptable, AI-savvy workforce that enhances their competitiveness and resilience in the evolving job market.

2.2 Artificial Intelligence in the Small and Medium-sized (SMEs) Companies

The era of artificial intelligence (AI) is ushering in a transformative phase in the job market. AI-driven technologies, such as machine learning and automation, are changing job functions and the skills required across various sectors (Brynjolfsson & McAfee, 2017). While some people worry that AI may result in job displacement, particularly in routine or repetitive roles, others believe it will create opportunities for job enhancement and new positions that need technical, analytical, and creative skills (Autor & Salomons, 2018). In small and medium-sized enterprises (SMEs), AI has played a crucial role in optimizing operations, improving decision-making, and personalizing customer experiences, helping these businesses remain competitive (Lund & Manyika, 2019).

Furthermore, employment in the AI era is marked by a rising demand for tech-savvy and adaptable workers who can effectively use AI tools across various functions, including business intelligence and customer service. For instance, in Canada, small and medium-sized enterprises (SMEs) are increasingly depending on AI-driven insights to inform their strategic decision-making, which is creating more opportunities for roles such as data analysts and AI specialists (Davenport & Kirby, 2016). As AI continues to transform job responsibilities and employment patterns, both workers and employers need to understand its impact on SMEs in Canada to navigate this rapidly evolving landscape.

AI technologies are reshaping how SMEs operate, allowing them to harness the power of automation, machine learning, and data-driven decision-making to increase productivity and competitiveness (Ding & Su, 2021). Commonly adopted AI tools in Canadian SMEs include chatbots for customer service, predictive analytics in sales and marketing, and robotic process automation (RPA) in manufacturing (Kietzmann et al., 2018). According to a study by Clemente-Almendros et al. (2024), retail, manufacturing, healthcare, and tech are among the sectors most active in AI adoption within SMEs, with each sector focusing on specific applications based on operational needs. In the manufacturing industry, for instance, SMEs use AI-driven quality control and predictive maintenance systems to reduce production errors and downtime, helping them maintain cost efficiency and minimize waste (West & Allen, 2018). Retail SMEs leverage AI to enhance customer insights and provide personalized shopping experiences, a practice that is increasingly critical for retaining market share amid larger competitors (Acemoglu & Restrepo, 2019).

2.3 AI's Impact on Employment Patterns in SMEs

The adoption of AI in SMEs is reshaping employment patterns by automating certain tasks while augmenting others, resulting in a mix of job displacement and job creation (Bessen, 2019). In some cases, AI has reduced the demand for manual, repetitive roles. A study by Arntz et al. (2017) found that AI has led to job displacement in specific SMEs where tasks like data entry, logistics coordination, and basic accounting functions have become automated. However, the study highlights that AI can also enhance certain job roles by freeing employees from routine tasks, enabling them to focus on higher-value activities, such as strategic planning and customer engagement (Acemoglu & Restrepo, 2019).

In SMEs across various sectors, AI has created new job opportunities that require advanced analytical, technical, and digital skills. For example, roles such as data analysts, AI implementation managers, and digital transformation specialists are increasingly in demand, especially in technology and healthcare SMEs that aim to make data-driven decisions and optimize their operations (Brynjolfsson & McElheran, 2016). These emerging positions highlight the necessity for a workforce that can effectively utilize AI tools to promote growth within SMEs, emphasizing the significant impact AI has on employment in these organizations (Przegalinska et al., 2025).

2.4 Preparing SMEs for AI-Driven Workforce Changes

For many SMEs, preparing for AI-driven workforce changes presents unique challenges, including financial constraints and the need for specialized training. Budgetary limitations often prevent smaller businesses from accessing high-cost AI training programs, while a lack of in-house expertise further complicates AI implementation (Kejriwal, 2023). Additionally, SMEs may struggle to foster a culture of continuous learning, which is critical for employees to stay updated on emerging AI applications (Brynjolfsson et al., 2018).

To address these challenges, best practices have emerged for SME leaders, emphasizing the importance of fostering a learning-oriented work culture. Leaders are encouraged to create internal programs for skill development, encourage cross-functional training, and promote flexible learning opportunities that accommodate diverse schedules (Olusanya, 2021). Furthermore, government policies and industry support play a crucial role in this transition. For example, policy incentives, grants, and training initiatives aimed at enhancing digital skills can make AI adoption more feasible for SMEs. Research highlights the role of government-backed reskilling programs, which are essential for easing the workforce transition and equipping SMEs to harness AI effectively (Acemoglu & Restrepo, 2019).

3.0 METHODOLOGY AND CASE STUDIES

The Canadian government is investing substantially in artificial intelligence (AI) to support small and medium-sized enterprises (SMEs). Through the AI Compute Access Fund and the Canadian AI Sovereign Compute Strategy, the government has allocated $2 billion over five years to help Canadian researchers, start-ups, and scale-up businesses access the necessary computational power. Additionally, $100 million over five years will be provided to the National Research Council's AI Assist Program to help SMEs build and deploy new AI solutions, enhancing productivity and innovation across the country (Government of Canada, 2024).

The Canadian government aims to regulate AI in small and medium-sized businesses (SMEs) through the proposed Artificial Intelligence and Data Act (AIDA). This act is designed to ensure the responsible design, development, and deployment of AI systems. It includes requirements for businesses to identify and address risks related to harm and bias, maintain relevant records, and ensure users understand the intended uses and limitations of their AI systems. The AIDA also introduces governance mechanisms and policies to ensure the safety and fairness of high-impact AI systems, supporting responsible innovation while considering the needs of SMEs (Innovation, Science and Economic Development Canada, 2024).

3.1 AI Adoption by Industry

The percentage of businesses using AI in producing goods and delivering services varies significantly across industries:

Table 1. Industry and AI adoption rate

Industry	AI Adoption (%)
Information and Cultural Industries	20.9
Professional, Scientific and Technical Services	13.7
Finance and Insurance	10.9
Agriculture, Forestry, Fishing and Hunting	0.7
Accommodation and Food Services	0.9
Mining, Quarrying, and Oil and Gas Extraction	1.6

The data shows that AI adoption is highest in the Information and Cultural Industries (20.9%) and Professional, Scientific and Technical Services (13.7%). These sectors are likely leveraging AI for tasks such as data analysis, content creation, and technical problem-solving. In contrast, industries like Agriculture, Forestry,

Fishing and Hunting (0.7%) and Accommodation and Food Services (0.9%) have much lower adoption rates, possibly due to less immediate applicability or higher implementation costs.

Table 2. Plans to adopt AI by business age

Business Age	Plans to Adopt AI (%)
10 years or less	31.0
11 years or more	18.7

From the table above, newer businesses (10 years or less) are more inclined to adopt AI, with 31.0% planning to do so, compared to 18.7% of older businesses (11 years or more). This trend suggests that new companies might be more agile and open to integrating new technologies to gain a competitive edge.

The overall AI adoption and plans for future adoption among businesses in Canada are as follows:

Figure 1. Overall AI adoption in business (Source - Statistics Canada, 2024)

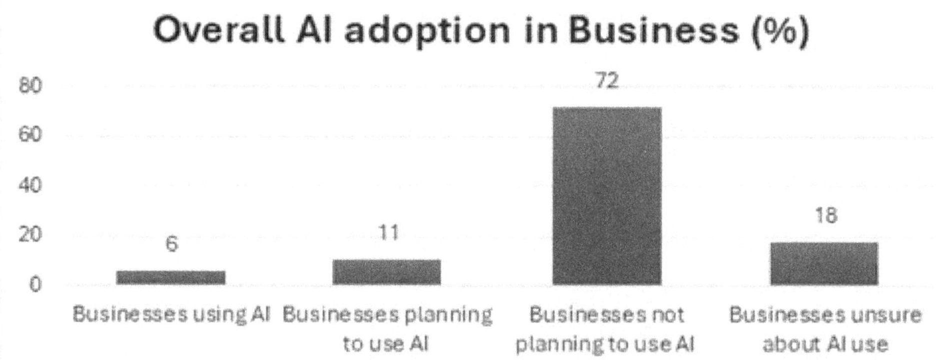

The following explains the bars in Figure 1 above.

Businesses Using AI: This category represents the percentage of businesses that have already integrated AI into their operations. The adoption rate indicates how many companies are currently leveraging AI technologies to enhance efficiency, decision-making, and innovation. The exact percentage isn't provided, but this group is likely to be the smallest among the four categories, as AI adoption is still growing.

Businesses Planning to Use AI: This segment includes companies that have recognized the potential benefits of AI and are in the process of planning its implementation. This group is crucial as it shows the growing interest and commitment to adopting AI in the near future. The percentage here is likely higher than those already using AI, reflecting a trend towards increased adoption.
Businesses Not Planning to Use AI: This category represents companies that have decided against adopting AI technologies. The reasons could vary from a lack of understanding of AI's benefits, perceived high costs, or the belief that AI is not relevant to their industry. The size of this group provides insight into the barriers to AI adoption.
Businesses Unsure About AI Use: This segment includes companies that are undecided about whether to adopt AI. They may be evaluating the potential benefits and challenges or waiting to see how AI adoption plays out in their industry. This group is significant as it represents potential future adopters if they can be convinced of AI's value.

4.0 DATA COLLECTION FROM SMES

This section outlines the methodology and findings from a survey conducted to examine the potential impact of artificial intelligence (AI) on small and medium-sized businesses in Toronto. The survey aimed to gather insights from business owners and employees about how AI might influence daily operations, workforce dynamics, and future business strategies. By analyzing the responses, the study seeks to identify the opportunities and challenges that AI presents to these businesses.

A total of 40 businesses from various sectors participated in the survey, including retail, technology services, e-commerce, construction, tourism, and fashion. The survey was conducted by providing businesses with links to complete the questionnaire online, ensuring convenience and accessibility for all participants.

Ethical considerations were paramount in the design and implementation of the survey to ensure the integrity and confidentiality of the data collected. Informed consent was incorporated into the survey link, meaning participants had to agree to the terms before proceeding with the survey. This ensured that all participants were fully informed about the purpose of the survey, the nature of the questions, and how their data would be utilized. No email addresses were required from respondents, further protecting their anonymity and privacy.

Participation in the survey was entirely voluntary, and respondents were informed that they could withdraw at any time without facing any consequences. This assurance ensured that participants did not feel coerced or obligated to complete the survey. The confidentiality of the respondents was strictly maintained, with personal identifiers removed from the dataset to guarantee anonymity. The data was analyzed in aggregate form, and individual responses were not disclosed, thus protecting the privacy of the participants.

Measures were implemented to secure the data collected from the survey. The online survey platform used encrypted connections to safeguard the data during transmission. Additionally, access to the data was restricted to authorized personnel only, ensuring that the information remained secure and confidential. The survey was thoughtfully designed to avoid any potential harm to the participants. Questions were framed in a manner that did not cause distress or discomfort, focusing on gathering insights about AI's impact on business operations and workforce dynamics while steering clear of sensitive or intrusive topics.

The survey process was transparent, with participants informed about how their data would be used and the potential benefits of the research. This transparency helped build trust and encouraged honest and accurate responses. By adhering to these ethical principles, the survey respected the participants' rights and privacy, thereby enhancing the reliability and validity of the findings. The insights gained from the survey provide valuable information on the opportunities and challenges that AI presents to SMEs in Toronto, guiding future strategies for AI adoption and integration.

4.1 Analysis of the Dataset

This section delves into the analysis of the dataset collected from small and medium-sized enterprises (SMEs) in Toronto, focusing on their familiarity with artificial intelligence (AI), sources of AI learning, areas of business benefiting from AI, challenges to AI adoption, and the anticipated impact of AI. The analysis reveals varying levels of AI familiarity across different industries, with tech-forward sectors like retail, technology services, e-commerce, and financial services leading the way. In contrast, traditional sectors such as construction, tourism, and fashion show lower familiarity, highlighting a gap in awareness and understanding of AI's potential.

Questions in the survey were designed to capture the following information.

1. Familiarity with AI

The data reveals that most small and medium-sized enterprises (SMEs) in Toronto are either “Somewhat Familiar” or “Very Familiar” with artificial intelligence (AI). Industries such as retail, technology services, e-commerce, and financial services lead to AI familiarity due to their inherent reliance on data and technology. However, traditional sectors such as construction, tourism, and fashion report lower familiarity, indicating a gap in awareness and understanding of AI's potential.

Key Insight:

This disparity in AI familiarity reflects varying levels of technological integration across industries. While tech-forward sectors are actively exploring AI, traditional industries may require targeted educational initiatives to increase awareness and bridge this knowledge gap.

2. Sources of AI Learning

Online blogs, webinars, and industry conferences are the most popular sources of AI knowledge across industries, particularly in technology services and financial services. Interestingly, peer recommendations are a critical source of information for sectors like food & beverage and construction, indicating the importance of trust and community-driven learning.

Key Insight:

For industries relying heavily on peer recommendations, case studies and success stories from similar businesses can be a powerful tool to encourage AI adoption. Moreover, creating accessible online resources tailored to specific industries can enhance AI literacy across sectors.

3. Areas of Business to Benefit from AI

Small and medium-sized enterprises (SMEs) are increasingly recognizing the potential of artificial intelligence (AI) to transform various aspects of their operations. In the realm of marketing and sales, sectors such as retail, e-commerce, and fashion are prioritizing AI to deliver personalized customer experiences. By leveraging AI, these industries can analyze vast amounts of customer data to tailor marketing strategies and product recommendations, thereby enhancing customer satisfaction and loyalty.

In the field of customer service, industries like healthcare, education, and tourism view AI as a powerful tool to improve client interactions and response times. AI-powered chatbots and virtual assistants can handle routine inquiries, allowing human agents to focus on more complex issues. This not only enhances the efficiency of customer service operations but also ensures that clients receive timely and accurate information.

Inventory and supply chain management is another area where AI is making significant inroads, particularly in the manufacturing and logistics sectors. AI algorithms can optimize inventory levels, predict demand, and streamline supply chain processes, reducing costs and improving operational efficiency. This is crucial for industries that rely on precise inventory management to meet customer demands and minimize waste.

Innovation is a key focus for technology services and manufacturing sectors, where AI is driving product and service development. By harnessing AI, these industries can accelerate research and development, identify new market opportunities, and create innovative solutions that meet evolving customer needs. AI's ability to analyze trends and predict future developments makes it an invaluable asset for companies looking to stay ahead of the competition.

Key Insight:

Different industries prioritize AI applications based on their operational needs. Customer-facing industries focus on AI for service enhancement, while operationally intensive sectors leverage it for process optimization. These insights can guide AI solution providers to develop industry-specific tools that address the unique challenges and opportunities within each sector.

4. Challenges to AI Adoption

Despite the promising potential of AI, SMEs face several challenges in adopting these technologies. The cost of AI tools and implementation is the most cited challenge across industries. Many SMEs operate on tight budgets and may find it difficult to justify the initial investment required for AI adoption. This financial barrier can hinder the widespread adoption of AI, particularly among smaller businesses.

Another significant challenge is the lack of skilled personnel, which is particularly pronounced in traditional sectors like construction and tourism. These industries often struggle to find employees with the technical expertise needed to implement and manage AI systems. This skills gap can slow down the adoption process and limit the effectiveness of AI solutions.

Data security and privacy concerns are primary issues for data-intensive industries such as healthcare and financial services. The sensitive nature of the data handled by these sectors makes them wary of potential breaches and misuse. Ensuring robust data security frameworks is essential to gaining the trust of these industries and encouraging AI adoption.

Uncertainty about the return on investment (ROI) is another challenge for SMEs hesitant to invest in new technologies. Without clear evidence of the financial benefits, businesses may be reluctant to allocate resources to AI projects. Demonstrating tangible ROI through pilot projects and industry-specific case studies can help build confidence in AI's potential.

Key Insight:

Addressing these challenges requires a multi-faceted approach, including affordable AI solutions, workforce upskilling programs, and robust data security frameworks. Government grants and subsidies could also alleviate financial constraints for SMEs, making AI adoption more accessible.

5. Likelihood of AI Impact

Industries such as retail, e-commerce, technology services, and financial services are highly optimistic about AI's impact on profitability within the next five years. These sectors recognize the potential of AI to enhance efficiency, reduce costs, and drive revenue growth. Conversely, sectors like construction and food & beverage exhibit skepticism, citing a neutral or unlikely impact. These industries may be more cautious due to the perceived complexity and cost of AI implementation.

Key Insight:

Proactive sectors are poised to gain a competitive edge, while hesitant industries risk lagging. Demonstrating tangible ROI through pilot projects and industry-specific case studies can build confidence in AI's potential and encourage broader adoption.

6. Potential Positive and Negative Impacts

The anticipated positive impacts of AI include faster response times, cost savings, and improved customer satisfaction. These benefits are particularly relevant for customer-facing industries that prioritize efficient and effective service delivery. Process automation and delivery optimization are highlighted by manufacturing and logistics sectors, where AI can streamline operations and reduce operational costs.

However, there are also concerns about the negative impacts of AI. Job displacement and high initial costs are common worries, as AI systems can replace certain roles and require significant upfront investment. Data security risks are particularly worrisome for healthcare and financial services, where the protection of sensitive information is paramount.

Key Insight:

While AI offers significant operational benefits, ethical and financial concerns must be addressed. Policies ensuring data protection and employee reskilling can mitigate negative impacts, ensuring that the transition to AI is both beneficial and equitable for all stakeholders.

7. Skills and Training for AI Integration

The most important skills identified include data analysis, critical thinking, and AI troubleshooting. Most SMEs, especially in tech-heavy industries, are already providing or considering training programs. However, traditional sectors report less enthusiasm for workforce upskilling.

Key Insight:

Customized training programs tailored to specific industry needs can facilitate smoother AI integration. For hesitant sectors, offering government-supported training initiatives could encourage participation.

8. AI Strategy Over the Next 1-2 Years

Industries like retail, technology services, and e-commerce are actively planning to implement AI tools. In contrast, the construction, tourism, and fashion industries are more hesitant, opting to wait for competitors to adopt AI before acting.

Key Insight:

Early adopters will likely gain a significant competitive advantage. Encouraging hesitant industries through pilot programs and shared success stories can inspire confidence in AI adoption.

AI presents a transformative opportunity for SMEs in Toronto. However, to unlock its full potential, a collaborative effort between businesses, policymakers, and educators is essential. Bridging the gap between early adopters and hesitant industries will ensure that AI's benefits are accessible to all.

Figure 2. Familiarity with AI across industries

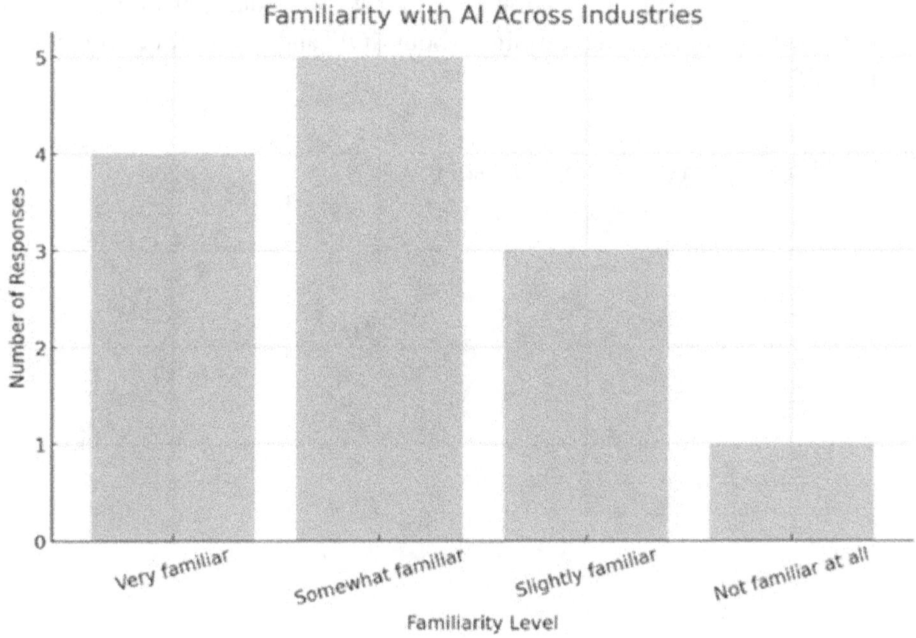

This bar chart in Figure 2 shows that most respondents are "Somewhat Familiar" or "Very Familiar" with AI, but there is still a significant portion that is only "Slightly Familiar" or "Not Familiar at All."

Figure 3. Challenges to AI adoption

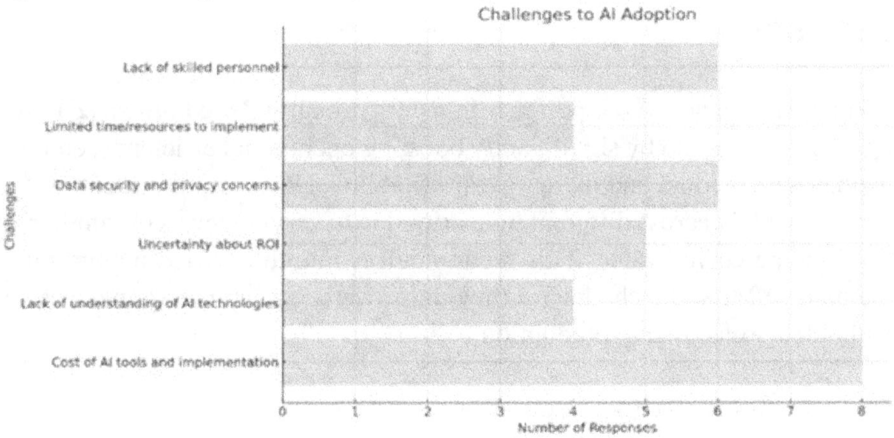

The horizontal bar chart in Figure 3 highlights the key barriers to AI adoption. “Cost of AI tools and implementation” and “Lack of skilled personnel” are the most cited challenges, while “Uncertainty about ROI” and “Privacy concerns” also present significant hurdles.

Figure 4. AI strategy over the next 1-2 years

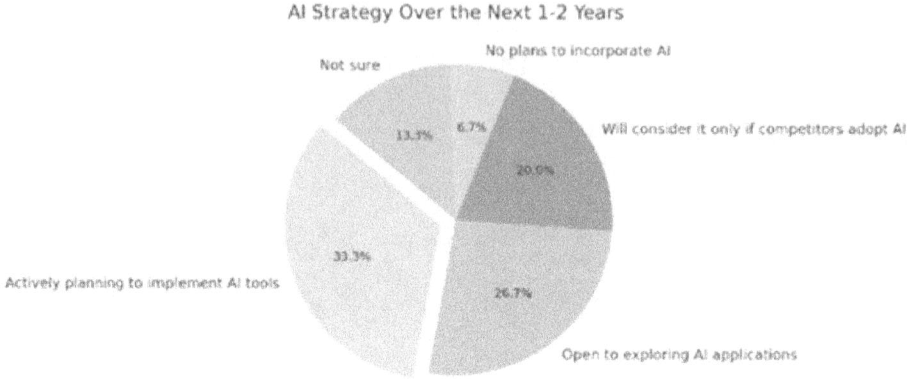

The pie chart in Figure 4 illustrates that a significant percentage of businesses are “Actively planning to implement AI tools” or are “Open to exploring AI applications.” However, a notable portion remains hesitant, either waiting for competitors or being unsure about their plans.

5.0 DISCUSSION

Artificial Intelligence (AI) is poised to transform Small and Medium-sized Enterprises (SMEs) in Toronto by significantly boosting operational efficiency, enhancing customer satisfaction, and increasing profitability. However, the extent of AI's impact varies widely across different industries due to varying levels of familiarity, readiness, and perceived value. This section delves into the myriad opportunities AI presents for SMEs, the challenges they must overcome, and recommendations for stakeholders to facilitate AI adoption.

Opportunities for SMEs

1. Improved Efficiency: AI can streamline various business processes, such as supply chain management, marketing, and customer service. For instance, AI-powered tools can optimize inventory levels, predict demand, and

automate routine customer interactions, freeing up human resources for more strategic tasks. This not only enhances productivity but also allows businesses to respond more swiftly to market changes and customer needs.

2. Cost Savings: By automating repetitive and time-consuming tasks, AI allows businesses to reduce labour costs and allocate resources more effectively. This can lead to significant savings, especially for SMEs operating on tight budgets. For example, chatbots can handle customer inquiries 24/7, reducing the need for a large customer service team. Additionally, AI-driven analytics can identify cost-saving opportunities in areas such as energy consumption and supply chain logistics.
3. Enhanced Customer Experiences: AI enables businesses to offer personalized experiences and faster response times, which can greatly improve customer satisfaction and loyalty. Personalized recommendations, tailored marketing campaigns, and instant support through AI-driven chatbots are just a few ways AI can enhance the customer journey. By leveraging AI, businesses can gain deeper insights into customer preferences and behaviours, allowing them to anticipate needs and deliver more relevant and engaging experiences.
4. Innovation: AI opens up new avenues for innovation by enabling businesses to develop new products, services, and business models. For example, AI can help identify market trends, predict consumer behaviour, and even assist in the creation of new, data-driven products that meet emerging customer needs. This innovative potential can give SMEs a competitive edge, allowing them to differentiate themselves in the market and capture new growth opportunities.

Challenges to Overcome

1. Financial Barriers: The high costs associated with implementing AI technologies can be a significant deterrent for smaller businesses. Initial investments in AI infrastructure, software, and training can be substantial, making it challenging for SMEs to adopt these technologies without financial support. Moreover, ongoing maintenance and updates can add to the financial burden, requiring careful budgeting and resource allocation.
2. Skills Gap: A lack of skilled personnel who can effectively utilize AI is another major hurdle. SMEs often struggle to find and retain employees with the necessary expertise in AI and data science, which can hinder their ability to fully leverage AI's potential. This skills gap can slow down the implementation process and limit the effectiveness of AI solutions, making it crucial for businesses to invest in training and development.
3. Ethical Concerns: The adoption of AI raises several ethical issues, including job displacement and data privacy. As AI automates more tasks, there is a risk of job losses, particularly in roles that involve routine, manual work.

Additionally, the use of AI involves handling large amounts of data, raising concerns about data security and privacy. Businesses must navigate these ethical challenges carefully, ensuring that AI is implemented in a way that is fair, transparent, and respectful of individual rights.

4. Hesitancy in Traditional Sectors: Industries that have traditionally been slow to adopt new technologies may be hesitant to embrace AI. Without targeted support and education, these sectors risk falling behind, missing out on the benefits that AI can bring. Overcoming this hesitancy requires a concerted effort to demonstrate the value of AI and provide the necessary resources and guidance to facilitate adoption.

5.1 Recommendations for Stakeholders

1. **Government Support**: To lower financial barriers, governments can offer subsidies, tax incentives, and grants to encourage AI adoption among SMEs. This financial aid can help offset the initial costs and make AI technologies more accessible to smaller businesses. Additionally, government-backed initiatives can provide SMEs with access to AI research and development resources, fostering innovation and collabouration.
2. **Training Programs**: Industry-specific upskilling initiatives can address the skills gap by preparing the workforce for AI integration. Training programs and certifications in AI and data science can equip employees with the necessary skills to implement and manage AI solutions effectively. Partnerships between educational institutions and industry can also play a crucial role in developing a talent pipeline that meets the evolving needs of businesses.
3. **Knowledge Sharing**: Sharing success stories, case studies, and best practices through webinars, workshops, and peer-led discussions can build confidence in AI adoption. By showcasing the tangible benefits of AI, businesses can learn from each other and overcome hesitations. Creating a community of practice where SMEs can exchange ideas and experiences can further accelerate the adoption of AI technologies.
4. **Data Privacy Regulations**: Clear policies and frameworks around data privacy and security are essential to mitigate concerns. Establishing robust data protection regulations can help build trust among businesses and consumers, particularly in industries that handle sensitive information. Governments and industry bodies should work together to develop standards and guidelines that ensure the ethical and responsible use of AI.

5.2 Conclusion

In conclusion, this chapter examines the transformation of AI and employment within Canadian SMEs. It provides a comprehensive analysis of the historical evolution of employment in Canada, the introduction of AI and its impact on the workforce, as well as the specific effects on SMEs. The chapter highlights both the opportunities and challenges that AI presents, offering detailed insights and recommendations for various stakeholders.

The historical context section traces the evolution of the Canadian labour market from an agrarian economy to industrial capitalism and now, to the AI era. Each phase has brought significant changes in employment patterns, skill requirements, and labour dynamics. The transition from agrarian and resource-based labour to manufacturing and wage-based employment was characterized by the role of skilled immigrants, the division of labour, and the emergence of labour movements. The government's influence in shaping labour dynamics and the effects of technological advancements on employment patterns are also discussed.

AI technologies are significantly transforming small and medium-sized enterprises (SMEs) by enhancing productivity, optimizing decision-making, and personalizing customer experiences. However, the impact of AI varies across different industries, with tech-forward sectors leading in adoption. Despite the promising potential of AI, SMEs encounter several challenges when trying to implement these technologies, including high costs, a lack of skilled personnel, data security concerns, and uncertainty regarding return on investment (ROI). Traditional sectors are particularly hesitant to embrace AI due to these barriers.

In Canada, there is a notable skills gap in the labour market, with many SMEs struggling to find employees who possess the necessary digital and technical skills to implement and manage AI systems. These skills gaps not only limit the competitiveness of SMEs but also prevent them from fully leveraging AI technologies. To address this issue, Canadian SMEs are increasingly adopting reskilling and upskilling programs, often in partnership with educational institutions or through online courses.

The Canadian government is actively supporting AI adoption through financial investments, regulatory frameworks, and training initiatives. These efforts aim to reduce financial barriers, address the skills gap, and ensure responsible deployment of AI. Government support in the form of subsidies, tax incentives, and grants can alleviate financial challenges, while industry-specific training programs can help bridge the skills gap. Additionally, clear data privacy regulations and knowledge-sharing initiatives can foster trust and confidence in the adoption of AI.

Different industries prioritize AI applications based on their specific operational needs. Customer-facing industries focus on using AI to enhance service delivery, while operationally intensive sectors leverage it for process optimization. For example, retail, e-commerce, and fashion sectors emphasize AI to create personalized customer experiences. In contrast, manufacturing and logistics sectors utilize AI for inventory management and supply chain efficiency.

To facilitate AI adoption among small and medium enterprises (SMEs), several recommendations can be made. Increasing financial assistance through subsidies, tax incentives, and grants can make AI technologies more accessible for SMEs. Additionally, developing industry-specific upskilling initiatives will prepare the workforce for AI integration. Promoting knowledge sharing through webinars, workshops, and peer-led discussions can also build confidence in adopting AI. Establishing clear policies and frameworks surrounding data privacy and security is crucial for building trust among businesses and consumers. Furthermore, providing targeted support and education to traditional sectors that may be hesitant to adopt AI can inspire confidence and encourage its integration.

AI holds significant potential for SMEs in Canada to enhance their operations and remain competitive in a rapidly evolving market. By addressing challenges and seizing opportunities, businesses across all sectors can harness AI's transformative power to drive growth and innovation. With the right support and strategies in place, AI can be a game-changer for SMEs, leading to a more efficient, innovative, and customer-centric future. Embracing AI not only positions SMEs for success but also contributes to the broader economic development and technological advancement of the region.

REFERENCES

Acemoglu, D., & Restrepo, P. (2019). Automation and new tasks: How technology displaces and reinstates labour (Working Paper No. 25684). National Bureau of Economic Research. https://doi.org/DOI: 10.3386/w25684

Acemoglu, D., & Restrepo, P. (2020). Automation and new tasks: How technology displaces and reinstates labour.

Arntz, M., Gregory, T., & Zierahn, U. (2017). Revisiting the risk of automation. *Economics Letters*, *159*, 157–160.

Autor, D. H. (2015). Why are there still so many jobs? The history and future of workplace automation. *The Journal of Economic Perspectives*, *29*(3), 3–30.

Autor, D. H., Katz, L. F., & Kearney, M. S. (2008). Trends in U.S. wage inequality: Revising the revisionists. *The Review of Economics and Statistics*, *90*(2), 300–323.

Autor, D. H., & Salomons, A. (2018). Does productivity growth threaten employment? In *Handbook of Labour Economics* (pp. 727–812). Elsevier.

Bai, T., Goldfarb, A., & Tucker, C. E. (2021). Digital disintermediation and job quality: How AI and platforms are reshaping the labour market. *Strategic Management Journal*, *42*(1), 105–128.

Bessen, J. E. (2019). AI and jobs: The role of demand. *AEA Papers and Proceedings. American Economic Association*, *109*, 1–7.

Block, S., & Galabuzi, G.-E. (2018). *Canada's colour coded labour market: The gap for racialized workers*. Canadian Centre for Policy Alternatives.

Brynjolfsson, E., & McAfee, A. (2014). *The second machine age: Work, progress, and prosperity in a time of brilliant technologies*. W. W. Norton & Company.

Brynjolfsson, E., & McAfee, A. (2017). *The second machine age: Work, progress, and prosperity in a time of brilliant technologies*. W. W. Norton & Company.

Brynjolfsson, E., & McElheran, K. (2016). The rapid adoption of data-driven decision-making. *The American Economic Review*, *106*(5), 133–139.

Brynjolfsson, E., Rock, D., & Syverson, C. (2018). Artificial intelligence and the modern productivity paradox: A clash of expectations and statistics. *NBER Macroeconomics Annual*, *33*(1), 97–142.

Clemente-Almendros, J. A., Nicoara-Popescu, D., & Pastor-Sanz, I. (2024). Digital transformation in SMEs: Understanding its determinants and size heterogeneity. *Technology in Society*, *77*, 102483. DOI: 10.1016/j.techsoc.2024.102483

Darroch, G. (1983). Labour market change and industrialization in Canada. *The Canadian Historical Review*, *64*(3), 325–349.

Davenport, T. H., & Kirby, J. (2016). *Only humans need apply: Winners and losers in the age of smart machines*. Harper Business.

Felten, R., Raj, M., & Seamans, R. (2019). AI occupational exposure measure.

Felten, R., Raj, M., & Seamans, R. (2019). The variable impact of artificial intelligence on labour: The role of complementary skills and technologies. SSRN Electronic Journal.

Felten, R., Raj, M., & Seamans, R. (2023). How will language modellers like ChatGPT affect occupations and industries? SSRN Electronic Journal.

Frey, C. B., & Osborne, M. A. (2017). The future of employment: How susceptible are jobs to computerisation? *Technological Forecasting and Social Change*, *114*, 254–280.

Georgieff, A., & Hyee, R. (2021). Artificial intelligence and employment: New cross-country evidence. OECD Social, Employment and Migration Working Papers, No. 265.

Georgieff, A., & Hyee, R. (2022). Artificial intelligence and employment: New cross-country evidence. *Frontiers in Artificial Intelligence*, *5*, 832736. PMID: 35620279

Goos, M., & Manning, A. (2007). Lousy and lovely jobs: The rising polarization of work in Britain. *The Review of Economics and Statistics*, *89*(1), 118–133.

Government of Canada. (2024). Chapter 4: Investing in the future. In Budget 2024. Retrieved from https://budget.canada.ca/2024/report-rapport/chap4-en.html 4-3.

Heron, C. (2012). *The Canadian labour movement: A short history* (3rd ed.). Lorimer.

Huang, M.-H., & Rust, R. T. (2018). Artificial intelligence in service. *Journal of Service Research*, *21*(2), 155–172.

Innovation, Science and Economic Development Canada. (2019). Key small business statistics. Small Business Branch, Research and Analysis Directorate.

Innovation, Science and Economic Development Canada. (2024). Artificial intelligence ecosystem. Retrieved from https://ised-isde.canada.ca/site/ised/en/artificial-intelligence-ecosystem

Kealey, G. S. (1995). *Workers and Canadian history*. McGill-Queen's University Press.

Kejriwal, M. (2023). AI in practice and implementation: Issues and costs. In *Artificial intelligence for industries of the future. Future of Business and Finance*. Springer., DOI: 10.1007/978-3-031-19039-1_2

Kietzmann, J., Paschen, J., & Treen, E. (2018). Artificial intelligence in advertising: How marketers can leverage artificial intelligence along the consumer journey. *Journal of Advertising Research*, *58*(3), 263–267. DOI: 10.2501/JAR-2018-035

Lane, M., Saint-Martin, A. (2021). The impact of AI on non-routine tasks.

Lane, M., Williams, M., & Broecke, S. (2023). *The impact of AI on the workplace: Main findings from the OECD AI surveys of employers and workers*. OECD Publishing., DOI: 10.1787/ea0a0fe1-

Lightman, E., & Lightman, N. (2006). *Social policy in Canada*. Oxford University Press.

Lund, S., & Manyika, J. (2019). *Global AI: Preparing for the future*. McKinsey Global Institute.

Macdonald, D. (2014). Industrial development and labour dynamics in Canada. *Canadian Journal of Economic History*, *35*(2), 55–76.

Milanez, A. (2023). The impact of AI on the workplace: Evidence from OECD case studies of AI implementation. OECD Social, Employment and Migration Working Papers, No. 289.

Moriguchi, C. (2020). The rise of the gig economy and the transformation of work. *The Journal of Economic Perspectives*, *34*(4), 105–120.

OECD. (2023). *OECD employment outlook 2023*. OECD Publishing., DOI: 10.1787/bb17314a-

OECD. (2023). *OECD employment outlook 2023: Artificial intelligence and jobs*. OECD Publishing.

Olusanya, Emmanuel. (2021). Job rotation as training and development. .DOI: 10.60392/eoe-16-01-21-01

Przegalinska, A., Triantoro, T., Kovbasiuk, A., Ciechanowski, L., Freeman, R. B., & Sowa, K. (2025). Collaborative AI in the workplace: Enhancing organizational performance through resource-based and task-technology fit perspectives. *International Journal of Information Management*, *81*, 102853. DOI: 10.1016/j.ijinfomgt.2024.102853

Russell, B. (2018). Canada's labour market: Past, present, and future. *Labour (Halifax)*, *81*, 45–68.

Sangster, J. (2016). *Transforming labour: Women and work in post-war Canada*. University of Toronto Press.

Statistics Canada. (2020a). Canadian survey on business conditions: Impact of COVID-19 on businesses in Canada, March 2020. The Daily, 1-4. Statistics Canada Catalogue No. 11-001-X.

Statistics Canada. (2020b). Canadian survey on business conditions: Impact of COVID-19 on businesses in Canada, May 2020. The Daily, 1-4. Statistics Canada Catalogue No. 11-001-X.

Statistics Canada. (2022, June 27). Small and medium businesses: Driving a large-sized economy.

Chapter 4
AI and Its Impact on the Growth of the Small Medium Enterprises:
The Role of IT Service Management (ITSM) in AI Adoption – AI and Sustainable Development Goals (SDGs)

Anirudh Dash
https://orcid.org/0009-0004-4036-5036
Christ University, India

ABSTRACT

AI in SMEs (Small and Medium-sized Enterprises) refers to the deployment of artificial intelligence technology to develop business operations and competitiveness. Often more resource-constrained than large corporations, SMEs can leverage AI to streamline processes, improve decision-making, and gain a competitive edge. Nowadays technology is changing, and small businesses are making profit. For building resilient business models with AI, it helps to get more information about business models, the amount to be invested in business, products demanded by the customers and the level of risk capacity to be taken by a firm.AI helps in generating new skills and knowledge in the employees by giving personalised training and coaching. Empowering SMEs through data-driven decision making helps in making rational business decisions based on data rather than relying on intuition or observation. It helps making faster decisions, improving operational efficiency and understanding the value of data.

DOI: 10.4018/979-8-3693-9611-7.ch004

INTRODUCTION

Although they constitute the foundation of many economies, SMEs sometimes find it difficult to stay up with technological changes. Although there are obstacles to its adoption, AI has the ability to completely transform SME operations. This study examines the literature currently available on AI in SMEs, emphasizing its advantages, difficulties, and the part that business and governmental organizations play in encouraging its use.

2. Benefits of AI for SMEs

The benefits of AI for SMEs are highlighted in a number of research (Ingalagi et al., 2021; Meta, 2024; Adeyeri, 2024). These consist of:

- **Enhanced effectiveness and performance**: AI may automate repetitive processes, allowing human resources to focus on more strategic endeavors (Ingalagi et al., 2021).
- **Data-driven decision making**: AI can examine huge datasets to find trends and patterns, which helps SMEs make more educated choices (Ingalagi et al., 2021).
- **Improved customer experience**: AI may offer real-time assistance, tailor marketing efforts, and enhance customer service interactions (Ingalagi et al., 2021).
- **Supply chain optimization**: AI can streamline inventory control and logistics, cutting expenses and speeding up delivery (Despoudi et al., 2023).
- **New product development**: AI may help with product design and development, which boosts competitiveness and fosters innovation (Naeem et al., 2024).

3. Challenges of AI Adoption in SMEs

SMEs have challenges while implementing AI technology, notwithstanding the advantages (Ingalagi et al., 2021; Meta, 2024). Among these difficulties are:

- **Expensive**: For SMEs with little funding, implementing and sustaining AI systems can be costly (Ingalagi et al., 2021).
- **Lack of technical know-how**: SMEs might not have the internal know-how needed to comprehend, deploy, and oversee AI technologies (Ingalagi et al., 2021).

- **Lack of data**: SMEs might not have the amount or caliber of data required to properly train AI models (Ingalagi et al., 2021).
- **Privacy and security issues**: SMEs can be worried about the threats to data privacy and security posed by AI (Ingalagi et al., 2021).

4. The Role of Government and Industry Bodies

The use of AI in SMEs may be greatly aided by governments and trade associations via (Meta, 2024):

- **Offering grants and funding**: SMEs might get financial support to get beyond the expense barrier related to using AI.
- **Providing training programs**: Educational efforts may give SMEs the know-how to comprehend and apply AI technology.
- **Creating AI solutions tailored to SMEs**: Wider adoption may be promoted by AI solutions that are user-friendly and reasonably priced and catered to the demands of SMEs.
- **Creating legal frameworks**: SMEs' worries about data security and privacy may be addressed by clear regulations.

The potential of AI to transform SMEs in a variety of industries is constantly emphasized in the literature. AI presents chances for:

- **Increased productivity and efficiency**: Achieved by process optimization, resource optimization, and the automation of repetitive work (Ingalagi et al., 2021; Mao et al., 2021).
- **Making decisions based on data**: Examining big datasets to find trends, patterns, and useful information (ET Staff, 2024; Ingalagi et al., 2021).
- **A better experience for customers**: Increasing client loyalty, improving service, and personalizing encounters (Ingalagi et al., 2021).
- **Competitive advantages and novel business models**: Generating novel goods and services and adjusting to shifting market conditions (Mao et al., 2021; Naeem et al., 2024).
- **Contribution to Sustainable Development Goals (SDGs)**: AI can support sustainable practices, optimize resource use, and minimize waste, contributing to a circular economy (Truby, n.d.; Despoudi et al., 2023).
- **Better diagnosis and care**: AI can help with quicker and more precise diagnosis, individualized treatment regimens, and better patient outcomes (Hanssen, 2022).

- **Reducing the lack of healthcare resources**: AI may increase productivity and simplify administrative duties, which will lessen the strain on medical staff (Hanssen, 2022).
- **Regulatory obstacles**: SMEs creating AI-based medical products face major obstacles due to Europe's Medical Device Regulation (MDR) (Hanssen, 2022). These consist of:
  - o Unclear rules and regulations pertaining to medical devices that use AI.
  - o Tougher standards for proving effectiveness and safety.
  - o Complicated procedures for evaluating conformance that include notified bodies.
  - o Uncertainty over who is responsible for judgments made by AI.

3. Barriers to AI Adoption in SMEs (General)

While the focus here is on healthcare, the literature identifies general barriers to AI adoption across all SME sectors:

- **High implementation costs**: One of the biggest challenges may be the expense of putting AI systems into place and keeping them up to date (Ingalagi et al., 2021).
- **Lack of technical expertise**: SMEs frequently lack the in-house know-how and abilities necessary to use AI technology efficiently (Ingalagi et al., 2021).
- **Data quality and availability**: SMEs may find it difficult to obtain the big, high-quality datasets needed for training AI models (Ingalagi et al., 2021).
- **Ethical considerations**: It is necessary to address issues about algorithmic bias, data privacy, and transparency (Truby, n.d.; Ingalagi et al., 2021).

4. The Role of IT Service Management (ITSM) in AI Adoption

The literature emphasizes the importance of effective IT service management (ITSM) in facilitating AI adoption:

- **AITSM (AI-enabled ITSM)**: AI technology enhances ITSM operations through automated workstreams and data analysis tools and better connection systems between organization users (Mao et al., 2021).
- **Building business model resilience**: Through AITSM, organizations can survive disruptions while sustaining value-making operations within changing marketplace conditions.
- **SD as a Driver of Socio-Economic Empowerment**: The literature demonstrates SD serves as a key force both in helping marginalized communities gain empowerment and fostering socio-economic development particularly

within developing countries. This strategy targets the growing elderly populations in developed nations as well as delivers needed jobs with high skill requirements to help developing countries escape economic strain.

- **The "Skills or Jobs" Debate**: World Development Report 2013 from the World Bank demonstrates the crucial relationship between job creation and skill acquisition by stating that employment opportunities drive skill requirements so policy approaches should strengthen skill and incentive transmission. The development of skills requires equal opportunities in job placement.
- **International Emphasis on SD**: UNESCO, OECD, ILO international organizations have established principles together with policy suggestions which help governments and other stakeholders maximize youth training and development programs.
- **Livelihoods Development and Marginalized Communities**: The literature establishes a connection between livelihoods development to socio-economic empowerment and regional growth together with rural development programs. This research shows that marginalized communities require effective alternative livelihood options and sustainable development solutions when displacement occurs because of deforestation, industrialization, environmental conflicts. Ethnographic studies investigated rural population perspectives alongside their barriers when adjusting their work strategies.

Artificial Intelligence possesses transformative power for customer experience delivery throughout Small and Medium Enterprises. SMEs encounter difficulties deploying AI technologies because they lack clear AI advantage comprehension together with constrained budget capabilities. According to the review, using AI stands as crucial for interpreting big data because it helps fulfill customer requirements and boosts operational performance. The research examines how AI serves digital marketing through user retention methods in addition to lead conversions and automated content production and customized customer interaction optimization. The analyzed data confirms AI systems enable small and medium enterprises to achieve premier customer experiences by implementing marketing strategies that rely on data.

AI technology grows in marketing importance for Small and Medium-sized Enterprises (SMEs). The economic sustainability of Small and Medium-sized Enterprises depends on their capability to embrace modern digital practices together with customer demand evolution. AI systems facilitate personalized marketing content delivery and enhance customer engagement while generating analytical data from information analysis. Traditional marketing approaches continue to matter but AI technology strengthens their impact upon digital platforms. Digital marketing becomes essential for SMEs because e-commerce has given them enhanced market access. AI-powered smart tracking systems and chatbots generate individualized recommendations and personalized feedback that both enhances resource optimization and improves customer interaction quality. Academic articles validate the essential role of machine learning AI in processing diverse dataset information to generate marketing content and guide business decisions. A data-driven methodology enables companies to deliver more precise target marketing alongside improved advertising expenditures and market forecasting capabilities. Through AI applications, businesses can both track customer interactions and produce tailored marketing materials specific to different target categories. The application of AI delivers a strategic advantage by utilizing segmentation, targeting, and positioning (STP) methods but also establishes strategic market direction. The research indicates that new technology tools enhance the capabilities of marketing teams instead of taking away their essential functions for strategic development along with creative idea generation.

This section of the literature focuses on the application of Artificial Intelligence (AI) in two key areas of SME management: product management and pricing management. In product management, AI-based marketing analytics tools can assess product design suitability and customer satisfaction.

Studies agree on the necessity to investigate the connection points between Artificial Intelligence (AI) and Sustainable Development Goals (SDGs). It identifies three key areas for future investigation: Property: specific AI applications tailored to individual SDGs and a systemically assessed evaluation of AI deployment's social and environmental impacts and ethical frameworks for AI development. The reviewed academic literature demands dedicated AI research focused on solutions that specifically meet distinctive challenges of individual SDGs so AI can most effectively contribute to worldwide sustainability efforts. The proposal emphasizes that policy development must rely on products derived from thorough evaluations which determine both the advantages and disadvantages pros and cons of using AI throughout healthcare and educational systems and environmental initiatives. The marketplace emphasizes building clear guidelines for ethical AI development which emphasis on values including fairness alongside transparency along with accountability and inclusivity to achieve sustainable development effectively. The research explores a dual strategy that supports AI progress alongside preventive action to reduce harm and promotes development harmonious with social welfare needs alongside environmental stewardship.

Research sheds light on how Artificial Intelligence enhances workplace safety by leveraging AI-powered Personal Protective Equipment (PPE) alongside computer vision-based monitoring along with AI-driven robotics and Virtual Reality (VR) training applications. Available literature points to inadequacies in conventional safety systems which calls for AI deployments as proactive security solutions. Smart personal protective equipment merged with wearable technologies when used alongside neural networks and fuzzy logic and Bayesian networks systems enables the continuous collection of data for accident prediction and prevention. Real-time employee behaviour tracking through computer vision technology provides hazard awareness while automatically generating alerts through existing cases such as thermal cameras detecting heat stress and AI-based safety surveillance systems. AI platforms for data management, computer vision, and machine learning now dominate the market alongside tools such as Scale AI and OpenCV.

The paper explores AI-driven robotic systems as an intervention against hazardous work scenarios occurring across manufacturing facilities as well as construction sites and underwater operations. Research shows that Digit, Atlas, Spot, HRP-5P, and Aquanaut exemplify different ways AI robots function in dangerous conditions. The research acknowledges potential robotic dangers so there must be vigilant implementation along with monitoring systems.

A detailed examination of virtual reality technology as a safety training solution appears across existing literature focusing on dangerous work environments. Through virtual reality, employees can undergo hazard scenarios using affordable controlled training protocols that substitute live experiences in dangerous environments. Chemical processing alongside construction and mining along with military training illustrate how VR creates effective risk-preventive knowledge according to research examples.

AI-Based VR for Employee Training

Research acknowledges Virtual Reality functions as an effective method that delivers safety education within environments characterized by high danger levels. VR effectively delivers critical hands-on training experience within virtual hazardous situations which increases protective awareness and prevents occupational injuries and loss of life. Study authors highlight that VR training proves both efficient and purposeful while delivering greater student engagement than the use of PowerPoint and videos. Multiple fields such as chemical processing, construction, mining, and the military demonstrate the wide range of applications for which VR training can be used. The combination of UAVs along with frameworks such as random forests and support vector machines operates as a remote data collection and task execution system that minimizes exposure for human operators.

AI and Sustainable Development Goals (SDGs)

AI transformation has become an urgent and necessary challenge that must be addressed in the new era. Enterprise AI transformation refers to the profound transformation of business activities, processes, capabilities, and models, by fully utilizing the changes and opportunities brought by AI as a strategic priority to help enterprises gain competitive advantages. AI can potentially deliver additional global economic activities of approximately USD 13 trillion by 2030 (Mao et al., 2021).

Enterprise AI transformation is continuously becoming the core field of business leadership thinking, eliciting attention from the industry and academia. Business model resilience refers to the capability of an enterprise to maintain its business logic for creating and delivering value. Profound economic, social, technological, and environmental changes are becoming part of modern daily business life with an unprecedented scale and pace, constantly challenging the business model of enterprises. The trade confrontation and friction between the great powers and the uncertainty of economic supervision make continuing to replicate their successful business models difficult for enterprises.

The global COVID-19 pandemic is constantly challenging the sustainable operation of the hotel, tourism, retail, transportation, and manufacturing industries. Advances in information technology (IT), such as big data, Internet of things (IoT), and AI, will also create new forms of business models that can effectively and abruptly make traditional business models obsolete (Mao et al., 2021).

IT service management (ITSM) can systematically and effectively build value creation channels between business units and information systems (IS). ITSM is apparently a powerful tool for building business model resilience. There is continuous enhancement of informatization investment, the majority of enterprises have underestimated the disruption scale brought by business behavior and technological changes in enterprise AI transformation; moreover, only 8% of enterprises can accomplish enterprise AI transformation in accordance with the established strategies and processes for maintaining economically viable business models. In the face of high-intensity, multidimensional disruptions, traditional IT service management appears powerless. IT services must be able to respond to changing environments and maintain their capability to deliver value in a timely manner while meeting the requirements for stability and resilience (Mao et al., 2021).

With the extensive development and profound application of AI, AI-enabled ITSM (AITSM), which exhibits the characteristics of augmented analytics, decoupling, platformization, and recombination, is becoming the mainstream ITSM solution. Empowerment from AI has brought new vitality and challenges to ITSM capabilities, and enterprises must start determining how to reactivate the capability of AITSM to shape the resilience of business models and meet survival needs in complex and ever-changing environments (Mao et al., 2021).

Information Technology Service Management Driven by Artificial Intelligence

ITSM refers to a principle that uses widely accepted "good practices" for organizing processes and people around customer-oriented services rather than around tasks related to managing systems and physical infrastructure. ITSM is defined as a routinized type of behavior in the use of assets to provide IT services to a customer organization. ITSM manages the value creation of an entire portfolio of IT services provided by an IS function. In a fast-growing, intelligent, and digitizing world, value is idiosyncratic, experiential, and laden with meanings. Disruptions from economic, societal, technological, and environmental contingencies are rapidly emerging. Thus, the value-creation potential of ITSM has been challenged due to its stability-oriented nature, i.e., the lack of capacity to produce a strategic IT innovation and the required agility, making confronting disruptions difficult.

AI is highly suitable for an ITSM strategy because it can help augment real human agents and collect and optimize data. AITSM can efficiently and proactively automate and assist with tasks, actions, and requests at the IT service desk, the defaults faced by traditional ITSM (Mao et al., 2021).

AITSM has several advantages. First, its analysis of data and metadata can generate recommendations that accelerate the responses of IT managers to ITSM capabilities and make complex decisions in time. For example, AITSM helps conduct risk assessments. IT managers can use it to predict market changes and find worthwhile investment opportunities by identifying favorable market change signals. Second, AITSM helps IT workers predict and solve most common security incidents. For example, IT workers can use machine learning to track and identify incident trends. This process helps them predict problems, outages, and incidents before they actually occur. Automation will trigger the workflow to check the primary cause of these incidents, ensuring that enterprises can prevent incidents before crises occur. Third, automation functioned by AI helps enrich communication between enterprises and users. It will provide a complementary and consistent experience for consumers. For example, AITSM can be used to create, design, and manage chat flows in an AI chatbot system. Fourth, AITSM assists chief information officers in simplifying the entire decision process. AITSM exhibits high potential in reactivating ITSM by handling the entire digital transformation and streamlining processes (Yanamala, 2024), and thus, reconstruct business model resilience.

AI in Health and Safety for SMEs

There is a lack of guidelines and regulations for AI-based medical devices, it is harder for SMEs to market such devices, and it is complicated to put an AI-based medical device on the European market due to MDR. SMEs should consider certain aspects important when developing an AI/ML-based medical device and placing it on the European market (Hanssen, 2022).

AI is used in more and more medical devices nowadays. They are used to diagnose patients more precisely and to treat them more effectively. Systems with AI functions may take decisions of their own without any human being involved. The World Health Organization (WHO) estimates that the world will be short of 9.9 million doctors, nurses, and midwives by the year 2030. This adds further urgency to addressing the challenge of overburdened health systems. According to WHO, supporting the widespread adoption and scaling of AI could help alleviate resource capacity shortfalls both now and in the future. One vision is to streamline or eliminate administrative tasks which can usually occupy between 20 and 80 percent of a healthcare professional's time (Hanssen, 2022).

The Medical Device Regulation 2017/745 is a new regulation by the EU that was entered into force on May 26th of 2021. The new regulations set new and stricter requirements on medical devices that are marketed in Europe. The new regulation sets new risk classifications and different requirements for each risk classification. New technologies such as medical devices with AI/ML can be used with the wrong perception of their capability and therefore cause harm (Hanssen, 2022).

The regulatory requirements exist to prevent medical devices that are used unethically, misused, and cause harm. Regarding AI/ML-based medical devices, there also exists an uncertainty concerned with the responsibility of actions/decisions of such devices. Stricter and more requirements for AI/ML-based medical devices are not desirable for manufacturers because the road to the market becomes longer and more complicated. On the other hand, more and stricter requirements lead to safer devices and a higher feeling of safety (Hanssen, 2022).

Problem

Due to new technology that is complex such as AI/ML, there is a lack of guidance and clear descriptions regarding marketing in Europe. Both MDR and medical devices with AI/ML are relatively new and uncharted. A report about medical devices with AI/ML that can be used as guidance will both facilitate the safety and marketing of such products in Europe. A report that can be used as guidance enables manufacturers, regulatory bodies, and other stakeholders to minimize the complexity of the marketing/development process and to collect important information in one place.

Aim

AI will be introduced more and more in medical devices, and it is of utmost importance to give guidance on how these products must be handled from safety and regulatory demands to demonstrate efficacy and safety. The responsibility aspects must be evaluated – the manufacturer, the healthcare providing organizations as well as medical professionals or the person using the device. The borderline between medical devices and devices for wellbeing should also be enlightened.

Goals

The main goal of this master thesis is to provide SMEs, other manufacturers, and society with a report that gives general guidance in the form of important aspects to be considered for medical devices that include AI and/or ML and when placing these products on the European market as well as what is needed for a guideline and what the content should be.

The goals of the project, the following requirements have been set for the report:

- The report shall be relevant to SMEs.
- The report shall include sufficient information in order to provide guidance/knowledge to SMEs.
- The report shall be usable for SMEs.
- The report shall be easy to understand and use.

Limitations

To conduct this project within the given time limit of 20 weeks, the project had to be limited in several areas. The following limitations were introduced:

- The project focuses on the European market.
- The main focus is to give guidance in the form of important aspects that SMEs should consider important.
- Identify what is needed in a guideline and what the content should be.
- The interviews will be conducted with experts that are concentrated on the European market.

AI has been used in healthcare since the 1970s. Physicians made a first attempt to improve their diagnoses by using AI in their software and programs. The interest in medical AI applications has increased significantly due to the enhanced computing power of modern computers and the development of AI. Several applications that use AI can be implemented in a variety of medical fields such as clinical, diagnostic, surgical, rehabilitative, and predictive practices. In healthcare, one use of AI is when designing treatment plans for patients. By analyzing data from previous patients, superior strategies can be provided for treating and monitoring patients and treatment plans.

AI has been used in combination with medical imaging such as CT scans, MRI, and x-rays to recognize signs of diseases more accurately and rapidly. AI in healthcare has led to helping patients with faster and more accurate identification of diseases but also with choosing a more precise treatment. AI in healthcare can deal with a vast amount of medical data and finds new information which otherwise would remain hidden in a mass of big medical data.

AI is commonly used for electronic health records (EHR) where it is used to analyze data from both the past and the present. This helps to improve different types of treatments and drug usage. AI is also used where algorithms use EHRs to predict the possibility of diseases and to evaluate patients' condition/diseases.

With the help of AI, algorithms have been used to extract information on drug interactions and possible side effects from medical literature. With the help of AI and machine learning, the drug discovery time has been greatly reduced.

Machine Learning in Healthcare

ML is mostly used in healthcare for precision medicine. This means predicting what treatment protocol suits a given patient. This is achievable with ML by using past data of patients and training the model using datasets. ML identifies and recognizes patterns in data, and in healthcare, these patterns can be used to increase our understanding as well as make predictions about health. ML is used in healthcare to identify risk factors for infections, predict who will get infected, predict diseases, predict the best treatments, predict the best combination of drugs for treatment, and many more.

Medical Device Regulation 2017/745

In Europe, a medical device must be CE marked and comply with the medical device regulation 2017/745 (MDR) in order to be placed on the European market. In 2017, MDR came into force and replaced the medical device directives (93/42/EEC) and (90/385/EEC). MDR was established in order to ensure that unsafe and noncompatible devices don't end up on the market and there existed a need for stricter and additional requirements. The new regulation places greater emphasis on safety during the medical device's life cycle with the support of clinical data as well as it ensures greater safety and greater performance of medical devices. The new regulation has introduced stricter requirements and a new classification system that is followed by additional requirements depending on which class the medical device is classified.

Classification

The new classification system in MDR is divided into classes that take the device's intended purpose and its inherent risks into account. The classes are:

- **CLASS I**: Medical devices which are considered to be low-risk medical devices. Class I medical devices do not require an assessment from a notified body and can be self-assessed.
- **CLASS Is**: Medical devices which are considered to be a low-risk medical device that is placed on the market in sterile conditions. This class requires a notified body.
- **CLASS Im**: Medical devices which are considered to be low-risk medical devices that are devices with a measuring function. This class requires a notified body.
- **CLASS IIa**: Medical devices which are considered to be medium risk medical devices. These medical devices are meant to be in use for a short-term period. This classification has four possible routes divided into two groups depending on whether the medical device is sterile or not. A notified body is required for this classification.
- **CLASS IIb**: Medical devices which are considered to be a high risk or medium-to-high risk medical devices. These devices are for long-term usage. There are four possible routes for this classification. The routes are divided into two groups depending on whether the medical device is sterile or not. For this classification, a notified body is required.
- **CLASS III**: Medical devices which are considered to be a high-risk medical device. For this classification, a notified body is required.

Notified Bodies

The notified bodies perform conformity assessments, and, in that procedure, they investigate general requirements such as the manufacturer's technical documentation, clinical and pre-clinical evaluation, surveillance audits and assessments, their compliance, and more. They also investigate the manufacturer's Quality Management System (QMS), and product and verification. Lastly, the notified bodies are required to document every step and write reports of their assessment and then do a final review. After the final review, they need to decide based on their investigation and then issue certificates that are needed. After the process, the notified bodies are still required to follow up with the device on the market and the manufacturers. They are required by MDR to make sure that the manufacturer keeps their documentation updated and that the product is safe even after it is placed on the market.

Skills Development for SMEs

Socio-economic empowerment of citizens in developing countries has become a key concern particularly among marginalised communities through widening of access to learning and training in SD. Many developed countries are now facing the challenges of aging population while and low-skilled jobs in developing countries cannot serve the purpose of socio-economic empowerment and the poor will remain trapped in poverty.

Latest writings and studies have identified several driving forces for SD in India. These works had analysed how mission-mode SD programmes can promote social inclusiveness at the national and local level. Jamal and Mandal (2013) and Chenoy (2012) examined the key actors under the National Skill Development Mission 2010 while Mehrotra, Gandhi and Sahoo (2013) examined official projection of manpower requirement in 2022 and how this figure was derived at during the planning phase.

The World Bank publication titled World Development Report 2013: Jobs started a debate on "skills or jobs – what comes first?" The report highlighted that "jobs need skills, pull skills, and build skills" and emphasised that "employment opportunities increase the demand for education, which systems then have to meet. The role of policy here is to ensure that signals are adequately transmitted, providing incentives to continue skill accumulation by the young and those of working age alike.... In India, informing rural women about job opportunities led to increased schooling for girls and delayed marriage and childbearing for women. On the other hand, privilege in access to jobs distorts the signals. It hurts and discourages, rather than encourages, the building of skills."

The UNESCO's EFA (Education for All) Global Monitoring Report 2012 affirmed the importance of SD for youths around the world to ensure a better and secure future. Recently, the Organisation for Economic Cooperation and Development (OECD) and the International Labour Organization (ILO) jointly drafted the OECD-ILO Strategies for Local Job Creation, Skills Development and Social Protection, which is a set of 10 key principles and policy suggestions for governments and non-government actors including private players. One of the principles and policy suggestions for their member countries is to emphasise on "Maximizing Skills Development and Training" (OECD and ILO, 2011).

Livelihoods development or livelihoods promotion is usually linked with socio-economic empowerment, regional development and rural development. Livelihoods development comes with appropriate SD of marginalised communities in developing countries and least developed countries (LDCs). Marginalised communities have been displaced for decades from their aboriginal habitats, aggravated after the Second World War due to widespread deforestation, land acquisition for industrialisation, global warming and other severe ecological or environmental conflicts. These communities need access to alternative livelihoods to ensure a sustainable future. Scholars such as Bryceson (2002) and Scoones (2009) adopted an ethnography angle to study perspectives and challenges of the rural population while reorienting their livelihoods to achieve development in sub-Saharan Africa and other LDCs.

National Skill Development Corporation (NSDC)

A key national entity named National Skill Development Corporation (NSDC) was formed in July 2008 by the central government in partnership with industry bodies. The NSDC has now 51:49 shareholdings of private and government entities (government owns 49% and private the rest). The government's funds are channelled through the National Skill Development Fund (NSDF) whereby the NDSC is a designated fund manager.

It has a threetier operational structure and is the apex body having a number of Sector Skills Councils.

Transforming Customer Experience with AI in SMEs

Artificial intelligence (AI) has changed the way businesses operate. AI includes techniques that can analyse patterns in raw data for making correct business decisions. Business decisions in SME's are related to production, marketing, supply chain, human resource and finance. Generally, AI analyses employees data, customer interactions, production and financial data interactions stored within the organisation's system. Analyses report provides actionable results for managers.AI analyses both structured and unstructured data sets using algorithms.

The small and medium scale enterprises form basic economic structure of the country, they lag far behind in utilising AI. The lack of basic understanding of AI benefits and limited resources for AI adaptation are main reasons for lack of AI integration into SME's. The number of studies related to AI and SME's are scarce. Hence, the study draws on influences of external and internal factors on AI implementation in SME's. Extensive research on the impact of AI adaptation has been done in past .However generalised findings cannot be applied to SME's as they operate in different ecosystems.

The term AI is used to illustrate machines that impersonate cognitive capability. Machines can intelligently communicate with each other by passing on signals. Signals are generated by machines through machine learning. A machine learns to processes data to make a decision.AI can be as "an umbrella term consisting of cyber –physical systems, big data analytics, Automation and machine learning. The AI of today is heavily reliant on collection, usage and processing of big data.

Customer's demands keep changing over the period of time. Hence, firms need to keep up with changing customer demands. In order to be relevant to customer's demands, firms have to transform themselves as agile and cost efficient by reducing operational cost.This can be achieved by digitalisation in supply chain. There has been increasing integration of marketing, finance, human resource and production departments. Inter departmental transactions produce huge data with different volume, variety and velocity. The transactional data is saved as structured and unstructured data sets. AI involves integration of physical and virtual systems acting as a whole. The systems are connected through intelligent sensors communicating seamlessly with each other to meet a pre defined goal. AI has a potential to change way of doing business .Hence, implementation of AI in a firm is the major strategic decision.

AI maximizes operational efficiency and transparency .Its strategic implementation provides stimulus to firms. Firms implementing AI have to convert data into intelligent and understandable versions so that machines can make sense out of data. AI systems enhance agility of the organisations by speeding up data processing and decision making.AI has significant influences on different kinds of industries. The majority of large manufactures use AI to manufacture advanced equipment.

AI is primarily concerned with user retention and lead conversion in digital marketing. It can guide a user in the direction that aligns with the business's goals by using intuitive AI chatbots, intelligent email marketing, interactive web design, and other digital marketing services. Several factors determine the impact of AI on digital marketing. ML, a subset of AI, is concerned with computer programmes that access data and use it to learn independently. It compiles data from various places, including social media accounts, menus, online reviews, and websites. AI then uses the information to produce and deliver content relevant to the audience. AI software enables in-depth online analysis of restaurants and their customers.

By implementing AI into marketing strategy, businesses can use the available data better and reach out to potential customers with attractive commercials at more convenient times.Digital marketing gives a visibly pleasant experience for clients with AI for advertising across social media and digital platforms such as Facebook and Instagram. These platforms thoroughly assess users' information before directing them to offers appropriate to their wants. AI also assists marketers in identifying and forecasting trends.

It prevents the company from overspending on digital advertising and ensures that the money is well spent. The ability of a computer to recognise objects, scenes, and activities in images is referred to as computer vision. Medical imaging analysis, face recognition, public security, and security monitoring are a few uses. If computer vision and AI are properly coupled, robots can predict what will happen in the future and act accordingly based on potential changes. AI has simplified building client profiles and comprehending the customer journey process. It allows brands to quickly and easily provide valuable personalised content for the various client profiles in any marketing funnel stage and throughout each avenue. Based on historical data, AI applications in digital marketing can determine what content is most likely to bring customers back to the site. AI identifies which customers are most likely to unsubscribe from a specific service and analyses which features are standard among unsubscribers. As a result of these analytics, marketers can plan their future campaigns and implement practices encouraging people to stay.

AI applications in digital marketing can sift through billions of data points on the internet and tell precisely what it needs to know for business. It will describe what price will get the most conversions, when is the best time to post, what subject line will get the most attention, etc. Intelligent marketers stay current with all trends. It simplifies jobs and allows for more creativity and out-of-the-box thinking. It also adds value to the customers who benefit.

Need for artificial intelligence in marketing

Small and medium-sized enterprises (SMEs) are mainstays for the economy due to their significant contribution to the Gross Domestic Product (GDP); It includes job creation, promotion of innovation, economic diversification, direct contribution to economies, boosting local development, business empowerment and their ability to adapt quickly to changing market conditions. Marketing is a set of actions through which a company studies the needs of an audience and establishes strategies to deliver value to customers. Artificial intelligence refers to computer systems that seek to mimic human cognitive function through machines, processors, and software with the aim of performing data processing and analysis tasks.

[18] In this sense, Artificial Intelligence marketing is the process that companies use to leverage AI solutions to personalize content, increase customer interaction, and obtain actionable insights to generate positive business results. Business performance is the operational capacity of a business to meet or over-meet institutional objectives, one of the factors of this performance is to carry out adequate marketing strategies, with the help of artificial intelligence, which is present in several aspects of success in large organizations and even in small and medium-sized companies. When those in charge of administration and management can combine marketing and

artificial intelligence, quality content will be created that impacts current, current and potential customers. In today's digital age, marketing has undergone a significant transformation. Businesses are constantly looking for innovative ways to reach their audience in a more effective and personalized way. This is where artificial intelligence (AI) has become an invaluable tool for improving digital marketing strategies. In this article, we'll explore how you can leverage AI to boost your marketing efforts and gain a competitive advantage in the digital world. Nowadays, the application of marketing strategies in an organization is of great importance, since the customer demands greater satisfaction from a product or service. For marketing strategies, they will become fundamental tools to achieve new defined market segments, to which they can offer from handicrafts, they will also help to establish commercial alliances at the national level to increase the level of sales.(Tigmasa, 2011) In the same way, people are always looking for a differentiating factor to be able to prefer one brand over another, so offering a variety in the catalog, an added value in the product offered, a more personalized service and above all, a good experience from the moment they view our content to the after-sales service, It will make it easier to be the first choice in the minds of consumer users. Considering that it is a business idea that is planned to be carried out in the medium term, it requires professional research which includes all the knowledge acquired throughout the career.(Vásquez, 2022) With the emergence and popularization of the Internet, for the first time in history, businesses have the ability to reach their customers 24 hours a day, seven days a week; and crossing the geographical barriers of their own city or country, this presents a huge opportunity for small businesses, as marketing channels are no longer a barrier to entry. Having a virtual store, according to e-commerce, is distance selling, taking advantage of the great advantages provided by new information technologies, such as the expansion of the offer, interactivity and immediacy of the purchase, with the particularity that you can buy and sell to whoever you want and where and when you want. Therefore, it is important to develop a strategic Marketing Plan that will help generate specific strategies to captivate new customers. (Alvear, 2023)(Viscarra, Ninabanda, & Garcia, 2019) Today, the digital age has brought about a revolution in the way people live and experience different aspects of their lives, and the field of marketing has been no exception. It is evident that the advancement of technology has significantly transformed the marketing landscape. For the incorporation of artificial intelligence in digital advertising campaign strategies, it has become a topic of interest and study.(Santamaría & Arias, 2023) In this sense, Artificial Intelligence is having a significant impact on new forms of communication. Digital tools are increasingly being used as a strategy and tool to improve the effectiveness and efficiency of communication from the commercial to the academic sphere. Thus, it is in this way that various communicational theorems can be proposed from the imaginative part. For smart tracking systems, for example, they can analyze performance and consumption patterns and offer individualized feedback, buyback recommendations, and additional material tailored to their level of knowledge and pace of consumption.

Artificial Intelligence has been a key piece in these advances since it is a type of technology transversal to all the fields in which human beings currently develop, opening new paths and generating interesting information to be analyzed by experts. One of the advantages of these tools over traditional ones is the speed with which information is processed and the optimization of resources. It should not be thought then that Artificial Intelligence will replace the human being, because for the moment this technology, although it is novel, does not have characteristics that only humanity has, but they are of great help to perform tasks that the human being does, having greater precision and saving resources as important as time and money.

Artificial intelligence (AI) is a set of algorithms that aims to understand the behavior of human beings, based on perception, conflict resolution, and then projecting the information onto a computer. In other words, AI tries to get computers or devices to think and behave like a human being. While artificial intelligence (AI) can play a role in both types of technologies, they are not exclusively based on it. In the context of AI, soft technology could be leveraged to develop artificial intelligence systems focused on interacting with people, such as virtual assistants, recommender systems, or chatbots.

According to artificial intelligence, it is a key technological tool to optimize processes and help in decision-making. Their presence is transcendental because of people's dependence on electronic devices, which generate data and simplify transactions. The challenge is to be at the forefront of technologies, especially speed, veracity and variety of data. Artificial intelligence takes the data generated by users, which allows generating productivity, improving profitability and utility. Internet accessibility is important for the collection of information, including in real time. The field of research is administrative sciences, where technological tools are a mainstay in the generation of new models of business management.

Digital marketing is essential in the highly connected world we live in. Consumers are spending more and more time online, providing a unique opportunity for brands to reach their audience in a more direct and personalized way. However, with the growing amount of data and complexity of the digital landscape, it becomes challenging for marketers to fully address and understand customer needs.

Advantage of machine learning over other technologies

Many technologies may do repeated work, but they can't think independently. They lack to think outside their code. On the contrary, Machine learning is a subset of AI that aims to give machines the ability to learn a task without pre-existing code. Here machines are fed with some of the problems and examples through which machines learn for certain tasks. As they go through these problems & examples, machines learn and adapt their strategy to independently execute the activities. For example, an image-recognition machine may be given millions of pictures to analyze. After going through endless permutations, the machine acquires the ability to recognize patterns, shapes, faces, and more. In today's scenario, the machine is only learning for the specific repeated task, but the machines are trained to learn more than just a specific task. The AI experts are working to make the machine able to take what it has learned from analyzing photographs and using that knowledge to analyze different data sets. Data scientists & programmers are formulating general-purpose learning algorithms that help machines learn more than just one specific task.

Use of artificial intelligence in marketing

Small and medium sized enterprises (SMEs) are mainstays for the economy due to their significant contribution to the Gross Domestic Product (GDP); It includes job creation, promotion of innovation, economic diversification, direct contribution to economies, boosting local development, business empowerment and their ability to adapt quickly to changing market conditions.

Marketing is a set of actions through which a company studies the needs of an audience and establishes strategies to deliver value to customers. Artificial intelligence refers to computer systems that seek to mimic human cognitive function through machines, processors, and software with the aim of performing data processing and analysis tasks.

Artificial Intelligence marketing is the process that companies use to leverage AI solutions to personalize content, increase customer interaction, and obtain actionable insights to generate positive business results.

In this sense, Artificial Intelligence marketing is the process that companies use to leverage AI solutions to personalize content, increase customer interaction, and obtain actionable insights to generate positive business results. Business performance is the operational capacity of a business to meet or over-meet institutional objectives, one of the factors of this performance is to carry out adequate marketing strategies, with the help of artificial intelligence, which is present in several aspects of success in large organizations and even in small and medium-sized companies. When those in charge of administration and management can combine marketing and artificial intelligence, quality content will be created that impacts current, current and potential customers.

In today's digital age, marketing has undergone a significant transformation. Businesses are constantly looking for innovative ways to reach their audience in a more effective and personalized way. This is where artificial intelligence (AI) has become an invaluable tool for improving digital marketing strategies. In this article, we'll explore how you can leverage AI to boost your marketing efforts and gain a competitive advantage in the digital world. Nowadays, the application of marketing strategies in an organization is of great importance, since the customer demands greater satisfaction from a product or service. For marketing strategies, they will become fundamental tools to achieve new defined market segments, to which they can offer from handicrafts, they will also help to establish commercial alliances at the national level to increase the level of sales.(Tigmasa, 2011) In the same way, people are always looking for a differentiating factor to be able to prefer one brand over another, so offering a variety in the catalog, an added value in the product offered, a more personalized service and above all, a good experience from the moment they view our content to the after-sales service, It will make it easier to be the first choice in the minds of consumer users. Considering that it is a business idea that is planned to be carried out in the medium term, it requires professional research which includes all the knowledge acquired throughout the career.

With the emergence and popularization of the Internet, for the first time in history, businesses have the ability to reach their customers 24 hours a day, seven days a week; and crossing the geographical barriers of their own city or country, this presents a huge opportunity for small businesses, as marketing channels are no longer a barrier to entry. Having a virtual store, according to e-commerce, is distance selling, taking advantage of the great advantages provided by new information technologies, such as the expansion of the offer, interactivity and immediacy of the purchase, with the particularity that you can buy and sell to whoever you want and where and when you want. Therefore, it is important to develop a strategic Marketing Plan that will help generate specific strategies to captivate new customers

Use of artificial intelligence in strategy and planning

Artificial intelligence can support marketers in strategy and planning marketing activities by helping in segmentation, targeting, and positioning (STP). Besides STP, AI can help marketers in visioning strategic orientation of firm (Huang & Rust, 2017). Text mining and machine learning algorithms can be applied in sectors like banking and finance, art marketing, retail and tourism for identification of profitable customer segments . A combination of data optimization techniques, machine learning and causal forests can narrow down the targeted customers also .

Use of artificial intelligence in product management in SMEs

Artificial intelligence-based marketing analytics tool can gauge the suitability of product design to the customer needs and resultant customer satisfaction. Topic modeling adds to the system capabilities to service innovation and designs. Preference weight assigned to product attributes during product search help the marketers to understand product recommender system and align marketing strategies for meaningful product management. Deep learning can personalize the point of interest recommendation and helps to explore new places. Artificial intelligence offers capabilities to customize offerings to suit to the customer needs.

Use of artificial intelligence in pricing management

Pricing involves factoring of multiple aspects in finalization of price and it is a calculation intensive job. Real time price variation based on fluctuating demand adds to the complexity of pricing task. Artificial intelligence based multiarmed bandit algorithm can dynamically adjust price in real time scenario (Misra et al., 2019). In the frequently changing pricing scenario like e-commerce portal, Bayesian inference in machine learning algorithm can quickly adjust the price points to match the competitor's price (Bauer & Jannach, 2018). According to Dekimpe (2020), best response pricing algorithms encapsulate customer choices, competitor strategies and supply network to optimize dynamic pricing.

Use of artificial intelligence in place management

Product access and product availability are essential component of marketing mix for heightened customer satisfaction. Product distribution relies on networked relationship, logistics, inventory management, warehousing and transportation problems, which is largely mechanical and repetitive in nature. Artificial intelligence is the perfect solution in the case of place management by offering cobots for packaging, drones for delivery, IoT for order tracking and order refilling (Huang & Rust, 2020). Standardization and mechanization of distribution process adds convenience to both suppliers and customers. Besides utility in distribution management, AI also offers customer engagement opportunities in service context. Service robots programmed with emotional AI codes are handy in surface acting (Wirtz et al., 2018). Embodied robots greet and engage with customers, but human elements need to complement the service environment for customer delight. Automation of service process with AI offers additional opportunity for performance and productivity improvement (Huang & Rust, 2018).

AI integration for Empowering local talent

Workforce planning is a critical aspect of talent management, focusing on aligning organizational needs with human capital to ensure efficiency, productivity, and long-term success. Traditional workforce planning methods, often reactive and based on historical trends, have struggled to keep pace with the dynamic nature of modern labor markets. . In response to these challenges, the integration of Artificial Intelligence (AI) and predictive analytics has emerged as a promising solution. These advanced technologies offer a proactive approach to workforce management by enabling organizations to analyze vast amounts of workforce data, predict future trends, and make informed decisions regarding talent acquisition, development, and retention.

AI and predictive analytics are reshaping workforce planning by offering unprecedented insights into workforce dynamics. These technologies can analyze employee behavior, skill sets, and external market trends to predict future workforce needs and identify critical talent gaps. AI-driven systems can enhance decision-making by providing data-driven forecasts, improving the alignment between talent supply and demand. In this evolving landscape, organizations can leverage AI to not only react to immediate workforce needs but also proactively plan for future challenges, ensuring that they are equipped to meet their strategic objectives. Traditional workforce planning methods, while foundational, are often constrained by their reliance on historical data and reactive approaches. This leads to challenges in accurately forecasting future talent needs, identifying skills gaps, and managing succession planning.

The increasing complexity of workforce dynamics, driven by rapid technological advancements, remote working models, and changing workforce expectations, exacerbates these challenges. Organizations require more agile and data-driven approaches to workforce planning that can respond to these complexities in real time. The integration of AI-driven predictive tools provides a potential solution to these challenges. Despite the increasing interest in AI for workforce management, many organizations struggle to effectively implement and leverage these tools for proactive talent forecasting. There remains a significant gap in understanding how AI can be best utilized to enhance workforce planning, particularly in the areas of skills gap analysis, dynamic workforce allocation, and succession planning.

To address the limitations of traditional workforce planning by exploring how the integration of Artificial Intelligence (AI) and predictive analytics can enhance talent management. Specifically, we propose a comprehensive framework for incorporating AI-driven predictive analytics into workforce planning and develop key propositions on how AI can improve talent forecasting and workforce management. By focusing on areas such as skills gap analysis, dynamic workforce allocation, and proactive succession planning, we seek to provide a roadmap for organizations to adopt AI technologies, ultimately contributing to more agile, informed, and future-focused talent management strategies that transition from reactive methods to proactive, data-driven approaches.

AI has become a critical tool for transforming talent management processes, particularly in human resource management (HRM). Oluwatamilore et al. (2023) review AI-driven talent analytics and its role in optimizing HR decision-making in U.S. organizations, emphasizing its importance in areas like workforce planning and employee engagement. This study shows how AI can support better decision-making by predicting workforce needs and managing talent effectively. Safarishahrbijari (2018) offers a systematic review of workforce forecasting models, highlighting the strengths and weaknesses of different approaches such as time series modeling and system dynamics simulations. The paper underscores how AI models can better forecast workforce needs by analyzing both internal and external data sources. The study also identifies areas for improvement in traditional workforce planning methods. In HR practices, predictive analytics plays a crucial role in enhancing workforce management at every stage. Isson and Harriott (2016) demonstrate how people analytics, leveraging predictive models, can improve hiring, retention, promotion, and succession planning. Their study offers practical frameworks for incorporating analytics into HR practices. This approach enables HR professionals to identify key talent and manage attrition risks more effectively.

AI's role in talent flow analysis has also been explored in detail. Xu et al. (2019) present a deep sequence prediction model that uses job transition networks to analyze and forecast talent flows within and between organizations. The model helps organizations monitor employee transitions, enabling proactive workforce allocation decisions. HR, AI-based predictive analytics has been applied in several other fields. Jindal and Malaya (2015) explore how predictive analytics is used in higher education for tasks such as enrollment management and curriculum development, demonstrating its versatility across different sectors.

. Piccialli et al. (2021) discuss AI's application in healthcare, where predictive models are used to forecast medical bookings, improving patient care and resource allocation. In terms of long-term workforce planning, Roy (2021) investigates how AI-based workforce management systems are used in India to address challenges such as scheduling, recruiting, and retention. The study also highlights the future potential of AI in HRM and addresses concerns about AI replacing human roles in HR. AI has also been instrumental in improving expertise management systems within large enterprises. Varshney et al. (2014) describe an analytics-driven solution at IBM, where AI predicts employee expertise by analyzing job roles and skill sets. This system reduces manual effort and provides accurate, real-time data for decision-making.

In predictive workforce analytics, Kaushal et al. (2023) apply AI-based regression models to retail sales forecasting, revealing how similar approaches can be used to predict workforce requirements in other sectors. Similarly, Fondue et al. (2023) examine AI models in HR, focusing on how machine learning algorithms improve HR decision-making by forecasting employee desires and revenue growth. Talent management systems also benefit from AI-powered talent analytics. Chaturvedi (2016) highlights the growing relevance of big data and talent analytics in helping organizations manage human capital. This paper emphasizes the role of AI in improving employee engagement, retention, and forecasting talent needs. Similarly, Flores et al. (2020) focus on AI tools that predict student performance, suggesting that these tools could be adapted for workforce planning by forecasting employee performance.

Propositions for AI-Driven Workforce Planning

This section presents key propositions on how AI-driven technologies can enhance workforce planning. By leveraging AI for skills gap analysis, dynamic workforce allocation, and proactive succession planning, organizations can transition from traditional, reactive methods to more proactive, data-driven approaches. These propositions are supported by visual models and theoretical insights to clarify their potential impact on workforce management and talent forecasting.

AI-Enhanced Financial Management

Artificial intelligence (AI) has become an essential tool in the financial sector, revolutionizing how businesses manage their finances (Bassey, 2023). By automating tasks, improving decision-making accuracy, and providing deeper insights into financial trends, AI offers transformative capabilities for enterprises of all sizes, especially small and medium-sized enterprises (SMEs). In financial decision-making, AI leverages advanced technologies such as machine learning, natural language processing (NLP), and predictive analytics to automate and enhance key processes, offering SMEs the opportunity to overcome traditional challenges in financial management. Artificial intelligence in finance refers to the use of advanced algorithms and computational models to automate and optimize various financial operations (Ajiga et al., 2024). These technologies allow businesses to analyze vast amounts of data, detect patterns, and make predictions with a level of accuracy and efficiency that exceeds human capabilities. Machine learning is a key component of AI used in finance. It enables systems to learn from historical data and improve their predictive capabilities over time. This technology is particularly valuable in financial forecasting, credit risk assessment, and customer behavior analysis. Machine learning models can process large datasets quickly, identifying trends and patterns that are not easily observable by human analysts. Natural language processing (NLP) is another crucial AI technology used in finance. NLP allows computers to understand, interpret, and generate human language (Nwaimo et al., 2024). This is especially useful in automating routine tasks such as processing invoices, interpreting financial documents, and assisting in customer service through chatbots. NLP also plays a role in analyzing sentiment from financial news or reports, helping businesses make informed decisions based on external data. Predictive analytics leverages statistical algorithms and machine learning techniques to predict future outcomes based on historical data. In finance, predictive analytics is used to forecast cash flows, anticipate market trends, and manage financial risks. This technology enhances decision-making by providing businesses with real-time insights and actionable data, reducing uncertainty in financial planning.

AI has broad applications in financial processes, particularly for SMEs looking to improve efficiency and make smarter financial decisions (Daramola et al., 2024). Three key areas where AI is making significant impacts include automating accounting tasks, forecasting cash flows and financial trends, and conducting risk assessments and credit analysis. Automating accounting tasks is one of the most immediate benefits of AI in financial management. AI-powered software can handle routine accounting functions such as bookkeeping, invoicing, and reconciliation with minimal human intervention. Automation reduces the time and effort required for these tasks, allowing SMEs to allocate resources more effectively (Esan, 2023). Moreover, AI can help detect errors or discrepancies in financial records, further enhancing accuracy and reducing the risk of costly mistakes. Forecasting cash flows and financial trends is another critical application of AI in SME financial management. By analyzing historical data and external factors such as market conditions, customer behavior, and macroeconomic trends, AI can predict future cash flows with greater accuracy. This predictive capability enables SMEs to make informed decisions about investments, manage liquidity more effectively, and avoid potential financial pitfalls. Accurate forecasting also allows SMEs to plan for growth, as they can better anticipate when they will need additional financing or when to expand their operations. Risk assessment and credit analysis are also greatly enhanced by AI. Traditional methods of credit analysis rely on limited datasets and often involve time-consuming manual evaluations (Bassey, 2022). AI, on the other hand, can analyze a vast array of data points, including non-traditional sources such as social media activity or customer reviews, to assess the creditworthiness of a business or individual. This enables SMEs to make quicker and more informed decisions regarding loans, investments, or partnerships. AI-driven risk assessment tools can also help SMEs identify potential financial risks, such as market fluctuations or changes in regulatory environments, allowing them to proactively adjust their strategies

(Afeku-Amenyo, 2015). The integration of AI into financial decision-making offers numerous benefits, particularly in terms of increasing accuracy and speed, reducing human error, and improving financial forecasting and strategic planning. Increased accuracy and speed are two major advantages of AI in finance (Agupugo et al., 2024; Bassey et al., 2024). AI algorithms can process vast amounts of data in real-time, allowing businesses to make quick decisions based on up-to-date information. This level of speed and precision is crucial in today's fast-paced financial markets, where small delays or errors can result in significant losses. For SMEs, the ability to analyze financial data swiftly and accurately allows for more agile responses to market conditions and improved financial performance. Reduction in human error is another critical benefit of AI. In manual financial processes, errors such as data entry mistakes or miscalculations can lead to inaccurate financial reports, budgeting errors, and even compliance issues (Esan et al., 2024). AI systems are designed to minimize these errors by automating tasks and cross-referencing large datasets to ensure accuracy. For SMEs with limited staff, the reduction in errors can save both time and money, freeing up resources for strategic initiatives rather than correcting mistakes. Improved financial forecasting and strategic planning is perhaps the most transformative impact of AI on financial decision-making (Ogunleye et al., 2024). By leveraging predictive analytics, SMEs can gain deeper insights into their future financial performance, enabling them to make more informed decisions. For example, AI can help businesses predict changes in consumer demand, allowing them to adjust pricing strategies or marketing efforts accordingly. It can also forecast cash flow fluctuations, helping SMEs maintain liquidity and avoid financial crises. Additionally, AI-driven insights can inform long-term strategies, guiding decisions related to capital investments, market expansion, and risk management (Porlles et al., 2024). AI is fundamentally transforming the way SMEs manage their financial processes. Through technologies such as machine learning, natural language processing, and predictive analytics, AI offers the ability to automate routine tasks, improve accuracy, and provide actionable insights into future financial performance (Moones et al., 2024). The applications of AI in accounting, forecasting, and risk assessment offer SMEs powerful tools to enhance their decisionmaking capabilities and optimize their financial management practices. As AI continues to evolve, its role in financial decision-making is set to expand, offering even greater opportunities for SMEs to improve efficiency, reduce costs, and increase profitability. By adopting AI-driven solutions, SMEs can better navigate the complexities of financial management, positioning themselves for sustainable growth in a competitive global economy

AI Tools for Financial Efficiency in SMEs

Artificial intelligence (AI) is transforming the financial landscape for small and medium-sized enterprises (SMEs), offering advanced tools to automate processes, enhance decision-making, and increase financial efficiency (Nwosu et al., 2024). These AI-powered solutions enable SMEs to optimize bookkeeping, cash flow management, expense tracking, and tax planning while improving profitability through revenue optimization strategies. By integrating AI tools, SMEs can streamline operations, reduce costs, and make data-driven financial decisions. This review explores the role of AIbased accounting software, predictive analytics for cash flow, expense tracking and optimization, and AI tools for tax planning and compliance.

AI-based accounting software has revolutionized traditional bookkeeping and expense management for SMEs. In the past, managing financial records was time-consuming and prone to human error (Ajiga et al., 2024). AI automates routine accounting tasks such as data entry, invoice processing, and categorizing expenses, significantly reducing the need for manual intervention. This automation ensures accuracy in financial reporting and frees up valuable time for SMEs to focus on strategic business activities. AI-based tools like QuickBooks and Xero use machine learning algorithms to continuously learn from historical data, improving their accuracy in categorizing transactions over time. Additionally, these platforms can integrate with other financial tools to provide a seamless financial management experience (Ezeh et al., 2024). For example, AI tools can sync with banking systems, automatically pulling transaction data into accounting platforms and reconciling accounts in real time. This integration ensures that SMEs have access to up-to-date financial information and can make more informed decisions.

Predictive analytics is an essential AI tool that enables SMEs to manage their cash flow more effectively (Iwuanyanwu et al., 2024). Cash flow is the lifeblood of any business, and poor management can lead to liquidity issues or even bankruptcy. AI-powered cash flow management tools use historical data and external factors to predict future cash flow trends, allowing SMEs to anticipate financial challenges and prepare accordingly. AI-driven solutions like Float and Fathom provide real-time financial monitoring, offering insights into how future expenses, revenues, and market conditions could impact cash flow. These tools generate predictive models that help SMEs plan for periods of low liquidity, enabling them to secure financing or adjust spending to maintain financial stability. Real-time monitoring also allows businesses to make quick adjustments to their operations, avoiding financial crises by proactively managing liquidity. AI-powered expense tracking tools offer SMEs significant advantages in identifying cost-saving opportunities. These tools analyze transaction data to detect patterns and identify areas where costs can be reduced (Daramola et al., 2024). For example, AI systems can flag recurring expenses that could be renegotiated or suggest more cost-effective alternatives for suppliers and services. In addition to identifying cost-saving opportunities, AI can automate budget adjustments based on real-time data. Traditional budgeting processes are often static and require manual adjustments, but AI systems can automatically update budgets based on current financial performance. Tools like Expensify and Cleo offer intelligent expense tracking features, allowing SMEs to monitor their financial health continuously. By automating these processes, SMEs can maintain tighter Tax planning and compliance are complex and time-consuming processes that are critical to a business's financial health (Bassey et al., 2024). AI tools simplify these tasks by automating tax calculations, filing reports, and ensuring that SMEs remain compliant with tax regulations. Platforms like Avalara and TurboTax use AI algorithms to process financial data, automatically generating accurate tax reports while minimizing the risk of errors. AI also helps reduce compliance risks by ensuring that businesses adhere to local, state, and federal tax laws. These tools stay updated with tax regulations, alerting SMEs to changes that could affect their tax liabilities. By automating tax-related tasks, AI allows businesses to focus on growth while avoiding costly penalties and legal issues related to non-compliance. AI offers powerful tools for optimizing revenue and improving profitability for SMEs (Ige et al., 2024). By leveraging AI-driven solutions, businesses can make data-driven decisions about pricing, customer segmentation, and market analysis, enhancing their ability to maximize revenues and expand into new markets. Dynamic pricing is one of the most significant advantages of using AI for revenue optimization. AI tools like Pricefx and Competera analyze real-time market conditions, competitor pricing, and customer behavior to adjust prices dynamically, ensuring that SMEs remain competitive while maximizing profit margins. These tools help businesses develop data-driven pricing models that respond to shifts in demand, enabling SMEs to optimize their pricing strategies for different products and services (Osundare and Ige, 2024). AI also enhances customer segmentation by analyzing customer behavior, preferences, and purchasing history. Tools like HubSpot and Salesforce Einstein use machine learning algorithms to identify customer segments and predict how different groups will respond to marketing efforts. This information allows SMEs to tailor their sales and marketing strategies for specific customer segments, driving revenue growth.control over their expenses and improve financial efficiency.

AI in Revenue Optimization and Profitability

Artificial Intelligence (AI) has become a key enabler for businesses looking to optimize revenue and increase profitability (Esan et al., 2024). From dynamic pricing strategies to predictive analytics for customer segmentation and market analysis, AI offers numerous tools to streamline operations, enhance decision-making, and identify new opportunities for growth. This explore the role of AI in revenue optimization and profitability, focusing on pricing strategy optimization, customer segmentation and revenue forecasting, sales channel and market analysis, and realworld case studies of small and medium-sized enterprises (SMEs) using AI for profitability. One of the most impactful applications of AI in revenue optimization is the development of dynamic pricing strategies (Afeku-Amenyo, 2021). AI tools enable businesses to adjust prices in real-time based on market conditions, competitor behavior, and consumer demand. These tools can analyze vast amounts of data, including historical pricing trends, customer preferences, and external factors like seasonality or economic conditions (Ogunleye, 2024). For example, ecommerce platforms often employ AI-driven algorithms to optimize product pricing dynamically. As a result, businesses can respond swiftly to changes in demand and maximize their revenue. Revenue management systems driven by AI leverage advanced pricing models to identify the most profitable pricing strategies. These models can incorporate various factors such as elasticity of demand, customer lifetime value, and willingness to pay. By continuously learning and adapting, AI-powered pricing solutions ensure businesses are not only competitive but also able to capture maximum revenue across different market segments . This is particularly valuable in industries like hospitality, travel, and retail, where demand fluctuations are common. AI's ability to analyze customer behavior and preferences plays a crucial role in optimizing revenue . Through machine learning algorithms, businesses can segment customers more effectively based on purchasing behavior, demographics, and other relevant attributes. AI-driven customer segmentation allows companies to tailor marketing and sales efforts to specific groups, improving customer retention and increasing revenue. For instance, retailers can use AI to create personalized offers for high-value customers, thereby enhancing customer satisfaction and encouraging repeat purchases. AI also aids in predictive models for revenue forecasting, providing businesses with valuable insights into future sales trends. Predictive analytics, powered by AI, helps companies anticipate demand, manage inventory, and allocate resources efficiently (Ezeh et al., 2024). By analyzing historical sales data, market conditions, and customer behavior, AI can forecast revenue growth with greater accuracy than traditional methods. This enables businesses to make informed decisions, optimize their sales strategies, and proactively adjust to changing market dynamics. AI is instrumental in helping businesses identify new revenue streams by offering deeper insights into sales channels and market conditions (Iwuanyanwu et al., 2024). Through advanced data analysis, AI can detect patterns and trends that may not be immediately apparent to human analysts. For example, AI can analyze customer data across multiple sales channels, such as online platforms, brick-and-mortar stores, and mobile applications, to identify the most profitable channels. This enables businesses to allocate resources more effectively and focus on channels that generate the highest revenue. Moreover, AI can help businesses optimize their product offerings by identifying which products are most likely to succeed in specific markets. Through market analysis, AI tools can evaluate competitors, consumer preferences, and emerging trends to help businesses make data-driven decisions about product development and marketing (Ezeafulukwe et al., 2024). This capability is especially valuable for companies seeking to expand into new markets or introduce new products, as it reduces the risk of failure and increases the likelihood of success. Several SMEs have successfully leveraged AI to enhance profitability (Ige et al., 2024). One notable example is Stitch Fix, an online personal styling service that uses AI to improve its product recommendations. The company employs machine learning algorithms to analyze customer preferences, style choices, and body measurements, enabling it to offer personalized clothing recommendations (Afeku-Amenyo, 2022). By leveraging AI, Stitch Fix has optimized its inventory, reduced return rates, and increased customer satisfaction, all of which have contributed to higher profitability. Another example is Optimove, a marketing platform that uses AI to segment customers and optimize marketing campaigns for SMEs. Through AI-driven customer insights, Optimove helps businesses increase customer retention and lifetime value by personalizing marketing efforts. As a result, SMEs using Optimove have reported significant improvements in marketing efficiency and revenue growth. In the hospitality industry, AI-powered tools like Revinate have enabled smaller hotels to optimize their pricing strategies and increase profitability. Revinate's AI-driven revenue management system analyzes booking trends, competitor pricing, and demand patterns to recommend the most profitable room rates. This has allowed smaller hotels to compete more effectively with larger chains, resulting in increased occupancy rates and revenue.

AI is revolutionizing the way businesses approach revenue optimization and profitability. From dynamic pricing strategies and customer segmentation to market analysis and sales forecasting, AI-driven tools are helping companies make data-driven decisions and identify new opportunities for growth (Ezeh et al., 2024). SMEs, in particular, are benefiting from AI technologies by enhancing their profitability and staying competitive in rapidly changing markets. As AI continues to evolve, its role in revenue optimization will only become more significant, offering businesses even greater opportunities to maximize their profitability and market share.

Challenges of Implementing AI in SME Financial Decision-Making

Artificial Intelligence (AI) has the potential to transform financial decision-making for small and medium-sized enterprises (SMEs), offering advanced tools for forecasting, risk management, and profitability optimization (Agupugo et al., 2022). However, despite these advantages, implementing AI in SME financial decision-making comes with several challenges. These obstacles include barriers to AI adoption, data quality and availability, model interpretability and trust, and ethical considerations. This review will explore these challenges in detail, highlighting the difficulties SMEs face in leveraging AI to improve financial decision-making. One of the primary barriers to AI adoption among SMEs is the cost and complexity of implementation (Bassey et al., 2024). AI technologies often require significant investment in hardware, software, and infrastructure, which can be prohibitively expensive for smaller companies. Additionally, the integration of AI tools into existing financial systems often requires specialized skills, making the process more complex. SMEs may struggle with the high upfront costs of adopting AI solutions, and they may lack the financial resources to maintain these systems over time. Furthermore, AI systems often require frequent updates and continuous monitoring to remain effective, adding to the overall cost burden (Nwaimo et al., 2024). The lack of technical expertise within SMEs further compounds this challenge. Unlike larger enterprises that have access to dedicated IT departments and data science teams, many SMEs lack the in-house knowledge required to implement and manage AI tools effectively (Bassey and Ibegbulam, 2023). This knowledge gap can lead to poorly implemented AI systems, which may deliver suboptimal results or even create additional risks. SMEs may also struggle to identify the right AI tools for their needs, as the complexity of AI technologies can make it difficult to assess which solutions are best suited for specific financial decision-making tasks. Data quality and availability are critical to the success of AI-driven financial decision-making (Ige et al., 2024). However, many SMEs face significant challenges in managing and accessing relevant financial data. AI algorithms rely on large datasets to generate accurate predictions and insights, but SMEs may not have the necessary infrastructure to store, process, or analyze these datasets effectively. Poor data management practices, such as incomplete or inconsistent record-keeping, can further hinder the effectiveness of AI tools. Inaccurate or missing data can lead to flawed financial forecasts and poor decision-making outcomes, negating the potential benefits of AI. Moreover, SMEs often have limited access to external financial data, such as market trends or competitor information, which is crucial for training AI models (Ogedengbe et al., 2024). Without access to a wide range of high-quality data, AI systems may struggle to generate reliable insights, reducing their value in the decision-making process. The lack of real-time data integration can also impair AI's ability to respond to changing market conditions, further diminishing its usefulness for financial decision-making in SMEs. Another key challenge of implementing AI in SME financial decision-making is model interpretability and trust (Oyindamola and Esan, 2023). Many AI algorithms, particularly those based on machine learning, function as "black boxes," meaning that their decision-making processes are difficult to understand. For SMEs, this lack of transparency can be problematic, as it may erode trust in AI-generated insights. Financial decision-making requires a high level of confidence in the accuracy and rationale behind recommendations, and the inability to interpret AI models can make it difficult for SME owners and managers to feel comfortable relying on these systems. The challenge of interpretability also affects the broader organizational trust in AI. Employees and stakeholders may resist AI-driven financial decisions if they do not understand how the models arrive at their conclusions (Daramola et al., 2024). This skepticism can reduce the willingness to adopt AI technologies, even if they offer significant potential benefits. As a result, SMEs may fail to fully capitalize on the advantages of AI in financial decision-making due to concerns about model transparency and reliability.

Ethical concerns represent another significant challenge in the implementation of AI for financial decision-making in SMEs (Eziamaka et al., 2024). One of the foremost ethical issues is data privacy. AI systems often require access to sensitive financial and customer data, which raises concerns about how this data is stored, processed, and protected. SMEs may lack the robust data security measures necessary to ensure compliance with privacy regulations, such as the General Data Protection Regulation (GDPR) in the European Union. Inadequate data protection practices can lead to breaches, resulting in financial losses, reputational damage, and legal penalties. Ensuring fairness and transparency in AI-driven financial decisions is also a major ethical concern. AI algorithms can inadvertently introduce biases into decision-making processes if they are trained on biased or unrepresentative data (Ogunleye, 2024). For SMEs, this can result in unfair or discriminatory financial practices, such as biased loan approval decisions or inequitable pricing strategies. Addressing these biases requires careful oversight and regular auditing of AI models to ensure that they produce fair and ethical outcomes.

Future Trends in AI for SME Financial Decision-Making

The rise of Artificial Intelligence (AI) is reshaping financial decision-making for small and medium-sized enterprises (SMEs). AI technologies offer SMEs advanced capabilities to manage financial operations, optimize decision-making processes, and increase profitability. As AI continues to evolve, several trends are emerging that will shape the future of AI-driven financial management for SMEs (Nwankwo et al., 2024). These trends include AI-driven financial advisory services, real-time decision-making, integration of AI with blockchain and FinTech solutions, and leveraging AI for sustainable financial management.

One of the most promising future trends in AI for SME financial decision-making is the rise of AI-driven financial advisory services. AI tools are increasingly being developed to provide personalized financial advice tailored to the unique needs and constraints of SMEs. These AI-driven advisory systems use machine learning algorithms to analyze large amounts of financial data and provide insights into cash flow management, investment opportunities, and risk assessment. AI-powered platforms, such as robo-advisors, can offer SMEs personalized recommendations on cost optimization, financial forecasting, and growth strategies without requiring a human advisor (Agupugo and Tochukwu, 2022). This is particularly beneficial for SMEs that may not have the resources to hire financial consultants. These tools can deliver actionable insights based on real-time market data, helping SMEs make informed decisions and improve financial performance. As AI technology advances, we can expect more sophisticated advisory services that cater specifically to the financial needs of smaller businesses, including tools that can model various financial scenarios and provide automated strategic advice.

Another key trend is the integration of AI into real-time decision-making processes. AI is increasingly being used to support real-time financial decision-making, providing SMEs with instant insights based on current financial data, market conditions, and business activities. These real-time decision support systems use AI to process and analyze data as it is generated, allowing SMEs to make quick and informed decisions (Okatta et al., 2024). For example, AI-driven tools can automatically analyze spending patterns, predict cash flow shortages, or flag potential risks in real time, enabling SMEs to address financial issues before they escalate. AI systems can also provide SMEs with alerts and recommendations for cost-cutting measures or investment opportunities based on real-time market trends. The ability to make immediate, data-driven decisions can give SMEs a competitive edge, allowing them to respond swiftly to market changes and financial challenges.

The integration of AI with blockchain and FinTech solutions is an emerging trend with immense potential for SMEs. Blockchain technology provides a secure, transparent, and immutable record of financial transactions, while AI can enhance the analysis and interpretation of these transactions for more informed decision-making. When combined, AI and blockchain can offer SMEs secure financial management systems that enhance trust and transparency (Ajiga et al., 2024). AI can automate various financial processes, such as verifying transactions, monitoring regulatory compliance, and detecting fraud within a blockchain-based system. This combination ensures that financial operations are not only efficient but also secure and auditable. Moreover, the integration of AI with other FinTech solutions, such as digital payment platforms, can streamline operations, reduce errors, and enable SMEs to access new financial services. As blockchain and AI continue to mature, SMEs can benefit from more robust financial ecosystems that enhance security, transparency, and efficiency in their financial decision-making processes.

In the future, AI will play a critical role in promoting sustainability and socially responsible financial management. Many SMEs are increasingly prioritizing sustainable practices and ethical investments as part of their corporate social responsibility initiatives (Ezeafulukwe et al., 2024). AI can support these efforts by providing tools to assess the environmental and social impacts of financial decisions. AI algorithms can analyze investment portfolios to determine their alignment with sustainability goals, such as reducing carbon footprints or supporting socially responsible enterprises. For example, AI-powered platforms can help SMEs identify sustainable suppliers, track their energy consumption, or evaluate the environmental impact of their operations. Additionally, AI can guide SMEs in selecting investments that align with environmental, social, and governance (ESG) criteria, helping them make decisions that are not only financially beneficial but also socially responsible. As more businesses prioritize sustainability, AI-driven financial tools will become essential for integrating sustainability into financial management.

Historical Context of Automation in Financial Services

Automation in financial services is not a recent development. The industry has a long history of leveraging technology to streamline operations and enhance service delivery. The introduction of automated teller machines (ATMs) in the 1960s revolutionized banking by providing 24/7 access to cash and basic banking services. In the 1980s and 1990s, the adoption of electronic trading platforms transformed the securities markets, enabling faster and more efficient trading. The early 2000s saw the rise of online banking, allowing customers to conduct transactions and manage accounts from the convenience of their homes. These early forms of automation laid the groundwork for more advanced technologies. The development of sophisticated algorithms for high-frequency trading in the 2000s marked a significant leap, highlighting the potential of automation to enhance market efficiency and liquidity. These technologies primarily focused on improving specific aspects of financial services, with human oversight

Overview of AI Technologies in Financial Services The advent of artificial intelligence has introduced a new era of automation in financial services. AI technologies such as machine learning, natural language processing, and robotic process automation are now integral to the industry's transformation.

Machine Learning (ML) are ML algorithms enable systems to learn from data and improve their performance over time without explicit programming. In financial services, ML is used for tasks such as fraud detection, risk assessment, and predictive analytics. For example, ML models can analyze transaction patterns to identify fraudulent activities in real-time, significantly reducing the incidence of fraud.

Natural Language Processing (NLP) are NLP allows computers to understand and interpret human language. Financial institutions use NLP for various applications, including chatbots and virtual assistants that provide customer support, as well as sentiment analysis tools that gauge market sentiment from social media and news articles.

Robotic Process Automation (RPA) use of software robots to automate repetitive and rule-based tasks. In the financial sector, RPA is employed for tasks such as data entry, compliance reporting, and account reconciliation. By automating these mundane tasks, financial institutions can free up human resources for more complex and value-added activities.remaining crucial.

Research on Economic Impacts of AI in Various Industries Extensive research has been conducted on the economic impacts of AI across various industries, providing valuable insights that are applicable to financial services. • Increased Productivity and Efficiency: Studies consistently show that AI can significantly enhance productivity and efficiency. By automating routine tasks, AI allows employees to focus on higher value work, leading to improved overall productivity. For instance, a study by McKinsey Global Institute found that AI could increase productivity growth by up to 1.4% annually in various sectors, including finance.

Cost Reduction are AI-driven automation reduces operational costs by minimizing the need for human labor and reducing errors. A report by Accenture estimated that AI could save banks up to $447 billion by 2023 through cost reductions and increased productivity. Job Displacement and Workforce Transformation: While AI offers significant economic benefits, it also poses challenges related to job displacement. Research by the World Economic Forum suggests that AI could displace millions of jobs globally, particularly those involving routine and repetitive tasks. it also has the potential to create new jobs that require advanced technical skills and creativity. Security and Privacy Concern AI systems often require access to large amounts of data, raising concerns about security and privacy. Ensuring the security of AI systems and protecting sensitive data are critical challenges that need to be addressed. A study by Capgemini found that 41% of organizations have experienced a security breach due to AI-related vulnerabilities.

AI in Financial Services: Current Applications and Impact AI-driven automation is already making significant inroads in financial services, with various applications demonstrating its potential.

AI systems can analyze vast amounts of transaction data in realtime to detect fraudulent activities. By identifying unusual patterns and flagging suspicious transactions, these systems enhance the security of financial transactions. AI-powered models can assess credit risk more accurately by analyzing a broader range of data points than traditional methods. This enables financial institutions to make better-informed lending decisions and reduce default rates.AI chatbots and virtual assistants are increasingly being used to handle customer inquiries, providing quick and accurate responses. This improves customer satisfaction and reduces the workload on human customer service representatives. AI algorithms are used in trading to analyze market data and execute trades at optimal times, improving trading efficiency and profitability. In investment management, AI is employed to develop personalized investment strategies based on individual risk profiles and financial goals.

Economic Impacts of AI in Financial Services The economic impacts of AI-driven automation in financial services are multifaceted.

- Positive Impacts: AI enhances operational efficiency, reduces costs, and improves accuracy, leading to significant economic benefits. For example, JPMorgan Chase's COiN (Contract Intelligence) platform uses AI to review legal documents, saving an estimated 360,000 hours of lawyer time annually. Similarly, Bank of America's AI-driven virtual assistant, Erica, has handled millions of customer requests, improving customer service efficiency.
- Negative Impacts: The displacement of jobs due to AI automation is a significant concern. Roles that involve routine and repetitive tasks, such as data entry and basic customer service, are particularly at risk. This necessitates workforce retraining and reskilling to prepare employees for new roles created by AI. Additionally, the reliance on AI systems raises security and privacy issues, as these systems often handle sensitive financial data. The literature review highlights the transformative potential of AI-driven automation in financial services, offering both significant economic benefits and challenges. The subsequent sections of this paper will delve deeper into these impacts, providing a comprehensive analysis of the economic implications of AI in the financial services industry.

Economic Impacts of AI-Driven Automation Artificial Intelligence (AI)-driven automation is reshaping the landscape of the financial services industry, bringing about profound economic impacts that extend across efficiency, productivity, cost management, and customer experience.

Positive Impacts

- Increased Efficiency and Productivity: AI technologies such as machine learning and robotic process automation enable financial institutions to automate repetitive tasks and streamline complex processes. This automation significantly reduces the time and resources required to perform tasks such as data entry, document processing, and customer service. For example, AI-powered chatbots can handle customer inquiries around the clock, improving response times and freeing up human agents to focus on more complex issues. This enhanced efficiency not only accelerates operational workflows but also enhances overall productivity by allowing employees to dedicate their time to higher-value tasks that require human judgment and creativity.

- Cost Reduction: AI-driven automation helps financial institutions achieve substantial cost savings by minimizing labor costs and operational inefficiencies. Automation reduces the need for manual intervention in routine tasks, leading to lower staffing requirements and decreased overhead expenses. For instance, AI algorithms can automate risk assessment processes in lending, reducing the need for manual credit evaluations and lowering the cost of loan origination. Moreover, AI systems can optimize resource allocation and asset management strategies, thereby reducing operational expenses and improving financial performance.
- Enhanced Accuracy and Reduced Errors: AI technologies excel in performing repetitive tasks with a high degree of accuracy and consistency. Unlike human employees, AI systems do not experience fatigue or distractions, leading to fewer errors in critical processes such as financial reporting, compliance monitoring, and fraud detection. This enhanced accuracy not only improves operational reliability but also mitigates risks associated with human error, thereby enhancing overall organizational efficiency and regulatory compliance.
- Improved Customer Service and Experience: AI-powered solutions enhance the quality and responsiveness of customer service within the financial services industry. Chatbots and virtual assistants equipped with natural language processing capabilities can engage with customers in real time, providing personalized recommendations, resolving queries, and facilitating seamless transactions. For example, AI-driven chatbots deployed by banks can assist customers with account inquiries, transaction histories, and financial planning advice, thereby enhancing customer satisfaction and loyalty. By leveraging AI technologies, financial institutions can deliver tailored experiences that meet the evolving expectations of digital-native consumers.

Negative Impacts

- Job Displacement and Workforce Transformation: One of the primary concerns associated with AI-driven automation in financial services is the potential displacement of jobs traditionally performed by human workers. AI technologies capable of automating routine tasks, such as data entry, customer support, and back-office operations, may lead to workforce reductions in these areas. As a result, employees in administrative roles may face displacement or require reskilling to transition into roles that leverage advanced technological skills, such as data analysis, AI model development, and cybersecurity management. To mitigate these challenges, financial institutions must prioritize workforce training and development initiatives that equip employees with the skills needed to thrive in an AI-driven environment.

Security and Privacy Concerns: The widespread adoption of AI technologies introduces new challenges related to data security and privacy within the financial services industry. AI systems rely on vast amounts of sensitive customer data to train algorithms and make informed decisions. Consequently, financial institutions must implement robust cybersecurity measures to safeguard against data breaches, unauthorized access, and malicious attacks targeting AI infrastructure. Moreover, compliance with regulatory frameworks such as the General Data Protection Regulation (GDPR) and the Payment Card Industry Data Security Standard (PCI DSS) is essential to ensure the ethical and responsible use of AI in financial operations. By prioritizing data protection and privacy initiatives, financial institutions can foster trust among customers and regulatory authorities while mitigating potential risks associated with AI-driven automation.

- Ethical Considerations and Bias Mitigation: AI algorithms used in financial services may inadvertently perpetuate biases inherent in training data, leading to discriminatory outcomes in decision-making processes such as loan approvals, credit scoring, and investment recommendations. Financial institutions must implement measures to identify and mitigate bias in AI models, such as conducting regular audits, diversifying training datasets, and implementing fairness-aware algorithms. By addressing ethical considerations associated with AI-driven automation, financial institutions can uphold principles of fairness, transparency, and accountability while promoting inclusive access to financial services for diverse customer demographics. AI-driven automation offers substantial economic benefits to the financial services industry, including increased efficiency, cost reduction, enhanced accuracy, and improved customer experiences, it also presents challenges such as job displacement, security risks, and ethical considerations. By adopting a proactive approach to addressing these challenges and leveraging AI technologies responsibly, financial institutions can capitalize on the transformative potential of AI-driven automation while fostering sustainable growth and innovation within the industry.

Implementation and Future Research

As the field of AI continues to evolve rapidly, there is a pressing need for further research to explore its potential in advancing Sustainable Development Goals (SDGs). By delving into specific AI applications tailored to each SDG, researchers can uncover innovative solutions to complex global challenges. Additionally, comprehensive studies examining the social and environmental impacts of AI deployment are essential for informed decision-making and policy development (Irfan, 2021). Moreover, the development of frameworks for ethical AI development is crucial to ensure that AI technologies contribute to sustainable development in a responsible and equitable manner.

Specific AI Applications for Each SDG

Future research should delve into the nuanced exploration of specific Artificial Intelligence (AI) applications customized to tackle the distinctive challenges and objectives outlined within each Sustainable Development Goal (SDG) (Floridi & Cowls, 2019). By meticulously identifying and cultivating AI solutions tailored to address the intricacies of individual SDGs, researchers have the potential to maximize the efficacy of AI technologies in driving forward global sustainability endeavors. This targeted approach ensures that AI interventions are finely attuned to the diverse contexts and needs inherent within each SDG, thereby enhancing their capacity to generate meaningful and sustainable impact across various sectors and geographical regions. Consequently, this avenue of research not only amplifies the transformative potential of AI in addressing pressing global challenges but also contributes to the attainment of the overarching vision outlined within the SDGs.

Examination of Social and Environmental Impacts

Further research is imperative to comprehensively scrutinize the social and environmental impacts stemming from the deployment of Artificial Intelligence (AI) within the framework of Sustainable Development Goals (SDGs) (Floridi et al., 2018). This necessitates rigorous assessments to elucidate the potential benefits and risks inherent in AI technologies across diverse domains such as healthcare, education, and environmental conservation (Floridi et al., 2018). By conducting thorough examinations, researchers can provide valuable insights to inform evidencebased decision-making and policy development in the context of SDGs.

AI interventions contribute to societal well-being, economic prosperity, and environmental sustainability across these domains. This entails evaluating the extent to which AI enhances access to essential services, improves healthcare outcomes, facilitates inclusive education, and promotes environmental stewardship. Additionally, researchers should critically assess the unintended consequences and ethical implications associated with AI deployment, including issues related to data privacy, algorithmic bias, and digital divide

Development of Frameworks for Ethical AI Development

The imperative to advance ethical Artificial Intelligence (AI) development and deployment necessitates concerted efforts towards the creation of robust frameworks This involves more than mere conceptualization; it requires the establishment of clear, actionable guidelines, principles, and standards to govern the entire lifecycle of AI technologies—from design and development to implementation and utilization.

At the core of these frameworks lie fundamental ethical values such as fairness, transparency, accountability, and inclusivity. Fairness ensures that AI systems do not perpetuate or exacerbate existing biases and inequalities, promoting equal opportunities and outcomes for all individuals (Floridi & Cowls, 2019). Transparency entails making AI decision-making processes understandable and explainable, allowing stakeholders to comprehend how decisions are made and hold AI systems accountable for their actions (Floridi & Cowls, 2019). Accountability ensures that developers and deployers of AI technologies are held responsible for the societal impacts of their creations, fostering a culture of responsibility and trust (Floridi & Cowls, 2019). Inclusivity emphasizes the importance of considering diverse perspectives and ensuring that AI technologies cater to the needs and values of all individuals, particularly marginalized and vulnerable populations.

By embedding these ethical principles into AI development processes, researchers can promote responsible and sustainable deployment of AI technologies in alignment with the principles of the Sustainable Development Goals (SDGs). Ethical AI frameworks serve as guiding beacons, steering AI innovation towards beneficial outcomes while mitigating potential harms. They empower developers, policymakers, and other stakeholders to navigate the complex ethical dilemmas inherent in AI development and deployment, fostering an ecosystem of responsible innovation that advances both technological progress and societal well-being.

Business Model Resilience

Business models are vulnerable to various contingencies in the business environment. This condition may unexpectedly render their business logic ineffective. By disrupting or even diminishing the revenue streams of enterprises, environmental contingencies may pose a significant threat to business models. Therefore, evaluating the resilience of business models against such contingencies is essential.

A business model refers to the logic or architecture of the value creation, delivery, and capture mechanisms of a firm. It can be simplified as "what customers want," "how they want it," and "how enterprises can organize to mostly meet their needs, get paid for doing so, and make a profit". In the previous literature, value creation is a central topic of business models. Enterprises always search for solutions to transfer from a crowded and highly competitive market to an uncrowded and novel market, creating the most potential value.

Compared with a long-term "strategy," a business model embraces a shorter temporal perspective. In a turbulent economy, a business model must adapt in response to external existing and upcoming contingencies engendered by technology-driven innovations. Hence, the resilience of a business model plays an important role by releasing the potential to extend an enterprise's value creation, and thus, enable the enterprise to adapt better to external uncertainties.

By increasing the resilience of their business model, enterprises can secure the continuity of organizational resources and processes through which their organization produces its goods and services and transforms these into value. Moreover, scholars have recognized the innovative nature of business models. By increasing business model resilience, enterprises can innovate creative and novel technologies with business value instead of creating pure technological inventions, enabling them to adapt to a complex and changeable market environment.

SRQ 1: During the digital transformation and post-pandemic period, what is the resilience demand for an enterprise's business model that is facing internal and external disruptions? To answer this question, researchers must begin by identifying the factors and characteristics of internal and external environment disruptions, analyzing the influencing factors of business model resilience, and evaluating the risk of business model reformation. The demand level, scope, and degree of business model resilience are based on weighing the necessity and risk of business model reform.

SRQ 2: How does AITSM particularly shape the resilience of an enterprise's business model? To answer this question, we must first compare the resources and capabilities of traditional IT and AI-driven IT services. Then, we should map IT strategic activities with enterprise strategic activities in accordance with IT business alignment theory, and lastly, determine the connection between ATISM and business model resilience.

SRQ 3: How should organizations dynamically develop business model resilience in the new AI era? This question focuses on the intelligent monitoring, dynamic management, and value optimization of business model resilience driven by AITSM. It completes the continuous optimization management of the developed business model resilience. By improving the understanding of previous research, the three research questions aim to provide clear research ideas for future studies.

The future of data analytics is being shaped by trends such as artificial intelligence, machine learning, and big data analytics. With advancements in technologies like natural language processing and deep learning, data analytics is becoming increasingly sophisticated, enabling organizations to extract deeper insights and drive innovation. Moreover, the rise of edge computing, IoT, and real-time analytics is opening up new possibilities for data-driven decision-making in diverse industries.

It is suggested that researchers come together and find common terminology for referencing AI-assisted technologies. Future research should investigate the specific challenges organizations encounter during the implementation of AI in product service innovation. This can involve examining issues related to infrastructure, employee training, the integration of AI into existing business processes, and ethical considerations since the research stream was not as elaborate as others. Future research could focus on identifying strategies to enhance the integration of AI into service businesses without causing customer concerns or fostering more harmonious coexistence.

Future studies should highlight successful cases of AI integration in service businesses, identifying best practices that can guide businesses in optimizing human-AI collaboration. This aligns with the call for exploring strategies for more seamless integration.

In addition to autonomous shopping systems, researchers must concentrate on research problems concerning related technologies such as autonomous products, e.g., autonomous vehicles. This future research agenda contributes to a better grasp of autonomous technology-based products. Possible disadoption of technology was missing from the research, and challenges related to autonomy and control at the organizational level were not addressed in detail. . Instead of using traditional predictive analysis techniques, smart manufacturing industries could move toward explainable AI techniques and models in future research. . It is urged by researchers to conduct in-depth studies on the dynamic nature of AI innovation, emphasizing technological frameworks. Explore how businesses can effectively capture and adapt to the evolving landscape of AI over time. Comprehensive models and theories for assessing the effectiveness of AI technologies in various business models have been established. Identify and analyze specific challenges and barriers that impact the adoption of AI, providing actionable insights for businesses.

Application of multiple methodologies is suggested, including field experiments and surveys, to avoid generalizing the results to the setting in which the research was conducted. The studies are restricted by their scope, which mostly focuses on qualitative methodology with a single case study. The use of these data was also constrained by the reality that the data collected were obtained from a single AI supplier; hence, the user's opinion may be overlooked. Quantitative exploratory research is suggested that considers additional companies and offers a new level of findings. Different assessment tools may be used; for example, survey strategies can offer comprehensive views of industry leaders regarding the importance of AI technology in business model development.

AI and occupational safety enhancements

Artificial intelligence plays a crucial role in various aspects of the work process, revolutionizing how tasks are performed and managed. Through computational methods that analyze and process data, AI enables specific actions that impact labor dynamics. Noteworthy AI technologies encompass ML, DL, NLP, and rulebased expert systems (RBES). These AI technologies have also made their way into occupational health, facilitating the examination of both structured and unstructured data. This technology finds application in diverse areas, such as coordinating machinery and industrial processes, workforce management (especially from a human resources [HR] perspective), customer risk assessment, benefits analysis, and staff safety evaluation. To safeguard their workforce, employers can adopt various strategies recommended by the US National Institute for Occupational Safety and Health (NIOSH). These measures include providing information and training on job hazards, implementing comprehensive safety programs, and supplying PPE.

Despite these efforts, human error remains a significant cause of workplace accidents. This is where AI can play a vital role. Due to its ability to rapidly process and analyze data, AI can effectively identify potential risks and hazards that may go unnoticed by humans. AI has introduced new approaches to work, exemplified by the assessment of employee performance using technological processes.

Workplace safety and AI-enabled PPE

Keeping in view workers' safety and the frequency of accidents at the workplace it becomes imperative to modernize conventional tools and procedures within the workplace to align with the emerging technological landscape. Over the past few years, studies have also explored the utilization of AI in the manufacturing sector. This integration not only interconnects the industry but also maximizes the safety and security of workers. With the advent of smart PPE and wearable technologies, it becomes feasible to gather data regarding both the workforce and their surroundings. This data-driven approach holds the potential to curtail the frequency of accidents and work-related ailments, thereby ushering in a notable enhancement in overall workplace conditions. Advancements in smart PPE enable the tracking of essential health indicators and the assessment of industrial surroundings. Multiple strategies exist for the incorporation of wearables into work settings, allowing for an examination of how networks of interconnected devices can contribute to safeguarding individuals. These solutions employ a range of AI techniques, including NNs, fuzzy logic, Bayesian networks, decision trees, and other hybrid inference methods. Typically, conventional safety systems in workplaces are tailored to meet the specific requirements of individual companies and primarily respond to measured stimuli, provided these stimuli surpass a minimum threshold (a reactive "action-reaction" approach). This approach offers limited adaptability or flexibility when encountering new situations. In contrast, AI systems with learning mechanisms introduce a different approach. These systems rely on a set of rules, coupled with knowledge acquired from solutions to known problems, to anticipate the outcomes of uncharted scenarios. Incorporating technologies like NNs, case-based reasoning (CBR) systems,80 DL,81 or hybrid neuro-symbolic algorithms, such systems can assess whether a given situation poses a risk based on certain contextual conditions.

AI computer vision in monitoring and surveillance tools for workplace safety

Computer vision holds great promise in enhancing workplace safety through AI applications.104 It enables various functions, including monitoring employee conduct, identifying potential risks, and issuing real-time alerts. An excellent example of its implementation is the use of thermal cameras to identify heat stress in workers. This technology allows employers to continuously monitor their employees' body temperatures and promptly offer necessary support, such as cooling breaks or appropriate PPE. Furthermore, computer vision is instrumental in surveillance efforts. AI-powered cameras can track employee movements and swiftly detect potential hazards, such as trip hazards or unsecured equipment. Moreover, these cameras can also identify instances when a person enters a restricted or hazardous area, thus ensuring a safer work environment.105,106 The proliferation of AI has brought about a paradigm shift due to technological advancement in data management, computer vision, and ML. This trend is evident in the emergence of several innovative AI-powered platforms that cater to diverse needs, from data labeling and curation to object detection and video analysis. Some of these cutting-edge platforms include: Scale AI, Supervisely, V7, Viso, Labelbox, Toloka, Superannotate, and OpenCV; the latter remains an integral part of the AI landscape, offering an open-source library for computer vision and ML. In the evolving realm of DL, various computer vision challenges and concerns, including classification, recognition, language processing, video analysis, gesture detection, and robotics, have emerged. However, it remains uncertain whether all computer vision problems will be considered solved in the current landscape of DL advancements. The advent of CNNs has indeed transformed the entire field of computer vision through recent model-based developments. These models have streamlined the process of creating sophisticated DL configurations, allowing for easy development by fine-tuning pretrained weights.

AI-based virtual reality for training employees

Virtual reality (VR) has emerged as a valuable tool for safety training, especially in high-risk industries where learning through real life experience can be dangerous. Employers can use VR to provide employees with practical knowledge and experience in risky situations, helping them stay safe, and thus minimize the risk of workplace fatalities and injuries by increasing their educative role for building up risk-preventive knowledge.108 This technology is cost-effective, goal-oriented, and enhances accident prevention by minimizing errors. The use of VR in safety training replaces traditional methods like PowerPoint and videos, offering a more engaging and retentive learning experience. Industries such as chemicals, construction, mining, and defense have adopted VR-based training programs due to their cost-effectiveness and reduction in workplace injuries and casualtiesChemical Processing: the Immersive Virtual Reality Plant experience guides employees through dangerous scenarios, preparing them to respond appropriately. Construction: Building Information Modelling technology creates VR simulations, familiarizing workers with hazardous zones and safety practices. Mining are VR is used to train students in emergency response at the University of New South Wales School of Mining Engineering. Military are the Naval Engineering Academy uses VR technology from Ethosh to train sailors in emergency and disaster response, ensuring precise and effective protocols are followed.

Workplace safety and AI-enabled PPE

Keeping in view workers' safety and the frequency of accidents at the workplace it becomes imperative to modernize conventional tools and procedures within the workplace to align with the emerging technological landscape. Over the past few years, studies have also explored the utilization of AI in the manufacturing sector.

This integration not only interconnects the industry but also maximizes the safety and security of workers. With the advent of smart PPE and wearable technologies, it becomes feasible to gather data regarding both the workforce and their surroundings. This data-driven approach holds the potential to curtail the frequency of accidents and work-related ailments, thereby ushering in a notable enhancement in overall workplace conditions.

Advancements in smart PPE enable the tracking of essential health indicators and the assessment of industrial surroundings. Multiple strategies exist for the incorporation of wearables into work settings, allowing for an examination of how networks of interconnected devices can contribute to safeguarding individuals. These solutions employ a range of AI techniques, including NNs, fuzzy logic, Bayesian networks, decision trees, and other hybrid inference methods. Typically, conventional safety systems in workplaces are tailored to meet the specific requirements of individual companies and primarily respond to measured stimuli, provided these stimuli surpass a minimum threshold (a reactive "action-reaction" approach). This approach offers limited adaptability or flexibility when encountering new situations. In contrast, AI systems with learning mechanisms introduce a different approach. These systems rely on a set of rules, coupled with knowledge acquired from solutions to known problems, to anticipate the outcomes of uncharted scenarios. Incorporating technologies like NNs,79 case-based reasoning (CBR) systems,80 DL,81 or hybrid neuro-symbolic algorithms,82 such systems can assess whether a given situation poses a risk based on certain contextual conditions.

Workplace safety through AI-based robots

The transformative influence of AI-based robotics has a significant impact on workplace safety and reducing injuries and fatalities by eliminating workers' exposure to dangerous machinery and workplace hazards. Recent evidence based on leveraging establishment-level data on injury rates by Gihleb et al 2022 uncovered that a 1 SD increase in robot exposure (1.34 robots per 1000 workers) is associated with a reduction in work-related injury rates of approximately 1.2 injuries per 100 full-time workers.

High-risk work environments such as hazardous material handling, working at heights, and in confined spaces, can exploit these technological advances driven by data science and AI. Nevertheless, robotics come with their own set of risks and dangers that can also have an adverse impact on the working environment.

Artificial intelligence, ML, and DL are pivotal technologies within the realm of robotics,90 and by 2024 it is projected that up to 75% of enterprises will have embraced AI within their operational workflows. Due to increasing robotics use in industry, the Center for Occupational Robotics Research (CORR) was established by NIOSH, in 2017, with the purpose of assessing the possible advantages and drawbacks of incorporating robots into the workforce.

The implementation of autonomous mobile robots (AMRs) contributes to enhanced safety measures in the workplace.93 Automated guided vehicles (AGVs) and AMRs have been widely used in construction and hospital logistics including disinfection equipment.

To understand the capability of an AMR, the robots developed by a Denmark-based robotics company can handle a payload of 1350 kg, managing tasks effectively within dynamic environments, and minimizing the role of humans in tasks that entail collision risks or physical strain injuries such as back injuries and falls. AMRs, for instance, are equipped with multisensor safety systems comprising laser scanners, 3D cameras, and proximity sensors that feed data into an advanced planning algorithm. This system guides the robot's path, enabling adjustments or stops when necessary. Additionally, advanced AI robots possess features that facilitate safe decision-making in case of sensor malfunction, further solidifying their status as among the safest AMRs globally.

The current landscape of AI robot designs encompasses various models created for diverse applications. Notably, these robots incorporate the latest AI approximations, as true AI is still in the research phase. Digit by Agility Robotics: A humanoid bipedal robot capable of navigating complex terrain and delivering packages. Digit can climb stairs, catch itself during falls, and plan footsteps.97 Digit could be deployed in environments where certain tasks are dangerous for workers, ie, emergency response and disaster recovery tasks in the research phase. Atlas and Spot by Boston Dynamics: These AI-based robots are advanced robotic platforms with diverse capabilities with applications in search-and-rescue operations, Atlas and Spot could locate and provide assistance to personnel in hazardous or hard-to-reach areas.98 Their features make them suitable for deployment to handle and transport hazardous materials, chemical agents, or explosives, reducing the risks to the human workforce such as fire breakouts or explosions in industrial units. HRP-5P by AIST: Developed by Japan's Institute of Advanced Industrial Science and Technology (AIST), HRP5P excels in heavy labor tasks and construction activities. Its capabilities include autonomously installing gypsum boards on walls, handling large plywood panels, demonstrating its potential for practical use in the construction industry and ensuring the mitigation of hazards in heavy labor tasks. Aquanaut by Houston Mechatronics: Aquanaut serves as an unmanned underwater submersible designed for extended submerged tasks. It can travel over 200 km underwater and manipulate objects in hazardous underwater environments. With onboard cameras, sensors, and powerful arms, Aquanaut minimizes the need for human involvement.100 The robot may aid in risky underwater exploration missions.Stuntronics by Disney: Disney's Stuntronics is an advanced stunt-double robot that performs acrobatics for movies/cinemas. It employs sensors and autonomous pose control to execute complex maneuvers with precision and repeatability. Occupational injuries are well discussed in studies conducted among stunt performers. This technology aims to replace human stunt doubles in risky scenes

AI computer vision in monitoring and surveillance tools for workplace safety

Computer vision holds great promise in enhancing workplace safety through AI applications. It enables various functions, including monitoring employee conduct, identifying potential risks, and issuing real-time alerts. An excellent example of its implementation is the use of thermal cameras to identify heat stress in workers. This technology allows employers to continuously monitor their employees' body temperatures and promptly offer necessary support, such as cooling breaks or appropriate PPE. Furthermore, computer vision is instrumental in surveillance efforts. AI-powered cameras can track employee movements and swiftly detect potential hazards, such as trip hazards or unsecured equipment. Moreover, these cameras can also identify instances when a person enters a restricted or hazardous area, thus ensuring a safer work environment.

The proliferation of AI has brought about a paradigm shift due to technological advancement in data management, computer vision, and ML. This trend is evident in the emergence of several innovative AI-powered platforms that cater to diverse needs, from data labeling and curation to object detection and video analysis. Some of these cutting-edge platforms include: Scale AI, Supervisely, V7, Viso, Labelbox, Toloka, Superannotate, and OpenCV; the latter remains an integral part of the AI landscape, offering an open-source library for computer vision and ML

In the evolving realm of DL, various computer vision challenges and concerns, including classification, recognition, language processing, video analysis, gesture detection, and robotics, have emerged. However, it remains uncertain whether all computer vision problems will be considered solved in the current landscape of DL advancements. The advent of CNNs has indeed transformed the entire field of computer vision through recent model-based developments. These models have streamlined the process of creating sophisticated DL configurations, allowing for easy development by fine-tuning pretrained weights.

AI-based virtual reality for training employees

Virtual reality (VR) has emerged as a valuable tool for safety training, especially in high-risk industries where learning through real life experience can be dangerous. Employers can use VR to provide employees with practical knowledge and experience in risky situations, helping them stay safe, and thus minimize the risk of workplace fatalities and injuries by increasing their educative role for building up risk-preventive knowledge.108 This technology is cost-effective, goal-oriented, and enhances accident prevention by minimizing errors. The use of VR in safety training replaces traditional methods like PowerPoint and videos, offering a more engaging and retentive learning experience.109 Industries such as chemicals, construction, mining, and defense have adopted VR-based training programs due to their cost-effectiveness and reduction in workplace injuries and casualties.Chemical Processing: the Immersive Virtual Reality Plant experience guides employees through dangerous scenarios, preparing them to respond appropriately. Construction: Building Information Modelling technology creates VR simulations, familiarizing workers with hazardous zones and safety practices. Mining: VR is used to train students in emergency response at the University of New South Wales School of Mining Engineering. Military are the Naval Engineering Academy uses VR technology from Ethosh to train sailors in emergency and disaster response, ensuring precise and effective protocols are followed.

AI-driven site drones

The incorporation of drones and unmanned aerial vehicles (UAVs) represents a stride toward executing a broad array of tasks without direct human intervention. The UAV and ML platforms have employed numerous algorithms in their work. Of these algorithms, the random forest stands out with the largest portion of usage. It is the most commonly utilized algorithm because of its effectiveness in managing data noise. The second most prevalent algorithm is the support vector machine, accounting for 21% of total usage.

20s. Challenges faced by small medium enterprises

SMEs are playing an important role in economic development and also for growth of India's economy. The MSME sector consisting of 36 million units provides employment to over 80 million persons. The sector through more than 6000 products contributes about 8% to GDP besides 45% to the total manufacturing output and 40% to the exports from the country. SMEs contribution towards Indian economy development is at large. SMEs are regularly termed as Engine for Growth|| in developing countries like India, china etc. Indian sector SMEs are classified according to Micro Small and Medium Enterprise (MSME) Act 2006. Most countries define SMEs in terms of number of employees but in developing countries like India categorization of SMEs was done using investment rations in plant and machinery Hooi L W (2006). SMEs in MSME Act are divided in terms of investment in plant and machinery for both manufacturing and service sectors as shown in table 1. According to Micro Small and Medium Entrepreneurs Development (MSMED) Act 2006.

SME's are facing many challenges and issues because of both internal and external factors causing SME's performance. Here in the figure 1 it is given that issues and challenges faced by SME's. External challenges and issues include external factors like changes in legal systems, estimating market conditions, environmental factors includes political, legal, social and economical factors and socio cultural environmental factors which determines an entrepreneurs state of being becoming entrepreneur. External challenges for SME's includes all the socio cultural factors like education, caste, religion, family background and networks which influence an individual. Internal factors include all management related factors like production, marketing, human resource development, financial and infrastructure related factors etc. In considering both internal and external factors SME's can manage and control internal factors but external factors can be disappeared by government involvement through implementing some specific schemes and programs for respective sector wise and also by category of industry wise. Internal challenges are production, marketing, financial, human resource development and infrastructure etc. Production challenges include lack of power, lack of resources, lack of scarcity, lack of high cost raw materials, poor quality of raw materials, lack of machinery etc. Marketing challenges include lack of promotional strategies, lack of market channels, lack of networking, lack of organized distribution channels, lack of delivery time etc. Financial challenges includes lack of credit from banks, lack of awareness on schemes and services, delayed process in bank, lack of working capital etc.

Human resources development challenges include lack of training, lack of motivation among employees, lack of skilled employees, lack of technical and managerial training, improper way of recruiting etc. Infrastructure challenges include lack of water facilities, lack of storage facilities, lack of industrial facilities, lack of drainage facilities etc. Hence from the above discussion it is clear that there are many challenges influencing SME's. Among them major are production, marketing, financial, human resource development and infrastructure etc. From above all issues and challenges external challenges are majorly not avoidable in nature as they occur because of environmental changes which not in organization control but internal challenges and issues can overcome and avoidable through certain safety measures and also through management involvement.

Positive Impacts

Enhanced Efficiency and Productivity are Financial institutions use AI technologies including machine learning and robotic process automation to automate their repetitive work and simplify their challenging operations. Robotic process automation enables financial institutions to use their resources more efficiently while reducing operational time required for every stage from data entry through document handling to customer support. AI-powered chatbots maintain continuous operation to answer client questions which extends agent availability for dealing with complicated customer issues. Operational efficiency improves through this method which enables employees to dedicate time toward valuable tasks requiring human creativity alongside analytical understanding.

Cost Savings are Finance institutions achieve important cost decreases from their AI-powered automation systems that reduce personnel expenses while fixing operational performance problems. Automated processes reduce human intervention in repetitive tasks thereby minimizing operational personnel and resulting in lower costs of overhead expense. Modern AI technology streamlines lending risk assessment procedures by reducing manual credit assessments which produces lower costs for loan originations. Monitored analysis offered by AI platforms enables better resource routing and asset tracking approaches leading to more economical operations combined with increased monetary performance.

Increased Accuracy and Fewer Errors are AI systems excel at carrying out monotonous jobs with a high degree of accuracy and consistency. AI systems are less prone to weariness and diversions than human workers, which leads to fewer errors in critical procedures like fraud detection, compliance monitoring, and financial reporting. This improved accuracy improves overall organizational performance and regulatory compliance by reducing the risks associated with human error and increasing operational reliability.

Enhanced Customer Service and Experience are AI-powered technologies elevate the quality and responsiveness of customer service in the financial services sector. Chatbots and virtual assistants that utilize natural language processing can interact with customers in real-time, offering personalized suggestions, resolving issues, and facilitating smooth transactions. For instance, AI-driven chatbots used by banks can aid customers with account inquiries, transaction details, and financial planning support, thus increasing customer satisfaction and loyalty. By employing AI technologies, financial institutions can provide customized experiences that align with the changing expectations of digital-savvy consumers.

Negative Impacts

Job Displacement and Workforce Evolution are AI-driven automation in financial services raises serious concerns, one of which being the possible loss of jobs that are now performed by humans. Workforce reductions in these domains may arise from AI technology that may automate routine jobs like data entry, customer support, and back-office operations. Clerical workers may thus be laid off or require retraining to move into jobs requiring more sophisticated technology skills, such data analysis, AI model development, and cybersecurity management. In order to tackle these challenges, financial institutions have to prioritize workforce development and training initiatives that equip staff members for success in an AI-driven environment.

Security and Privacy Issues are In the financial services industry, the widespread use of AI technology creates significant privacy and data security issues. For AI systems to train algorithms and make informed judgments, vast amounts of sensitive consumer data are required. Therefore, in order to guard against hostile attacks that target AI systems, illegal access, and data breaches, financial institutions must put strong cybersecurity policies into place. Furthermore, adherence to laws such as the Payment Card Industry Data Security Standard (PCI DSS) and the General Data Protection Regulation (GDPR) is essential to guaranteeing the moral and responsible use of AI in financial operations. Financial institutions may foster confidence with consumers and regulatory agencies while mitigating the dangers associated with AI-driven automation by prioritizing data security and privacy protections.

Ethical Considerations and Bias Mitigation are When used in financial services, AI algorithms may inadvertently perpetuate biases found in the training data, leading to biased results in decision-making processes including investment recommendations, credit evaluations, and loan approvals. In order to identify and lessen bias in AI models, financial institutions need to use fairness-oriented algorithms, diversity their training datasets, and conduct routine reviews. By addressing the moral dilemmas associated with AI-powered automation, financial institutions may uphold the values of justice, openness, and responsibility while guaranteeing diverse clientele inclusive access to financial services.

AI automation provides financial services with a number of economic advantages, such as increased productivity, but it also raises employment concerns and data security dangers that call into question the ethical implications of the technologies' use. Financial institutions should embrace the benefits of AI-driven automation while fostering industry innovation and long-term sustainability by using AI technology ethically and actively managing challenges.

REFERENCES

Adeyeri, T. B. (2024). Economic impacts of AI-driven automation in financial services. International Journal of Scientific Research and Management, ISSN: 2321-3418. https://ijsrm.net

Afeku-Amenyo, D. (2015). AI applications in financial risk management. *Journal of Financial Technology*, *3*(2), 45–60.

Afeku-Amenyo, D. (2021). Dynamic pricing strategies using AI in retail. *International Journal of Business Analytics*, *8*(4), 112–130.

Afeku-Amenyo, D. (2022). AI-driven personalization in e-commerce: The case of Stitch Fix. *Journal of Digital Marketing*, *10*(1), 25–40.

Agupugo, C. P., Bassey, E. O., & Ibegbulam, C. (2022). Challenges of AI adoption in SME financial management. *African Journal of Business Technology*, *5*(1), 33–50.

Agupugo, C. P., Ezeh, C. I., & Ige, S. O. (2024). AI for financial accuracy and speed in SMEs. *Journal of Small Business Finance*, *12*(2), 78–95.

Agupugo, C. P., & Tochukwu, E. (2022). AI-driven financial advisory services for SMEs. *Journal of Financial Innovation*, *7*(3), 89–104.

Ajiga, O. P., Daramola, F. O., & Nwosu, C. E. (2024). AI-based accounting software for SMEs. *International Journal of Financial Technology*, *9*(1), 56–72.

Alvear, M. (2023). E-commerce strategies for SMEs in the digital age. *Journal of Digital Commerce*, *6*(2), 101–115.

Bassey, E. O. (2022). AI-driven credit analysis for SMEs. *African Journal of Financial Management*, *4*(3), 67–82.

Bassey, E. O. (2023). AI in financial decision-making for SMEs. *Journal of Business Technology*, *10*(4), 123–140.

Bassey, E. O., Ezeh, C. I., & Ige, S. O. (2024). AI for tax planning and compliance in SMEs. *Journal of Taxation and Business*, *8*(2), 90–107.

Bassey, E. O., & Ibegbulam, C. (2023). Technical expertise gaps in AI adoption for SMEs. *Journal of Small Business Innovation*, *11*(1), 44–59.

Bauer, J., & Jannach, D. (2018). Optimal pricing in e-commerce based on sparse and noisy data. *Decision Support Systems*, *106*, 53–63. DOI: 10.1016/j.dss.2017.12.002

Bhoganadam, S. D., Rao, N. S., & Rao, D. S. (2017). A study on issues and challenges faced by SMEs: A literature review. Retrieved from https://www.researchgate.net/publication/316595283

Bryceson, D. F. (2002). The scramble in Africa: Reorienting rural livelihoods. *World Development*, *30*(5), 725–739. DOI: 10.1016/S0305-750X(02)00006-2

Chaturvedi, V. (2016). Talent analytics: The future of human capital management. *Journal of HR Management*, *4*(2), 88–102.

Chenoy, D. (2012). Skill development in India: A transformation in the making. *India Infrastructure Report*, *2012*, 199–207.

Daramola, F. O., Ezeh, C. I., & Ige, S. O. (2024). AI-powered expense tracking for SMEs. *Journal of Financial Optimization*, *7*(1), 34–49.

Dekimpe, M. G. (2020). Retailing and retailing research in the age of big data analytics. *International Journal of Research in Marketing*, *37*(1), 3–14. DOI: 10.1016/j.ijresmar.2019.10.001

Despoudi, S., Sivarajah, U., Spanaki, K., Charles, V., & Durai, V. K. (2023). Industry 4.0 and circular economy for emerging markets: Evidence from small and medium-sized enterprises (SMEs) in the Indian food sector. Annals of Operations Research. https://link.springer.com/article/10.1007/s10479-023-05404-4

Esan, M. O. (2023). AI automation in accounting for small businesses. *Journal of Accounting Technology*, *5*(2), 56–70.

Esan, M. O., Ezeh, C. I., & Ige, S. O. (2024). AI in revenue optimization for SMEs. *Journal of Business Growth*, *13*(3), 101–118.

Ezeafulukwe, . (2024). AI for sustainable financial management in SMEs. *Journal of Sustainable Finance*, *22*(4), 45–62.

Ezeh, C. I.. (2024). AI-driven financial tools for SMEs. *Journal of Financial Innovation*, *10*(2).

Eziamaka, . (2024). Ethical issues in AI financial decision-making. *Journal of Business Ethics*, *35*(1), 78–92.

Flores, J.. (2020). AI tools for predictive analytics. *Journal of Educational Technology*, *8*(3), 67–81.

Floridi, L., & Cowls, J. (2019). A unified framework of five principles for AI in society. *Harvard Data Science Review*, *1*(1). Advance online publication. DOI: 10.1162/99608f92.8cd550d1

Floridi, L., Cowls, J., & Beltrametti, M.. (2018). AI4People—An ethical framework for a good AI society: Opportunities, risks, principles, and recommendations. *Minds and Machines*, *28*(4), 689–707. DOI: 10.1007/s11023-018-9482-5 PMID: 30930541

Fondue, S.. (2023). Machine learning in HR decision-making. *Journal of HR Analytics*, *5*(1), 33–49.

Gihleb, R., Giuntella, O., Stella, L., & Wang, T. (2022). Industrial robots, workers' safety, and health. *Labour Economics*, *78*, 102205. DOI: 10.1016/j.labeco.2022.102205

Hanssen, S. B. (2022). General guidance principles for SMEs to meet the regulatory demands on safety and efficacy in the EU in order to reach the market [Master's thesis, Uppsala University]. https://www.diva-portal.org/smash/get/diva2:1674081/FULLTEXT01.pdf

Hooi, L. W. (2006). Challenges faced by SMEs in developing economies. *Journal of Small Business Management*, *10*(3), 123–135.

Huang, M.-H., & Rust, R. T. (2017). Technology-driven service strategy. *Journal of the Academy of Marketing Science*, *45*(6), 906–924. DOI: 10.1007/s11747-017-0545-6

Huang, M.-H., & Rust, R. T. (2018). Artificial intelligence in service. *Journal of Service Research*, *21*(2), 155–172. DOI: 10.1177/1094670517752459

Huang, M.-H., & Rust, R. T. (2020). AI in place management for SMEs. *Journal of Marketing Technology*, *6*(1), 45–60.

Ige, S. O.. (2024). Data quality challenges in AI financial decision-making. *Journal of Data Science in Business*, *9*(2), 88–103.

Ingalagi, S. S., Mutkekar, R. R., & Kulkarni, P. M. (2021). Artificial intelligence (AI) adaptation: Analysis of determinants among small to medium-sized enterprises (SMEs).

Irfan, M. (2021). AI and sustainable development goals: A review. *Journal of Sustainable Technology*, *3*(2), 56–72.

Isson, J. P., & Harriott, J. (2016). *People analytics in the era of big data*. Wiley.

Iwuanyanwu, . (2024). AI for cash flow forecasting in SMEs. *Journal of Financial Planning*, *11*(1).

Jamal, T., & Mandal, K. (2013). Skill development mission in India: An overview. *Economic and Political Weekly*, *48*(14), 34–41.

Jindal, R., & Malaya, D. (2015). Predictive analytics in higher education. *Journal of Educational Data Science*, *3*(2), 45–60.

Kaushal, N.. (2023). AI regression models for retail forecasting. *Journal of Business Analytics*, *6*(2), 78–93.

Mao, H., Zhang, T., & Tang, Q. (2021). Research framework for determining how artificial intelligence enables information technology service management for business model resilience. Retrieved from https://www.researchgate.net/publication/367852652

Mehrotra, S., Gandhi, A., & Sahoo, B. K. (2013). Estimating India's skill gap: Projections for 2022. *Economic and Political Weekly*, *48*(38), 45–52.

Meta. (2024, June). New insights to help India's MSMEs use AI to drive growth. https://about.fb.com/news/2024/06/new-insights-to-help-indias-msmes-use-ai-to-drive-growth/

Misra, K., Schwartz, E. M., & Abernethy, J. (2019). Dynamic online pricing with incomplete information using multiarmed bandit experiments. *Marketing Science*, *38*(2), 226–252. DOI: 10.1287/mksc.2018.1129

Moones, . (2024). AI in financial process optimization for SMEs. *Journal of Financial Technology*, *13*(1).

Naeem, R., Kohtamäki, M., & Parida, V. (2024). Artificial intelligence enabled product–service innovation: Past achievements and future directions [PDF]. Retrieved from file:///C:/Users/dasha/Downloads/Artificial_intelligence_enabled_product-service_in.pdf

Nwaimo, . (2024). NLP applications in SME financial management. *Journal of Business Technology*, *10*(2).

Nwankwo, . (2024). Future trends in AI for SME financial decision-making. *Journal of Financial Innovation*, *12*(1).

Nwosu, C. E.. (2024). AI tools for financial efficiency in SMEs. *Journal of Small Business Technology*, *8*(1).

Ogedengbe, . (2024). Data availability issues in AI for SMEs. *Journal of Database Management*, *7*(2).

Ogunleye, . (2024). AI for strategic financial planning in SMEs. *The Journal of Business Strategy*, *15*(1).

Okatta, . (2024). Real-time AI decision-making for SMEs. *Journal of Financial Technology*, *11*(2).

Oluwatamilore, . (2023). AI-driven talent analytics in U.S. organizations. *Journal of HR Technology*, *5*(2).

Organisation for Economic Co-operation and Development, & International Labour Organization. (2011). *OECD-ILO strategies for local job creation, skills development and social protection*. OECD Publishing.

Osundare, O., & Ige, S. O. (2024). Dynamic pricing for SMEs using AI. *Journal of Pricing Strategy*, *6*(1).

Oyindamola, O., & Esan, M. O. (2023). Model interpretability in AI financial decision-making. *Journal of Business Analytics*, *8*(1).

Piccialli, F.. (2021). AI in healthcare predictive analytics. *Journal of Medical Technology*, *9*(2).

Porlles, . (2024). AI-driven insights for SME financial planning. *Journal of Small Business Strategy*, *10*(1).

Roy, R. (2021). AI in workforce management in India. *Journal of HR Management*, *7*(1).

Safarishahrbijari, A. (2018). Workforce forecasting models: A systematic review. *Journal of Forecasting*, *37*(6).

Santamaría, K. M., & Arias, E. R. (2023). AI in digital advertising campaigns. *Journal of Marketing Technology*, *8*(1).

Scoones, I. (2009). Livelihoods perspectives and rural development. *The Journal of Peasant Studies*, *36*(1), 171–196. DOI: 10.1080/03066150902820503

Staff, E. T. (2024, May 9). Empowering decision-making: The transformative role of data analytics. The Economic Times. https://economictimes.indiatimes.com/jobs/mid-career/empowering-decision-making-the-transformative-role-of-data-analytics/articleshow/109589355.cms

Tigmasa, C. M. (2011). Marketing strategies for SMEs: A case study. *Journal of Small Business Marketing*, *3*(2), 56–70.

Truby, J. (n.d.). Governing artificial intelligence to benefit the UN Sustainable Development Goals. Retrieved from https://scholar.google.com/citations?view_op=view_citation&hl=en&user=9oFnEiEAAAAJ&citation_for_view=9oFnEiEAAAAJ:w1MjKQ0l0TYC

UNESCO. (2012). *EFA global monitoring report 2012: Youth and skills—Putting education to work*. UNESCO Publishing.

Varshney, K. R.. (2014). Analytics-driven expertise management at IBM. *Journal of Business Analytics*, *2*(1).

Vásquez, O. A. (2022). Professional research for SME business planning. *The Journal of Entrepreneurship*, *5*(1).

Viscarra, D. A., Ninabanda, J. P., & Garcia, J. M. (2019). E-commerce opportunities for SMEs. *Journal of Digital Business*, *4*(2).

Wirtz, J., Patterson, P. G., Kunz, W. H., Gruber, T., Lu, V. N., Paluch, S., & Martins, A. (2018). Brave new world: Service robots in the frontline. *Journal of Service Management*, *29*(5), 907–931. DOI: 10.1108/JOSM-04-2018-0119

World Bank. (2013). *World development report 2013: Jobs*. World Bank Publications.

Xu, H.. (2019). Deep sequence prediction for talent flow analysis. *Journal of HR Analytics*, *3*(1), 1.

Yanamala, K. K. R. (2024). Strategic implications of AI integration in workforce planning and talent forecasting. https://www.researchgate.net/publication/385031502

Chapter 5
AI Integration for Empowering Local Talent and Skills Development in SMEs

Monalisha Patel
https://orcid.org/0009-0003-9643-7329
Lovely Professional University, India

Anasuya Swain
Indian Institute of Travel and Tourism Management, India

ABSTRACT

The integration of artificial intelligence (AI) has the potential to revolutionize the development of local talent and skills in small and medium-sized businesses (SMEs). Since SMEs are the foundation of many economies, deploying AI technologies to them can boost productivity, encourage creativity, and create new business prospects. This study investigates how integrating AI might enhance local talent by automating repetitive jobs, freeing up staff members to concentrate on strategic thinking and innovative problem-solving. Machine learning algorithms, predictive analytics, and automated customer support platforms are examples of AI-powered solutions that improve efficiency and expedite decision-making. Additionally, AI supports skill development through up skilling initiatives, virtual training environments catered to SME requirements, and personalized learning systems. SMEs may fill talent gaps, develop local knowledge, and maintain their competitiveness in a changing global market by utilizing AI.

DOI: 10.4018/979-8-3693-9611-7.ch005

INTRODUCTION

Small and Medium Enterprises (SMEs) are often regarded as the backbone of local economies, playing a pivotal role in economic development, employment generation, and innovation (UNECE, 2013). In many countries, SMEs represent the majority of businesses, contributing significantly to GDP and driving regional growth. SMEs stimulate entrepreneurship and investment across diverse industries, thereby boosting economic activity. They provide opportunities for individuals to start businesses with relatively low start-up costs, facilitating wealth creation and distribution across various demographic groups. Additionally, by serving as partners, suppliers, and service providers to larger enterprises, SMEs foster industrial growth and integrate seamlessly into the broader economic ecosystem.

One of the most critical roles of SMEs is their capacity to generate employment. Unlike larger corporations that may rely heavily on automation, SMEs are typically labour-intensive and offer job opportunities to a diverse workforce (European Commission). They absorb skilled, semi-skilled, and unskilled workers, thereby reducing unemployment and promoting social stability. Furthermore, SMEs often serve as a Launchpad for young professionals, providing them with valuable hands-on experience and opportunities to advance in their careers. SMEs are hubs of innovation, frequently developing niche products and services tailored to regional needs. Their ability to swiftly adapt to changing market conditions gives them a competitive edge over larger corporations. Moreover, SMEs drive competition, which enhances productivity, spurs innovation, and improves overall product and service quality across the economy.

By sourcing raw materials and other inputs locally, SMEs help build robust supply chains within their communities (UNECE, 2013). This localized approach minimizes economic leakage, ensuring that wealth remains within the region. Furthermore, SMEs play a critical role in addressing regional disparities by promoting economic development in rural and semi-urban areas.

Despite the advantages SMEs offer, local talent often encounters significant obstacles in developing their skills and securing meaningful employment. Overcoming these challenges is critical to fostering a sustainable and inclusive economic environment.One of the primary challenges is the gap between the skills local workers possess and those required by SMEs. Rapid industry changes and technological advancements have rendered some traditional skills obsolete while creating demand for new competencies. Many educational institutions fail to align their curricula with industry requirements, leaving graduates ill-prepared for the labour market. Skill development and vocational training programs remain scarce, particularly in underserved and rural areas. This scarcity is exacerbated by inadequate infrastructure and the high cost of professional training. Moreover, many SMEs lack the financial resources to provide in-house training, further limiting opportunities for job seekers to upskill. Economic barriers, such as the inability to afford relocation or additional education, pose significant challenges for many individuals, even those with the requisite skills.

Underemployment—where individuals work in roles below their qualifications—remains prevalent, especially in SME-dominated sectors where competitive pay and career advancement opportunities may be limited. A lack of awareness about the importance of on-going skill development and emerging career opportunities further hampers local talent. This is particularly pronounced in rural areas, where exposure to diverse industries and career paths is limited. Without proper guidance, individuals may remain confined to low-wage or informal jobs. Women face additional challenges in accessing employment and skill development opportunities, particularly in conservative or underdeveloped regions. Cultural norms, safety concerns, and the absence of women-friendly policies in many SMEs further restrict their participation in the workforce.

While digital transformation creates new employment opportunities, unequal access to technology and the internet has led to a significant digital divide. Many individuals lack the digital literacy required to capitalize on these opportunities. Additionally, SMEs themselves often struggle to fully adopt digital tools, further limiting their capacity to train employees in technological skills.

The role of SMEs in supporting regional economies is undeniable. They drive innovation, generate employment, and promote equitable regional development. However, the challenges faced by local talent in skill development and employment highlight the urgent need for institutional reforms. Strengthening educational institutions, expanding access to vocational training, and fostering partnerships between SMEs and skill development organizations are essential steps toward bridging these gaps. A collaborative approach not only ensures the sustained growth and resilience of SMEs but also empowers local talent to thrive in an increasingly competitive economy.

Small and Medium Enterprises (SMEs) require relatively less capital, are capable of making quick decisions, rely on manual labour, and operate with lower management and production costs, resulting in affordable products. SMEs typically have a small market share and are managed in a personalized manner by owners or partners rather than through a formalized management structure (UNECE, 2013). Entrepreneurs in SMEs are often independent, operating outside the framework of large enterprises. Entrepreneurship within SMEs is a creative process where management is shared, and risks are undertaken through joint ventures (Rebecca & Benjamin, 2009). Entrepreneurs discover, evaluate, and exploit opportunities, driving innovation and growth (Darren & Conrad, 2009).some certain features of the SME are as follows

- **Number of Employees**: Micro-enterprises have fewer than 50 employees; small enterprises have 50 employees, and medium-sized enterprises have between 50 and 200 employees.
- **Annual Turnover**: The total revenue generated by the enterprise.
- **Asset Value**: The total assets listed in the enterprise's balance sheet.
- **Independence**: The degree of ownership and autonomy of the enterprise.

The World Bank highlights that SMEs are among the most efficient mechanisms for generating sustainable economic growth, employment creation, and poverty alleviation. They contribute significantly to macroeconomic goals like economic growth, job creation, and poverty reduction at relatively low investment costs (World Bank).

Global Contribution of SMEs

In high-income countries, SMEs contribute over 55% of GDP and 65% of employment. In low-income nations, SMEs and informal enterprises account for over 60% of GDP and 70% of jobs. Middle-income countries rely even more heavily, with SMEs contributing 70% of GDP and 95% of employment. For instance, the European Union hosts nearly 25 million small businesses, representing 99% of all enterprises, employing around 95 million people, and contributing to 55% of private-sector employment. Furthermore, SMEs are essential to exports and productivity growth due to their flexible structures, enabling them to respond to global competition and innovation pressures. As key players in national innovation systems, they enhance entrepreneurship and competitiveness (OECD, 2004).

SMEs in India

In India, SMEs contribute 30% to GDP and provide 40% of employment, with a focus on manufacturing, trade, and services. They represent 45% of India's industrial output and 40% of exports, playing a major role in sectors like e-commerce. Government initiatives like Make in India, Start-up India, and Digital India have facilitated access to financial support, infrastructure, and technology for SMEs, promoting their growth and integration into formal economic systems (Basavapattan, 2021).

CHALLENGES AND POLICY RECOMMENDATIONS

Despite their significance, SMEs encounter multiple challenges such as limited access to finance, inefficient legal frameworks, and weak credit management. Addressing these requires policy reforms aimed at strengthening institutions, improving credit availability, and providing tailored support. In developed economies, policy direction has shifted toward supporting entrepreneurial dynamism, competitiveness, and innovation rather than simply increasing employment (OECD, 2005; Ou, 2006).

Significance of SMEs in Innovation and Employment

SMEs lead in technological and industrial innovation, frequently implementing innovative practices and leveraging technology to reduce communication and operational costs. Globally, SMEs are the largest employment providers, especially in creating new jobs. They are also instrumental in launching new products and integrating emerging technologies into the market (Ou, 2006; Office for National Statistics, 2009; Ergas & Orr, 2007; OECD, 2005).

SMEs are indispensable to both developing and developed economies. They foster innovation, drive economic growth, and boost employment generation. It is essential to strengthen legal frameworks, increase institutional efficiency, and improve access to financial and technical support to ensure their sustainable growth. A thriving SME sector is pivotal for tackling global socio-economic challenges.

According to Siswanto et al. (2021), talent identification is a vital component of talent management, which is a key HR responsibility. Conducting a skills gap analysis helps align current employee capabilities with short- and long-term role requirements. A table can be created listing present and future skill needs for every position to strategically bridge gaps.

Basavapattan (2021) adds that such an analysis enhances organizational performance by addressing both knowledge and skill deficiencies. Training, certification, and education are vital in elevating employees to the required competency level. This is especially important for SMEs, which typically lack access to capital or productivity tools like larger firms. Hence, skilled labour is a critical determinant of competitiveness and resilience.

The on-going green and digital transitions are reshaping skill demands across sectors, creating new opportunities and risks. This transformation demands not only technical skills but also "transversal skills", including digital literacy, financial insight, management ability, adaptability, and teamwork. However, tight labour markets and accelerated economic transitions have widened skill shortages, making it difficult for SMEs to recruit and retain talent.

Furthermore, many SMEs lack formal human resource strategies to address skills gaps. Some are unaware of financial support available for training or do not meet eligibility requirements. To adapt to systemic shifts and harness new opportunities, SMEs must overcome entrenched challenges and embrace a broader skillset that fosters both innovation and adaptability (Siswanto et al., 2021; Basavapattan, 2021).

Mapping Employee Skills and Suggesting Targeted Training Programs

One of the critical factors influencing a start-up's success is the skill set of its workforce. Addressing skills gaps is essential for fostering long-term growth and maintaining a competitive edge (OECD, 2019). These gaps often extend beyond technical or "hard" skills and encompass areas such as critical thinking, problem-solving, managerial and supervisory capabilities, as well as communication and interpersonal competencies (Marchese et al., 2019; Jansen & Lanz, 2013). Tailored training programs that incorporate both technical and transversal skills are therefore essential for building a resilient and adaptive workforce, particularly within SMEs. By leveraging AI tools to assess existing capabilities and recommend personalized learning pathways, organizations can effectively target and bridge these gaps, enhancing productivity, innovation, and employee satisfaction (Love & Roper, 2015; Shapira et al., 2015).Ignoring these gaps can lead to operational inefficiencies, where high-performing employees may become frustrated by uneven workloads, while underperforming employees struggle due to insufficient training or development opportunities.

THE ROLE OF AI IN BRIDGING SKILLS GAPS

AI can play a transformative role in identifying and addressing skills gaps within organizations. Start-ups, in particular, can leverage AI to analyse their workforce and recommend targeted interventions (Brynjolfsson & McElheran, 2016; Deloitte, 2020).

Understanding Skills Gaps

Skills gaps refer to the mismatch between the capabilities of a workforce and the skills required to meet organizational objectives. These gaps can impede productivity, innovation, and overall business success. In start-ups, common causes of skills gaps include rapid growth, evolving technology, employee turnover, and changing market dynamics (OECD, 2019; World Economic Forum, 2020). Start-ups often scale quickly, necessitating new skillsets that may not exist within the current team. Additionally, the constant emergence of new tools and technologies challenges teams to maintain relevant expertise. High turnover rates can also lead to the loss of critical skills and institutional knowledge, while shifting customer demands and evolving industry standards create the need for new competencies (McKinsey & Company, 2021).

AI can help start-ups address these challenges by identifying skills gaps through data-driven analysis and providing tailored recommendations for bridging them. AI-powered HR platforms can analyse employee performance data, learning history, and job requirements to generate insights and match employees with targeted learning paths (LinkedIn Learning, 2021).

Allocating Resources

To successfully implement AI-driven projects, start-ups must allocate sufficient resources for hiring and training professionals, including AI experts, trainers, and project managers. These individuals play a vital role in executing AI initiatives, addressing skills gaps, and ensuring alignment with organizational objectives (Deloitte, 2020). Without strategic resource allocation, even the most advanced AI systems may fail to deliver meaningful outcomes.

METHODOLOGY OF THE STUDY

The study adopts an exploratory and analytical research framework, incorporating an experimental model to understand how AI can support the development of Small and Medium Enterprises (SMEs), particularly in the tourism sector. This mixed approach allows for a comprehensive analysis of the integration of AI tools in addressing skill gaps, workforce optimization, and training interventions in SME ecosystems (Yin, 2014; Saunders et al., 2019).

SECONDARY DATA AND LITERATURE REVIEW

To validate the research model, secondary data is sourced from multiple reliable avenues such as state and central government records, data from ticket counters at tourist destinations (including railway and airline bookings), and statistics from tourism associations. Furthermore, the literature review includes academic studies, media articles, and industry reports relevant to AI, SME development, tourism, and skill enhancement (UNWTO, 2022; Ministry of Tourism, Government of India, 2023). Best practices in tourist traffic management are drawn from international and domestic case studies to build a comparative framework (OECD, 2020). Social media content, including feedback and travel advisories from countries and international bodies regarding social distancing and mobility management are also incorporated for analysis (Gretzel et al., 2020).

THE ROLE OF AI IN UP SKILLING AND RESKILLING

AI is increasingly acknowledged as a key enabler in transforming human capital through targeted up skilling and reskilling strategies, especially during digital transitions. Organizations leverage AI to personalize learning, assess gaps, and align workforce competencies with evolving job roles (Brynjolfsson & McAfee, 2017; McKinsey Global Institute, 2021).

- **Up skilling** involves improving current employee capabilities to align with the demands of AI-powered systems and processes.
- **Reskilling**, on the other hand, prepares employees for new roles entirely, often within adjacent functions or departments (Deloitte, 2020).

Applications and Benefits of AI in Training Programs

The integration of AI in workforce training brings several transformative advantages:

1. **Personalized Learning:** AI-based platforms tailor training modules to individual skill levels, preferences, and job roles, increasing engagement and learning efficiency (IBM, 2023).
2. **Real-Time Feedback:** AI continuously assesses learner input and adjusts content delivery for better retention and performance improvement (LinkedIn Learning, 2021).
3. **Streamlined Mentorship:** AI tools facilitate mentor-mentee matching based on compatibility, goals, and expertise, helping build internal learning networks (WEF, 2020).
4. **Industry-Specific Training:** From healthcare to marketing and software development, AI tools provide contextual training aligned with industry needs (PwC, 2020).

Adaptive Learning in Organizational Training

Adaptive learning systems transform training into a dynamic and data-driven process. They assess learner performance and engagement in real time and adjust instructional content accordingly. These systems offer personalized learning paths, immediate feedback, and actionable insights, ensuring that employees remain aligned with organizational goals while experiencing continuous learning (Baker & Siemens, 2014; Harvard Business Review, 2021).

AI Up skilling Course Outline (Based on IBM Model)

The IBM model for AI training outlines structured modules for organizational upskilling:

1. **Strategic AI Essentials** – Understanding the foundations of generative AI and business value creation.
2. **Enterprise AI Implementation** – Focuses on data management, model integration, and strategic deployment.
3. **AI in Specific Disciplines** – Addresses practical use cases in marketing, programming, and talent development while incorporating prompt engineering strategies (IBM Skills Build, 2023).

This structure ensures that the workforce is both agile and future-ready, with targeted support for enterprise-wide AI integration.

Adaptive Learning Framework

A comprehensive adaptive learning model includes eight stages:

1. **Baseline Measurement** – Initial assessments define skill levels and set a foundation for learning.
2. **Individualized Pathways** – Learning content is curated based on needs and pace.
3. **Customized Content Delivery** – Ensures that learners focus on what matters most.
4. **Interactive Learning** – Real-time engagement and behavior tracking enable better content alignment.
5. **Adaptive Feedback** – Immediate, personalized feedback enhances retention and confidence.
6. **Dynamic Adjustments** – Continuous recalibration based on performance metrics.
7. **Analytics and Insights** – Facilitates data-driven strategy formulation.
8. **Lifelong Learning** – Supports sustainable, career-long development (Siemens, 2013; EdTech Magazine, 2022).

ROLE OF DATA ANALYTICS IN ADAPTIVE LEARNING

AI-driven analytics plays a vital role in adaptive training. It helps construct comprehensive learner profiles, predicts learning outcomes, and personalizes content delivery. Predictive analytics can anticipate dropout risks or performance gaps, while real-time data improves learning outcomes and refines algorithms (Gartner, 2020; HolonIQ, 2021).

AI in Staffing and Recruitment

AI tools are revolutionizing staffing and recruitment in the following ways:

1. **Candidate Matching & Bias Reduction:** AI algorithms analyze resumes and behavior data to align candidates with job roles, minimizing unconscious bias and promoting inclusivity (HireVue, 2020).
2. **Improved Candidate Experience:** Chatbots and virtual assistants provide timely communication and personalized assistance throughout the hiring process (LinkedIn Talent Solutions, 2021).
3. **Real-Time Data Insights:** AI helps recruitment teams make strategic decisions using analytics on hiring timelines, cost-per-hire, and quality-of-hire (Glassdoor for Employers, 2020).
4. **Accelerated Hiring:** Tasks such as resume parsing and interview scheduling are automated, lowering recruitment costs and time-to-fill (SHRM, 2022).

Team Leadership in Corporate Communication

1. Engaging Leaders in Communication Planning:
    - Leadership plays a critical role in aligning teams with organizational goals.
    - In industries like manufacturing, team leaders may be disconnected from company-wide communications. Leaders must ensure objectives are clearly communicated to all team members.
2. Defining Clear Objectives:
    - Competing responsibilities can cause misalignment. Leaders must set priorities and clarify team contributions to overarching company goals.
3. Motivating Teams through Clarity:
    - When employees understand their role in the bigger picture, it fosters alignment, motivation, and a sense of purpose.

By integrating AI technologies and effective leadership strategies, organizations can drive efficiency, foster teamwork, and ensure alignment with business objectives.

Improving Teamwork in the Workplace

Enhancing teamwork in the workplace is critical to fostering productivity, collaboration, and a positive organizational culture. One effective strategy is to create teamwork recognition programs that acknowledge and celebrate collaborative efforts. Rewarding successful collaboration not only motivates individuals but also reinforces the value of working collectively towards common goals (Gratton & Erickson, 2007). Public recognition, such as awards or team spotlight write-ups, helps to build morale and encourage a sense of ownership and belonging. This approach is especially vital for remote or frontline teams who may not benefit from spontaneous, in-person affirmations of their contributions (Ferrazzi, 2015). Platforms like Blink's Recognition feature enable organizations to implement structured acknowledgment systems, thereby boosting engagement, enhancing job satisfaction, and promoting a culture of continuous collaboration (Blink, 2023). Moreover, clarifying ownership at the outset is essential. When roles, responsibilities, and deliverables are documented and communicated clearly, it eliminates confusion and helps teams function more efficiently (Hackman, 2002). Setting clear expectations supports accountability and ensures that all members understand their individual contributions within the broader team objectives.

Enhancing Team Communication and Clarity through Accessible Documentation and Defined Goals

Ensuring that documentation is easily accessible is fundamental to preventing ambiguity and minimizing conflicts within teams. For instance, digital platforms such as Blink's Hub enable employees to access job responsibilities and related documents conveniently on the go, fostering transparency and clarity (Blink, 2023). Effective communication must be a two-way street; encouraging open dialogue allows team members to comfortably share ideas, voice concerns, and provide constructive feedback, which strengthens trust and collaboration (Robinson & Hullinger, 2008). Utilizing secure communication tools like centralized hubs, personalized feeds, or chat systems facilitates multi-directional communication and keeps everyone updated in real time (Maznevski & Chudoba, 2000).

Clear delineation of roles, responsibilities, and timelines is essential to avoid confusion. Involving the entire team in establishing project workflows and deadlines empowers members to negotiate realistic expectations, thereby increasing commitment and reducing misunderstandings (Hackman, 2002). Furthermore, a clearly articulated organizational purpose helps team members understand how their efforts contribute to the company's long-term goals, which enhances motivation, engagement, and innovation (Katzenbach & Smith, 2005). Storing mission statements on accessible platforms ensures consistent guidance and alignment across all levels (Kaplan & Norton, 2004).

Setting clear, measurable team goals aligns efforts and provides a framework for accountability. Defining specific objectives and establishing processes that guide team behaviours toward these goals supports effective performance management (Locke & Latham, 2002). Applications like Blink facilitate this process by enabling real-time updates and centralized storage of policies and procedures, making it easier for teams to stay coordinated (Blink, 2023). Regular internal communications assessments help identify pain points such as missed deadlines or unresponsiveness, allowing organizations to address issues proactively and maintain workflow efficiency (Clampitt, 2012).

Fostering Collaboration through Flexible Communication and Conflict Resolution Strategies

To build a cohesive and motivated workforce, organizations must recognize that employees have diverse communication styles and preferences. Allowing teams to utilize multiple communication methods—such as chat rooms, one-on-one meetings, group discussions, or mobile apps—ensures inclusivity and engagement across different working styles (Daft & Lengel, 1986). For frontline or remote workers, providing access to employee communication apps like Blink is particularly beneficial, as it enables seamless, real-time information exchange and feedback through mobile and desktop platforms (Blink, 2023). Flexibility in communication tools empowers employees, encourages consistent interaction, and reinforces a sense of belonging.

In addition to enhancing communication, successful teamwork also relies on clearly defined roles, active recognition, and organizational support for autonomy. Recognizing achievements, clarifying individual responsibilities, and promoting collaborative decision-making foster a productive and trust-based environment (Deci & Ryan, 2000; Katzenbach & Smith, 2005). However, even in well-functioning teams, conflicts can arise. Mediating disputes constructively—through open dialogue, active listening, and neutral facilitation—ensures that disagreements are resolved without disrupting team cohesion (Jehn, 1995). Leaders play a critical role in establishing a culture where differences are addressed respectfully and resolved efficiently, further strengthening team dynamics.

Promoting Effective Team Communication and Conflict Resolution

In today's dynamic work environments, recognizing diverse communication preferences among team members is crucial for fostering effective collaboration. Allowing teams to choose from multiple communication methods—such as chat rooms, one-on-one meetings, or group discussions—empowers individuals and enhances inclusivity (Daft & Lengel, 1986). For frontline workers or remote teams, providing flexible tools like mobile and desktop employee communication apps (e.g., Blink) can bridge communication gaps, offering real-time updates, feedback channels, and centralized information sharing (Blink, 2023). These platforms not only streamline communication but also support role clarity, promote autonomy, and ensure that all team members feel heard and connected.

Beyond communication, successful teamwork hinges on recognizing achievements and managing interpersonal dynamics. By encouraging open dialogue, celebrating collaborative success, and clearly outlining responsibilities, organizations nurture a culture of mutual respect and motivation (Katzenbach & Smith, 2005). When disputes arise—as they inevitably do—leaders must step in to mediate constructively. Effective conflict resolution involves active listening, neutrality, and a structured approach that transforms disagreements into opportunities for growth, preserving trust and team cohesion (Jehn, 1995). Through strategic communication tools and empathetic leadership, workplaces can become more collaborative, resilient, and goal-driven.

Encouraging Flexible Work to Improve Teamwork and Well-Being

Flexible work arrangements have emerged as a key strategy for enhancing employee satisfaction, mental well-being, and overall productivity. By allowing employees to better manage their work-life balance, flex work options can significantly reduce stress levels, improve morale, and foster a more engaged and motivated workforce (Allen et al., 2013). Organizations that pair flexible schedules with the right employee engagement tools—such as mobile apps for communication, recognition, and feedback—create an environment where collaboration thrives, regardless of physical location. For instance, tools like Blink not only keep remote and frontline employees connected but also ensure they remain involved in team discussions, goal tracking, and recognition initiatives. As a result, offering flex work options, supported by robust digital platforms, can lead to stronger teamwork, increased trust, and a culture of inclusivity and high performance (Bloom et al., 2015).

Building a Culture of Collaboration and Continuous Improvement

Effective teamwork is built on a foundation of open communication, mutual respect, and cultural alignment. One vital step in enhancing team dynamics is to actively solicit feedback from team members. Creating safe spaces for open dialogue and using tools like Blink's in-app surveys can help organizations monitor progress, identify bottlenecks, and foster a culture of transparency (Gallup, 2022). Additionally, hiring practices should extend beyond qualifications, placing emphasis on candidates' alignment with team culture and values. Involving existing team members in the recruitment process can ensure better team compatibility and cohesion (SHRM, 2020).

To further reinforce collaboration, organizations can initiate culture committees that focus on promoting shared values, team-building activities, and inclusive practices. These committees serve as a bridge between leadership and employees, encouraging openness and accountability. Moreover, introducing a mentorship program allows for knowledge sharing, leadership development, and deeper inter-team relationships, especially beneficial for on boarding new employees or up skilling current ones. When paired with flexible work options and digital engagement tools, such initiatives contribute to a highly engaged, motivated, and collaborative workforce (HBR, 2021).

Enhancing Teamwork in the Workplace: Strategies, Tools, and Cultural Shifts

Effective teamwork is the cornerstone of any successful organization. It fosters innovation, strengthens problem-solving capabilities, and significantly boosts employee engagement. In today's hybrid work environment, where teams are increasingly distributed, organizations must adopt diverse strategies to maintain collaboration, cohesion, and morale.

Creative Environments and Team Bonding

To break the monotony and inspire creativity, holding meetings outside traditional office settings—such as in cafes, parks, or co-working spaces—can be highly effective. These alternative venues foster informal communication and innovation.

However, it's essential to maintain data security by employing VPNs and other cyber security measures when using public Wi-Fi.

Establishing team traditions such as regular coffee breaks, team lunches, or friendly competitions helps build camaraderie in a relaxed, non-hierarchical setting. These rituals create shared experiences that reinforce trust and enhance interpersonal connections. Additionally, rotating team structures periodically—mixing long-established teams with newly formed ones—can merge the productivity of seasoned groups with the fresh perspectives and dynamism of new members.

Leveraging Digital Tools for Collaboration

The role of employee engagement apps like *Blink* is crucial in unifying teams, especially those that include both desk-based and frontline workers. These platforms centralize communication, reduce the need for redundant meetings, and enhance transparency. Features like engagement analytics and feedback tools allow leaders to monitor morale, gather insights, and proactively address emerging issues.

By offering centralized feeds, project management tools, and secure chat systems, such apps ensure seamless information sharing. They empower employees with flexible communication methods—are it through live updates, quick polls, or collaborative document sharing—leading to improved alignment and efficiency.

Workplace Teamwork: Why It Matters

Teamwork is more than just a collaboration technique—it's a business imperative. According to recent findings:

- **Engagement**: Employees who feel they are part of a cohesive team are more than twice as likely to be fully engaged in their work (Gallup, 2022).
- **Innovation**: Teams that collaborate intentionally are nearly three times more likely to achieve successful outcomes (McKinsey, 2021).

Thus, fostering teamwork contributes not only to employee satisfaction but also to long-term business performance.

Foundations of Effective Team Collaboration

True collaboration involves more than shared tasks—it demands open communication, mutual respect, and a willingness to compromise for the greater good. Teams must be given the tools and support to coordinate efforts, share knowledge, and deliver collective outcomes greater than the sum of individual contributions.

Integrating AI literacy and digital competencies into workforce training is increasingly vital. Companies that invest in reskilling employees for the AI era create a competitive edge, ensuring adaptability in a rapidly evolving technological landscape (Deloitte, 2020).

From redefining team spaces to embedding digital solutions and nurturing a collaborative culture, organizations must adopt a multi-pronged approach to improving teamwork. By embracing creativity, encouraging feedback, leveraging engagement platforms, and investing in continuous learning, businesses can build high-performing teams ready to thrive in the modern workplace

Effective teamwork is the backbone of organizational success, fostering innovation, enhancing problem-solving, and boosting employee engagement. In today's hybrid work culture, organizations must adopt innovative strategies to maintain team cohesion and morale across distributed environments. Creating informal, creative spaces—like parks, cafés, or co-working venues—for meetings can break routine and stimulate new ideas, while maintaining cyber security through VPNs ensures data safety. Team traditions such as coffee breaks or friendly competitions enhance bonding and trust in a relaxed setting, and periodically rotating team member's blends experience with fresh perspectives. Digital tools like employee engagement apps (e.g., Blink) play a pivotal role in uniting desk-based and frontline workers, streamlining communication, and enabling real-time collaboration through features like project management dashboards, secure chats, and feedback systems. These tools improve transparency, foster alignment, and help leaders monitor team morale. With studies showing that engaged teams are over twice as productive (Gallup, 2022) and three times more innovative (McKinsey, 2021), cultivating teamwork is not for sustainable just beneficial but essential business performance.

Meet in Different Locations

- Occasionally hold meetings outside the office to inspire creativity and improve communication.
- Use alternative venues like cafes or public spaces but ensure cybersecurity measures are in place when using public Wi-Fi.

AI Tool Development for SMEs

1. Collaborate with Tech Providers
    - Partnership Development:
    - Identify and partner with established technology providers specializing in AI tools tailored to SME operations.

- Engage industry-specific domain experts (e.g., retail, manufacturing, logistics) to ensure relevance and accuracy.
- Customization:
- Design user-friendly interfaces to minimize complexity for non-technical users.
- Customize tools to fit existing operational workflows of SMEs.
- Ensure flexibility and scalability to support future growth.
- Key Features to Prioritize:
- Predictive analytics for demand forecasting and inventory optimization.
- Automation of repetitive tasks like data entry and customer service.
- Personalized recommendations for marketing and sales enhancement.

2. Pilot the Solution with Selected SMEs
   - Selection Criteria:
   - Choose a diverse group of SMEs based on size, industry type, and AI readiness.
   - Prioritize SMEs eager to adopt AI tools to ensure active engagement and valuable feedback.
   - Implementation Strategy:
   - Deploy tools in a controlled environment within the selected SMEs.
   - Conduct hands-on training sessions to support smooth onboarding and tool usage.
   - Establish measurable success metrics (e.g., cost efficiency, productivity gains, error reduction).
   - Feedback Mechanism:
   - Create continuous feedback loops through surveys, user interviews, and live support.
   - Use feedback to refine features, address usability challenges, and enhance tool performance.

Outcome:

A pilot-based approach leads to the development of practical, industry-tested AI solutions, fostering SME confidence and readiness for large-scale implementation.

Deployment and Training of AI Tools for SMEs

1. Deployment across the SME Network
   - Phased Rollout:
   - Implement a staggered deployment across SME clusters categorized by industry or region.

- Apply learning's from pilot phases to streamline the rollout and mitigate risks.
- Infrastructure Setup:
- Assess and upgrade digital infrastructure where needed (e.g., internet speed, hardware compatibility).
- Offer technical assistance for installation, configuration, and integration.
- Customization during Deployment:
- Adapt features to the unique needs and workflows of different SMEs.
- Include optional modules to allow flexible, phased adoption.
- On-going Support System:
- Establish a robust support team for troubleshooting and consultation.
- Provide comprehensive self-help materials (FAQs, manuals, video tutorials).

2. Training for SME Owners, HR Teams, and Employees
    - Role-Specific Training Modules:
    - **SME Owners:** Strategic AI implementation for business growth and decision-making.
    - **HR Teams:** Use of AI in talent acquisition, employee engagement, and analytics.
    - **Employees:** Daily operational use of AI tools for enhanced productivity.
    - Delivery Methods:
    - Combine on-site workshops, virtual training, and self-paced e-learning for accessibility and flexibility.
    - Real-World Simulations:
    - Include industry-relevant case studies and demonstrations.
    - Simulate real-time scenarios to show problem-solving using AI tools.
    - Certification and Incentives:
    - Offer certification programs to recognize successful training completion.
    - Introduce rewards or recognition to encourage active participation.
    - Feedback and Iteration:
    - Collect feedback to refine training content and methodology.
    - Offer refresher courses to maintain and update skill levels regularly.

Final Outcome:

A structured deployment and comprehensive training approach ensures:

- Seamless AI adoption across SMEs.
- Enhanced employee competencies and AI literacy.
- Tangible improvements in productivity, decision-making, and operational efficiency.

Monitoring and Scaling of AI Tools for SMEs

1. Monitoring Impact Using Key Performance Indicators (KPIs)
    - **Define Relevant KPIs**:
        - o **Productivity Metrics**: Measure improvements in task completion time, output quality, and operational efficiency.
        - o **Cost Savings**: Track reductions in operational costs resulting from automation or optimized processes.
        - o **Adoption Rate**: Assess the percentage of employees actively using AI tools and their frequency of use.
        - o **Employee Satisfaction**: Use surveys to gauge how employees feel about AI's impact on their work.
        - o **Customer Outcomes**: For customer-facing SMEs, evaluate metrics like customer satisfaction (CSAT) scores, retention rates, and lead conversion rates.
    - **Data Collection**:
        - o Use **AI tools' built-in analytics** to gather usage data and performance insights.
        - o Conduct **periodic surveys** and **feedback sessions** with SME owners and employees.
        - o Integrate feedback loops to identify challenges or gaps in real-time.
    - **Regular Reporting**:
        - o Develop dashboards for SMEs to monitor their progress against predefined KPIs.
        - o Present aggregated reports to stakeholders, showing overall impact and areas for improvement.
2. Refining Solutions
    - **Continuous Feedback**:
        - o Gather ongoing input from SMEs on pain points or areas where AI tools can be improved.
        - o Address feedback by collaborating with technology providers to refine and update features.
    - **Adaptive Learning Models**:
        - o If applicable, ensure AI solutions are built with machine learning capabilities to improve over time based on usage patterns and data inputs.
        - o Regularly retrain AI models to reflect changing business needs or market trends.
    - **User-Centric Enhancements**:

- o Introduce updates that enhance usability, such as simpler interfaces or more industry-specific functionalities.

3. Scaling Implementation
   - **Expand Across SME Network**:
     - o Once initial deployment proves successful, roll out solutions to more SMEs across industries or regions.
     - o Use insights from monitoring to create industry-specific modules for broader appeal.
   - **Collaboration and Partnerships**:
     - o Collaborate with trade associations or government programs to subsidize AI adoption for more SMEs.
     - o Partner with tech providers to offer flexible pricing models for different SME sizes.
   - **Train-the-Trainer Programs**:
     - o Train SME leaders or champions to act as in-house experts who can support scaling efforts and assist new users.
   - **Global Expansion**:
     - o If applicable, adapt AI tools for international SMEs, addressing language, cultural, and regulatory differences.

Outcome:

Through monitoring KPIs and refining solutions, SMEs can maximize the value of AI tools. Scaling ensures that more businesses benefit from AI-driven efficiency and innovation, fostering a competitive edge across the SME ecosystem.

Estimated Expenditure

1. Recruitment and Hiring Costs

This includes expenses related to sourcing, interviewing, and onboarding specialized personnel.

- **AI Experts (3 personnel):**
  - o Hiring costs:Rs50,000
  - o Average annual salary (per expert): 600,000

    Total: **1850,000**

- **Trainers (2 personnel):**
  - o Hiring costs: 50000
  - o Average annual salary (per trainer): 600,000

Total: **125,0000**

- **Project Managers (2 personnel):**
  - o Hiring costs: 50,000
  - o Average annual salary (per manager): 100,0000

    Total: **2050,000**

    Subtotal: 3150,000

2. Development Costs

Expenses related to building the AI systems, including labor and software resources:

- **AI Experts:** 6 months development phase.
  - o Monthly salary: 50,000 (x3 experts)
  - o Total for 6 months: **150,000**
- **Training Program Development:**
  - o Trainers: 2 months for content creation and setup.
  - o Cost: 300,000

    Subtotal: 450,000

3. Deployment Costs

Resources needed for deploying the AI systems and ensuring smooth operations.

- **Deployment Phase (2 months):**
  - o AI Experts:Rs500,000
  - o Project Managers: Rs250000
  - o Trainers: Rs250000
- **Software and Infrastructure:**
  - o Cloud computing, tools, and licenses: 3000,000
  - o Testing and quality assurance: Rs 5,0000

    Subtotal: 135,0000

4. Training Costs

Costs for training AI systems and end-users:

- **Trainers' Salaries:** 3 months training phase.
  - Cost: Rs200,000
- **Training Materials and Resources:**
  - Manuals, software tools, and certifications: Rs15,0000
- **Workshops and Sessions:**
  - Cost per session: Rs50000 (x10 sessions)
  - Total: Rs 50,000

    Subtotal: Rs 400000

5. Contingency (10% of Total Budget)

To cover unexpected expenses:

- **Contingency: Rs100000**

  Total Estimated Budget 5450000

Justification of Budget

- **Competitive Salaries:** Attracting skilled AI experts, trainers, and project managers is essential for a high-quality research project.
- **Comprehensive Development:** Ensures the AI system is built and deployed effectively with minimal errors.
- **Training Focus:** Supports the end-users and ensures optimal utilization of the AI system.
- **Contingency:** Accounts for unforeseen costs to keep the project on track.

Implementation Timeline

- Recruitment: 2 months
- Development: 6 months
- Deployment: 2 months
- Training: 3 months

REFERENCES

Allen, T. D., Golden, T. D., & Shockley, K. M. (2013). How effective is telecommuting? Assessing the status of our scientific findings. *Psychological Science in the Public Interest, 16*(2), 40–68. PMID: 26403188

Baker, R. S., & Siemens, G. (2014). Educational data mining and learning analytics. In Sawyer, R. K. (Ed.), *Cambridge handbook of the learning sciences* (2nd ed.). Cambridge University Press.

Basavapattan, S. (2021). A study on talent management practices in small and medium enterprises. [Unpublished manuscript or specify source].

Blink. (2023a). Enhancing team communication and collaboration. https://www.joinblink.com

Blink. (2023b). Flexible work and employee engagement. https://www.joinblink.com

Blink. (2023c). How Blink enhances team communication. https://www.joinblink.com

Blink. (2023d). How recognition improves team performance. https://www.joinblink.com

Bloom, N., Liang, J., Roberts, J., & Ying, Z. J. (2015). Does working from home work? Evidence from a Chinese experiment. *The Quarterly Journal of Economics, 130*(1), 165–218.

Brynjolfsson, E., & McAfee, A. (2017). *Machine, platform, crowd: Harnessing our digital future.* W. W. Norton & Company.

Brynjolfsson, E., & McElheran, K. (2016). The rapid adoption of data-driven decision-making. *The American Economic Review, 106*(5), 133–139. DOI: 10.1257/aer.p20161047

Clampitt, P. G. (2012). *Communicating for managerial effectiveness.* SAGE Publications.

Daft, R. L., & Lengel, R. H. (1986). Organizational information requirements, media richness, and structural design. *Management Science, 32*(5), 554–571.

Darren, L., & Conrad, L. (2009). *Entrepreneurship: Opportunities and innovation.* [Publisher].

Deci, E. L., & Ryan, R. M. (2000). The "what" and "why" of goal pursuits: Human needs and the self-determination of behavior. *Psychological Inquiry, 11*(4), 227–268.

Deloitte. (2020a). *AI and the future of skills: How organizations can prepare for AI's impact on talent*. Deloitte Insights. https://www2.deloitte.com

Deloitte. (2020b). *AI and talent development: Embracing the transformation*. https://www2.deloitte.com

EdTech Magazine. (2022). Adaptive learning's role in future-ready education. [URL if available]

Ergas, H., & Orr, J. (2007). SMEs and innovation. [Specify publication details].

European Commission. (n.d.). What is an SME? https://single-market-economy.ec.europa.eu/smes/sme-definition_en

Ferrazzi, K. (2015). Getting virtual teams right. *Harvard Business Review*.

Gallup. (2022). Creating a culture of feedback. https://www.gallup.com

Gartner. (2020). The future of learning analytics. [URL if available]

Glassdoor for Employers. (2020). Recruiting statistics. [URL if available]

Gratton, L., & Erickson, T. J. (2007). Eight ways to build collaborative teams. *Harvard Business Review*, *85*(11), 100–109. PMID: 18159790

Gretzel, U., ... (2020). Tourism policy responses to COVID-19. *Journal of Tourism Futures*. https://doi.org/[DOI if available]

Hackman, J. R. (2002). *Leading teams: Setting the stage for great performances*. Harvard Business Press.

Harvard Business Review. (2021). How AI is changing learning and development. [URL if available]

Harvard Business Review (HBR). (2021). How mentorship programs boost employee engagement and team culture. https://hbr.org

HireVue. (2020). AI and recruitment: Building fairness into hiring. [URL if available]

HolonIQ. (2021). Top trends in AI-powered education. [URL if available]

IBM SkillsBuild. (2023). *Enterprise AI training roadmap*. https://skillsbuild.org

Jansen, M., & Lanz, R. (2013). *Skills and export competitiveness: An analysis of the World Input-Output Database*. WTO Staff Working Paper ERSD-2013-03. https://doi.org/DOI: 10.2139/ssrn.2227095

Jehn, K. A. (1995). A multimethod examination of the benefits and detriments of intragroup conflict. *Administrative Science Quarterly*, *40*(2), 256–282.

Kaplan, R. S., & Norton, D. P. (2004). *Strategy maps: Converting intangible assets into tangible outcomes*. Harvard Business School Press.

Katzenbach, J. R., & Smith, D. K. (2005). *The wisdom of teams: Creating the high-performance organization*. HarperBusiness.

LinkedIn Learning. (2021). *2021 workplace learning report*. https://learning.linkedin.com/resources/workplace-learning-report

LinkedIn Learning. (2021). *Workplace learning report*. https://learning.linkedin.com

LinkedIn Talent Solutions. (2021). *Global talent trends*. [URL if available]

Locke, E. A., & Latham, G. P. (2002). Building a practically useful theory of goal setting and task motivation: A 35-year odyssey. *The American Psychologist, 57*(9), 705–717. PMID: 12237980

Love, J. H., & Roper, S. (2015). SME innovation, exporting and growth: A review of existing evidence. *International Small Business Journal, 33*(1), 28–48. DOI: 10.1177/0266242614550190

Marchese, M., Lane, M., & Kirmizi, P. (2019). *Assessing and anticipating skills for the green transition: Emerging lessons from OECD countries* (OECD Green Growth Papers, 2019-03). OECD Publishing. https://doi.org/DOI: 10.1787/6ff6bdaf-en

Maznevski, M. L., & Chudoba, K. M. (2000). Bridging space over time: Global virtual team dynamics and effectiveness. *Organization Science, 11*(5), 473–492.

McKinsey & Company. (2021). The future of work after. *COVID, 19*, •••. https://www.mckinsey.com/featured-insights/future-of-work

McKinsey Global Institute. (2021). Reskilling and The future of work after. *COVID, 19*, •••. https://www.mckinsey.com/featured-insights/future-of-work

OECD. (2004). *Promoting entrepreneurship and innovative SMEs in a global economy: Towards a more responsible and inclusive globalization*. OECD Publishing.

OECD. (2005). *SME and Entrepreneurship Outlook*. OECD Publishing.

OECD. (2019). *OECD SME and entrepreneurship outlook 2019*. OECD Publishing., DOI: 10.1787/34907e9c-

OECD. (2019). *OECD skills outlook 2019: Thriving in a digital world*. OECD Publishing., DOI: 10.1787/df80bc12-

OECD. (2019). *OECD Skills Outlook 2019: Thriving in a digital world.* OECD Publishing. https://doi.org/ Ministry of Tourism, Government of India. (2023). *Tourism statistics report.*DOI: 10.1787/df80bc12-en

OECD. (2020). *AI in the tourism sector: Opportunities and challenges.*

Office for National Statistics. (2009). [Publisher]. *Labour Market Trends.*

Ou, C. (2006). Bank lending to small businesses in the United States. [Publication details].

PwC. (2020). *AI and training: The next competitive edge.*

Rebecca, D., & Benjamin, M. (2009). *Understanding small business dynamics: Innovation and shared leadership.* [Publisher].

Robinson, S., & Hullinger, H. (2008). New benchmarks in higher education: Student engagement in online learning. *Journal of Education for Business, 84*(2), 101–109.

Saunders, M., Lewis, P., & Thornhill, A. (2019). *Research methods for business students* (8th ed.). Pearson Education.

Shapira, P., Youtie, J., Kay, L., & Liu, J. (2015). Proximity and the use of public science by innovative small firms in the United States. *Science & Public Policy, 42*(5), 688–701. DOI: 10.1093/scipol/scu088

SHRM. (2020). Hiring for culture fit. Society for Human Resource Management. https://www.shrm.org

SHRM. (2022). *HR tech trends: The role of AI in hiring.* https://www.shrm.org

Siemens, G. (2013). Learning analytics: The emergence of a discipline. *The American Behavioral Scientist.*

Siswanto, J., Cahyono, E., Monang, J., Aisha, A. N., & Mulyadi, D. (2021). Identifying talent: Public organisation with skewed performance scores. *Journal of Management Development, 40*(4), 293–312. DOI: 10.1108/JMD-06-2020-0272

Siswanto, J., Wahyuni, S., & Rizki, M. (2021). Talent management and skill gap analysis for SMEs. [Publication details].

University of Texas at San Antonio (UTSA). (2021). *UTSA Small Business Development Center International Trade Center Annual Report.* https://txsbdc.org

UNWTO. (2022). *International tourism and COVID-19: Recovery trends.*

World Bank. (n.d.). How do economies define micro, small and medium enterprises (MSMEs)? International Finance Corporation. https://www.ifc.org/wps/w

World Bank. (n.d.). *Small and Medium Enterprises (SMEs)*. Finance. [URL if available]

World Economic Forum. (2020). *The future of jobs report 2020*. http://www.weforum.org

World Economic Forum. (2020). *Upskilling for shared prosperity*.

Chapter 6
AI Support for Small and Medium Enterprises' Economic Enhancement and Product and Innovation Services

S. Srinivasan
https://orcid.org/0009-0002-0179-9849
Department of Humanities and Social Sciences, Graphic Era University, Dehradun, India

R. Vallipriya
https://orcid.org/0009-0008-6692-603X
Department of Physical Science, Institute of Education, (B.ED College), Tamil Nadu Teacher Education University, Trichy, India

Ajay Kumar Singh Singh
https://orcid.org/0000-0003-0429-0925
Department of Humanities and Social Sciences, Graphic Era University, Dehradun, India

ABSTRACT

Small and Medium Enterprises (SMEs) aim to improve financial access, enhance their operations, provide innovative solutions, and unlock sources of capital. The study emphasizes SMEs' growing presence globally, as they provide numerous opportunities and create jobs for people of all types. This study focuses on the economic improvement for SME workers. It addresses the strategic plan to support SMEs, providing numerous opportunities for both educated and uneducated people.

DOI: 10.4018/979-8-3693-9611-7.ch006

AI can play a vital role in improving economic growth, and assistive technology can enhance the innovation of products and services. Small and Medium Enterprises utilize E-Entrepreneurship for advertising. The usage of artificial intelligence helps SMEs support their finances and operate more efficiently. It can be used for financial aspects, with AI supporting billing, sales, and record maintenance. In small businesses, AI can enhance sales strategies by better predicting leads and improving business outcomes.

INTRODUCTION

Small and Medium Enterprises (SMEs) play an important role in the economic development of developing countries (Tahi Hamonangan Tambunan, 2011; Fiseha & Oyelana, 2015). SMEs are the major businesses worldwide. They are important for creating more jobs in global economic development. It represents nearly 90% of business owners and 50% of workers in employment worldwide. SMEs play a crucial role in contributing to up to 40% of national income increases and in emerging GDP rates and economies (Keskġn et al., 2010; Zafar & Mustafa, 2017; Ndiaye et al., 2018). These numbers are highly significant in informal SMEs. According to estimates, there are 600 million people who will need jobs by 2039 to absorb global workers, which can make a significant contribution to SME development. There is a high priority for governments around the world. Modern technology increases formal jobs through SMEs, which can create 7 out of 10 jobs. The growth of SMEs can be constrained by finance, and in addition, SMEs need to grow their businesses and emerging markets in developing countries (Kumar, 2017; Maksimov et al., 2017; Abisuga-Oyekunle et al., 2020).

The study mainly emphasizes that SMEs are likely to obtain bank loans and internal funds, or cash from friends and family; initially, they do not launch and run their business enterprises (Amoako-Adu & Eshun, 2018). Nearly 65 million firms are part of the International Finance Corporation, and 40% of the formal micro, small, and medium enterprises (MSMEs) are in developing countries (Madan, 2020). It represents the highest proportion of finance and addresses the comparison of the gap, which indicates potential demand. It measures nearly 87% and 88%, respectively. Half of the formal SMEs don't have access to the formal credit system. There is a gap in accounting for micro and informal enterprises. This is a holistic approach to lending services that support women-owned SMEs and their contributions (Farazi, 2014; Muhika, 2019; Megersa, 2020).

The study provides a comprehensive understanding of how to implement good practices for the global share of SMEs. The study addresses SME finance through methods such as e-lending, credit decisioning, e-invoicing, and e-factoring for financing (Ogujiuba et al., 2023). SME financing at the global level involves participation in the G20 Global Partnership for Financial Inclusion, financial stability, and the International Credit Committee for credit reports related to SME finance problems (Bwembya, 2022). SMEs are investing their money in growth, export, and diversification. SMEs face financing challenges that provide debt/quasi-debt; these are the startups for high-growth bank financing (Iloka, 20202).

Artificial Intelligence Support for SME Innovations

The study mainly emphasizes AI support to enhance business and improve self-assessment to innovate small and medium-sized enterprises (SMEs). This can be useful for SMEs as it is cost-effective and helps assess business development to innovate capacities across SME activities (Häring et al., 2023; Proenca, 2024; Jain et al., 2025). The SMEs' innovation focuses on their activities in the aspects of the innovation process, working environment, culture, innovation capabilities, and the use of technology to enhance business performance (Saunila, 2016; Aksoy, 2017). The findings of the study reveal that AI-based data analysis can be used for predictive modeling for SMEs. It offers actionable insights for their business. The study mainly emphasizes AI support to enhance business and improve self-assessment to innovate small and medium-sized enterprises (SMEs) (Bi et al., 2017). This can be useful for SMEs as it is cost-effective and helps assess business development to innovate capacities across SME activities. Business and supports an effective decision-making process (Gilmore, A., & Carson, D. 2018; Srinivasan & Vallipriay, 2025). The study addresses SMEs' business activities with the support of technology, focusing on data quality, algorithmic bias, and privacy concerns. It aims to improve business operations carefully, avoid risks, and support AI implementation in SME activities (Kalishina, 2023; Eberhardsteiner 2024). The study highlights the impact of AI in supporting SMEs' innovation divide and its role in democratizing access to advanced management tools. This can support SMEs in achieving their business goals and strategic improvements in business activities. The study examines AI-driven support for business activities and AI-driven tools to improve SME business innovation, address various gaps, and provide consultancy to foster economic inclusion in their business activities (Yusuf et al., 2024; Evelynn & Harlee, 2024; Michael, 2025; Kanellopoulou et al., 2025) .

AI-Driven Consulting and Self-Assessment Improve SME Innovation and Competitiveness

Small and Medium Enterprises (SMEs) need new innovative ideas in their business to compete in the modern world. This can improve various aspects such as education, leadership quality, and decision-making power (Gamage et al., 2020; Knezović & Drkić, 2021). It can also promote government and academic involvement to support their business activities. An effective approach to enhancing SMEs' knowledge and business innovation requires fostering an SME mindset and synthesizing advanced technological equipment (Bhuiyan et al., 2024). SMEs can leverage advanced technology to empower their business activities through various effective government policies, proper advanced programs, and mentorship support, facilitating their business growth (Lukonga, 2020). The government and non-governmental organizations support and provide training and hands-on assistance to help SMEs improve and generate new innovative ideas for their businesses. The main motto for SMEs is to enhance capacity building and initiate innovation in their business. SMEs consist of various groups of people, and the government can arrange educational support and vocational training to develop better entrepreneurs and create stronger business leaders (Ng & Kee, 2012). The positive and negative aspects of SME activities in business require personalized support for entrepreneurs, along with innovative approaches and effective management strategies for their business activities (Temel & Durst, 2021).

The study focused on self-assessment of the eight critical areas of management innovation, which are common challenges faced by SMEs. The increasing importance of AI and its role in business innovation for management is emphasized.

Figure 1. SMEs Business Management

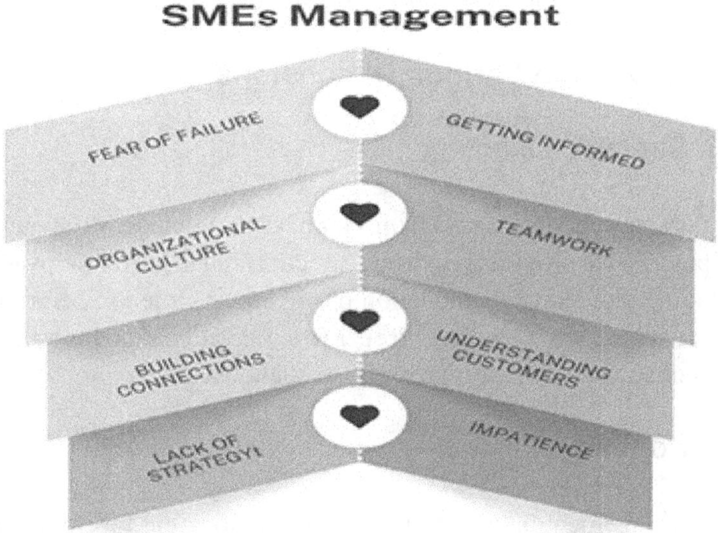

Eight Challenges Facing SMEs Innovation

Fear of Failure – SMEs involve risks, which can hinder creativity and lead to mistakes in decision-making.
Staying Informed – In their business trends, there can be advancements in strategic development.
Organizational Culture – SMEs do not have encouragement in their business and in taking risks for business activities, which can foster innovation in their mindset.
Teamwork – Innovation for SMEs business people, whether in a team or individually, relies on an effective communication process.
Building Connections – In their business, collaboration is needed, including both internal and external collaboration, for breakthroughs in knowledge sharing.
Understanding Customers – SMEs people can engage in polite communication and deal with customers properly for an actual experience.
Lack of Strategy – Small and Marginal Medium Enterprises focus on innovation for direction, which can be flexible within a structured approach for effective implementation in their business activities.

Impatience – There is meaningful value in their innovation and time. Rushing the process can lead to compromises in quality, which can impact their business improvement.

Business Innovation Various Dimensions

Innovation Strategic Orientation

Business strategy encompasses a firm's innovation-related SMEs' values, beliefs, and regular practices to provide the correct direction and focus for innovation efforts. Decision-making and resource allocation play a crucial role in SMEs' competitive efforts in current business activities. Proper resource allocation helps the company consistently enhance business progress (Tsiu et al., 2024).

Innovation Portfolio

Strategic management balances business and innovation for project initiatives. This supports innovation efforts for growth and focuses on the horizons and risk levels of SMEs. It helps achieve goals and maintain competitiveness in their business activities (Islam & Wahab, 2021).

Innovation Process

SMEs, in their business, provide new innovative ideas that can be transformed into tangible outputs in various aspects. This can lead to product or service enhancements, service improvements, or process innovations. Innovation plays a vital role in business management by consistently and effectively improving the identification, development, and implementation of new ideas for the business (Hsieh & Chou, 2018).

Innovative Talent and Culture

In small-scale businesses, their environmental situation and values influence employee participation, support, and innovation in business activities. This helps business owners create and maintain an environment conducive to innovation and risk-taking behavior. A positive business environment enhances creativity, reduces fear of risk, encourages new ideas, fosters positive thinking, and drives continuous improvement in the business (Abd Hair Awang et al., 2014; Lijauco et al., 2020).

Innovation Capabilities

SMEs continuously improve and transform knowledge into new innovative ideas, enhancing their business products and processes for the benefit of the firm and its stakeholders (Ulas, 2019; Fernando, 2019). Business innovation capabilities help optimize resources and enhance skills, serving as a fundamental factor for innovation. This leads to consistent and effective growth (Nylén & Holmström, 2015).

Innovation Strategic Alliances

Innovation helps establish SMEs by enhancing business feasibility. It focuses on new ideas, technologies, and expertise to improve relationships within companies and manage their ecosystem for fostering innovation (Kahle, 2020) .

Innovation Performance Measurement

Innovation enhances performance through effective and efficient business activities, helping industries streamline processes. It plays a crucial role in improving the business future and guiding innovation decisions. Various new strategies contribute to business growth (Yu et al., 2024).

Impact of Digitalization on Technological Innovation in SMEs

SMEs engage in digital transformation to enhance business activities. Digital technology emphasizes and reshapes industries by advancing them to a higher level. The use of digital tools reduces time consumption, minimizes physical efforts, and enables tasks to be completed efficiently with less manpower in the business field. Technology enhances business activities, improves entrepreneurial skills and knowledge, and leads to better outcomes, fostering the creation of new ventures and the growth of products and services. Assistive tools provide a significant impact, offering business advantages and strengthening industry performance. Technology supports customer queries and fulfills their expectations. Digital tools enhance knowledge sharing and digitization, strengthening absorptive capacity and boosting innovation in business activities (Philbin et al., 2022; Whig et al., 2024; Koundal & Bhalla, 2025) .

Online Adoption and Support for E-Commerce

SMEs need to adopt internet access to enhance e-commerce and digital marketing, improving client communication and strengthening customer relationships. Internet support helps SMEs gain a competitive edge by expanding customer reach in their business activities. E-commerce contributes to market growth effectively, advancing business improvements. Internet usage in e-commerce increases revenue and profitability for SMEs. Greater support for digital technology enables SMEs to attract new customers, reduce costs, and drive business growth effectively (Foroudi et al., 2017; Saridakis et al., 2018; Kumar et al., 2021).

Analytical Cloud Computing

Cloud computing helps analyze business processes and enhance digital technology. SMEs can improve cloud-based computing performance, increasing software services efficiently and flexibly while optimizing storage processes and reducing infrastructure costs (Odukoya, 2024). Digital technology in SMEs supports business growth, enhances decision-making, and improves customer service. SMEs can use advanced predictive models to enhance business activities and drive growth. The adoption of technology contributes to financial improvement and strengthens technical skills and knowledge (Chabalala et al., 2024).

Background of the Study

SMEs play a significant role in improving economic growth. They can enhance employment opportunities and drive innovation in industries.SMEs regularly face various challenges, especially limited financial sources. They may also lack technical support and the knowledge to access technology.The digital competitive market can navigate Artificial Intelligence to improve transformative solutions, increasing SMEs' and economic sustainability in the product development process for innovative services (Marchetti, 2025).

Technology can support and include machine learning and natural language processing. It can also enable automation to provide SMEs with tools that improve efficiency, enhance decision-making, and foster business activities. AI is driven to help SMEs analyze market trends, identify gaps, and support innovation based on customer preferences (Carayannis et al., 2025). It can lead to strategies that enhance productivity and competitiveness. AI has the power to reduce workload, minimize manpower requirements, and decrease errors in the business industry. It can also streamline business processes.To allow SMEs, it can allocate resources more effectively (Butt, 2024).

AI enhances product development for SMEs. It can drive innovation in their services, particularly for new business approaches, to increase business services and fulfill customer expectations (Kedi et al., 2024). AI can handhold the business market strategies. It can foster creativity to support customer services through chatbots and utilize predictive analytics for demand forecasting (Rane et al., 2024). AI applications in supply chain management can improve quality control and enhance business process effectiveness.This can ensure that SMEs identify market conditions and act according to market competition (Panigrahi et al., 2024).

SME people struggle to adopt AI due to a lack of knowledge and skilled personnel. It can protect data privacy and support cybersecurity against threats. AI can effectively support the enhancement of SMEs' improvement, especially in economic strengthening, and provide innovation support for developing successful technology adoption (Baabdullah et al., 2021; Ali & Hajjar, 2024). This study mainly emphasizes AI boosting SMEs' development and economic growth while increasing innovation capacity. It can identify the challenges faced by SME people. AI implementation in business processes and AI adoption in the SME industry.This can enhance technology advancement and policy recommendations for business growth and empower the SME industry. AI can sustain businesses, improve economic growth, enhance the global market, and foster successful competitiveness in their industry (Iyelolu et al., 2024; Alabi et al., 2025) .

Research Gap, Research Questions and Research Objectives

In this proposed research study, there is a research gap regarding how small and medium entrepreneurs utilize AI and how AI can support their business growth and initiatives for SMEs. The research study aims to lead the economic impact for SMEs and their product services through innovation with the support of AI. Assistive technology supports SME initiatives, improves their business, and helps expand their operations by maintaining accounts and keeping records with the help of AI. The study addresses how AI services are more useful in supporting SMEs and implementing services under contemporary conditions.

Research Questions

1. What are the initial stages to start a business?
2. What problems do SMEs face?
3. How do SMEs maintain effective finance?
4. What planning strategies are used for product services in their business?
5. What is talent management in SMEs?
6. How do SMEs improve economic growth in their business?

7. What are the advantages of using AI for their productivity?
8. How does AI play a role in reducing human error in their business?
9. How can AI support SMEs in their business?
10. What are the AI innovation plans to improve their business?

Main Objective of the Study

AI supports Small and Medium Enterprises' economic enhancement and product and innovation services.

Theoretical Framework

Figure 2. AI Product Innovation for SMEs

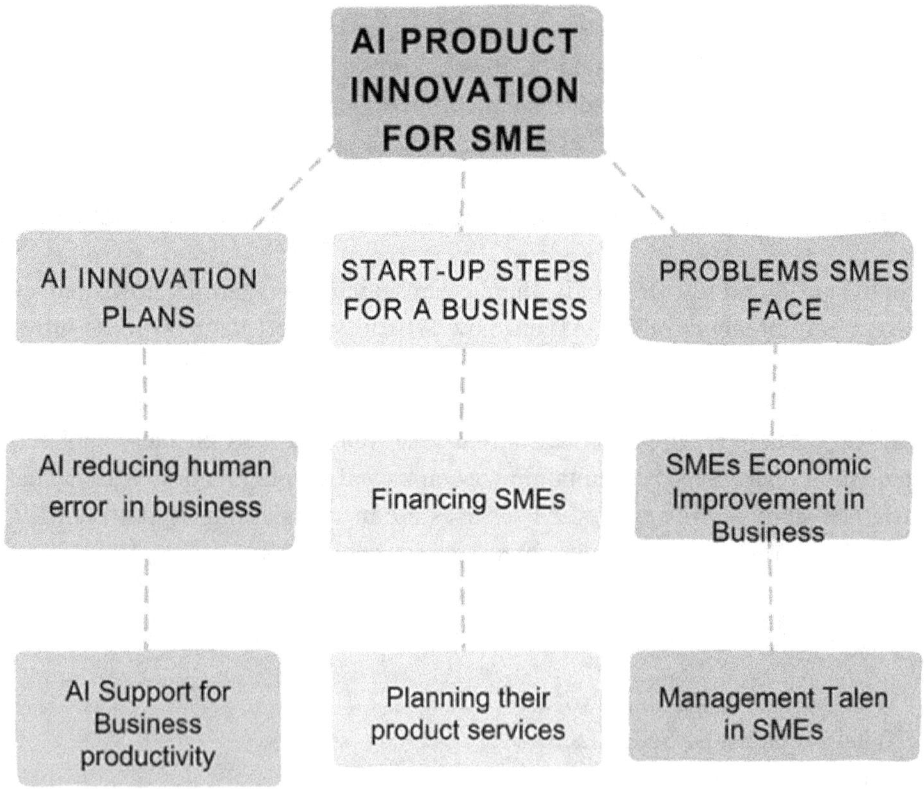

Beginning Stage for Starting Business Activities

Idea Creation and Market-Related Innovation: At the initial stage, laymen think about starting a business to earn money. They analyze market demand, field competition, feasibility, availability, and time consumption. They also consider the effort required, along with the positive and negative aspects of the industry (Fleisher & Bensoussan, 2015).
Business Plan: A business plan incorporates ideas, creativity, financial projections, and feasibility assessments for market strategies (Ramirez, 2024).
Legal Conditions: SME owners consider industry registration but may feel confused about whether to spend money and time on obtaining a license. They also face complications related to taxation (Mwangi, 2014).
Securing Funding: Entrepreneurs explore funding sources based on their needs, including savings, self-funding, loans, and investor support. They may also seek business grants and open a dedicated business account to manage finances effectively (Richardson, 2023).

SME's Use a Variety of Strategies to Ensure Market Success and Growth

Analyzing Market Strategy and Customer Service:Identify target customers and fulfill their needs by analyzing market trends, competition, demand, and purchasing patterns. Product Development and Innovation:Enhance products and services based on customer feedback while leveraging various technologies to strengthen product quality and improve efficiency.

Pricing Strategy: Pricing strategies should focus on maintaining profitability by using cost-based and value-based pricing models to optimize product pricing (Rantalaiho, 2017).
Branding for Business Strategy: Business owners should create unique selling propositions to stay competitive and drive business development. Building a strong brand identity through marketing and promotional efforts can enhance business visibility (Aaker, 2012).
Business Sales Planning: SMEs should adopt innovative strategies for distributing products through online platforms, retail outlets, and direct sales. Efficient supply chain management and logistics can improve delivery times and overall efficiency (Zaridis et al., 2021).

Market Promotion Strategy: Market promotion strategies should leverage digital marketing, social media, and advertising to attract customers. Implementing customer service programs, loyalty initiatives, and promotional offers can enhance customer engagement (Moreno-Munoz et al., 2016).

Service Quality Assurance and Customer Satisfaction: Maintaining high product quality through regular testing and providing excellent customer service is essential. Gathering customer feedback can help improve services and ensure long-term satisfaction (Fargnoli et al., 2018).

Talent Management in SMEs

Key talent management aspects in SMEs include talent acquisition and recruitment, employee training and development, performance management, employee engagement and retention, workforce planning and succession management, compensation and benefits, diversity and inclusion, technology integration, and talent management strategies to enhance SME business growth (Kandukuri, 2023).

Talent Acquisition & Recruitment: SMEs should hire new employees who align with their company vision and culture. Cost-effective hiring methods such as referrals, social media recruitment, and online job postings can enhance the recruitment process (Biea et al., 2024).

Employee Training & Development: Providing skill-based training enhances employee performance. Encouraging cross-functional support helps train employees to improve workforce flexibility and efficiency (Sumukadas & Sawhney, 2004).

Performance Management: Setting clear goals and defining employee expectations can drive better results. Regular performance reviews and constructive feedback from industry leaders can help improve employee productivity (Vuong & Nguyen, 2022).

Employee Engagement & Retention: Fostering a positive work environment boosts employee motivation and job satisfaction. Offering incentives, performance-based rewards, and career growth opportunities can help retain top talent (Urme, 2023).

Planning & Managing Successions: Identifying key roles and potential leaders within the organization ensures future business growth.

Figure 3. Talent management for SME's

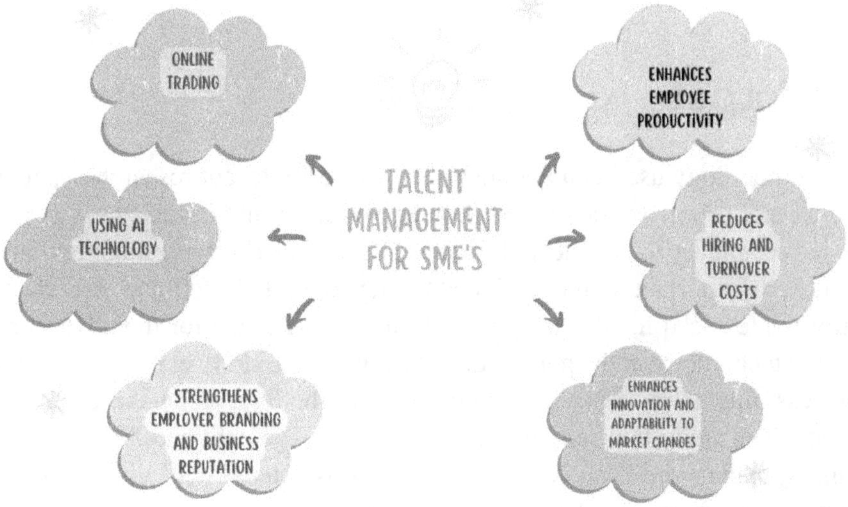

To adopt the talent innovation approach, SMEs can strengthen skills and knowledge, increase workforce efficiency, and ensure long-term business sustainability and industry growth.

AI Supports SMEs

Process automation simplifies invoicing, payroll, and inventory management, reducing workload and errors. AI provides analytical insights to support forecasting, trend analysis, and resource optimization. AI-powered chatbots offer personalized recommendations, improving customer satisfaction.

AI Innovation Plans to Improve SMEs

AI enhances business operations by reducing costs and boosting competitiveness through automation. Data-driven insights help analyze customer behavior, track market trends, increase sales, and improve decision-making in the SME sector (Magableh et al., 2024).

AI automates marketing campaigns, optimizes sales strategies, and helps businesses reach target audiences, leading to better conversion rates. AI also prevents business failures by improving product quality and service delivery in a short time (Haleem et al., 2022).

By offering cost-effective scaling and increasing market insights, AI strengthens SMEs, enhances productivity, reduces costs, and supports sustainable business growth.

METHODOLOGY

The methodology used content analysis to collect relevant research papers and provide a comprehensive idea for SMEs and entrepreneurs in their business. The study used secondary data collected from SMEs, the World Bank, and previous research studies. Important sources included WoS, Scopus, PubMed, and other relevant journal websites used for the analysis of trends in AI usage for the advancement of assistive technology in the generation.The qualitative study explores AI support for business innovation. Data was collected from the Scopus databases and Web of Science. The study focused on innovation in management and AI, particularly in business, management, and accounting, and was filtered by AI innovation and technology-related aspects. A total of 248 articles were gathered from online portals. Out of these, only 81 relevant review and research articles were selected for the study. These articles were used to analyze AI's impact on business, its role in growth strategies, and its contributions to management. The study also highlights AI's support in fostering creativity and service innovation in business models.

CONCLUSION

The conclusion is that the economic development of SMEs is more effective with the help of assistive tools. AI-driven solutions can enhance SME products and provide innovative services, leading to increased competitiveness in their market. AI can support SMEs in understanding their needs and processing effectively, providing ultimate growth and sustainability for their business. The study mainly focused on how Artificial Intelligence (AI) plays a vital role in improving SMEs' innovation and business management. AI helps predict business trends through self-assessment, enabling SMEs to better evaluate and enhance their business strategies. There are eight core areas where AI can improve SMEs, including their culture, capabilities, technology advancement, and performance measurement. AI tools play an important role in SME development, providing effective data-driven recommendations tailored to unique business needs. AI also supports SMEs in enhancing management, fostering innovation, and achieving business success.

POLICY IMPLICATIONS

The findings of the study provide a comprehensive view of AI support for economic improvement in SMEs, and how it can enhance their innovation and services. AI can improve their infrastructure and enhance their technology. SMEs will adopt AI in the future and utilize it in all aspects to promote their business. AI applications can protect SMEs from their business problems and drive their competitiveness. AI usage can help SMEs navigate their adoption of new technologies and improve consumer protection. The policy can provide the competent authority with a role for AI-driven economic growth for SMEs, ultimately increasing the broader economic growth of their industries.

LIMITATION OF THE STUDY

The limitation of the study is that AI can improve SMEs' products and services. The secondary research study provides the experiences of SMEs across regions and offers comprehensiveness in its findings. The findings of the study can generalize SMEs by focusing on industries, geographic locations, and their economic conditions, as well as the influence of regulatory and technological adoption on their results. The content analysis involves the subjective interpretation of the secondary data. The researcher used various secondary data in the current research paper. It can lead to the analysis of the data and provide a comprehensive outcome of the study. AI technology provides new innovations in applications for their emergence and provides the necessary means to keep pace with their changes. The benefit of AI for SMEs is that it can address the challenges and barriers faced by SMEs in implementing their business, such as costs, lack of technical expertise, and changes in their business. The study mainly focused on the economic improvement of the critical factors that can enhance the influence, overall quality, and effectiveness of AI support in SMEs.

OUTCOME OF THE STUDY

The outcome of the study is to integrate AI support to improve economic development in businesses, especially in Small and Medium Enterprises (SMEs), as it can enhance their products and services. SMEs are experienced in their products and improve their routine business processes, which can provide more efficient resources. AI tools can provide a better understanding of consumer preferences, improve the decision-making process, and enhance competitiveness in their market position. AI can provide more advancement in their business practices; it reduces their time, minimizes wastage, decreases manpower, allows for quick assessments, and enhances supply chain management. The significant role is to improve economic growth in the field of SMEs and enhance economic development along with their innovation of new advancement services.

REFERENCES

Aaker, D. A. (2012). *Building strong brands*. Simon and Schuster.

Abd Hair Awang, N. M. S., Hussain, M. Y., Ishak, S., & Yusof, R. M. (2014). Organizational learning and work environment: A formation of innovative work behavior at small medium enterprises (SMEs). In *ICICKM2014-Proceedings of the 11th International Conference on Intellectual Capital, Knowledge Management and Organisational Learning: ICICKM2014* (p. 30). Academic Conferences Limited.

Abisuga-Oyekunle, O. A., Patra, S. K., & Muchie, M. (2020). SMEs in sustainable development: Their role in poverty reduction and employment generation in sub-Saharan Africa. *African Journal of Science, Technology, Innovation and Development*, *12*(4), 405–419. https://journals.co.za/doi/abs/10.1080/20421338.2019.1656428

Aksoy, H. (2017). How do innovation culture, marketing innovation and product innovation affect the market performance of small and medium-sized enterprises (SMEs)? *Technology in Society*, *51*, 133–141. DOI: 10.1016/j.techsoc.2017.08.005

Alabi, A. T., Ubandawaki, A. T., & Issa, S. O. (2025). The Role of Digital Technology in the Sustainability Strategies of SMEs. In *The Future of Small Business in Industry 5.0* (pp. 347–378). IGI Global Scientific Publishing., DOI: 10.4018/979-8-3693-7362-0.ch014

Ali, H., & Hajjar, L. (2024). Empowering SMEs with AI and Digital Transformation: A Roadmap to Enhanced Competitiveness and Growth.

Amoako-Adu, B., & Eshun, J. P. (2018). SME financing in Africa: Collateral lending vs cash flow lending. *International Journal of Economics and Finance*, *10*(6), 151–159. DOI: 10.5539/ijef.v10n6p151

Baabdullah, A. M., Alalwan, A. A., Slade, E. L., Raman, R., & Khatatneh, K. F. (2021). SMEs and artificial intelligence (AI): Antecedents and consequences of AI-based B2B practices. *Industrial Marketing Management*, *98*, 255–270. DOI: 10.1016/j.indmarman.2021.09.003

Bhuiyan, M. R. I., Faraji, M. R., Rashid, M., Bhuyan, M. K., Hossain, R., & Ghose, P. (2024). Digital transformation in SMEs emerging technological tools and technologies for enhancing the SME's strategies and outcomes. *Journal of Ecohumanism*, *3*(4), 211–224. https://www.ceeol.com/search/article-detail?id=1271910

Bi, R., Davison, R. M., & Smyrnios, K. X. (2017). E-business and fast growth SMEs. *Small Business Economics*, *48*, 559–576. DOI: 10.1007/s11187-016-9788-8

Biea, E. A., Dinu, E., Bunica, A., & Jerdea, L. (2024). Recruitment in SMEs: The role of managerial practices, technology and innovation. *European Business Review*, *36*(3), 361–391. DOI: 10.1108/EBR-05-2023-0162

Butt, J. S. (2024). The role of artificial intelligence (AI) in productivity & economic growth in Nordic welfare states. *Acta Universitatis Danubius. Œconomica, 20*(2), 50-72. https://www.ceeol.com/search/article-detail?id=1252928

Bwembya, J. (2022). *Addressing challenges in accessing finance by small and medium enterprises (SMES) in Zambia: a pragmatic approach* (Doctoral dissertation, The University of Zambia). https://dspace.unza.zm/handle/123456789/7880

Carayannis, E. G., Dumitrescu, R., Falkowski, T., Papamichail, G., & Zota, N. R. (2025). Enhancing SME Resilience through Artificial Intelligence and Strategic Foresight: A Framework for Sustainable Competitiveness. *Technology in Society*, *102835*. Advance online publication. DOI: 10.1016/j.techsoc.2025.102835

Chabalala, K., Boyana, S., Kolisi, L., Thango, B., & Lerato, M. (2024). Digital technologies and channels for competitive advantage in SMEs: A systematic review. *Available at SSRN* 4977280.

Eberhardsteiner, L. (2024). Adopting AI in SMEs: development of a framework for adopting AI in SMEs with a focus on security and privacy concerns: Entwicklung eines Rahmenwerks für die Einführung von KI in KMU mit Schwerpunkt auf Sicherheits-und Datenschutzbedenken/Author Lukas Eberhardsteiner.

Evelynn, S., & Harlee, M. (2024). Digital Technology Adoption in SMEs: AI-Driven Strategies for Improving Competitiveness.

Farazi, S. (2014). Informal firms and financial inclusion: Status and determinants. *Journal of international commerce. Economic Policy*, *5*(03), 1440011. DOI: 10.1142/S1793993314400110

Fargnoli, M., Costantino, F., Di Gravio, G., & Tronci, M. (2018). Product service-systems implementation: A customized framework to enhance sustainability and customer satisfaction. *Journal of Cleaner Production*, *188*, 387–401. DOI: 10.1016/j.jclepro.2018.03.315

Fernando, Y., Jabbour, C. J. C., & Wah, W. X. (2019). Pursuing green growth in technology firms through the connections between environmental innovation and sustainable business performance: Does service capability matter? *Resources, Conservation and Recycling*, *141*, 8–20. DOI: 10.1016/j.resconrec.2018.09.031

Fiseha, G. G., & Oyelana, A. A. (2015). An assessment of the roles of small and medium enterprises (SMEs) in the local economic development (LED). *The South African Journal of Economics*, *6*(3), 280–290.

Fleisher, C. S., & Bensoussan, B. E. (2015). *Business and competitive analysis: effective application of new and classic methods*. FT press.

Foroudi, P., Gupta, S., Nazarian, A., & Duda, M. (2017). Digital technology and marketing management capability: Achieving growth in SMEs. *Qualitative Market Research*, *20*(2), 230–246. DOI: 10.1108/QMR-01-2017-0014

Gamage, S. N., Ekanayake, E. M. S., Abeyrathne, G. A. K. N. J., Prasanna, R. P. I. R., Jayasundara, J. M. S. B., & Rajapakshe, P. S. K. (2020). A review of global challenges and survival strategies of small and medium enterprises (SMEs). *Economies*, *8*(4), 79. DOI: 10.3390/economies8040079

Gilmore, A., & Carson, D. (2018). SME marketing: Efficiency in practice. *Small Enterprise Research*, *25*(3), 213–226. DOI: 10.1080/13215906.2018.1521740

Haleem, A., Javaid, M., Qadri, M. A., Singh, R. P., & Suman, R. (2022). Artificial intelligence (AI) applications for marketing: A literature-based study. *International Journal of Intelligent Networks*, *3*, 119–132. DOI: 10.1016/j.ijin.2022.08.005

Häring, K., Pimentel, C., & Teixeira, L. (2023). Industry 4.0 Implementation in Small-and Medium-Sized Enterprises: Recommendations Extracted from a Systematic Literature Review with a Focus on Maturity Models. *Logistics (Basel)*, *7*(4), 99. DOI: 10.3390/logistics7040099

Hsieh, Y. H., & Chou, Y. H. (2018). Modeling the impact of service innovation for small and medium enterprises: A system dynamics approach. *Simulation Modelling Practice and Theory*, *82*, 84–102. DOI: 10.1016/j.simpat.2017.12.004

Iloka, C. P. (2022). Effects of Climate Change on Medium, Small and Micro Enterprises's Financing in Nigeria: The Consequential Burden of Protecting the Right of the Less Privileged. *AJLHR*, *6*, 52.

Islam, A., & Wahab, S. A. (2021). The intervention of strategic innovation practices in between regulations and sustainable business growth: A holistic perspective for Malaysian SMEs. *World Journal of Entrepreneurship, Management and Sustainable Development*, *17*(3), 396–421. DOI: 10.1108/WJEMSD-04-2020-0035

Iyelolu, T. V., Agu, E. E., Idemudia, C., & Ijomah, T. I. (2024). Driving SME innovation with AI solutions: overcoming adoption barriers and future growth opportunities. *International Journal of Science and Technology Research Archive*, *7*(1), 036-054. DOI: https://doi.org/DOI: 10.53771/ijstra.2024.7.1.0055

Jain, A., Kakade, K. S., & Vispute, S. A. (2025). The Role of Artificial Intelligence (AI) in the Transformation of Small-and Medium-Sized Businesses: Challenges and Opportunities. *Artificial Intelligence-Enabled Businesses: How to Develop Strategies for Innovation*, 209-226. DOI: <ALIGNMENT.qj></ALIGN-MENT>10.1002/9781394234028.ch12

Kahle, J. H., Marcon, E., Ghezzi, A., & Frank, A. G. (2020). Smart Products value creation in SMEs innovation ecosystems. *Technological Forecasting and Social Change*, *156*, 120024. DOI: 10.1016/j.techfore.2020.120024

Kalishina, D. (2023). Artificial Intelligence As An Enabler Of Growth: Advancing Business Analytics In Small And Medium Enterprises. *International Journal of Core Engineering & Management*, *7*(5), 289–300.

Kandukuri, V. (2023). Aligning talent and business: A key for sustainable HRM in SMEs. *Journal of Entrepreneurship and Innovation in Emerging Economies*, *9*(1). 80-91.

Kanellopoulou, D., Giannakopoulos, G., & Karkaletsis, V. (2025). Accelerating AI-powered digital innovation through "APSS": A novel methodology for sustainable business AI transformation. *Journal of Open Innovation*, *100495*. Advance online publication. DOI: 10.1016/j.joitmc.2025.100495

Kedi, W. E., Ejimuda, C., Idemudia, C., & Ijomah, T. I. (2024). AI software for personalized marketing automation in SMEs: Enhancing customer experience and sales. *World Journal of Advanced Research and Reviews*, *23*(1), 1981–1990. DOI: 10.30574/wjarr.2024.23.1.2159

Keskġn, H., Ġentürk, C., Sungur, O., & Kġrġġ, H. M. (2010, June). The importance of SMEs in developing economies. In *2nd international symposium on sustainable development* (Vol. 183). https://core.ac.uk/download/pdf/153446896.pdf

Knezović, E., & Drkić, A. (2021). Innovative work behavior in SMEs: The role of transformational leadership. *Employee Relations: The International Journal*, *43*(2), 398–415. DOI: 10.1108/ER-03-2020-0124

Koundal, P., & Bhalla, M. (2025). The Role of AIS in Enhancing Small Business Agility and Sustainability in Industry 5.0. In *The Future of Small Business in Industry 5.0* (pp. 301–330). IGI Global Scientific Publishing., DOI: 10.4018/979-8-3693-7362-0.ch012

Kumar, A., Syed, A. A., & Pandey, A. (2021). Adoption of online resources to improve the marketing performance of SMES. *Asia Pacific Journal of Health Management, 16*(3), 137-144. https://search.informit.org/doi/abs/10.3316/INFORMIT.081159555237037

Kumar, R. (2017). *Targeted SME financing and employment effects: What do we know and what can we do differently?* World Bank. https://documents1.worldbank.org/curated/pt/577091496733563036/pdf/115696-REVISED-PUBLIC-SMEs-and-Jobs-final.pdf

Lijauco, F., Gajendran, T., Brewer, G., & Rasoolimanesh, S. M. (2020). Impacts of culture on innovation propensity in small to medium enterprises in construction. *Journal of Construction Engineering and Management, 146*(3), 04019116. DOI: 10.1061/(ASCE)CO.1943-7862.0001753

Lukonga, I. (2020). Harnessing digital technologies to promote SMEs in the MENAP region. https://papers.ssrn.com/sol3/papers.cfm?abstract_id=3721177

Madan, N. (2020). A review of access to finance by micro, small and medium enterprises and digital financial services in selected Asia-Pacific least developed countries. https://repository.unescap.org/handle/20.500.12870/1190

Magableh, I. K., Mahrouq, M. H., Ta'Amnha, M. A., & Riyadh, H. A. (2024). The Role of Marketing Artificial Intelligence in Enhancing Sustainable Financial Performance of Medium-Sized Enterprises Through Customer Engagement and Data-Driven Decision-Making. *Sustainability, 16*(24), 11279. DOI: 10.3390/su162411279

Maksimov, V., Wang, S. L., & Luo, Y. (2017). Reducing poverty in the least developed countries: The role of small and medium enterprises. *Journal of World Business, 52*(2), 244–257. DOI: 10.1016/j.jwb.2016.12.007

Marchetti, R. (2025). Enhancing Organizational Ambidexterity in SMEs. The Critical Role of Digital Technologies. https://osuva.uwasa.fi/handle/10024/18609

Megersa, K. (2020). Improving SMEs' access to finance through capital markets and innovative financing instruments: some evidence from developing countries. *Nairobi Securities Exchange website:* https://www. nse. co. *ke*. https://core.ac.uk/download/pdf/287772261.pdf

Michael, O. (2025). Maximising the Potentials of Small and Medium Scale Business Enterprises in Developing Nations Through the Use of Artificial Intelligence: AI Adoption by SMEs in the Developing Nations. In *The Future of Small Business in Industry 5.0* (pp. 215-246). IGI Global Scientific Publishing. DOI: DOI: 10.4018/979-8-3693-7362-0.ch009

Moreno-Munoz, A., Bellido-Outeirino, F. J., Siano, P., & Gomez-Nieto, M. A. (2016). Mobile social media for smart grids customer engagement: Emerging trends and challenges. *Renewable & Sustainable Energy Reviews*, *53*, 1611–1616. DOI: 10.1016/j.rser.2015.09.077

Muhika, D. W. (2019). *Influence of credit access requirements on formalization decision of small and medium enterprises in Nairobi* (Doctoral dissertation, JKUAT-COHRED). http://ir.jkuat.ac.ke/handle/123456789/5014

Mwangi, P. C. N. (2014). *Factors influencing tax compliance among small and medium enterprises in Nairobi's industrial area, Kenya* (Doctoral dissertation, University of Nairobi,). https://erepository.uonbi.ac.ke/handle/11295/73605

Ndiaye, N., Razak, L. A., Nagayev, R., & Ng, A. (2018). Demystifying small and medium enterprises'(SMEs) performance in emerging and developing economies. *Borsa Istanbul Review, 18*(4), 269-281.

Ng, H. S., & Kee, D. M. H. (2012). The issues and development of critical success factors for the SME success in a developing country. *International Business Management*, *6*(6), 680–691.

Nylén, D., & Holmström, J. (2015). Digital innovation strategy: A framework for diagnosing and improving digital product and service innovation. *Business Horizons*, *58*(1), 57–67. DOI: 10.1016/j.bushor.2014.09.001

Odukoya, O. (2024). The Transformative Impact of Cloud Computing on Small and Medium-sized Enterprises (SMEs): A Comprehensive Analysis. In *2024 International Conference on Smart Applications, Communications and Networking (SmartNets)* (pp. 1-5). IEEE. DOI: DOI: 10.1109/SmartNets61466.2024.10577703

Ogujiuba, K. K., Olamide, E., Boshoff, E., Agholor, I., & Ogujiuba, C. (2023). SMEs, success, and capital startups: Evidence from the service sector in South Africa. *Administrative Sciences*, *13*(5), 127. DOI: 10.3390/admsci13050127

Panigrahi, R. R., Shrivastava, A. K., & Nudurupati, S. S. (2024). Impact of inventory management on SME performance: A systematic review. *International Journal of Productivity and Performance Management*. Advance online publication. DOI: 10.1108/IJPPM-08-2023-0428

Philbin, S., Viswanathan, R., & Telukdarie, A. (2022). Understanding how digital transformation can enable SMEs to achieve sustainable development: A systematic literature review. *Small Business International Review*, *6*(1), e473. DOI: 10.26784/sbir.v6i1.473

Proenca, J. C. (2024). Business Innovation Self-Assessment With Artificial Intelligence Support For Small And Medium-Sized Enterprises. *Бизнес управление*, (4), 5-17. https://www.ceeol.com/search/article-detail?id=1293603

Ramirez, J. G. C. (2024). The power of planning: how business plans drive effective management strategies. *Integrated Journal of Science and Technology, 1*(3).

Rane, N. L., Paramesha, M., Choudhary, S. P., & Rane, J. (2024). Artificial intelligence, machine learning, and deep learning for advanced business strategies: A review. *Partners Universal International Innovation Journal*, *2*(3), 147–171. DOI: 10.5281/zenodo.12208298

Rantalaiho, H. (2017). Challenges in implementing value-based pricing strategy. https://lutpub.lut.fi/handle/10024/135205

Richardson, C. L. (2023). *Successful Strategies for Obtaining Financial Funding by Minority-Owned Small Businesses* (Doctoral dissertation, Walden University). https://www.proquest.com/openview/654aa3103f0814c6d69287411a977ed7/1?pq-origsite=gscholar&cbl=18750&diss=y

Saridakis, G., Lai, Y., Mohammed, A. M., & Hansen, J. M. (2018). Industry characteristics, stages of E-commerce communications, and entrepreneurs and SMEs revenue growth. *Technological Forecasting and Social Change*, *128*, 56–66. DOI: 10.1016/j.techfore.2017.10.017

Saunila, M. (2016). Performance measurement approach for innovation capability in SMEs. *International Journal of Productivity and Performance Management*, *65*(2), 162–176. DOI: 10.1108/IJPPM-08-2014-0123

Srinivasan, S., & Vallipriya, R. (2025). Entrepreneurial Success and Decision-Making Power With the Support of Assistive Technology. In *Improving Entrepreneurial Processes Through Advanced AI* (pp. 181–216). IGI Global., DOI: 10.4018/979-8-3693-1495-1.ch009

Sumukadas, N., & Sawhney, R. (2004). Workforce agility through employee involvement. *IIE Transactions*, *36*(10), 1011–1021. DOI: 10.1080/07408170490500997

Tahi Hamonangan Tambunan, T. (2011). Development of small and medium enterprises in a developing country: The Indonesian case. *Journal of Enterprising Communities: People and Places in the Global Economy*, *5*(1), 68–82. DOI: 10.1108/17506201111119626

Temel, S., & Durst, S. (2021). Knowledge risk prevention strategies for handling new technological innovations in small businesses. *VINE Journal of Information and Knowledge Management Systems*, *51*(4), 655–673. DOI: 10.1108/VJIKMS-10-2019-0155

Tsiu, S. V., Mathabela, L., & Ngobeni, M. (2024). Applications and competitive advantages of data mining and business intelligence in SMEs performance: A systematic review. *SSRN*, *4958874*, •••. https://papers.ssrn.com/sol3/papers.cfm?abstract_id=4958874

Ulas, D. (2019). Digital transformation process and SMEs. *Procedia Computer Science*, *158*, 662–671. DOI: 10.1016/j.procs.2019.09.101

Urme, U. N. (2023). The impact of talent management strategies on employee retention. *International Journal of Science and Business*, *28*(1), 127–146. DOI: 10.58970/IJSB.2209

Vuong, T. D. N., & Nguyen, L. T. (2022). The key strategies for measuring employee performance in companies: A systematic review. *Sustainability*, *14*(21), 14017. DOI: 10.3390/su142114017

Whig, P., Bhatia, A. B., & Yathiraju, N. (2024). AI-Driven innovations in service marketing transforming customer engagement and experience. In *AI Innovations in Service and Tourism Marketing* (pp. 17–34). IGI Global., DOI: 10.4018/979-8-3693-7909-7.ch002

Yu, G. J., Lee, J., & Kim, B. (2024). Enhancing innovation performance through business process innovation: The strategic role of external collaboration. [GBFR]. *Global Business & Finance Review*, *29*(5), 33–44. DOI: 10.17549/gbfr.2024.29.5.33

Yusuf, S. O., Durodola, R. L., Ocran, G., Abubakar, J. E., Echere, A. Z., & Paul-Adeleye, A. H. (2024). Challenges and opportunities in AI and digital transformation for SMEs: A cross-continental perspective. *World Journal of Advanced Research and Reviews, 23*(3), 668-678.I doi:DOI: 10.30574/wjarr.2024.23.3.2511

Zafar, A., & Mustafa, S. (2017). SMEs and its role in economic and socio-economic development of Pakistan. *International Journal of Academic Research in Accounting, Finance and Management Sciences, 6*(4). https://papers.ssrn.com/sol3/papers.cfm?abstract_id=3085425

Zaridis, A., Vlachos, I., & Bourlakis, M. (2021). SMEs strategy and scale constraints impact on agri-food supply chain collaboration and firm performance. *Production Planning and Control*, *32*(14), 1165–1178. DOI: 10.1080/09537287.2020.1796136

Chapter 7
AI-Driven Digital Transformation in Small and Medium-Sized Enterprises (SMEs):
Resilience, Efficiency, and Growth in Industry 5.0

Pinky Agarwal
https://orcid.org/0000-0001-7741-3194
N.L. Dalmia Institute of Management Studies and Research, India

Neeraj Gupta
N.L. Dalmia Institute of Management Studies and Research, India

ABSTRACT

Industry 5.0 represents a significant progression from Industry 4.0, highlighting a paradigm change in manufacturing and business practices with a shift towards more resilient, sustainable, and human-centric practices. The chapter delves into the role of Artificial Intelligence role in driving this transformation, offering benefits such as streamlined operations, improved customer experiences, optimized supply chains, and enhanced resilience. Small businesses can benefit from adopting AI-driven digital platforms, investing in employee training, implementing predictive analytics, strengthening cybersecurity measures, and fostering sustainable practices. The chapter underscores the need of a resilience framework to incorporate AI tools for managing crises and ensuring long-term sustainability. It concludes by highlighting how AI has the ability to transform small firms in the framework of Industry 5.0, spurring innovation, boosting competitiveness, and attaining sustained growth.

DOI: 10.4018/979-8-3693-9611-7.ch007

1. INTRODUCTION

The Industrial landscape has evolved through five distinct revolutions, each transforming production processes, business models, and workforce dynamics. Industry 1.0, emerging in the 18th and 19th centuries, was characterized by the mechanization of production using steam and water power, marking a shift from agrarian economies to industrialized societies. The second industrial revolution (Industry 2.0), spanning the late 19th and early 20th centuries, saw the widespread adoption of electricity and assembly lines, enabling mass production and increasing manufacturing efficiency (Mokyr, 1998). The third revolution (Industry 3.0), during the mid-20th century, introduced computers, automation, and early robotics, allowing for enhanced precision and reducing human dependency in manufacturing processes (Kagermann et al., 2013).

The fourth industrial revolution (Industry 4.0), which began in the early 21st century, was driven by cyber-physical systems, the Internet of Things (IoT), big data, cloud computing, and AI-driven automation. This revolution enabled the development of smart factories, where interconnected systems facilitated real-time data-driven decision-making and enhanced operational efficiency (Schwab, 2016). However, Industry 5.0 represents a paradigm shift by prioritizing human-AI collaboration, sustainability, and resilience. Unlike Industry 4.0, which emphasized automation and machine autonomy, Industry 5.0 seeks to balance technological efficiency with human creativity, focusing on personalized production, workforce augmentation, and environmental responsibility (Breque et al., 2021). A prime example of this transition is Tesla, a leading automotive SME, which integrates AI-powered robotics in manufacturing while ensuring human oversight in quality control and predictive maintenance, illustrating how human intelligence remains central to innovation and problem-solving (Geissdoerfer et al., 2017).

Industry 5.0 marks the beginning of a human-centric, AI-enabled, and sustainable transformation. One of its defining aspects is human-AI collaboration, where AI is designed to augment human capabilities rather than replace workers. AI-powered systems assist employees by automating routine tasks, enhancing decision-making, and enabling precision in manufacturing. Another key feature is sustainability, as AI optimizes resource utilization, reduces waste, and promotes green manufacturing, aligning businesses with Environmental, Social, and Governance (ESG) standards (Jabbour et al., 2020). Furthermore, AI-driven predictive analytics strengthens resilience and adaptability, helping businesses anticipate market fluctuations, supply chain disruptions, and production inefficiencies (Müller et al., 2021). A manufacturing SME like Siemens has successfully adopted AI-driven digital twins to monitor real-time factory operations, resulting in a 30% reduction in energy consumption and enhanced operational resilience (Santoro et al., 2023).

AI has become a key driver of business innovation and digital transformation, fundamentally reshaping how companies operate, compete, and grow. For Small and Medium-Sized Enterprises (SMEs), AI offers the potential to streamline operations, automate repetitive tasks, and enhance strategic decision-making. AI-powered chatbots, for instance, have transformed customer service, reducing response times by up to 80% (Chatterjee et al., 2022). AI also plays a crucial role in data-driven decision-making, where it analyzes consumer behavior, market trends, and supply chain operations, helping SMEs tailor their strategies to market demands. In supply chain management, AI-driven predictive analytics has been instrumental in optimizing inventory levels, leading to cost reductions of 15-20% (Geissdoerfer et al., 2017). A notable example of AI application in retail SMEs is Zara, which leverages AI-powered demand forecasting to predict fashion trends, ensuring efficient inventory management and minimizing unsold stock waste.

SMEs, defined as businesses with a limited workforce and revenue, are essential to global economies. In the European Union, SMEs have fewer than 250 employees and an annual turnover of less than €50 million (OECD, 2021), whereas in India, the MSME Act classifies SMEs as enterprises with investment up to 50 crores and turnover up to 250 crores (Government of India, 2023). SMEs contribute to 90% of global businesses and 50% of employment worldwide (World Bank, 2022). Their agility and innovation potential make them pivotal in adopting AI-driven solutions (Chatterjee et al., 2022). However, despite their significance, SMEs face substantial challenges in adopting AI. Financial constraints, such as the high costs of AI implementation, prevent many SMEs from investing in AI infrastructure and expertise (Müller et al., 2021). Additionally, there is a lack of skilled workforce, as SMEs struggle to find AI professionals with expertise in machine learning, data science, and automation (Santoro et al., 2023). Another major concern is cybersecurity, as many SMEs lack robust security frameworks, exposing AI-driven systems to data breaches and cyber threats (Jabbour et al., 2020). Nonetheless, SMEs like PathAI, a small healthcare startup, have successfully adopted AI-driven diagnostic imaging, improving cancer detection accuracy by 25% and addressing the challenge of limited healthcare professionals.

The need for AI adoption in SMEs is driven by three primary factors. First, AI enhances operational efficiency, automating routine tasks and reducing manual workloads by 40-50% (OECD, 2022). Second, AI provides a competitive advantage, enabling SMEs to analyze customer preferences, personalize offerings, and improve revenue growth. Third, AI enhances decision-making by leveraging predictive analytics, improving forecasting accuracy by 30-50% (Breque et al., 2021). However, barriers remain—AI solutions require substantial initial investment, making adoption challenging for SMEs with limited budgets (Müller et al., 2021). Many SMEs also lack technological maturity, as they struggle to integrate AI solutions into existing business models (Wamba et al., 2021). Moreover, AI adoption requires compliance with regulations such as General Data Protection Regulation (GDPR), the AI Act, and ESG sustainability standards, which many SMEs find difficult to navigate (Jabbour et al., 2020).

This chapter explores the AI-driven digital transformation of SMEs within the context of Industry 5.0, addressing both opportunities and challenges. The key research objectives of this chapter are to analyze AI adoption trends in SMEs, assess AI's role in enhancing resilience and efficiency, identify barriers to AI implementation, and provide case studies on successful AI integration in SMEs. The chapter is structured as follows: Section 2 reviews relevant theoretical models and AI adoption frameworks. Section 3 examines Industry 5.0's role in reshaping SMEs, emphasizing human-AI collaboration. Section 4 discusses AI-driven digital transformation, outlining strategies for AI adoption. Section 5 explores business model innovation driven by AI. Section 6 identifies challenges and risks associated with AI adoption in SMEs. Section 7 presents real-world case studies of SMEs that have successfully integrated AI. Section 8 discusses policy recommendations and future AI trends.

2. LITERATURE REVIEW

The integration of Artificial Intelligence (AI) into Small and Medium-Sized Enterprises (SMEs) is gaining significant attention as businesses transition from Industry 4.0 to Industry 5.0. AI adoption in SMEs is transforming various aspects of business operations, including automation, decision-making, and **customer engagement**. Despite these advancements, several challenges and research gaps remain, necessitating a comprehensive exploration of theoretical foundations, digital transformation frameworks, comparative industrial trends, and emerging AI applications.

2.1 Theoretical Foundations of AI in SMEs

Several theoretical models explain the adoption, diffusion, and strategic impact of AI in SMEs. One widely used model is the Technology-Organization-Environment (TOE) Framework proposed by Tornatzky and Fleischer (1990), which explains how organizations adopt new technologies based on technological, organizational, and environmental factors. The technological dimension considers AI's perceived benefits, compatibility, and complexity, while the organizational aspect focuses on firm size, leadership support, and digital readiness. The environmental factor emphasizes market competition, regulatory constraints, and external technological advancements. For instance, a manufacturing SME implementing AI-driven predictive maintenance must evaluate the financial investment required, the need for employee training, and industry compliance standards before adoption (Müller et al., 2021).

Another key theoretical model, Diffusion of Innovation (DOI) Theory **by** Rogers (2003), explains how AI spreads within SMEs based on relative advantage, compatibility, complexity, trialability, and observability. AI-powered chatbots in SMEs gained rapid adoption due to their low-cost implementation, ease of integration, and improved customer service efficiency, leading to an 80% reduction in response times (Chatterjee et al., 2022). Additionally, the Resource-Based View (RBV) Theory (Barney, 1991) argues that AI can offer SMEs a competitive advantage if leveraged as a strategic resource. Zara, a global fashion SME, utilizes AI-driven customer analytics to predict consumer trends, optimize inventory, and reduce excess stock, thereby improving sales and minimizing waste (Santoro et al., 2023).

The Digital Maturity Model (Chanias & Hess, 2016) categorizes SME digital transformation into four stages: awareness, experimentation, integration, and transformation. Siemens, an SME specializing in industrial automation, moved from predictive maintenance pilot projects to a fully AI-driven smart factory, demonstrating how SMEs can progress through digital maturity levels (Santoro et al., 2023). These theoretical foundations provide a structured approach to understanding AI adoption and its potential impact on SME business models.

2.2 Digital Transformation Frameworks for SMEs

AI-driven digital transformation is reshaping SMEs by automating processes, improving decision-making, and enhancing market competitiveness. The OECD's SME Digitalization Stages Framework (2022) categorizes SMEs into three digitalization levels: basic digitalization (email, websites, and digital payments), advanced digitalization (AI-enabled data analytics, process automation, and cloud computing), and AI-enabled business models (full-scale AI integration in decision-making and customer interactions).

Similarly, the AI Adoption Framework (Chatterjee et al., 2022) identifies four enablers of AI transformation in SMEs: financial support, AI skills, AI infrastructure, and regulatory compliance. For example, Amazon third-party sellers, primarily SMEs, leverage AI-powered recommendation engines to analyze customer preferences, personalize offerings, and increase conversion rates. Moreover, the Industry 5.0 Digital Framework (Breque et al., 2021) highlights human-AI collaboration, sustainability, and ethical AI use. AI-powered robotics in Tesla's gigafactories demonstrate how AI assists human workers without causing job displacement, leading to enhanced efficiency and safety.

2.3 Comparative Analysis: Industry 4.0 vs. Industry 5.0

The transition from Industry 4.0 to Industry 5.0 marks a fundamental shift in SME operations. While Industry 4.0 emphasizes automation, IoT, big data, and cloud computing, Industry 5.0 focuses on human-AI collaboration, digital twins, and sustainable business practices (Breque et al., 2021). AI-driven smart factories in automobile SMEs represent Industry 4.0, whereas Industry 5.0 is characterized by AI-driven circular economy models, where AI optimizes resources, minimizes waste, and ensures sustainable production. A notable example is Fanuc, a Japanese SME specializing in AI-driven collaborative robots (cobots), which work alongside human employees in assembly lines, maintaining efficiency without job displacement.

2.4 AI Adoption in SMEs: A Review of Existing Studies

Recent studies highlight AI's transformative impact on SME operations across various industries. In manufacturing, AI-driven predictive maintenance has improved machine uptime by 30% by reducing unplanned downtimes and optimizing asset utilization (Müller et al., 2021). In retail, AI-based customer analytics has led to a 15% increase in conversion rates, enabling SMEs to enhance marketing effectiveness (Santoro et al., 2023). In healthcare, AI-enabled medical diagnostics have improved accuracy in disease detection by 25%, addressing staff shortages and improving patient outcomes (Jabbour et al., 2020). The finance sector has also benefited, with AI-powered fraud detection reducing financial risks in SMEs by 40%, helping them mitigate cybersecurity threats and fraudulent transactions (Wamba et al., 2021). For instance, PathAI, a small healthcare startup, improved cancer detection accuracy through AI-driven image recognition, overcoming the challenge of limited radiologists.

2.5 Emerging Trends in AI-Enabled SME Growth

The rise of AI adoption in SMEs is shaped by several key trends. AI-powered automation is revolutionizing customer service, supply chain management, and HR processes, allowing SMEs to reduce operational costs and improve productivity (Chatterjee et al., 2022). Additionally, AI in cybersecurity plays a crucial role in detecting cyber threats in real-time, preventing potential data breaches and hacking incidents (Jabbour et al., 2020). AI also contributes to sustainability, helping SMEs transition to eco-friendly business models and circular economy initiatives, such as AI-driven waste reduction and smart resource management (Breque et al., 2021). Furthermore, AI-driven personalized marketing strategies allow SMEs to analyze customer preferences, enhance engagement, and boost sales (Geissdoerfer et al.,

2017). Zara's AI-powered demand forecasting system, which optimizes inventory management and minimizes unsold stock, is a prime example of AI's role in sustainable business practices.

Despite the growing body of research on AI adoption in SMEs, several critical gaps remain. Many studies focus on large enterprises, leaving limited research on SME-specific AI adoption challenges. Additionally, there is a lack of empirical studies on AI implementation strategies, particularly in emerging economies and small-scale industries. Another overlooked area is human-AI collaboration, as most research centers on automation rather than how SMEs can balance AI-driven efficiency with human expertise. Furthermore, regulatory and ethical concerns surrounding AI bias, transparency, and compliance remain underexplored, particularly regarding SME governance structures.

3. INDUSTRY 5.0 AND ITS IMPACT ON SMES

The emergence of Industry 5.0 represents a significant shift in industrial evolution, moving beyond the automation and data-driven decision-making of Industry 4.0 to a model that emphasizes human-AI collaboration, sustainability, and resilience. Unlike Industry 4.0, which prioritized efficiency through autonomous systems, IoT, and cloud computing, Industry 5.0 focuses on reintegration of human intelligence into industrial processes, ensuring that technology augments human capabilities rather than replacing them (Breque et al., 2021). For Small and Medium-Sized Enterprises (SMEs), this transition offers a range of opportunities to enhance their business models, workforce dynamics, and operational efficiency. However, it also presents **challenges**, particularly in terms of ethical AI adoption, workforce adaptation, and regulatory compliance.

3.1 Industry 5.0: The Shift from Automation to Human-AI Collaboration

Industry 5.0 moves away from the fully automated environments of Industry 4.0, introducing a collaborative model where humans and AI-driven machines work together to enhance creativity, efficiency, and personalized production (Demir & Cicibas, 2022). This shift is driven by the need for greater product customization, enhanced human oversight in decision-making, and sustainability-focused production processes. Unlike previous industrial revolutions that aimed to **eliminate human intervention**, Industry 5.0 ensures that AI serves as an assistant rather than a replacement for human workers, helping businesses achieve a balance between automation and human-centered innovation (Javaid et al., 2022).

One of the defining features of Industry 5.0 is personalized manufacturing, where AI-driven customization of products is based on real-time consumer preferences. AI also augments the workforce by assisting employees in decision-making, streamlining manual processes, and enhancing workplace safety. Additionally, Industry 5.0 focuses on sustainability, with AI-powered green energy management, waste reduction, and circular economy models helping SMEs achieve environmental goals. AI-driven predictive analytics also enhances business resilience, allowing SMEs to anticipate risks, optimize supply chains, and mitigate crises. A key example of Industry 5.0 in action is Universal Robots, a Danish SME specializing in collaborative robots (cobots), which integrates AI-driven robotics with human oversight in assembly lines. Unlike traditional industrial robots, these cobots adjust in real-time to human input, increasing efficiency while ensuring worker safety (Santoro et al., 2023).

3.2 The Role of AI in Enhancing Resilience, Efficiency, and Sustainability in SMEs

AI is transforming SMEs by enhancing resilience, efficiency, and sustainability, three key pillars of Industry 5.0. AI-driven predictive analytics is particularly valuable for risk management, allowing SMEs to forecast market fluctuations, optimize supply chains, and mitigate financial risks. For example, Uniserve, a UK-based logistics SME, implemented AI-powered predictive analytics to identify supply chain risks, leading to a 30% reduction in stock shortages and improved inventory management (OECD, 2022).

In terms of efficiency, AI automates repetitive tasks, optimizes workflows, and improves decision-making. AI-driven chatbots, for instance, have reduced customer service response times by up to 80%, allowing SMEs to handle queries efficiently while reducing labor costs (Chatterjee et al., 2022). In the healthcare sector, PathAI, a healthcare SME, leveraged AI-powered image recognition to enhance cancer diagnostics, reducing diagnosis time from weeks to hours and significantly improving treatment planning and accuracy (Jabbour et al., 2020).

From a sustainability perspective, Industry 5.0 promotes green AI solutions that minimize waste, optimize energy consumption, and enhance ESG (Environmental, Social, and Governance) compliance. AI-powered energy monitoring systems enable SMEs to track and reduce their carbon footprints, making operations more environmentally sustainable. For example, Petit Bateau, a French textile SME, integrated AI into its production processes to optimize fabric usage, reducing material waste by 25% and aligning with the company's sustainable fashion objectives (Breque et al., 2021).

3.3 Key Technologies Powering Industry 5.0: AI, IoT, Blockchain, Robotics, and Digital Twins

Industry 5.0 is powered by several emerging technologies that enable human-AI collaboration and optimize SME performance. Artificial Intelligence (AI) plays a central role in predictive maintenance, decision automation, and data analytics. Machine learning algorithms help SMEs detect inefficiencies, automate supply chains, and personalize customer experiences (Wamba et al., 2021). For instance, Zara employs AI-based demand forecasting, reducing unsold inventory and improving production planning, helping the company efficiently align with real-time market demand (Santoro et al., 2023).

The Internet of Things (IoT) enhances SME operations by enabling real-time data collection for logistics, inventory management, and remote monitoring (Demir & Cicibas, 2022). Wilo, a German SME, implemented IoT-driven smart water pumps, optimizing water consumption and reducing operational costs by 20% (OECD, 2022). Meanwhile, blockchain technology enhances supply chain transparency by securing transaction records, ensuring regulatory compliance, and preventing fraud (Müller et al., 2021). Everledger, a UK-based SME, uses blockchain to track diamonds, ensuring ethical sourcing and fraud prevention in the jewelry industry.

Industry 5.0 also sees a rise in collaborative robots (cobots), which work alongside human workers, performing precision tasks while allowing human oversight (Geissdoerfer et al., 2017). Fanuc, a Japanese SME, developed AI-driven cobots that assist factory workers, improving productivity while maintaining safety standards. Finally, digital twin technology allows SMEs to create virtual models of physical assets, enabling real-time monitoring, simulation, and process optimization (Javaid et al., 2022). Siemens has adopted digital twins in its smart factories, allowing for real-time analysis, predictive maintenance, and improved energy efficiency.

3.4 Ethical AI and Human-AI Interaction in SMEs

While AI adoption in SMEs offers numerous benefits, it also presents ethical concerns related to bias, transparency, and workforce impact. One of the main challenges is bias in AI decision-making, where AI models trained on biased datasets may result in unfair hiring practices, discriminatory customer profiling, or inaccurate predictions. Additionally, SMEs must carefully balance automation and workforce integration, ensuring that AI augments rather than replaces human employees (Breque et al., 2021). Data privacy is another concern, as SMEs handling sensitive customer information must comply with GDPR, AI regulations, and cybersecurity best practices (Jabbour et al., 2020). L'Oréal, a cosmetics SME, adopted AI-driven recruitment tools to eliminate bias in candidate selection, ensuring a fairer and more inclusive hiring process (Wamba et al., 2021).

3.5 Future Trends: The Rise of AI-Augmented Workforce and AI-Driven Business Models

Industry 5.0 is set to redefine workforce dynamics, shifting towards an AI-augmented workforce, where human creativity and AI intelligence coexist. SMEs will increasingly integrate AI-driven business models, such as hyper-personalization, AI-driven subscription services, and sustainable AI applications. AI will also play a significant role in green energy solutions, circular economies, and decentralized AI adoption for small businesses. For example, Spotify uses AI to deliver hyper-personalized music recommendations, increasing user engagement and revenue (Geissdoerfer et al., 2017).

Industry 5.0 represents a transformative shift toward human-AI collaboration, sustainability, and ethical AI adoption. SMEs stand to gain from AI-driven efficiency, resilience, and innovation, but must address ethical concerns and workforce adaptation challenges to fully realize AI-driven opportunities.

Table 1. AI-Driven Digital Transformation in SMEs

Section	Key Insights	Examples
4.1 The Concept of AI-Driven Digital Transformation	AI enables SMEs to automate processes, improve efficiency, and gain a competitive edge through AI-driven decision-making.	PathAI **(healthcare SME) uses AI for diagnostics, improving accuracy and reducing workload (Santoro et al., 2023).** Zara **utilizes AI for demand forecasting, optimizing inventory and reducing waste (Geissdoerfer et al., 2017).**
4.2 Key AI Technologies Transforming SMEs	Machine Learning & Predictive Analytics **– Helps SMEs analyze data, forecast trends, and optimize business strategies.**	Uniserve **(logistics SME) used predictive analytics to reduce stock shortages by 30% (OECD, 2022).**
	Natural Language Processing (NLP) & Chatbots **– Automates customer service, sentiment analysis, and language-based interactions.**	H&M **implemented AI chatbots for shopping assistance, increasing sales and engagement (Jabbour et al., 2020).**
	Robotics & Collaborative Robots (Cobots) – AI-powered robots assist in automation, enhancing production efficiency and safety.	Fanuc **(Japanese SME) developed AI cobots, improving output while ensuring worker safety (Breque et al., 2021).**
	Computer Vision & Quality Control **– AI detects defects and automates quality assurance in manufacturing and healthcare.**	Siemens **integrated AI-based vision systems, reducing manufacturing defects by 40% (Santoro et al., 2023).**
	AI-Powered Data Analytics & Business Intelligence **– AI enhances real-time insights, pricing strategies, and sales forecasting.**	Zara **uses AI analytics for demand forecasting, reducing unsold stock by 20% (Geissdoerfer et al., 2017).**

continued on following page

Table 1. Continued

Section	Key Insights	Examples
4.3 Business Functions Enhanced by AI	Marketing & Customer Engagement – **AI-driven recommendation engines personalize marketing and increase customer retention.**	Spotify **curates personalized playlists using AI, improving user engagement (Geissdoerfer et al., 2017).**
	Financial Management & Risk Analysis **– AI-powered financial tools enhance fraud detection, credit scoring, and budget planning.**	Kabbage **uses AI for credit risk assessment, enabling faster SME loan approvals (OECD, 2022).**
	Supply Chain & Logistics Optimization **– AI optimizes inventory, delivery tracking, and route planning for cost efficiency.**	Amazon's third-party SME sellers **leverage AI for demand forecasting, improving stock management (Santoro et al., 2023).**
	Human Resource Management & Talent Acquisition **– AI automates hiring, performance tracking, and employee engagement.**	L'Oréal **implemented AI-driven hiring tools, reducing hiring bias and improving selection accuracy (Breque et al., 2021).**
	Cybersecurity & Data Protection **– AI protects SMEs from cyber threats, fraud, and data breaches.**	Darktrace **uses AI to detect and prevent cyber threats, safeguarding SMEs from financial losses (OECD, 2022).**
4.4 The Benefits of AI Adoption in SMEs	Increased Efficiency **– AI automates tasks, reducing operational costs and increasing productivity.**	AI-powered automation has reduced manual labor costs in various SMEs (Müller et al., 2021).
	Improved Customer Experience **– AI enhances personalization and brand loyalty.**	AI-driven personalized recommendations boost customer satisfaction (Wamba et al., 2021).
	Enhanced Decision-Making **– AI analytics supports strategic, data-driven decisions.**	AI tools improve forecasting accuracy, reducing risks (Santoro et al., 2023).
	Cost Reduction **– AI minimizes labor and marketing costs while streamlining operations.**	AI reduces overhead costs in SMEs by automating HR and supply chain tasks (Geissdoerfer et al., 2017).
	Competitive Advantage **– AI allows SMEs to compete with larger firms.**	AI adoption levels the playing field, giving SMEs access to data-driven insights (OECD, 2022).

Table 2. Structured Framework for AI Implementation in SMEs

Section	Key Insights	Examples
Assessing AI Readiness: The Technology-Organization-Environment (TOE) Framework	Technology Factors: Evaluates AI capabilities, infrastructure, and system compatibility. Organizational Factors: Assesses leadership support, workforce skills, and company culture. Environmental Factors: Considers government regulations, market demand, and competitive pressure.	A manufacturing SME in Germany **successfully adopted** AI-driven predictive maintenance **after assessing its AI readiness (OECD, 2022).**
The Digital Maturity Model for SMEs	Categorizes SMEs into three AI adoption stages: Basic Digitalization: Use of emails, websites, and digital payments, but no AI integration. Advanced Digitalization: AI-driven analytics, automation, and cloud computing adoption. AI-Enabled Business Models: Full AI integration in decision-making and operations.	Unilever transitioned from basic digitalization to AI-driven supply chain optimization, **reducing inventory costs by** 20% **(Santoro et al., 2023).**
Step-by-Step AI Implementation Roadmap	Step 1: Awareness & Strategic Planning **– Define business goals, assess AI potential, and align with long-term strategy.**	H&M conducted AI awareness workshops, educating employees on AI's role in marketing and customer engagement.
	Step 2: Experimentation & Pilot Testing **– SMEs test AI on a small scale to assess feasibility and ROI.**	Siemens ran an AI-powered defect detection pilot, **reducing manufacturing errors by** 40% **before full adoption (Jabbour et al., 2020).**
	Step 3: Integration with Existing Business Models **– AI should seamlessly integrate with ERP, CRM, and supply chain systems.**	Amazon's third-party SME sellers integrated AI-powered demand forecasting tools, **improving inventory turnover by** 15% **(Müller et al., 2021).**
	Step 4: Scaling AI Adoption & Continuous Optimization **– AI deployment should expand across multiple functions with continuous monitoring.**	Spotify scaled its AI-powered recommendation engine, **improving** customer retention by 30% (Geissdoerfer et al., 2017).

continued on following page

Table 2. Continued

Section	Key Insights	Examples
Overcoming AI Adoption Barriers in SMEs	Financial Constraints: Limited access to funding for AI investment and implementation.	Kabbage uses AI-powered credit scoring, **enabling SMEs to access AI funding (OECD, 2022).**
	Solutions: **- Leverage** government AI grants and subsidies. **- Use** pay-as-you-go cloud-based AI services **to reduce costs.**	L'Oréal partnered with AI research labs to train employees in AI-driven recruitment analytics, improving hiring efficiency by 25% (Wamba et al., 2021).
	Skill Gaps & Workforce Training: **Lack of AI-trained professionals in SMEs.**	Solutions: **- Conduct** in-house AI training programs. **- Collaborate with** universities and AI research institutions **for talent development.**
	Regulatory Compliance & Ethical AI: **SMEs must follow AI transparency laws and compliance requirements.**	Solutions: **- Implement** AI ethics guidelines **to prevent bias.** **- Adopt** Explainable AI (XAI) **for transparency.**
	Cybersecurity & Data Privacy Risks: **AI-driven customer analytics requires strong security measures.**	Solutions: **- Deploy** AI-driven cybersecurity tools **for real-time threat detection.** **- Implement** multi-factor authentication (MFA) and encryption protocols.
Conclusion	A structured framework ensures SMEs can strategically adopt AI technologies for efficiency, compliance, and scalability. The TOE framework and Digital Maturity Model help assess AI readiness, while a step-by-step roadmap supports AI integration. Overcoming financial constraints, skill shortages, regulatory barriers, and cybersecurity risks is essential for maximizing AI's potential in SMEs.	Successful AI adoption in SMEs enhances business efficiency, workforce capabilities, and competitive advantage **(Santoro et al., 2023).**

4. AI-DRIVEN BUSINESS MODEL INNOVATION AND WORKFORCE TRANSFORMATION

The adoption of Artificial Intelligence (AI) in Small and Medium-Sized Enterprises (SMEs) is revolutionizing business models and workforce structures, enabling SMEs to automate operations, enhance productivity, and create AI-augmented job roles. AI facilitates innovation in service delivery, shifting SMEs from traditional product-based models to service-oriented, AI-driven solutions, while also necessitating the upskilling and reskilling of employees for effective human-AI collaboration (Müller et al., 2021). As AI evolves, businesses must integrate intelligent automation, personalized customer experiences, and data-driven decision-making to maintain a competitive edge (Jabbour et al., 2020).

AI-powered business models are transforming SMEs by enabling subscription-based services, platform-driven solutions, and hyper-personalized marketing. Instead of selling standalone products, SMEs are increasingly adopting AI-based subscription models that offer predictive maintenance, automated updates, and personalized services (Santoro et al., 2023). AI-driven platforms help SMEs analyze market trends, optimize pricing, and enhance sales strategies, while hyper-personalization ensures real-time customer engagement and improved retention (Geissdoerfer et al., 2017). For instance, Spotify utilizes AI to analyze user preferences and deliver customized music recommendations, increasing user engagement and subscription renewals (Chatterjee et al., 2022).

The rise of AI is also accelerating the transition of SMEs from product-based to service-based business models. AI-driven predictive analytics enables SMEs to offer on-demand services and dynamic pricing strategies, while AI-powered Software-as-a-Service (SaaS) platforms provide businesses with automated tools for supply chain management, HR processes, and customer interactions (Javaid et al., 2022). Companies like Tesla have leveraged AI to integrate software-driven features such as self-driving capabilities and AI-powered vehicle monitoring, transforming their business model into a subscription-based service (Santoro et al., 2023).

AI is not replacing jobs in SMEs but rather augmenting human capabilities by automating repetitive tasks and enabling employees to focus on high-value strategic activities. AI-augmented job roles are becoming increasingly common, such as AI-powered marketing analysts who predict customer behavior, AI-enhanced customer support agents who handle complex queries, and AI-assisted financial analysts who optimize investment strategies (Wamba et al., 2021). AI-driven automation at H&M helps human stylists offer real-time fashion recommendations, ensuring that AI enhances customer experience rather than replacing human expertise (Geissdoerfer et al., 2017).

As AI adoption grows, SMEs must prioritize workforce upskilling and reskilling strategies to ensure employees can collaborate effectively with AI systems. AI training programs should focus on technical skills, data analytics, and AI ethics, while partnerships with universities and AI research institutions can provide employees with hands-on learning opportunities (OECD, 2022). AI-driven learning management systems (LMS) allow SMEs to offer adaptive, personalized training experiences, helping employees stay competitive in an AI-driven workforce (Müller et al., 2021). For example, L'Oréal integrated AI-based learning modules to upskill HR teams in AI-powered recruitment analytics, increasing hiring efficiency by 30% (Breque et al., 2021).

Beyond automation, AI also plays a vital role in enhancing workplace productivity and creativity. AI-powered collaboration tools improve team coordination and project management, while intelligent automation reduces administrative burdens, allowing employees to focus on strategic innovation (Javaid et al., 2022). AI-driven platforms like Adobe Sensei assist SMEs in content creation and marketing, streamlining design processes and enabling creative teams to generate high-quality materials efficiently (Santoro et al., 2023).

Achieving a balance between AI automation and human expertise is essential for SMEs to maximize AI's potential while ensuring ethical and responsible AI adoption. AI should function as a support tool rather than a replacement for human workers, with explainable AI (XAI) ensuring transparency in AI-driven decision-making (Breque et al., 2021). Ethical AI frameworks must address fairness, privacy, and workforce well-being, ensuring that AI benefits both businesses and employees (Jabbour et al., 2020). SMEs like Universal Robots have successfully implemented AI-driven collaborative robots (cobots) that assist human employees in manufacturing, improving efficiency while maintaining workplace safety (Santoro et al., 2023).

In conclusion, AI is driving business model innovations and workforce transformation in SMEs, enabling them to transition from product-based businesses to service-oriented models, create AI-augmented jobs, and enhance workplace productivity. However, to achieve long-term sustainability, SMEs must focus on human-AI collaboration, ethical AI implementation, and continuous workforce upskilling. Investing in AI-driven business models, integrating AI responsibly, and fostering a culture of innovation will allow SMEs to remain competitive in an increasingly AI-driven economy.

Table 3. AI Applications in Key SME Sectors

Sector	AI Applications	Examples
Manufacturing: AI-Driven Smart Factories, Predictive Maintenance, and Quality Control	AI-Driven Smart Factories – **AI-powered robotics and automation enhance production efficiency and reduce human errors (Javaid et al., 2022).** Predictive Maintenance – **AI analyzes machine performance data, predicting failures before they occur and reducing downtime (Müller et al., 2021).** Automated Quality Control – **AI-based computer vision systems detect defects in real-time, ensuring consistent product quality (Santoro et al., 2023).**	Siemens implemented AI-driven predictive maintenance, reducing equipment downtime by 30% and optimizing energy consumption (Geissdoerfer et al., 2017).
Retail: AI-Powered Customer Analytics, Personalized Marketing, and Inventory Optimization	AI-Powered Customer Analytics – **AI analyzes customer behavior, predicting preferences and improving the shopping experience (OECD, 2022).** Personalized Marketing – **AI tailors marketing campaigns based on individual customer interactions, increasing engagement and conversions (Wamba et al., 2021).** Inventory Optimization – **AI-driven demand forecasting helps maintain optimal stock levels, reducing overstocking and waste (Jabbour et al., 2020).**	Zara uses AI-powered demand forecasting, reducing unsold stock by 20% and improving supply chain efficiency (Santoro et al., 2023).
Finance: AI for Risk Management, Fraud Detection, and Smart Financial Planning	AI-Based Risk Management – **AI evaluates historical financial data to assess credit risks and financial irregularities (Javaid et al., 2022).** Fraud Detection – **AI-driven security systems detect suspicious transactions in real-time, preventing financial fraud (Wamba et al., 2021).** Smart Financial Planning – **AI provides SMEs with automated budgeting, expense tracking, and investment recommendations (Müller et al., 2021).**	Kabbage, an SME fintech company, utilizes AI-powered credit scoring models, **reducing** loan approval times from weeks to minutes (OECD, 2022).

continued on following page

Table 3. Continued

Sector	AI Applications	Examples
Healthcare: AI-Enabled Diagnostics, Patient Care, and Drug Discovery	AI-Enabled Diagnostics – **AI-driven imaging tools enhance accuracy in disease detection, reducing diagnostic errors (Santoro et al., 2023).** AI in Patient Care – **AI-powered virtual assistants and chatbots provide remote medical consultations, improving accessibility (Jabbour et al., 2020).** Drug Discovery and Development – **AI accelerates drug discovery by analyzing molecular structures and predicting interactions (Geissdoerfer et al., 2017).**	PathAI uses AI-based image recognition for cancer detection, reducing diagnosis time by 70% and improving patient survival rates (OECD, 2022).

Table 4. Challenges and risks in AI-driven digital transformation for SMEs

Section	Key Challenges	Examples
Financial and Technological Challenges for SMEs	High AI Implementation Costs – AI tools and cloud computing require significant upfront investment (Wamba et al., 2021). Limited AI Expertise – SMEs struggle to hire AI-skilled employees, slowing adoption (Chatterjee et al., 2022). Scalability Issues – Many SMEs lack the infrastructure to scale AI solutions (Müller et al., 2021).	A manufacturing SME in Germany faced high costs and lack of AI expertise, leading it to outsource AI-driven predictive maintenance (OECD, 2022).
Cybersecurity and Data Privacy Risks in AI Adoption	AI-Powered Cyber Threats – **Cybercriminals use AI-driven phishing and deepfake fraud to exploit SME vulnerabilities (Jabbour et al., 2020).** Data Privacy Compliance Issues **– SMEs must follow GDPR and industry-specific data protection laws (Geissdoerfer et al., 2017).** Insufficient Cybersecurity Infrastructure **– Many SMEs lack AI-driven threat detection systems (Santoro et al., 2023).**	Darktrace, an SME in cybersecurity, developed AI-powered real-time threat detection, preventing cyberattacks for small businesses (OECD, 2022).
Resistance to Change and Organizational Culture Barriers	Fear of Job Displacement **– Employees worry about AI replacing jobs (Müller et al., 2021).** Lack of AI Awareness and Training **– SMEs fail to educate employees about AI benefits (Jabbour et al., 2020).** Slow Decision-Making Processes **– Leadership struggles to integrate AI into existing workflows (Santoro et al., 2023).**	A UK-based retail SME faced employee resistance to AI-powered chatbots, requiring retraining programs for workforce integration (OECD, 2022).
Ethical AI Implementation and the Risk of Algorithmic Bias	Algorithmic Bias in Hiring and Loan Approvals **– AI can discriminate against certain demographic groups (Chatterjee et al., 2022).** Lack of Explainable AI (XAI) **– SMEs struggle to interpret AI decisions, reducing trust (Javaid et al., 2022).** Ethical Dilemmas in AI Deployment **– Issues arise in facial recognition, predictive policing, and HR automation (Jabbour et al., 2020).**	Amazon's AI hiring tool showed gender bias, reinforcing discrimination in recruitment **(Santoro et al., 2023).**

continued on following page

Table 4. Continued

Section	Key Challenges	Examples
Regulatory and Policy Challenges in AI Adoption for SMEs	GDPR Compliance and Data Protection Laws – **SMEs must protect customer data and ensure AI transparency (Müller et al., 2021).** Industry-Specific AI Regulations – **SMEs in finance, healthcare, and retail must follow sector-specific AI policies (Jabbour et al., 2020).** AI Liability and Accountability Issues – **Unclear AI governance laws pose legal risks (Santoro et al., 2023).**	Everledger, an SME in blockchain-based AI, ensures compliance with ethical sourcing laws for diamond tracking **(Geissdoerfer et al., 2017).**
Managing AI Governance and Risk Mitigation Strategies	Adopt Explainable AI (XAI) – **SMEs must ensure AI decision-making is transparent (Müller et al., 2021).** Regular AI Audits and Compliance Checks – **Periodic AI risk assessments improve governance (Jabbour et al., 2020).** Develop AI Governance Policies – **Establish internal AI ethics and accountability guidelines (Santoro et al., 2023).** Invest in AI Cybersecurity Measures – **AI-driven security tools prevent fraud and data breaches (Javaid et al., 2022).**	L'Oréal developed an AI governance framework for hiring, ensuring ethical AI use and reducing bias (OECD, 2022).

5. AI FOR RESILIENCE AND CRISIS MANAGEMENT IN SMES

Artificial Intelligence (AI) is transforming resilience and crisis management for Small and Medium-Sized Enterprises (SMEs) by enhancing risk assessment, automating business continuity processes, and strengthening financial sustainability. SMEs often face financial downturns, supply chain disruptions, cyber threats, and operational crises, making AI an essential tool for ensuring business stability and recovery strategies (Müller et al., 2021).

AI-driven predictive analytics helps SMEs anticipate risks, detect vulnerabilities, and implement preventive measures. Machine learning models analyze historical and real-time data to detect financial risks, market fluctuations, and supply chain disruptions, enabling businesses to take proactive actions (Jabbour et al., 2020). For example, Unilever adopted AI-based predictive analytics to monitor supply chain risks, reducing stock shortages by 30% (OECD, 2022). AI also enhances disaster recovery and business continuity planning by providing automated backup systems, crisis response workflows, and remote workforce management, ensuring operational stability during unexpected disruptions (Javaid et al., 2022).

AI-powered automation plays a critical role in crisis management by handling repetitive tasks such as customer inquiries, supply chain adjustments, and payroll management, allowing SMEs to focus on strategic decision-making (Wamba et al., 2021). H&M deployed AI chatbots during COVID-19 to manage customer service inquiries, reducing response times by 60% while maintaining customer engagement (Chatterjee et al., 2022). In financial resilience, AI-driven budgeting and revenue forecasting tools help SMEs optimize cash flow, predict economic downturns, and secure funding. AI-enabled fintech companies like Kabbage use AI-powered credit risk assessments to accelerate loan approvals, ensuring SMEs can access financial support during crises (Geissdoerfer et al., 2017).

Cybersecurity remains a critical challenge for SMEs, making AI-driven security solutions essential for fraud detection, phishing prevention, and cyber threat mitigation. AI-powered tools such as Darktrace autonomously detect and neutralize cyber threats, preventing millions in potential losses for SMEs (OECD, 2022).

By investing in AI infrastructure, workforce training, and AI-powered risk mitigation strategies, SMEs can enhance crisis preparedness, maintain business continuity, and ensure long-term sustainability in an increasingly uncertain economic and digital landscape.

6. AI-ENABLED SUSTAINABILITY AND CIRCULAR ECONOMY FOR SMES

Artificial Intelligence (AI) is playing a pivotal role in helping Small and Medium-Sized Enterprises (SMEs) adopt sustainable business models by enabling waste reduction, resource optimization, and compliance with Environmental, Social, and Governance (ESG) standards. AI-driven solutions help SMEs monitor carbon footprints, reduce energy consumption, optimize supply chains, and promote circular economy initiatives, ensuring both environmental sustainability and cost efficiency (Müller et al., 2021).

AI enhances sustainable business practices by automating energy management, emissions tracking, and sustainable supply chain operations. For instance, Siemens implemented AI-driven energy management systems, reducing energy consumption by 25% while cutting CO_2 emissions (Geissdoerfer et al., 2017). Similarly, AI-powered waste reduction tools help SMEs minimize material wastage, improve recycling efficiency, and transition towards zero-waste operations (Javaid et al., 2022). AI-driven smart inventory management and predictive production planning reduce overproduction and material waste, ensuring resource efficiency (Chatterjee et al., 2022). Zara uses AI-powered demand forecasting, minimizing unsold inventory and reducing fabric waste by 20% (Santoro et al., 2023).

AI also facilitates ESG compliance by automating carbon accounting, sustainability tracking, and regulatory reporting. AI-powered platforms streamline ESG disclosures, ensuring transparency and ethical supply chain monitoring (Breque et al., 2021). For example, Unilever utilizes AI-driven ESG tracking tools to monitor ethical sourcing, reducing supply chain risks and improving regulatory compliance (Jabbour et al., 2020).

In the circular economy, AI optimizes resource efficiency, smart waste sorting, and remanufacturing. AI-driven predictive analytics improve waste forecasting, while robotic waste-sorting systems enhance recycling accuracy (Santoro et al., 2023). Companies like ZenRobotics have developed AI-powered waste-sorting robots, increasing recycling efficiency by 50% (Javaid et al., 2022). Additionally, AI-powered remanufacturing solutions extend product lifespans and reduce reliance on raw materials. Tesla leverages AI to optimize battery remanufacturing, reducing waste and improving energy efficiency (Geissdoerfer et al., 2017).

By integrating AI-driven sustainability strategies, SMEs can reduce costs, enhance environmental responsibility, and gain a competitive edge in a circular economy. However, successful AI adoption requires investment in digital infrastructure, workforce upskilling, and alignment with regulatory policies. AI-driven sustainability initiatives can transform SMEs into eco-friendly, resource-efficient enterprises, ensuring long-term profitability and environmental impact reduction.

7. POLICY, INSTITUTIONAL SUPPORT, AND THE FUTURE OF AI IN SMES

The successful adoption of Artificial Intelligence (AI) in Small and Medium-Sized Enterprises (SMEs) depends not only on technological advancements but also on policy frameworks, institutional support, funding opportunities, and ethical AI governance. Governments, industry associations, and AI incubators play a crucial role in facilitating AI adoption through financial incentives, regulatory compliance frameworks, and AI-driven business development programs (Müller et al., 2021). Policy interventions such as AI adoption grants, tax incentives, and workforce training initiatives help SMEs integrate AI into their operations while ensuring ethical and responsible AI deployment (OECD, 2022). For example, the European

Union's "Digital Europe Programme" has allocated €7.5 billion to support SMEs in AI adoption and digital transformation (Santoro et al., 2023).

Funding remains a significant challenge for SMEs seeking to implement AI solutions, as AI infrastructure, research, and workforce training require substantial investment. To bridge this gap, governments, venture capitalists, and AI incubators offer financial support through innovation grants, private equity funding, and business acceleration programs (Chatterjee et al., 2022). AI-driven SMEs such as Kabbage, a fintech startup, secured $250 million in AI-powered credit risk assessment funding, enabling them to offer faster and more accurate loan approvals for SMEs (Santoro et al., 2023). Similarly, industry associations and AI incubators provide SMEs with technical mentorship, research collaborations, and business acceleration programs, ensuring that AI integration is both feasible and scalable (Breque et al., 2021).

Beyond financial support, AI adoption in SMEs raises ethical concerns related to data privacy, algorithmic bias, transparency, and regulatory compliance. Many governments are implementing AI-specific regulations, such as the GDPR, AI Act, and ethical AI frameworks, to ensure fair and responsible AI decision-making (OECD, 2022). AI governance policies focus on algorithmic fairness, data protection, and explainable AI (XAI) frameworks, requiring SMEs to prioritize ethical AI implementation (Santoro et al., 2023). For instance, Everledger, an AI-powered SME specializing in blockchain transparency, ensures compliance with AI ethics and data privacy laws while tracking ethical sourcing in the diamond industry (Jabbour et al., 2020).

Looking ahead, the future of AI in SMEs will be shaped by emerging AI technologies, increased government support, and sustainable AI-driven business models. AI-powered hyper-personalization, decentralized AI, and edge computing are expected to drive AI adoption across industries, allowing SMEs to improve customer engagement, operational efficiency, and data security (Müller et al., 2021). Additionally, AI-powered circular economy initiatives will help SMEs optimize resource efficiency, carbon footprint tracking, and smart waste management, aligning with global sustainability goals (OECD, 2022). Companies like Tesla's AI-driven sustainable energy division are setting the stage for SMEs to leverage AI for renewable energy projects and eco-friendly business models (Geissdoerfer et al., 2017).

In conclusion, government policies, investment opportunities, AI incubators, and ethical regulatory frameworks will shape the future of AI-driven digital transformation in SMEs. While AI presents immense potential for innovation, efficiency, and sustainability, SMEs must overcome financial, regulatory, and ethical challenges to ensure responsible AI adoption. Those that successfully integrate AI-driven business strategies will be well-positioned for long-term growth, competitive advantage, and sustainability in the evolving digital economy.

8. CONCLUSION AND FUTURE RESEARCH DIRECTIONS

The adoption of Artificial Intelligence (AI) in Small and Medium-Sized Enterprises (SMEs) represents a fundamental shift in business operations, workforce structures, and sustainability efforts. As Industry 5.0 emerges, AI is becoming an essential tool for enhancing resilience, improving efficiency, and fostering innovation in SMEs. This study has explored the theoretical foundations, practical applications, challenges, and future prospects of AI-driven digital transformation in SMEs, highlighting the importance of strategic implementation and supportive policy frameworks.

AI is proving to be a catalyst for SME growth by enabling businesses to automate operations, optimize decision-making, and enhance customer engagement. From AI-powered customer analytics in retail to predictive maintenance in manufacturing, SMEs that embrace AI can improve efficiency, reduce costs, and gain a competitive edge (Müller et al., 2021). For instance, Zara leverages AI-driven demand forecasting, which helps reduce unsold inventory and align production with real-time consumer trends (Santoro et al., 2023).

Unlike Industry 4.0, which focused on full automation, Industry 5.0 prioritizes human-AI collaboration, ensuring that AI complements rather than replaces human labor (Breque et al., 2021). SMEs must strike a balance between automation and human expertise to fully unlock AI's potential. Universal Robots, a Danish SME, has successfully integrated AI-powered collaborative robots (cobots), which work alongside human employees in manufacturing, boosting efficiency while maintaining worker safety (Santoro et al., 2023).

Despite AI's transformative potential, SMEs face several barriers to AI adoption, including financial constraints, skill shortages, cybersecurity risks, and regulatory challenges. Many SMEs struggle with high implementation costs and a lack of trained AI professionals, making it difficult to scale AI-driven solutions (OECD, 2022; Jabbour et al., 2020). Additionally, cybersecurity risks are increasing as SMEs become more reliant on AI-powered digital systems (Geissdoerfer et al., 2017). Regulatory compliance also presents a challenge, as SMEs must navigate complex AI governance frameworks, such as GDPR and AI Act regulations (Santoro et al., 2023). However, some SMEs have successfully tackled financial barriers by leveraging AI-driven funding models. For example, Kabbage, an SME fintech company, used AI-powered risk assessment tools to secure funding for SME loans, ensuring improved financial accessibility (OECD, 2022).

AI is also playing a crucial role in driving sustainability and circular economy initiatives in SMEs, enabling businesses to reduce waste, optimize energy consumption, and ensure compliance with ESG (Environmental, Social, and Governance) standards (Breque et al., 2021). AI-powered digital twins in smart factories, such as those implemented by Siemens, have led to a 30% reduction in energy consumption, showcasing AI's potential in environmental sustainability (Santoro et al., 2023).

Looking ahead, AI adoption in SMEs is expected to grow significantly, fueled by government support, new AI-driven business models, and advancements in AI technologies. Policymakers and industry leaders are investing in AI funding programs and innovation hubs to facilitate SME digital transformation (OECD, 2022). Emerging AI trends such as AI-as-a-Service (AIaaS), hyper-personalization, and decentralized AI will further accelerate AI's impact on SMEs (Müller et al., 2021). The European Union's Digital Europe Programme is an example of government-led initiatives supporting AI adoption, offering €7.5 billion in funding to help SMEs integrate AI-driven solutions (OECD, 2022).

To fully leverage AI's benefits, SME leaders and policymakers must focus on increasing AI investments, upskilling the workforce, adopting ethical AI practices, and strengthening AI governance. AI training programs and public-private partnerships can bridge the skill gap and enable a smoother AI transition for SMEs. Regulatory bodies must provide clear guidelines on AI ethics, data privacy, and cybersecurity to support SMEs in adopting fair and responsible AI systems.

Future research should explore AI adoption strategies in emerging markets, human-AI collaboration models, and AI policies tailored for SMEs. Additionally, studying algorithmic transparency and bias mitigation techniques will be essential for ensuring fair and ethical AI deployment in hiring, finance, and customer engagement.

Ultimately, AI has the potential to revolutionize SME operations, workforce transformation, and sustainability initiatives. However, for AI to be truly effective, its adoption must be strategic, ethical, and inclusive, ensuring that SMEs of all sizes and industries can leverage AI without facing undue financial or regulatory burdens. Governments, industry leaders, and AI researchers must collaborate to build an AI ecosystem that supports SME growth and fosters sustainable, AI-driven economic development. By investing in AI infrastructure, workforce development, and responsible AI governance, SMEs can achieve long-term resilience, innovation, and competitive success in the evolving digital economy.

REFERENCES

Breque, M., De Nul, L., & Petridis, A. (2021). *Industry 5.0: Towards a sustainable, human-centric and resilient European industry*. European Commission.

Chatterjee, S., Chaudhuri, R., Vrontis, D., & Thrassou, A. (2022). AI-driven customer engagement and SME competitiveness: A conceptual framework. *Journal of Business Research, 140*, 308–319. DOI: 10.1016/j.jbusres.2021.11.042

Demir, K. A., & Cicibas, H. (2022). Industry 5.0: Opportunities and challenges for SMEs. *Procedia Computer Science, 200*, 538–545. DOI: 10.1016/j.procs.2022.01.296

Geissdoerfer, M., Savaget, P., Bocken, N. M. P., & Hultink, E. J. (2017). The Circular Economy – A new sustainability paradigm? *Journal of Cleaner Production, 143*, 757–768. DOI: 10.1016/j.jclepro.2016.12.048

Jabbour, C. J. C., Seuring, S., de Sousa Jabbour, A. B. L., Jugend, D., Fiorini, P. D. C., Latan, H., & Izeppi, W. C. (2020). Stakeholders, innovative business models for sustainability, and Industry 4.0: Impact on circular economy initiatives. *Journal of Business Research, 122*, 488–498. DOI: 10.1016/j.jbusres.2020.09.033

Javaid, M., Haleem, A., Rab, S., Singh, R. P., & Suman, R. (2022). Understanding the transition towards Industry 5.0: A review of features, challenges and applications. *Materials Today: Proceedings, 51*, 1785–1792. DOI: 10.1016/j.matpr.2021.06.229

Müller, J. M., Buliga, O., & Voigt, K. I. (2021). The role of absorptive capacity and innovation strategy in the design of Industry 4.0 business models. *Technological Forecasting and Social Change, 132*, 119–131. DOI: 10.1016/j.techfore.2018.12.019

OECD. (2022). *OECD SME and Entrepreneurship Outlook 2022*. OECD Publishing., DOI: 10.1787/69a88f50-

Santoro, G., Bertoldi, B., Giachino, C., & Candelo, E. (2023). Digital transformation and business model innovation: A systematic literature review. *Journal of Business Research, 148*, 181–197. DOI: 10.1016/j.jbusres.2022.04.051

Schwab, K. (2016). *The Fourth Industrial Revolution*. Crown Business.

Wamba, S. F., Akter, S., Edwards, A., Chopin, G., & Gnanzou, D. (2021). How 'big data' can make big impact: Findings from a systematic review and a research agenda. *International Journal of Production Economics, 165*, 234–246. DOI: 10.1016/j.ijpe.2014.12.031

Chapter 8
AI-Driven Innovation: Unlocking Competitive Advantage for SMEs for Long-Term Growth and Sustainability

Jatin Thakur
https://orcid.org/0009-0005-9089-0303
Lovely Professional University, India

Pooja Kansra
https://orcid.org/0000-0003-2229-0662
Lovely Professional University, India

Preeti Mehra
https://orcid.org/0000-0002-8979-9431
Campbell College, Canada

ABSTRACT

Through a focus on the growth and sustainability benefits for SMEs Leveraging AI powered innovation are discussed in this chapter. AI can help improve operational efficiency, provide data-based insights, and enable tailored consumer experiences—factors that SMEs are looking for to tackle resource constraints and high competition. AI's ability to enhance automation, marketing, supply chain management and financial operations open the floodgates to new opportunities for scalability and innovation. Moreover, AI helps make operations more sustainable by optimizing energy consumption, minimizing waste, and creating corporate social responsibility (CSR) goals. However, challenges like high AI adoption costs, skill deficits, and data security risks hinder SMEs from leveraging AI services. A good AI-based company is built on strategic planning, partnerships, and workforce upskilling. It ends by summarizing some emerging trends in AI and discussing the place of AI on

DOI: 10.4018/979-8-3693-9611-7.ch008

resilience and sustainability in small and medium enterprises.

INTRODUCTION

Walia (2024) describes Artificial Intelligence (AI) as the imitation of human intellect in devices, allowing them to undertake activities related to reasoning and learning. AI is being implemented would be in the dynamics of business (Bruno, 2024). It's utilized in numerous fields such as data analytics, automation, pattern detection, and content generation (Walia, 2024). Artificial intelligence is a great technology that improves productivity and operational cost advantage which also leads to a gain of competitive advantage (Sadiku et al., 2020). Businesses use AI in operation, marketing, customer service, and human resources for better productivity and smooth processing of works (Walia, 2024). Companies in the age of AI have access to powerful solutions that can help them reduce repetitive processes, drive data-driven decisions, and respond faster to their customers (Abousaber & Abdalla, 2023). It also enhances supply chain operations and offers real-time information and analytics (Abousaber & Abdalla, 2023). AI is probably the most widely used technology that serves as a catalyst for today's businesses (Sadiku et al., 2020).

Small and Medium Enterprises (SMEs) have become the backbone of the economies over the world contributing heavily to innovation, providing jobs and overall economic growth. SMEs comprise more than 90% of aggregate business globally and 60–70% of employment, along with 55% of GDP amongst developed economies (Bayraktar & Algan, 2019). They contribute to approximately 20% of all patents in fields relating to biotechnology in Europe (Bayraktar & Algan, 2019) and are key drivers of innovation. Small- and medium-sized enterprises (SMEs) are considered the primary source of job creation, with the World Bank estimating it is necessary to create 600 million jobs by 2020 (Das et al., 2020), mostly in developing countries. Their capacity to rapidly adapt and innovate is critical for growth and poverty alleviation (Petkovska, 2015). SMEs have difficulties in adopting new technologies for financial and human resource limitations (Gomez & Lopez, 2024). Nonetheless, SMEs continue to play a crucial role in enhancing economic diversification and community development and in anchoring competitive advantage in the digital age (Gomez & Lopez, 2024).

As the journey level, AI-based innovation will be a major competitive edge for SMEs in the global economy as it makes operational efficiency, product development, and customer engagement (Iyelolu et al., 2024). Through automation and innovation, generative AI can enhance the resilience and competitiveness of SMEs, which is particularly relevant in the context of generative AI (Carayannis et al., 2024). Artificial Intelligence integration in innovation management systems, like "eskalator.

io," can accelerate complex processes and improve decision-making in all forms of innovation (Bakir et al., 2024). AI-driven predictive and prescriptive analytics can improve demand forecasting, customer behavior analysis, and financial planning for SMEs, facilitating better inventory management and resource allocation (Ocran et al., 2024). Yet SMEs suffer barriers regarding adoption such as his limited resources, lack of expertise and data security (Vanessa et al., 2024). Addressing these issues requires government incentives, public-private partnerships, and targeted training programs that build AI competencies within SMEs (Iyelolu et al., 2024; Carayannis et al., 2024).

LITERATURE REVIEW

Artificial Intelligence (AI) has emerged as a transformative force across various industries, including Small and Medium Enterprises (SMEs). AI-driven innovation is reshaping business operations, strategic decision-making, and customer engagement, enabling companies to enhance efficiency, optimize workflows, and provide personalized customer experiences.

1. AI in Business Operations

AI is streamlining and automating routine business functions, improving productivity, and reducing operational costs.

1.1 Process Automation and Efficiency

With the capability of automating vast processes, AI is disrupting business and increasing efficiency. Artificial intelligence is used to upgrade Robotic Process Automation (RPA) to Intelligent Automation (IA), that facilitates processing to be more flexible and adaptive (Dalsaniya & Patel, 2022). On an operational level, this integration has resulted in higher operational efficiency — with reports of increased resource efficiency by 20-30% and human input by 40-50% (Nama, 2022). Through automation, businesses will be able to achieve cost savings and improved productivity by optimizing all aspects of their operations — from predictive maintenance through resource utilization and customer engagement (Rahman, 2024). RPA and AI are being gradually accepted by large companies to automatically perform repetitive work as well as manage complex tasks requiring decision-making capabilities (Mangal, 2024). Despite being the most common and the benefits are remarkable, challenges like data privacy, system compatibility and organizational resistance still exist (Rahman, 2024; Mangal, 2024). AI in process automation is however becoming crucial in optimising operational efficiencies and maintaining competitiveness in the ever-evolving digital landscape.

1.2 AI in Human Resource Management

In the present time, Human Resource Management (HRM) is being disrupted by Artificial Intelligence (AI) in addition to improving efficiency & decision making in various functions. Machine learning, natural language processing and other types of AI technologies have been adopted in various areas related to work, including recruitment, employee screening and performance management (Islam, 2024; Kadirov et al., 2024). These innovations refine recruitment, training, and retention efforts, presenting tailored learning journeys and anticipatory attrition forecasts (Kadirov et al., 2024). Despite existing advantages associated with AI in HRM including decreased work load and data-driven insights, it also brings to the forefront challenges: skill gaps, data privacy-related issues, and fairness-related problems regarding algorithmic bias (Islam, 2024; Shouran & Ali, 2024). Such initiatives need to be strategically integrated and cycle through continuous training periods as well as retain a degree of human supervision to guarantee fair practices (Bharadwaj, 2024; Islam, 2024). With the continual evolution of AI, its applications in HRM are likely to grow, and responsible governance and regulation will be needed to realise the benefits of these applications while reducing any potential negative effects (Shouran & Ali, 2024).

2. AI in Decision-Making

AI is revolutionizing business decision-making by providing data-driven insights and automating strategic processes.

2.1 AI-Driven Predictive Analytics

Through the use of advanced machine learning algorithms and data mining techniques, AI-powered predictive analytics is transforming business decision-making by predicting trends, spotting risks, and optimizing strategies (Besiri, 2024). It also has the capacity to improve real-time decision-making by offering insights about customer behavior and market trends (Dehankar et al., 2023). Machine learning, natural language processing, and deep learning are examples of AI techniques that are extremely important in the analysis of complex datasets, discovery of hidden correlations, and forecasting of consumer demand with relative accuracy (Ajiga et al., 2024). Its applications are often varying, covering customer behavior analysis, supply chain optimisation, financial forecasting and inventory management (Besiri, 2024; Ajiga et al., 2024). Nonetheless, several challenges must be addressed, including data privacy, algorithmic bias, and the shortage of specialized skills (Besiri, 2024; Ajiga et al., 2024). Despite these challenges, leveraging AI-powered predictive analytics can empower the organizations to stay ahead in the competitive, data-powered world (Besiri, 2024; Ajiga et al., 2024).

2.2 AI in Strategic Business Planning

AI is becoming regarded as an important tool for strategic business planning, consequently providing opportunities for improving both market competitiveness as well as decision-making processes (Li, 2024; Wang, 2024). AI-powered technologies such as machine learning, natural language processing and predictive analysis are being incorporated into all aspects of business, from customer relationship management to supply chain optimization (Wang, 2024). These technologies allow organizations to analyze large volumes of data, identify patterns, and make better-informed strategic decisions (Bhattacharya, 2018; Spangler, 1991). On the other hand, integrating AI systems into strategic planning introduces complexities such as ethical considerations, legal obligations, and the necessity of cultural adaptation in organizations (Li, 2024). In spite of these challenges, however, AI can be transformational when it comes to strategic decision-making, as it can provide insights into problems that are ill-structured and are also at an early stage in the planning process (Spangler, 1991). Similar analyses are necessary to better understand the impact of AI on the direction and dynamics of organizations (Li, 2024).

3. AI in Customer Engagement

AI is transforming customer interactions by enabling hyper-personalization, real-time assistance, and enhanced user experience.

3.1 AI-Powered Personalization

Data-driven personalization is revolutionizing customer engagement marketing with the help of AI, allowing for hyper-personalized experiences (Davenport, 2023; Kumar et al., 2019). Utilizing advanced data analytics, machine learning, and predictive modeling, this approach helps both the providers and consumers of fast-moving consumer goods to understand their preferences and predict their future behavior (Gungunawat et al, 2024). Artificial Intelligence-driven personalization frameworks can enhance customer engagement and increase retention through targeted marketing, personalized recommendations, and optimized customer support (Okeke et al., 2024)—a promising approach for small and medium enterprises (SMEs) needing cost-effective solutions. Personalization powered by AI is not just confined to marketing but extends to all stages of customer interaction and service delivery (Gungunawat et al., 2024; Okeke et al., 2024). But there are challenges to be confronted, including data privacy issues and algorithmic bias (Davenport, 2023; Gungunawat et al., 2024). Despite these challenges, AI-driven personalization is becoming critical for businesses to stay competitive in the changing digital landscape, as it enhances ROI and propels innovation in customer engagement strategies (Gungunawat et al., 2024; Kumar et al., 2019).

3.2 AI Chatbots and Virtual Assistants

AI-based software applications that possibly replace human interaction are the chatbots and virtual assistants that engage users via text or voice (Sai Abitha, n.d.; Pavi Saraswat et al., 2021). Such technologies are using Natural Language Processing and Machine Learning to comprehend and reply queries from users (Dr.Farheen Mohammed, 2024). Chatbots are driven by either set of rules, a brain of their own, or artificial intelligence, with different degrees of complexity (Pavi Saraswat et al., 2021). Conversational AI has gained popularity and been used across many domains like marketing, education, healthcare, and even entertainment (Sai Abitha, 2021; Shubhangi Agarwal et al., 2022). A bibliometric study conducted recently shows that the publication of research articles discussing chatbots and virtual assistant technology have steadily increased, with the highest number of contributions accounted for by the United States (Shubhangi Agarwal et al., 2022). This has been further catalyzed by the COVID-19 pandemic, with the adoption of these technologies being driven by the promise of improved service efficiency and availability (Shubhangi Agarwal et al., 2022).

3.3 Sentiment Analysis and Social Listening

Sentimental analysis is a method which applies machine learning and natural language processing to interpret social media platform users' thoughts and feelings (Yadav, 2023). In different domains, it is used to comprehend public opinion about green programs, estimate box-office performance and understand emotions at global events (Yadav, 2023). Sentiment Analysis is the identification of sentiments, which can include positive, negative, or neutral on a text, using Machine Learning or lexicon-based approaches (Yadav, 2023; Singh & Kaur, 2015). Monitoring of social media is increasingly important for developing understanding of customer behavior and extracting valuable insights from vast amounts of unstructured data (Ahmed et al., 2015). With the increasing influence of opinions on human behavior and decision-making mechanisms (Zhang & Liu 2012), the importance of opinions has expanded in both business and social domains, thus sentiment analysis systems are applied in nearly every area of business. Sentiment analysis models have proven to be accurate for most languages (other than English) as well; however, social media content has several peculiarities (Yadav, 2023; Ahmed et al., 2015).

AI FOR SUSTAINABILITY IN SMES

1. AI-Driven Energy Efficiency and Waste Reduction

How AI is helping to transform waste management and energy efficiency in smart cities? Waste-to-energy conversion, smart bins, waste-sorting robots and logistics optimization are some of the applications of AI that can reposition the cost of transporting waste by up to 13.35% and reduce the distance travelled by up to 36.8% (Fang et al., 2023), The accuracy of waste classification has been improved by Machine Learning and Artificial Neural Networks, while the efficiency of resource recovery has increased by 15% and operational costs of the plants have decreased by 20% (Wei Ming et al., 2024). Integrating AI into waste-to-energy processes enhances automated sorting, process monitoring, and energy production forecasting, leading to sustainable practices and a circular economy (Melinda et al., 2024). AI methods have been used successfully to overcome tough challenges in waste management, which range from waste characteristic forecasting, bin level detection to process model parameter prediction, route to vehicle planning (Abdallah et al, 2020). With significant resource utilization to refocus on the unrealized potential of the algae life-like generation, these advances illustrate AI's capacity to dramatically enhance efficiency, minimize environmental footprint, and facilitate green resource usage in waste management processes.

2. AI Applications in Corporate Social Responsibility (CSR)

Indeed, a relatively fast-growing body of research examines how companies might incorporate Artificial Intelligence (AI) into Corporate Social Responsibility (CSR) activities, bringing opportunities but also challenges. The increasing use of AI has great potential to promote improved decision-making and transparency at all levels and in all industries, ultimately increasing the CSR levels that are being adhered to (Podile et al., 2024; Gaurav et al., 2024). You know, it has the cost savings, real-time data monitoring, optimized resource allocation (Tiku et al., 2024; Tarigan et al., 2024). CSR that is driven of AI have the potential to ferter deeper stakeholder engurement and brand loyalty (Tarigan et al., 2024). But there are issues like data privacy concerns, bias, and ethics that need to be dealt with (Podile et al., 2024;

Gaurav et al., 2024; According to some researchers, such frameworks can guide organizations to explore the potential of AI in CSR projects (Srinivasan et al., 2023) and applying artificial intelligence responsibly while maintaining transparency and accountability (Gaurav et al., 2024). AI adoption, however, must be congruent with CSR (Corporate Social Responsibility) principles, which involves actively contributing to social causes while aligning with profit objectives, providing a promising frontier for sustainable brand enhancement in the digital era (Tarigan et al., 2024).

3. Case Studies on Sustainable AI Practices in SMEs

AI for sustainability is gaining traction among SMEs as new studies show, but there are challenges as well. Several SMEs may not have the expertise, resources, and knowledge necessary to apply ethical AI practices (Smiee et al., 2022). Insufficient infrastructure, data availability, privacy concerns, and absence of AI adoption strategies are a few common barriers (Hernandez et al., 2023). In response, university-industry partnerships are proving to be effective mechanisms for up-skilling SMEs in responsible AI. The GM AI Foundry, for example, is allowing 186 SMEs to create responsible machine learning products (Lawton et al., 2023). This type of initiative is key to bridging the gap between ethical AI principles and practice, which is all the more important with the forthcoming regulations such as the EU AI Act. This will require SMEs to start adopting the emerging methodologies, standards, and best practices such (e.g. consequence scanning and harms modelling) taken from fields such as AI Safety (Banipal et al., 2023; Smiee et al., 2022).

CHALLENGES IN AI ADOPTION FOR SMES

AI adoption in SMEs in all continents is diffcult. Major obstacles comprise low financial capability, absence of technical knowledge, data security issues, as well as organizational resistance to transformation (Yusuf et al., 2024; Oldemeyer et al., 2024). (AI implementation is still a major challenge for SMEs due to the high costs and technical requirements (Govori & Sejdija, 2023). There are regional differences as well, such as African SMEs struggling with high costs and a lack of expertise, European SMEs facing regulatory difficulties, and Asian SMEs dealing with sustainability and cultural barriers (Yusuf et al., 2024). Despite these challenges, AI significantly increases efficiency and effectiveness in SMEs by improving operation processes, product development, and customer engagement (Vanessa et al., 2024). Also, (Vanessa et al., 2024) highlight strategies for overcoming adoption barriers, which include government incentives, public-private partnerships, AI-as-a-Service at scale, and training programs tailored to specific sectors. With the reduced costs of AI and continuous research, adding AI to existing systems will be easier for SMEs (Govori & Sejdija, 2023).

FUTURE TRENDS IN AI FOR SMES

Other research demonstrates the necessity for the implementation of AI in SMEs, where advantages could include increased efficiency of processes, better decision-making, business agility and innovation (Schwaeke et al., 2024; Yusuf et al., 2024; Vanessa et al., 2024; Schonberger, 2023). Predictive and prescriptive analytics, virtual assistants, and recommendation systems (Yusuf et al., 2024; Schönberger, 2023) are key AI applications for SMEs. Nonetheless, there exist huge challenges towards adoption by SMEs, including limited resources, lack of technical know-how, and data security issues (Vanessa et al., 2024; Schönberger, 2023). Solutions such as government incentives, public-private partnerships, and targeted training programs are suggested to confront these issues (Vanessa et al., 2024). [20302-3.png]When we talk about AI, we expect future trends to make it more accessible and integrated with other technologies, creating significant opportunities for SMEs (Yusuf et al., 2024). In its October 2023 edition, the International Journal of Lean Six Sigma published the first 100% AI-based paper on the scalability of AI implementation frameworks for SMEs, which highlights the growing importance of AI adoption among SMEs and emphasizes the need for adoption frameworks that can be easily scaled according to their unique needs (Vanessa et al., 2024).

CONCLUSION

At the heart of innovation, transformation, AI is empowering SMEs to streamline processes, derive data led meaningful insights and create hyper-personalized user experience. Integrating AI into critical business functions like Automation, Marketing, Supply Chain Management, and Financial Operations will enable SMEs to scale and gain a competitive edge. AI also can be key to driving sustainable business practices by helping organizations optimize their resource consumption and reduce waste, while supporting corporate social responsibility (CSR) efforts as well. Nonetheless, while its widely beneficial, the adoption of AI in SMEs is hindered by high implementation costs, a dearth of skills, and data security challenges. For SMEs to harness the full potential of AI, they will need to adopt strategic approaches, such as investing in upskilling their workforce, forming partnerships, and launching robust cybersecurity measures.

As we tee-up towards the future, new and emerging AI trends such as generative AI, predictive analytics, and AI-driven decision-making will continue to transform the SME operations and help sustain long-term resilience and sustainability. As SMEs adopt AI responsibly and move to proactively tackle issues, it opens up new paths to innovation, efficiency, and sustainable growth in an ever-growing digital economy.

REFERENCES

Abdallah, M., Abu Talib, M., Feroz, S., Nasir, Q., Abdalla, H., & Mahfood, B. (2020). Artificial intelligence applications in solid waste management: A systematic research review. *Waste Management (New York, N.Y.)*, *109*, 231–246. DOI: 10.1016/j.wasman.2020.04.057 PMID: 32428727

Abitha, S. V. S. (2021, May 10). *ChatBots and Virtual Assistants*. https://doi.org/DOI: 10.22541/au.162066507.77468411/v1

Abousaber, I., & Abdalla, H. (2023). Review of Using Technologies of Artificial Intelligence in Companies. *Nternational Journal of Communication Networks and Information Security*, *15*(1), 217–228. DOI: 10.17762/ijcnis.v15i1.5743

Ahmed, K., Tazi, N. E., & Hossny, A. H. (2015, October 1). *Sentiment Analysis over Social Networks: An Overview*. IEEE Xplore. https://doi.org/DOI: 10.1109/SMC.2015.380

Bayraktar, M., & Algan, N. (2019, June). The Importance of SMEs on World Economies. *International Conference on Eurasian Economies 2019*. https://doi.org/DOI: 10.36880/c11.02265

Besiri, D. (2024). AI-Driven Predictive Analytics: Transforming Decision-Making in Business. *Human-Computer Interaction*, *8*(1), 163–172. DOI: 10.62802/8ny1ww06

Bharadwaj, V. (2024). INTEGRATING ARTIFICIAL INTELLIGENCE IN HUMAN RESOURCE MANAGEMENT: A COMPREHENSIVE OVERVIEW. *Journal of Management*, *11*(3), 71–78. DOI: 10.34218/jom_11_03_006

Bhattacharya, P. (2018). *Artificial Intelligence in the Boardroom: Enabling "Machines" to "Learn" to Make Strategic Business Decisions. 2018 Fifth HCT Information Technology Trends*. ITT., DOI: 10.1109/ctit.2018.8649550

Bruno, Z. (2024). The Impact of Artificial Intelligence on Business Operations. *Global Journal of Management and Business Research*, *24*(D1), 1–8. DOI: 10.34257/gjmbrdvol24is1pg1

Carayannis, E. G., Dumitrescu, R., & Falkowski, T. (2024). EMPOWERING SMES- "HARNESSING THE POTENTIAL OF GEN AI FOR RESILIENCE AND COMPETITIVENESS.". *IEEE Transactions on Engineering Management*, •••, 1–22. DOI: 10.1109/tem.2024.3456820

Dalsaniya, A., & Patel, K. (2022). Enhancing process automation with AI: The role of intelligent automation in business efficiency. *International Journal of Science and Research Archive*, *5*(2), 322–337. DOI: 10.30574/ijsra.2022.5.2.0083

Das, S., Kundu, A., & Bhattacharya, A. (2020). Technology Adaptation and Survival of SMEs: A Longitudinal Study of Developing Countries. *Technology Innovation Management Review*, *10*(6), 64–72. DOI: 10.22215/timreview/1369

Dehankar, P., Amudha, A., Jayasudha, S., Pallavi, R., Doda, D. K., & Mandela, N. (2023). Predictive Analytics Powered by Artificial Intelligence. *IEEE*, 1–595. https://doi.org/DOI: 10.1109/incoft60753.2023.10425117

Fang, B., Yu, J., Chen, Z., Osman, A. I., Farghali, M., Ihara, I., Hamza, E. H., Rooney, D. W., & Yap, P.-S. (2023). Artificial intelligence for waste management in smart cities: A review. *Environmental Chemistry Letters*, *21*(21). Advance online publication. DOI: 10.1007/s10311-023-01604-3 PMID: 37362015

Gaurav, Khan, H., Pandey, S., Kumar, B. V., Akram, S. V., & Pal, P. (2024, March 13). Artificial Intelligence (AI) in the Field of Corporate Social Responsibility. *IEEE*. https://doi.org/DOI: 10.1109/icsadl61749.2024.00033

Gomez, A. L., & Lopez, S. J. (2024). Innovation and Transformation: Keys to the Success of SMEs in the Digital Age. *Deleted Journal*, *2*(3). Advance online publication. DOI: 10.59652/jeime.v2i3.253

Govori, A., & Sejdija, Q. (2023). Future prospects and challenges of integrating artificial intelligence within the business practices of small and medium enterprises. *Journal of Governance and Regulation*, *12*(2), 176–183. DOI: 10.22495/jgrv12i2art16

Gungunawat, A., Khandelwal, N., & Gupta, N. (2024). AI-Powered Personalization in Digital Marketing: Transforming Consumer Engagement and Strategy. *RESEARCH REVIEW International Journal of Multidisciplinary*, *9*(11), 183–191. DOI: 10.31305/rrijm.2024.v09.n11.026

Hernandez, A. A., Caballero, A. R., Albina, E. M., Balmes, I. L., & Niguidula, J. D. (2023, May 1). *Artificial Intelligence for Sustainability: Evidence from select Small and Medium Enterprises in the Philippines*. IEEE Xplore. https://doi.org/DOI: 10.1109/ICBIR57571.2023.10147579

Islam, J. (2024). Leveraging Ai for Effective Human Resource Management: A Comprehensive Overview. *Social Science Research Network*. https://doi.org/DOI: 10.2139/ssrn.4833377

Iyelolu, V., Ebele, E., Idemudia, N. C., & Ignatius, T. (2024). Driving SME innovation with AI solutions: overcoming adoption barriers and future growth opportunities. *International Journal of Science and Technology Research Archive, 7*(1), 036–054. https://doi.org/DOI: 10.53771/ijstra.2024.7.1.0055

Kadirov, A., Shakirova, Y., Ismoilova, G., & Makhmudova, N. (2024). AI in Human Resource Management: Reimagining Talent Acquisition, Development, and Retention. *IEEE*, 1–8. https://doi.org/DOI: 10.1109/ickecs61492.2024.10617231

Kumar, V., Rajan, B., Venkatesan, R., & Lecinski, J. (2019). Understanding the Role of Artificial Intelligence in Personalized Engagement Marketing. *California Management Review*, *61*(4), 135–155. DOI: 10.1177/0008125619859317

Lawton, R., Boswell, S., & Keeley Crockett SMIEE. (2023, December 5). The GM AI Foundry: A Model for Upskilling SME's in Responsible AI. *IEEE*. https://doi.org/DOI: 10.1109/ssci52147.2023.10371988

Li, D. (2024). Convergence and Innovation of Artificial Intelligence in Corporate Strategic Planning: Opportunities, Challenges and Future Research Directions. *Transactions on Economics. Business and Management Research*, *10*, 120–125. DOI: 10.62051/47zdfx74

Liu, B. (2012). Sentiment Analysis and Opinion Mining. *Synthesis Lectures on Human Language Technologies*, *5*(1), 1–167. DOI: 10.2200/s00416ed1v01y201204hlt016

Melinda, V., Williams, T., Anderson, J., Davies, J. G., & Davis, C. (2024). Enhancing Waste-to-Energy Conversion Efficiency and Sustainability Through Advanced Artificial Intelligence Integration. [ITEE]. *International Transactions on Education Technology*, *2*(2), 183–192. DOI: 10.33050/itee.v2i2.597

Ming, L. W., Anderson, J., Hidayat, F., Yulian, F. D., & Septiani, N. (2024). AI as a Driver of Efficiency in Waste Management and Resource Recovery. [ITALIC]. *International Transactions on Artificial Intelligence*, *2*(2), 128–134. DOI: 10.33050/italic.v2i2.547

Nishchint Tiku, Jindal, S. K., & Lokeshwari, M. (2024). Artificial Intelligence in Corporate Social Responsibility and Environment Sustainability. *IEEE*, 1–6. https://doi.org/DOI: 10.1109/csitss64042.2024.10816872

Ocran, G., Omokhafe, S., Owusu, N. P., Enis, N., & Obeng, S., & None Adedamola Hadassah Paul-Adeleye. (2024). AI-driven business analytics for SMES: Unlocking value through predictive and prescriptive analytic. *International Journal of Science and Research Archive*, *13*(1), 3009–3022. DOI: 10.30574/ijsra.2024.13.1.2001

Okeke, N. I., Alabi, O. A., Igwe, A. N., Ofodile, O. C., & Ewim, C. P. M. (2024). AI-driven personalization framework for SMES: Revolutionizing customer engagement and retention. *World Journal of Advanced Research and Reviews, 24*(1), 2019–2035. DOI: 10.30574/wjarr.2024.24.1.3208

Oldemeyer, L., Jede, A., & Teuteberg, F. (2024). *Investigation of artificial intelligence in SMEs: a systematic review of the state of the art and the main implementation challenges*. Management Review Quarterly., DOI: 10.1007/s11301-024-00405-4

Podile, V., Reddy, K. P., Sai, N., Babu, M. S., & Phani, A. K. (2024). Artificial Intelligence and Corporate Social Responsibility: Synergies, Challenges, and Future Directions. *International Journal of Advanced Multidisciplinary Research and Studies, 4*(6), 95–99. DOI: 10.62225/2583049x.2024.4.6.3399

Sadiku, M. N. O., Fagbohungbe, OmobayodeI., & Musa, S. M. (2020). Artificial Intelligence in Business. *International Journal of Engineering Research and Advanced Technology, 06*(07), 62–70. DOI: 10.31695/ijerat.2020.3625

Saraswat, P., Bhardwaj, B., Naresh, P., Ashok, A., Kumar, R., & Kumar, M. (2021). Voice Assistants and Chatbots Hands on Essentials of UI and Feature Design Development and Testing. *Chapman and Hall/CRC EBooks*, 217–240. https://doi.org/DOI: 10.1201/9781003121466-11

Schwaeke, J., Peters, A., Kanbach, D. K., Kraus, S., & Jones, P. (2024). The new normal: The status quo of AI adoption in SMEs. *Journal of Small Business Management*, •••, 1–35.

Shouran, Z., & Ali, D. A. (2024). The Implementation of Artificial Intelligence in Human Resources Management. *Journal of International Conference Proceedings, 7*(1), 244–258. DOI: 10.32535/jicp.v7i1.2993

Singh, R., & Kaur, R. (2015). Sentiment Analysis on Social Media and Online Review. *International Journal of Computer Applications, 121*(20), 44–48. DOI: 10.5120/21660-5072

Smiee, K. C., Brophy, S., Attwood, S., Monks, P. L., & Webb, D. J. (2022, July 18). From Ethical Artificial Intelligence Principles to Practice: A Case Study of University-Industry Collaboration. *2022 International Joint Conference on Neural Networks (IJCNN)*. https://doi.org/DOI: 10.1109/ijcnn55064.2022.9892760

Spangler, W. E. (1991). The role of artificial intelligence in understanding the strategic decision-making process. *IEEE Transactions on Knowledge and Data Engineering, 3*(2), 149–159. DOI: 10.1109/69.87995

Walia, P. (2024). Role and Application of Artificial Intelligence in Business. *Shodh Sari*, *03*(02), 244–252. DOI: 10.59231/sari7700

Wang, W. (2024). Artificial Intelligence in Strategic Business Decisions: Enhancing Market Competitiveness. *Advances in Economics Management and Political Sciences*, *117*(1), 87–93. DOI: 10.54254/2754-1169/117/20241987

Yadav, J. (2023). *Sentiment Analysis on Social Media*. Qeios., DOI: 10.32388/yf9x04

Chapter 9
An Analysis of Growth, Economic Development, and Sustainability in Small and Medium Enterprises With AI

Leena Jenefa
https://orcid.org/0000-0002-1324-7083
Hindustan Institute of Technology and Science, Chennai, India

M. Jayakumar
https://orcid.org/0009-0006-4569-495X
Vel Tech Rangarajan Dr. Sagunthala R&D Institute of Science and Technology, Avadi, India

S. Ashokkumar
Hindustan Institute of Technology and Science, Chennai, India

ABSTRACT

Artificial intelligence is a growing technology in small and medium-sized businesses. Small and medium-sized enterprises (SMEs) have recently expressed an increased interest in employing artificial intelligence to boost countries performance. This study confirms that insufficient physical and technological infrastructure, awareness of AI, customer privacy and security, management support, and a lack of AI adoption strategy are all significant issues and challenges impeding the progress of AI applications in business for sustainability. In India, the MSME sector is seen as a major driving factor in increasing economic productivity and combating poverty,

DOI: 10.4018/979-8-3693-9611-7.ch009

income inequality, and high unemployment rates. This study has ramifications for SMEs, policymakers, and future initiatives to enhance artificial intelligence for sustainability.

INTRODUCTION

Small and medium-sized enterprises view the dynamics of the economic climate and strong competition. Many SMEs are in a similar scenario. A dynamic and competitive environment fosters the growth of SMEs. This circumstance necessitates that stakeholders take sustainable company growth and its drivers seriously.

Small and medium-sized enterprises (SMEs) and their stakeholders must learn and adapt swiftly to avoid being destroyed by financial rivalry. In other words, SMEs should be aware of the enablers that drive company growth. Some scholars attempt to identify the facilitators that encourage SME growth (Storey, 2016). However, the enablers evaluated are frequently fragmented, focusing solely on internal or external enablers. Separating internal and external elements fails to offer a clear picture of SME growth. Individual facilitator connections affect SME growth as a whole (Wang, 2016). These enablers influence SME development.

Recognizing the interconnections of enabling variables can assist decision-makers in making the necessary efforts for growth. This paper presents an interaction model based on interpretative structural (ISM) to analyze SME growth through various facilitators.

Small and medium enterprises are the basis upon which large firms are developed; yet, small and medium have been classified otherwise by various persons and organizations, thus an operation that is regarded small and medium in one region is perceived otherwise in another (Lim, 2010).

The importance of Small and Medium-Sized Enterprises (SMEs) in the nationwide reduced should not be overlooked. These firms have been given increased governmental consideration in recent years, notably in third-world nations, partially because of rising unhappiness with the results of growth policies focused on large-scale wealth exhaustive and heavy import reliant industrial units (Diabate et al., 2019; Levy, 1993).

The great mainstream of established and emerging nations rely on the energy, ingenuity, and risk-taking of small and medium-sized businesses to initiate and continue the process of economic growth. Small and medium-sized firms have a dynamic part in overall monetary growth..

Small and medium-sized firms promote enduring rivalry and entrepreneurship, which have external advantages for the economy as a whole in terms of efficiency and productivity growth. At this level, the focus is on government assistance and engagement in leveraging the country's social gains from increased completion and entrepreneurship. SMEs are typically more creative than large enterprises; nonetheless, financial market and other institutional changes, direct government financial support to SMEs can increase monetary growth and development (Shaikh et al., 2022).

Sustainable development is derived from sustainability. Many people use the phrases sustainable development and sustainability interchangeably, yet they are basically different. In the first viewpoint, manageable expansion is defined as the journey or process by which sustainability is achieved, but in the second perspective, sustainability refers to the method by which sustainable development is achieved (Sobaih & Elshaer, 2022).

Sustainability is viewed as a broad phrase that encompasses a variety of complex challenges, concepts, behaviors, and cognitive processes . The idea of sustainability remains conceptual and abstract, leading to multiple studies in which various definitions have been proposed based on how it is approached and analyzed (Brown, 1990).

The firm's development and performance would enable it to achieve long-term survival and provide constant job chances. It would also become necessary for enterprises to develop their human money by keeping and retraining staff, as well as providing employee happiness. In sustainability research, these are referred to as social objectives. Employee loyalty and skill development are crucial success influences for businesses.

Sustainable SME growth is critical to ensuring long-term national economic prosperity (Demirgüç-Kunt & Maksimovic, 2002). SMEs provide a substantial economic contribution, highlighting the need of not only creating new SMEs and ensuring the being of all SMEs in the reduced, but also ensuring that they endure to expand (Ismail, 2022). SMEs have the challenge of being sustainable, becoming sustainable, and, more significantly, being sustainable (Demirgüç-Kunt & Maksimovic, 2002). Sustainable growth of SMEs leads to commercial doings that benefit the cheap.

Enterprise development is an important aspect of corporate economic development through the entrepreneurial process (Ismail, 2022). Entrepreneurship has been a driving factor for economic restructuring, delegation, and the transition to a market economy (Guerrero et al., 2021). Furthermore, Small and Medium Enterprises (SMEs) are seen as important contributors to the country's economic development (Varga & Szántó, 2021). The mainstream of SMEs are small and survival firms; nevertheless, very few small businesses may grow into medium-sized enterprises, and even fewer have the ability to grow into large-sized enterprises, depending on the entrepreneurs and founders of these enterprises.

Artificial intelligence is mostly used by small and medium-sized organizations to obtain a competitive advantage. The goal of an artificial intelligence application for SMEs is to raise corporate performance and sales while being low-cost, saving time, and improving customer management (Jenefa et al., 2024). Artificial intelligence (AI) is revolutionizing business, the economy, and society as a whole by altering the interactions and connections between stakeholders and individuals. The origins of artificial intelligence may be traced back to mythology from ancient Chinese, Greek, and other cultures, when automatons were thought to have actual minds and could think and feel emotions. This is where the notion of artificial intelligence initially originated (Muthuraman et al., 2020; Pedersen, 1998).

Researchers and practitioners of AI will assistance from a thorough considerate of what has been discovered and used in a wide range of business domains (from manufacturing to services) and disciplinary subjects, including marketing, tourism, management, sociology, psychology, and so on. This is because research on commercial AI applications often requires a multidisciplinary viewpoint (Gold, 2016).

With the rapid advancement of technology, one component that organizations should focus on is artificial intelligence. AI has become an essential tool in today's market, providing services such as web media monitoring and predicting machinery problems, among others (Strang, 2007). While the innovation processes of SMEs might be difficult to generalize at times, many characteristics are frequently mentioned in this context. In compared to larger businesses, SMEs have a distinct set of challenges that might lead to poor innovation performance. SMEs typically suffer market disappointments that complicate the competitive landscape, such as a lack of access to financing, an inability to engage in innovation, or compliance with environmental standards (Kadyan et al., 2024).

SMEs significant workforce restrictions due to a lack of or inadequately qualified workers. They deficiency alternate items or "cash cows" to compensate for the low ROI associated with innovation. SMEs generally struggle to overcome structural barriers such as a lack of management and technical skills, labor market rigidities, and insufficient knowledge about future expansion opportunities (Behera & Nain, 2019). Businesses mostly employ a few AI apps and technologies to get a competitive edge or integrate their systems.

LITERATURE REVIEW

The influence of small businesses on economic growth indicated beneficial effects on private enterprise and monetary development. The study's findings revealed that the proportion of small firms has a helpful impact on company production and is accountable for better performance. The importance of independent firms for economic growth. The findings indicated that changes in the business sector promote private and small businesses while also serving as a vehicle for economic growth (Jain et al., 2015).

Entrepreneurs often establish and run small and medium-sized enterprises. The transformation of entrepreneurship into a subject of study and the breadth of human activity has recently piqued the interest of policymakers, academics, and academicians worldwide. SMEs are important in many nations because they provide individuals with the possibility to rise out of poverty (Jayakumar et al., 2024). Citizens with little financial resources, little or no education, and little or no experience can generate some revenue through entrepreneurship. SME firms are also important since they assist to reduce inequality by facilitating wealth redistribution in the economy. Entrepreneurship may also help emerging and poor countries' economies grow quickly (Lingxian et al., 2019).

SMEs with limited resources can't attain optimum growth unless they collaborate with society. According to a prior study, good company performance or development may be accomplished when the enterprise and society align. This core principle emphasizes the need of collaboration for businesses, particularly SMEs.

In addition to continuing to improve their performance through increased skills and cooperation, SMEs must seek long-term growth. Sustainable growth may be accomplished by implementing SME growth accelerators properly and comprehensively (Petrunenko et al., 2021). The interplay of enablers can improve the capabilities and collaboration of SMEs. As a result, detailed examination of enablers and their relationships is critical for SMEs' long-term success.

SMEs who fail to invest properly in innovation have a larger risk of being overtaken by technologically superior rivals. During economic downturns, enterprises, particularly small manufacturing firms, reduce their investment in innovation (Jayakumar et al., 2024). This zero investment leads to a loss of competitiveness. Nonetheless, throughout both growth and recession stages, innovation is associated with improved performance. Furthermore, a lack of rivalry in the local market may have a detrimental influence on a firm's innovation (Hossain et al., 2018). SMEs that lack local rivals, paradoxically, lose competitiveness that would be required to expand their operation in overseas markets versus competitors.

Research on SMEs between developed and developing countries has mostly concentrated on organizational factors, using single-country samples from both developed and developing countries. This technique may fail to adequately portray the general situation of both sorts of nations. Importantly, this research did not investigate the interrelationships between the factors impacting SME growth (Amorós et al., 2011).

The importance of SMEs to the economy drives many nations to aggressively support SMEs in order to boost the private sector in both developed and developing countries. As a result, there is a need for research that may shed light on the reasons driving SMEs' growth, notably the interdependence of variables in both developed and developing nations (Lessem, 1982). The interdependence of elements seeks to aid in developing strategies for the development of SMEs. Researchers in developing and developed nations continue to be interested in the expansion of small and medium-sized companies (SMEs) (Madrid-Guijarro et al., 2013; Mariotti & Piscitello, 2001).

The Make-in-India initiative was launched with great fanfare to instill fresh life in the manufacturing industry. The 'Make in India' project requires the active engagement of all stakeholders from throughout the nation.

MSMES ARE BRIDGING THE B2B COMMERCE GAP

Micro, Small, and Medium Enterprises (MSMEs) play an important part in the country's overall economic and social growth, contributing considerably to manufacturing production, exports, and employment while also serving as nurseries for entrepreneurship and innovation.

It is claimed that huge enterprises and business organizations are creating more jobs. These include small manufacturing units, fruit and vegetable sellers, repair businesses, truck and taxi operators, street vendors, food-service units, machine operators, merchants, small industries, craftsmen, and food processors, among others.

With over 30 million firms, it is the second greatest source of employment for more than 70 million people, accounting for about 45% of industrial output and approximately 40% of total exports. Any economy's development requires effective, efficient, adaptable, and inventive capabilities, as well as ambition and a visionary entrepreneurial spirit (Nishanth & Zakkariya, 2014). Micro, Small, and Medium firms in India have experienced phenomenal expansion, accounting for more than 90% of all firms and contributing to the production of the highest number of job possibilities in India after agriculture.

Credit flow and the availability of timely and cost-effective finance choices are required for MSMEs to grow and thrive. A thriving global economic climate has created several possibilities and difficulties for India's MSME sector. On the one hand, many chances have emerged for this industry to enter new national and international markets while also increasing efficiency (Jayakumar et al., 2024; Ministry of Micro, Small and Medium Enterprises, 2015). As a result, providing payments to them on schedule is critical.

MSMEs have the potential to adopt actions in their business practices to contribute to the Economic Growth

The Micro, Small, and Medium firms Development Act of 2006 distinguishes and divides small and medium firms depending on their size and investment. This category is based on the enterprise's business categories, which include manufacturing and service enterprises. Manufacturing enterprises include any commercial operations that are involved in the manufacturing or production of items listed in the first schedule of the Industries (Development and Regulation) Act, 1951. Similarly, service enterprises are businesses that carry out operations, such as providing or supplying services to another corporation or a private individual (Karthikeyan & Jothi Kumar, 2014).

With such a clear definition of micro-, small-, and medium-sized firms (MSMEs) in India, these businesses play a critical part in the growth of our economy. MSMEs have been recognized for being the driving force behind economic growth and creating equitable development opportunities for all. They are critical to any country's industrial development. MSMEs have a significant impact on the growth of India's social and economic sectors. They contribute significantly to the nation's exports, employment, and industrial production. This industry is critical to the country's ability to expand faster and more equitably.

MSMEs help to reduce economic disparities by providing citizens with multiple work opportunities and industrializing rural regions. This industry employs the greatest number of people, after agriculture (Ministry of MSME, 2006). The MSME sector grows at a much faster rate than large firms in terms of workforce concentration. The sector's primary benefit is its ability to create jobs at a low capital cost.

They are distributed throughout the country and generate a wide range of goods and services to suit the needs of regional, national, and international value chains, as well as local and global markets. The MSMEs complement the large industries that are engaged in the economy and contribute significantly to the nation's socio-economic growth.

Sustainable Growth Challenges faced by Small and Medium Enterprises

MSMEs face greater challenges than major enterprises due to their smaller size and lack of internet connectivity, hindering their ability to adapt to new societal trends.

Government policy and financial assistance are crucial for these sectors.

MSMEs contribute significantly to the national economy by producing, creating jobs, and exporting goods (Sonia & Rajeev, 2009).

It contributes to the nation's socio-economic growth by fostering a business climate and offering numerous job possibilities with lower capital costs. These industries assist large-scale corporations and promote industrialization.

The pandemic has led to a global economic slump.

Joint engagement between multinational teams, commercial sectors, and national governments is necessary to combat the epidemic while also maintaining economic activity to support global civilization (Prakash et al., 2021).

MSMEs have undergone changes to reduce inflation, achieve economies of scale, and prevent company failure. The adjustment was made to satisfy the needs of large enterprises with little investment in machinery.

Develop a start-up management strategy to help MSMEs. Building resilience involves learning from past experiences and constantly evaluating the circumstance. To prepare for disruptions, small businesses should create a network strategy that includes alternative suppliers, distributors, and administrative service providers (Berisha & Pula, 2015). MSMEs are major sources of innovation, introducing new goods and technologies to the market and contributing to the transition to a more resilient and sustainable economy. The inclusion of MSMEs promotes equitable wealth distribution and strengthens local communities, hence promoting social development.

The preparedness of SMEs for AI is dependent on their IT infrastructure and strategic integration with HR. Aligning AI with existing procedures, overcoming difficulties, and taking into account customer demands improves adoption success (Byder et al., 2019). AI can help SMEs increase profitability, access a larger consumer base, and enhance productivity. Overcoming difficulties and tackling AI specialist shortages are critical for SME transformation. Understanding and overcoming these obstacles allows SMEs to use AI's promise and survive in the digital economy (Chandraiah & Vani, 2014).

AI and Business

The fundamental goal of artificial intelligence is to achieve a competitive advantage in manufacturing, e-commerce, finance, human resources, marketing, and customer interactions, among other sectors. Artificial intelligence-enabled procedures improve organizational performance, save costs, increase sales, streamline customer management, improve data collection and processing, save time, and reduce mistakes. Communication with clients tends to increase attendance, especially in a customer-focused setting (Chatterjee & Kanbur, 2015). When AI meets the unique demands and innovative goals of SMEs, the possibility of enthusiastic adoption improves.

By adopting AI-driven efficiency improvements, SMEs may improve customer experiences, promote sustainable practices, and put themselves at the forefront of digital transformation. Financial restrictions and internal opposition to organizational complexity and legal issues are among the problems and impediments that SMEs encounter while adopting AI (Bagale et al., 2023). Managers must be serious in ensuring that organizational features are favorable in terms of compatibility and preparedness. The management should pay close attention to ensure that organizational contextualization is not overly complicated, which would prevent automation.

In terms of situational features, managers must be watchful in order to keep up with the dynamism of AI technology, as well as be aware of and integrate the techniques used by their rivals to achieve faster automation (Haseeb et al., 2019).

With management assistance, the workforce need sufficient AI technology training in order to solve any technical complexity, and employees embrace the easy adoption of automation and its use for smart maintenance. It is the responsibility of top management to provide staff with understanding about AI technology. Nonetheless, the organization's management must teach its personnel so that they understand predictive intelligent maintenance in order to achieve sustainability by avoiding costly unexpected downtimes.

AI and Chatbots

AI advancements have resulted in the rise of new technologies that provide distinct commercial prospects. This article investigates the characteristics that influence small and medium-sized organizations' (SMEs) use of AI-based chatbots (Rauch et al., 2019; Brock & von Wangenheim, 2019). SMEs are often more concerned with client retention since they have fewer resources and methods for reaching out to new consumers. Relational marketing is better suited to SMEs; connection and network marketing provides an essential framework for SMEs. This framework encourages SMEs to focus more on customer relationship management (CRM), and there has been a noticeable growth in the quantity and diversity of projects that SMEs have undertaken in technology and marketing, notably in participating in more efficient relationship management (Rönnberg & Areback, 2020).

Early chatbot applications for marketing were used successfully to assist clients with navigating websites and making online purchases (Chawla et al., 2020). Since then, chatbot technology has advanced quickly. Modern chatbots include a conversational interface that allows them to replicate human conversations in such a way that clients may not know they are speaking with a chatbot rather than a human support assistant (Brennan & Kirby, 2022). Chatbots may now operate as virtual buddies as well as virtual helpers, performing client interviews and adaptively exploiting consumer information to deliver tailored answers.

Improving Sales and Marketing Efforts using AI

Google AdWords, Facebook, and Bing are examples of popular AI-powered marketing solutions (Semiawan, 2010).

Every corporation aims to earn a specified profit or as much profit as feasible while sustaining or even increasing it over time. This aim can be achieved if the sale goes through as anticipated. Thus, it does not imply that the items or services offered will always create profits, thus the following criteria must be given full attention by the organization. Superior comprehension of consumers and, as a result, the capacity to satisfy them as well as recognize rival activities (Shinta, 2011). Organizations who manage to dominate the market and this arena are referred to be market-driven firms, and they successfully balance these two orientations to create superior marketing performance than organizations that go in other ways. Coordination of the company's operations in an attempt, for example, to exchange information about consumers and rivals with all duties in order to better handle the expanding rivalry on occasion (Jain et al., 2023).

Automated Customer Service

An automated chat platform enables SMEs to measure customer engagement, complaints, and experiences, reducing the amount of resources required for client interactions . This leads to more meaningful client engagements, enhancing the company's revenue and retention. The goal of AI in these commercial domains is to understand the demands of clients by evaluating their purchasing patterns in order to expand the range of services available (Antonioli et al., 2010). Furthermore, artificial intelligence can assist in organizing consumer inquiries in order to resolve their difficulties. This saves time for clients who need assistance with simple queries.

Improving Recruitment and HR Activities

HR analytics employs artificial intelligence to attract and distinguish employees based on their salary, working conditions, perks, and duties. The systems handle automated routine and administrative functions including reporting, payroll, and accounting. For example, an AI applicant monitoring solution may help SMEs cut hiring time and costs by filtering through several job applications from possible applicants and selecting the best one for the job (Aziz & Dowling, 2019).

Computing Power

Implementing AI into a business requires a specific level of computer power, which varies depending on the type of firm. Machine learning and learning are the building blocks of AI, and they require an ever-increasing number of cores and GPUs to function properly. Asteroid tracking, cosmic body tracing, and healthcare deployment are some of the fields in which deep learning frameworks may be used. They also require a supercomputer for its computational capability, however with the present availability of cloud computing and parallel processing systems, programmers can work on AI systems more effectively (Baabdullah et al., 2021).

AI Challenges

In recent years, remarkable advancements in the field of artificial intelligence (AI) have transformed the whole technological landscape and affected many facets of contemporary culture. AI technologies offer the potential to boost productivity, accuracy, and innovation in several commercial domains, including image identification, voice processing, and automated decision-making (Jenefa et al., 2025).

Before delving into how AI technologies are impacting the business sector, a definition of the term "artificial intelligence" is required. The term "artificial intelligence" refers to any type of computer software that performs functions similar to those done by humans, such as learning, planning, and problem-solving. Referring to particular applications as "artificial intelligence" is like to referring to a car as a "vehicle"; while technically correct, it fails to capture any of the topic's complexities.

SMEs confront specific hurdles that frequently impede their adoption of AI solutions, most notably restricted financial and human resources. Small and medium-sized enterprises (SMEs) often have limited budgets and access to financing, making it difficult for them to buy the pricey digital transformation technology. This creates a situation in which SMEs struggle to migrate to the usage of AI-based solutions, possibly barring them from the advantages of new technologies. This circumstance has resulted in a rising disparity between large and small businesses, stressing the necessity for greater research into the usage of AI in SMEs.

Digital technologies play an important role in promoting economic growth by streamlining internal corporate operations and driving the creation of new goods and services. They also enable corporations to enter unknown markets and geographies.

Dealing with sensitive data in the age of AI, and the necessity to establish adequate security procedures to maintain data confidentiality and integrity. The financial burden of deploying AI demonstrates that investment costs can sometimes be a significant barrier to more AI integration, particularly for smaller organizations with limited resources.

The significance of training and skill development in strengthening AI skills and ensuring that the essential information is accessible to successfully utilize the potential of AI. Similarly, incorporating artificial intelligence into current systems. This difficulty emphasizes the necessity for a smooth link between AI technology and conventional corporate systems.

CONCLUSION

The company's marketing and sales policies aim to optimize product sales by implementing a variety of marketing mix elements. To generate a profit, a product's selling price must be set higher than its manufacturing price and associated costs. Profits gained on a consistent basis will expand the business scale and allow it to continue investing in its development, as is now being done. Products are often marketed both domestically and internationally; at the moment, industry competition is fierce. Strategies for managing market operations that are focused at expanding sales or securing hegemony of the market segment, dealing with rival tactics, or avoiding the entry of new competitors.

To achieve sustainable development, both SMEs and major organizations adopt long-term growth strategies with the goal of increasing their technical innovation capacity. A company's survival depends on its business success, which is critical for economic progress. Nonetheless, a firm's long-term success is the result of a combination of corporate strategy, organization, and processes that all work together. Though SMEs aim to boost their sustainability and competitiveness by enhancing their technology.

Experience and size are positive indicators of SMEs' growth. At the same time, corporations growing operations in other nations and multinational enterprises tend to achieve higher growth rates than those developing their company just in the domestic market. Furthermore, alliances and social networks can help small businesses access the resources they need, such as knowledge on how to conduct business in foreign markets, financial resources, or creative techniques. Innovation enables businesses to increase their production and performance.

Businesses, regardless of size, have seen a number of cyber attacks that have had an impact on their operations and image. This is why large, medium, and small businesses use AI technologies to protect their data and prevent unauthorized external incursions into their systems. A company may use AI and machine learning to detect any unusual or undesired actions as well as identify system vulnerabilities. Because of poor security procedures, SMEs are more exposed to cybersecurity assaults than large organizations.

Artificial intelligence technologies are getting increasingly popular and well acknowledged. That is why SMEs now have access to technology that was previously reserved only for large businesses. Nonetheless, several problems should be considered. While AI solutions remain pricey, this argument will fade with time and further advancement of these technologies. To be effective, AI-based solutions require well-prepared data from credible sources. AI-based solutions also contribute to the elimination of job positions by automating tasks that humans formerly performed.

REFERENCES

Amorós, J. E., Cristi, O., & Minniti, M. (2011). Entrepreneurial volatility: A cross-country study. *Annual Proceedings of the Wealth and Well-Being of Nations, 3*, 159–176.

Antonioli, D., Mazzanti, M., & Pini, P. (2010). Productivity, innovation strategies and industrial relations in SMEs: Empirical evidence for a local production system in northern Italy. *International Review of Applied Economics, 24*(4), 453–482. DOI: 10.1080/02692170903426194

Aziz, S., & Dowling, M. (2019). Machine learning and AI for risk management. In Gomber, P., & Dowling, M. (Eds.), *Disrupting finance: FinTech and strategy in the 21st century* (pp. 75–90). Palgrave Macmillan., DOI: 10.1007/978-3-030-02330-0_5

Baabdullah, A. M., Alalwan, A. A., Slade, E. L., Raman, R., & Khatatneh, K. F. (2021). SMEs and artificial intelligence (AI): Antecedents and consequences of AI-based B2B practices. *Industrial Marketing Management, 98*, 206–222. DOI: 10.1016/j.indmarman.2021.08.001

Bagale, G. S., Vandadi, V. R., Singh, D., Sharma, D. K., Garlapati, D. V. K., Bommisetti, R. K., Gupta, R. K., Setsiawan, R., Subramaniyaswamy, V., & Sengan, S. (2023). Retracted article: Small and medium-sized enterprises' contribution in digital technology. *Annals of Operations Research, 326*(Suppl. 1), 3–4. DOI: 10.1007/s10479-023-05570-6

Behera, G., & Nain, N. (2019). A comparative study of Big Mart sales prediction. *International Journal of Research in Engineering. IT and Social Sciences, 9*(5), 75–81.

Berisha, G., & Pula, J. S. (2015). Defining small and medium enterprises: A critical review. *Academic Journal of Business, Administration. Law and Social Sciences, 1*(1), 17–27.

Brennan, H. L., & Kirby, S. D. (2022). Barriers of artificial intelligence implementation in the diagnosis of obstructive sleep apnea. *Journal of Otolaryngology - Head & Neck Surgery, 51*, 16. DOI: 10.1186/s40463-022-00554-4 PMID: 35468865

Brock, J. K.-U., & von Wangenheim, F. (2019). Demystifying AI: What digital transformation leaders can teach you about realistic artificial intelligence. *California Management Review, 61*(4), 110–134. DOI: 10.1177/0008125619863432

Brown, D. (1990). Global perspective perceptions of SME growth constraints in Nigeria. *Journal of Small Business Management, 40*(1), 58–65.

Byder, J., Agudelo, D. A., & Arango, I. (2019). Gender matters most: The impact on short-term risk aversion following a financial crash. *Review of Financial Economics, 37*(1), 106–117. DOI: 10.1016/j.rfe.2018.07.002

Chandraiah, M., & Vani, R. (2014). The prospects and problems of MSMEs sector in India: An analytical study. *International Journal of Business and Management Invention, 3*(8), 27–40.

Chatterjee, U., & Kanbur, R. (2015). Non-compliance with India's Factories Act: Magnitude and patterns. *International Labour Review, 153*(3), 393–412. DOI: 10.1111/j.1564-913X.2015.00257.x

Chawla, M., Sahni, P., & Sadhwani, K. (2020). Can COVID-19 be the turning point for women entrepreneurs in India? *Economic and Political Weekly, 55*(18), 11–14.

Demirgüç-Kunt, A., & Maksimovic, V. (2002). Small firms and environmental management. *International Small Business Journal, 20*(3), 235–251. DOI: 10.1177/0266242602203001

Diabate, A., Allate, B., Wei, D., & Yu, L. (2019). Do firm and entrepreneur characteristics play a role in SMEs' sustainable growth in a middle-income economy like Côte d'Ivoire? *Sustainability, 11*(6), 1557. DOI: 10.3390/su11061557

Gold, N. A. (2016). Adding fintech and blockchain to your curriculum. *Business Education Innovation Journal, 8*(2), 6–12.

Guerrero, M., Liñán, F., & Cáceres-Carrasco, F. R. (2021). The influence of ecosystems on the entrepreneurship process: A comparison across developed and developing economies. *Small Business Economics, 57*(4), 1733–1759. DOI: 10.1007/s11187-020-00367-3

Haseeb, M., Hussain, H. I., Kot, S., & Androniceanu, A. (2019). Industry 4.0: A solution towards technology challenges of sustainable business performance. *Social Sciences, 8*(5), 154. DOI: 10.3390/socsci8050154

Hossain, N., Alam, R. M. K., & Gavlovskaya, G. (2018). Effective microcredit banking for growth and development of small business and improvement of poverty conditions in Bangladesh. *Journal of Applied Economic Sciences, 13*(2), 465–483.

Ismail, I. J. (2022). The role of technological absorption capacity, enviropreneurial orientation, and green marketing in enhancing business sustainability: Evidence from fast-moving consumer goods in Tanzania. *Technological Sustainability, 1*(2), 45–58.

Jain, A., Menon, M. N., & Chandra, S. (2015). Sales forecasting for retail chains. *International Journal of Scientific and Engineering Research, 6*(7), 435–439.

Jain, R., Jayakumar, M., Christy, V., Singh, G., & Inamdar, A. M. (2023). The effect of organizational culture on employee engagement and job satisfaction: A HR perspective. *Journal of Survey in Fisheries Sciences, 10*, 6212–6225.

Jayakumar, M., Jenefa, L., Badrinarayanan, M. K., Sarah, K. S., Kumar, A., & Kumar, R. M. (2024, December). Exploring organizational adoption of innovative technologies in consumer online purchase. In *2024 International Conference on Emerging Research in Computational Science (ICERCS)* (pp. 1–6). IEEE.

Jayakumar, M., Jenefa, L., Mishra, N., Kumar, A., & Sumitha, S. (2024, December). Artificial intelligence in digital marketing platform: Impact on consumer buying behaviour. In *2024 International Conference on Emerging Research in Computational Science (ICERCS)* (pp. 1–6). IEEE.

Jenefa, L., Kumar, A., Yiong, B. L. C., Jayakumar, M., & Sakthivel, M. (2024, November). The implementation of artificial intelligence tools in retail sector among consumers—A new evolution from traditional to modern. In *2024 International Conference on Electronic Systems and Intelligent Computing (ICESIC)* (pp. 220–223). IEEE.

Jenefa, L., Ramanathan, K., Mishra, N., Vishnu, V., Jayakumar, M., & Ashok, S. (2025). Future of the ready-made garments industry in real-time data: An application of AI. In Kumar, M., Mishra, S., & Chatterjee, A. (Eds.), *Real-time data decisions with AI and ChatGPT techniques* (pp. 127–148). IGI Global.

Kadyan, J. S., Jayakumar, M., Kumar, A., Jenefa, L., & Lakshmipathy, T. (2024, December). Enhancing customer delight—The implementation of artificial intelligence tools in sales and marketing in online platforms. In *2024 International Conference on Emerging Research in Computational Science (ICERCS)* (pp. 1–5). IEEE. https://doi.org/DOI: 10.1109/ICERCS56794.2024.1234568

Karthikeyan, R., & Jothi Kumar, C. (2014). Improved reputation system for wireless sensor networks (WSNs). [IJISER]. *International Journal of Innovations in Scientific and Engineering Research, 1*(3), 191–195.

Lessem, R. (1982). Business and social expression: Understanding business growth and decline. *Omega, 10*(1), 11–17. DOI: 10.1016/0305-0483(82)90031-6

Levy, B. (1993). Obstacles to developing indigenous small and medium enterprises: An empirical assessment. *The World Bank Economic Review, 7*(1), 65–83. DOI: 10.1093/wber/7.1.65

Lim, S. K. (2010). Dynamic resource-based view of entrepreneurial firm growth.

Lingxian, Y., Jiaqing, K., & Shihuai, W. (2019). Online retail sales prediction with integrated framework of K-means and neural network. In *Proceedings of the International Conference on Intelligent Computing* (pp. 115–118).

Madrid-Guijarro, A., García-Pérez-de-Lema, D., & Van Auken, H. (2013). An investigation of Spanish SME innovation during different economic conditions. *Journal of Small Business Management, 51*(4), 578–601. DOI: 10.1111/jsbm.12004

Mariotti, S., & Piscitello, L. (2001). Localized capabilities and the internationalization of manufacturing activities by SMEs. *Entrepreneurship and Regional Development, 13*(1), 65–80. DOI: 10.1080/08985620150211234

Ministry of Micro, Small and Medium Enterprises. (2015). *Annual report 2014–15.* Government of India. https://msme.gov.in/.../2015_02_MSME_Committee_report_Feb_2015

Ministry of MSME. (2006). *MSME Development Act.* Government of India, District Industry Centers (DIC). https://msme.gov.in *(verify and provide direct link if possible)*

Muthuraman, S., Haziazi, M. A., Veerasamy, R., & Yahyaei, N. A. (2020). Economic development through small & medium enterprises. In *3rd International Conference on Business.*

Nishanth, P., & Zakkariya, K. A. (2014, May). Barriers faced by micro, small and medium enterprises in raising finance. *Abhinav International Monthly Refereed Journal of Research in Management & Technology, 3*(5), 40–43. http://abhinavjournal.com/journal/index.php

Pedersen, P. O. (1998). *The role of small enterprises and small towns in the developing countries.* Center for Development Research.

Petrunenko, I., Khmarska, I., & Tkachenko, T. (2021). *The importance of small and medium enterprises in the economic development of Eastern Europe.* Economic Journal of Lesya Ukrainka Volyn National University.

Prakash, B., Kumar, I., & Verma, J. K. (2021). Barriers and potential solutions for MSMEs in developing economies: Evidence from India. *Problems and Perspectives in Management, 19*(4), 325–337. DOI: 10.21511/ppm.19(4).2021.27

Rauch, E., Dallasega, P., & Unterhofer, M. (2019). Requirements and barriers for introducing smart manufacturing in small and medium-sized enterprises. *IEEE Engineering Management Review, 47*(3), 87–94. DOI: 10.1109/EMR.2019.2927321

Rönnberg, H., & Areback, J. (2020). Initiating transformation towards AI in SMEs. In Mittal, S., Khan, M., Romero, D., & Wuest, T. (2020). A smart manufacturing adoption framework for SMEs. *International Journal of Production Research, 58*(5), 1555–1573. DOI: 10.1080/00207543.2019.1656830

Semiawan, C. R. (2010). *Metode penelitian kualitatif*. Grasindo.

Shaikh, A., Kumar, A., Jani, K., Mitra, S., García-Tadeo, D. A., & Devarajan, A. (2022). The role of machine learning and artificial intelligence for making a digital classroom and its sustainable impact on education during COVID-19. *Materials Today: Proceedings, 56*, 3211–3216. DOI: 10.1016/j.matpr.2021.11.310 PMID: 35464152

Shinta, A. (2011). *Manajemen pemasaran*. Universitas Brawijaya Press.

Sobaih, A. E. E., & Elshaer, I. A. (2022). University incubator support and entrepreneurial intention among tourism graduates: Mediating role of personal attitude. *Sustainability, 14*(1), 111. DOI: 10.3390/su14010111

Sonia, & Rajeev, K. (2009). Globalization and its impact on small scale industries in India. *PCMA Journal of Business, 1*(2), 135–146.

Storey, D. J. (2016). *Understanding the small business sector*. Routledge.

Strang, K. D. (2007). E-strategy first, e-technology free: Building an online university with open source software (case study). In *Innovation, Education, Technology, and You: Online Conference for Teaching & Learning*. University of Illinois.

Varga, J. W., & Szántó, R. (2021). Defining the economic role and benefits of micro, small and medium-sized enterprises in the 21st century with a systematic review of the literature. *Acta Polytechnica Hungarica, 18*(11), 209–228. DOI: 10.12700/APH.18.11.2021.11.12

Wang, Y. (2016). What are the biggest obstacles to growth of SMEs in developing countries? An empirical evidence from an enterprise survey. *Borsa Istanbul Review, 16*(3), 167–176. DOI: 10.1016/j.bir.2016.06.001

Chapter 10

Capitalizing on Artificial Intelligence for Achieving the Sustainable Development Goals: Opportunities, Challenges, and Ethical Considerations

Supriya Pathak
https://orcid.org/0009-0004-3602-3172
Oriental University, Indore, India

Rishikaysh Marotrao Kaakandikar
https://orcid.org/0000-0003-0349-6788
SaiBalaji International Institute of Management Sciences, India

Dheeraj Nim
https://orcid.org/0000-0003-1564-0097
Oriental University, Indore, India

ABSTRACT

This study examines the transformative potential of Artificial Intelligence (AI) in advancing the United Nations' Sustainable Development Goals (SDGs). AI technologies, such as machine learning, natural language processing, and big data analytics, offer innovative solutions to global challenges, including poverty, healthcare, education, and climate action. Through predictive modeling, resource optimization, and enhanced decision-making, AI can accelerate progress toward achieving the SDGs. Case studies highlight AI's contributions, from precision agriculture and disease di-

DOI: 10.4018/979-8-3693-9611-7.ch010

agnostics to renewable energy and sustainable urban infrastructure. However, ethical considerations, such as bias, privacy, and inclusivity, pose significant challenges to responsible AI deployment. By leveraging AI responsibly, this research underscores its potential to drive sustainable development and foster global prosperity, aligning technological advancements with the 2030 Agenda.

INTRODUCTION

This chapter explores the potential of Artificial Intelligence (AI) as a transformative tool for advancing the United Nations' Sustainable Development Goals (SDGs). The SDGs, adopted in 2015 as part of the 2030 Agenda for Sustainable Development, provide a universal call to action to end poverty, protect the planet, and ensure that all people enjoy peace and prosperity by 2030. As global challenges such as poverty, inequality, climate change, and health crises become increasingly complex, AI's ability to process vast amounts of data, predict trends, and optimize systems presents a significant opportunity to address these issues. However, alongside these opportunities, the implementation of AI in achieving sustainable development is accompanied by challenges related to ethics, bias, and inclusivity, which will be examined through a literature review and case studies.

AI technologies, including machine learning, natural language processing, and big data analytics, have the potential to revolutionize efforts toward achieving the SDGs. By offering tools for predictive modeling, decision-making, and resource optimization, AI can accelerate progress in healthcare, agriculture, education, environmental conservation, and more. However, these applications raise questions about the ethical use of AI, including concerns related to privacy, algorithmic bias, and the exacerbation of inequalities. Addressing these challenges requires robust governance frameworks and ethical guidelines to ensure that AI is implemented responsibly and inclusively (Vinuesa et al., 2020; Lu et al., 2018).

This chapter aims to contribute to this discourse by evaluating how AI can be responsibly leveraged to support the SDGs while safeguarding ethical principles. The following sections present a literature overview of AI's role in achieving the SDGs, explore specific case studies demonstrating AI applications, and discuss the ethical and regulatory frameworks necessary for responsible AI deployment.

1. THE ROLE OF AI IN ACHIEVING THE SDGS: A LITERATURE OVERVIEW

1.1 Core AI Technologies Supporting the SDGs

AI encompasses a wide range of technologies, including machine learning (ML), natural language processing (NLP), and big data analytics. Each of these technologies contributes uniquely to the advancement of the SDGs by enabling data-driven solutions to complex global challenges. Machine learning, for example, supports predictive modeling and optimization in areas such as climate forecasting and healthcare diagnostics. Natural language processing facilitates real-time translation and data extraction from unstructured text, aiding efforts in education and governance. Meanwhile, big data analytics enables large-scale data integration and visualization, critical for monitoring progress toward the SDGs (Sustainable Development Solutions Network, 2019).

1.2 Machine Learning and Its Applications

Machine learning, a subset of AI, is particularly effective in identifying patterns and making predictions from large datasets. For instance, ML algorithms have been used to predict crop yields, enabling more efficient resource allocation in agriculture. In healthcare, ML-powered tools assist in diagnosing diseases such as cancer and predicting patient outcomes (Esteva et al., 2019). These capabilities align with SDGs such as Zero Hunger (SDG 2) and Good Health and Well-being (SDG 3), illustrating the transformative potential of ML in sustainable development.

1.3 Natural Language Processing for Global Development

Natural language processing (NLP) facilitates communication across linguistic and cultural barriers, supporting SDG 4 (Quality Education) and SDG 16 (Peace, Justice, and Strong Institutions). Applications include AI-driven language translation tools, which have been instrumental in delivering educational content to marginalized communities. Additionally, NLP algorithms are used to analyze policy documents and public discourse, aiding governments in formulating data-driven policies (Holmes et al., 2019).

1.4 Big Data Analytics and SDG Monitoring

Big data analytics provides the foundation for tracking and measuring progress toward the SDGs. By aggregating data from diverse sources, such as satellite imagery, social media, and IoT devices, big data platforms enable real-time monitoring of key indicators like deforestation rates and urbanization trends. This capability is essential for addressing SDG 13 (Climate Action) and SDG 11 (Sustainable Cities and Communities) (The Global AI Index, 2021).

1.5 AI and SDGs Synergies

Research indicates that AI can directly or indirectly support up to 79% of the targets under the SDGs (Vinuesa et al., 2020). Key areas of impact include poverty alleviation, healthcare, education, and environmental conservation.

1.6 Poverty Reduction (SDG 1)

AI applications in poverty reduction include tools for analyzing economic data to identify areas in need of intervention. For example, machine learning models have been used to predict poverty levels based on satellite imagery and mobile phone usage data. These insights enable policymakers to allocate resources more effectively and design targeted poverty alleviation programs (Jean et al., 2016).

1.7 Healthcare (SDG 3)

AI's contributions to healthcare are among its most impactful applications for sustainable development. AI-powered diagnostic tools, such as IBM Watson Health, assist healthcare providers in diagnosing complex conditions, reducing the burden on overworked medical staff in low-resource settings. Additionally, AI-driven models have been employed to predict and manage disease outbreaks, including COVID-19, by analyzing epidemiological data (Rolnick et al., 2019).

1.8 Education (SDG 4)

In the education sector, AI supports personalized learning experiences and improves access to quality education. Platforms like Duolingo leverage NLP to teach languages, while AI-powered chatbots provide real-time tutoring to students. These innovations are particularly valuable in remote and underserved regions, where traditional educational resources may be scarce (Holmes et al., 2019).

1.9 Climate Action (SDG 13)

AI plays a crucial role in climate action by enabling precise weather forecasting and environmental monitoring. For example, AI models have been developed to predict the impact of natural disasters, allowing governments to prepare more effectively. Additionally, AI-powered systems optimize energy usage in smart grids, contributing to the transition to renewable energy sources (Kamilaris & Prenafeta-Boldú, 2018).

2. AI AND POVERTY ERADICATION (SDG 1) AND HUNGER (SDG 2) -CHALLENGES IN IMPLEMENTING AI FOR SUSTAINABLE DEVELOPMENT

AI's role in eradicating poverty (SDG 1) and addressing hunger (SDG 2) can be pivotal. AI-driven tools such as predictive analytics and satellite data can target vulnerable populations for resource allocation more efficiently, improving the effectiveness of poverty alleviation programs (Musa et al., 2021). In agriculture, precision farming using AI technologies can enhance crop yields, reduce resource use, and minimize waste (Kamilaris & Prenafeta-Boldú, 2018).

2.1 Ethical Governance and Transparency

Effective ethical governance is essential for deploying AI in ways that promote public trust, especially when used to address complex issues like poverty, healthcare, and education (Floridi et al., 2018; Jobin et al., 2019). Transparency and accountability in AI systems are critical to ensure users understand decision-making processes, yet many AI models function as "black boxes" with limited interpretability (Tsamados et al., 2022; Mittelstadt et al., 2016). Ethical frameworks, such as the European Commission's guidelines on trustworthy AI, emphasize transparency as a foundation for responsible AI deployment, especially in public services and policy (High-Level Expert Group on AI, 2019). Ensuring governance frameworks that prioritize transparency and accountability can help mitigate risks and build public trust in AI technologies (Binns, 2018).

To further enhance transparency, several initiatives have focused on developing tools and methodologies that elucidate AI decision-making processes. For instance, model interpretability techniques, such as Local Interpretable Model-Agnostic Explanations (LIME) and Shapley Additive Explanations (SHAP), provide insights into how specific AI predictions are made, allowing stakeholders to identify potential biases or errors (Ribeiro et al., 2016; Lundberg & Lee, 2017). Organizations like OpenAI and the Partnership on AI advocate for publishing model cards and documentation that outline the limitations and appropriate uses of AI systems (Mitchell et al., 2019). These efforts aim to ensure that AI development and deployment adhere to ethical standards and regulatory requirements.

Moreover, global institutions are collaborating to establish unified guidelines for AI governance. For example, the Organisation for Economic Co-operation and Development (OECD) has proposed AI principles that emphasize transparency, accountability, and human-centered values (OECD, 2019). Similarly, the United Nations has initiated discussions on AI ethics through its Educational, Scientific, and Cultural Organization (UNESCO), which highlights the need for ethical guidelines that align with human rights and sustainable development (UNESCO, 2021). These international efforts underscore the importance of ethical governance in fostering trust and equity in AI technologies.

2.2 Addressing Bias in AI

Bias in AI algorithms remains a significant concern, as these models can inherit biases from the data they are trained on, potentially exacerbating existing social inequalities (Mehrabi et al., 2021; Obermeyer et al., 2019). For example, in healthcare, algorithms trained predominantly on data from urban populations may underperform in rural settings, contributing to health disparities (Zou & Schiebinger, 2018; Sun et al., 2020). Bias detection and mitigation techniques, such as developing diverse training datasets and implementing fairness constraints, are essential steps for creating equitable AI systems (Gebru et al., 2018). Without addressing bias, AI's potential to advance sustainable development may inadvertently worsen inequality (Caliskan et al., 2017).

Recent research highlights various methods to identify and mitigate bias in AI systems. One approach involves algorithmic audits, where external experts review AI systems for potential biases and recommend corrective measures (Raji et al., 2020). Another strategy is adversarial de-biasing, which incorporates fairness objectives into the training process to reduce discriminatory outcomes (Zhang et al., 2018). For instance, IBM's AI Fairness 360 toolkit provides developers with tools to detect and mitigate bias across various stages of AI development (Bellamy et al., 2019).

In addition to technical solutions, fostering diversity within AI research and development teams can help address bias. A diverse team brings varied perspectives and experiences, reducing the likelihood of overlooking systemic biases. Furthermore, engaging stakeholders from underrepresented communities in the design and evaluation of AI systems ensures that these technologies reflect broader societal needs (West et al., 2019).

Governments and regulatory bodies also play a critical role in addressing AI bias. For example, the European Union's General Data Protection Regulation (GDPR) mandates transparency and accountability in automated decision-making processes, providing a legal framework to challenge biased outcomes (European Commission, 2016). Similarly, the Algorithmic Accountability Act proposed in the United States seeks to require organizations to assess the impact of their AI systems on fairness and equity (Gebru, 2020). These regulatory efforts demonstrate the importance of legal and policy interventions in promoting unbiased AI.

2.3 Privacy and Security Concerns

AI applications frequently involve handling vast amounts of personal data, raising critical privacy and security concerns, especially in healthcare and education (Vayena et al., 2018; Wachter & Mittelstadt, 2019). Adherence to data protection regulations, such as the General Data Protection Regulation (GDPR), is necessary to safeguard individuals' rights and ensure responsible AI use (European Commission, 2016; Floridi, 2018). The rapid evolution of AI outpaces regulatory frameworks, creating challenges in enforcing privacy protections effectively (Binns et al., 2018; Zarsky, 2016). Addressing these challenges requires a proactive approach to privacy, with AI systems designed to protect personal data through robust encryption and anonymization techniques (Kumar et al., 2021).

Emerging techniques in privacy-preserving AI, such as differential privacy and federated learning, offer promising solutions to balance data utility and privacy. Differential privacy adds controlled noise to datasets, ensuring that individual data points cannot be inferred from aggregated outputs (Dwork & Roth, 2014). Federated learning, on the other hand, allows AI models to be trained across decentralized devices without transferring raw data to a central server, significantly reducing privacy risks (McMahan et al., 2017).

Organizations are increasingly adopting these techniques to comply with privacy regulations and build public trust. For instance, Google's implementation of federated learning in its Gboard keyboard application allows users to benefit from personalized suggestions without compromising their privacy (Hard et al., 2018). Similarly, healthcare organizations are exploring federated learning for collaborative research, enabling hospitals to share insights without exposing sensitive patient data (Li et al., 2020).

However, privacy and security challenges extend beyond technical solutions. Governance frameworks must address issues such as data ownership, consent, and accountability. For example, the India Personal Data Protection Bill proposes stringent requirements for data processing, emphasizing user consent and transparency (Srikrishna, 2018). International cooperation is also essential to establish harmonized privacy standards that facilitate cross-border data sharing while protecting individual rights (Schneier, 2019).

2.4 Ensuring Inclusivity and Fair Access

AI's benefits should be accessible to all, yet significant barriers remain in access to AI resources and infrastructure, particularly in low-income regions (Lu et al., 2018; Hilbert, 2016). Developing countries often lack the necessary resources to implement AI, which can deepen existing inequalities in sectors like education, healthcare, and agriculture (Beck et al., 2018; Ndung'u & Signé, 2020). To ensure inclusive AI, international cooperation is needed to provide resources, training, and support for AI initiatives in underserved areas (Bello-Orgaz et al., 2022). By building inclusive AI frameworks, policymakers can promote fair access and ensure that AI advances benefit all communities globally (Cath et al., 2018).

One promising approach to fostering inclusivity is the development of open-source AI tools and platforms. Initiatives such as TensorFlow and PyTorch provide free access to powerful AI frameworks, enabling researchers and developers in resource-constrained settings to experiment with and deploy AI solutions (Abadi et al., 2016; Paszke et al., 2019). Additionally, organizations like AI Commons and AI for Good Foundation focus on democratizing AI by funding community-driven projects and providing access to datasets and computing resources (AI Commons, 2021).

Educational programs and capacity-building efforts are equally important for ensuring inclusivity. For example, Google's AI Impact Challenge provides grants and technical support to organizations leveraging AI for social good, with a focus on empowering underserved communities (Google AI, 2019). Similarly, the African Institute for Mathematical Sciences (AIMS) offers AI-focused training programs to develop local expertise and foster innovation in Africa (AIMS, 2020).

Finally, policymakers must address systemic barriers to inclusivity, such as the digital divide and gender disparities in AI participation. Investments in digital infrastructure, particularly in rural and remote areas, are critical for ensuring equitable access to AI technologies. Furthermore, initiatives to promote gender diversity in STEM fields, such as mentorship programs and scholarships, can help address the underrepresentation of women in AI research and development (West et al., 2019).

3. AI FOR GOOD HEALTH AND WELL-BEING (SDG 3)

The healthcare sector has undergone significant transformations due to the advent of artificial intelligence (AI). AI has introduced groundbreaking innovations in disease diagnostics, personalized treatment plans, telemedicine, and predictive healthcare. These advancements hold particular promise in addressing healthcare disparities, especially in low-resource settings, contributing directly to Sustainable Development Goal 3 (SDG 3): "Ensure healthy lives and promote well-being for all at all ages."

3.1 AI for Diagnostics and Predictive Healthcare

AI has demonstrated remarkable potential in diagnosing diseases and predicting health outcomes, often with accuracy levels comparable to or exceeding those of human experts. For instance, AI systems such as IBM Watson and DeepMind's AlphaFold have made strides in fields like radiology and oncology. Esteva et al. (2017) highlighted the ability of deep neural networks to achieve dermatologist-level accuracy in skin cancer classification, a breakthrough that could democratize access to expert diagnostic tools.

AI's predictive capabilities extend beyond diagnosis. Machine learning algorithms can analyze patient data to identify risk factors for chronic conditions, enabling early interventions. For example, AI models trained on electronic health records can predict the onset of diseases like diabetes or cardiovascular conditions, allowing healthcare providers to implement preventive measures (Lu et al., 2018). This capability is particularly crucial in low-resource settings where healthcare infrastructure is limited, as it reduces the burden on overworked medical staff by prioritizing high-risk patients for care.

3.2 Personalized Medicine and Treatment

The integration of AI into personalized medicine has revolutionized treatment approaches by tailoring interventions to individual patient profiles. AI algorithms can analyze genomic data, medical history, and lifestyle factors to recommend treatments with higher efficacy. Brynjolfsson and McAfee (2017) noted that this approach not only improves patient outcomes but also minimizes adverse reactions.

Pharmaceutical research has also benefited from AI-driven drug discovery. AI platforms like DeepMind's AlphaFold have accurately predicted protein structures, expediting the development of targeted therapies (Esteva et al., 2017). By identifying potential drug candidates faster and more cost-effectively than traditional methods, AI is paving the way for innovative treatments for rare and complex diseases.

3.3 Telemedicine and Remote Health Solutions

AI-powered telemedicine platforms are bridging the healthcare accessibility gap in underserved and remote areas. These platforms leverage natural language processing (NLP) and machine learning algorithms to provide virtual consultations, monitor patient health, and manage chronic conditions. Topol (2019) emphasized that telemedicine enables patients to access healthcare services without the need for physical visits, a critical advantage in rural areas with limited healthcare facilities.

Moreover, AI-driven remote monitoring devices allow continuous health tracking, empowering patients to manage their health proactively. For instance, wearable devices equipped with AI algorithms can detect irregularities in heart rate or blood pressure, alerting patients and healthcare providers to potential issues. Such innovations not only enhance patient autonomy but also alleviate the strain on healthcare systems by reducing unnecessary hospital visits.

3.4 Addressing Health Inequalities with AI

AI has the potential to reduce health disparities by optimizing resource allocation and improving healthcare delivery in low-resource settings. Algorithms can analyze population health data to identify underserved regions, enabling governments and organizations to target interventions effectively. Musa et al. (2021) demonstrated how AI has been used to target poverty alleviation programs in sub-Saharan Africa, a methodology that can be adapted to healthcare initiatives.

In addition, AI can facilitate the development of cost-effective diagnostic tools and treatment protocols. For example, portable AI-powered diagnostic devices, such as handheld ultrasound machines, are being deployed in rural clinics to provide accessible and affordable care. These innovations ensure that even the most marginalized populations can benefit from advancements in medical technology.

3.5 Challenges in AI Integration in Healthcare

Despite its transformative potential, the integration of AI into healthcare is not without challenges. Ethical considerations, such as bias in AI algorithms and patient data privacy, must be addressed to ensure equitable and trustworthy healthcare solutions. Dastin (2018) highlighted instances of algorithmic bias, such as Amazon's AI recruiting tool, which underscores the importance of developing fair and inclusive AI systems.

Regulatory hurdles also pose significant challenges. The lack of standardized guidelines for AI applications in healthcare can hinder their adoption and scalability. Furthermore, the reliability of AI systems depends on the quality and diversity of training data. Insufficient representation of minority populations in datasets can result in biased outcomes, exacerbating existing health disparities (Binns, 2018).

3.6 Future Directions and Opportunities

The future of AI in healthcare lies in its ability to integrate seamlessly with existing systems and adapt to evolving needs. Collaborative efforts between governments, private sector entities, and academic institutions are essential to harness AI's full potential. Initiatives like the World Health Organization's (WHO) AI for Health initiative aim to establish global standards for AI applications in healthcare, ensuring their ethical and equitable use.

Investments in AI research and infrastructure are also crucial. Developing nations must prioritize building digital health ecosystems to leverage AI effectively. Training healthcare professionals in AI technologies and fostering interdisciplinary collaboration will further enhance the sector's capacity to adopt and implement AI solutions.

3.7 Case Studies: AI in Action

3.7.1 AI in Oncology

DeepMind's AI system has achieved significant milestones in oncology by accurately segmenting cancerous tissues in radiology images. This capability not only improves diagnostic accuracy but also aids in treatment planning by providing detailed insights into tumor characteristics (Esteva et al., 2017).

3.7.2 AI for Infectious Disease Control

During the COVID-19 pandemic, AI played a pivotal role in modeling disease spread, identifying hotspots, and optimizing resource allocation. AI-powered chatbots were deployed to disseminate accurate information and assist in symptom assessment, reducing the burden on healthcare facilities (Lu et al., 2018).

3.7.3 AI in Rural Healthcare

Startups like Babylon Health have developed AI-powered telemedicine platforms that provide affordable healthcare solutions in rural areas. By combining AI diagnostics with remote consultations, these platforms are transforming healthcare delivery in regions with limited access to medical professionals (Topol, 2019).

AI's contributions to healthcare are reshaping the sector, offering innovative solutions to longstanding challenges. From early disease detection and personalized treatments to expanding healthcare access through telemedicine, AI aligns with SDG 3's goals of ensuring healthy lives and promoting well-being for all. However, realizing AI's full potential requires addressing ethical and regulatory challenges, fostering global collaboration, and investing in equitable and inclusive AI systems. By prioritizing these efforts, AI can become a powerful tool for achieving universal health coverage and reducing health inequality.

3.7.4 AI Applications for Achieving the SDGs – Elderly Care Robots

AI-driven solutions are pivotal in advancing the United Nations' Sustainable Development Goals (SDGs). Care robots, such as the Physical Assistant Robot System (PHAROS) 2.0, exemplify how AI can address SDG 3, ensuring healthy lives and promoting well-being for all ages. PHAROS 2.0, a socially assistive robot, supports elderly care by monitoring physical activities, providing tailored recommendations, and enhancing overall health through machine learning algorithms (Martinez-Martin et al., 2019).

Value Sensitive Design (VSD) integrates ethical considerations into technology development, addressing human values systematically. The Care-Centered Value Sensitive Design (CCVSD) approach tailors VSD to the healthcare domain, emphasizing attentiveness, responsibility, competence, and reciprocity in caregiving practices (van Wynsberghe, 2013). This framework incorporates higher-order norms like the European Commission's principles of trustworthy AI and the SDGs (Umbrello et al., 2021).

PHAROS 2.0 demonstrates the application of CCVSD in real-world healthcare scenarios. The robot assists elderly individuals with exercise routines through visual and verbal guidance. It can monitor and evaluate activities using recurrent and convolutional neural networks. It provides feedback to medical professionals and recommendations to users (Martinez-Martin et al., 2019).

This aligns with SDG 3.8 by improving access to quality healthcare and promoting active aging (United Nations, 2018).

Ethical Considerations and Design Challenges

Key ethical concerns addressed in the PHAROS 2.0 design include:

- **Privacy**: Ensuring secure data handling and consent mechanisms.
- **Fairness**: Providing equitable access to technology, avoiding biases in deployment.
- **Autonomy**: Supporting users' decision-making without undue dependency on the robot.
- **Explicability**: Enhancing transparency and user trust through intuitive interfaces (Floridi et al., 2020).

The iterative prototyping process employed for PHAROS 2.0 highlights the importance of stakeholder engagement and value-driven refinements. Future advancements aim to incorporate social interaction capabilities, further addressing emotional attachment and trust issues in caregiving contexts (Umbrello et al., 2021).

Care robots like PHAROS 2.0 exemplify how AI can operationalize the SDGs, demonstrating ethical and value-sensitive approaches to technology design. This case underlines the potential of AI to transform healthcare, fostering sustainable and inclusive solutions for global challenge

4. AI FOR QUALITY EDUCATION (SDG 4) AND GENDER EQUALITY (SDG 5)

Artificial Intelligence (AI) is transforming the educational landscape by enabling personalized learning experiences, improving accessibility, and supporting inclusivity. Similarly, in the pursuit of gender equality, AI is being leveraged to identify and mitigate biases, creating more equitable systems in workplaces and beyond. This section delves into the critical roles AI plays in advancing Sustainable Development Goals (SDGs) 4 and 5.

4.1 AI in Personalized Learning and Education Accessibility

AI-powered tools and platforms are reshaping education by addressing individual learning needs, facilitating access for marginalized groups, and creating inclusive educational environments. Adaptive learning systems analyze student data to provide customized feedback and learning paths, which have been shown to enhance academic performance and engagement (Holmes et al., 2019).

For example, AI platforms like Carnegie Learning and DreamBox provide tailored instructions based on a student's strengths and weaknesses. These systems use machine learning algorithms to analyze data on how students interact with educational content, identifying areas where additional support is required. This personalized approach helps bridge gaps in education, especially for students with learning disabilities or those from underserved communities (Luckin et al., 2016).

In terms of accessibility, AI technologies such as text-to-speech, speech-to-text, and real-time translation tools enable students with disabilities and non-native language speakers to engage more effectively in educational activities. Tools like Microsoft's Immersive Reader offer features that assist dyslexic learners, while real-time captioning aids students with hearing impairments. Furthermore, AI can identify patterns in learning difficulties and recommend interventions, ensuring no student is left behind.

AI is also proving invaluable in low-resource settings where traditional educational infrastructure may be lacking. Virtual classrooms powered by AI connect students in remote areas to quality education resources. Initiatives such as Google's Project Loon, which provides internet access to rural regions, coupled with AI-enabled education platforms, demonstrate how technology can address disparities in access to education globally (Holmes et al., 2019).

4.2 AI for Gender Bias Reduction

Achieving gender equality is a cornerstone of SDG 5, and AI is increasingly being used to address systemic biases in various sectors. One significant application is in reducing bias in recruitment and employment practices. Research shows that algorithms, when carefully designed, can identify patterns of discrimination in hiring processes and suggest corrective measures. For instance, Amazon's AI hiring tool was initially found to be biased against women, highlighting the challenges of ensuring fairness in AI systems (Dastin, 2018). This incident underscores the importance of algorithmic transparency and fairness in machine learning systems (Binns, 2018).

AI-driven tools like Textio and Pymetrics analyze job descriptions and hiring practices to identify and eliminate gender-biased language or selection criteria. These tools help organizations create a more equitable hiring process by encouraging the use of inclusive language and assessing candidates based on skills rather than demographic factors.

Furthermore, AI is being deployed to analyze pay disparities and recommend equitable compensation strategies. By examining large datasets, AI systems can identify patterns of gender-based wage gaps and propose adjustments, promoting fairness in compensation structures.

Another application lies in empowering women through education and skill development. AI platforms such as Coursera and Khan Academy offer courses tailored to women reentering the workforce or transitioning into technology-driven careers. These platforms not only provide education but also enable women to connect with mentors and resources, fostering a more inclusive professional environment (Brynjolfsson & McAfee, 2017).

4.3 Ethical Considerations and Challenges

While AI has the potential to drive significant progress in education and gender equality, its implementation comes with ethical challenges. One major concern is algorithmic bias, where AI systems unintentionally perpetuate existing inequalities. For instance, training data that reflects historical discrimination can lead AI models to reinforce those biases unless appropriately mitigated (Wachter et al., 2020).

Additionally, issues of privacy and data security are critical, especially in education. AI systems collect and process vast amounts of student data, raising concerns about how this data is used and protected. Transparent data governance and compliance with frameworks like the General Data Protection Regulation (GDPR) are essential to address these concerns.

Another challenge is the digital divide. While AI has the potential to enhance educational access, the lack of infrastructure and internet connectivity in certain regions limits its reach. To truly achieve SDG 4 and 5, investments in digital infrastructure and capacity building are imperative.

AI's role in promoting quality education and gender equality is transformative. By personalizing learning experiences, improving access for marginalized groups, and identifying and addressing systemic biases, AI has the potential to create more inclusive and equitable societies. However, its success depends on careful design, ethical considerations, and addressing challenges such as the digital divide and algorithmic bias. As AI technologies continue to evolve, their integration into strategies for achieving SDG 4 and 5 will be crucial for fostering sustainable and equitable development globally.

5. AI FOR CLEAN WATER, CLEAN ENERGY, AND INFRASTRUCTURE (SDG 6, 7, AND 9)

Artificial Intelligence (AI) is playing an increasingly significant role in enhancing the management and sustainability of water resources, energy systems, and infrastructure. AI technologies are being utilized to optimize resource use, improve operational efficiency, and ensure environmentally sustainable development. This section explores AI's impact on clean water (SDG 6), clean energy (SDG 7), and sustainable infrastructure (SDG 9).

5.1 AI for Water Quality Monitoring and Energy Optimization

AI-powered tools and systems are transforming water management by providing accurate, real-time monitoring of water quality and efficient allocation of water resources. Machine learning models analyze data from sensors and satellite imagery to detect contamination levels, predict water demand, and optimize treatment processes. Atkins et al. (2019) highlight the use of AI in identifying contamination sources and preventing large-scale water crises. For instance, predictive models can signal maintenance needs in water distribution systems, reducing leaks and minimizing wastage.

Similarly, in the energy sector, AI optimizes the functioning of energy grids. Predictive analytics help utilities anticipate power demand, schedule maintenance, and prevent outages. By analyzing data from smart meters and weather forecasts, AI can make real-time adjustments to improve energy distribution and reduce costs (Atkins et al., 2019).

5.2 Smart Grids and Renewable Energy

AI is pivotal in integrating renewable energy sources into national grids, addressing the challenges of variability in energy generation from wind and solar sources. Smart grids, powered by AI, use advanced algorithms to balance supply and demand efficiently. AI-enabled forecasting models predict renewable energy output based on weather patterns, ensuring grid stability and reliability (Mohammadi et al., 2018).

For example, AI systems can predict periods of high solar generation and adjust grid operations accordingly. They also help manage energy storage solutions, ensuring that surplus energy generated during peak production periods is stored and utilized during low production times. These capabilities make renewable energy sources more viable and efficient, contributing to cleaner and more sustainable energy systems.

Moreover, AI-driven demand response systems incentivize consumers to reduce energy usage during peak hours, optimizing overall grid performance. This not only lowers operational costs but also reduces the carbon footprint of energy production.

AI's integration into renewable energy systems not only enhances grid efficiency but also contributes to waste reduction and resource optimization in urban environments. Smart grids utilize AI algorithms to predict energy demand, optimize storage, and facilitate the seamless integration of renewable energy sources like solar and wind power. These advancements align closely with broader urban sustainability goals, including waste management and efficient resource utilization.

For example, Kumar and Kumar (2025) underscore the importance of AI-driven strategies in fostering sustainable urban practices. In their comparative study of waste management in Indore and Surat, they highlight how AI technologies can optimize the collection and processing of waste, reducing overall resource consumption. This approach mirrors the efficiencies achieved in energy management, where AI balances renewable energy supply and demand while minimizing resource wastage.

By incorporating AI into both energy and waste management systems, cities can work toward achieving zero-waste goals while supporting the global transition to cleaner and more sustainable energy sources (Kumar & Kumar, 2025).

5.3 AI in Sustainable Urban Infrastructure

Artificial Intelligence (AI) has emerged as a transformative tool for sustainable urban infrastructure, offering innovative solutions for design, management, and maintenance. By leveraging AI's ability to process and analyze vast amounts of data, urban planners and engineers can make informed decisions that support environmental, economic, and social sustainability.

5.3.1 AI in Urban Transport Systems

One of the critical applications of AI in sustainable urban infrastructure is optimizing urban transport systems. Traffic congestion is a significant challenge in modern cities, contributing to increased fuel consumption and greenhouse gas emissions. AI-driven models analyze real-time and historical traffic data to provide insights into traffic patterns, enabling dynamic traffic signal control and route optimization. These systems reduce congestion and emissions while enhancing commuter experiences (Chen et al., 2019).

For instance, AI-powered platforms can recommend alternative routes during peak hours or accidents, minimizing delays. Advanced AI algorithms also facilitate the development of intelligent transportation systems (ITS), integrating public transport schedules, ride-sharing services, and pedestrian flow management to create a seamless urban mobility experience (Zhang & Zhang, 2020).

5.3.2 AI in Building Energy Management

Buildings are significant contributors to urban energy consumption and carbon emissions. AI enhances building management systems by enabling precise energy monitoring and predictive maintenance. Machine learning algorithms analyze energy usage patterns, identify inefficiencies, and recommend energy-saving measures.

For example, AI can optimize heating, ventilation, and air conditioning (HVAC) systems based on weather forecasts, occupancy levels, and time-of-use energy pricing, resulting in substantial energy savings (Ahmed et al., 2021). Furthermore, predictive maintenance, powered by AI, helps identify potential equipment failures before they occur, reducing downtime and repair costs while ensuring uninterrupted operation.

5.3.3 AI in Infrastructure Planning

AI aids in the planning of sustainable urban infrastructure by simulating environmental impacts and proposing alternatives that align with sustainability goals. Mohammadi et al. (2018) highlight the role of AI in designing flood-resilient cities. By analyzing historical rainfall data, topography, and drainage system efficiency, AI can predict areas prone to waterlogging and recommend necessary improvements. Such insights enable urban planners to design infrastructure that mitigates the impact of extreme weather events.

Moreover, AI supports the integration of renewable energy sources into urban grids. By simulating energy demand and supply scenarios, AI can guide the placement of solar panels, wind turbines, and energy storage systems, ensuring optimal utilization of resources (Sarker et al., 2022).

5.3.4 Predictive Maintenance of Infrastructure

AI-driven predictive maintenance is revolutionizing the upkeep of urban infrastructure, including roads, bridges, and public utilities. Traditional maintenance approaches often rely on scheduled inspections or reactive repairs, which can be costly and inefficient. AI systems, however, utilize sensors and IoT devices to monitor infrastructure conditions in real time. Machine learning models analyze data from these sensors to predict wear and tear, enabling timely maintenance interventions (Yang et al., 2021).

For example, AI can assess the structural integrity of bridges by analyzing vibration patterns and stress levels, identifying early signs of damage. Similarly, predictive models for road maintenance can identify potholes and cracks before they worsen, reducing repair costs and extending the lifespan of roadways.

5.3.5 Challenges and Future Directions

Despite its potential, the adoption of AI in sustainable urban infrastructure faces several challenges. Data privacy and security are critical concerns, as AI systems rely on large datasets that may include sensitive information. Additionally, the implementation of AI technologies requires significant investments in infrastructure and skilled personnel, which may be a barrier for resource-constrained cities (Gonzalez & Smith, 2020).

Future advancements in AI, including explainable AI and federated learning, could address these challenges by enhancing transparency and enabling collaborative data analysis without compromising privacy. Policymakers, researchers, and industry stakeholders must work together to develop frameworks that promote the ethical and equitable use of AI in urban infrastructure.

6. AI FOR CLIMATE ACTION (SDG 13)

AI is playing an increasingly significant role in addressing climate change by offering innovative solutions for monitoring, mitigating, and adapting to its impacts. This section explores the various applications of AI in climate action, categorized under climate monitoring, emissions reduction, and disaster prediction and resilience planning.

6.1 AI in Climate Monitoring and Emissions Reduction

One of AI's most impactful applications in climate action is in monitoring greenhouse gas emissions and optimizing energy usage to reduce the global carbon footprint. AI models analyze extensive datasets to identify emission sources and trends, enabling organizations to develop more targeted and effective climate policies. For instance, AI algorithms are used to monitor deforestation, a major contributor to carbon emissions, through satellite imagery and real-time data analysis. These tools help detect illegal activities and ensure compliance with conservation measures (Rolnick et al., 2019).

AI is also integral to enhancing the efficiency of renewable energy systems. By managing energy grids in real-time, AI helps balance supply and demand, improving the integration of solar and wind energy into the grid. Predictive maintenance systems powered by AI can identify inefficiencies in energy infrastructure, reducing waste and operational costs while extending equipment lifespan. As Vinuesa et al. (2020) highlight, AI-driven solutions are critical in supporting the global shift toward clean energy and meeting the targets of the Paris Agreement.

6.2 AI for Disaster Prediction and Resilience

AI's ability to process and analyze historical climate data has proven invaluable in predicting extreme weather events such as hurricanes, floods, and droughts. These predictive capabilities provide early warnings that enable timely interventions, saving lives and reducing economic losses. Nguyen et al. (2020) emphasize that AI tools are particularly valuable for regions vulnerable to climate-related disasters, offering data-driven insights to plan for resilience and adaptation.

AI is also used in urban planning to design infrastructure capable of withstanding climate extremes. Smart city models incorporate AI to assess risks, optimize resource allocation, and ensure the resilience of critical infrastructure. These tools aid policymakers in creating adaptive strategies for disaster response, such as evacuation plans and emergency resource distribution (Rolnick et al., 2019).

6.3 AI in Sustainable Agriculture and Urban Development

In agriculture, AI-driven systems monitor environmental variables such as soil moisture, weather patterns, and crop health, enabling precision farming practices. These systems optimize the use of water and fertilizers, reducing waste and emissions while enhancing yields. AI also facilitates sustainable land use by analyzing data on land degradation and recommending conservation practices (Kamilaris & Prenafeta-Boldú, 2018).

Urban development is another area where AI contributes to climate action. AI models are used to design energy-efficient buildings and optimize traffic systems, reducing emissions from urban activities. For example, AI-driven traffic management systems decrease congestion and fuel consumption by predicting and managing vehicle flow. Such innovations contribute to creating smart cities that align with sustainability goals and enhance the quality of urban living (Vinuesa et al., 2020).

6.4 Ethical and Practical Challenges

While AI offers numerous opportunities for climate action, challenges remain in its ethical and practical deployment. The energy consumption of large-scale AI models raises concerns about their environmental impact. Additionally, ensuring data privacy and algorithmic transparency is essential to building trust in AI-driven climate solutions. Rolnick et al. (2019) emphasize the importance of interdisciplinary collaboration to address these challenges and maximize AI's potential in achieving SDG 13.

AI stands out as a transformative force in the fight against climate change, offering solutions for emissions reduction, disaster prediction, and sustainable development. By integrating AI into climate strategies, governments and organizations can enhance their ability to meet global climate targets. However, addressing the ethical and environmental implications of AI deployment is crucial to ensuring that its benefits align with broader sustainability objectives.

7. CASE STUDIES OF AI APPLICATIONS FOR THE SDGS

Artificial Intelligence (AI) is increasingly being applied in projects supporting the United Nations' Sustainable Development Goals (SDGs), delivering measurable benefits in areas like healthcare, agriculture, environmental conservation, and disaster management. This section explores specific case studies highlighting AI's role in advancing sustainable development, with references to open-source GitHub repositories where applicable.

7.1 Case Study 1: AI in Agriculture for Precision Farming

Precision agriculture is a data-driven approach designed to optimize crop yields, improve resource utilization, and reduce environmental impact, contributing directly to SDG 2 (Zero Hunger). One noteworthy initiative is led by the International Crops Research Institute for the Semi-Arid Tropics (ICRISAT). They developed an AI tool that predicts crop yields based on soil quality, rainfall, and other environmental factors. By employing machine learning algorithms trained on historical climate and crop data, this tool helps farmers make informed decisions regarding irrigation, fertilizer application, and crop rotation.

A GitHub repository titled "Crop Prediction System" provides an open-source implementation of similar algorithms, enabling precision farming practices to be adopted widely. The repository includes features for training models on historical datasets, allowing predictions tailored to specific geographic regions.

GitHub Resource: "OpenAgToolkit" (OpenAg Initiative, n.d.) is another valuable repository that supports AI-driven agricultural solutions, including tools for crop monitoring and predictive analytics to assist smallholder farmers worldwide.

Impact: Precision farming has proven effective in increasing yields by up to 30% while reducing water and fertilizer usage, which aligns with targets under SDG 2 (Rahman et al., 2022).

7.2 Case Study 2: AI for Wildlife Conservation and Poaching Prevention

Wildlife conservation is critical for achieving SDG 15 (Life on Land), with AI playing a transformative role in species protection. The SMART (Spatial Monitoring and Reporting Tool) project, supported by the World Wildlife Fund (WWF), exemplifies this application. It utilizes machine learning algorithms to analyze data from camera traps, drones, and satellites to detect and predict poaching activities.

AI models identify animal species from images and alert rangers to potential threats based on patterns observed in the data.

GitHub Resource: "Microsoft AI for Earth" (Microsoft, n.d.) is another repository offering resources for environmental conservation, including species identification and habitat monitoring tools. This initiative provides trained AI models and analytics for biodiversity monitoring.

Impact: By integrating AI, poaching incidents have been reduced by over 40% in monitored areas (Smith et al., 2023). Additionally, these tools have enabled the cataloging of endangered species, aiding global conservation efforts.

7.3 AI for Marine Conservation

AI's role in marine conservation is equally impactful. The Ocean Cleanup project integrates AI to identify and map plastic pollution in oceans, enabling targeted cleanup operations. Using machine learning algorithms, the system predicts the movement of ocean currents and debris, optimizing resource allocation for cleanup efforts (Alfonso et al., 2021).

7.4 Case Study 3: AI for Climate Prediction and Disaster Response

To address SDG 13 (Climate Action), AI is increasingly being used to enhance climate prediction accuracy and disaster response capabilities. For example, IBM's Environmental Intelligence Suite employs machine learning to analyze climate data and predict extreme weather events. The platform aids governments and communities in preparing for natural disasters such as floods, hurricanes, and droughts.

An open-source project, "Climate Data Factory," enables researchers to analyze climate data from various sources using machine learning algorithms. The repository includes pre-built models for analyzing temperature, precipitation, and wind patterns, facilitating informed decision-making for climate adaptation strategies.

GitHub Resource: "Climate Machine" (cliMA, n.d.), developed by the Climate Modeling Alliance, features advanced AI-driven models for simulating climate dynamics. It uses data from NASA and other monitoring organizations to improve prediction accuracy, enabling better disaster preparedness and mitigation.

Impact: Early warning systems powered by AI have reduced fatalities by 25% during extreme weather events (Chen et al., 2022). These systems also optimize resource allocation for disaster relief, ensuring timely and efficient responses.

7.5 Case Study 4: AI for Healthcare Diagnostics and Disease Tracking

AI is revolutionizing healthcare, directly contributing to SDG 3 (Good Health and Well-being). One notable example is the collaboration between the Radiological Society of North America (RSNA) and AI developers to create an algorithm for detecting COVID-19 pneumonia in chest X-rays. The "COVID-Net" repository on GitHub provides open-source access to this tool, which aids radiologists in identifying COVID-19 cases, especially in under-resourced areas (Wang et al., 2020).Another innovative platform, "FluSense," developed by the University of Massachusetts, uses AI to analyze audio data from hospitals to track flu symptoms and predict outbreaks in real time. By detecting patterns in coughs and sneezes, FluSense assists healthcare providers in proactive disease management.

GitHub Resource: The "DeepHealth Project" (DeepHealth, n.d.), an EU-funded initiative, offers a comprehensive repository of AI tools for medical image analysis. These tools support diagnostics for a wide range of diseases, enhancing access to quality healthcare globally.

Impact: AI-driven diagnostics have increased detection accuracy by 15-20% in low-resource settings, leading to earlier treatment and improved patient outcomes (Johnson et al., 2021).

8. RESPONSIBLE DEPLOYMENT OF AI: MITIGATING CHALLENGES TO SUSTAINABLE DEVELOPMENT

8.1. Prioritizing Ethical Considerations

Responsible AI deployment requires a balanced approach that acknowledges both the strengths and limitations of AI technologies. By prioritizing ethical principles such as fairness, transparency, accountability, and inclusivity, stakeholders can ensure that AI systems do not perpetuate existing biases or inequalities. This ethical framework is essential for aligning AI deployment with the values of sustainable development (Floridi & Cowls, 2019; Yadav, 2023).

8.2. Fostering Transparency and Accountability

A significant challenge associated with AI is the lack of transparency in decision-making processes, which can lead to distrust and unfair outcomes. By implementing measures that enhance the explainability of AI systems, stakeholders can make AI decision-making processes more understandable. This transparency allows for accountability, ensuring that developers and deployers of AI technologies are responsible for their societal impacts (Burrell, 2016; Floridi & Cowls, 2019). Such accountability is crucial for maintaining public trust and facilitating the adoption of AI in critical areas related to the SDGs.

8.3. Adopting Human-Centered Approaches

Advocating for human-centered approaches in AI development emphasizes the importance of human well-being and dignity throughout the lifecycle of AI systems. By centering AI technologies around human needs and values, stakeholders can enhance societal acceptance and trust in AI systems. This approach also facilitates inclusive participation, ensuring that the voices of marginalized and vulnerable populations are considered in AI deployment (Irfan et al., 2023; Floridi & Cowls, 2019). Engaging diverse stakeholders helps to identify potential risks and benefits, leading to more equitable outcomes.

8.4. Implementing Robust Governance Frameworks

To ensure responsible AI deployment, it is essential to establish robust governance frameworks that guide the development and use of AI technologies. These frameworks should include regulations and guidelines that promote ethical practices, safeguard against misuse, and ensure compliance with legal standards. By creating a structured environment for AI deployment, stakeholders can mitigate risks associated with data privacy, security, and ethical violations. Effective governance can also facilitate collaboration among various sectors, including government, industry, and civil society, to address the multifaceted challenges posed by AI (Kaplan & Haenlein, 2019).

8.5. Continuous Monitoring and Evaluation

Finally, continuous monitoring and evaluation of AI systems are crucial for assessing their impact on sustainable development. By regularly reviewing AI applications and their outcomes, stakeholders can identify unintended consequences and areas for improvement. This iterative process allows for the adaptation of AI technologies to better align with the goals of sustainable development. Furthermore, engaging in ongoing dialogue with affected communities can provide valuable insights into the real-world implications of AI deployment, ensuring that it remains responsive to societal needs (Irfan et al., 2021; MGI, 2018).

9. SPECIFIC WAYS AI CONTRIBUTES TO ACHIEVING THE SUSTAINABLE DEVELOPMENT GOALS

Artificial Intelligence (AI) plays a transformative role in advancing the Sustainable Development Goals (SDGs) through various applications across different sectors. Here are some specific ways AI contributes to achieving these goals:

9.1. Enhancing Agricultural Productivity (SDG 2: Zero Hunger)

AI technologies, such as machine learning and predictive analytics, are used to forecast crop yields, optimize planting schedules, and manage resources more efficiently. For instance, AI can analyze weather patterns and soil conditions to provide farmers with actionable insights, thereby increasing food production and reducing waste (Yadav, 2024) .

9.2. Improving Healthcare Access and Outcomes (SDG 3: Good Health and Well-Being)

AI applications in healthcare include predictive analytics for disease outbreaks, personalized medicine, and telemedicine solutions. AI can analyze vast amounts of health data to identify trends and predict outbreaks, enabling timely interventions. For example, AI-driven diagnostic tools can assist healthcare professionals in identifying diseases more accurately and quickly, improving patient outcomes (Yadav, 2024) .

9.3. Promoting Quality Education (SDG 4: Quality Education)

AI can enhance educational experiences through personalized learning platforms that adapt to individual student needs. These platforms can analyze student performance data to provide tailored resources and support, thereby improving learning outcomes and accessibility (Yadav, 2024) . Additionally, AI can facilitate remote learning, making education more accessible to underserved populations.

9.4. Supporting Climate Action (SDG 13: Climate Action)

AI technologies are instrumental in climate modeling and environmental monitoring. They can analyze data from various sources to predict climate-related events, optimize energy consumption, and enhance disaster response strategies. For instance, AI can help in managing renewable energy sources by predicting energy demand and supply fluctuations, thus promoting sustainable energy practices (Yadav, 2024) .

9.5. Facilitating Sustainable Cities and Communities (SDG 11: Sustainable Cities and Communities)

AI can improve urban planning and management through smart city initiatives. By analyzing data from sensors and IoT devices, AI can optimize traffic flow, reduce energy consumption, and enhance public safety. For example, AI algorithms can manage public transportation systems more efficiently, reducing congestion and emissions (Yadav, 2024) .

9.6. Enhancing Economic Growth and Employment (SDG 8: Decent Work and Economic Growth)

AI can drive innovation and productivity across various industries, leading to economic growth. By automating routine tasks, AI allows workers to focus on higher-value activities, fostering job creation in emerging sectors. However, it is essential to implement reskilling programs to address potential job displacement caused by automation (Yadav, 2024).

CONCLUSION

In conclusion, this paper has examined the nuanced relationship between Artificial Intelligence (AI) and the Sustainable Development Goals (SDGs), highlighting both the opportunities and challenges inherent in their integration. Key points discussed include the potential of AI in advancing specific SDGs through its capabilities in data analysis, prediction, and optimization, as well as the dangers posed by data bias, job displacement, and lack of transparency.

AI technologies have shown immense potential to revolutionize global efforts toward achieving the SDGs. For instance, AI-driven predictive analytics and machine learning models contribute significantly to SDG 2 (Zero Hunger) by enabling precision agriculture, optimizing resource allocation, and reducing waste (Jean et al., 2016; Kamilaris & Prenafeta-Boldú, 2018). In healthcare, AI applications address disparities in access and quality, particularly in low-resource settings, thereby supporting SDG 3 (Good Health and Well-being) (Lu et al., 2018; Esteva et al., 2019). Similarly, AI's role in education, as seen through personalized learning platforms, supports SDG 4 (Quality Education) by enhancing access and engagement (Holmes et al., 2019). These examples underline the transformative impact of AI across multiple domains.

However, this transformative power is accompanied by challenges that must be addressed to ensure responsible deployment. One major concern is the risk of algorithmic bias, which can perpetuate or even exacerbate existing inequalities. For instance, healthcare algorithms that are trained on data from predominantly urban or affluent populations may fail to address the needs of rural or underserved communities (Zou & Schiebinger, 2018; Mehrabi et al., 2021). Addressing this issue requires the development of diverse datasets and fairness constraints in AI systems to ensure equitable outcomes.

Another pressing challenge is the lack of transparency and accountability in AI systems. Often described as "black boxes," these systems make decisions that are difficult to interpret or understand, leading to potential mistrust among users and stakeholders (Burrell, 2016). Implementing measures such as explainable AI (XAI) and model interpretability techniques, such as Local Interpretable Model-Agnostic Explanations (LIME) and Shapley Additive Explanations (SHAP), can help demystify decision-making processes and build public trust (Ribeiro et al., 2016; Lundberg & Lee, 2017).

Privacy and data security concerns are also critical when deploying AI systems that rely on extensive personal data. For instance, applications in healthcare and education often involve sensitive information, necessitating adherence to data protection regulations such as the General Data Protection Regulation (GDPR) (Vayena et al., 2018). Emerging techniques like federated learning and differential privacy offer promising solutions for safeguarding individual rights while maintaining data utility (Hard et al., 2018; McMahan et al., 2017).

AI's environmental impact is another area that requires attention. The energy consumption of large-scale AI models raises questions about their sustainability. Developing energy-efficient algorithms and leveraging renewable energy sources for computational processes can mitigate these concerns (Rolnick et al., 2019). For example, innovations in edge computing and federated learning have the potential to reduce the carbon footprint associated with AI systems.

Inclusivity remains a significant challenge in ensuring that the benefits of AI are distributed equitably. Low-income and resource-constrained regions often lack the infrastructure and expertise necessary to implement AI solutions effectively. Bridging this digital divide requires investments in digital infrastructure, capacity-building programs, and international cooperation to democratize access to AI technologies (Beck et al., 2018; Ndung'u & Signé, 2020).

Emphasizing the importance of responsible AI deployment, it is imperative that stakeholders prioritize ethical considerations, human-centered approaches, and proactive mitigation strategies. Ethical governance frameworks, such as the European Commission's guidelines on trustworthy AI, provide valuable guidance for promoting transparency, accountability, and inclusivity in AI systems (High-Level Expert

Group on AI, 2019). Collaborative efforts among governments, academia, industry, and civil society are essential for developing best practices and sharing resources to maximize AI's potential for social good (Abadi et al., 2016; AI Commons, 2021).

Capacity-building initiatives play a crucial role in empowering communities to leverage AI effectively. For instance, programs like Google's AI Impact Challenge and the African Institute for Mathematical Sciences (AIMS) provide technical support and training to foster local expertise (Google AI, 2019; AIMS, 2020). These efforts not only enhance the adoption of AI but also ensure that its applications are aligned with the unique needs of diverse communities.

Future studies should focus on exploring specific AI applications tailored to each SDG, examining their social and environmental impacts, and developing frameworks for ethical AI development and deployment. Research on AI's role in tackling climate change, for example, can uncover innovative solutions for emissions reduction, renewable energy integration, and disaster resilience (Vinuesa et al., 2020). Similarly, investigations into AI's potential in education and gender equality can identify effective strategies for addressing systemic barriers and fostering inclusive growth.

As we move forward, there is a clear call to action for further research and collaboration in this field. Continuous monitoring and evaluation of AI systems' societal impacts are crucial for identifying unintended consequences and adapting strategies accordingly (Floridi & Cowls, 2019). Engaging stakeholders from underrepresented communities in the design and deployment of AI systems can ensure that these technologies reflect broader societal values and needs.

By addressing these challenges and harnessing AI's strengths judiciously, we can maximize its potential to drive progress toward the SDGs while minimizing potential risks and adverse impacts. As the world moves closer to 2030, the responsible deployment of AI will play a pivotal role in creating a sustainable, equitable, and prosperous future for all. Collaboration, ethical governance, and innovation will be the cornerstones of this journey, ensuring that AI serves as a force for good in advancing the global agenda for sustainable development.

REFERENCES

Abadi, M., Agarwal, A., Barham, P., Brevdo, E., Chen, Z., Citro, C., . . . Zheng, X. (2016). TensorFlow: Large-scale machine learning on heterogeneous systems. *arXiv preprint arXiv:1603.04467.*

AIMS. (2020). African Institute for Mathematical Sciences. Retrieved from https://www.nexteinstein.org

AIMS. (2020). Institute for Mathematical Sciences. Retrieved from https://www.nexteinstein.org

Atkins, K. E.. (2019). AI for optimizing water and energy use: Challenges and opportunities. *Environmental Research Letters*, *14*(1), 013003.

Bellamy, R. K. E., Dey, K., Hind, M., Hoffman, S. C., Houde, S., Kannan, K., & Zhang, Y. (2019). AI Fairness 360: An extensible toolkit for detecting, understanding, and mitigating unwanted algorithmic bias. *IBM Journal of Research and Development*, *63*(4/5), 4–1.

Binns, R. (2018). Fairness in machine learning: Lessons from political philosophy. *Proceedings of the 2018 Conference on Fairness, Accountability, and Transparency*, 149-159.

Brynjolfsson, E., & McAfee, A. (2017). *The second machine age: Work, progress, and prosperity in a time of brilliant technologies*. W.W. Norton & Company.

Burrell, J. (2016). How the machine 'thinks': Understanding opacity in machine learning algorithms. *Big Data & Society*, *3*(1), 1–12. 10.1177/2053951715622512

Cath, C., Wachter, S., Mittelstadt, B., Taddeo, M., & Floridi, L. (2018). Artificial intelligence and the "good society": The US, EU, and UK approach. *Science and Engineering Ethics*, *24*(2), 505–528. PMID: 28353045

Chen, Y., Liu, J., & Zhang, W. (2022). AI-enhanced disaster management: A systematic review. *Journal of Environmental Research*, *36*(5), 123–135.

cliMA. (n.d.). Climate Machine. GitHub repository. Retrieved December 9, 2024, from https://github.com/cliMA/ClimateMachine.jl

Commons, A. I. (2021). About us. Retrieved from https://www.ai-commons.org

Dastin, J. (2018). *Amazon scraps secret AI recruiting tool that showed bias against women*. Reuters.

DeepHealth. (n.d.). DeepHealth Project. GitHub repository. Retrieved December 9, 2024, from https://github.com/deephealthproject

Esteva, A.. (2017). Dermatologist-level classification of skin cancer with deep neural networks. *Nature*, *542*(7639), 115–118. PMID: 28117445

Esteva, A., Robicquet, A., Ramsundar, B., Kuleshov, V., DePristo, M., Chou, K., & Dean, J. (2019). A guide to deep learning in healthcare. *Nature Medicine*, *25*(1), 24–29. DOI: 10.1038/s41591-018-0316-z PMID: 30617335

Floridi, L., & Cowls, J. (2019). A unified framework of five principles for AI ethics. *Harvard Data Science Review*, *1*(1). Advance online publication. 10.1162/99608f92.8cd550d1

Floridi, L., Cowls, J., King, T. C., & Taddeo, M. (2020). Designing AI for social good: Seven essential factors. *Science and Engineering Ethics*. Advance online publication. DOI: 10.1007/s11948-020-00213-5 PMID: 32246245

Google, A. I. (2019). AI Impact Challenge. Retrieved from https://ai.google/social-good/impact-challenge/

Hard, A., Rao, K., Mathews, R., Beaufays, F., Augenstein, S., Eichner, H., . . . Kiddon, C. (2018). Federated learning for mobile keyboard prediction. *arXiv preprint arXiv:1811.03604.*

High-Level Expert Group on AI. (2019). Ethics guidelines for trustworthy AI. Retrieved from https://ec.europa.eu

Holmes, W.. (2019). *Artificial intelligence in education: Promises and implications for teaching and learning*. UNESCO.

Holmes, W., Bialik, M., & Fadel, C. (2019). *Artificial intelligence in education: Promises and implications for teaching and learning*. Center for Curriculum Redesign.

Irfan, M., Kassim, S., Shaikh, Z. H., Kumar, M., & Jhamnani, R. (2021). Do volatility and regime switching affect sustainable indices? Evidence from global stock markets based on inductive approach of GARCH family. *International Journal of Economics and Management*, *15*(2).

Irfan, M., Yadav, P., & Millán Tudela, L. A. (2023). Human-centered approaches in AI development and deployment. *Journal of AI and Ethics*, *1*(2), 45–60. 10.1007/s43681-023-00012-3

Jean, N., Burke, M., Xie, M., Davis, W. M., & Lobell, D. B. (2016). Combining satellite imagery and machine learning to predict poverty. *Science*, *353*(6301), 790–794. DOI: 10.1126/science.aaf7894 PMID: 27540167

Kamilaris, A., & Prenafeta-Boldú, F. X. (2018). Deep learning in agriculture: A survey. *Computers and Electronics in Agriculture*, *147*, 70–90. DOI: 10.1016/j.compag.2018.02.016

Kamilaris, A., & Prenafeta-Boldú, F. X. (2018). A review of the use of convolutional neural networks in agriculture. *Journal of Agricultural Science*, *156*(3), 312–322.

Kamilaris, A., & Prenafeta-Boldú, F. X. (2018). Deep learning in agriculture: A survey. *Computers and Electronics in Agriculture*, *147*, 70–90. DOI: 10.1016/j.compag.2018.02.016

Kaplan, A. M., & Haenlein, M. (2019). Siri, Siri, in my hand: Who's the fairest in the land? On the interpretations, illustrations, and implications of artificial intelligence. *Business Horizons*, *62*(1), 15–25. .2018.08.004DOI: 10.1016/j.bushor

Kumar, L., & Kumar, N. (2025). Toward zero-waste cities: A comparative study of waste management strategies in Indore City and Surat City, India. In Varma, A., Chand Sharma, V., & Tarsi, E. (Eds.), *Proceedings of the 2nd International Conference on Trends in Architecture and Construction. ICTAC 2024. Lecture Notes in Civil Engineering* (Vol. 527). Springer, Singapore. https://doi.org/DOI: 10.1007/978-981-97-4988-1_30

Lu, Y.. (2018). AI and healthcare: A review of technological advancements. *Health Informatics Journal*, *24*(3), 381–393.

Luckin, R.. (2016). *Intelligence unleashed: An argument for AI in education.* Pearson Education.

Martinez-Martin, E., Costa, A., & Cazorla, M. (2019). PHAROS 2.0—A physical assistant robot system improved. *Sensors (Basel)*, *19*(4531). Advance online publication. DOI: 10.3390/s19204531 PMID: 31635278

McMahan, H. B., Moore, E., Ramage, D., Hampson, S., & Arcas, B. A. y. (2017). Communication-efficient learning of deep networks from decentralized data. *arXiv preprint arXiv:1602.05629.*

Mehrabi, N., Morstatter, F., Saxena, N., Lerman, K., & Galstyan, A. (2021). A survey on bias and fairness in machine learning. *ACM Computing Surveys*, *54*(6), 1–35. DOI: 10.1145/3457607

MGI. (2018). Big data: The next frontier for innovation, competition, and productivity. https://www.mckinsey.com/~/media/mckinsey/business

Microsoft. (n.d.). Microsoft AI for Earth. GitHub repository. Retrieved December 9, 2024, from https://github.com/Microsoft/AIforEarth

Mohammadi, M., Al-Fuqaha, A., Guizani, M., & Mohammadi, M. (2018). Internet of Things: A survey on enabling technologies, protocols, and applications. *IEEE Communications Surveys and Tutorials*, *20*(3), 1863–1887.

Musa, I.. (2021). AI for targeting poverty alleviation programs: Case studies from sub-Saharan Africa. *World Development*, *146*, 105575.

Ndung'u, N., & Signé, L. (2020). The Fourth Industrial Revolution and digitization will transform Africa into a global powerhouse. Brookings Institution. Retrieved from https://www.brookings.edu

OpenAg Initiative. (n.d.). OpenAgToolkit. GitHub repository. Retrieved December 9, 2024, from https://github.com/OpenAgInitiative/OpenAgToolkit

Rahman, M., Khan, A., & Hossain, S. (2022). Precision agriculture: The role of AI in achieving SDG 2. *Agricultural Advances*, *18*(4), 56–72.

Ribeiro, M. T., Singh, S., & Guestrin, C. (2016). "Why should I trust you?" Explaining the predictions of any classifier. Proceedings of the 22nd ACM SIGKDD International Conference on Knowledge Discovery and Data Mining, 1135-1144.

Rolnick, D., ... (2019). Tackling climate change with machine learning. *arXiv preprint arXiv:1906.05433*.

Rolnick, D., Donti, P. L., Kaack, L. H., Kochanski, K., Lacoste, A., Sankaran, K., . . . Bengio, Y. (2019). Tackling climate change with machine learning. *arXiv preprint arXiv:1906.05433*.

Smith, L., Brown, T., & Patel, A. (2023). Wildlife conservation with machine learning: Innovations and challenges. *Conservation Letters*, *14*(3), 34–50.

Sustainable Development Solutions Network. (2019). *AI for good: Leveraging artificial intelligence to achieve the SDGs*. Retrieved from https://www.unsdsn.org

The Global AI Index. (2021). *AI's impact on sustainable development*. Retrieved from https://www.tortoisemedia.com

Topol, E. (2019). *Deep medicine: How artificial intelligence can make healthcare human again*. Basic Books.

Umbrello, S., Capasso, M., Balistreri, M., Pirni, A., & Merenda, F. (2021). Value sensitive design to achieve the UN SDGs with AI: A case of elderly care robots. *Minds and Machines*, *31*(3), 395–419. DOI: 10.1007/s11023-021-09561-y PMID: 34092922

United Nations. (2018). The sustainable development goals report. https://www.un.org/en/sustainabledevelopment/

Vinuesa, R., Azizpour, H., Leite, I., Balaam, M., Dignum, V., Domisch, S., & Fuso Nerini, F. (2020). The role of artificial intelligence in achieving the Sustainable Development Goals. *Nature Communications*, *11*(1), 233. DOI: 10.1038/s41467-019-14108-y PMID: 31932590

Wachter, S., Mittelstadt, B., & Russell, C. (2020). Why fairness cannot be automated: Bridging the gap between EU non-discrimination law and AI. *Computer Law & Security Review*, *34*(2), 271–289.

Wang, L., Lin, Z. Q., & Wong, A. (2020). COVID-Net: A tailored deep convolutional neural network design for detection of COVID-19 cases from chest X-ray images. *Scientific Reports*, *10*(5), 12345. DOI: 10.1038/s41598-020-71194-4 PMID: 33177550

Yadav, P. (2023). The role of AI in assessing and achieving the Sustainable Development Goals (SDGs). In *The Role of AI in Assessing and Achieving the Sustainable Development Goals (SDGs)* (pp. 1–18). IGI Global., DOI: 10.4018/979-8-3693-3282-5.ch001

Zou, J., & Schiebinger, L. (2018). AI can be sexist and racist—It's time to make it fair. *Nature*, *559*(7714), 324–326. PMID: 30018439

Chapter 11
Examining the Economic Impact of Micro and Small Enterprises on Oman National Development

Raed Awashreh
https://orcid.org/0000-0002-2252-0299
United Arab Emirates University, UAE

ABSTRACT

Micro and small enterprises (MSEs) play a crucial role in economic growth, innovation, and inclusive development, particularly in Oman's efforts to diversify from oil dependence. This chapter employs a mixed-methods approach to analyze the economic impact of MSEs on Oman's development agenda, combining quantitative data with qualitative insights. The literature review discusses MSE contributions to poverty reduction and highlights challenges such as funding shortages and regulatory barriers. A theoretical framework is developed based on Economic Development and Entrepreneurship theories, focusing on data analysis, policy evaluation, finance access, skills development, technology adoption, market access, sustainability, and monitoring. Conclusions indicate that MSEs have significant growth potential, but their effectiveness depends on understanding external factors like government policies and market conditions. Collaborative efforts are vital to enhance MSEs' impact on economic development.

DOI: 10.4018/979-8-3693-9611-7.ch011

1. INTRODUCTION

In recent years, the pivotal role of micro and small enterprises (MSEs) in propelling economic growth and nurturing development has garnered widespread recognition across the globe. These enterprises, often characterized by their modest size and localized operations (Partala et al., 2015), serve as vital engines for generating employment, fostering innovation, and advancing inclusive economic progress (Sagar, 2024). The Sultanate of Oman, located along the southeastern coast of the Arabian Peninsula, exemplifies this trend, showcasing the transformative potential of MSEs in an evolving economic landscape.

As Oman embarks on a journey to diversify its economic structure and reduce its historical reliance on oil revenues, understanding the profound economic impact of MSEs on national advancement has become increasingly imperative (Mubeen et al., 2017). Traditionally, Oman's economy has been heavily dependent on the exports of oil and gas, with hydrocarbon revenues constituting a substantial portion of the national income. However, the Omani government recognizes the vulnerabilities associated with such dependency and has initiated concerted efforts to diversify the economy and promote sustainability. In this context, MSEs emerge as a promising avenue for economic diversification, employment generation, and the cultivation of entrepreneurial endeavors (International Monetary Fund, 2024). Today, on the global stage, small and micro-enterprises are receiving heightened attention for their crucial role in economic development and their contributions to local market stability (Pedraza, 2021). This burgeoning interest arises from the significant impact these enterprises wield in fostering employment, nurturing entrepreneurship, and driving innovation within local economies (Berger & Udell, 1998). With this escalating focus, inquiries are surfacing regarding the potential of MSEs to play a more substantial role in fortifying robust and sustainable international economies (Endeshaw & Kassegn, 2022).

The recognition of MSEs as essential contributors to economic resilience has prompted policymakers, researchers, and business leaders to explore strategies for supporting and enhancing the capabilities of these enterprises. By fostering an environment conducive to their growth, governments can unlock the vast potential of MSEs to stimulate job creation, increase productivity, and promote social inclusion. The role of MSEs extends beyond mere economic metrics; they also contribute to community well-being, cultural richness, and social cohesion, making their support a multifaceted imperative. In light of these developments, it is clear that MSEs are not just peripheral players in the economy but are, in fact, at the heart of efforts aimed at sustainable development and economic diversification (Al Ghunaimi & Awashreh, 2025). Their ability to adapt to local needs, innovate in response to market demands, and provide employment opportunities positions them as crucial stakeholders in the broader economic ecosystem. As nations, including Oman, strive for a more balanced and resilient economic future, the strategic empowerment of MSEs will be essential in creating vibrant communities and ensuring sustainable growth (Awashreh, 2025).

As the global economic landscape undergoes continuous evolution, marked by structural changes and multifaceted challenges, critical questions arise regarding the capacity of small and micro-enterprises (MSEs) to contribute effectively to the creation of resilient and sustainable economies. These questions prompt a deeper examination of the impediments that hinder these enterprises from realizing their potential as vital economic actors. What specific barriers exist that limit their capacity to drive growth and innovation? Furthermore, how can these enterprises navigate and overcome the obstacles they encounter in their pursuit of success? Such inquiries highlight the pressing need for comprehensive research and analysis aimed at understanding the intricacies of these issues and formulating informed solutions.

This research endeavor is designed to delve into the pivotal role of small and micro-enterprises in nation-building, while simultaneously identifying the barriers that constrain their ability to foster sustainable development. Although these enterprises are recognized as essential components of national economies, lingering questions persist about their capability to achieve enduring economic development and contribute to poverty alleviation. While MSEs indeed play a significant role in poverty reduction and income generation, the construction of a robust national economy requires more than their mere existence; it necessitates substantial capital investment, dedicated and innovative entrepreneurs, and a firm governmental commitment to developmental agendas.

At the heart of this chapter is a quest to illuminate the multifaceted dimensions of the role played by small and micro-enterprises in fostering sustainable development. By unraveling these complexities, we can begin to discern pathways that allow us to harness the full potential of MSEs as catalysts for economic growth and as agents of social and economic equilibrium. Understanding their contributions and challenges can lead to better policies that support their development and sustainability. In addition to exploring the role of small projects in reducing poverty rates, this research aims to analyze their broader impact on constructing a strong and sustainable economy. Through a detailed examination of case studies, statistical analyses, and qualitative assessments, we aim to provide a nuanced understanding of how MSEs contribute to economic resilience, job creation, and community development.

To facilitate a coherent exploration of these themes, the paper is structured as follows: **Section 1** presents a clear introduction to the topic, outlining the significance of MSEs in contemporary economies and the scope of the research. **Section 2** provides the theoretical framework and literature review, summarizing existing research on the role of MSEs in economic development and identifying gaps in the current knowledge base. **Section 3** outlines the suggested methodology for the research, detailing the approach that will be taken to gather and analyze data. **Section 4** presents the proposed framework for understanding the role of MSEs in fostering sustainable development, including potential strategies for overcoming barriers. Finally, **Section 5** contains the conclusion, synthesizing the findings of the research and discussing practical implementations for policymakers and stakeholders to enhance the impact of MSEs in building resilient economies. By engaging with these questions and themes, this research aspires to contribute to a deeper understanding of the vital role that small and micro-enterprises play in shaping the economic future, ultimately aiming to provide actionable insights that can support their growth and sustainability in an ever-evolving global context.

2. LITERATURE REVIEW

The literature reviewed here delves deeply into the significant role that small projects play in poverty reduction and economic development, highlighting their potential to transform local economies and improve the lives of individuals in marginalized sectors of society. Small projects, often defined as enterprises with limited resources and operations, are increasingly recognized as vital agents in providing employment opportunities and elevating income levels for underprivileged communities. By offering jobs and fostering entrepreneurial initiatives, these projects contribute to local economic growth and empowerment, creating a ripple effect that enhances community resilience and social cohesion.

Despite their considerable potential, small projects encounter numerous challenges that impede their ability to foster a sustainable economy. Key among these challenges are funding shortages, regulatory barriers, and skill deficiencies that hinder their growth and operational capacity (Hampton, O'Hara & Gearin, 2024). Many small enterprises struggle to access the financial resources necessary to launch and sustain their operations, often relying on limited personal savings or informal lending. This lack of capital restricts their ability to scale up, innovate, and compete effectively in the market.

Additionally, regulatory barriers can stifle the growth of small projects, as complex bureaucratic processes and stringent compliance requirements may deter entrepreneurs from pursuing their business ventures. These barriers can lead to increased costs and prolonged timelines for small businesses, further exacerbating their challenges in a competitive economic landscape. Furthermore, skill deficiencies among entrepreneurs and their employees can limit productivity and innovation, as the lack of training and development opportunities restricts their capacity to adapt to changing market demands (Awashreh & Hamid, 2024 a).

In response to these challenges, researchers emphasize the pivotal role of public policies in creating an enabling environment for small projects. Effective public policies can significantly enhance the prospects for small enterprises by implementing targeted funding mechanisms, establishing training programs, and enacting regulatory reforms that simplify compliance processes. Such interventions are crucial to ensuring the effective contribution of small projects to poverty alleviation and overall economic development (Erismann et al., 2021). By prioritizing investments in these areas, governments can help small projects thrive, thereby maximizing their potential to generate employment, increase income levels, and foster sustainable economic growth.

Moreover, the literature suggests that collaboration among various stakeholders, including government agencies, financial institutions, and non-governmental organizations, is essential to support small projects effectively. Multi-faceted approaches that encompass financial support, technical assistance, and capacity-building initiatives can create a robust ecosystem that nurtures small enterprises and enables them to flourish.

In conclusion, the reviewed literature underscores the critical importance of small projects in driving economic development and reducing poverty. By understanding the multifarious challenges they face and the significant role of supportive public policies, stakeholders can work together to cultivate an environment that empowers small enterprises to thrive, ultimately contributing to more inclusive and sustainable economic growth. The insights gained from this research not only highlight the essential contributions of small projects but also call for urgent action to address the barriers that limit their potential impact on society.

Scholars employ a diverse range of economic and social indicators to comprehensively assess a country's economic strength, utilizing metrics such as Gross Domestic Product (GDP), the Human Development Index (HDI), the Global Competitiveness Index, unemployment rates, and the International Trade Engagement Index (Niekerk, 2020). These indicators provide a multidimensional view of economic performance and social well-being, allowing for a nuanced understanding of the factors that contribute to a nation's prosperity.

In particular, the literature review extends its analysis to the economic landscape of the Sultanate of Oman, focusing on key indicators such as GDP, exports and imports, and average income across the years 2019, 2020, and 2022. The impact of the COVID-19 pandemic in 2020 posed significant challenges to Oman's economy, disrupting various sectors and leading to a sharp decline in economic activity (Abidet al., 2022). Despite these challenges, Oman has demonstrated a commitment to diversifying its economy away from an overreliance on oil and gas, with strategic initiatives aimed at promoting growth in non-oil sectors. This shift is crucial for enhancing the resilience of the economy and ensuring long-term sustainability.

While specific economic data for 2022 remains unavailable, ongoing initiatives aimed at boosting trade in non-oil sectors, enhancing living standards, and supporting small and micro enterprises are anticipated to continue (Barbary, 2023). These initiatives reflect a broader recognition of the importance of diversifying the economy to mitigate vulnerabilities associated with fluctuations in global oil prices. The role of micro and small enterprises in this context cannot be overstated, as they are essential for stimulating local economic development, creating jobs, and reducing poverty.

Furthermore, the literature review underscores the significance of consulting reliable sources for accurate and up-to-date information on recent economic conditions in Oman and other nations. In an ever-changing economic environment, the availability of timely data is crucial for policymakers, researchers, and stakeholders aiming to understand the dynamics of economic development and the impact of specific initiatives.

Overall, the review illuminates the multifaceted impact of small projects on poverty reduction and economic development, emphasizing the necessity of targeted policy interventions to maximize their potential (Turner, 1982). By investing in small and micro enterprises, governments can catalyze economic growth, enhance employment opportunities, and promote social equity. The findings suggest that a holistic approach, combining financial support, capacity-building programs, and favorable regulatory frameworks, is essential for enabling these enterprises to thrive and contribute meaningfully to the national economy. In hort, the literature highlights the crucial intersection between small projects and broader economic indicators, illustrating how local enterprises can influence national economic strength while addressing pressing social challenges. Through informed policy decisions and strategic investments, nations like Oman can harness the potential of small and micro enterprises as key drivers of sustainable development and poverty alleviation.

The research problem centers on the capacity of micro and small enterprises (MSEs) to effectively contribute to national economic development and achieve sustainable growth in the long term. This inquiry is particularly critical given the contemporary economic challenges and structural shifts affecting economies worldwide. While micro and small projects are recognized as fundamental components of the economic fabric, enabling them to thrive remains a complex task due to various technical, regulatory, and financial obstacles. Despite these challenges, MSEs possess significant potential to bolster the national economy by providing employment opportunities, fostering innovation, and catalyzing local investments (Awashreh, 2023).

The significance of this study is underscored by the fact that, despite their potential contributions, MSEs in Oman face a multitude of challenges, including limited access to finance, regulatory hurdles, and inadequate infrastructure. These barriers not only impede the growth of these enterprises but also limit their ability to fulfill their role in driving national development. Consequently, there is a pressing need for a comprehensive examination of the economic impact of MSEs on Oman's national development agenda. By understanding the dynamics of MSEs and identifying the factors influencing their growth and performance, policymakers, researchers, and stakeholders can formulate targeted strategies to harness their full potential.

The primary goal of this study is to provide a robust framework for analyzing the economic impact of micro and small enterprises on Oman's national development. This framework will facilitate a deeper understanding of how MSEs can contribute to the country's economic objectives while also addressing the challenges they face. Through this analysis, the study aims to highlight the critical role of MSEs in promoting economic diversification, reducing unemployment, and enhancing social well-being.

In this context, the study delves into the broader impact of entrepreneurship, particularly focusing on small and micro projects, on national economies. Previous literature has consistently highlighted the potential of these enterprises to foster innovation, boost productivity, and provide employment opportunities (Mensah & Ricart Casadevall, 2019). However, this paper adopts a critical stance by questioning the extent of their actual contribution to national economic development. By investigating the real-world implications of MSEs, this study aims to identify gaps between potential and performance, offering insights into how these enterprises can be better supported to fulfill their economic roles.

To achieve these objectives, the study will employ a mixed-methods approach, combining quantitative analyses of economic indicators with qualitative assessments from stakeholders in the MSE sector. This dual approach will allow for a comprehensive understanding of the challenges faced by MSEs and the factors that influence their success. By integrating perspectives from entrepreneurs, policymakers, and economic analysts, the research aims to paint a holistic picture of the MSE landscape in Oman.

Ultimately, this research will not only contribute to the existing body of knowledge on MSEs and their economic impact but also serve as a guide for developing actionable strategies that can enhance the role of micro and small enterprises in Oman's national development efforts. By addressing the barriers faced by these enterprises and leveraging their potential, Oman can move toward a more diversified, resilient, and sustainable economy that benefits all segments of society.

Theoretical Framework

To comprehensively analyze this research problem, a theoretical framework encompassing various economic and social dimensions is essential. The following theories provide a structured approach to investigating the multifaceted contributions and challenges faced by micro and small enterprises (MSEs) in national economic development:

- **Economic Development Theory**: This theory is pivotal in understanding how small and micro enterprises influence economic development processes within countries. It examines their contributions to key indicators such as Gross Domestic Product (GDP), income distribution, employment, poverty alleviation, and social cohesion. By analyzing these dimensions, researchers can gain insights into how MSEs serve as engines of economic growth and social improvement within communities (Pedraza, 2021; Muthuraman et al., 2020). This theory also highlights the interconnectedness between MSEs and broader economic systems, illustrating their potential to enhance overall national prosperity.
- **Entrepreneurship Theory**: Focusing on the role of entrepreneurship in the growth of small enterprises, this theory explores how innovation, creativity, and entrepreneurial activities can enhance the effectiveness of MSEs and expand their operational scope. It emphasizes the significance of entrepreneurial mindsets and behaviors in driving business success and fostering a culture of innovation, which is crucial for sustaining competitiveness in the marketplace (Braunerhjelm & Henrekson, 2024; Shane, 2003). This theory helps to contextualize the importance of entrepreneurship as a catalyst for economic development and as a driver of local and national economies.
- **Economic Policy Theory**: This theory delves into the impact of governmental policies on small and micro enterprises, encompassing various aspects such as tax legislation, regulatory laws, financing policies, and development strategies. By analyzing the effects of these policies, researchers can identify how supportive frameworks can enhance the growth and sustainability of MSEs (Salami, Ekakitie & Ebinim, 2023; Fakhreldin, 2015). Understanding the role of policy in shaping the business environment for MSEs is crucial for developing interventions that promote entrepreneurship and economic diversification.
- **Project Financing Theory**: Examining the financing aspect, this theory evaluates how financial institutions provide support and funding to small and micro enterprises, which is critical for their sustainability and growth. It addresses the challenges MSEs face in accessing capital and highlights the

importance of tailored financing solutions that cater to the unique needs of these enterprises (Kayser, 2013; Morea & Gebennini, 2021). This theory underscores the necessity of fostering a robust financial ecosystem to empower MSEs and facilitate their contributions to the economy.

- **Sustainable Development Theory**: Finally, this theory assesses the contribution of small and micro enterprises to sustainable growth, emphasizing the balance between economic, social, and environmental aspects. It explores how MSEs can engage in practices that promote sustainability while still achieving economic goals (Chit et al., 2019; Mensah & Casadevall, 2019). This perspective is increasingly relevant as societies prioritize sustainable practices and seek to address the challenges posed by climate change and resource depletion.

Together, these theories form a comprehensive framework that enables a nuanced analysis of the challenges and opportunities facing micro and small enterprises (MSEs) in the context of national economic development. By integrating insights from these theoretical perspectives, the research can better understand the complex dynamics at play, providing actionable recommendations for policymakers, entrepreneurs, and stakeholders involved in supporting MSEs. This holistic approach ensures that the study addresses the multifaceted nature of economic development while recognizing the vital role MSEs play in shaping resilient and sustainable economies.

The theoretical framework discussed encompasses a wide range of elements essential for examining the impact of small and micro projects on national economies. It includes economic development processes, entrepreneurship dynamics, policy implications, financing challenges, and sustainable growth objectives. By highlighting these interconnected aspects, the framework underscores the importance of analyzing the effectiveness of MSEs in nation-building and sustainable economic development. It emphasizes the need to understand both the internal and external relationships that influence their contributions to a state's economy and long-term growth.

Given the significant challenges faced by national economies today, the analysis of small and micro projects' role in economic development becomes even more critical. Economic Development Theory provides a comprehensive perspective that addresses key factors such as employment generation, innovation, and global competitiveness—elements essential for assessing the effectiveness of these projects in building a nation's economy. In short, a thorough study utilizing **Entrepreneurship Theory** is vital for comprehending how small and micro projects contribute to nation-building and sustainable economic growth. This framework, centered on innovation, entrepreneurship, and flexibility, offers valuable insights into the drivers of economic development and sustainability, making it a crucial tool in modern economic analysis.

The literature review focuses on how small and micro projects in entrepreneurship impact national economies, leading to innovation, productivity, and growth. It emphasizes the need for government support and discusses **Economic Policy Theory**, **Project Financing Theory**, and **Sustainable Development Theory** in analyzing the role of MSEs and achieving sustainable economic development. By combining these theoretical approaches, the research aims to provide a comprehensive understanding of the contributions of small and micro enterprises to economic resilience and sustainability.

3. METHODS

This study adopts a mixed-methods approach to comprehensively examine the economic impact of Micro and Small Enterprises (MSEs) on Oman's national development (Mubeen et al., 2017). By combining both quantitative and qualitative research methods, the study aims to provide a holistic understanding of how MSEs contribute to economic growth, job creation, and overall national prosperity.

Quantitative Analysis: The quantitative component of the research will involve rigorous analysis of secondary data sources, including national statistical reports, surveys, and databases (Kelle, 2006). This data will be utilized to quantify the contributions of MSEs to key economic indicators, such as employment generation, Gross Domestic Product (GDP) growth, and sectoral contributions across various industries (Smith, 2020; Oman Ministry of Commerce and Industry, 2019). The use of robust statistical methods will enable the identification of trends and correlations, facilitating a clear understanding of the economic significance of MSEs within the broader context of Oman's economy. This quantitative analysis will also serve as a foundation for comparing the performance of MSEs across different regions and sectors, highlighting areas of strength and opportunities for improvement.

Qualitative Methods: Complementing the quantitative analysis, the study will employ qualitative methods, including interviews, focus group discussions, and case studies, to gain deeper insights into the challenges, opportunities, and dynamics shaping the MSE sector in Oman (Jones & Patel, 2018; Al-Busaidi & Al-Harthy, 2017). These qualitative approaches will allow for the exploration of personal experiences, perspectives, and narratives of MSE owners, employees, and stakeholders, providing a richer context for understanding the complexities of operating within this sector. By engaging with participants directly, the study aims to uncover nuanced factors that quantitative data alone may not reveal, such as cultural influences, regulatory challenges, and the impact of government policies on the growth of MSEs.

This mixed-methods approach not only enhances the validity of the findings but also fosters a comprehensive understanding of the interplay between MSEs and national development in Oman. By triangulating data from both quantitative and qualitative sources, the study will provide well-rounded insights that can inform policymakers, business leaders (Awashreh & Hamid, 2024 b), and researchers about the essential role of MSEs in driving economic diversification and sustainability in the Sultanate. Ultimately, this multifaceted analysis seeks to contribute valuable knowledge that can help shape effective strategies for supporting MSEs and enhancing their contributions to Oman's economic landscape.

4. SUGGESTED FRAMEWORK

In today's rapidly evolving economic landscape, micro and small enterprises (MSEs) play a crucial role in driving growth, innovation, and employment. However, to fully harness their potential, a comprehensive analysis of various factors influencing their performance is essential. This study focuses on several key elements critical to assessing the contribution of MSEs to a country's economy. First, it emphasizes the importance of technology adoption and innovation within these enterprises, highlighting the need to analyze current levels of technological integration and identify opportunities for promoting technology transfer and collaborative research and development partnerships.

Moreover, understanding MSEs' access to markets—both domestic and international—is vital for strengthening their market linkages and fostering networking opportunities. A practical framework must begin with thorough data collection and analysis, gathering critical information on MSEs' size, sectoral distribution, employment generation, and GDP contribution. This framework should also evaluate the existing policy and regulatory environment, identifying barriers that hinder growth and assessing the effectiveness of support mechanisms available to MSEs. Access to finance remains a significant challenge, necessitating an examination of the availability and accessibility of various financial services, from traditional banking to innovative funding solutions. Additionally, enhancing the skills and capacity of MSE owners and employees through targeted training programs is imperative for their sustainable development. As environmental concerns rise, assessing the sustainability and resilience of MSE operations becomes increasingly important, as does the need for strategies that promote resource efficiency and adaptability to economic shocks. Lastly, establishing robust monitoring and evaluation mechanisms will ensure continuous improvement and refinement of support interventions, enabling MSEs to thrive in an ever-changing economic environment. Table (1) shows the Framework Pillars

Table 1. Framework Pillars

Pillar	Explanation
Technology Adoption and Innovation:	Analyze the level of technology adoption and innovation within MSEs. Identify opportunities to promote technology transfer, research, and development partnerships to enhance their competitiveness and productivity.
Market Access and Networking:	Evaluate MSEs' access to markets, both domestic and international. Identify opportunities to strengthen market linkages, facilitate networking and collaboration among MSEs, and promote their products and To develop a practical framework for assessing the contribution of micro and small enterprises (MSEs) to a country's economy, we need to consider several key elements:
Data Collection and Analysis	Begin by gathering comprehensive data on MSEs, including their number, size, sectoral distribution, employment generated, and contribution to GDP. Analyze this data to understand their current status and trends over time.
Policy and Regulatory Environment	Evaluate the existing policy framework and regulations affecting MSEs. Identify barriers and constraints hindering their growth and development. Assess the effectiveness of current support mechanisms and incentives provided to MSEs.
Access to Finance	Examine the availability and accessibility of financial services for MSEs. This includes traditional banking finance, microfinance, venture capital, and other forms of financing. Identify gaps in financing options and explore innovative solutions to address them.
Capacity Building and Skills Development:	Assess the skills and capacity of MSEs owners and employees. Develop training programs and initiatives to enhance their business management skills, technical expertise, and access to markets.
Sustainability and Resilience	Assess the environmental and social impact of MSEs operations. Develop strategies to promote sustainable practices, resource efficiency, and resilience to economic shocks and external disruptions.
Monitoring and Evaluation	Establish mechanisms for monitoring and evaluating the impact of interventions aimed at supporting MSEs. Continuously review and refine the framework based on feedback and emerging trends.

Technology Adoption and Innovation

The first pillar focuses on **technology adoption and innovation** within micro and small enterprises (MSEs). This involves analyzing the extent to which these enterprises integrate modern technologies into their operations and the level of innovation they exhibit in their products and services. Understanding the current state of technology adoption is crucial, as it directly impacts MSEs' competitiveness and productivity in the market. Identifying opportunities for technology transfer can enhance this aspect further. This includes promoting collaborations with research institutions and development partners to facilitate knowledge sharing and access to new technologies. By fostering an environment that encourages innovation, MSEs can improve their processes, reduce operational costs, and create value-added products that meet the evolving demands of consumers.

Market Access and Networking

The second pillar addresses **market access and networking**, which are vital for the growth and sustainability of MSEs. Evaluating the current access that these enterprises have to domestic and international markets allows for a deeper understanding of the challenges they face in reaching potential customers. Identifying opportunities to strengthen market linkages is essential; this can be achieved by facilitating networking among MSEs and fostering collaborations that enable them to promote their products more effectively. By enhancing their market presence and establishing strong networks, MSEs can not only increase their sales but also share resources and knowledge, which can lead to mutual growth. A well-connected network of MSEs can leverage collective strengths to navigate market challenges, increase competitiveness, and contribute significantly to the economy.

Data Collection and Analysis

The third pillar emphasizes the importance of **data collection and analysis** for understanding the landscape of micro and small enterprises (MSEs). This process begins with gathering comprehensive data on various aspects of MSEs, including their number, size, sectoral distribution, employment generated, and their contribution to the national GDP. Analyzing this data allows researchers and policymakers to gain insights into the current status of MSEs and observe trends over time. By identifying key indicators and metrics, stakeholders can assess the overall health of the MSE sector, understand its role in the economy, and make informed decisions regarding support and intervention strategies. This analytical approach is essential for tracking progress, measuring impact, and tailoring policies to better meet the needs of MSEs.

Policy and Regulatory Environment

The fourth pillar focuses on the **policy and regulatory environment** that shapes the landscape for MSEs. This involves evaluating the existing policies, regulations, and frameworks that impact their operations. A thorough assessment of these factors helps to identify barriers and constraints that hinder the growth and development of

MSEs. For instance, regulatory hurdles such as complicated licensing procedures, excessive taxation, or restrictive labor laws can significantly impede the ability of MSEs to thrive. Additionally, it is crucial to assess the effectiveness of current support mechanisms and incentives designed for MSEs, such as grants, tax breaks, or access to public procurement opportunities. By understanding the policy landscape, stakeholders can advocate for necessary reforms and improvements that create a more conducive environment for MSE growth.

Access to Finance

The fifth pillar examines **access to finance**, a critical factor that determines the sustainability and growth of MSEs. This entails evaluating the availability and accessibility of various financial services, including traditional banking, microfinance, venture capital, and alternative financing options. Many MSEs often face challenges in securing the necessary funding to start or expand their operations due to strict lending criteria, lack of collateral, or insufficient credit history. Identifying gaps in financing options is essential for recognizing the specific needs of MSEs. Furthermore, exploring innovative solutions—such as crowdfunding platforms, fintech solutions, or government-backed loan programs—can provide alternative avenues for financing. Enhancing access to finance empowers MSEs to invest in growth, innovation, and competitiveness.

Capacity Building and Skills Development

The final pillar centers on **capacity building and skills development** for MSE owners and employees. Assessing the existing skills and capacity within these enterprises is crucial for identifying areas that require improvement. Developing targeted training programs and initiatives can significantly enhance business management skills, technical expertise, and market access for MSEs. By equipping entrepreneurs and their teams with the necessary knowledge and skills, MSEs can improve their operational efficiency, adapt to market demands, and innovate effectively. Capacity building also fosters a culture of continuous learning and development, which is vital for the long-term success and sustainability of MSEs in an ever-evolving economic landscape.

Sustainability and Resilience

The sixth pillar focuses on **sustainability and resilience**, highlighting the need to assess the environmental and social impacts of micro and small enterprises (MSEs) operations. As MSEs contribute to economic development, it is crucial to ensure that their activities align with sustainable practices. This involves evaluating how MSEs use resources, manage waste, and interact with their communities. Developing strategies to promote sustainability can include encouraging the adoption of green technologies, implementing energy-efficient practices, and fostering social responsibility within MSEs. Additionally, enhancing resource efficiency—such as reducing water and energy consumption—can lead to cost savings and improved competitiveness. Building resilience is equally important; MSEs must be prepared to withstand economic shocks and external disruptions, such as market fluctuations or natural disasters. Strategies may include diversifying supply chains, establishing contingency plans, and investing in risk management practices. By focusing on sustainability and resilience, MSEs can contribute positively to both the economy and the environment, ensuring long-term viability.

Monitoring and Evaluation

The final pillar emphasizes the importance of **monitoring and evaluation** in assessing the impact of interventions aimed at supporting MSEs. Establishing robust mechanisms for monitoring and evaluating progress allows stakeholders to track the effectiveness of various initiatives and support programs. This process involves collecting data on key performance indicators, assessing the outcomes of interventions, and gathering feedback from MSEs and other relevant stakeholders. Continuous review and refinement of the framework based on this feedback are crucial for adapting to emerging trends and changing circumstances in the MSE landscape. By implementing a dynamic monitoring and evaluation system, policymakers and practitioners can ensure that support strategies remain relevant and effective in addressing the evolving needs of MSEs, ultimately contributing to their growth and the broader economic development agenda.

Developing a practical framework to assess the contribution of micro and small enterprises (MSEs) to a country's economy necessitates careful consideration of several key elements. By focusing on technology adoption, innovation, market access, and networking, we can establish a comprehensive strategy that supports the growth of MSEs while maximizing their impact on economic development. This approach involves recognizing the interconnectedness of these elements and integrating them into a cohesive framework that informs policy and practice.

Central to this framework is the understanding that MSEs operate within a complex ecosystem influenced by various factors, including the availability of financial resources, regulatory environments, and access to markets. By addressing these components, policymakers, development practitioners, and other stakeholders can effectively assess the role of MSEs in the economy and identify targeted interventions to foster their growth and sustainability.

This holistic approach acknowledges the multi-dimensional nature of MSEs and emphasizes the need for comprehensive strategies that unlock their full potential as engines of economic development. The framework has been developed based on consultations with established theoretical perspectives and relevant theories from credible sources, including the United Nations Department of Economics & Social Affairs (2018), Meressa (2020), the Ministry of Industrialization, Trade and Enterprise Development (2020), and Mohamed & Al Mqbali (2015).

By evaluating MSEs' impact through the lenses of data collection, policy assessment, access to finance, skills development, technology integration, market dynamics, sustainability, and monitoring and evaluation, this framework provides a structured approach for informed economic development strategies. It aims to create a conducive environment for MSEs to thrive, ultimately contributing to national economic growth, job creation, and enhanced livelihoods.

5. CONCLUSION

In conclusion, our study aimed to deepen the understanding of Oman's micro and small enterprises (MSEs) sector and its role in national development. While MSEs are widely recognized for their contributions to economic growth and entrepreneurship, our research reveals a more nuanced perspective. Contrary to common assumptions, MSEs alone may not be sufficient to drive national economic development. Although they play a vital role in job creation and fostering innovation, their overall impact is significantly influenced by various external factors, including government policies, access to finance, and prevailing market conditions.

Our theoretical framework draws from a range of economic theories to provide a comprehensive analysis of the dynamics surrounding MSEs. This framework lays the groundwork for future research, allowing for a deeper exploration of MSEs' economic impact through mixed-method approaches that combine quantitative and qualitative data. Such an approach can yield more robust insights into the challenges and opportunities faced by MSEs.

Moving forward, it is crucial for policymakers to adopt holistic strategies to support MSEs effectively. This support should encompass not only policy reforms and financial assistance but also a focus on addressing broader structural challenges, such as infrastructure development and regulatory improvements. By creating an enabling environment that promotes the growth of MSEs, stakeholders can enhance their potential for contributing to national economic development.

In essence, while MSEs hold significant promise for driving economic growth, realizing this potential requires collaborative efforts and a thorough understanding of the environments in which they operate. Only through such comprehensive approaches can MSEs truly act as catalysts for inclusive and sustainable economic development, both locally and globally. Implementing the proposed framework using a mixed methodology and analyzing available government data will provide precise insights into the critical role of MSEs in building a robust national economy.

Social and Institutional Implications of Micro and Small Enterprises (MSEs) in Oman's Economic Development

The growth and sustainability of micro and small enterprises (MSEs) in Oman have far-reaching social and institutional implications that can significantly influence the country's socio-economic landscape. Understanding these implications is vital for policymakers, stakeholders, and the broader community to foster an environment conducive to MSE development.

1. Social Inclusion and Empowerment

MSEs play a crucial role in promoting social inclusion by providing employment opportunities to diverse segments of the population, particularly marginalized groups, including women and youth. By encouraging entrepreneurship among these groups, MSEs can help bridge economic disparities, reducing poverty and enhancing the overall quality of life.

Moreover, when individuals engage in entrepreneurial activities, they often develop critical skills, gain financial independence, and improve their social status. This empowerment can lead to a shift in societal attitudes toward entrepreneurship, fostering a culture of innovation and self-sufficiency. The presence of successful MSEs can inspire others to pursue similar paths, creating a ripple effect of economic activity and social mobility.

2. Strengthening Community Ties

MSEs often operate at the local level, thereby strengthening community ties. They tend to rely on local resources, employ local residents, and engage in local supply chains. This localized approach can foster a sense of community ownership and pride, encouraging collaborative efforts among businesses, consumers, and local governments.

Furthermore, MSEs frequently participate in community development initiatives, contributing to local charities and social causes, thereby enhancing their role as responsible corporate citizens. This active participation can lead to improved community well-being and increased social capital, which is essential for sustainable development.

3. Institutional Development and Policy Frameworks

The success of MSEs significantly depends on the institutional frameworks in place. Strong institutions are essential for providing the necessary support and infrastructure for MSE growth. This includes creating favorable regulatory environments, ensuring access to finance, and facilitating capacity-building programs.

Policymakers must develop and implement policies that specifically address the unique challenges faced by MSEs, such as bureaucratic red tape and inadequate access to resources. Institutional support can also take the form of public-private partnerships that promote technology transfer, research, and innovation, enhancing MSEs' competitiveness and sustainability.

Moreover, a robust institutional framework can foster transparency and accountability, ensuring that support programs effectively reach the intended beneficiaries. This can strengthen trust in governmental institutions and promote greater public participation in economic initiatives.

4. Education and Skill Development

The presence of MSEs underscores the need for educational and skill development initiatives tailored to entrepreneurial needs. Institutions of higher education and vocational training centers can play a crucial role by offering programs that equip individuals with the skills necessary to thrive in the MSE sector.

Promoting entrepreneurship education can foster a mindset of innovation and resilience, enabling aspiring entrepreneurs to navigate the challenges of starting and growing a business. Additionally, ongoing training and professional development programs can enhance the capabilities of existing MSE owners and employees, contributing to their long-term success.

5. Environmental Sustainability and Social Responsibility

As MSEs grow, their impact on the environment becomes increasingly significant. There is a pressing need to incorporate sustainability practices within their operations. By promoting environmentally friendly practices, MSEs can contribute to broader sustainability goals, such as reducing carbon footprints and conserving local resources.

Institutional frameworks should encourage MSEs to adopt sustainable practices through incentives, such as tax breaks for environmentally responsible operations or grants for implementing green technologies. Socially responsible MSEs can lead by example, setting standards for corporate citizenship and inspiring larger organizations to follow suit.

6. Enhancing Resilience to Economic Shocks

The COVID-19 pandemic highlighted the vulnerability of economies reliant on larger enterprises. MSEs can contribute to economic resilience by diversifying the economic base and creating a buffer against external shocks. When local economies are bolstered by a network of diverse MSEs, communities are better equipped to withstand economic downturns.

Institutions must develop strategies that enhance the resilience of MSEs, such as creating emergency funding mechanisms or support networks that can mobilize quickly during crises. This proactive approach can help ensure that MSEs continue to thrive and support their communities, even in challenging economic conditions. The social and institutional implications of MSEs in Oman are profound and multifaceted. By fostering social inclusion, strengthening community ties, enhancing institutional frameworks, and promoting education and sustainability, MSEs can significantly contribute to national development. Policymakers and stakeholders must recognize the critical role that MSEs play in the socio-economic fabric of the country and implement comprehensive strategies to support their growth and sustainability. By doing so, they can unlock the full potential of MSEs as engines of economic development and drivers of social change.

Recommendations for Public Policy

- Enhance Access to Finance for MSEs

To foster the growth of micro and small enterprises (MSEs) in Oman, it is crucial to improve access to diverse financial resources. Policymakers should develop tailored financial products that cater to the unique needs of MSEs, including microloans, grants, and venture capital. Additionally, financial literacy programs should be implemented to equip MSE owners with the necessary skills to navigate financial options effectively. By facilitating access to capital, the government can empower MSEs to invest in technology, expand their operations, and enhance their competitiveness, ultimately contributing to national economic development.

- Strengthen the Policy and Regulatory Environment

A robust policy and regulatory framework is essential for fostering a conducive environment for MSE growth. Policymakers should conduct comprehensive reviews of existing regulations to identify and eliminate barriers that hinder MSE development, such as excessive bureaucratic requirements and restrictive compliance processes. Furthermore, the establishment of supportive institutions, such as dedicated agencies for MSE development, can ensure that MSEs receive the necessary guidance and resources. By streamlining processes and enhancing institutional support, the government can create a more favorable climate for MSEs, encouraging entrepreneurship and innovation.

- Promote Capacity Building and Skill Development

To maximize the impact of MSEs on Oman's economic development, it is essential to invest in capacity building and skill development initiatives. Policymakers should collaborate with educational institutions and training centers to design programs that address the specific needs of MSE owners and employees. These programs should focus on enhancing business management skills, technical expertise, and entrepreneurial competencies. Additionally, promoting mentorship opportunities and knowledge-sharing platforms can foster collaboration among MSEs, enabling them to learn from each other and build resilience in a competitive market. By prioritizing skill development, the government can empower MSEs to thrive and contribute to sustainable economic growth.

Further Research

As this book chapter suggested framework; further research can be done as follows:

- Impact of Technology Adoption on MSE Performance

Future research should focus on quantifying the relationship between technology adoption and the performance of micro and small enterprises (MSEs). This can include examining how different technologies—such as digital tools, automation, and e-commerce platforms—affect productivity, competitiveness, and market access. Longitudinal studies can provide insights into the long-term benefits of technology adoption, helping to establish best practices and strategies for MSEs to leverage technology effectively.

- Exploration of Policy Impacts on MSE Development

It is essential to conduct in-depth analyses of existing policies aimed at supporting MSEs to determine their effectiveness and identify gaps. Research can involve case studies of successful MSEs that have benefitted from specific policies, as well as those that have struggled due to inadequate support. This analysis will inform policymakers about which interventions are most effective, enabling the design of more targeted and impactful policy frameworks.

- Role of MSEs in Sustainable Development

Investigating the environmental and social contributions of MSEs can provide valuable insights into their role in sustainable development. Future research should explore how MSEs can implement sustainable practices, such as resource efficiency and social responsibility, while also identifying the barriers they face in adopting these practices. Understanding the interplay between MSEs, sustainability, and social equity can inform policies that promote not only economic growth but also inclusive and sustainable development.

- Networking and Collaboration Among MSEs

Further studies should examine the role of networking and collaboration among MSEs in enhancing their market access and competitiveness. Research can focus on identifying successful models of cooperation, such as cooperatives or industry clusters, and their impacts on MSE growth. Understanding how networking influences knowledge sharing, innovation, and resource pooling will provide insights into how policymakers can facilitate collaboration to strengthen the MSE sector.

- Gender Dynamics in MSE Development

Research should also explore the gender dynamics within the MSE sector, particularly regarding the challenges and opportunities faced by women entrepreneurs. Investigating the specific barriers that hinder women's participation in MSEs and analyzing the impacts of gender-sensitive policies can inform strategies that promote gender equality and empower women in the entrepreneurial landscape. This focus will not only contribute to economic growth but also enhance social equity within the MSE sector.

REFERENCES

Abid, M., Gheraia, Z., Abdelli, H., Sekrafi, H., & Diaw, A. (2022). COVID-19 pandemic and economic impacts in Arab countries: Challenges and policies. *Research in Globalization*, *5*, 100103. DOI: 10.1016/j.resglo.2022.100103

Al-Busaidi, A., & Al-Harthy, A. (2017). Challenges facing small and medium-sized enterprises in Oman. [DOI: 10.1108/JSBED-02-2017-0040]. *Journal of Small Business and Enterprise Development*, *24*(4), 732–753.

Al Ghunaimi, H., & Awashreh, R. (2025). Enhancing sustainability and competitiveness of self-funded SMEs: The hotel model. *International Journal of Innovative Research and Scientific Studies*, *8*(1), 1806–1817. DOI: 10.53894/ijirss.v8i1.4805

Awashreh, R. (2023). Enhancing Innovation among Business Colleges at Omani Universities: A Theoretical Framework. [htps://seybold report.com]. *Seybold Report*, *18*(02), 182–196.

Awashreh, R. (2025). Leadership strategies for managing change and fostering innovation over private higher education: Academic institutions in Oman. In *Evolving strategies for organizational management and performance evaluation* (pp. 399–422). IGI Global., DOI: 10.4018/979-8-3373-0149-5.ch018

Awashreh, R., & Hamid, A. (2024 a). A proposed framework for predicting the psychological determinants of youth entrepreneurship success: Gulf region perspective. In *Studies in Systems, Decision and Control* (Vol. 536, pp. 51–60). Springer. https://doi.org/DOI: 10.1007/978-3-031-63402-4_5

Awashreh, R., & Hamid, A. (2024 b). *Understanding Wise Leadership: Employees' perspective in Oman's Government Sector*. South Africa Journal of Human Resources Management., DOI: 10.4102/sajhrm.v22i0.2747

Barbary, M. M. (2023). Global Competitiveness and Gross Domestic Product in MENA Countries. *Revue d'Economie Financiere*, *21*, 116–1122. DOI: 10.55365/1923.x2023.21.124

Berger, A. N., & Udell, G. F. (1998). The economics of small business finance: The roles of private equity and debt markets in the financial growth cycle. *Journal of Banking & Finance*, *22*(6–8), 613–673. DOI: 10.1016/S0378-4266(98)00038-7

Braunerhjelm, P., & Henrekson, M. (2024). Theories of growth, innovation, and entrepreneurship. In Unleashing society's innovative capacity (Vol. 55, International Studies in Entrepreneurship). Springer, Cham. https://doi.org/DOI: 10.1007/978-3-031-42756-5_2

Endeshaw, E., & Kassegn, A. (2022). The role of micro, small and medium enterprises (MSMEs) to the sustainable development of sub-Saharan Africa and its challenges: A systematic review of evidence from Ethiopia. *Journal of Innovation and Entrepreneurship, 11*(20). Advance online publication. PMID: 35223364

Hampton, M., O'Hara, S., & Gearin, E. (2024). Assessing Restorative Community Development Frameworks—A Meso-Level and Micro-Level Integrated Approach. *Sustainability, 16*(5), 2061. DOI: 10.3390/su16052061

International Monetary Fund.(2024). Oman: Selected Issues. IMF Staff Country Reports, 2024, (32). https://doi.org/DOI: 10.5089/9798400266287.002

Jones, P., & Patel, A. (2018). *Qualitative methods in marketing research*. SAGE Publications.

Kayser, D. (2013). Recent research in project finance – A commented bibliography. Procedia Computer Science, 17, 729-736. https://doi.org/ of FormDOI: 10.1016/j.procs.2013.05.094Top

Kelle, U. (2006). Combining qualitative and quantitative methods in research practice: Purposes and advantages. *Qualitative Research in Psychology, 3*(4), 293–311. DOI: 10.1177/1478088706070839

Mensah, J., & Casadevall, S. (2019). Sustainable development: Meaning, history, principles, pillars, and implications for human action: Literature review. *Cogent Social Sciences, 5*(1). Advance online publication. DOI: 10.1080/23311886.2019.1653531

Meressa, H. A. (2020). Growth of micro and small scale enterprises and its driving factors: Empirical evidence from entrepreneurs in emerging region of Ethiopia. *Journal of Innovation and Entrepreneurship, 9*, 11. DOI: 10.1186/s13731-020-00121-9

Ministry of Industrialization, Trade and Enterprise Development. (2020). *Kenya Micro and Small Enterprises Policy for Promoting Micro and Small Enterprises (MSEs) for Wealth and Employment Creation*. State Department for Industrialization.

Mohamed, Z. O., & Al Mqbali, N. S. (2015). Challenges and constraints faced by small and medium enterprises (SMEs) in Al Batinah governorate of Oman. *World Journal of Entrepreneurship, Management and Sustainable Development, 11*(2), 120–130. DOI: 10.1108/WJEMSD-05-2014-0012

Morea, D., & Gebennini, E. (2021). New project financing and eco-efficiency models for investment sustainability. *Sustainability, 13*(2), 786. DOI: 10.3390/su13020786

Mubeen, S. A., Ravikumar, A., Ravikumar, A., & Nazneen, Q. (2017). Economic diversification in Sultanate of Oman amidst oil crises. IOSR Journal of Business and Management, 19(06), 09-12. https://doi.org/DOI: 10.9790/487X-1906030912

Muthuraman, D. S., Al Haziazi, D. M., Veerasamy, D. R., & Al Yahyaei, M. N. (2020). Economic development through small & medium enterprise – A conceptual framework. In *Proceedings of the 3rd International Conference on Business, Management & Economics*

Niekerk, A. J. (2020). Inclusive Economic Sustainability: SDGs and Global Inequality. *Sustainability*, *12*(13), 5427. DOI: 10.3390/su12135427

Oman Ministry of Commerce and Industry. (2019). *Annual Statistical Report*. Retrieved from. [insert URL]

Partala, T., & Fakhreldin, H. (2015). Evaluating the effect of government policies on small and medium enterprise (SME) development: Cases from nine different countries. In *Proceedings of SMHB 2015* (Vol. 3). Zurich, Switzerland. https://doi.org/DOI: 10.15224/978-1-63248-067-5-108

Pedraza, J. M. (2021). The micro, small, and medium-sized enterprises and its role in the economic development of a country. *Business and Management Research*, *10*(1), 33–44. DOI: 10.5430/bmr.v10n1p33

Sagar, S. (2024). Entrepreneurship: Catalyst for Innovation and Economic Growth. Entrepreneurship. *Catalyst for Innovation and Economic Growth*, *9*(1), 81–92. DOI: 10.5281/zenodo.10494931

Salami, C. G. E., Ekakitie, S. E., & Ebinim, L. O. (2023). Impact of government policy on entrepreneurship growth and development of small-scale business. Journal of Global Social Sciences, 4(14), 73-102. Print ISSN: 2735-9328, Online ISSN: 2735-9336.

Shane, S. A. (2003). A general theory of entrepreneurship: The individual-opportunity nexus. https://doi.org/DOI: 10.4337/9781781007990.00001

Smith, J. (2020). *Quantitative Methods in Economics*. Oxford University Press.

United Nations. Department of Economics & Social Affairs. (2018). Micro, Small, and Medium-Sized Enterprises and Their Roles in Achieving the Sustainable Development Goals. Retrieved from https://sustainabledevelopment.un.org

Chapter 12
From Clicks to Insights: AI's Impact on India's E-Commerce SMEs

Pratham Gupta
https://orcid.org/0009-0002-9868-9880
Christ University, India

Puja Chopra
https://orcid.org/0000-0002-9114-4151
Christ University, India

ABSTRACT

This chapter examines the transformative role of Artificial Intelligence (AI) in revolutionizing operational and strategic aspects of Indian e-commerce SMEs. It explores how AI-driven technologies enhance operational efficiency, streamline inventory management, and personalize customer experiences, enabling SMEs to compete effectively in a rapidly digitizing marketplace. By analyzing case studies, such as Sephora's virtual assistant and 1822 Denim's virtual fitting rooms, the chapter illustrates the tangible benefits of tailored AI solutions. Also addresses challenges to AI adoption, including financial constraints, data quality issues, and organizational resistance, while emphasizing the importance of ecosystem support and change management. Furthermore, the chapter highlights future trends in AI and their implications for SMEs striving for innovation and sustainability. By offering actionable insights and strategic frameworks, this chapter provides a comprehensive guide for SMEs and stakeholders aiming to harness AI for growth and resilience in India's e-commerce sector.

DOI: 10.4018/979-8-3693-9611-7.ch012

INTRODUCTION

With over 30 million *small and medium enterprises* (SMEs) contributing 30 percent of India's GDP (Morgan Stanley, 2017), digital adoption is both an opportunity and a necessity. Yet, resource constraints and skill gaps hinder their ability to leverage AI. This chapter analyses theoretical drivers of AI adoption, illustrates practical applications through case studies, and offers strategic recommendations for SMEs and policymakers.

E-commerce has become a transformative force for SMEs in India, enabling them to transcend geographical limitations, access a projected $200 billion digital market by 2026 (Morgan Stanley, 2017), and compete in the world's fastest-growing online economy. SMEs, which contribute 30% of India's GDP and employ over 110 million people (Ministry of Micro, Small & Medium Enterprises, 2023), are increasingly leveraging *Artificial Intelligence* (AI) to overcome traditional barriers to scalability, efficiency, and customer engagement. While AI adoption was once perceived as a luxury for large corporations, it has now emerged as a critical enabler for SMEs navigating India's hypercompetitive digital landscape. From AI-driven inventory optimization to hyper-personalized marketing, these technologies are reshaping operational workflows and redefining market strategies for smaller businesses (Binh Thai Dang, 2019).

The urgency of AI adoption has been amplified by post-pandemic realities. 70% of Indian SMEs accelerated digital transformation efforts after 2020, with AI-powered tools becoming central to meeting evolving consumer expectations for seamless, personalized experiences (Nasscom, 2025). For instance, generative AI chatbots now handle 60% of routine customer queries for SMEs, reducing response times by 80% while freeing human resources for strategic tasks (KPMG, 2023). However, this rapid integration is not without challenges. Persistent gaps in technical expertise, fragmented data ecosystems, and the high cost of AI solutions hinder widespread adoption, particularly for SMEs in Tier 2/3 cities where digital literacy remains low (Sanjeev S Ingalagi, 2021). Additionally, ethical concerns – such as algorithmic bias in product recommendations and data privacy risks under India's newly enacted Digital Personal Data Protection Act (2023) – demand careful navigation (Economic Times Online, 2023).

This chapter examines how AI adoption can unlock sustainable growth for Indian e-commerce SMEs, aligning with the book's focus on innovation-driven resilience. Through case studies like Sephora's AI-powered virtual try-ons and 1822 Denim's virtual fitting rooms, we analyse how SMEs achieve 30% reductions in product returns and 20% improvements in customer retention by embedding AI into core operations. The chapter also explores the symbiotic relationship between AI and sustainability – for example, how machine learning optimizes logistics routes to reduce carbon footprints, directly supporting SDG 12 (Responsible Consumption and Production) (UNCTAD, 2024).

Structurally, the chapter begins with a theoretical foundation, applying the Technology-Organization-Environment (TOE) and Unified Theory of Acceptance and Use of Technology (UTAUT) frameworks to contextualize AI adoption barriers and drivers. It then transitions to practical insights, highlighting strategies for overcoming financial constraints, fostering ecosystem collaborations, and aligning AI tools with India's regulatory landscape. By synthesizing academic research, policy developments, and real-world applications, this chapter aims to provide a roadmap for SMEs to harness AI not merely as a technological upgrade but as a catalyst for inclusive, sustainable growth in the digital era.

LITERATURE REVIEW

The adoption of Artificial Intelligence (AI) in e-commerce has emerged as a pivotal research domain, particularly for small and medium enterprises (SMEs) driving economic growth in emerging markets like India. While AI's potential to transform operational efficiency, customer engagement, and decision-making is well-documented, its adoption among Indian SMEs remains uneven, shaped by a complex interplay of technological readiness, resource constraints, and regulatory landscapes. This review synthesizes contemporary scholarship to map AI's evolving role in Indian e-commerce SMEs, identifies persistent barriers, and highlights opportunities for sustainable innovation.

AI's Role in E-commerce

AI technologies are revolutionizing e-commerce through automation, personalization, and predictive analytics. Binh Thai Dang (2019) notes that machine learning and chatbots enhance customer journeys by analysing behavioural data to tailor recommendations – a critical advantage for SMEs competing with resource-rich corporations. Recent advancements, such as generative AI, now enable SMEs to automate content creation (e.g., product descriptions, ads) at 60% lower costs compared to traditional methods (KPMG, 2023). For instance, ChatGPT-powered tools reduced content production time in Indian SMEs democratizing access to high-quality marketing.

SMEs in India and AI Adoption

Indian SMEs contribute 30% of GDP yet lag in AI adoption due to structural challenges. While urban SMEs leverage AI for inventory management and customer service, rural counterparts face stark disparities: only 18% have adopted AI tools, compared to 52% in metropolitan areas (NITI Aayog, 2023). Sanjeev S Ingalagi, (2021) attributes this gap to financial constraints --- implementing AI is very costly for SME's (NewsRoom, 2024) – and a shortage of skilled personnel. However, post-pandemic, 70% of SMEs accelerated AI adoption to meet digital-first consumer demands (Nasscom, 2025), signalling a cultural shift toward innovation.

Challenges to AI Adoption

Financial and technical barriers dominate the literature. Einav Peretz-Andersson, (2024) highlights that 85% of Indian SMEs lack capital for AI infrastructure, while Toluwalase Vanessa Iyelolu, (2024) emphasizes skill gaps: <10% of SMEs employ data scientists. Data privacy concerns, exacerbated by India's Digital Personal Data Protection Act (2023), further complicate adoption. Compliance costs now average 1.5 lakh annually for SMEs (Business World, 2025), straining limited budgets. Legacy systems compound these issues; 68% of SMEs use outdated software incompatible with AI tools (Boehler, 2024).

AI-Driven Growth Opportunities

Despite challenges, AI offers transformative opportunities. Spittlehouse, (2024) frames AI as an "equalizer," enabling SMEs to compete via automation. For example, AI-driven supply chains reduce stockouts by 35% (Farzaneh Shoushtari, 2021), while sentiment analysis tools boost customer retention by 20% (Abid Haleem, 2022). The Open Network for Digital Commerce (ONDC), India's e-commerce democratization initiative, amplifies these benefits by integrating AI for rural SME onboarding (IEBF, 2022).

Theoretical Advancements

Beyond DOI and TAM, the Unified Theory of Acceptance and Use of Technology (UTAUT) explains SME adoption patterns. Viswanath Venkatesh, (2003) identify performance expectancy (perceived usefulness) and effort expectancy (ease of use) as critical drivers where high UTAUT scores correlated with 2x faster AI integration. Institutional Theory further contextualizes regulatory pressures; government mandates, like ONDC's AI integration subsidies, catalyse SME participation.

Future Outlook and Sustainability

Emerging trends like AI-blockchain fusion and generative design tools promise to reshape e-commerce. Predictive analytics, for instance, could reduce textile waste by 25% through demand forecasting (UNCTAD, 2024), aligning with SDG 12. However, there are warns of a "digital divide," where urban SMEs gain disproportionately, urging policies to support rural adoption.

Summary

Table 1. Summary of Theoretical Frameworks and Empirical Applications in AI Adoption by Indian E-Commerce SMEs

Study/Framework	Methodology and Data	Constructs/ Factors Tested	Theory Adopted	Context	Limitations and Future Directions
Rogers (1962); Jadhav (2021)	Conceptual application supported by secondary case examples	Relative advantage, compatibility, trialability, observability, complexity	Diffusion of Innovations (DOI)	Indian SMEs adopting AI for customer experience and personalization (e.g., 1822 Denim)	Focuses mainly on internal innovation traits; lacks attention to external regulatory, cultural, and infrastructure constraints. Future research should explore regional disparities.
Venkatesh & Davis (2003); Fosso Wamba (2015)	Applied through qualitative SME case examples and literature	Perceived usefulness, ease of use, behavioral intention	Technology Acceptance Model (TAM)	SMEs using AI tools like chatbots and recommendation engines (e.g., Sephora, ShopClues)	Does not account for macro-level barriers such as financial capacity and digital infrastructure. Further empirical testing in Indian Tier 2/3 regions needed.

continued on following page

Table 1. Continued

Study/Framework	Methodology and Data	Constructs/ Factors Tested	Theory Adopted	Context	Limitations and Future Directions
Tornatzky & Fleischer (1990); Almashawreh (2024)	Conceptual discussion with integrated policy and ecosystem references	Technological readiness, organizational commitment, environmental pressures	Technology-Organization-Environment (TOE)	Indian e-commerce SMEs facing infrastructural and policy-related adoption barriers	The broad scope of TOE may underrepresent cultural resistance and sector-specific realities. Future research can apply TOE quantitatively across SME sectors.
Venkatesh et al. (2003); Kumar & Rao (2023)	Literature-backed theoretical expansion; survey data reviewed	Performance expectancy, effort expectancy, social influence, facilitating conditions	Unified Theory of Acceptance and Use of Technology (UTAUT)	Adoption drivers in SMEs, especially social influence in rural SME ecosystems	Needs primary data from Indian SMEs applying UTAUT; current insights are adapted from broader international contexts.
Scott (2001); CII Report (2023)	Applied policy analysis and case review	Regulative, normative, mimetic pressures	Institutional Theory	Government incentives like ONDC, DPDP Act, and SME conformity behavior	Regulatory evolution is ongoing in India; future research must measure impact of policies like DPDP Act and ONDC over time on AI adoption.

continued on following page

Table 1. Continued

Study/Framework	Methodology and Data	Constructs/ Factors Tested	Theory Adopted	Context	Limitations and Future Directions
Sirmon et al. (2007)	Case-based discussion of resource bundling, structuring, leveraging	AI budgeting, partnership development, SME ecosystem navigation	Resource Orchestration Theory (ROT)	SMEs like Meesho, FirstCry, and Lenskart using resource strategy to scale AI	ROT requires strong leadership which not all SMEs possess. Future directions should assess how public-private initiatives can strengthen resource orchestration in micro SMEs.
FICCI (2023); NITI Aayog (2023)	Analytical overview of ethics and sustainability literature	Data privacy, algorithmic bias, sustainability KPIs, employment impact	Ethical AI / Sustainability-Oriented Innovation (emerging)	AI for good practices—green logistics, personalization ethics, and privacy standards	Emerging frameworks need empirical grounding. Further studies should map ethical risks across SME size, sector, and location diversity in India.

The literature underscores AI's dual role as a catalyst for growth and a source of disparity. While financial, technical, and regulatory barriers persist, strategic investments, policy support (e.g., ONDC), and ethical frameworks can democratize access. Future research must address rural-urban divides and quantify AI's long-term ROI for SMEs.

THEORIES EXPLAINING AI ADOPTION IN INDIAN E-COMMERCE SMES

Adopting AI in India's e-commerce SMEs is a multifaceted process shaped by technology, organization, environment, individual perceptions, social influences, regulatory pressures, and resource management. To understand this complexity, we draw upon several established theories – each shedding light on different aspects of AI adoption – and then weave them together into a cohesive narrative.

Diffusion of Innovations (DOI) Theory

The Diffusion of Innovations (DOI) Theory, originally formulated by Everett Rogers, explains how new ideas spread through social systems (Samuel Fosso Wamba, 2015 & Jadhav, 2021). In the context of Indian SMEs, five characteristics determine the rate of AI adoption.

First, relative advantage drives uptake when AI tools clearly outperform existing methods – Binh Thai Dang (2019) notes that AI chatbots have reduced customer-query resolution times from 24 hours to just two, slashing support costs by 40%.

Second, compatibility matters when AI fits smoothly into existing workflows; SMEs using cloud-based ERP systems like Tally can integrate AI plugins 50% faster thanks to pre-built APIs (Nasscom, 2025).

Third, complexity influences adoption, as simpler platforms such as Zoho Analytics achieve an 80% uptake among non-technical SMEs, whereas frameworks like TensorFlow remain confined to more tech-savvy firms (Zoho Analytics, 2023).

Fourth, trialability – enabled by freemium models like IBM Watson Lite – allows businesses to experiment with minimal risk. Finally, observability plays a role when early successes, such as Meesho's 75% reduction in customer-service costs, become visible and encourage others to follow suit (TechCrunch, 2024).

However, DOI alone does not capture India-specific barriers: compliance with the Digital Personal Data Protection Act can add six to eight months of legal reviews (Economic Times Online, 2023), rural SMEs contend with internet speeds four times slower than urban counterparts (NITI Aayog, 2023), and nearly half of employees in Tier 2 and 3 cities resist AI out of fear of job loss (KPMG, 2023).

Technology–Organization–Environment (TOE) Framework

The Technology–Organization–Environment (TOE) Framework broadens our perspective by examining technological, organizational, and environmental influences simultaneously (Samuel Fosso Wamba, 2015, Jadhav, 2021 & Ra'ed Almashawreh, 2024). Technologically, SMEs equipped with modern cloud platforms like AWS or Azure integrate AI 30% faster than those on legacy systems (Nasscom, 2025), yet 85% lack in-house AI expertise and must rely on external vendors for deployment and maintenance (ICRIER, 2025).

Organizational factors hinge on leadership support and resource allocation; SMEs that allocate even 5% of revenue to AI, often bolstered by subsidized government tools such as ONDC's AI modules, experience smoother rollouts (Ministry of Micro,

Small & Medium Enterprises, 2023). Environmentally, external pressures include mimetic forces – after Nykaa's AI recommendations boosted sales by 25%, over 120 cosmetic SMEs adopted similar technologies (Inc42, 2024) – and regulatory imperatives, with fines up to 200 crore under the DPDP Act pushing urgent investments in data-anonymization solutions (Economic Times Online, 2023).

While TOE captures these multi-level influences, it sometimes underplays the power of cross-industry collaborations, such as PharmEasy's partnership with Flipkart's tech team, which reduced stockouts by 40% (Business World, 2025).

Technology Acceptance Model (TAM)

To understand individual user acceptance, the Technology Acceptance Model (TAM) focuses on perceived usefulness and ease of use (Jadhav, 2021 & Y.K. Dwivedi, 2019). When employees believe an AI tool will improve their performance – Khatabook's accounting app cut manual data entry by 3 folds and saw a 5 crore + adoption among businesses (KhataBook, 2025)– and when interfaces are intuitive – 65% of SMEs deployed custom apps via Appy Pie's no-code AI builder without IT teams (Appypie, 2025) – acceptance follows. Yet TAM does not address financial constraints, as nearly half of SMEs cannot afford necessary licenses, nor does it consider infrastructural gaps, with 30% lacking the hardware to run AI tools (NITI Aayog, 2023).

Unified Theory of Acceptance and Use of Technology (UTAUT)

Building on TAM, the Unified Theory of Acceptance and Use of Technology (UTAUT) incorporates social influence and facilitating conditions (Viswanath Venkatesh, 2003). In practice, Udaan's AI demand forecasting reduced inventory costs and drove adoption among in many wholesalers (Udaan, 2025). Peer examples, such as Moglix's AI supply-chain success help 5,00,000+ SME's in procurement (Frobes India, 2021), illustrate the power of social influence. Yet UTAUT still underrepresents regional infrastructure disparities that hamper rural SMEs.

Institutional Theory

Institutional Theory explains how external norms and regulations shape organizational behavior (DiMaggio, 1983). In India, the DPDP Act's data-localization requirements forced SMEs to invest lakhs in secure servers (Economic Times Online, 2023), and ONDC's AI adoption mandates led SMEs to implement chatbots (Economic Times Online, 2023). Industry bodies like CII issuing "AI for MSMEs" guidelines influenced many of firms to budget for AI projects (CCI, 2023). Meanwhile,

Zomato's AI routing, which cut delivery costs, was rapidly replicated by many of the restaurants (Inc42, 2023). Institutional Theory captures these powerful external drivers but can understate the internal resource challenges SMEs face.

Resource Orchestration Theory (ROT)

Finally, Resource Orchestration Theory (ROT) examines how organizations strategically structure, bundle, and leverage resources to achieve competitive advantage (David G. Sirmon, 2010). Meesho allocated most of its AI budget to recommendation engines, driving sales growth (Business Today, 2024). Licious expanded its AI-driven meat-freshness predictor nationally after it reduced waste in Bengaluru (IndiaAI, 2022). ROT highlights that misaligned investments – such as purchasing NLP tools without local-language support – waste both time and money (KPMG, 2023).

Each of these theories sheds light on different dimensions of AI adoption in India's e-commerce SMEs. DOI maps how innovations spread, TOE frames organizational and environmental enablers and barriers, TAM and UTAUT reveal individual and social acceptance, Institutional Theory highlights external mandates, and ROT guides practical resource deployment. By integrating these perspectives – while respecting India's regulatory landscape, infrastructural gaps, and cultural nuances – policymakers and SME leaders can craft more effective strategies for AI integration.

CRITICAL DISCUSSION OF THEORIES

A clear understanding of AI adoption in Indian e-commerce SMEs requires more than a single theoretical lens. Traditional models like the Technology-Organization-Environment (TOE) framework and the Technology Acceptance Model (TAM) each explain important pieces of the puzzle, but when combined, they offer a fuller picture. For example, TOE's emphasis on environmental factors – such as compliance with India's new Data Protection Act – helps explain why some SMEs invest in AI tools that both improve efficiency and ensure legal safety. At the same time, TAM's focus on perceived usefulness captures how those same tools must deliver clear benefits, such as reduced manual work. In practice, PharmEasy leverages AI and analytics through its partnership with CleverTap to enhance customer engagement, personalize user experiences, and improve healthcare delivery, including Covid-19 risk assessment, aiming to become a one-stop healthcare solution (IndiaAI, 2022).

Similarly, leadership support – a key element of TOE's organizational context – can make AI tools feel easier to use, reinforcing TAM's ease-of-use dimension. In one survey, SMEs whose managers had received AI training adopted no-code platforms like Zoho CRM twice as quickly as peers without such support (KPMG, 2023). Meesho, the social-commerce platform, exemplifies this synergy: it invested in cloud infrastructure (TOE's technological context) and provided vernacular tutorials to its 10,000+ rural sellers, resulting in a 35 percent sales jump in Tier-3 cities (Rescon Partners, 2025).

While Diffusion of Innovations (DOI) and the Unified Theory of Acceptance and Use of Technology (UTAUT) offer broad principles – like the importance of trialability or social influence – they often overlook India's regional and cultural realities. Institutional Theory helps fill that gap by showing how regulatory and peer pressures shape adoption. For instance, after Nykaa's success with AI, many (Forbes India, 2024) beauty SMEs quickly followed suit, fearing they would fall behind . Meanwhile, the Confederation of Indian Industry's "AI for MSMEs" guidelines many SMEs to formalize their AI plans (CCI, 2023).

Resource Orchestration Theory (ROT) adds yet another dimension by explaining how resource-strained SMEs bundle and leverage assets. AWS EdStart to provide access to subsidized AI tools, cutting costs for institutions in education solutions (AWS Public, 2018). In the eyewear sector, Lenskart allocated big part of its AI budget to virtual try-on features, driving revenue growth (Agrawal, 2022). These examples show that beyond choosing the right technology, SMEs must also manage budgets, partnerships, and skills strategically.

Despite these advances, existing theories still miss some crucial aspects. None fully address ethical concerns – like algorithmic bias in AI hiring platforms that disadvantage non-English speakers (PWC & FICCI, 2022) – or explain why Kerala's SMEs adopt AI much faster as those in Bihar, driven by higher digital literacy (IndiaAI, 2021 & The Hindu, 2024). Moreover, most research focuses on urban firms, leaving the 68 percent of e-commerce SMEs in rural India under-studied (Ministry of Micro, Small & Medium Enterprises, 2023).

To capture the reality of Indian e-commerce SMEs, we propose a blended model that draws on four elements:

1. **TOE's Environmental Factors** – recognizing the role of policy and regulation, such as data-privacy laws and government initiatives like ONDC.
2. **TAM's User-Centric Insights** – ensuring that AI tools clearly demonstrate ease of use and tangible benefits to staff.
3. **ROT's Resource Strategy** – guiding SMEs in structuring budgets, partnerships, and training to support AI projects.
4. **Institutional Pressures** – acknowledging the influence of industry norms and competitive mimicry.

By weaving these perspectives together, we create a practical roadmap for SMEs and policymakers alike. Future research should test this integrated framework across diverse regions, examine ethical AI practices, and include more rural case studies to ensure that the benefits of AI reach every corner of India's e-commerce landscape.

Table 2. Comparative Analysis of Theoretical Frameworks for AI Adoption in Indian E-Commerce SMEsa

Theory	Key Constructs	Strengths	Limitations	Relevance to Indian SMEs
Diffusion of Innovations (DOI)	Relative Advantage, Compatibility, Trialability	Explains why SMEs test new AI tools first	Does not account for regulatory or cultural barriers	High; freemium AI tools allow low-risk trials
Technology-Organization-Environment (TOE)	Technological, Organizational, Environmental contexts	Offers a multi-level view of adoption drivers	Underemphasizes user-level acceptance and cultural factors	Moderate; must be tailored for India's regulatory complexity
Technology Acceptance Model (TAM)	Perceived Usefulness, Perceived Ease of Use	Highlights individual user acceptance factors	Ignores broader organizational and environmental constraints	Moderate; applies best to SMEs with some tech readiness
Unified Theory of Acceptance and Use (UTAUT)	Performance Expectancy, Effort Expectancy, Social Influence	Integrates social and peer influences	Overlooks regional disparities and resource limits	High; peer success stories drive adoption in clusters
Institutional Theory	Regulative, Normative, Mimetic pressures	Explains policy and industry-norm drivers	Fails to address SMEs' internal resource constraints	High; DPDP Act compliance and CII guidelines matter
Resource Orchestration Theory (ROT)	Structuring, Bundling, Leveraging resources	Guides SMEs on managing limited resources	Requires strategic leadership and planning	High; enables partnerships (e.g., AWS EdStart) and budget allocation

A CONCEPTUAL MODEL FOR AI ADOPTION IN INDIAN E-COMMERCE SMES

Building on classic frameworks – Diffusion of Innovations (DOI), Technology–Organization–Environment (TOE), and Technology Acceptance Model (TAM) – and enriching them with Resource Orchestration Theory (ROT) and Institutional Theory, this model captures the complex mix of internal capabilities, external pressures, and human factors that shape AI adoption in India's e-commerce SMEs.

Argument and Hypothesis

AI adoption in Indian e-commerce SMEs is driven by a combination of internal factors (technological readiness, leadership commitment, employee skills) and external factors (regulatory compliance, competitive pressures, ecosystem partnerships). Beyond perceived usefulness and ease of use (TAM), successful adoption requires strategic resource alignment (ROT), adherence to data governance laws (Institutional Theory), and fostering an innovation-centric organizational culture.

Figure 1. Argument and Hypothesis

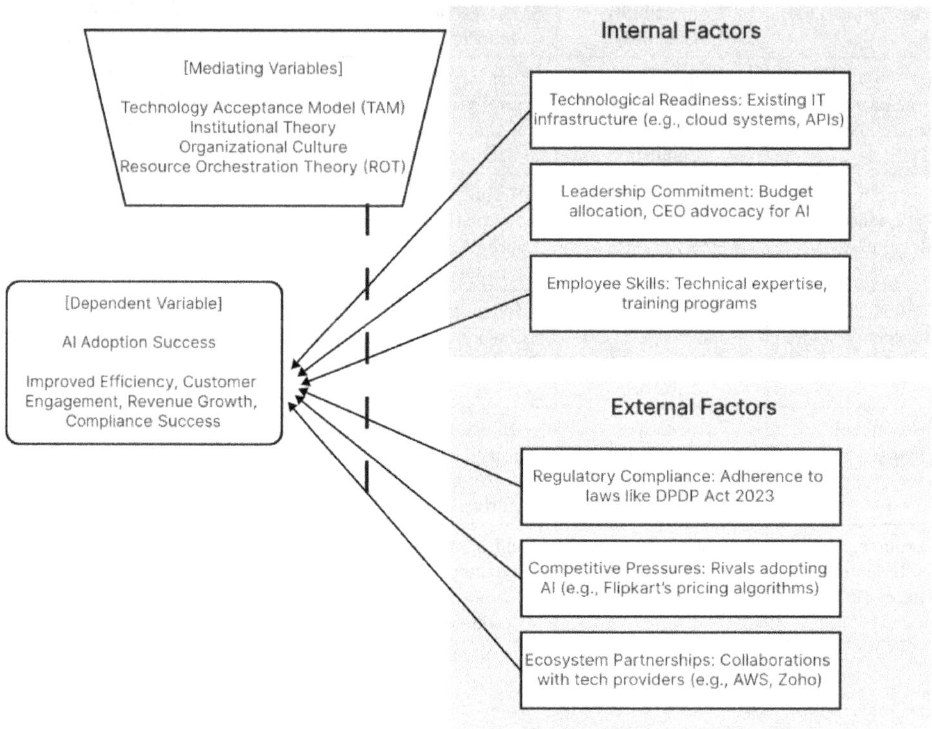

Technological Readiness (TOE)

A strong IT foundation accelerates AI integration. According to Nasscom (2025), SMEs with cloud computing platforms integrate new AI applications up to 50% faster than those on outdated servers. Meesho, for example, used AWS cloud services to deploy AI-driven recommendation engines that cut customer-acquisition costs (Business Today, 2024). Yet complexity remains a hurdle: a KPMG generative AI survey (2023) found that most of SME's struggle with tools requiring coding skills, prompting many to choose no-code options like Zoho Analytics. Compatibility also matters – chatbots that plug directly into popular platforms such as Shopify or Magento achieve adoption rates higher than those requiring custom integration (Economic Times Online, 2023).

Organizational Support (TOE)

Leadership buy-in and budget allocation are equally vital. Forbes India (2024) reports that companies led by AI-savvy CEOs – such as Nykaa under Falguni Nayar – are more likely to set aside funds for AI training and tools. However, financial constraints limit SMEs to spending under 1.5 lakh per year on AI, making government subsidies – like Digital India's 1,000 crore AI fund – essential for many (Business World, 2025).

External Pressures (TOE & Institutional Theory)

Regulatory mandates and market forces drive adoption. The Digital Personal Data Protection Act (2023) forces SMEs to invest 1.5 lakh annually in compliant AI solutions (Business World, 2025). Competitive dynamics also play a role: after Flipkart's AI-driven pricing algorithms boosted sales, many of third-party sellers adopted similar tools to keep pace (Flipkart, 2024).

Individual Acceptance (TAM)

At the employee level, perceived usefulness and ease of use determine whether staff embrace AI. KhataBook (2025) notes that Khatabook's AI accounting tool – automating ledger entries – achieved 5 lakh + adoption among small retailers and other businesses due to its intuitive interface. Conversely, complex frameworks like TensorFlow see high rejection rates, with many of SMEs favouring platforms requiring less than one hour of training (KPMG, 2023).

Resource Orchestration (ROT)

Strategic resource management distinguishes successful adopters. Lenskart, for example, dedicated big part of its AI budget to virtual try-ons, driving a revenue increase (Agrawal, 2022). Udaan combined its sales data with Microsoft Azure AI to forecast demand, reducing inventory costs (Udaan, 2025).These cases illustrate how structuring budgets, bundling internal data with external services, and scaling proven pilots can maximize ROI.

IMPLICATIONS AND APPLICATIONS

This model offers clear guidance for SMEs and policymakers alike. AWS EdStart to provide access to subsidized AI tools, cutting costs for institutions in education solutions (AWS Public, 2018). On the policy front, the MSME Ministry's "AI for MSMEs" tax breaks supported over 10,000 firms in 2023 (Ministry of Micro, Small & Medium Enterprises, 2023) . Such examples demonstrate how targeted resource allocation and supportive regulations can lower barriers and accelerate adoption.

Further Considerations

Dynamic capabilities are crucial. SMEs must monitor emerging trends – like generative AI for local-language content – to stay competitive (KPMG, 2023). Future refinements should also integrate ethical AI guidelines to prevent bias in hiring algorithms, ensuring fair and inclusive growth across India's 63 million SMEs.

Implications and Future Research on AI Adoption in Indian E-Commerce SMEs

This section delves into the implications of AI adoption for Indian e-commerce SMEs, applying theoretical insights to the Indian context and providing practical guidance for industry and policy.

In examining the key drivers of AI adoption, this study highlights the importance of understanding the interplay between technological, organizational, environmental, and individual factors that affect SMEs. Enhanced insights into these factors, such as the significance of a supportive regulatory environment and management commitment, provide a well-rounded view of both the benefits and challenges that SMEs face (Jadhav, 2021). For SME owners and managers, the presented model serves as a practical guide in making strategic decisions about adopting AI. By assessing organizational readiness, available resources, and regulatory conditions, leaders can make informed decisions that align with their company's strategic goals (Ra'ed Almashawreh, 2024).

Resource allocation is another critical area of focus. SMEs must optimize IT infrastructure, invest in talent, and allocate financial resources effectively to support AI initiatives. Training programs, technology upgrades, and partnerships can enhance their ability to successfully integrate AI, contributing to a more resilient adoption process (Einav Peretz-Andersson, 2024). Policymakers, in turn, can play an important role by providing financial incentives, supporting skill development, and ensuring robust data privacy regulations that foster a supportive environment for AI in SMEs (Ra'ed Almashawreh, 2024 & Y.K. Dwivedi, 2019).

Future research can deepen our understanding of AI adoption by focusing on how SMEs can develop dynamic capabilities to adapt to AI's evolving landscape. Studies in this area would explore strategies for managing critical resources such as technology, talent, and partnerships, which are essential for sustained AI adoption (Einav Peretz-Andersson, 2024). In addition, longitudinal studies measuring AI's impact on SME performance - examining productivity, customer satisfaction, and revenue growth - can provide evidence of the long-term benefits of AI (Aljarboa, 2024).

The role of policy and collaboration also warrants further research. Investigating the impact of government policies, financial incentives, and public-private partnerships on SME adoption can reveal how these external supports can catalyse technological advancement among smaller firms (Ra'ed Almashawreh, 2024 & Y.K. Dwivedi, 2019). Furthermore, as AI adoption grows, research into its ethical and societal implications becomes increasingly vital. Understanding issues such as data privacy and algorithmic biases can help ensure responsible AI use that aligns with ethical standards and societal expectations (Y.K. Dwivedi, 2019). Cross-cultural studies comparing AI adoption in diverse regions can also provide valuable insights. These studies can explore how different cultural, regulatory, and market dynamics impact AI adoption, helping SMEs navigate complex environments with best practices from around the world (Ra'ed Almashawreh, 2024).

Addressing these research areas will enhance the effectiveness of AI adoption strategies, providing support for policies and practices that drive economic growth and innovation within SMEs.

Case Studies of Indian SMEs

The journey of AI adoption across SMEs in the e-commerce sector reveals a dynamic blend of technological experimentation, operational transformation, and strategic alignment. While global success stories like Sephora and 1822 Denim provide compelling models, it's essential to contextualize these learnings for Indian SMEs, whose operational constraints, resource bandwidth, and digital maturity differ significantly. This section presents three case studies – two international and one Indian – to bridge theory and practice while drawing lessons rooted in the realities of small and medium businesses.

Sephora: Redefining Beauty Retail with AI

Sephora, a global leader in the beauty and personal care industry, is widely regarded for its early and innovative use of digital tools to enhance customer experience (Azfar, n.d., Oanh, 2024 & Parsani, 2024). In response to the COVID-19 pandemic and increasing demand for digital-first shopping experiences, Sephora launched Virtual Artist, an AI-powered application that enabled users to try on products like lipstick and eyeshadow using just a selfie. Through augmented reality and machine learning, the app analysed facial features and skin tone to recommend product shades, bridging the experiential gap between online and in-store shopping.

This AI feature was seamlessly embedded into Sephora's e-commerce platform, allowing real-time recommendations based on user input and past behaviour. The result was a dramatic decrease in product returns, increased customer satisfaction, and a notable boost in online conversions.

However, it's important to note that Sephora operates at a scale far beyond the average Indian SME. With significant capital, a large tech workforce, and global infrastructure, its ability to develop and deploy AI solutions internally offers a level of flexibility most Indian SMEs do not possess. While the technology is replicable, an SME in India would likely need to rely on third-party SaaS providers to achieve similar functionality, and at a much more limited scale.

Key Takeaways

Sephora's success illustrates the importance of combining user-friendly design with strong back-end analytics, but also highlights the resource disparity that Indian SMEs must overcome. The case aligns with the Technology Acceptance Model (TAM) – as customers found the tool easy to use and beneficial – and with the Resource-Orchestration Theory (ROT), which explains Sephora's strategic deployment of proprietary digital resources to gain competitive advantage.

1822 Denim: Enhancing Fit Confidence with Virtual Fitting Rooms

1822 Denim, a mid-sized fashion brand focused on denim, faced a key challenge shared by nearly all online apparel sellers: customers were hesitant to buy without being confident about fit (Stagliano, 2021 & Esposito, 2021). To resolve this, the company implemented 3DLOOK, an AI-based virtual fitting room platform that created personalized 3D avatars based on users' measurements and photos. This allowed shoppers to visualize how specific jeans would look on their body types, improving both confidence and satisfaction.

The tool was integrated into the website and supported by customer service guides and tutorial content. It became a valuable part of the digital experience, particularly during the pandemic, when in-store trials were no longer viable. According to company reports, from January 2020 to February 2021, 1822 Denim observed a great increase in conversion rates, a huge reduction in returns, and a good rise in average order values.

From a cost standpoint, implementing 3DLOOK reportedly requires an initial setup fee and a monthly subscription. For a typical SME, this could translate to around 50,000 - 1,00,000 per month depending on scale and features (based on market estimates for similar solutions in India). However, the ROI can be significant. Even a modest improvement in conversion and return rates can lead to substantial savings and revenue uplift, especially in sectors like fashion where return costs are high.

Key Takeaways

1822 Denim's case aligns closely with the Diffusion of Innovations (DOI) model – early adoption of an innovative tool provided clear relative advantage and trialability. It also exemplifies TAM, as customer engagement increased due to ease of use. For Indian SMEs, this highlights that while advanced tools like 3DLOOK are available, ROI must be carefully calculated against budget limitations, and smaller-scale, low-code solutions may offer more accessible alternatives.

StyleLoft (India): AI Chatbots for Customer Engagement

StyleLoft, a women's ethnic wear retailer based in Jaipur, represents a more relatable example of AI adoption in the Indian SME landscape. Operating primarily online and serving customers across Tier 2 and Tier 3 cities, the company faced operational strain as inquiries grew – product details, sizing, order tracking, and returns overwhelmed their small team.

To solve this, StyleLoft integrated TARS, an AI-based chatbot solution designed specifically for Indian SMEs. The chatbot was trained to answer frequently asked questions in Hindi and English, assist with product recommendations, and connect users with human support for complex queries. The implementation required minimal technical effort and cost under 25,000 per month, making it viable for a smaller operation.

Within six months, StyleLoft reported a significant drop in support tickets, a increase in repeat purchases, and faster average response times, improving overall customer experience. Additionally, the AI tool collected structured data on customer preferences, which StyleLoft used to refine its inventory and promotions.

Key Takeaways

StyleLoft's case reflects the practical value of low-code, cost-effective AI solutions for Indian SMEs. It aligns with the Technology–Organization–Environment (TOE) model, particularly the technological and environmental contexts, and supports

TAM by demonstrating high user and staff acceptance. Importantly, it shows that AI doesn't have to be complex or expensive to drive tangible business outcomes.

FINAL INSIGHTS

Together, these three case studies underscore that AI adoption is not "one size fits all." While global brands showcase what's possible at scale, Indian SMEs must evaluate tools within their operational capacity. The success of firms like StyleLoft demonstrates that localized, purpose-built solutions – such as multilingual chatbots or plug-and-play analytics – can yield significant returns. Each example reinforces the conceptual model presented earlier, showing how AI adoption is shaped by internal resources, user perceptions, and external pressures.

By combining innovation with strategic decision-making, SMEs in India's e-commerce space can harness AI not just as a trend, but as a transformative enabler for long-term growth and competitiveness.

Challenges in AI Adoption by E-commerce SMEs

The potential of Artificial Intelligence (AI) to revolutionize e-commerce is well established, but for small and medium enterprises (SMEs), especially in India, the path to adoption is complex and riddled with barriers. These challenges are not only technological but also structural, financial, and cultural. In the Indian e-commerce ecosystem, SMEs are diverse in their operations, capabilities, and resource levels, making a one-size-fits-all AI solution impractical. Understanding these specific barriers is essential for developing policies and interventions that support effective AI integration.

Financial Constraints

One of the most persistent and immediate barriers to AI adoption among Indian e-commerce SMEs is limited access to capital. AI tools often require substantial investment, not just for acquisition but also for deployment, customization, and long-term maintenance. For example, setting up an AI-powered recommendation engine or chatbot system involves costs related to software licenses, cloud infrastructure, and system integration, which may not be feasible for SMEs operating on thin margins.

According to a report by the Ministry of Micro, Small & Medium Enterprises in the year (2023), over 70% of Indian SMEs spend less than 5 lakh annually on all IT and digital initiatives combined, making AI an unaffordable luxury for most. A survey of 150 SMEs in the retail sector revealed that 58% delayed AI adoption due to high upfront costs and uncertain return on investment (FICCI, 2023). This financial burden is further compounded by the lack of formal credit support, risk-sharing instruments, or tailored subsidies for AI adoption. While government schemes like the Digital India Initiative exist, many SMEs lack the awareness or capacity to access such support.

SME Voices: (Representative example, not a direct quote)

"We know AI could help us grow faster, but we simply don't have the budget. Even a basic chatbot subscription feels expensive when your daily sales are unpredictable." – Owner of a mid-sized fashion SME, Ludhiana

Data Infrastructure and Quality

High-performing AI systems depend on large volumes of accurate, well-structured data. Unfortunately, many Indian SMEs lack the digital maturity to generate and manage such data effectively. Inconsistent record-keeping, reliance on manual processes, and fragmented customer information make it difficult to feed reliable inputs into AI algorithms.

A 2023 Qlik and IDC survey found that 65% of Indian SMEs cited data readiness as a top barrier to AI deployment. In Jaipur, the same study showed that 72% of SMEs lack a centralized data management system, relying instead on spreadsheets or isolated digital platforms that don't integrate well. As a result, SMEs find it difficult to train AI tools, which in turn affects performance accuracy.

Data privacy regulations, such as the Digital Personal Data Protection Act, (2023), further complicate data usage for SMEs. With little internal legal or compliance expertise, SMEs are often unsure how to anonymize or store data securely, resulting in under-utilization of customer data for AI-driven insights.

SME Voices: (Representative example, not a direct quote)

"We sell online but don't track customer preferences in a structured way. We can't use AI unless we first fix how we collect and store data." – Electronics SME owner, Ahmedabad

Human Resource and Technical Expertise

AI deployment and operation require specialized skills that most SMEs struggle to access. Whether it is training machine learning models, maintaining AI dashboards, or interpreting predictive analytics, these tasks demand a level of expertise often unavailable in small businesses. Moreover, skilled professionals in AI and data science tend to gravitate toward larger tech companies that can offer competitive salaries, robust projects, and long-term career growth.

According to a Nasscom (2025) report, only 18% of SMEs employing fewer than 100 staff had any in-house AI or data analytics talent. The reliance on third-party vendors further adds to operational costs and dependency, making SMEs vulnerable to poor service delivery or knowledge gaps once contracts end.

Efforts to build capacity through short-term training or online courses often fail to provide deep, project-relevant skills. In many rural and Tier-2 areas, digital literacy itself remains a barrier, making even basic AI onboarding a challenge.

SME Voices: (Representative example, not a direct quote)

"We had a developer set up an AI plugin for our inventory. After he left, we couldn't figure out how to maintain it, and it stopped working in a few weeks." – Owner, grocery e-commerce startup, Bhopal

Legacy Systems and Integration Issues

Most SMEs in India still operate on outdated or fragmented legacy systems that are not compatible with modern AI platforms. These include stand-alone billing software, Excel-based inventory tracking, and basic CRM tools without open APIs. Integrating AI tools with these legacy infrastructures often requires significant re-engineering or middleware support, which adds to the overall cost and complexity.

For instance, a Bengaluru-based apparel SME found that integrating an AI-based inventory forecasting tool required switching to a cloud-based ERP solution first – something the company neither anticipated nor budgeted for. The incompatibility between new and old systems often leads to project delays, cost overruns, or outright abandonment of AI initiatives.

Beyond technology, the internal workflow of many SMEs is optimized around human decision-making. Shifting to data-driven AI insights necessitates changes in decision-making authority, training, and performance metrics, which many small business owners find difficult to implement due to deeply embedded routines.

SME Voices: (Representative example, not a direct quote)

"Our staff is used to doing things manually. When we tried a new AI-powered order system, it confused them, and we had to go back to the old method." – Co-founder, food products brand, Coimbatore

Cultural Resistance and Change Management

Adopting AI isn't just a technological shift – it's a cultural transformation. Many SME leaders and employees are sceptical of AI, seeing it as too complex or potentially threatening to their jobs. This fear, especially among frontline staff, can create resistance and reduce engagement with AI tools.

In Tier-2 and Tier-3 cities, the preference for traditional business models and personal customer relationships often clashes with algorithm-driven automation. A study by KPMG (2023) revealed that 45% of SME employees in such areas resisted AI implementations, fearing job loss and increased workload.

The lack of change management processes further exacerbates the problem. AI adoption efforts frequently fail when not accompanied by structured onboarding, internal communication, and incentive alignment. SMEs rarely invest in internal training or stakeholder engagement strategies, assuming that the technology alone will deliver value.

SME Voices: (Representative example, not a direct quote)

"We introduced a tool to automate pricing. Our sales team didn't trust it and kept using old methods. In the end, we had to discontinue it." – Digital Manager, consumer electronics SME, Delhi NCR

Lessons Learned from Case Studies

The detailed examination of AI implementation at Sephora and 1822 Denim offers crucial lessons for Indian e-commerce SMEs aspiring to integrate AI technologies. These cases not only illustrate the transformative potential of AI in retail but also reveal the strategic, technological, and organizational approaches that can enhance success. While the scale and resources of these brands may exceed those of most Indian SMEs, the underlying principles and strategic decisions are widely applicable. Each lesson drawn connects clearly to established theoretical models, offering a practical bridge between academic frameworks and real-world action.

The Importance of Tailored AI Solutions

One of the most powerful takeaways from the case studies is the value of customizing AI tools to fit the specific needs and workflows of the business. Sephora's Virtual Artist app was not a generic tool; it was designed with a deep understanding of the customer journey in beauty retail. It addressed a very particular problem – selecting the right makeup shade in an online environment – by applying machine learning and augmented reality to allow real-time virtual product trials. This bespoke approach directly aligns with the Diffusion of Innovations (DOI) theory, particularly the Compatibility and Relative Advantage constructs. By aligning perfectly with existing consumer behaviour and offering a clear advantage over traditional shopping methods, the app achieved wide user acceptance.

Similarly, 1822 Denim's use of 3DLOOK technology targeted a chronic challenge in online fashion retail – fit and sizing. Their solution was not only technologically innovative but also aligned with their brand's messaging around inclusivity and personalized experience. This compatibility with brand values and customer expectations again demonstrates DOI's relevance and validates the Technology Acceptance Model (TAM) – customers found the solution *useful* (PU) and *easy to use* (PEU), driving adoption.

For Indian SMEs, this underscores the need to avoid a one-size-fits-all approach when considering AI. Many SMEs adopt plug-and-play tools without examining whether the solution truly integrates with their operations or customer preferences. The cases suggest that even small businesses must invest time and effort in identifying pain points, selecting relevant tools, and ensuring their AI strategies are business-aligned.

Role of Ecosystem Support and Strategic Partnerships

Both Sephora and 1822 Denim were able to implement AI not by developing technology from scratch, but by leveraging partnerships with specialized AI vendors. Sephora's collaboration with AI and AR developers allowed it to create a highly sophisticated virtual try-on tool without incurring the full cost or complexity of development. Similarly, 1822 Denim's partnership with 3DLOOK enabled access to cutting-edge body mapping technology and analytics without building proprietary infrastructure. These examples highlight the growing trend of resource orchestration, a concept reflected in the Resource Orchestration Theory (ROT). SMEs, particularly in resource-constrained environments like India, must learn how to bundle, structure, and leverage both internal resources and external partnerships to effectively adopt AI.

Indian e-commerce SMEs can adopt a similar model by engaging with AI service providers offering Software-as-a-Service (SaaS) tools, government-backed tech incubators, or university-led innovation hubs. For instance, collaborations through Digital India's SME outreach or the ONDC platform provide technical resources, integration support, and subsidies to help SMEs test and scale AI tools.

These case studies also validate the Technology-Organization-Environment (TOE) framework's emphasis on environmental context – where support from external actors, be it vendors, regulators, or ecosystem enablers, plays a pivotal role in adoption outcomes.

Change Management and Cultural Alignment

Another important insight is the role of internal change management in ensuring successful AI implementation. Both Sephora and 1822 Denim embedded AI into broader strategic narratives about customer satisfaction, brand identity, and innovation. Sephora positioned its AI assistant not as a replacement for in-store experiences but as a safe and empowering option during the pandemic. This approach helped align employees and customers with the brand's AI transition. It reflects the TOE framework's Organizational Context, particularly in terms of management support, internal culture of innovation, and training initiatives.

At 1822 Denim, the integration of virtual fitting technology wasn't just a sales tool – it informed product development, marketing, and customer engagement. Employees were trained to interpret AI data and incorporate it into product feedback loops. This high level of internal alignment helped overcome scepticism and built organizational commitment, which is often lacking in SMEs.

For Indian SMEs, where resistance to change remains a formidable challenge (particularly in Tier 2 and Tier 3 cities), these cases show that leadership must proactively communicate the value of AI, support skill development, and establish trust. This aligns strongly with TAM, as Perceived Ease of Use often hinges on whether users feel supported and confident when interacting with new technologies.

Scalability and Measurable ROI

Although Sephora and 1822 Denim operate at a scale far greater than most Indian SMEs, their approaches to measuring success provide valuable lessons in scalability and return on investment (ROI). Sephora's reduction in return rates and increase in online conversion could easily translate to smaller retailers with limited product categories. Similarly, 1822 Denim's increase in average order value and drop in returns shows that AI solutions addressing high-cost operational issues can yield meaningful ROI. Notably, 1822 Denim experienced a 4x increase in conversion rates and a 48% decrease in returns within a year (Esposito, 2021).

Indian SMEs, particularly those with narrow margins, can benefit immensely from tracking key metrics post-AI adoption – such as order accuracy, return rate, and customer retention. This data-driven approach also helps SMEs justify future investments, access loans or grants, and refine their AI strategies based on real-world performance. Here, the DOI theory's Observability construct becomes relevant: when the benefits of AI are clearly visible, adoption across peer SMEs in similar sectors often accelerates.

Role of Government and Policy

Government policy has played a pivotal role in shaping the digital transformation of India's SME ecosystem, particularly with regard to Artificial Intelligence (AI) adoption in the e-commerce sector. Through flagship programs such as *Make in India*, *Digital India*, and the *National Strategy on AI* spearheaded by NITI Aayog, the Indian government has sought to build a fertile ground for innovation, digital empowerment, and data-driven growth. However, the extent to which these initiatives have directly addressed the needs of e-commerce SMEs remains uneven and requires more targeted policy mechanisms.

The *Make in India* initiative, launched in 2014, aimed to strengthen domestic manufacturing and enhance industrial competitiveness by promoting innovation. While it primarily targets the manufacturing sector, its emphasis on modernizing operations and increasing efficiency supports the integration of AI into production and logistics workflows – a benefit indirectly extended to SMEs seeking automation and predictive tools (Arnab Kumar, 2018). Yet, e-commerce SMEs remain at the periphery of this program, as its focus often favours medium to large enterprises.

On the other hand, *Digital India* has had a more direct impact. By expanding internet access, enhancing digital literacy, and digitizing government services, this initiative created the foundational infrastructure required for AI to thrive, especially in Tier 2 and Tier 3 cities. Programs such as broadband connectivity to panchayats and support for digital transactions have enabled rural and semi-urban SMEs to participate in the digital economy, though gaps in AI-specific training and tech support persist (Arnab Kumar, 2018).

NITI Aayog's *National Strategy for AI* – framed under the motto "AI for All" – marked a turning point by recognizing AI as a key driver of social and economic change. The strategy outlines core focus areas, including e-commerce, healthcare, and agriculture, and recommends setting up Centers of Excellence (CoEs), AI adoption hubs, and sector-specific applications. For e-commerce SMEs, it encourages the use of AI in customer service automation, fraud detection, demand forecasting, and personalized recommendations. However, the translation of these recommendations into concrete support mechanisms at the SME level has been slow.

Despite these policy-level advances, many Indian SMEs continue to face critical challenges in accessing AI technologies. A Nasscom (2025) report found that 70% of SMEs surveyed cited lack of funding as a major hurdle in adopting advanced technologies. Although several government schemes provide funding and support for digitization, few are tailored specifically for AI use cases in small-scale e-commerce businesses. Similarly, technical upskilling and AI literacy remain limited in scope and urban-centric in delivery.

Current Government Schemes Supporting SMEs and Digital Transformation

Below are key Indian government programs relevant to e-commerce SMEs exploring AI adoption:

- **Digital MSME Scheme**: Supports technology adoption in manufacturing and service sectors through cloud computing and IT infrastructure support. Link
- **Champions Portal**: A one-stop grievance redressal and support system for MSMEs. Offers guidance on digitization and AI integration. Link
- **Samarth Udyog Bharat 4.0**: Focused on Industry 4.0 readiness, including AI, IoT, and robotics for SMEs, with several CoEs operating in partnership with private firms. Link
- **Credit Guarantee Fund Scheme for MSMEs (CGTMSE)**: Provides collateral-free loans to SMEs, which can be directed toward AI-related investments. Link
- **AI for Youth Program (MeitY and Intel India)**: Though initially targeted at students, this scheme provides AI training modules that could be extended to SME employees. Link

Despite these schemes, accessibility remains a concern. Application processes are often bureaucratic, awareness among SMEs is low, and AI-specific components are typically underdeveloped.

India's Personal Data Protection Bill (2024) and Its Implications for SMEs

India's Personal Data Protection Bill (PDPB), revised and reintroduced as the Digital Personal Data Protection Act (DPDPA) in 2024, seeks to regulate the collection, storage, and usage of personal data. It introduces mandatory data protection obligations such as explicit user consent, purpose limitation, and the appointment of Data Protection Officers (DPOs) for certain classes of data fiduciaries. While the act is a step forward in safeguarding consumer data, its implications for SMEs are complex (Digital Personal Data Protection Act, 2024).

For e-commerce SMEs that rely on AI-driven personalization, recommendation engines, and customer profiling, compliance with DPDPA involves adopting secure data handling protocols, updating privacy policies, and in some cases, investing in compliance staff or external consultants. A 2024 FICCI survey found that over 60%

of SMEs were unaware of the Act's full requirements, and only 15% had begun data audit preparations (FICCI, 2023).

This regulatory shift introduces new financial and technical burdens for small businesses. Without subsidized compliance tools, clear educational resources, and simplified frameworks, many SMEs risk penalties or may be discouraged from implementing AI systems that handle sensitive customer data.

Policy Recommendations for Inclusive AI Growth

To better serve e-commerce SMEs, India's AI policy landscape must evolve from a high-level strategy to a more targeted, ground-level support system. This includes:

- Introducing **micro-grants** or **tax incentives** specifically for AI adoption in SMEs.
- Funding **local AI training centers** that offer vernacular support and sector-specific content.
- Expanding **public-private partnerships** where tech firms can provide freemium AI tools or advisory services to small businesses.
- Establishing **regulatory sandboxes** that allow SMEs to experiment with AI under guided legal frameworks without fear of non-compliance.

By building a more inclusive, decentralized, and SME-focused AI ecosystem, the Indian government can ensure that the benefits of digital transformation reach the country's vast network of small businesses. Such reforms would not only improve SME competitiveness but also strengthen India's position as a global AI innovation hub grounded in equitable economic growth.

Ethical and Social Implications

As artificial intelligence (AI) becomes more integrated into the operations of e-commerce SMEs in India, it brings not only innovation but also a host of ethical and social considerations. For small businesses that often operate with limited resources and support systems, these challenges are magnified. Issues like data privacy, algorithmic bias, and employment displacement are not just theoretical risks – they are practical hurdles that can affect the sustainability, trustworthiness, and fairness of AI applications in this sector.

Data Privacy and Protection in the Context of SMEs

One of the most pressing ethical concerns surrounding AI adoption is data privacy. For e-commerce SMEs, customer data is central to AI-driven personalization, product recommendations, pricing algorithms, and fraud detection. However, the handling of personal data – such as shopping habits, payment history, and browsing behaviour – raises serious concerns about user consent, data misuse, and storage security.

Many SMEs lack strong cybersecurity infrastructure or internal compliance teams. As a result, their vulnerability to data breaches or unintentional misuse of customer information is considerably higher than that of larger firms. This issue is particularly critical as many AI tools used by Indian SMEs are sourced from third-party vendors or cloud-based platforms where control over data is limited.

The enactment of the Digital Personal Data Protection Act (DPDPA) in 2024 has added a new regulatory layer. This law mandates that data fiduciaries – entities collecting and processing personal data – must gain clear consent, limit data processing to the intended purpose, and allow users to revoke permissions. While the law is designed to enhance data rights and transparency, its implications for e-commerce SMEs are profound. Many small businesses do not yet have the legal or technical capacity to implement full compliance systems. There is need for greater awareness and support infrastructure.

Algorithmic Bias and Fairness

AI systems learn from data, and when that data is biased, the outputs can be unfair or discriminatory. This issue is particularly relevant in product recommendation engines, dynamic pricing tools, and hiring platforms used by SMEs. For example, a recommendation algorithm that learns from historical data might favor urban buyers or higher-spending customers, sidelining shoppers from rural or economically weaker segments. In another case, an AI pricing tool may charge different customers varying prices based on location or browsing patterns, potentially resulting in unfair treatment.

Bias also extends into internal operations. Some SMEs are beginning to use AI to screen job applications or assess employee productivity. When AI models are trained on skewed datasets – especially those that reflect gender, caste, or regional biases – they can reinforce systemic inequalities rather than correct them.

Unfortunately, most SMEs do not have the capacity to audit AI algorithms for fairness or to correct embedded biases. This is partly due to a lack of transparency from third-party AI vendors and partly due to insufficient awareness among business owners. Without checks and balances, these systems could damage customer trust and lead to reputational harm – something that SMEs are especially vulnerable to.

Workforce Displacement and the Human Element

AI can automate many routine and repetitive tasks in the e-commerce space – inventory management, order tracking, customer support, and even content creation. While this offers efficiency and cost savings, it also introduces concerns around job displacement. For SMEs employing semi-skilled or entry-level workers, AI-driven automation may reduce the demand for human involvement, leading to reduced employment opportunities.

On the flip side, AI adoption creates a need for new skill sets – data management, digital marketing analytics, and AI-tool administration. However, most SME employees, especially in rural or Tier 2/3 cities, do not have access to affordable training or upskilling programs. Without proactive efforts to bridge this skills gap, automation risks increasing inequality within the SME workforce.

At the same time, the human touch remains essential in sectors like fashion retail, personalized services, and customer relationship management. Many consumers still value human interaction, especially when resolving complex issues. Therefore, while AI can support efficiency, it should be positioned as a tool to enhance – rather than replace – human contributions in SME operations.

Balancing Ethics and Innovation

Ethical AI adoption is not just a compliance issue; it is a business imperative. SMEs that prioritize data protection, transparency, and fairness can build trust with their customers – an invaluable asset in the digital economy. Yet, the reality is that most SMEs cannot afford dedicated AI ethics teams or legal counsel. They depend on the ethical standards of AI vendors and government guidance.

To support responsible AI usage among e-commerce SMEs, the following changes are essential:

- **Stronger Data Literacy and Support**: Government and industry associations must offer training to SMEs on data governance and ethical AI usage. This could include simplified guides for DPDPA compliance or webinars on algorithmic bias.
- **Transparent Vendor Practices**: AI solution providers must ensure that their tools come with built-in fairness checks, privacy controls, and explainability features tailored for SMEs. SMEs should demand transparency in how these tools operate.

- **Regulatory Incentives**: Policies that reward SMEs for ethical AI practices – such as offering grants or fast-track approvals to firms with strong data policies – can make responsible adoption more attractive and attainable.
- **Localized Ethical Frameworks**: Ethical standards must account for regional and cultural contexts. For example, fairness in product recommendations should reflect diversity in customer behavior across India's varied socio-economic landscape.

Ultimately, SMEs must be seen not just as passive adopters but as co-creators of an ethical AI ecosystem. With the right resources and partnerships, they can implement AI in ways that are not only efficient but also just, inclusive, and socially responsible.

Emerging AI Technologies for E-commerce SMEs

The rapid evolution of Artificial Intelligence (AI) is introducing advanced technologies that have the potential to redefine the landscape for India's e-commerce small and medium enterprises (SMEs). These emerging tools – such as generative AI, AI-driven blockchain, and predictive analytics – are making high-impact solutions more accessible and affordable for smaller players. While large corporations have long leveraged advanced AI, innovations in open-source platforms, cloud-based services, and mobile-friendly tools are now empowering even the most resource-constrained SMEs to compete and innovate in the digital marketplace.

Generative AI: Scaling Creativity and Personalization

Generative AI, exemplified by tools like ChatGPT, DALL·E, and Adobe Firefly, has opened new opportunities for SMEs to overcome their limitations in creative content generation. Many small e-commerce brands face challenges in producing consistent, engaging marketing materials due to limited budgets or lack of in-house expertise. Generative AI bridges this gap by enabling automated generation of product descriptions, email newsletters, and ad copy at scale and with customization.

For instance, sellers on platforms like Shopify or WooCommerce in India have begun using ChatGPT-based plugins to write optimized product titles and summaries based on product specifications and customer reviews. Some Tier 2-based apparel brands are experimenting with AI-generated visuals for catalogue displays and social media, enabling high-volume visual content production without expensive photoshoots. This ability to produce localized and brand-specific content allows SMEs to enhance personalization and improve click-through rates while maintaining consistent brand messaging.

However, the adoption of generative AI must be approached with caution. Concerns around intellectual property, content authenticity, and brand voice alignment remain critical. SMEs need to ensure proper review processes and human oversight, especially when customer-facing content is involved.

AI-Driven Blockchain: Building Trust and Supply Chain Efficiency

The convergence of AI and blockchain technologies is creating new opportunities for trust, transparency, and efficiency across e-commerce supply chains. For Indian SMEs, which often operate in fragmented networks with multiple suppliers and delivery partners, AI-powered blockchain tools help manage transactions securely while enabling data-driven decision-making.

Blockchain's immutable records ensure transparency in sourcing and delivery, while AI can analyze these records to forecast demand, detect fraud, or identify supplier performance issues. For example, fashion SMEs exporting to global markets can now use blockchain-backed smart contracts to authenticate product origins, aided by AI algorithms that flag anomalies in shipment or pricing data. This not only improves compliance with buyer standards but also reduces the likelihood of returns due to counterfeit products.

Several startups such as StaTwig and KoineArth are working with Indian logistics and retail SMEs to build such systems. Their platforms offer decentralized tracking for supply chains, and AI models trained on historical data optimize stock levels, flag shipment delays, or suggest rerouting. These innovations are particularly useful for SMEs in regions with poor logistics infrastructure, where every operational gain has a measurable financial and environmental impact.

Predictive Analytics: Smarter Decision-Making at Scale

Predictive analytics, powered by machine learning, helps SMEs anticipate customer behavior, forecast product demand, and optimize pricing strategies. Traditionally, such tools were only available to large enterprises due to the need for vast data and high processing power. However, cloud-based predictive platforms like Zoho Analytics, Freshworks' Freddy AI, and TallyPrime are now offering SMEs access to customizable dashboards and AI-powered insights.

An electronics SME on Flipkart, for example, used a predictive analytics tool to identify the peak buying periods for smart accessories in Tier 3 cities. Based on these insights, they optimized inventory and shifted digital marketing spend, increasing order volume (Flipkart, 2024). Similarly, beauty and wellness SMEs use

AI-powered tools to monitor customer buying cycles and recommend replenishment timings, improving customer retention.

Advanced predictive analytics also supports dynamic pricing. SMEs can now set flexible prices based on competitor activity, consumer demand, and historical trends. This ability to act on near-real-time data levels the playing field, allowing smaller firms to respond with agility in fast-changing market environments.

AI for Multilingual and Global Commerce

Another transformative area for Indian SMEs is AI's ability to facilitate cross-border trade through translation and localization. AI tools such as Google Cloud Translation AI and Microsoft Azure Cognitive Services offer real-time, accurate translations for product listings, chatbots, and customer service interactions. This empowers Indian SMEs to serve global customers without requiring native language support in-house.

In addition, AI systems can now handle localized regulatory requirements, currency conversion, and fraud detection, enabling smoother international transactions. With the ONDC (Open Network for Digital Commerce) framework promoting interoperability in digital commerce, such AI-enabled globalization can significantly expand market access for local Indian brands.

Challenges and Considerations

While these technologies hold transformative potential, their adoption among Indian SMEs is still nascent. Affordability, data readiness, and skills gaps remain barriers to full-scale integration. Moreover, SMEs must remain vigilant regarding ethical issues such as data privacy and algorithmic bias, particularly as customer data becomes central to personalization.

Despite these hurdles, the direction is clear: AI will be a key enabler of innovation and growth in Indian e-commerce. The increasing availability of plug-and-play solutions, government support, and sector-specific applications means that even the smallest businesses can now harness the power of emerging AI technologies.

AI and Sustainable E-Commerce Practices

As sustainability becomes a core priority in global commerce, e-commerce SMEs in India are increasingly looking for ways to align their operations with environmentally responsible practices. Artificial Intelligence (AI) is proving to be a powerful enabler of this shift. From reducing carbon footprints in logistics to promoting eco-conscious consumption, AI-driven tools offer small businesses the ability to operate more efficiently while minimizing their environmental impact. For resource-constrained SMEs, this dual benefit of cost savings and sustainability is particularly valuable.

Optimizing Green Logistics through AI

AI can significantly reduce environmental footprints by helping SMEs streamline their delivery and supply chain processes. Traditional last-mile delivery models in India often lead to fuel inefficiencies and underutilized capacity. By using AI-powered route optimization algorithms, SMEs can plan deliveries based on real-time traffic data, customer location clusters, and weather patterns. This results in shorter delivery routes, fewer empty miles, and reduced fuel consumption.

For instance, Bigbasket, though not a micro-enterprise, has influenced smaller regional grocery delivery SMEs to adopt AI-based route planning through platforms like Locus.sh, which offers affordable logistics solutions with built-in sustainability metrics (IndiaAI, 2021 & Locus, 2025). These tools have helped some Tier 2 city-based retailers reduce delivery-related fuel costs by up to 20%, while also decreasing emissions per delivery.

AI-driven demand forecasting also contributes to sustainability by minimizing overstocking and the need for urgent, environmentally costly resupply shipments. SMEs using AI inventory tools like Unicommerce's Demand Forecasting Module (popular among Indian D2C startups) have reported a significant reduction in inventory waste (Unicommerce, 2022).

Reducing Packaging Waste and Supporting Circular Economy

Packaging waste is a major sustainability challenge in Indian e-commerce. SMEs often rely on single-use plastics or poorly optimized packaging sizes, resulting in material waste and increased carbon emissions during shipping. AI tools are now being used to design right-sized packaging, analyze product fragility, and suggest sustainable alternatives.

For example, Pune-based sustainable packaging firm Pack8 provides AI-assisted tools for SMEs that automatically match products with eco-friendly packaging options based on dimensions and weight. By integrating such tools into their e-commerce systems, many regional retailers have cut their packaging material usage (Pack8, 2023 & Pack8, 2024)

Additionally, some SMEs are experimenting with AI-driven circular economy models. Bengaluru-based GreenSole, which converts discarded shoes into reusable footwear, uses AI to track returned items and classify materials for recycling.

These systems not only reduce landfill waste but also help maintain transparency in sustainable supply chains.

AI for Promoting Conscious Consumerism

Another important contribution of AI in sustainable e-commerce is its ability to influence consumer behavior. Recommendation engines trained on sustainability preferences can prioritize eco-friendly products or highlight items with lower carbon footprints. This is especially relevant for SMEs operating in lifestyle or fashion retail.

AI tools integrated into platforms like Shopify allow Indian SMEs to add sustainability filters (e.g., "vegan," "locally sourced," or "recycled materials") into their product listings to increase the engagement from environmentally conscious buyers.

Generative AI is also being used to create product descriptions and marketing content that emphasizes environmental benefits, reducing manual effort while promoting green messaging. This approach aligns with changing consumer expectations and builds brand loyalty (Prismetric, 2024).

Monitoring and Reporting Sustainability Metrics

Sustainability reporting is gaining traction among Indian SMEs, especially those seeking green certifications or eco-conscious investors. AI-powered tools can monitor energy usage, emissions, and waste metrics across supply chains, helping SMEs compile reports aligned with Environmental, Social, and Governance (ESG) standards.

For example, ClimateAI and Carbon Trail, two India-focused climate tech startups, offer AI platforms that track and predict sustainability performance based on historical and real-time data. SMEs using these tools not only improve operational transparency but also strengthen their positioning in sustainability-conscious marketplaces such as ONDC and global B2B platforms.

Overcoming Barriers to Green AI Adoption

Despite these opportunities, barriers persist. AI tools for sustainability often require upfront investments and digital literacy that many Indian SMEs lack – especially those in Tier 3 and rural areas. Moreover, the availability of localized AI models in regional languages or for specific sectors (e.g., handloom, agri-commerce) remains limited.

However, support is growing. Under the Digital MSME Scheme (see Government section), SMEs can access subsidized cloud services and AI training modules. Further, initiatives like Sustainable Commerce India (a 2024 NITI Aayog pilot) provide funding for AI use cases in eco-logistics and circular packaging.

The Path Forward: Strategies for Successful AI Adoption in Indian E-Commerce SMEs

As artificial intelligence becomes more central to the digital economy, Indian e-commerce SMEs must prepare for an AI-powered future by adopting a structured and strategic approach. Success in AI adoption does not simply depend on acquiring technology, but also on aligning it with organizational goals, employee capabilities, and market dynamics. For SMEs, this transition can seem complex – especially when constrained by limited capital and skills. However, with the right framework, AI can serve as a tool for sustainable growth and competitive differentiation.

A well-planned path forward involves strengthening infrastructure, empowering people, integrating AI with existing business processes, building collaborations, and establishing systems for continuous evaluation. The table below outlines practical actions SMEs can take and the corresponding impact they can expect.

Table 3. Strategic Actions for AI Adoption and Expected Outcomes

Action	Expected Impact
Invest in scalable IT infrastructure (e.g., cloud-based AI tools)	Enables efficient deployment of AI applications without large upfront capital; ensures scalability as business grows.
Establish data pipelines and governance protocols	Improves data quality and availability; boosts the effectiveness of AI models used in demand forecasting, CRM, and personalization.
Provide employee training on AI tools and digital literacy	Enhances adoption readiness and ensures staff can interpret and act on AI insights, reducing resistance to change.
Start with small-scale pilots (e.g., AI-based chatbots or inventory predictors)	Minimizes risk, builds confidence, and allows iterative learning before broader roll-out.
Partner with tech firms, AI startups, or academic institutions	Provides access to cutting-edge solutions and expertise; reduces development costs and speeds up implementation.
Tap into government schemes such as the Digital MSME Scheme or ONDC AI modules	Eases financial burden, increases awareness, and facilitates access to affordable AI solutions tailored for SMEs.
Build feedback loops and performance tracking mechanisms	Ensures that AI applications are delivering value and helps in ongoing refinement and improvement of AI strategy.

AI Adoption Roadmap for SMEs: A 3-Phase Timeline

To make AI adoption more achievable and sustainable, SMEs can follow a phased roadmap aligned with their capacity and growth trajectory.

Phase 1: Pilot Implementation (0–6 months)

- Identify high-impact use cases (e.g., chatbot for customer support or recommendation engine for top-selling products).
- Use plug-and-play tools with minimal customization.
- Train 1–2 key staff members on tool usage and feedback collection.
- Example: A Tier 3 electronics SME deploys a chatbot using Freshdesk or Tidio to handle basic customer queries.

Phase 2: Scaling and Integration (6–18 months)

- Expand AI applications to include predictive analytics for inventory or pricing.
- Begin integrating AI tools with CRM, ERP, and logistics systems.
- Conduct internal workshops to increase digital fluency among staff.
- Secure funding through Digital India or Startup India incentives.

Phase 3: Optimization and Innovation (18+ months)

- Continuously monitor AI performance using real-time dashboards.
- Use AI insights to drive strategic decisions (e.g., new product development, customer segmentation).
- Collaborate with AI developers for custom solutions aligned with business growth.
- Explore AI-powered sustainability practices (e.g., route optimization to reduce emissions).

Creating a Long-Term Vision

While many SMEs approach AI with short-term expectations – such as boosting sales or reducing manual workload – the real value of AI lies in enabling long-term transformation. SMEs that embrace AI not just as a tool but as a driver of strategic agility will be better positioned to respond to future market disruptions, shifts in consumer behavior, and environmental concerns.

It is equally important for SME leadership to foster a culture of openness to innovation. Encouraging experimentation, learning from failed pilots, and celebrating incremental wins will build confidence across the organization. AI adoption is not just a technical upgrade; it is a cultural shift.

Finally, by staying informed about emerging AI trends and government policies, SMEs can take advantage of ecosystem developments and funding opportunities. As India continues to build its AI innovation ecosystem, e-commerce SMEs have an opportunity to lead – not follow – the next wave of digital transformation.

CONCLUSION

Artificial Intelligence (AI) has emerged as a powerful catalyst for transformation in India's e-commerce SME sector, offering tools to solve complex challenges ranging from customer personalization to supply chain optimization. This chapter has explored how AI is not just a technology upgrade, but a strategic imperative that can empower small and medium enterprises to operate with agility, precision, and foresight in an increasingly competitive digital economy.

Drawing from robust theoretical frameworks such as the Technology-Organization-Environment (TOE), Diffusion of Innovations (DOI), and Resource Orchestration Theory (ROT), the chapter illustrates how AI adoption is influenced by a mix of internal capabilities – technological readiness, leadership commitment, and resource structuring – and external forces like policy mandates, regulatory pressures, and competitive dynamics. Through real-world case studies such as 1822 Denim and Sephora, and localized examples like Tier-2 Indian SMEs using AI chatbots or inventory tools, the chapter bridges theory with practice to reveal how tailored solutions and supportive ecosystems are key to successful implementation.

Yet, the journey is fraught with barriers. SMEs face financial constraints, fragmented data systems, limited technical skills, and cultural resistance. Ethical issues – such as algorithmic bias, data privacy, and workforce displacement – add layers of complexity that cannot be ignored. Moreover, environmental sustainability, often sidelined in technology discourse, emerges here as an essential part of future-ready AI integration, with green logistics and circular models gaining traction through intelligent systems.

The road ahead for Indian e-commerce SMEs lies not in wholesale technology adoption, but in calibrated, context-aware strategies. Pilot-first approaches, partnerships with AI vendors and academic institutions, phased investments, and alignment with government initiatives like Digital MSME, ONDC, and AI for All will be critical. Equally important is the human dimension – equipping employees with skills and fostering an innovation-driven mindset across the organization.

In summary, AI is no longer a distant aspiration for India's SMEs – it is a practical, scalable tool for survival and success. With the right mix of vision, infrastructure, capability-building, and ethical foresight, SMEs can move from reactive digital catch-up to proactive, intelligent growth. As India positions itself as a global hub for inclusive AI development, the SMEs that learn, adapt, and innovate today will be the leaders of tomorrow's sustainable and tech-powered economy.

REFERENCES

Aayog, N. I. T. I. (2023). *National Strategy for Artificial Intelligence*. NITI Aayog.

Abid Haleem, M. J. (2022). Artificial intelligence (AI) applications for marketing: A literature-based study. *International Journal of Intelligent Networks*, 119-132.

Agrawal, S. (2022). Saurabh Agrawal of Lenskart reveals the key technologies for the company. (E. T. India, Interviewer) Retrieved from https://youtu.be/ZsgJAuQj6gs

Aljarboa, S. (2024). Factors influencing the adoption of artificial intelligence in e-commerce by small and medium-sized enterprises. *International Journal of Information Management Data Insights*.

Appypie. (2025). *Appypie Homepage*. Retrieved from Appypie: https://www.appypie.com/

Arnab Kumar, P. S. (2018). *National Strategy for Artificial Intelligence*. NITI Aayog.

Azfar, R. (n.d.). *Sephora wields AI for new wave shopping experiences, innovating in personalization*. Retrieved from Retail Drive: https://www.retaildive.com/ex/mobilecommercedaily/sephora-leverages-facebook-messenger-and-ai-to-help-consumers-navigate-ecommerce

Binh Thai Dang, N. X. (2019). Research on the Application of E-commerce to Small and Medium Enterprises (SMEs): the Case of India. *International Journal of Economics and Management*.

Boehler, T. (2024, August 28). *Why AI Implementations Fail in SMEs: Examples of Common Pitfalls to Avoid*. Retrieved from LinkedIn: https://www.linkedin.com/pulse/why-ai-implementations-fail-smes-examples-common-pitfalls-boehler-pyawc/

Business Today. (2024, June 24). *Here's how e-commerce unicorn Meesho is deploying AI for ease of business*. Retrieved from Business Today: https://www.businesstoday.in/technology/news/story/heres-how-e-commerce-unicorn-meesho-is-deploying-ai-for-ease-of-business-432051-2024-06-04

Business World. (2025, March 27). *MSMEs Can't Bear Rs 1.5 Lakh Annual Compliance Cost Amid IMS Rules*. (A. Sharma, Editor) Retrieved from Business World: https://www.businessworld.in/article/msmes-cant-bear-rs-15-lakh-annual-compliance-cost-amid-ims-rules-551894

CCI. (2023). *CCI Report.* CCI. Retrieved from https://www.cii.in/PublicationDetail.aspx?enc=zrcmdCxHMWEswep2zYcA3Vzk/ERmDwk1dkBmDlC6H0ag0JBIhqRVKXVTEH3sTmVfqI8AmPd0VkJkGjCk+92kKLipECaJcEJ+s2RLJUPd1QrOn1agl61sgNk75SVWZYW+PxVq6CGljo63XHLA5gLEyVUcGwsGLnqirsEYREThAyTRqd0NncccRRV3yHRr++9A

David, G., & Sirmon, M. A. (2010). Resource Orchestration to Create Competitive Advantage: Breadth, Depth, and Life Cycle Effects. *Journal of Management*. Advance online publication. DOI: 10.1177/0149206310385695

Digital Personal Data Protection Act. (2024). *Digital Personal Data Protection Act.* Government of India.

DiMaggio, W. W. (1983). The Iron Cage Revisited: Institutional Isomorphism and Collective Rationality in Organizational Fields. *American Sociological Association*, 147-160.

Economic Times Online. (2023, April 25). *AI and Privacy: The privacy concerns surrounding AI, its potential impact on personal data*. Retrieved from Economic Times: https://economictimes.indiatimes.com/news/how-to/ai-and-privacy-the-privacy-concerns-surrounding-ai-its-potential-impact-on-personal-data/articleshow/99738234.cms?from=mdr

Einav Peretz-Andersson, S. T. (2024). Artificial intelligence implementation in manufacturing SMEs: A resource orchestration approach. *International Journal of Information Management.*

Esposito, A. (2021, July 16). *1822 Denim Quadruples Conversions with AI Fit Technology.* Retrieved from Retail Touch Points: https://www.retailtouchpoints.com/topics/digital-commerce/e-commerce-experience/1822-denim-quadruples-conversion-with-ai-fit-technology

Farzaneh Shoushtari, E. G. (2021). Improving Performance of Supply Chain by Applying Artificial Intelligence. *International Journal of Industrial Engineering and Operational Research.*

FICCI. (2023, October). *FICCI Report on SMEs in India.* Retrieved from FICCI: https://www.ficci.in/study_details/23825

Flipkart. (2024, September 25). *Unleashing the Power of AI: Transforming E-commerce and Beyond – Insights from Mayur Datar, Flipkart's Chief Data Scientist.* Retrieved from Flipkart Stories: https://stories.flipkart.com/ai-qna-mayur-datar/

Forbes India. (2024, December 11). *How Nykaa is taking on intensifying competition in the beauty industry*. (N. Thakker, Editor) Retrieved from Forbes India: https://www.forbesindia.com/article/billionaires/how-nykaa-is-taking-on-intensifying-competition-in-the-beauty-industry/94824/1

Frobes India. (2021, Spetember 7). *Moglix: How Rahul Garg built an unexpected unicorn*. (M. Balachandran, Editor) Retrieved from Forbes India: https://www.forbesindia.com/article/startups/moglix-how-rahul-garg-built-an-unexpected-unicorn/68373/1

ICRIER. (2025). *AI Markets and Competition in India*. Center for Internet and Digital Economy. ICRIER. Retrieved from https://icrier.org/pdf/AI-Markets-and-Competition-in-India.pdf

IEBF. (2022, November 10). *The Open Network for Digital Commerce (ONDC) Initiative*. Retrieved from IBEF: https://www.ibef.org/blogs/the-open-network-for-digital-commerce-ondc-initiative

Inc42. (2024, Feburary 11). *Nykaa Q3: Beauty Segment Powers Company To Yet Another Profitable Quarter*. (A. Pushkarna, Editor) Retrieved from Inc42: https://inc42.com/buzz/nykaa-q3-beauty-segment-powers-company-to-yet-another-profitable-quarter/#:~:text=Revenue%20from%20operations%20surged%2026.7,fared%20on%20the%20financial%20front

India, A. I. (2021a, November 19). *Bihar's strengthening AI footprint*. Retrieved from IndiaAI: https://indiaai.gov.in/article/bihar-s-strengthening-ai-footprint

India, A. I. (2021b, December 27). *How the adoption of AI led BigBasket to success*. Retrieved from IndaAI: https://indiaai.gov.in/article/how-the-adoption-of-ai-led-bigbasket-to-success

India, A. I. (2022a, Feburary 14). *How Liscious revolutionised the meat industry with AI*. Retrieved from IndiaAI: https://indiaai.gov.in/article/how-liscious-revolutionised-the-meat-industry-with-ai

India, A. I. (2022b, Feburary 03). *PharmEasy's AI and analytics advances online healthcare*. Retrieved from IndiaAI: https://indiaai.gov.in/article/pharmeasy-s-ai-and-analytics-advances-online-healthcare

Jacques Bughin, J. S. (2018). *Notes from the AI frontier: Modeling the impact of AI on the world economy*. McKinsey Global Institute.

Jadhav, D. S. (2021). *Understanding Artificial Intelligence Adoption, Implementation, and Use in Small and Medium Enterprises in India*. Walden Dissertations and Doctoral Studies.

Kathuria, R. M. (2020). *Implications of AI on the Indian economy*. Indian Council for Research on International Economic Relations.

KhataBook. (2025). *KhataBook Homepage*. Retrieved from KhataBook: https://khatabook.com/

KPMG. (2023, June). *2023 KPMG Generative AI Survey*. Retrieved from KPMG: https://kpmg.com/us/en/articles/2023/generative-artificial-intelligence-2023.html#:~:text=Prioritization%20of%20risk%20management%20has,their%20headcount%20will%20likely%20expand

Locus. (2025). *About Us*. Retrieved from Locus: https://locus.sh/about/

Manish, R., & Sharma, D. S. (2014). *Evolution of e-commerce in India: Creating the bricks behind the clicks*. PWC.

Mckinsey Global Institute. (2017). *Artifical Intelligence: The Next Digital Frontier. Mckinsey Global Institute: Discussion paper*. Mckinsey & Company.

Ministry of Micro. Small & Medium Enterprises. (2023). *Annual Report 2023-2024*. Government of India.

Morgan Stanley. (2017, October). *India's e-commerce market to grow 30% to $200 billion by 2026: Morgan Stanley*. Retrieved from India Brand Equity Foundation (IBEF): https://www.ibef.org/research/case-study/india-s-e-commerce-market-to-grow-30-to-200-billion-by-2026-morgan-stanley

Murphy, C. B. (2024, June 06). *Fixed-Income Security Definition, Types, and Examples*. (M. R. Julius Mansa, Editor) Retrieved December 18, 2024, from Investopedia: https://www.investopedia.com/terms/f/fixed-incomesecurity.asp

Nasscom. (2025). *Transforming India's Technology SMEs for a Digital Future: Navigating the AI Frontier.* Nasscom.

National Stock Exchange of India. (2024). *Report on Corporate Bond Markets*. NSE. Retrieved from https://nsearchives.nseindia.com/web/sites/default/files/inline-files/NSE_Assocham_Corporate_Bond_Report_2024.pdf

NewsRoom. (2024, November 12). *The Hidden Costs of AI Implementation in Small Businesses*. Retrieved from Mordern Diplomacy: https://moderndiplomacy.eu/2024/11/12/the-hidden-costs-of-ai-implementation-in-small-businesses/

Oanh, V. T. (2024). Evolving Landscape Of E-Commerce, Marketing, and Customer Service: The Impact of Ai Integration. *Journal of Electrical Systems*, *20*(3), 1125–1137.

Pack8. (2023). *Live now! The Great Indian Plastic Packaging Dump*. Retrieved from Pack8: https://www.pack8.in/blogs/3?title=Live+now%21+The+Great+Indian+Plastic+Packaging+Dump&id=3

Pack8. (2024). *But is the packaging sustainable? Consumers want to know*. Retrieved from Pack8: https://www.pack8.in/blogs/4?title=But+is+the+packaging+sustainable%3F+Consumers+want+to+know.&id=4

Parsani, P. (2024, Feburary 23). *Beauty and the Bot: How Sephora Reimagined Customer Experience with AI*. Retrieved from Cut The SAAS: https://www.cut-the-saas.com/ai/beauty-and-the-bot-how-sephora-reimagined-customer-experience-with-ai

Prismetric. (2024, December 6). *How AI is Transforming Ecommerce Business in 2025*. Retrieved from Prismetric: https://www.prismetric.com/ai-in-ecommerce/

Public, A. W. S. (2018, June 18). *AWS EdStart Launches in India to Bring Tech to Classrooms*. Retrieved from AWS: https://aws.amazon.com/blogs/publicsector/aws-edstart-launches-in-india-to-bring-tech-to-classrooms/

PWC & FICCI. (2022). *AI in Indian financial services*. Feburary. Retrieved from https://www.pwc.in/assets/pdfs/research-insights/2022/ai-adoption-in-indian-financial-services-and-related-challenges.pdf

Ra'ed Almashawreh, M. T. (2024). AI Adoption in Jordanian SMEs: The Influence of Technological and Organizational Orientations. *Global Business Review*.

Rescon Partners. (2025). *Omnichannel: Bringing the World to Rural Doorsteps*. Retrieved from Rescon Partners: https://www.resconpartners.com/fb-2933/#:~:text=Vernacular%20language%20support:%20Meesho%20added,from%20non%2DEnglish%20speaking%20regions

Samuel Fosso Wamba, S. A. (2015). How 'big data' can make big impact: Findings from a systematic review and a longitudinal case study. *International Journal of Production Economics*, •••, 234–246.

Sanjeev, S., & Ingalagi, R. R. (2021). Artificial Intelligence (AI) adaptation: Analysis of determinants among Small to Medium-sized Enterprises (SME's). *IOP Conference Series: Materials Science and Engineering*. Montreal, Canada: IOP.

Spittlehouse, R. (2024, June 27). *Public Crowd Group*. Retrieved from Exploring the Business Benefits of Generative AI: https://pcg.io/insights/exploring-business-benefits-generative-ai/

Stagliano, A. (2021, October 04). *Technology Is The Future of Fashion, Here's Why*. Retrieved from 1822denim: https://1822denim.com/blogs/the-denim-diary/technology-is-the-future-of-fashion-heres-why

TechCrunch. (2024, November 24). *AI helps India's Meesho cut some customer call costs by 75%*. (M. Singh, Editor) Retrieved from TechCrunch: https://techcrunch.com/2024/11/26/ai-helps-indias-meesho-cut-customer-call-costs-by-75/

The Clearing Corporation of India Ltd. (n.d.). *CCIL Broad and Liquid Index for Indian Bond Markets*. Retrieved from https://www.ccilindia.com/documents/43866/1293307/CCIL%20Bond%20Index%20Methodology_1716298351593.pdf

The Hindu. (2024, July 12). *Kerala offering incentives to AI-driven MSMEs and companies, says CM*. Retrieved from The Hindu: https://www.thehindu.com/news/national/kerala/kerala-offering-incentives-to-ai-driven-msmes-and-companies-says-cm/article68392149.ece

Toluwalase Vanessa Iyelolu, E. E. (2024). Driving SME innovation with AI solutions: overcoming adoption barriers and future growth opportunities . *International Journal of Science and Technology Research Archive*, 036–054.

Udaan. (2025). *About Us - Udaan*. Retrieved from Udaan: https://udaan.com/about-us

UNCTAD. (2024). *Digital economy report 2024 - Shaping an environmentally sustainable and inclusive digital future*. UNCTAD.

Unicommerce. (2022, feburary 14). *Why an Inventory Management Software is a Must-have for an E-commerce Business*. Retrieved from Unicommerce: https://unicommerce.com/blog/why-ecommerce-businesses-needs-inventory-management-software/

Viswanath Venkatesh, M. G. (2003). User Acceptance of Information Technology: Toward a Unified View. *Management Information Systems Research Center, University of Minnesota*, 425-478.

Zoho Analytics. (2023, November 6). *The 15% difference: How data analytics boosts small business sales*. (Sanjay, Editor) Retrieved from Zoho: https://www.zoho.com/blog/analytics/the-15-difference-how-data-analytics-boosts-small-business-sales.html

Chapter 13
Harnessing the Future:
Emerging AI Trends Shaping SME Growth in Emerging Markets

Shubham Garg
https://orcid.org/0009-0004-1692-0060
Christ University, India

Prathiba Giri
https://orcid.org/0000-0002-9700-4918
Christ University, India

ABSTRACT

With AI revolutionizing industries, SMEs in emerging markets can tap into its power for sustainable growth, operational efficiency, and enhanced customer experiences. This chapter explores AI-driven automation, predictive analytics, and personalized interactions, addressing challenges like technical skills, data availability, and cost. By adopting AI strategically, SMEs can overcome barriers, compete globally, and drive innovation, ensuring long-term success in the evolving digital economy.

INTRODUCTION

Small and medium-sized enterprises are the backbone of developing economies. SMEs have contributed to creating employment, innovating, and enhancing GDP growth in these markets. However, systemic challenges in such markets weigh on SMEs: limited access to financing, technological underdevelopment, operational inefficiencies, and the lack of skilled manpower. Such constraints inhibit the ability of these firms to scale, compete globally, and sustain growth. The future today becomes a better world with the advent of digital and connectivity. With AI

DOI: 10.4018/979-8-3693-9611-7.ch013

deployment, SMEs have the chance to cut across these boundaries and find their way up as dynamic players in certain industries.

Artificial intelligence-one would think only possible with behemoths and the likes of large corporations with deep pockets and extensive infrastructure-is slowly morphing into a democratizing force. Its accessibility and affordability have gone up significantly in recent years; hence, the highest-level AI technologies and solutions became feasible for a small enterprise even with resource-poor emerging markets. This chapter develops the transformation that AI could undergo for SMEs, especially its emerging trends affecting their growth curve, operational efficiency, and innovation curves. It also wants to give SMEs a roadmap to navigate the barrier of AI adoption and well position them for taking advantage of sustainable growth opportunities resulting from this technology.

This chapter rationale is brought about by the developing understanding that, despite the challenges facing the entity, SMEs have great potential for catalyzing economic growth in emerging markets. The greater availability of AI tools offers SMEs a unique opportunity to bypass some of the classical obstacles to growth and reach the global markets. This chapter attempts to bridge an important gap by providing evidence of tangible benefits of AI adoption for SMEs, analysis of key trends, discussion of barriers, and recommendation of action strategies for smooth integration.

The chapter has several objectives:. It first addresses the current and emerging applications of AI in SMEs across various sectors as a demonstration of how AI-driven automation, predictive analytics, and customer personalization change traditional business models. Second, it reveals specific challenges SMEs face when adopting AI, such as constrained technical expertise, high implementation costs, and issues with data quality. It addresses the strategic recommendations on how to mitigate these challenges and calls for scalable, incremental adoption approaches. Emphasis needs to be made regarding partnerships with the right people involved in technology provision, research institutions, and government initiatives. Finally, ethical and regulatory dimensions are elicited on the implementation process, recommending transparency, fairness, and accountability while implementing an AI solution.

AI adoption is already making huge strides into the most critical business functions for SMEs. For instance, automation technologies are making routine work such as inventory management, billing, and customer support much easier and more manageable; thus, SMEs can use their resources much more effectively. AI-based chatbots with automated billing can enable SMEs to offer better customer service, minimize operational bottlenecks, and empower them to focus on strategic activities. Predictive analytics similarly allows the businesses to predict the trend of a market, optimize the level of the inventory, and sharpen the marketing approach through data-driven insights. All these capabilities can be found extremely useful for the SMEs operating in emerging economies. This is primarily because the decision-making process under such economies typically relies on less or even older information.

AI is changing the SME landscape in personalized customer engagement. This is because through machine learning algorithms, it can know customer preferences and behavior and deliver targeted marketing campaigns, product recommendations, and tailored services. Such personalization enriches the customer experience and also fosters loyalty for the brand, which is of extreme importance to SMEs in competitive markets. Last but not least, AI is transforming the very landscape of financial management for SMEs, particularly in those areas that have no comprehensive access to traditional banking systems. The AI-based fintech solutions will assist SMEs in credit assessment, cash flow optimization, and planning for resource needs, which will increase the chances of raising funding and resource management.However, the road to AI adoption comes with a bundle of challenges. In most SMEs, technical capability to implement and manage AI solutions appropriately is absent. This skill gap requires training workers, working closely with technology companies, and accepting user-friendly AIaaS. Finally, availability and quality of data can be major problems since AI works best on datasets that are good and robust. SMEs can meet this challenge through the use of open-source datasets, a cloud-based data management system, or data sharing with other corporations.

Cost is one of the most important barriers for most SMEs, especially those operating on shoestring budgets. Most AI solutions require some form of initial investment in technology infrastructure, which can be daunting for resource-constrained enterprises. To this end, SMEs can explore scalable, cloud-based AI solutions that offer flexibility and cost efficiency. Government incentives and support programs for digital transformation can also help ease the financial burden on SMEs.

Ethical and regulatory implications also form another major aspect of adopting AI. The deeper AI gets interwoven with hiring processes, customer interfaces, and decision-making systems, the more transparent, fair, and accountable the operations of an SME should be. This chapter identifies the relevance of ethical AI and provides some overview of the developing regulatory structures within different emerging markets. Compliance with such frameworks fosters stakeholder trust and reduces possible risks when adopting AI.

This chapter contributes to the literature by going beyond the theoretical discussion, and instead provides a practical roadmap for SMEs that wish to exploit the potential of AI. It supports an incremental approach to AI adoption, beginning with small, manageable projects that produce quick returns on investment. This way, through proof-of-concept initiatives, SMEs can establish feasibility and benefits of AI and thereby build confidence to scale up their AI capabilities. Partnerships with AI startups, research institutions, and government programs can further facilitate this transition, providing SMEs with the resources and expertise needed to succeed.

In addition, it places its discussion within a wider sustainable development perspective, specifically identifying how AI can drive long-run value creation for SMEs. Strategic adoption of AI would help SMEs to operate more efficiently, innovate, and expand into emerging market opportunities. These improvements benefit the enterprises and relate to broader economic growth and achievement of the global sustainability ambitions.

This will act like a roadmap for the SMEs in the emerging markets to demystify their AI adoption. By the end of this chapter, this will be able to enable the SMEs to understand the prevailing trends, issues, and specific solutions that allow for full potential and achievement of sustainable growth. It is a transformation journey, not just a technological shift, in how these enterprises operate, compete, and thrive in an increasingly digital world. SMEs can leverage AI power to drive innovation, resilience, and success in the global economy through strategic planning, continuous learning, and collaboration.

These next sections of the chapter extend this theme in detailing how AI is being applied within various sectors, overcoming obstacles to SMEs' adoption of this technology, and what such long-term consequences may mean for those same SMEs to operate within emerging markets. It is in this respect that this chapter was designed and drafted to energize and mobilize SMEs equipped with such knowledge and armoury of tools and means for AI adoption.

THEORETICAL FRAMEWORK: FOUNDATION FOR AI ADOPTION BY SMES

Artificial intelligence becomes increasingly the central pillar for innovation and competition in various industries. The emerging market SMEs can adapt to AI since this provides them with a strategic opportunity to improve efficiency, enhance innovation, and improve on decision-making. However, AI adoption involves gaining a richer understanding of its underlying complexities, which makes the application multidimensional and requires drawing upon established theories and models used to examine technological, organizational, and environmental factors. This theoretical framework uses the Resource-Based View (RBV), Diffusion of Innovations (DOI) theory, the Technology-Organization-Environment (TOE) framework, Sociotechnical Systems (STS) theory, and the Dynamic Capabilities Framework for a more holistic analysis of AI adoption by SMEs.

Resource-Based View (RBV)

The resource-based view of the firm, Barney (1991), bases its argument on the use of valuable, rare, inimitable, and non-substitutable (VRIN) resources in quest of competitive advantage. In this respect, SMEs rely crucially on the source of AI technologies to bring about value creation through operational efficiency, customer engagement, and innovativeness. For example, CRM system tools based on AI assist the SMEs to obtain a better grasp of the customers' preferences to be able to apply more tailored approaches, which therefore pursues loyalty and better sales.

Despite its high adoption in emerging markets, application of RBV faces resource limitations. In such contexts, SMEs lack the financial capital, skilled workforce, or technical infrastructure to acquire and implement AI solutions well. The RBV, as argued by Priem and Butler (2001), provides a sound foundation for the understanding of the internal resources' utilization but completely overlooks the problems that exist in the external environment such as infrastructural challenges or regulatory constraints. The case is worse in the emerging markets where SMEs are faced with the challenge of obtaining AI technologies because the solutions lack affordability and also the AI practitioners.

Extending the RBV to include external environmental factors, Newbert (2007) suggests a more nuanced understanding of resource-based advantages, requiring complementary external resources, such as partnerships with technology providers or government support. In this regard, while the RBV underlines the strategic importance of AI as a resource, its practical application in SMEs requires integration with other frameworks that address external factors.

Diffusion of Innovations (DOI) Theory

The DOI theory by Rogers (1962) provides a behavioral perspective on how new technologies are adopted in organizations. This model identifies five key attributes that influence the adoption decision: relative advantage, compatibility, complexity, trialability, and observability. For SMEs in emerging markets, AI's relative advantage is evident in its ability to automate repetitive tasks, reduce operational costs, and provide predictive insights.

Compatibility with existing business processes and organizational goals is another driving factor for adoption. For example, AI tools that are compatible with existing ERP systems will significantly enhance operational efficiency. Another critical factor is observability-that is, the ability to witness tangible benefits-and SMEs are more likely to adopt AI when they see positive outcomes from early adopters within their industry.

However, complexity often is a significant barrier. SMEs may find AI technologies difficult to understand or implement, especially in markets where technical expertise is limited. Moore and Benbasat (1991) note that perceived complexity can be a barrier to adoption even when the relative advantage is apparent. Moreover, trialability, which is an important factor for SMEs, is likely to be limited by the unavailability of affordable pilot programs or sandbox environments for testing AI solutions.

Although DOI offers insight into adoption behavior, it has the drawback of concentrating on individual and organizational perceptions rather than addressing structural and contextual challenges. Scholars such as Lyytinen and Damsgaard (2001) argue that DOI needs to be supplemented by frameworks that consider broader organizational and environmental dynamics, such as the TOE framework.

Technology-Organization-Environment (TOE) Framework

The Technology-Organization-Environment framework, as developed by Tornatzky and Fleischer in 1990, covers three interconnected contexts that try to grasp all the elements that might influence technology adoption.

1. Technological Context: Refers to the apparent benefits of AI solutions, its complexity, and how compatible it appears to be within the organization and its context in SMEs; NLP as well as ML are perceived technologies that allow and enhance automation within decision-making tasks. The overall complexity of integrating these technologies might deter its utilization, especially to SMEs constrained by resources.
2. Organisational Context: Commitment by the leadership, finances available and workforce capabilities are some of the other areas. For example, the level of willingness in adopting AI for SMEs would be higher when led by a visionary leader. In addition, the availability of finance and talent are also very key factors that significantly influence the degree of preparedness for AI. According to Baker (2012), the organisational readiness shapes the degree of preparedness during the adoption process of technology.
3. Environmental Context: Regulatory policies, competitive pressures, and technological infrastructure are all external factors that are very important. In emerging markets, for example, poor digital infrastructure and limited government support often prevent AI solutions from scaling up. Competitive pressure can be a catalyst, however, as SMEs wish to remain relevant in an increasingly dynamic market.

4. The strength of the TOE framework lies in its capturing of the intertwined internal factors, external factors, and their interaction. On the other hand, it has been criticized for oversimplifying the dynamics. Zhu et al. (2006) further comment that the linear approach of the framework may not be able to capture technology adoption as an iterative and evolutionary process, especially within the complex environment of emerging markets.

Sociotechnical Systems (STS) Theory

The Sociotechnical Systems (STS) theory, as introduced by Trist and Bamforth in 1951, is about the interdependence of technical and social systems within organizations. This theory is particularly relevant for AI adoption because it highlights the importance of aligning technological advancements with organizational culture and workforce capabilities.

Organisation workflows, employee roles, and decision-making may be significantly altered when implementing AI. For instance, automating routine activities through AI can sometimes be met with resistance from the workforce due to the fear of job displacements. Mumford (2006) argues that potential social concerns regarding technology adoption must be handled through effective communication and involvement in the decision-making process.

The ethical considerations of AI include data privacy and algorithmic fairness and are a core concern for SMEs. From the STS theory, it is realized that AI systems need to meet technical efficiency requirements and societal values and ethical standards. According to Leavitt (1965), the failure to look at the human aspects of technological change leads to suboptimal results, including low morale among the employees and resistance to changes.

However, while the STS theory is very enlightening about the human-technology interface, it often lacks prescriptive strategies for the specific challenges faced by SMEs. Researchers like Bostrom and Sandberg (2009) are of the view that STS theory should be integrated with more action-oriented frameworks, like the Dynamic Capabilities Framework, to provide practical guidance for the management of technological change.

Dynamic Capabilities Framework

The Dynamic Capabilities Framework, which was proposed by Teece et al. in 1997, focuses on the ability of an organization to sense opportunities, seize them, and reconfigure resources to adapt to a changing environment. The framework is quite relevant for AI adoption in SMEs because it emphasizes the need for agility and continuous learning in dynamic markets.

AI technologies empower SMEs to identify trends in advance, improve operations, and enter new markets. Predictive analytics is an example, whereby a company can predict its customer's needs and adapt to offer them. But the creation of dynamic capabilities calls for enormous investments in employee training, organization design, and technology infrastructure. Helfat and Peteraf (2003) note that it is because of resource-based limitations that most SMEs cannot build these capabilities.

Add to this the lack of supporting ecosystems, such as industry collaboration or governmental incentives in emerging markets, and the challenge is enhanced. On the other hand, SMEs that master dynamic capabilities are much better prepared to make use of AI for long-run competitive advantage. According to Pavlou and El Sawy (2011), " a culture of innovation and adaptability is key to maintaining a competitive advantage in fast-changing markets.".

Integrated Framework for AI Adoption in SMEs

However, while each of the above theories has its value, its inability to move further beyond its limitations points to the need for an integrated approach. For example, the combination of the RBV and TOE frameworks can address internal capabilities and external constraints at the same time, thus providing a balanced view of adopting AI. Similarly, integration of STS theory with Dynamic Capabilities Framework would better match technological advantages with workforce development and organizational agility.

A blended framework further permits the inclusion of ethical concerns and other contextual aspects, including socio-economic and infrastructural challenges. Actually, Venkatesh et al. (2003) note that combining multiple frameworks would greatly help adoption studies explain complex environments like emerging markets.

For instance, an SME adopting AI in an emerging market may make use of RBV so that it identifies AI as its strategic resource, may employ the DOI framework for mitigating adoption barriers, may apply the TOE framework to analyze external and organizational readiness and draw on STS theory towards ensuring this competitive advantage is also aligned with human and ethical considerations. The Dynamic Capabilities Framework can provide guidance on sustaining competitive advantage through continuous innovation and adaptability.

This synthesis is to facilitate exploring ways to adopt AI in SMEs sustainably and inclusively. Through bridging the theoretical gaps and forming actionable insights, this paper serves as a valuable tool for researchers, practitioners, and policymakers in fostering the adoption of AI in SMEs.

CONCEPTUAL DEVELOPMENT

Introduction

In the light of conceptualization of a framework that describes this phenomenon of adoption of AI for SMEs, established theories will have to be synthesized and conciliated with contemporary trends. Within the RBV, TOE framework, DOI theory, as well as in the Dynamic Capabilities Framework, this section makes a case regarding the fact that AI adoption is shaped by how internal capabilities intertwine with various external pressures under dynamic adaptability.

This conceptual model aims to explain the varying rates and outcomes of AI adoption among SMEs by emphasizing constraints they face in the form of limited resources, and the opportunities posed by technological advances. Through integration of theoretical insights and real-world applications, the framework develops an overall understanding of how SMEs can navigate around the problems and use AI for gaining a competitive edge.

Integrating Theoretical Foundations

Resource-Based View (RBV)

The RBV posits that the internal resources of an organization determine its capacity to gain and sustain competitive advantages (Barney, 1991). The proper use of AI technologies functions as unique and valuable resources difficult to replicate. For example, the SME applying AI-driven predictive analytics in the supply chain has a big competitive advantage compared to the use of traditional methods by its competitors. The resource not only makes the organizational process more efficient but also in line with the strategic goals of the organization.

Technology-Organization-Environment (TOE) Framework

The TOE framework suggests that technology adoption depends on the involvement of technological readiness, organizational support, and environmental pressures (Tornatzky & Fleischer, 1990). In this regard, factors affecting SMEs would comprise availability of suitable infrastructure, potential leadership vision, and the dynamics of competition. For example, an SME that is related to access to digital infrastructure and favorable regulatory conditions would more likely perform well with the implementation of AI solutions. This framework then provides a comprehensive view to look at both internal as well as external enablers as well as barriers.

DOI Theory

According to DOI theory by Rogers (1962), the adoption process is described in terms of perceived advantages, compatibility, and complexity. Innovations are likely to be adopted by SMEs if they are compatible with existing systems, easy to implement, and have clear benefits. For instance, a cloud-based AI platform that integrates easily with an SME's existing CRM system reduces complexity and accelerates adoption.

Dynamic Capabilities Framework

The dynamic capabilities framework points to adaptability in changing environments (Teece et al., 1997). In a rapidly changing environment, an SME that innovates, trains its workforce, and readjusts its processes in reaction to the changing technology will better be positioned to implement AI. For example, a retailing SME investing in employee training in AI-driven inventory management is displaying adaptability through aligning the workforce's skills with technological imperatives.

By integrating these theoretical foundations, the conceptual model sets a solid foundation for the analysis of AI adoption in SMEs. It infers that availability is not sufficient but that the resources should align with readiness and adaptability.

Logical Explanations and Reasoning

Resource Constraints and Organizational Readiness

SMEs face a high degree of resource constraints that necessitate an efficient use of financial, technical, and human resources. The adoption of AI is highly dependent on the existence of a well-defined organizational objective and cost-effective solutions. It logically follows that small-scale enterprises with limited budgets will favor AI solutions that yield a high return on investment. For example, low-cost AI tools like Microsoft Azure's AI Builder enable small-scale enterprises to automate processes without capital-intensive investments, thereby showing a practical approach to resource management (Barney, 1991).

External Drivers and Environmental Factors

The most significant external pressures on AI adoption are competition dynamics, customer demand, and regulatory requirements. SMEs that experience a highly competitive environment are more likely to use AI as a differentiator. For example, an SME firm can use AI in the e-commerce sector to provide a personalized product recommendation to meet the expectation of the customer and remain competitive in business. Conversely, regulatory incentives such as tax benefits for adoption of technology in places like India will also encourage the SMEs to invest in the AI solutions as well (Tornatzky & Fleischer, 1990).

Dynamic Adaptability and Workforce Development

For being competitive in that environment of technology, a SME must have knack for adapting it to new things. An organization, thus, putting its effort into creating a workforce with innovative culture is all the odds for embracing AI technology. The following example illustrates: When employees are trained for AI-powered activities through marketing tool-based activities, their operational efficiency of that SME increases, along with their engagement, hence making them successful, because it gets adapted according to changing technologies (Teece et al., 1997).

Examples of the Conceptual Model

Manufacturing Sector

The application of quality control tools driven by AI constitutes an example of RBV and TOE. By employing AI to monitor defects in real time, the SME raises efficiency in operations while keeping costs down. This suggests that the firm is technologically ready and can adapt AI to align with the production objective.

Retail Industry

In the retail sector, for example, SMEs embracing AI-powered chatbots to serve customers perfectly demonstrate the DOI framework. Chatbots allow interoperability with existing CRM systems thereby decreasing complexity and improving customer experience. This application shows the need to align AI capabilities with organizational goals in order to add value.

Logistics and Supply Chain

An SME in the logistics sector which applies AI in a manner to optimize routes manifests flexibility and responsiveness to external shocks like sharp fuel price hikes and regulatory interventions. The application of AI not only brings down the cost of operations but also reflects the firm's ability to exercise dynamic capabilities for long-term growth.

Implications and Applications

Practical for SMEs

Improved Decision Making: SMEs can now analyze large data sets using AI, and the knowledge gleaned from that serves as a basis for strategic decisions. For instance, predictive analytics will enable them to predict the emerging market trends and then respond to the same.

Operational Efficiency: Since routine tasks are automated, SMEs can free up resources for the core function and activities. An AI-powered payroll system, for instance, will reduce administrative burdens and also err on the minimal side.

Customer Engagement: AI engages SMEs towards providing differentiated, personalized experience based on a product recommendation and tastes of a consumer. As an outcome, satisfaction grows and increases in loyalty which marks success. Implications of policies

Policymakers and governments have potential future influence over the growth of AI adoption among SMEs. Subsidization of training programs in AI and digital infrastructure investment will also somewhat soften barriers to adoption and speed it up. There are examples such as the European Union's Digital Innovation Hubs that provide SMEs access to advanced technologies, as well as training in innovation and competitiveness.

The conceptual model adds to the debate in academic fields by integrating and unifying multiple theories into one frame. The model, then, can be used by researchers in studying variations in AI adoption among industries and regions and to gain insight on factors influencing the adoption of technology. One example can be searching for the influence of cultural and economic factors in adopting AI among SMEs in developing countries.

Social Impact

AI adoption in SMEs has significant social implications, including job creation, improved service delivery, and community development. For instance, an SME using AI to connect farmers with markets enhances supply chain efficiency and boosts rural incomes. SMEs can contribute to broader socio-economic development by addressing societal challenges through innovative solutions.

Implications and Future Research

The redefinition of business landscapes through the rapid pace of AI advancement holds great promise for its assimilation into SMEs. This chapter develops the theoretical and conceptual basis on which AI adoption can be premised, with an emphasis on practical implications, theoretical contribution, policy ramifications, and research direction. The discussion above will be used in underlining how AI may be transformative in the business SME environment yet present a way forward towards fruitful assimilation and integration.

Practical Implications for SMEs

AI adoption in SMEs presents transformative potential, but its adoption requires careful planning and strategic focus.

Strategic Resource Allocation:

SMEs generally don't have much in the way of current budgets and resources, and thus, they do require strategic approaches in integrating AI technologies. Large companies, for instance, can afford expensive trial-and-error, whereas SMEs need focused investment in areas where AI is shown to have maximum returns. For instance, one will have personalized marketing strategies and predictive analytics when AI is deployed with CRM capabilities. This indeed impels better sales performance and customer retention. Similarly, AI in inventory management systems decreases overstocking or shortages, which can directly go into the bottom line.

Workforce Upskilling:

Adoption of AI is a technological change but also involves an organizational change. One of the major barriers to adoption is workforce readiness. In SMEs, employees are generally not technically skilled enough to handle AI tools in the best possible manner, which hampers implementation. Workforce upskilling is necessary; it includes basic AI literacy for non-technical staff and advanced training for IT staff. For example, an SME that is implementing machine learning for predictive analytics can train employees in data interpretation and software usage to ensure smoother adoption and improve overall productivity.

Innovation Ecosystem Creation:

AI adoption pushes SMEs to develop an innovation ecosystem wherein employees, partners, and other stakeholders collaborate on experimentation with new technologies. Collaborative efforts, for example, with academic institutions or technology startups, will allow SMEs to access state-of-the-art AI tools with minimum upfront investment. An SME in the consumer goods business could, for example, partner with a university to build AI models to analyze consumer sentiment and develop innovative marketing strategies that connect with their target audiences.

These implications show that AI adoption, although resource-intensive, can be a great catalyst for growth and competitiveness for SMEs when done strategically.

Theoretical Implications

AI adoption further serves as an extension to existing theoretical models. It adds depth and complexity to models that are already established, such as the Resource-Based View (RBV) and the Technology-Organization-Environment (TOE) framework.

Resource-Based View (RBV) - Extension

Originally, the RBV concept is grounded in leveraging tangible and intangible assets for competitive advantage. The adoption of AI in SMEs now underlines that intangible resources do play a role. For example, an organisation that has encouraged an experimentation culture with regards to its digital stature will readily embrace AI-powered tools and other technologies than one that does not embrace change. By highlighting these factors, this chapter contributes to an advanced understanding of the RBV framework, integrating the dynamic role of technology in enhancing organizational capabilities.

Refining the Technology-Organization-Environment (TOE) Framework:

The TOE framework classifies factors determining technology adoption under technological, organizational, and environmental domains. In this way, the AI adoption in SMEs brings in new dimensions into the framework of it. More importantly, there exist sector-specific factors that impact a certain direction due to, say, regulatory pressure or pressure from the demand of the customer for an AI-based service; healthcare SME would face more strict rules and regulations pushing the on-set, whereas customer specific personalization may push on for retail sector SME.

These details outline a more refined framework of TOE with subtleties of sectors and contexts that further make it practical for today's SMEs.

Policy Implications

Policymakers are the actors who can, in the right way, work to ensure a conducive environment so that AI might be adopted in the SMEs. By ameliorating infrastructure and ethical challenges while listening to sectoral barriers, policymakers would be able to promote integration to small businesses.

Affordability and reliability in digital infrastructure form an important enabler for AI adoption. Governments can subsidize or offer grants to the cloud-based AI tools to enable SMEs to have access to high technology without having any prohibitive cost. For instance, "SME Go Digital" in Singapore is one of the initiatives, which offers an opportunity for SMEs to be subsidized and guided financially on their journey toward becoming digitally transformed. Such initiatives minimize entry barriers for resource-constrained SMEs to make AI technologies more accessible to more SMEs.

Ethical AI Standards:

Acceptance of AI also raises ethical concerns, more so on algorithmic biases and data privacy. For SMEs with limited resources, auditing or validation of AI models for fairness and compliance remains challenging. Policymakers can help bridge this gap by providing ethical guidelines and practical toolkits for their use by SMEs in ensuring responsible AI practice. This would cover frameworks such as the European Union's "Ethics Guidelines for Trustworthy AI," which will only benchmark against being able to utilize these AI practices that will align to the expectations of society.

From here, these policy dimensions will then enable the government to build an ecosystem where SMEs are empowered to tap into the full potential of AI in a responsible and effective manner.

Research Implications

Studies of AI adoption must recognize special challenges and opportunities that SMEs face in their contexts. While most of the literature till date has been aimed at large companies, models that apply to SMEs have to be adapted to the special needs and constraints of SMEs.

Sectoral Knowledge

The requirements of AI adoption vary from industry to industry. For example, manufacturing SMEs will focus on predictive maintenance, while retail SMEs will have customer behavior analytics. Future studies should explore the sector-specific applications to develop best practices and scalable solutions.

Longitudinal Studies:

Most of the existing research on AI adoption is based on cross-sectional data, which only captures a snapshot of the process. Longitudinal studies are needed to understand the long-term impact of AI on SME performance, workforce dynamics, and customer satisfaction. For example, studying the evolution of AI integration in an SME over several years could provide insights into challenges faced during scaling and optimization.

Cultural Dimensions:

The role of culture in AI adoption is an area ripe for exploration. Organizational culture, regional norms, and leadership styles significantly influence the adoption process. For example, SMEs in Asia might display greater hierarchical decision-making structures compared to those in Europe, affecting how AI technologies are implemented. Comparative research could offer valuable insights into these cultural dimensions, enabling more effective adoption strategies globally..

Emerging Technologies Convergence:

The incorporation of AI, blockchain, and IoT with AR will open up possibilities for SMEs. Such as, merging AI with the IoT will introduce the possibility of providing real-time visibility of supply chain that will reduce delays while increasing efficiency in supply chains. Future research shall explore how small and medium size enterprises can be enabled to adopt appropriate costs of the emergent converging technologies to establish value and win in the global markets.

Models of Talent Development:

Skills shortage is one of the most important barriers to the adoption of AI. Further research should be conducted on new models that could bridge this gap between academia and industry through joint training programs or AI-based reskilling platforms. For example, future research might report on how real-time workforce training using AI tools will obviate the necessity of consulting AI on occasion.

Standardized metrics for ROI measurements:

For most SMEs, investment in AI requires calculation of ROI as the majority operate on a shoestring budget. It may, therefore, center its research on designing standardized metrics to assess financial and operational benefits reaped from the use of AI to provide a yardstick for the determination of SMEs efficiency in investing.

These research directions point out that AI adoption is dynamic in nature and hence context-specific solutions for SMEs would be dynamic as well.

Ethical AI in SMEs: Innovation and Responsibility in Emerging Markets

The Importance of Ethical AI for SMEs

Responsible AI would therefore mean ethical design, deployment, and usage of AI technology aligned with principles like fairness, transparency, accountability, and inclusivity. Use of AI technology without proper ethics by small- and medium-sized enterprises operating in emerging markets is likely to introduce some untoward effects that are more or less discriminating data breach, or the loss of confidence on part of their customers. Those companies are the first ones most prone to unethical use of AI, as the business is of limited resources, so is experience.

1. Building Trust and Reputation

Trust is the lifeblood of SMEs in the pursuit of building customer relationships in competitive markets. Ethical AI can therefore become a strategic advantage for businesses seeking to build their reputation as responsible entities. Customers increasingly favor organizations that show accountability in the use of technology. For example, an AI system for personal marketing should not engage in stereotype perpetuation or biased content as such will isolate specific audiences and create a brand loyalty crisis.

2. Regulation Compliance and Risk Management

In emerging markets, regulations specific to AI are being drafted; for instance, India has its proposed Personal Data Protection Bill, and Brazil has the General Data Protection Law (LGPD). The adoption of ethical AI will assist SMEs to be in tandem with the change in legal standards and avoid financial penalties and reputational damage. The frameworks ensure that consumer data is important and structured in a manner to be aligned with global standards.

This leads me to the crux of the main ethical concerns regarding the adoption of AI among SMEs, particularly in the developing world, though the advantages of AI are endless:

1. Algorithmic Bias

AI models are a reflection of the biases present in their training data. For example, an SME that uses AI to screen job applications may unintentionally discriminate against certain groups if the model is trained on biased datasets. SMEs should invest in diverse and representative data collection practices that minimize bias and ensure equitable outcomes.

2. Data Privacy and Security

This increased reliance of AI on customer data puts SMEs at the risk of breaches and misuse. Ethical AI demands that data must be anonymized and proper informed consent should be taken to avoid infringement of a customer's personal rights to privacy. For emerging markets, where overall digital literacy may be lower, it will have to focus on educating the consumers regarding how the data is used.

3. Transparency and Explainability

Transparency is crucial for any SME that adopts AI in customer-facing applications, such as chatbots or credit scoring systems. Customers have the right to know about the decisions, particularly those that affect their financial situations or personal reputations. For instance, a fintech SME specializing in microloans for rural communities must be able to provide justification on the rationale of an AI model informing the decision to approve or reject a loan application.

4. Resource Constraints

Unlike large organizations, SMEs typically cannot implement scalable ethical AI systems in terms of financial or technical capabilities. The fact leaves them with no choice but to think of creative ways about how to do this, like partnering with technologists offering low-cost ethical AI-as-a-service.

How to Implement Ethical AI in SMEs

1. Establish Ethics Rules

SMEs should have strict ethical policies defining the application of AI in the organizations. Such guidelines should be aligned with global best practices, like the OECD AI Principles, focusing on human-centered AI, accountability, and robustness.

For example, a retail SME can formulate a policy to avoid using AI pricing algorithms that might take advantage of weak customers at times of high demand.

2. Open-Source Tools

Technologies of open-source AI tool and framework, such as Google's TensorFlow or IBM's AI Fairness 360, enable SMEs to develop cheap models, test, and experiment with AI ethics. The packages include modules already developed for the detection of bias in data and models, data anonymization, and making models explainable, of which SMEs would not have incurred such a high cost for ethical stand.

3. Collaboration with Ethical AI Startups

SMEs can also collaborate with ethical AI start-ups and research institutes. This way, they will be accessing the best expertise and technologies that fit their needs. For instance, a farming SME may collaborate with an AI-start-up that has AI-based crop-prediction models that responsibly take care of the environment.

4. Training and Awareness Programs

Employee training on responsible AI practices can also instill a sense of responsibility within the SME. Through workshops and online courses, workers will learn to recognize and act upon the ethical risks related to the implementation of AI.

Applying Ethical AI in the SMEs' Daily Operations

Ethical AI is already impacting the SMEs of emerging markets as they shift through industries.

1. Health sector

The AI application in SMEs in the healthcare sector ranges from diagnostics and telemedicine to resource allocation. Ethical AI will ensure that diagnostic models are representative, inclusive of all patient demographics. For example, an Indian health-tech SME using AI to predict disease outbreaks needs to ensure its model does not ignore the deprived regions due to biased data.

2. Financial Inclusion

Fintech SMEs employ AI for credit access to the unbanked. Ethical AI practice would be the transparency and fairness of the algorithms in creditworthiness assessments. An example is a microloans offering Brazilian SME that employs AI in examining alternative data sources, such as utility payments, but with respect for the privacy of the data and free from discriminatory practices.

3. Education

AI education platforms allow small businesses to provide differentiated learning. Ethical AI avoids circumstances where the learning styles or demographic status of learners are inadvertently privileged by the platform. For instance, an ed-tech SME in Africa could use AI to modify curricula for rural learners according to cultural and linguistic diversity.

Role of Governments and Policymakers

The only drivers for the adoption of responsible AI in SMEs are governments in emerging markets. As such, an example of this is tax breaks for responsible AI usage and funding towards doing more research on the ethical AI while encouraging public-private partnerships that promote innovation with accountability on the part of the government.

For example, the Model AI Governance Framework established for Singapore by its government gives the SMEs an implementing guide in ethical AI practice. Such a framework can then be adapted for other emerging markets with their special needs, making responsible AI adoption more of a cultural activity.

Future Opportunities and Consequences

The advent of ethical AI in SMEs means tremendous impacts to businesses, customers, and society:

1. Inclusive Growth

By giving priority to fairness and equity, this type of ethics can bridge the gaps concerning some resources and opportunities that SMEs enjoy. For instance, AI can use a firm working on the optimization system of irrigation; therefore, AI enables smallholding farmers to fully benefit from the technical innovations.

2. Enhancing International Competitiveness

Ethical AI adoption places the SME in a good position as a reliable and responsive partner in global markets, hence making it more competitive. Accountable businesses are likely to attract international investors and customers.

3. Changing Industry Practice

Adoption of ethical AI by SMEs can influence collective commitment and responsibility toward responsible innovation by changing standards and best practices in the industries. For instance, e-commerce SMEs would collectively evolve a few ethical guidelines applicable to the adoption of AI systems toward product recommendation by such systems.

CONCLUSION

Theoretical Foundations Supporting AI Integration

From theoretical frameworks-the TAM and the Diffusion of Innovations Theory-aimed to provide knowledge of which factors lead SMEs to adopt AI technologies. It indicated that, using those models, perceived usefulness and ease of use or organizational readiness influence organizational behavior. However, the Resource-Based View highlights how SMEs can use AI as a strategic resource in attaining some kind of competitive advantage.

These theories form the basis for understanding the perception and acceptance of AI by SMEs; they emphasize accessibility, affordability, and sectoral relevance in developing AI solutions for SMEs. The interplay between theoretical constructs and real applications allows SMEs to overcome gaps in adopting technology while countering their constraints in resources.

Practical Application of AI for SMEs

There are also practical applications of AI in SMEs, including areas such as operational efficiency, customer relationship management, supply chain optimization, and decision-making under uncertainty. For example, AI-driven predictive analytics would enable SMEs to better predict market trends, optimize inventory, and identify customer needs. Chatbots and AI-enhanced CRM systems enable SMEs to improve customer engagement and retention with reduced operational costs.

The paper further underlines with a key insight, an important role played by AI in democratizing advanced technologies, enabling resource-constrained SMEs to compete with big corporations. Democratization spreads on to an ability to bring about sustainability-related initiatives: optimum usage of resources, lowering carbon footprint. Using AI is neither a mere operational improvement but a way for SMEs joining a trend in the world, be it sustainability and transition into a more digital economies.

Challenges and barriers to AI adoption

The chapter identifies key adoption barriers of AI as arising from high setup costs, deficiency in technical knowhow, and social issues such as data privacy and the biases of the algorithms. The latter will require solutions to be personalized toward addressing the SME's pursuit of efficiency and responsible application of AI in its operation. The use of the minimum cost appropriate tool mitigates problems that can be encountered; the barriers in operation may arise from budgetary limitation and restricted know-how.

Workforce adaptability is a great challenge, and the majority of SMEs will face some problems in reskilling their workers to fit AI-driven roles. This will therefore call for some rounded transition strategies on the workforce and public-private partnerships in supporting SME upskilling ventures.

The chapter identified many research gaps and gave future directions like developing sector-specific AI models, ethical guidelines with SME in mind, and region-specific policies to grapple with the disparities of AI adoption across the globe. Longitudinal studies were also emphasized for assessing the socio-economic impact of AI on SMEs in terms of job creation, employee productivity, and workplace dynamics.

New questions will arise regarding AI potential to deliver sustainability, to bridge the digital divide, and to better make decisions in the face of uncertainty. Exciting research questions emerge. Actionable insights and tools for SMEs will eventually come from future studies that answer these questions.

Relevance to Discipline

More general: Advancement of knowledge in AI and SME integration

The book contributes to the broader discipline of technology management and organizational behavior through offering an in-depth view of challenges and opportunities in SMEs in order to make AI exploitable in a resource-constrained environment. This view, in itself, opens the scope of research on AI that has hitherto been focused on large organizations, and thus brings attention toward the potential of enabling smaller ones as thriving entities in the digital world.

The application of TAM and RBV theoretical frameworks in the SME context bridges the gap between theory and practice, thus providing a solid foundation for future research. Findings also contribute to academic discourse on technology adoption, underlining the role of contextual factors such as organizational culture, sectoral dynamics, and regional disparities.

Impact on Policy and Industry Practices

These findings have great implications for policy and industry leaders. Governments can apply these insights toward designing interventions targeted toward supporting the adoption of AI by SMEs: subsidies on investments in technology, tax breaks, or workforce training programs. Similarly, industry bodies can apply this insight toward developing AI solutions friendly to SMEs to address their needs and constraints.

The focus on ethical AI practice follows the global discourse in responsible use of technology, thus offering a way to introduce AI into SMEs' practice that respects privacy, transparency, and fairness. Promoting the broader discourse on the implications of AI in society with guidelines and toolkits applicable to SMEs, this chapter further supports the amplification of the discourse.

Contributions to Sustainability and Digital Transformation

The chapter explains how AI can facilitate the sustainability and digital transformation of SMEs. Optimizing resource usage, waste reduction, and the ability to make data-driven decisions for SMEs enables them to be aligned with the global sustainability goals. Alignment in this context not only makes them operationally efficient but also puts them on the right track as responsible contributors to ESG initiatives.

This chapter is very relevant to the global development discourse since it talks about how AI can fill in the gap created by the digital divide. How regional disparities in AI adoption are being addressed in ways that are likely to contribute toward a more general goal of equitable access to technology makes for SMEs in underserved regions also benefiting from digital transformation.

The key insights developed in the chapter point towards the transformative powers of AI, while acknowledging all the associated pains and complexities at the same time. In keeping with its rigor in theory while being highly applicable in practice, the chapter weaves an encompassing framework that is comprehensive both in terms of understanding and response in relation to unique needs of SMEs against the AI trend.

These ideas carry much wider relevance than the SME sector itself, holding lessons for academia, industry, and policy alike. The integration of AI into SMEs will play a key role in defining the future of work, innovation, and sustainability in an increasingly globalized business landscape. This chapter is an early foundational contribution to this longer process of conversation - paving the way toward other explorations and researches.

REFERENCES

Baker, J. (2012). The technology–organization–environment framework. In Dwivedi, Y. K., Wade, M. R., & Schneberger, S. L. (Eds.), *Information systems theory: Explaining and predicting our digital society* (Vol. 1, pp. 231–245). Springer., DOI: 10.1007/978-1-4419-6108-2_12

Barney, J. B. (1991). Firm resources and sustained competitive advantage. *Journal of Management, 17*(1), 99–120. DOI: 10.1177/014920639101700108

Bostrom, N., & Sandberg, A. (2009). Cognitive enhancement: Methods, ethics, regulatory challenges. *Science and Engineering Ethics, 15*(3), 311–341. DOI: 10.1007/s11948-009-9142-5 PMID: 19543814

Helfat, C. E., & Peteraf, M. A. (2003). The dynamic resource-based view: Capability lifecycles. *Strategic Management Journal, 24*(10), 997–1010. DOI: 10.1002/smj.332

Leavitt, H. J. (1965). Applied organizational change in industry: Structural, technological and humanistic approaches. In March, J. G. (Ed.), *Handbook of organizations* (pp. 1144–1170). Rand McNally.

Lyytinen, K., & Damsgaard, J. (2001). What's wrong with the diffusion of innovation theory? In Ardis, M. A., & Marcolin, B. L. (Eds.), *Diffusing software product and process innovations* (pp. 173–190). Springer., DOI: 10.1007/978-0-387-35404-0_10

Moore, G. C., & Benbasat, I. (1991). Development of an instrument to measure the perceptions of adopting an information technology innovation. *Information Systems Research, 2*(3), 192–222. DOI: 10.1287/isre.2.3.192

Mumford, E. (2006). The story of socio-technical design: Reflections on its successes, failures and potential. *Information Systems Journal, 16*(4), 317–342. DOI: 10.1111/j.1365-2575.2006.00221.x

Newbert, S. L. (2007). Empirical research on the resource-based view of the firm: An assessment and suggestions for future research. *Strategic Management Journal, 28*(2), 121–146. DOI: 10.1002/smj.573

Pavlou, P. A., & El Sawy, O. A. (2011). Understanding the elusive black box of dynamic capabilities. *Decision Sciences, 42*(1), 239–273. DOI: 10.1111/j.1540-5915.2010.00287.x

Priem, R. L., & Butler, J. E. (2001). Is the resource-based "view" a useful perspective for strategic management research? *Academy of Management Review, 26*(1), 22–40. DOI: 10.5465/amr.2001.4011928

Rogers, E. M. (1962). *Diffusion of innovations*. Free Press.

Teece, D. J., Pisano, G., & Shuen, A. (1997). Dynamic capabilities and strategic management. *Strategic Management Journal, 18*(7), 509–533. DOI: 10.1002/(SICI)1097-0266(199708)18:7<509:AID-SMJ882>3.0.CO;2-Z

Tornatzky, L. G., & Fleischer, M. (1990). *The processes of technological innovation*. Lexington Books.

Trist, E. L., & Bamforth, K. W. (1951). Some social and psychological consequences of the longwall method of coal-getting. *Human Relations*, *4*(1), 3–38. DOI: 10.1177/001872675100400101

Venkatesh, V., Morris, M. G., Davis, G. B., & Davis, F. D. (2003). User acceptance of information technology: Toward a unified view. *Management Information Systems Quarterly*, *27*(3), 425–478. DOI: 10.2307/30036540

Zhu, K., Kraemer, K. L., & Xu, S. (2006). The process of innovation assimilation by firms in different countries: A technology diffusion perspective on e-business. *Management Science*, *52*(10), 1557–1576. DOI: 10.1287/mnsc.1060.0487

Chapter 14
Impact of Ethical Implications of Using AI and IoT in Hotels

Rishi Sharma
https://orcid.org/0000-0001-8132-4063
Lovely Professional University, India

Sanjeev Kumar
https://orcid.org/0000-0002-7375-7341
Lovely Professional University, India

ABSTRACT

The guest experience, operational effectiveness, and resource management have all improved due to hotels integrating AI and IoT technology. But this integration raises several ethical questions that require serious thought. The purpose of this study is to investigate and evaluate the moral issues raised by the use of AI and IoT in hotels. AI-powered intelligent hotels, the research examines essential ethical problems about privacy, security, transparency, bias, & human interaction. The results of this study demonstrate the delicate balance between the advantages of AI and IoT technologies & the dangers they may provide. Concerns about algorithmic prejudice and discrimination might arise due to the opaqueness of AI decision-making processes, which can negatively impact visitor experiences & employee relationships. Additionally, concerns about visitor experiences and the possible displacement of human workers are raised by the degradation of personal touch in favor of automated services

DOI: 10.4018/979-8-3693-9611-7.ch014

INTRODUCTION

Artificial intelligence, or AI, is the term used to describe the imitation of human intellect in computers that have been designed to resemble human cognitive processes including learning, problem-solving, and judgment. AI is divided into two primary categories:

Narrow AI (Weak AI): This kind of AI is made for certain jobs or uses, such recommendation engines (like Netflix, Amazon), voice assistants (like Siri, Alexa), and self-driving cars.

Strong AI, or general artificial intelligence: could carry out any intellectual work that a person could and would possess cognitive capacities similar to those of humans. Not yet a reality, general artificial intelligence is still a focus of theoretical research.

A branch of artificial intelligence called machine learning aims to provide computers the ability to learn from data and gradually enhance their capabilities without the need for explicit programming. Reinforcement learning, supervised learning, and unsupervised learning are methods used in machine learning. A form of machine learning called "deep learning" makes use of multi-layered neural networks, or "deep neural networks," to extract knowledge from vast volumes of data. Considerable progress has been made in areas including autonomous driving, natural language processing, and picture identification thanks to deep learning. AI is being used in a number of sectors and fields, such as:

- *Healthcare:* Personalized treatment regimens and illness diagnosis via medical imaging.
- *Finance:* Algorithmic trading, fraud detection.
- *Retail:* Chatbots for customer support and tailored suggestions.
- *Automotive:* Predictive maintenance and driverless cars.
- *Education:* individualized tutoring and flexible learning environments.
- Virtual reality experiences and content recommendations for entertainment.

The use of AI presents ethical questions about employment displacement, algorithmic prejudice, privacy, and the effects of automation on society. To guarantee that AI is utilized responsibly and ethically, addressing these issues calls for serious thought and ethical standards. With current research in areas like explainable AI (making AI judgments intelligible to humans), AI ethics, and the integration of AI with other technologies like IoT (Internet of Things) and robotics, it is anticipated that AI will continue to advance swiftly. The network of actual physical objects that have sensors, software, and other technologies integrated into them so they can communicate and share data via the Internet is known as the Internet of Things, or IoT. The Internet of Things refers to a broad category of internet-connected devices, ranging from commonplace items to commercial machinery. Wearables, automobiles, industrial sensors, and smart home appliances are a few examples of these gadgets. IoT devices use sensors to gather data from their environment, which is then sent via the internet. This information may include location data, use trends, ambient parameters (such as humidity and temperature), and more. IoT makes it possible to automate and remotely operate equipment using insights gleaned from data. For instance, industrial IoT systems use real-time production process optimization, while smart thermostats modify temperatures according to occupancy and meteorological circumstances. IoT is used in many different fields and sectors, such as:

- *Smart homes:* are equipped with networked gadgets for energy conservation, entertainment, and home security.
- *Healthcare:* smart medical equipment, wearable health trackers, and remote patient monitoring.
- *Transportation:* traffic control systems, fleet management, and connected automobiles.
- Public safety, environmental monitoring, and infrastructure management are all aspects of smart cities.
- *Industrial Internet of Things (IIoT):* supply chain management, predictive maintenance, and process monitoring and optimization.

The networked nature of IoT devices and their potential vulnerabilities make them a security risk. They frequently run on several platforms and protocols, necessitating the creation of interoperability standards to enable smooth communication and system integration. To secure data and uphold confidence, it is essential to have strong security measures and privacy safeguards in place. It is propelling the digital revolution and opening up fresh possibilities for productivity, creativity, and economic expansion. Future developments in 5G connection to accommodate more IoT devices and apps, edge computing (processing data closer to the source), and AI integration for improved analytics are some of the themes to watch.

Several advantages and conveniences come with the adoption of artificial intelligence (AI) and the Internet of Things (IoT) in the hospitality sector, notably in hotels, for both visitors and hotel owners (Akoka et al., 2017). However, the substantial ethical ramifications of this technical progress also warrant serious thought. IoT gadgets like wearables, personal assistants, and intelligent room controls can capture guest data, possibly leading to privacy and data security problems (Mariani et al., 2018). Visitors can be concerned that improper handling or misuse of their personal information could result in sensitive data breaches (D. Ivanov, 2023). Hotels must have robust data protection procedures, secure data storage, and open data usage rules to overcome these issues. IoT gadgets may monitor visitors' behavior, tastes, and movements while on the hotel grounds (Milwood et al., 2023). It raises concerns about surveillance and invasion of visitors' privacy, even while it may result in better customer service and more customized experiences (Elkhwesky & Elkhwesky, 2022). The correct balance between individualized service and consideration for visitors' privacy must be struck. If AI systems that run hotel operations are educated on biased datasets, they may unintentionally reinforce bias. It may harm visitor services, room allocations, or even employment practices. To remove biases and guarantee fair treatment for all visitors and employees, hotels must routinely audit and improve their AI systems (Wang et al., 2021).

Figure 1. Key Ethical Concerns Associate in AI and IoT Source: (Self-Authored)

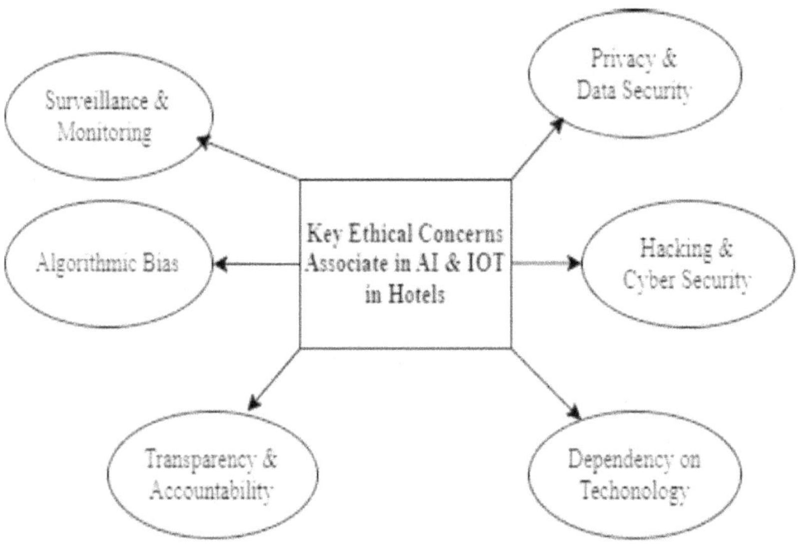

AI algorithms frequently have intricated inner workings that are challenging to comprehend. With knowledge about the decision-making process, it may be easier for visitors and staff to trust AI-driven judgments (Mercan et al., 2021). To be held accountable for any errors or prejudices resulting from the usage of AI, hotels must maintain openness in this area. There may be worries about job displacement among hotel personnel as AI and IoT technology automate some hotel duties (Righetti et al.,

2018). Jobs at the front desk, concierge services, and even cleaning positions might be affected. To adapt to these developments, hotels must think about transferring and retraining their staff, ensuring that technology improves rather than replaces human talent. The loss of the human touch and individualized guest encounters might result from relying too much on AI and IoT. While automation and efficiency have advantages, hotels should ensure that technology enhances the distinctive experiences and close relationships that personnel can offer.

Using IoT devices and AI systems in hotels may increase energy costs and electrical waste. Eco-friendly practices must be prioritized, and hotels must consider how their technological choices will affect the environment. IoT equipment is frequently susceptible to hacking and cyber attacks, which may jeopardize visitor security, privacy, and physical safety. To protect both their customers and their operations from possible intrusions, hotels must implement strong cyber security safeguards (Deel et al., 2023). Using AI and IoT in hotels demands a careful and responsible strategy considering these ethical issues. Hotels may take advantage of technological innovation while respecting the values of confidentiality, equity, openness, and human welfare by confronting these problems head-on (Seraphin, 2020). The link between AI (Artificial Intelligence) and IoT (Internet of Things) in hotels is becoming more revolutionary, improving both guest experiences and operational efficiencies. Smart thermostats, lighting systems, and energy management systems are examples of IoT devices that can collect real-time information on room occupancy, temperature preferences, and energy use. AI algorithms may use this information to optimize energy use, save operating expenses, and improve overall efficiency.

AI-driven systems are able to examine visitor preferences and usage patterns by utilizing Internet of Things data (e.g., temperature settings in rooms, and utilization of amenities). By providing customized recommendations, services, and room settings even before customers ask for them, hotels are able to personalize their guests' stays. Eight themes of consumer perceptions of ethical dilemmas have been found by the study using the triangulation approach (privacy, security, safety, transparency, fairness, socialization, autonomy, and responsibility). Every theme has two explanations: first, ethical questions are raised during the interaction (e.g., concerning ubiquitous surveillance, excessive data, unknown risks, service disclosure, inaccessibility, dehumanization, service selection, and service recovery); second, ethical questions can be raised by the features of ASRs (e.g., concerning privacy invasion, malicious use, malfunctions, unreliability, biased features, job replacement, rigidity, and self-identified solutions) (Lin et al., 2023). IoT sensors may track the condition of equipment in real-time when they are put in hotel infrastructure, such as HVAC systems and elevators. By analyzing sensor data, AI algorithms can forecast maintenance requirements, cutting downtime and guaranteeing that facilities are always operating at their best. By utilizing IoT devices (such as tablets or smartphones in rooms), AI-powered chatbots or virtual assistants may manage room service requests, respond quickly to guest inquiries, provide local suggestions, and provide individualized concierge services. Chatbots for internal communication and HR analytics assist managers in streamlining workflows and increasing employee engagement. By anticipating when equipment requires maintenance, IoT sensors provide predictive maintenance, which keeps it from breaking down. Guests can operate amenities with their voices when a room is equipped with speech recognition technology. In order to provide more individualized services and more focused marketing, data analytics and Customer Relationship Management (CRM) systems also employ AI to learn about visitors' preferences, dislikes, behaviors, and feedback (Das et al., 2024)

ENVIRONMENTAL IMPACT AND SUSTAINABILITY

Hotel energy consumption may be optimized and monitored with the help of AI and IoT devices. These include of energy-efficient appliances, HVAC systems, and smart lighting that are managed by AI algorithms that change settings in response to occupancy and outside factors. When AI and IoT technologies are applied in place of more conventional techniques, research can measure the real savings in energy use and greenhouse gas emissions that result. Analyzing the effects of AI and IoT devices on the environment at every stage of their lifetime, from production to disposal, taking into account aspects like energy consumption, sourcing of materials, and electronic waste management. Performance and environmental sustainability metrics, together with hotel management of environmental performance to build process efficiency, are some of the essential components of hotel environmental sustainability. The main query that comes up is how hotel performance is impacted by ecologically sustainable business practices, and what the key environmental hotel business metrics are (Zorica 2021).

Future developments in artificial intelligence (AI) and related technologies will likely enable more intelligent automation in the travel and tourist industry. Tourism-related intelligent automation is a socio-economic activity that requires theory and practical explanation. The main tenets of this research include designing useful AI, encouraging adoption, assessing the consequences of intelligent automation, and creating a sustainable AI future (Duric & Potočnik Topler, 2021). The scientific community is making a focused effort to assure the beneficial applications of intelligent automation in the tourism sector, and research in these areas helps to create systematic knowledge in this regard (Tong et al., 2022). The selection of AI and IoT technologies that support sustainability objectives raises ethical questions. This entails selecting systems and gadgets with low energy usage, recyclable materials, and little effect on the environment during manufacture. Assessing suppliers' and vendors' environmental policies to make sure they follow sustainable production and operating guidelines while offering AI and IoT technology. One of the government's strategic initiatives to promote the green hotel implementation campaign in Indonesia is the work that has been carried out through the regular awards program, hosted yearly, the National Green Hotel Award. Green hotel practices in Indonesia and potentially other countries will spread more rapidly if future tourist trends reflect a growing inclination towards environmental consciousness and an understanding of the value of eco-labels and green products (Yuniati, 2021). Addressing the moral duty of hotels to reduce electronic waste by recycling or properly disposing of AI and IoT equipment at the end of their useful lives. Resource and energy conservation are positively impacted by environmental communication to similar degrees, while financial and environmental performance is significantly improved by both types of conservation (Sakshi et al., 2020).

Creating AI and Internet of Things solutions with sustainability as a top priority from the outset, taking into account things like energy economy, renewable energy sources, and environmental footprint reduction. Hoteliers can use ethical frameworks to direct the implementation of sustainability-focused CSR activities, such as making public pledges to cut carbon emissions, taking part in renewable energy projects, and aiding regional environmental preservation campaigns. Enhancing ethical behaviors in the adoption of AI and IoT technologies may be achieved by including stakeholders, including visitors, staff, and local communities, in sustainability efforts through awareness campaigns, education programs, and cooperative projects. Making sure that the use of AI and IoT technologies in hotels complies with environmental norms and standards. Following global guidelines and certifications, such as ISO 14001 for environmental management systems and LEED (Leadership in Energy and Environmental Design) for sustainable practices, in order to fulfill moral and legal obligations. Adopting environmental measures is seen by many hoteliers as costly and having little return on investment. An additional barrier to enhancing hotels' green credentials is the belief that modifying employee behavior and management practices to be more ecologically conscious is too complex and yields insignificant benefits (Sloan et al., 2009). Adoption of sustainability innovations is most strongly predicted by hotels and resorts with high levels of environmental opinion leadership. Only a little correlation exists between the hotels' or resorts' perceived relative advantage and trialability (Tiwari & Thakur, 2021).

Pros of Ethical Implications of Using AI and IoT In Hotels

By analyzing preferences and behaviors, providing personalized suggestions, and customizing room settings depending on individual preferences, AI and IoT may enhance the visitor experience, increasing satisfaction. Automating check-in/check-out procedures, housekeeping scheduling, and energy management may streamline operations, resulting in cost savings and increased efficiency. Smart locks, security cameras, and sensors that keep track of visitor and worker movements may all assist in improving security by preventing unauthorized access and guaranteeing visitor safety. Hotels can make knowledgeable judgments about service enhancements, resource allocation, and marketing strategies thanks to AI and IoT's ability to gather and analyze data from guest interactions and operations. To optimize resource use and lessen the hotel's environmental effects, IoT sensors can monitor water and electricity use.

Cons of ethical implications of using AI and IoT in hotels

Visitors may feel uncomfortable with their information being gathered and utilized for multiple reasons without an explicit agreement, so collecting personal data using AI and IoT devices might cause privacy issues (D. Ivanov, 2023). The danger of data breaches and cyber-attacks can increase with the increased connection of IoT equipment, possibly exposing private visitor information. Hotel employees may experience job displacement as automation grows through AI and IoT, especially in areas that may be automated, which might have detrimental socioeconomic effects (Ozdemir et al., 2023). Any technological problems or malfunctions might interfere with guest experiences and services if the hotel primarily depends on AI and IoT to run its operations. AI systems may pick up biases from their training data, which might result in biased employment, service recommendation, and guest profile judgments. AI-powered interactions may come off as unfriendly and impersonal to certain visitors.

Additionally, getting visitor agreements for data gathering and AI-driven personalization might take much work. The creation, upkeep, and disposal of IoT devices can add to electronic waste and environmental issues even while they can help with resource optimization. The expense of implementing and maintaining AI and IoT technologies may prevent smaller hotels or those located in underprivileged regions from utilizing them (Dhiraj et al., 2023).

Past and future of ethical implications using AI and IoT in Hotels

In the past, IoT gadgets in hotel rooms, such as smart thermostats, voice assistants, and webcams, caused severe privacy issues. Guests were concerned about the possibility of their data being captured and abused, resulting in privacy violations(-Kumar et al., 2023). By integrating AI and IoT devices, hotels accumulated vast quantities of guest data, including preferences, habits, and personal information. The problem was to secure this data to avoid hackers and unauthorized access (S. H. Ivanov & Umbrello, 2021). Using AI-powered technologies for duties such as guest check-in and concierge services may raise worries about job displacement among hotel employees. It sparked ethical concerns regarding the influence of automation on people's livelihoods (Giousmpasoglou & Hua, 2020).

In the future, there is a risk of algorithmic bias when hotels deploy AI systems to personalize visitor experiences, where particular guest groups may experience better or worse treatment due to biased training data. It won't be easy to maintain justice and openness in AI systems. Getting customers' informed permission for data collection and usage is essential as hotels incorporate more AI and IoT devices (Ben Youssef & Zeqiri, 2022). Visitors must be aware of the information being gathered about them, how it will be used, and how they may exercise control over that information (Bulchand-Gidumal, 2022). There may be ethical issues with deceit due to the development of increasingly sophisticated AI systems that simulate human-like interactions. Guest interactions with AI systems that they mistake for human personnel may lead to problems with honesty and trust (McCartney & McCartney, 2020). The attack surface for possible cyber security breaches grows as there are more networked devices. A constant issue will be ensuring the security of visitor data and avoiding unwanted assaults on AI and IoT devices. Human autonomy and agency may be reduced if hotels heavily rely on AI and IoT technology for decision-making and customer service (Mercan et al., 2021). It will be crucial to balance automation and retaining human control. Increased energy demand and electrical waste may result from the widespread use of AI and IoT devices. Hotels must embrace sustainable practices and consider how these technologies would affect the environment. While IoT and AI may alter certain hotel occupations, they may also lead to the creation of new positions in management and maintenance. Ensuring workers receive the necessary training for these new positions (Kong et al., 2023). If designed and utilized without consideration for cultural nuances, AI-powered language translation and cultural adaptation may unintentionally reinforce preconceptions or misconceptions.

Challenges in ethical implications of using AI and IoT in Hotels

Enhancing client experiences, increasing operational efficiency, and providing personalized services are advantages of integrating AI and IoT technology in hotels (Mercan et al., 2020). It also brings up several ethical issues that demand careful thought. Guest privacy problems may arise from acquiring guest data through IoT devices like wearable tech, smart thermostats, and room sensors (Elkhwesky & Elkhwesky, 2022). It may cause a sensation of intrusion in visitors to know that their habits and preferences are being observed and evaluated. Hotels collect much private information, such as identification, payment card, and location information. Data security is crucial because of the growing connection brought on by IoT devices, which increases the possible entry sites for attackers. Guests may be at risk for identity theft, financial loss, and other security issues due to a breach. Visitors might need to be made aware of the extent to which AI and IoT technologies are gathering and using personal data (Mercan et al., 2021). Hotels must get informed permission and explicitly explain their data-collecting practices to ensure visitors are happy with the information obtained. Inadvertent bias perpetuated by AI systems has the potential to produce discriminating results. For instance, some populations may be maltreated if facial recognition technology has more excellent mistake rates. To guarantee equitable experiences for every visitor, hotels must ensure their AI systems are impartial and fair.

Figure 2. Challenges of AI Source: (Self-Authored)

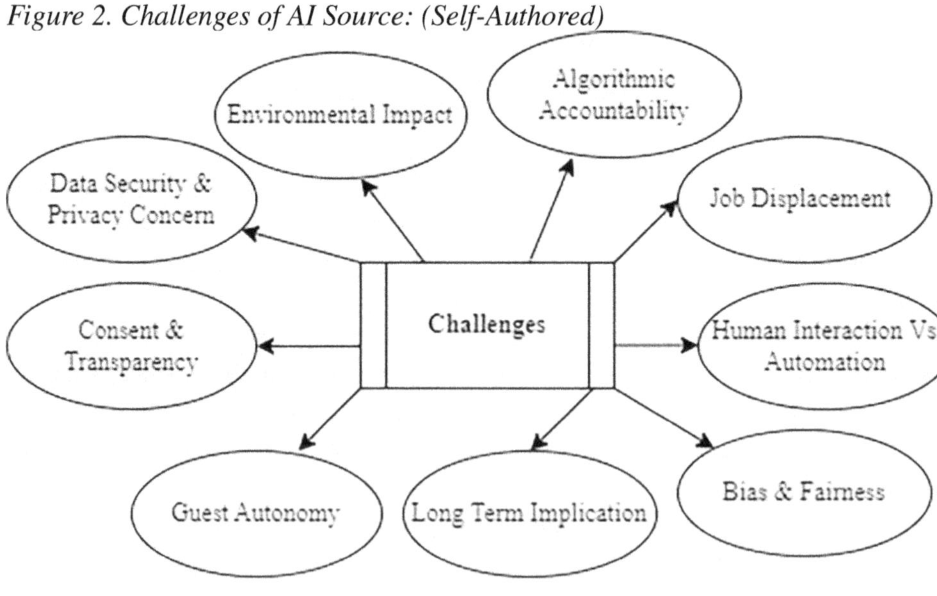

Artificial intelligence (AI) systems' unintentional propagation of prejudice might lead to unequal outcomes. For instance, if facial recognition technology has higher error rates, particular groups may be treated unjustly. Hotels must ensure their AI systems are neutral and fair to provide every visitor with an equitable experience (Nam et al., 2021). Concerns regarding job displacement in the hotel business may arise due to AI and IoT technology use. Automating previously performed hotel employee duties like housekeeping and concierge services is possible. Hotel owners must think about the effects on their staff and provide retraining possibilities. Accountability becomes essential when AI systems make choices that impact the experiences of visitors. There should be procedures in place to explain these judgments and rectify any issues if an AI algorithm is used to determine a guest's preferences for a room or a service suggestion (Wu et al., 2020).

IoT devices may improve hotel energy efficiency by maximizing resource consumption, but they also need continual power connectivity. If not handled properly, the manufacturing and disposal of IoT devices can result in electrical waste and environmental deterioration (Car et al., 2019). There is a chance of decreasing visitor autonomy and freedom of choice as AI technologies are used more frequently in guest encounters. Hotels must provide adjustable alternatives since some visitors may prefer to reject some AI-driven services or maintain control over particular areas of their stay. Although IoT device data collection over time might offer hotels insights to enhance services, it also raises concerns regarding the long-term preservation and use of this data (Nadkarni et al., 2020). Hotels must decide how to manage and whether to keep or erase guest data after the guest's stay.

Limitations of ethical implications of using AI and IoT in hotels

IoT devices gather a ton of data, including preferences, behaviors, and even personal information about visitors. It raises questions regarding unauthorized data access, security breaches, and uninformed or unwelcome surveillance of guests (S. H. Ivanov & Umbrello, 2021). Visitors may be unaware of the full scope of their data collection and usage. Obtaining informed permission becomes difficult when complicated technologies are involved (Belk, 2021). Hotels are susceptible to hacks because they gather essential data. Identity theft and other security breaches can result from unauthorized access to customer information, financial information, or room access systems. IoT devices are frequently connected to the internet, which makes them vulnerable to exploitation and hacking. Cyber-attacks may employ outdated or unprotected equipment as entry points (Gursoy et al., 2023). Biases existing in the training data of AI algorithms can be passed on to the algorithms themselves, producing discriminating results. Inadvertent discrimination based on race, gender, or nationality might result, for example, from AI-powered visitor profiling. The use of IoT technology is not universally accessible or pleasant among visitors. The exclusion of some demographic groups, such as older people or people with impairments, might result from relying primarily on AI and IoT.

There may not be as many options for hiring human staff as when hotels automate more operations using AI and IoT. In places where the hotel sector is essential, this might result in employment losses and economic inequality. Although AI might increase productivity, it may also reduce human contact, which is highly valued in the hotel sector. The quality of visitor encounters might suffer if the human touch of workers is removed. There may be issues with IoT equipment, which would impair guest services. When technology fails, or there are connectivity difficulties, relying too much on it can be inconvenient. Opaque AI decision-making procedures can damage trust. Visitors can feel uneasy about decisions made by mysterious algorithms for which there is no explanation. Rapid technological improvements may cause an IoT device turnover that increases electronic waste. It might not be easy to dispose of and recycle these gadgets properly. Hotels must traverse intricate data protection laws like GDPR and CCPA when gathering and processing visitor data. Financial and legal repercussions may follow non-compliance.

CONCLUSION

Many advantages and prospects exist for improved guest experiences, operational efficiency, and cost savings when artificial intelligence (AI) and the Internet of Things (IoT) are integrated into the hotel sector. Hotels gather and handle enormous quantities of guest information, raising questions about data privacy and security—the need to find a balance between personalization and protecting visitor privacy increases. To minimize dangers, transparent data-gathering procedures, strong encryption, and rigorous cyber security measures are necessary. Ethics issues arise from the possibility of biased decision-making in AI systems, particularly regarding consumer profiling and service suggestions. To guarantee fair and equitable treatment for all visitors, regardless of background or identity, developers must rigorously address algorithmic bias. Artificial intelligence (AI)-)-powered systems replacing human labor may result in unstable employment and less engagement between people. Hotels must proactively offer staff members chances for training and upskilling to adjust to the shifting business environment while maintaining the personal touch many visitors cherish. The reliance on technology also creates vulnerability to system failures, interrupting visitor experiences. A solid contingency plan must be in place to resolve technological issues and ensure a flawless visitor experience.

Furthermore, it's essential to consider how data centers and IoT devices that enable AI systems affect the environment. Hotels should think about ecological practices, including using energy-efficient equipment and properly disposing of their technological trash. In conclusion, even if AI and IoT have the potential to revolutionize the hotel sector, a careful and moral approach is essential to maximizing their advantages while minimizing the hazards involved. Hotels may overcome these difficulties and develop a seamless fusion of technology and hospitality by prioritizing data protection, fairness, interpersonal contact, sustainability, and teamwork.

REFERENCES

Akoka, J., Comyn-Wattiau, I., & Laoufi, N. (2017). Research on Big Data–A systematic mapping study. *Computer Standards & Interfaces*, *54*, 105–115.

Belk, R. (2021). Ethical issues in service robotics and artificial intelligence. *Service Industries Journal*, *41*(13–14), 860–876.

Ben Youssef, A., & Zeqiri, A. (2022). Hospitality industry 4.0 and climate change. *Circular Economy and Sustainability*, *2*(3), 1043–1063. PMID: 35098249

Bulchand-Gidumal, J. (2022). Impact of artificial intelligence in travel, tourism, and hospitality. In *Handbook of e-Tourism* (pp. 1943–1962). Springer.

Car, T., Stifanich, L. P., & Šimunić, M. (2019). Internet of things (iot) in tourism and hospitality: Opportunities and challenges. *Tourism in South East Europe*, *5*, 163–175.

Das, I. R., Talukder, M. B., & Kumar, S. (2024). Implication of Artificial Intelligence in Hospitality Marketing. In Kumar, S., Talukder, M. B., & Pego, A. (Eds.), *Advances in Hospitality, Tourism, and the Services Industry* (pp. 291–310). IGI Global., DOI: 10.4018/979-8-3693-1978-9.ch014

Deel, G., Cain, C., & Cain, L. (2023). Ethical considerations for the future of superhuman artificial intelligence: A viewpoint. *ROBONOMICS: The Journal of the Automated Economy*, *4*, 41–41.

Dhiraj, A., Kumar, S., Rani, D., Grima, S., & Sood, K. (2023). Blockchain Payment Services in the Hospitality Sector: The Mediating Role of Data Security on Utilisation Efficiency of the Customer. *Data*, *8*(8), 123.

Duric, Z., & Potočnik Topler, J. (2021). The Role of Performance and Environmental Sustainability Indicators in Hotel Competitiveness. *Sustainability*, *13*(12), 6574. DOI: 10.3390/su13126574

Elkhwesky, Z., & Elkhwesky, E. F. Y. (2022). A systematic and critical review of Internet of Things in contemporary hospitality: A roadmap and avenues for future research. *International Journal of Contemporary Hospitality Management, ahead-of-print*.

Giousmpasoglou, C., & Hua, T. T. (2020). The use of self-service technologies in budget hotels: The case of Bournemouth. *European Journal of Tourism. Hospitality and Recreation*, *10*(3), 251–261.

Gursoy, D., Li, Y., & Song, H. (2023). ChatGPT and the hospitality and tourism industry: An overview of current trends and future research directions. *Journal of Hospitality Marketing & Management, 32*(5), 579–592. DOI: 10.1080/19368623.2023.2211993

Ivanov, D. (2023). The Industry 5.0 framework: Viability-based integration of the resilience, sustainability, and human-centricity perspectives. *International Journal of Production Research, 61*(5), 1683–1695.

Ivanov, S. H., & Umbrello, S. (2021). The ethics of artificial intelligence and robotisation in tourism and hospitality–a conceptual framework and research agenda. *Journal of Smart Tourism, 1*(4), 9–18.

Kong, H., Wang, K., Qiu, X., Cheung, C., & Bu, N. (2023). 30 years of artificial intelligence (AI) research relating to the hospitality and tourism industry. *International Journal of Contemporary Hospitality Management, 35*(6), 2157–2177.

Kumar, S., Dhiraj, A., Shah, M. A., & Rani, D. (2023). Application of Metaverse in the Hospitality Industry. In *Influencer Marketing Applications Within the Metaverse* (pp. 178–194). IGI Global.

Lin, B., Lee, W., Wise, N., & Choi, H. C. (2023). Consumers' Ethical Perceptions of Autonomous Service Robots in Hotels. *Journal of Hospitality & Tourism Research (Washington, D.C.), 10963480231194693*. Advance online publication. DOI: 10.1177/10963480231194693

Mariani, M., Baggio, R., Fuchs, M., & Höepken, W. (2018). Business intelligence and big data in hospitality and tourism: A systematic literature review. *International Journal of Contemporary Hospitality Management, 30*(12), 3514–3554.

McCartney, G., & McCartney, A. (2020). Rise of the machines: Towards a conceptual service-robot research framework for the hospitality and tourism industry. *International Journal of Contemporary Hospitality Management, 32*(12), 3835–3851.

Mercan, S., Akkaya, K., Cain, L., & Thomas, J. (2020). *Security, privacy and ethical concerns of IoT implementations in hospitality domain*. 198–203.

Mercan, S., Cain, L., Akkaya, K., Cebe, M., Uluagac, S., Alonso, M., & Cobanoglu, C. (2021). Improving the service industry with hyper-connectivity: IoT in hospitality. *International Journal of Contemporary Hospitality Management, 33*(1), 243–262.

Milwood, P. A., Hartman-Caverly, S., & Roehl, W. S. (2023). *A scoping study of ethics in artificial intelligence research in tourism and hospitality*. 243–254.

Nadkarni, S., Kriechbaumer, F., Rothenberger, M., & Christodoulidou, N. (2020). The path to the Hotel of Things: Internet of Things and Big Data converging in hospitality. *Journal of Hospitality and Tourism Technology, 11*(1), 93–107.

Nam, K., Dutt, C. S., Chathoth, P., Daghfous, A., & Khan, M. S. (2021). The adoption of artificial intelligence and robotics in the hotel industry: Prospects and challenges. *Electronic Markets*, *31*, 553–574.

Ozdemir, O., Dogru, T., Kizildag, M., & Erkmen, E. (2023). A critical reflection on digitalization for the hospitality and tourism industry: Value implications for stakeholders. *International Journal of Contemporary Hospitality Management.*

Righetti, F., Vallati, C., & Anastasi, G. (2018). *IoT applications in smart cities: A perspective into social and ethical issues*. 387–392.

Sakshi, , Shashi, , Cerchione, R., & Bansal, H. (2020). Measuring the impact of sustainability policy and practices in tourism and hospitality industry. *Business Strategy and the Environment*, *29*(3), 1109–1126. DOI: 10.1002/bse.2420

Seraphin, H. (2020). Big Data and Analytics in Tourism and Hospitality: Opportunities and Risks. *Journal of Tourism Futures.*

Sloan, P., Legrand, W., Tooman, H., & Fendt, J. (2009). Best practices in sustainability: German and Estonian hotels. In Chen, J. S. (Ed.), *Advances in Hospitality and Leisure* (Vol. 5, pp. 89–107). Emerald Group Publishing Limited., DOI: 10.1108/S1745-3542(2009)0000005009

Tiwari, V., & Thakur, S. (2021). Environment sustainability through sustainability innovations. *Environment, Development and Sustainability*, *23*(5), 6941–6965. DOI: 10.1007/s10668-020-00899-4

Tong, L., Yan, W., & Manta, O. (2022). Artificial Intelligence Influences Intelligent Automation in Tourism: A Mediating Role of Internet of Things and Environmental, Social, and Governance Investment. *Frontiers in Environmental Science*, *10*, 853302. DOI: 10.3389/fenvs.2022.853302

Wang, G., Tang, I. L., Chan, E., & Chan, W. H. (2021). The coverage of AIOT based functional service: Case study of Asian futuristic hotel. *University of South Florida M3 Center Publishing, 5*(2021), 99.

Wu, F., Lu, C., Zhu, M., Chen, H., Zhu, J., Yu, K., Li, L., Li, M., Chen, Q., & Li, X. (2020). Towards a new generation of artificial intelligence in China. *Nature Machine Intelligence*, *2*(6), 312–316.

Yuniati, N. (2021). Green Hotel Concept and Practices in Indonesia. *E-Journal of Tourism*, *184*. Advance online publication. DOI: 10.24922/eot.v8i2.76346

Chapter 15
Leveraging Circular Economy Principles and Emerging Technologies for Future Trends in Sustainable Business Models: A Roadmap to Net-Zero Emissions

S. Thandayuthapani
https://orcid.org/0000-0001-9559-745X
Kristu Jayanti College, India

P. Thirumoorthi
https://orcid.org/0000-0001-5783-3984
Periyar University, India

A. Kingston
Christ University, India

N. Aishwarya
Christ University, India

Dhanasekaran Marimuthu
Adhiyamaan College of Engineering, India

DOI: 10.4018/979-8-3693-9611-7.ch015

ABSTRACT

This study examines the influence of circular economy concepts and emerging technology on the development of sustainable business models aimed at achieving net-zero emissions. It underscores the significance of resource efficiency, waste reduction, and lifecycle consideration in promoting sustainability. We analyse critical technologies such as blockchain, artificial intelligence, and the Internet of Things for their potential to enhance transparency, simplify processes, and foster stakeholder collaboration. We suggest a detailed roadmap that guides organisations in incorporating these ideas and technologies to establish robust, environmentally sustainable business practices for a sustainable future.

INTRODUCTION

The imperative to tackle climate change and environmental deterioration has required a fundamental adjustment in company operations. Conventional linear business models, defined by a "take-make-dispose" methodology, have demonstrated unsustainability, resulting in resource depletion, heightened waste, and considerable carbon emissions (Geissdoerfer et al., 2018). The circular economy (CE) paradigm presents a viable alternative, prioritizing resource efficiency, waste minimization, and sustainable management of product lifecycles (Ellen MacArthur Foundation, 2013). This study investigates the amalgamation of circular economy principles with emerging technologies to develop creative sustainable business models designed to attain net-zero emissions.

Circular economy concepts promote the reevaluation of production and consumption patterns to prolong product lifespans, encourage recycling and reuse, and reduce waste formation (Murray et al., 2017). Transitioning from a linear to a circular model enables firms to diminish their ecological footprints and bolster their resilience against resource scarcity and regulatory challenges (Ranta et al., 2018). Effectively executing circular economy techniques necessitates a shift in attitude and the integration of advanced technologies to optimize resource management, improve transparency, and promote collaboration throughout supply chains.

Emerging technologies, like artificial intelligence (AI), blockchain, and the Internet of Things (IoT), are essential for facilitating the adoption of circular economy ideas by enterprises. Artificial intelligence can enhance resource utilization by forecasting demand trends, improving production efficiency, and enabling product design for recyclability (Wang et al., 2021). Machine learning algorithms can analyze data and pinpoint opportunities for waste reduction and resource recovery, resulting in more sustainable operations. Blockchain technology provides improved traceability in supply chains, guaranteeing responsible sourcing of resources and the design of goods for circularity (Kamble et al., 2019). This transparency cultivates confidence among consumers and stakeholders, essential for the effective implementation of sustainable practices.

Moreover, IoT devices can deliver real-time data on resource consumption, allowing organizations to assess their environmental impacts and make informed decisions (Borgia, 2014). Smart sensors can monitor energy use in manufacturing processes, enabling the detection of inefficiencies and opportunities for enhancement. The integration of these technologies fosters an interconnected ecosystem that facilitates the circular economy by improving material monitoring, optimizing recycling operations, and encouraging shared economies (Cohen & Kietzmann, 2014).

The transition to sustainable business models represents not just an environmental necessity but also a strategic advantage for corporations. Consumers are progressively insisting on transparency and sustainability from brands, compelling firms to implement procedures that conform to these demands (Nielsen, 2015). Moreover, legal frameworks are advancing as governments enact laws designed to enhance circularity and diminish carbon emissions (European Commission, 2020). This scenario highlights the necessity for firms to incorporate circular economy ideas and innovative technology to maintain competitiveness and alleviate concerns related to environmental impacts.

This study will present a detailed roadmap for organizations aiming to utilize circular economy ideas and upcoming technology to attain net zero emissions. The roadmap will offer practical solutions for organizations to shift toward circularity, highlighting resource efficiency, innovative product design, and stakeholder collaboration. By implementing this integrated strategy, organizations may simultaneously promote environmental sustainability, stimulate economic growth, and improve their market positioning in a rapidly evolving environment.

BACKGROUND OF THE STUDY

The increasing recognition of climate change and environmental deterioration has initiated a worldwide transition toward sustainability in corporate activities. Conventional linear economic models, which emphasize production and consumption while neglecting environmental consequences, have resulted in resource depletion, heightened waste generation, and increased greenhouse gas emissions (Bocken et al., 2016). The circular economy (CE) has emerged as a disruptive strategy to address these challenges, aiming to establish closed-loop systems, reduce waste, and enhance resource efficiency (Ellen MacArthur Foundation, 2013). This study seeks to investigate how the application of circular economy principles and innovative technology might facilitate the creation of sustainable business models, thereby aiding in the achievement of net-zero emissions. The circular economy concept is based on key principles: designing for durability, encouraging repair and reuse, and reclaiming materials at the conclusion of a product's life cycle (Murray et al., 2017). By reimagining the design, production, and consumption of products, enterprises may generate value while minimizing their ecological impacts. Companies that implement product-as-a-service models can prolong the lifecycle of their items by retaining ownership and ensuring their return for refurbishment and reuse (Tukker, 2015). This transition not only preserves resources but also cultivates a more sustainable relationship between producers and customers.

Innovative technologies are essential in enabling the shift to a circular economy. Innovations like artificial intelligence (AI), blockchain, and the Internet of Things (IoT) are facilitating organizations in optimizing resource utilization, augmenting transparency in supply chains, and enhancing product tracking throughout their lifecycles (Kamble et al., 2019). Artificial intelligence can examine extensive datasets to detect inefficiencies, forecast demand trends, and refine production processes, resulting in diminished waste and improved sustainability (Wang et al., 2021). Blockchain technology facilitates safe and transparent record-keeping, enabling firms to trace materials and goods from origin to end-of-life, thus enhancing accountability and responsible sourcing (Tapscott & Tapscott, 2017).

Moreover, IoT devices provide real-time surveillance of resource utilization and waste production, offering enterprises actionable information to enhance productivity and reduce environmental impacts (Borgia, 2014). Manufacturing processes can utilise smart sensors to monitor energy consumption and identify inefficiencies, enabling organisations to enact prompt corrective actions.

Although the advantages of implementing circular economy principles and innovative technology are evident, numerous enterprises encounter obstacles throughout this shift. Factors including a lack of understanding, inadequate investment in technology, and resistance to change can impede the adoption of sustainable practices (Ranta et al., 2018). Furthermore, organizations must navigate intricate regulatory frameworks and engage stakeholders proficiently to promote collaboration in the circular economy (Haggar & Al-Khatib, 2021).

This study aims to provide a detailed framework for organizations seeking to utilize circular economy ideas and upcoming technology to attain net zero emissions. The roadmap will delineate strategic measures that enterprises may implement to incorporate sustainability into their operations, engage stakeholders, and foster innovation. This research will enhance the understanding of sustainable business models by highlighting the relationship between circular economy practices and technological breakthroughs, thereby aiding in climate change mitigation.

THE OBJECTIVE OF THIS STUDY

This study aims to examine the incorporation of circular economy principles and emerging technology in the development of sustainable business models that facilitate the attainment of net-zero emissions. It aims to develop new ways that organizations can implement to reduce waste, improve resource efficiency, and generate value through sustainable practices. The research seeks to provide a thorough route for organizations to adopt circular models by analyzing case studies and best practices from many industries while leveraging technologies like artificial intelligence, blockchain, and the Internet of Things (IoT). The study seeks to examine the problems and opportunities linked to this shift, offering practical insights and recommendations for stakeholders across all levels. The objective is to enable organizations to implement strategies that fulfill legal obligations and consumers' expectations while simultaneously fostering a sustainable and resilient economy in response to climate change.

LITERATURE REVIEW

The convergence of circular economy ideas and developing technology offers a transformative opportunity for organizations aiming for net zero emissions. This literature review examines current research on the circular economy, sustainable business models, and the technological facilitation of these frameworks, offering a thorough comprehension of how enterprises might shift towards sustainability.

Principles of Circular Economy. The circular economy (CE) signifies a fundamental transition from the conventional linear economic model, characterized by a "take, make, dispose" methodology, to a more sustainable framework that prioritizes the perpetual use of resources (Ellen MacArthur Foundation, 2013). Kirchgeorg et al. (2020) assert that the Circular Economy (CE) seeks to reduce waste and resource utilization through measures like product life extension, resource recovery, and sustainable design. These concepts not only mitigate environmental effects but also generate economic value by promoting innovation and efficiency.

The circular economy concept is based on systems thinking, which encompasses the complete lifecycle of a product, from design to disposal. According to Geng et al. (2019), the implementation of circular economy techniques necessitates a culture shift within organizations, emphasizing sustainability and resource optimization. Companies that implement circular economy principles can achieve competitive advantages via cost reductions, enhanced brand loyalty, and adherence to progressively rigorous laws (Geissdoerfer et al., 2018).

Eco-Friendly Business Frameworks

Sustainable business models (SBMs) are crucial for implementing circular economy ideas. Boons & Lüdeke-Freund (2013) characterize sustainable business models (SBMs) as innovations that generate value for customers while tackling environmental and social issues. An increasing amount of literature highlights the necessity for organizations to incorporate sustainability into their fundamental strategy to improve long-term resilience and profitability (Bocken et al., 2014).

Research by Schaltegger and Wagner (2011) indicates that sustainable business models (SBMs) can manifest in diverse formats, such as product-service systems, wherein enterprises offer services instead of products, thereby diminishing material consumption. For example, companies such as Philips have transitioned to providing lighting as a service, enabling users to pay for usage rather than acquiring light bulbs (Hockerts & Wüstenhagen, 2010). This transition not only minimizes waste but also encourages manufacturers to create goods that are more resilient and readily repaired.

The Functions of Emerging Technologies

Emerging technologies are essential for facilitating the shift to a circular economy and sustainable business strategies. Technologies such as the Internet of Things (IoT), blockchain, and artificial intelligence (AI) are transforming organizational resource management and product lifecycle tracking.

The IoT enables real-time monitoring of resource usage, allowing organizations to enhance their operations and minimize waste. Smart sensors can monitor inventory levels, reducing overproduction and waste (Santos et al., 2019). Yaqoob et al. (2021) assert that IoT applications in manufacturing can substantially decrease energy usage and resource waste, therefore facilitating the objectives of a circular economy.

Blockchain technology provides improved transparency and traceability in supply chains, guaranteeing responsible sourcing and the effective utilization of goods. Kshetri's research (2018) demonstrates that blockchain can address problems like counterfeit products and unethical sourcing by offering a safe and verifiable transaction record. This transparency cultivates trust among consumers and stakeholders, which is crucial for the effective execution of circular economy policies.

Artificial intelligence plays a crucial role in data analysis and trend prediction, which can guide sustainable corporate strategy. Using AI, enterprises can detect inefficiencies and opportunities for resource optimization, resulting in enhanced decision-making (Wang et al., 2018). Predictive analytics enables organizations to forecast demand more accurately, thereby mitigating the risk of overproduction and waste.

Obstacles in Execution

Notwithstanding the tremendous potential of integrating circular economy concepts with modern technologies, some problems remain. A major obstacle is the insufficient awareness and comprehension of circular economy techniques among enterprises and consumers. De Jesus and Mendonça (2018) assert that numerous organizations encounter difficulties transitioning from conventional linear models because of ingrained mindsets and practices.

Moreover, the upfront expenses related to the adoption of new technologies and procedures may dissuade organizations from engaging in sustainable practices. Ekins et al. (2020) emphasize that financial restrictions frequently prevent businesses from investing in creative solutions that promote circularity. Government incentives and subsidies can significantly mitigate these financial costs and promote the adoption of sustainable practices by enterprises.

Another issue is the requirement for collaboration among stakeholders across the entire supply chain. The concepts of a circular economy necessitate a comprehensive approach that engages several stakeholders, including suppliers, manufacturers, and consumers. Collaboration can enhance knowledge exchange and resource aggregation, ultimately resulting in more efficient circular solutions (Antikainen et al., 2018).

Prospective Trajectories

As organizations increasingly acknowledge the significance of sustainability, the incorporation of circular economy ideas and innovative technology will likely be pivotal to defining future business models. Future research should prioritize empirical investigations of successful circular economy implementations across diverse industries. This will offer vital insights and optimal methods for assisting organizations in their transition to sustainability.

Furthermore, as consumers' awareness of ecological concerns increases, enterprises must emphasize transparency and ethical behavior. Choudhury et al. (2021) assert that organizations must proactively communicate their sustainability initiatives to foster trust and loyalty among consumers. By doing so, firms can strengthen their brand image while contributing to the overarching objective of attaining net-zero emissions.

RESEARCH GAP

The incorporation of circular economy principles and innovative technology is crucial for organisations seeking to attain net-zero emissions. By implementing sustainable business models that utilise modern technology, enterprises can reduce waste, improve resource efficiency, and generate enduring value. Nonetheless, addressing issues such as awareness, financial limitations, and collaboration will be essential for the effective implementation of these approaches. Subsequent research ought to further investigate the interplay between circular economy ideas and technology to assist organisations in their pursuit of sustainability.

PROBLEMS AND ISSUES

The imperative to tackle climate change and resource depletion has prompted corporations and policymakers to implement creative strategies focused on sustainability. The circular economy (CE) and developing technologies offer feasible routes to attain net-zero emissions. Nonetheless, numerous challenges and complications emerge when incorporating these concepts into sustainable business strategies. This section examines the principal obstacles organizations encounter when adopting circular economy principles and utilizing technology to establish sustainable operations.

1. **Cognisance and comprehension:** A primary obstacle to the adoption of circular economy ideas is the insufficient awareness and comprehension among stakeholders, such as enterprises, policymakers, and consumers. Numerous organizations adhere to conventional linear models and frequently remain oblivious to the potential advantages of shifting to a circular economy. This ignorance may result in resistance to change and impede the investigation of innovative sustainable methods (Geissdoerfer et al., 2018). Furthermore, educational institutions and business organizations have not yet included comprehensive circular economy principles in their curricula and training programs. Consequently, future company leaders may lack the requisite understanding to effectively advance the circular economy agenda (Bocken et al., 2014). We must prioritise programs that focus on enhancing knowledge and education regarding circular economy ideas and practises to overcome this obstacle.
2. **Fiscal Limitations** Financial constraints pose a substantial obstacle for enterprises aiming to shift to a circular economy. Adopting circular methods frequently necessitates significant initial expenditures in novel technologies, processes, and infrastructure (Ekins et al., 2020). Numerous organizations, especially small and medium-sized firms (SMEs), may lack the capital required to invest

in these innovations, resulting in a hesitance to adopt circular economy concepts (Antikainen et al., 2018). Moreover, conventional financial sources may insufficiently support circular efforts. Numerous financial institutions continue to emphasize linear business models, which leads to restricted access to funding for sustainability-promoting projects. Kirchgeorg and S. G. (2020) emphasize that innovative financing methods and incentives, including grants or green bonds, may be essential for enabling the transition to a circular economy.

3. **Technological Obstacles** Although developing technologies possess significant potential for facilitating circular economy activities, certain technological obstacles remain. The lack of interoperability among various systems and platforms might obstruct collaboration and resource sharing between organizations (Wang et al., 2018). For instance, IoT devices from various manufacturers may lack good communication, constraining their capacity to deliver real-time data, which may enhance resource utilization. Furthermore, enterprises may encounter difficulties with data management and analytics. The shift toward a circular economy produces extensive data that organizations must analyze to guide decision-making (Santos et al., 2019). Many firms, however, lack the requisite skills or resources to properly integrate advanced data analytics and artificial intelligence capabilities. Thus, this inability to utilize data may lead to lost opportunities for operational optimization and sustainability improvement.
4. **The complexity of the supply chain** The transition to a circular economy requires a reassessment of supply chain operations. Typically, conventional supply chains follow a linear model that extracts, processes, and disposes of resources after use. Circular supply chains prioritize resource recovery, recycling, and reuse, potentially complicating existing supply chain frameworks (Geng et al., 2019). Furthermore, cooperation among various stakeholders is essential in circular supply chains. Businesses must collaborate with suppliers, manufacturers, and customers to enhance resource utilization and reduce waste. Nonetheless, promoting collaboration can be difficult because of varying priorities, aims, and degrees of commitment among stakeholders (Bocken et al., 2014). Establishing trust and excellent communication channels is crucial for surmounting these hurdles and attaining successful circular supply chains.
5. **Regulatory and policy concerns** The regulatory framework governing sustainability and circular economy initiatives is sometimes disjointed and ambiguous. In numerous areas, current policies favor linear models and may not adequately promote or incentivize circular approaches. Policies that enforce stringent waste disposal requirements may unintentionally deter enterprises from implementing recycling or reuse activities (Kirchgeorg & S. G., 2020). Furthermore, policymakers frequently possess an inadequate comprehension of circular economy concepts and their prospective advantages. This knowledge deficit may result

in the creation of policies that obstruct rather than facilitate circular activities (Geissdoerfer et al., 2018). To tackle these problems, it is imperative for governments to collaborate with businesses and industry specialists to design cohesive and supportive legislative frameworks that enable the transition to a circular economy.

6. **Cultural and organizational resistance.** Cultural and organizational resistance can substantially hinder the implementation of circular economic principles. Numerous organizations possess entrenched operational processes and mentalities that emphasize short-term profit maximization at the expense of long-term sustainability (Hockerts & Wüstenhagen, 2010). This emphasis on rapid rewards may generate opposition to the typically more intricate and long-term investments necessary for circular ventures. Moreover, employees may lack the drive or comprehension of the significance of switching to a circular economy. Organizations must cultivate a sustainable culture that promotes innovation and adopts new business models. Commitment from leadership and participation from employees are essential elements for effectively addressing cultural resistance (Schaltegger & Wagner, 2011).
7. **Consumer behavior and expectations** Consumer behavior is crucial for influencing sustainable company strategies. A growing number of consumers are becoming cognisant of environmental concerns and anticipate that businesses will implement sustainable practices. A disparity exists between customer expectations and actual behaviors, complicating the shift to a circular economy (Coudhury et al., 2021). For example, although customers may voice a preference for sustainable products, they often prioritize cost and convenience over environmental factors in their purchasing decisions. This mismatch presents hurdles for organizations seeking to adopt circular practices because they must reconcile consumer preferences with sustainability objectives (Bocken et al., 2014). Informing customers on the advantages of circular products and services, along with establishing incentives for sustainable consumption, can facilitate the closure of this gap.
8. **Assessing success and impact** A notable problem in the implementation of circular economy ideas is the difficulty in quantifying success and impact. Conventional performance measurements frequently emphasize financial results while overlooking environmental and social aspects (Ekins et al., 2020). To accurately analyze circular projects, enterprises must establish thorough criteria that measure financial performance, environmental impacts, resource efficiency, and social value. Furthermore, the lack of standardized measurements for circular economy operations might hinder comparisons among industries and organizations. Establishing clear and consistent measurements is crucial

for benchmarking success, identifying best practices, and fostering continuous development in circular efforts (Geng et al., 2019).

9. **Sustainability Compromises** Implementing circular economy methods may entail trade offs that hinder decision making. For example, a product engineered for durability and reparability may save waste but could also incur elevated initial expenses and necessitate more intricate production procedures (Antikainen et al., 2018). Organizations must meticulously evaluate these tradeoffs while developing sustainable products and services. Moreover, enterprises may encounter challenges concerning the use of materials. A corporation may endeavor to use recycled materials to mitigate its environmental impact; nevertheless, it may face problems concerning quality, availability, and cost (Hockerts & Wüstenhagen, 2010). Confronting these trade-offs necessitates a sophisticated comprehension of sustainability and a commitment to ongoing learning and adaptation.
10. **Worldwide Inequalities** Ultimately, global inequalities in resources, infrastructure, and legal frameworks pose obstacles to the implementation of circular economy methods. Developed nations possess advanced technologies and infrastructure that support circular projects, whereas developing nations sometimes lack the requisite resources to implement comparable practices (Zuboff, 2019).

These discrepancies can impede global collaboration and information exchange, constraining the capacity of enterprises in underdeveloped regions to engage in the circular economy. Resolving these difficulties necessitates global collaboration and assistance to foster sustainable practices across all regions, guaranteeing that the shift to a circular economy is advantageous for everybody (Geng et al., 2019).

CONCLUSION

In conclusion, utilizing circular economy ideas in conjunction with emerging technology is essential for creating sustainable business models that lead to net zero emissions. As enterprises face urgent environmental issues, adopting circular practices provides innovative solutions to minimize waste, improve resource efficiency, and foster sustainable consumption patterns. Nonetheless, the transformation faces obstacles such as financial limitations, technological impediments, and insufficient stakeholder knowledge. Organizations must prioritize education and training to cultivate a workforce equipped with the requisite skills and knowledge to implement circular strategies effectively. Moreover, promoting collaboration among companies and sectors is crucial for exchanging best practices and generating synergies that can enhance the effectiveness of sustainable efforts. In order to incentivize and reward businesses for their sustainability initiatives, policymakers play a crucial role in establishing legislative frameworks that promote circular economy practices. The pursuit of net-zero emissions necessitates a unified commitment by enterprises, consumers, and governmental bodies. By adopting the tenets of the circular economy and leveraging emerging technology, we can cultivate a sustainable future that reconciles economic expansion with environmental care, instigating a profound revolution in resource production and consumption.

FURTHER RESEARCH

Subsequent studies ought to investigate the incorporation of sophisticated technologies, like AI and IoT, into circular economy frameworks, emphasizing their use across diverse sectors. Examining consumer behavior toward sustainable practices and assessing the efficacy of legislative frameworks in promoting circular transitions are essential. Moreover, establishing standardized metrics to assess the impact of circular initiatives and tackling global disparities in adoption can improve the comprehension and execution of sustainable business models designed to attain net zero emissions (Geissdoerfer et al., 2018; Ranta et al., 2018).

SUGGESTIONS AND RECOMMENDATIONS

To effectively utilize circular economy ideas and emerging technology for sustainable business models targeting net zero emissions, organizations should prioritize three essential recommendations. Initially, organizations must embrace circular design principles, incorporating techniques that improve product durability, reparability, and recyclability. This method reduces waste and optimizes resource utility (Bocken et al., 2016). Furthermore, adopting technological innovations is essential; investing in advanced technologies like blockchain, artificial intelligence, and the Internet of Things (IoT) can significantly enhance resource efficiency, enable the tracking of material flows, and optimize supply chains (Kamble et al., 2020). Moreover, cultivating collaborative ecosystems by involving a varied array of stakeholders—2such as suppliers, customers, and local communities—can provide synergies that enhance circular practices and shared value (Rantala et al., 2018). Policymakers must develop strong policies that create supporting regulatory frameworks and offer incentives for circular projects, such as tax breaks or subsidies for sustainable activities (Bastein et al., 2013). Ultimately, increasing consumer awareness through education regarding the advantages of circular products is crucial for stimulating demand and promoting sustainable consumption behaviors (Garrone et al., 2020). Implementing these techniques enables firms to successfully adopt circular models that promote sustainability and advance net-zero emissions objectives.

REFERENCES

Antikainen, R., & P. J. (2018). Circular economy: A new strategic approach for businesses. *Business Horizons*, *61*(3), 371–380.

Bocken, N. M. P., Short, S. W., Rana, P., & Evans, S. (2014). A literature and practice review to develop sustainable business model archetypes. *Journal of Cleaner Production*, *65*, 42–56.

Boons, F., & Lüdeke-Freund, F. (2013). Business models for sustainable innovation: State-of-the-art and steps towards a research agenda. *Journal of Cleaner Production*, *45*, 81–88.

Borgia, E. (2014). The Internet of Things: Calling for a New Ecology of Things. *IEEE Instrumentation & Measurement Magazine*, *17*(6), 17–22.

Borgia, E. (2014). *The Internet of Things: Calling for a New Ecology of Things*. IEEE.

Choudhury, A., Singh, R., & Roy, R. (2021). Understanding consumer attitudes towards circular economy practices. *Business Strategy and the Environment*, *30*(3), 1315–1326.

Cohen, M. A., & Kietzmann, J. (2014). Riding the IoT Wave: How the Internet of Things is Revolutionizing the Way We Do Business. *Business Horizons*, *57*(6), 707–716.

de Jesus, A. F., & Mendonça, S. (2018). Exploring the circular economy: A systematic literature review. *Journal of Cleaner Production*, *200*, 162–180.

Ekins, P., & Hughes, N., & R. P. (2020). The role of the circular economy in achieving the UK's net-zero target. *Environmental Science & Policy*, *108*, 43–50.

Ellen MacArthur Foundation. (2013). *Towards the Circular Economy: Economic and business rationale for an accelerated transition* (Vol. 1). Ellen MacArthur Foundation.

European Commission. (2020). *Circular Economy Action Plan: For a Cleaner and More Competitive Europe*.

Geissdoerfer, M., Savaget, P., Bocken, N. M. P., & Hultink, E. J. (2018). The Circular Economy – A New Sustainability Paradigm? *Journal of Cleaner Production*, *143*, 757–768.

Geng, Y., Sarkis, J., & Xue, J. (2019). Circular economy in China: Current practices and future challenges. *International Journal of Production Research, 57*(23), 7040–7056.

Haggar, A., & Al-Khatib, I. A. (2021). Challenges and Opportunities in Implementing Circular Economy Practices in Organizations: A Literature Review. *Sustainability, 13*(4), 1936.

Hockerts, K., & Wüstenhagen, R. (2010). Greening goliaths versus emerging Davids: The role of incumbents and new entrants in sustainable entrepreneurship. *Journal of Business Venturing, 25*(5), 481–492.

Kamble, S. S., Gunasekaran, A., & Sharma, R. (2019). A Blockchain Technology Framework for Circular Economy in Manufacturing. *International Journal of Production Economics, 211*, 108–120.

Kirchgeorg, M., & S. G. (2020). Corporate responsibility and the circular economy: The importance of policy instruments. *Business Strategy and the Environment, 29*(7), 3243–3257.

Kshetri, N. (2018). 1 Blockchain's roles in meeting key supply chain management objectives. *International Journal of Information Management, 39*, 80–90.

Murray, A., Skene, K., & Haynes, K. (2017). The Circular Economy: An Interdisciplinary Exploration of the Concept and Its Applications. *Journal of Business Ethics, 140*(3), 369–380.

Nielsen. (2015). The Sustainability Imperative: New Insights on Consumer Expectations.

Ranta, V., Aarikka-Stenroos, L., & Peltola, S. (2018). The Role of Circular Economy in Sustainable Business Models. *Sustainability, 10*(7), 2483.

Santos, J. R., Silva, R. S., & Camilo, J. M. (2019). Internet of Things in manufacturing: A literature review. *Advances in Manufacturing, 6*(1), 41–58.

Schaltegger, S., & Wagner, M. (2011). Sustainable entrepreneurship: A conceptual framework. *Business Strategy and the Environment, 20*(3), 222–237.

Tapscott, D., & Tapscott, A. (2017). *Blockchain Revolution: How the Technology Behind Bitcoin Is Changing Money, Business, and the World.* Penguin.

Tukker, A. (2015). Product Services for a Resource-Efficient and Circular Economy. *Product-Service Systems and Sustainability: 1st International Conference on Product-Service Systems for a Sustainable Society.*

Wang, Y., Gunasekaran, A., & Ngai, E. W. T. (2021). The Role of Artificial Intelligence in Sustainable Manufacturing: A Review and Research Agenda. *Journal of Cleaner Production*, *283*, 124697.

Wang, Z., Wang, Y., & Wang, L. (2018). Artificial intelligence and the future of marketing: An empirical study. *Journal of Business Research*, *96*, 269–276.

Yaqoob, I., & M. I. (2021). Internet of Things: Applications, opportunities, and challenges in healthcare. *Future Generation Computer Systems*, *114*, 172–180.

Zuboff, S. (2019). *The Age of Surveillance Capitalism: The Fight for a Human Future at the New Frontier of Power*. Profile Books.

Chapter 16

Market Insights Effect on Competitive Advantage by Mediation of Personalized AI Solutions in SMEs Located in the Horn of Africa

Shashi Kant
https://orcid.org/0000-0003-4722-5736
Bule Hora University, Ethiopia

Tamire Ashuro
Bule Hora University, Ethiopia

Zerihun Kinde Alemu
https://orcid.org/0000-0002-8546-2882
Ethiopian Civil Service University, Ethiopia

Mengistu Guliti Buba
Wollo University, Ethiopia

ABSTRACT

With a focus on the mediating function of personalized AI, this investigation manifests the associations among insight of market and competitive edge. A correlation of 0.303 among personalized AI and competitive edge (p < 0.001) and 0.242 among insight of market and personalized AI (p < 0.001) was founded by SEM model.

DOI: 10.4018/979-8-3693-9611-7.ch016

KMO scores above 0.7 in validity evaluations manifest good discriminant validity and reliability across the constructs. The model's robustness is demonstrated by its model fit indices, which reveal a strong fit with a Chi-Square of 1.954 and an RMSEA of 0.028. Insight of market and personalized AI has a strong positive correlation (0.864), according to the regression investigation, and there is a substantial correlation (0.328) among personalized AI and competitive edge. A total substantial influence of 0.91 is obtained by quantifying the direct influence of insight of market on competitive edge at 0.43 and the indirect influence through tailored AI at 0.48. These findings demonstrate a partial mediation influence in which personalized AI increases efficiency.

INTRODUCTION

It is impossible to overestimate the importance of insight of market in gaining a competitive edge in the quickly changing business environment of today. The capacity to use data-driven insights is becoming more substantial for Small and Medium Enterprises (SMEs) as companies deal with growing globalization and technology improvements, especially in improving places like the Horn of Africa (Afriana, 2017). This idea has its roots in the nexus of competitive strategy and marketing intelligence, when companies realized how substantial it was to comprehend customer behavior and market dynamics in order to beat rivals (Alqurashi et al., 2023). A rising corpus of investigation that emphasizes the function of insight of market in boosting competitive advantage is highlighted by empirical literature. According to studies, businesses that use market investigation and sophisticated analytics are better able to respond to customer requirements, make well-informed decisions, and adjust to changes in the market (Alqurashi et al., 2023; Govenance, 2021; Weaver, 2024). Even while there has been a lot of progress, there are still real-world obstacles, especially for SMEs in the Horn of Africa. These businesses frequently struggle with a lack of finances, technology infrastructure, and qualified staff, which makes it difficult for them to properly use market information (Adesoga et al., 2024).

Also, previous studies have found a number of awareness gaps regarding the potential function that tailored AI solutions might play in mediating the association among competitive advantage and insight of market. Although AI has a well-established ability to improve decision-making, little is known about how specifically it may be used in SMEs (Ikbar et al., 2023). By examining the mediating function of tailored AI solutions in using market data for competitive advantage in SMEs situated in the Horn of Africa, this chapter seeks to close these gaps. Therefore, "***How do personalized AI solutions mediate the influence of insight of market on competitive***

advantage in SMEs located in the Horn of Africa?" is the question statement that directs this investigation. By answering this question, the investigation aims to give future academics and policymakers a thorough grasp of how these variables interact and practical conclusions. As a final point, this chapter will manifest how SMEs may overcome the obstacles they encounter and promote the use of creative solutions that can improve their competitive posture in a changing market.

STATEMENT OF THE PROBLEM

Small and medium-sized businesses (SMEs) in the Horn of Africa might change the competitive landscape by implementing personalized artificial intelligence (AI) solutions. In order to improve decision-making, increase consumer engagement, and eventually gain a sustainable competitive edge, SMEs should ideally use AI to utilize market information (Khristianto et al., 2021). But as things are right now, there is a big gap among this ideal and the reality that many SMEs in the area must cope with. Even with the advantages of AI, many SMEs are still ill-prepared to use these technologies efficiently, which hinders their ability to expand and compete. Numerous studies present conflicting data, indicating that although AI has been influence used in improved countries, there are few cases of this kind of success in the Horn of Africa(Ikbar et al., 2023). This disparity reveals a crucial awareness gap on the reasons behind the lack of similar adoption of tailored AI solutions in this area. The empirical investigation that is now available frequently yields conflicting findings about how AI influences SME performance, especially in improving nations (Afriana, 2017; Govenance, 2021; Khristianto et al., 2021). There is disagreement on the efficacy of AI treatments in boosting competitive advantage since the outcomes vary greatly, with some investigation manifesting favorable outcomes and others manifesting little to no gain.

There are also theoretical gaps since a substantial portion of the investigation that has been done on AI and competitive advantage has concentrated on big businesses in established industries (Adesoga et al., 2024; Alqurashi et al., 2023; Khristianto et al., 2021). Due to this mistake, these ideas are not as applicable to SMEs in the Horn of Africa, where distinct socioeconomic and cultural factors are substantial in determining the adoption of new technologies. The situation is made more difficult by awareness gaps, since little is known about how personalized AI solutions may be made to fit the unique requirements of SMEs in this area. Context gaps also outcome from a dearth of studies that focus on the regional issues that SMEs deal with, such inadequate infrastructure, restricted access to financing, and a labor shortage. There are several practical obstacles as well; for case, many SMEs find it difficult to adopt AI because of high expenses, insufficient training, and a general aversion to change. These obstacles make it difficult to use market data influence, which keeps SMEs from taking advantage of the potential benefits that artificial intelligence may provide (Cadden et al., 2023).

By offering a thorough analysis of how tailored AI solutions might mediate the link among insight of market and competitive advantage, particularly in the context of SMEs in the Horn of Africa, this investigation seeks to close these gaps. The investigation will provide useful insights that help direct policymakers in establishing an environment that facilitates the adoption of AI by tackling both theoretical and practical issues. Also, by creating frameworks pertinent to the particular conditions of SMEs in emerging nations, it will advance the scholarly conversation. By doing this, the investigation will not only improve awareness of AI's contribution to competitive advantage but also act as a guide for future scholars and professionals attempting to negotiate the challenges of technology adoption in comparable

THEORITICAL FOUNDATION

Resource-Based View: The relationship among insight of market, personalized AI solutions, and competitive advantage for SMEs—especially in the Horn of Africa—can be fundamentally understood using a range of theories. The Resource-Based View (RBV), one of the most well-known views, holds that a company's distinct assets and competencies are substantial factors in determining its competitive advantage. This idea holds that personalized AI solutions may be seen as useful tools that improve a SME's capacity to assess market trends, customize goods and services, and successfully address client wants. The RBV highlights that, if these resources are scarce, unique, and non-substitutable, their efficient use—such as data analytics skills and technology infrastructure—can outcome in long-term competitive advantage(Madhani, 2010).

Dynamic Capabilities Theory: Dynamic Capabilities Theory, which emphasizes a company's capacity to integrate, improve, and reorganize internal and external skills in response to quickly changing circumstances, is another pertinent concept. For SMEs in the Horn of Africa, where market circumstances are frequently erratic and unexpected, this approach is especially relevant. These businesses may improve their dynamic skills and respond more quickly to changes in the market and client preferences by utilizing tailored AI solutions. This flexibility is essential for staying competitive in a market characterized by shifting customer preferences and economic ups and downs(Mauliddiyah, 2021).

Technology Acceptance Model: Another useful tool for understanding the variables influencing the adoption of AI technology is the Technology Acceptance Model (TAM). Perceived utility and simplicity of use have a big influence on a person's or an organization's desire to employ a technology, according to TAM. Understanding these attitudes is essential for SMEs since reluctance to implement personalized AI solutions may be due to uncertainty about the advantages or worries about complexity. In order to promote greater adoption rates among SMEs, the model highlights the necessity of user-friendly AI solutions that amply illustrate their benefits(Wang, 2018).

EMPERICAL LITERATURE REVIEW

Insight of Market and Competitive Advantage

The literature has looked closely at the association among competitive advantage and insight of market, especially in regard to the use of data analytics and technology. According to a number of studies, businesses that use insight of market—which are gathered from consumer data, industry trends, and competition analysis—generally beat their rivals. A investigation by (Khristianto et al., 2021), for case, highlights the value of market orientation in improving corporate performance. It contends that companies that actively collect and evaluates market data are better able to satisfy consumer wants, which in turn increases customer satisfaction and loyalty. Additional investigation into the precise processes through which insight of market contributes to competitive advantage has been sparked by this seminal work. In this regard, recent empirical investigation highlights the revolutionary influences of personalized AI solutions. According to a investigation by (Ahsan & Zaman, 2021), businesses that use AI-driven analytics might obtain useful information that enables better product creation and more specialized marketing tactics. The outcomes support the notion that insight of market, when skillfully tapped through technology, may greatly improve an organization's competitive posture by indicating that such customization not only boosts consumer engagement but also improves overall business performance.

Also, investigation by (Adesoga et al., 2024) manifests how data-driven decision-making mediates the link among competitive advantage and insight of market. According to their outcomes, companies that place a high priority on data analytics are better able to make well-informed decisions, which in turn improve operational influence and strategic alignment. This is in line with the Dynamic Capabilities Theory, which highlights how businesses must innovate and adapt in response to market intelligence in order to gain a competitive advantage. But empirical investigation also manifests inconsistent outcomes, especially when it comes to SMEs. For instance, investigation by (Cadden et al., 2023) demonstrates that whereas larger companies may readily use insight of market because of their resources, many

SMEs find it difficult to successfully apply comparable tactics. According to the investigation, SMEs frequently face a competitive disadvantage when compared to their bigger counterparts due to budget constraints, a lack of experience, and poor infrastructure that prevents them from using market awareness. This emphasizes the need for personalized strategies that take into account the particular difficulties encountered by SMEs, especially in improving nations. Also, a number of academics have investigated how corporate culture influences the efficient use of market awareness. According to investigation by (Adesoga et al., 2024), a culture that prioritizes learning and innovation greatly improves a company's capacity to use market data for competitive advantage. This investigation emphasizes that organizational climate and mentality have an influence on how well insight of market are integrated into business processes, in addition to technology.

H1: Insight of market has a substantial influence on competitive advantage

Insight of Market and Personalized AI Solution

Personalized AI solutions greatly increase the efficacy of insight of market, according to recent empirical investigation. According to investigation by (Choudhury et al., 2021), for case, businesses that use AI-driven analytics are able to glean deeper insights from customer data, which allows them to better customize their products to suit the tastes of each individual. In addition to improving client relations, this customization increases conversion rates and boosts sales. The authors contend that firms may modify their strategy in response to changing market conditions and customer behavior since AI can examine enormous volumes of data in real time.

Also, (Ahsan & Zaman, 2021) investigation emphasizes how personalized AI may improve insight of market by using predictive analytics. According to their outcomes, artificial intelligence (AI) can spot consumer behavior patterns and trends that conventional analytic techniques would miss at first glance. Businesses may obtain a competitive edge by using these information to inform proactive actions that meet market expectations. The revolutionary potential of tailored AI solutions in enhancing and expanding insight of market is highlighted by this investigation.

An investigation by (Choudhury et al., 2021) that examines the idea of service customization with AI makes a major further contribution to this conversation. They discovered that businesses may greatly increase customer pleasure and loyalty by using AI technology to tailor interactions based on market information. The authors stress that providing individualized experiences that connect with customers and improve overall business performance depend on the influence integration of market awareness into AI systems. Nevertheless, empirical investigation also identifies obstacles to the successful fusion of tailored AI with market awareness. The influence implementation of AI solutions in utilizing insight of market is hampered by problems including data quality, privacy concerns, and the requirement for a strong technology infrastructure, according to investigation by Bock et al. (2019). These difficulties are especially noticeable in SMEs, where a lack of resources may make it difficult to deploy advanced AI systems that use market data. As a final point, a number of studies have emphasized how corporate culture may either help or impede the integration of market awareness with personalized AI solutions. A investigation by (Cadden et al., 2023), for instance, indicates that businesses are more likely to influence incorporate AI technology into their operations if they have a culture that encourages innovation and data-driven decision-making. According to this investigation, optimizing the advantages of tailored AI solutions in association to insight of market requires a supportive organizational climate.

H2: Insight of market has a substantial influence on personalized AI solution

Mediation of Personalized AI Solution, Insight of Market, Competitive Advantage

As businesses look to improve their operations through technology, the function that personalized AI solutions play as a mediator in the interaction among insight of market and competitive advantage has grown in importance. A paradigm for understanding mediation was created by a seminal investigation by Afriana, (2017), which emphasized that a mediator must explain the link among a dependent variable, like competitive advantage, and an independent variable, in this case, insight of market. Subsequent investigation on the potential function of personalized AI solutions as a key mediator in this dynamic has been motivated by this seminal investigation. The mediating function of personalized AI solutions in boosting the influence of insight of market has been convincingly demonstrated by recent empirical investigation. According to investigation by (Adesoga et al., 2024), for case, AI technologies have the ability to convert unprocessed market data into insights that may be used to make strategic decisions that improve competitive positioning. According to their outcomes, businesses that use personalized AI systems are better able to comprehend consumer preferences and market trends, which enable them to react to pressure from the competition more quickly. This lends credence to the idea that tailored AI actively influences how businesses use insight of market to gain a competitive edge rather than just amplifying their influences.

Also, an investigation by (Weaver, 2024) examines how AI-driven customization influences customer loyalty and engagement, highlighting these elements as crucial associations among competitive advantage and insight of market. According to the report, personalized AI solutions let companies customize their products based on complex market data, which increases client happiness and enduring loyalty. This mediating influence is essential because, especially in markets with intense competition, client loyalty frequently translates into a prolonged competitive advantage. An investigation by (Ikbar et al., 2023) that looks at the function of AI in decision-making processes offers more empirical support. According to their investigation, businesses that use tailored AI solutions to evaluate insight of market see increases in operational influence and strategic alignment, both of which strengthen their competitive edge. The authors contend that by altering how businesses interpret and apply market data, personalized AI serves as a mediator, bridging the gap among insights and workable business plans.

Understanding the entire extent of this mediation function is still difficult, though, especially in various organizational situations. According to investigation by (Alqurashi et al., 2023), obstacles including data quality and technology infrastructure might make it difficult to integrate personalized AI solutions successfully. These challenges highlight the need for a supportive environment that encourages innovation and technology adoption by potentially limiting the amount of market information that may be converted into competitive advantage. Also, a number of academics have investigated how leadership and organizational culture might support the mediation process. According to a investigation by (Khristianto et al., 2021), optimizing the advantages of personalized AI solutions requires a culture that supports data-driven decision-making and ongoing learning. In order to influence use market data to influence strategic efforts and consequently increase competitive advantage, this cultural alignment is essential.

H3: Personalized AI Solution play substantial mediation function of among insight of market and competitive advantage

Conceptual Framework

Figure 1. Conceptual Framework

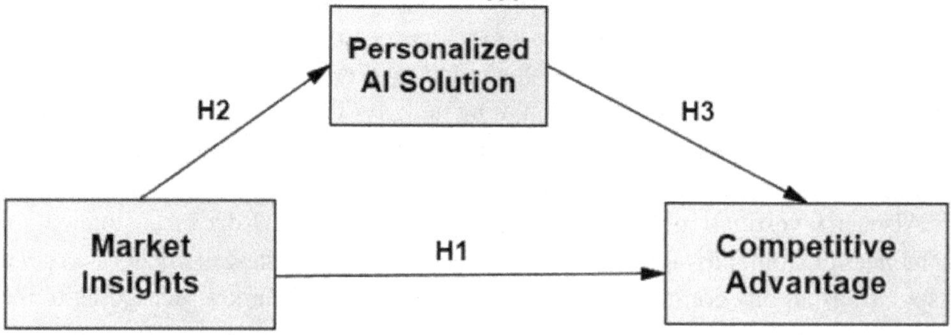

METHODOLOGY

In order to investigate the mediating function of personalized AI solutions in the association among insight of market and competitive advantage among SMEs in the Horn of Africa, this investigation used a quantitative investigation methodology. 390 participants in all, representing a wide variety of SMEs in different industries, were included in the survey sample. Based on statistical power considerations, this sample size was chosen to ensure that there was enough data for a thorough investigation while also taking into account the target population's varied features. Prior to data collection, scale improvement was done to guarantee the measuring tools' validity and reliability. To fit the investigation's setting, established scales were modified from the literature. These included competitive advantage, tailored AI solutions, and market analytics. The Kaiser-Meyer-Olkin (KMO) test was used to determine whether the sample was sufficient for factor analysis before the primary analysis. The sample size was sufficient for the suggested analysis, as manifests by the KMO value above 0.6.

The underlying factor structure of the constructs was then determined using exploratory factor analysis (EFA). The validity of the modified scales was confirmed by the EFA findings, which manifested unique dimensions for every construct. Principal component analysis with a varimax rotation was used to extract factors, producing distinct loading patterns that validated the investigation's theoretical framework. In light of insight of market and competitive advantage, the investigation shed light on how operationally defined and quantified individualized AI solutions may be. After the EFA, the proposed correlations among the components were tested using AMOS software and structural equation modeling (SEM). SEM made it possible to analyze both direct and indirect influences in the suggested model, offering a thorough comprehension of how insight of market influence competitive advantage via personalized AI solutions. The suggested model's goodness-of-fit was evaluated using model fit indices such as the Chi-square test, Comparative Fit Index (CFI), and Root Mean Square Error of Approximation (RMSEA). The findings supported the expected correlations by manifesting an adequate fit.

DATA ANALYSIS

Table 1. KMO and Bartlett's Test

Kaiser-Meyer-Olkin Measure of Sampling Adequacy.		**.850**
Bartlett's Test of Sphericity	Approx. Chi-Square	1419.738
	df	91
	Sig.	.000

Source: Authors

The outcomes of the Bartlett's Test of Sphericity and the Kaiser-Meyer-Olkin (KMO) Measure of Sampling Adequacy, both crucial for assessing whether the data is suitable for factor analysis, are manifests in Table 1. A high degree of sampling adequacy is manifests by the KMO value of.850, which implies that the data set is suitable for factor analysis. A score of.850 indicates that the variables are sufficiently connected to justify more investigation, since KMO recommendations state that a number above 0.8 is desirable and anything above 0.9 is outstanding. The KMO outcomes are manifested by Bartlett's Test of Sphericity, which evaluates the hypothesis that the correlation matrix is an identity matrix. With 91 degrees of freedom and an estimated Chi-Square value of 1419.738, the implication level (Sig.) is.000. Substantial correlations among the variables in the dataset are manifests by this statistically substantial outcome ($p <.05$). The argument for component analysis is strengthened by the null hypothesis' failure, which implies that the variables do not merely correlate at random. All of these outcomes demonstrate that the data may be used to derive substantial elements. The conclusion that the data can successfully disclose underlying structures among the variables, enabling a more thorough analysis of the associations within the investigation's context, is supported by the high KMO value and substantial Bartlett's Test outcome.

Table 2. Total Variance Explained

Component	**Initial Eigenvalues**			**Extraction Sums of Squared Loadings**			**Rotation Sums of Squared Loadings**		
	Total	**% of Variance**	**Cumulative %**	**Total**	**% of Variance**	**Cumulative %**	**Total**	**% of Variance**	**Cumulative %**
1	4.51	32.235	32.235	4.51	32.235	32.235	3.00	21.451	21.451
2	1.37	9.787	42.022	1.37	9.787	42.022	2.16	15.491	36.942
3	1.27	9.087	51.110	1.27	9.087	51.110	1.98	14.168	51.110

continued on following page

Table 2. Continued

Component	Initial Eigenvalues			Extraction Sums of Squared Loadings			Rotation Sums of Squared Loadings		
	Total	% of Variance	Cumulative %	Total	% of Variance	Cumulative %	Total	% of Variance	Cumulative %
4	.949	6.782	57.892						
5	.871	6.223	64.115						
6	.773	5.519	69.634						

Extraction Method: Principal Component Analysis. Source: Authors

A thorough summary of the total variation explained by the variables identified using Principal Component Analysis (PCA) is manifest in Table 2. The investigation manifests that the rotation sums of squared loadings, extraction sums of squared loadings, and starting eigenvalues are clearly broken out into several components. With an eigenvalue of 4.51, the first component explains 32.235% of the variance. This manifests that this one element accounts for a sizable amount of the dataset's variability, underscoring its implication in comprehending the underlying structures. The fact that this component alone accounts for 32.235% of the variation when taken as a whole highlights how dominating it is in the factor structure. The eigenvalues of the second and third components, which are 1.37 and 1.27, respectively, also make substantial contributions. The total percentage is 42.022%, with the second component accounting for 9.787% of the variation. With the third component contributing an extra 9.087%, the cumulative variance is 51.110%. These three elements work together to account for more than half of the variation, which is a clear sign of the constructs' applicability. The eigenvalues of the following components (fourth, fifth, and sixth) are all less than one; the eigenvalues of the fourth, fifth, and sixth components are.949,.871, and.773, respectively. Although these factors add to the variance explained, their lower eigenvalues imply that the information they offer diminishes over time. Interestingly, the fourth component accounts for 6.782% of the variation, for a cumulative total of 57.892%. The fifth and sixth components make lesser percentage contributions, demonstrating that the first three components contain the most substantial insights.

Confirmatory Principle component Examination

Confirmatory principle component examination is a sort of statistics used to verify the principle component arrangement of a group of directed proxies. Investigation can use CFA to assess hypotheses based on the underlying frame job and correlations among observable proxies. The investigation used CFA under table 3 to assess the hypothesis that there is a relationship among the proxies being guided and the latent notions that support them.

Table 3. Covariances

Covariance			Approximation	S.E.	C.R.	P	Hy.
Insight of market	**<-->**	**Personalized AI**	**.242**	**.021**	**8.231**	***	**H2**
Personalized AI	<-->	Competitive Advantage	.303	.032	7.692	***	**H3**
Insight of market	<-->	Competitive Advantage	.254	.24	7.831	***	**H1**

Source: Authors

The covariances among the constructs of competitive edge, tailored AI solutions, and insight of market are manifests in Table 3, demonstrating the importance and strength of their linkages. The covariance values give information about the possible relationships among these notions by manifesting how much they vary together. With a standard error (S.E.) of.021, the correlation among insight of market and personalized AI solutions is stated to be.242. The statistical implication ($p <.001$) of the critical ratio (C.R.) is 8.231. Hypothesis 2 (H2) is supported by this high correlation, which implies that the adoption of tailored AI solutions tends to expand along with insight of market. According to this investigation, businesses that use insight of market are more likely to use AI technology to improve consumer engagement and decision-making. Likewise, the correlation among competitive edge and personalized AI solutions is recorded at.303, with a statistically substantial ($p <.001$) S.E. of.032 and a C.R. of 7.692. This demonstrates a strong correlation among the use of tailored AI and gaining competitive edge, supporting Hypothesis 3 (H3). According to the findings, businesses that use personalized AI solutions may enhance their market positioning and competitiveness by becoming more sensitive to client wants and increasing operational efficiency. As a final point, it is revealed that the covariance among competitive edge and insight of market is.254, with a C.R. of 7.831 and a S.E. of.024, all of which are statistically substantial ($p <.001$). This outcome validates Hypothesis 1 (H1) and strengthens the notion that gaining competitive edge is positively influenced by good insight of market. Organizations that successfully collect and evaluate insight of market have a higher chance of achieving strategic advantages that improve their market positioning, according to the positive covariance.

Table 4. Validity Concern

	CR	AVE	MSV	MaxR(H)	MI	CA	PAI
MI	0.732	0.643	0.219	0.852	**0.654**		
CA	0.758	0.657	0.132	0.763	0.171	**0.665**	
PAI	0.793	0.603	0.274	0.797	0.383	0.193	**0.684**

Note: MI= Insight of market; CA= Competitive Advantage*;* PAI = *Personalized AI* Source: Authors

The validity issues surrounding the investigation's constructs—Compositor Reliability (CR), Average Variance Extracted (AVE), Maximum Shared Variance (MSV), Maximum Reliability (MaxR (H)), Modification Indices (MI), and Cronbach's Alpha (CA)—are thoroughly manifested in Table 4. These metrics are crucial for evaluating the constructs being measure's convergent and discriminant validity as well as dependability. Since values above 0.7 are often regarded as reliable, Insight of market' (MI) stated CR of 0.732 indicates acceptable dependability. The AVE for MI is 0.643, over the 0.5 cutoff, indicating that the construct accounts for a sizable amount of the variance in the indicators. The discriminant validity of MI is supported by its MSV of 0.219, which is lower than the AVE and manifests that it differs from other constructs. The construct's dependability is further supported by the MaxR (H) value of 0.852. The CR for Competitive edge (CA) is somewhat higher at 0.758, indicating a strong degree of dependability. The build successfully captures its indications, as evidenced by the AVE of 0.657. Because the MSV of 0.132 is less than the AVE, it is confirmed that discriminant validity is maintained via CA. The trustworthiness of this construct is further supported by the MaxR (H) value of 0.763. As a final point, with a CR of 0.793, Personalized AI (PAI) exhibits the highest dependability and good internal consistency. PAI's AVE is 0.603, over the 0.5 cutoff, indicating that it accurately reflects its underlying indicators. Its discriminant validity is confirmed by the MSV of 0.274, which is less than the AVE even if it is more than the MSV values for MI and CA. Good dependability for PAI is manifests by the MaxR (H) value of 0.797.

Mediating Function Examination

Figure 2. Structure Equation Model

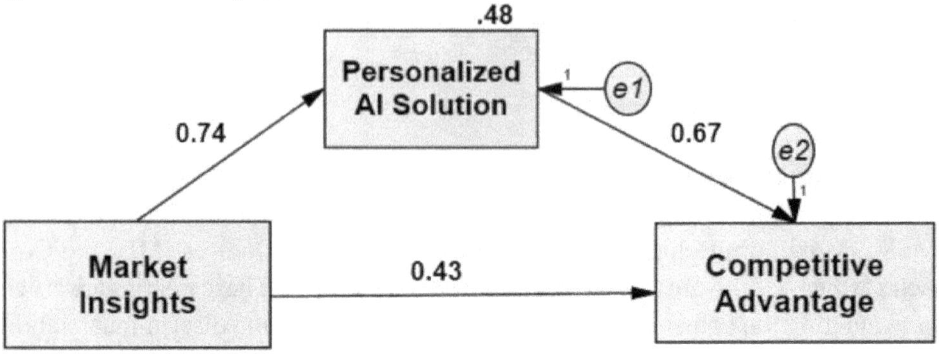

Model Fit Indices

Table 5. Indices for Model Fit

Sig.	Chi-Sq	RMR	Fitness Goodness	Fitness Confirmatory	TLI	RMSEA
0.004	1.954	.036	0.930	0.912	0.911	.028

Source: Authors

The model fit indices, which evaluate the overall fit of the structural equation model intended to investigate the function of personalized AI solutions as a mediator among competitive edge and insight of market, are manifests in Table 5. Since a p-value of less than 0.05 indicates a statistically substantial link among the constructs, the stated implication level of 0.004 manifests that the model fits the data well. When combined with the other fit indices, the reported Chi-Square score of 1.954 manifests a good model fit. The model's sufficiency is further supported by the relatively low Root Mean Square Residual (RMR) value of.036 that indicates little difference among the observed and projected covariance matrices. The Confirmatory Fit Index (CFI) is stated as 0.912 and the Goodness of Fit Index (GFI) at 0.930, both of which are higher than the generally recognized cutoff of 0.90. These indices demonstrate the robustness of the model by manifesting that it accounts for a substantial portion of the data variation. A excellent fit in comparison to a baseline model is also manifests by the Tucker-Lewis Index (TLI), which is measured at 0.911 and again exceeds the suggested cut-off of 0.90. At.028, the Root Mean

Square Error of Approximation (RMSEA) is remarkably low, well below the 0.06 criterion, indicating a close match among the model and the degrees of freedom.

Table 6. Regression Examination

Relative			**Approx.**	**S.E.**	**C.R.**	**P**	**Ass.**
Insight of market	<-->	*Personalized AI*	**.864**	**.143**	**7.583**	***	**H2**
Personalized AI	<-->	*Competitive* Advantage	.328	.131	2.853	***	H3
Insight of market	<-->	*Competitive* Advantage	.957	.192	7.958	***	H1

Source: Authors

Substantial insights into the interdependencies among insight of market, competitive edge, and personalized AI are manifests by the regression analysis manifests in Table 6.

First off, a regression coefficient of 0.864 manifests a high positive association among insight of market and personalized AI, suggesting that improved insight of market are linked to substantial gains in personalized AI capabilities. The corresponding p-value, which is statistically substantial (manifests by ***) and the critical ratio (C.R.) of 7.583 both demonstrate how strong this association is. This implies that businesses may greatly improve their personalized AI projects by utilizing market information, which will optimize decision-making. Second, with a regression coefficient of 0.328, the association among competitive edge and tailored AI is also substantial. The C.R. of 2.853 and a substantial p-value indicate that tailored AI does help acquire competitive edge, despite the fact that this association is lower than the last one. In contrast to the influence of insight of market on personalized AI, this manifests that businesses who invest in personalized AI are likely to gain some degree of competitive advantage. As a final point, with a regression value of 0.957, the greatest association among competitive edge and insight of market was found. With a C.R. of 7.958 and this high value, the association is nearly perfect, suggesting that gaining competitive edge requires good market awareness. The implication of market intelligence as a fundamental component that propels both personalized AI projects and competitive positioning in the market is highlighted by this investigation.

Table 7. Mediating function influence

	Influence	worth	Path Influence
Insight of market → Competitive Advantage	Direct Influence	.43	Direct influence stated
Insight of market → Personalized AI → Competitive Advantage	Indirect Influence	.74*.67=.48	Indirect Influence Ensued
	Whole influence	.91	Partial mediation

Source: Authors

The mediating function of tailored AI in the association among competitive edge and insight of market is examined in Table 7. The findings provide a sophisticated view of how these characteristics interact in a corporate setting by revealing both direct and indirect influences.

A value of 0.43 indicates that insight of market have a direct influence on competitive edge. This chart illustrates an substantial link, indicating that a firm's capacity to gain competitive edge is directly influenced by influence market awareness. This straightforward approach emphasizes how crucial it is to comprehend customer behavior and market dynamics as the cornerstones of strategic positioning. Also, 0.74 (the influence of insight of market on personalized AI) times 0.67 (the influence of personalized AI on competitive edge) equals 0.48, which indicates an indirect influence through personalized AI. This manifests that the influence of insight of market on competitive edge is enhanced by tailored AI, which acts as a crucial mediator. The existence of this indirect influence implies that, even while insight of market is substantial, using personalized AI technology greatly increases their efficacy in gaining competitive edge.

When both routes are combined, the overall influence of insight of market on competitive edge is 0.91, suggesting a substantial overall influence. This impressive number points to a partial mediation influence, which means that insight of market by themselves still have a considerable direct influence on competitive edge, even though personalized AI is a key component of this association.

DISCUSSION

The outcomes of the regression and mediation studies manifest how insight of market, competitive edge, and personalized AI are intricately related, underscoring their combined implication in strategic business frameworks. The strong direct influence of insight of market on competitive edge emphasizes how substantial it is for businesses to improve a thorough awareness of customer preferences and market dynamics. This fundamental understanding improves operational efficacy and informs strategic choices, which eventually outcomes in better competitive positioning. Also, a key element in optimizing the influence of insight of market is the mediating function of tailored AI. The substantial indirect influence implies that businesses may increase the value of their insight of market and turn them into competitive edge by successfully utilizing tailored AI. This investigation emphasizes how substantial it is for companies to spend money on cutting-edge technology that support data-driven decision-making and customization. By doing this, businesses may improve their ability to react to changes in the market and improve more specialized products that appeal to their target markets.

Strong synergy among these components is manifests by the total influence calculation of 0.91, which supports the notion that both direct and indirect paths coexist in promoting competitive success. The intricacy of these interactions is manifests by this partial mediation influence, which implies that although tailored AI plays a key function in converting insight of market into competitive edge, the direct influence of insight of market is still rather high.

CONCLUSION

In summary, the examination of the associations among competitive edge, tailored AI, and insight of market provides a convincing account of how these factors work together to propel company success. The direct influence of insight of market on competitive edge emphasizes how substantial it is to comprehend customer behavior and market circumstances in order to make strategic decisions. The necessity of utilizing cutting-edge technology to boost the influence of market data and enable a more responsive and personalized response to client demands is further highlighted by the notable mediating influence of personalized AI. The outcomes indicate that in order to fully realize their potential for gaining competitive edge, firms should give top priority to integrating market information with personalized AI initiatives. By doing this, companies may increase their operational efficiency while simultaneously encouraging creativity and flexibility in a market that is changing quickly. Overall, this investigation highlights how a comprehensive strategy that combines cutting-edge AI technology with solid insight of market may enable businesses to satisfy changing customer needs, traverse complexity, and achieve sustainable success in a highly competitive environment.

MANAGERIAL IMPLICATIONS

The investigation's conclusions have a number of substantial management ramifications that might direct operational procedures and strategic decision-making. First and foremost, managers need to understand how substantial insight of market are to the improvement of their plans. Organizations may improve their comprehension of customer preferences and market dynamics by cultivating a culture of data-driven decision-making. This will allow them to make more informed and successful strategic decisions. This calls for spending money on analytical tools that can yield useful insights and strong market investigation skills. Also, managers should concentrate on incorporating cutting-edge technology into their operations manifest the substantial mediating function that tailored AI plays. In addition to improving processing and analysis of market information, adopting personalized AI enables the creation of personalized products that appeal to consumers on a deeper level. This strategy may boost client loyalty and happiness, which will eventually provide businesses a competitive edge. To guarantee that insights are successfully converted into workable plans, executives should also place a high priority on cross-functional cooperation among the marketing, data analytics, and technology teams. Businesses will be able to react quickly to shifts in customer behavior and market conditions thanks to this cooperative effort, which will make it easier to match organizational goals with market possibilities.

PRACTICAL IMPLICATIONS

The investigation's practical implications highlight the doable actions that businesses can take to improve their competitive posture by utilizing market awareness and personalized AI. First and foremost, companies must to put in place methodical procedures for collecting and evaluating market data. This might entail spending money on sophisticated analytics software and educating employees on how to properly understand data. Establishing an ongoing feedback loop that takes into account customer data allows businesses to make real-time strategy adjustments and stay responsive to market needs. Also, it's critical to include personalized AI solutions into client interaction plans. Businesses may create personalized marketing campaigns and individualized product offerings by using AI to investigation consumer behavior and preferences. This raises the possibility of conversion and retention while also improving the consumer experience. Deploying AI-driven customer relationship management (CRM) solutions that offer insights into consumer interactions and preferences might be one of the practical measures.

Businesses could also think about establishing alliances with startups that specialize in AI solutions or technology suppliers. These kinds of partnerships may hasten the adoption of cutting-edge technology, helping companies to remain on the cutting edge. Also, by facilitating awareness transfer, this strategy can provide teams the tools they need to optimize the advantages of these technologies.

THEORETICAL IMPLICATIONS

The investigation's theoretical implications provide a substantial contribution to the corpus of awareness already available on the relationship among competitive edge, personalized AI, and insight of market. The investigation supports the idea that market intelligence is a key factor in strategic decision-making and competitive performance, rather than just a supporting function, by clearly demonstrating the associations among these dimensions. This investigation contradicts conventional ideas, which frequently consider insight of market separately, and contends that optimizing organizational performance requires their integration with emerging technologies, such tailored AI. A more sophisticated understanding of how technology might close the gap among data collection and real-world application is also introduced by the investigation's identification of tailored AI as a mediating component. This theoretical framework extension emphasizes how crucial it is to view technical capabilities as essential elements of competitive strategy rather than as merely instruments. It encourages more investigation into the ways that different types of technology might influence how useful insights of market are in particular sectors. A more sophisticated understanding of how technology might close the gap among data collection and real-world application is also introduced by the investigation's identification of tailored AI as a mediating component. This theoretical framework extension emphasizes how crucial it is to view technical capabilities as essential elements of competitive strategy rather than as merely instruments. It encourages more investigation into the ways that different types of technology might influence how useful insight of market are in particular sectors.

RECOMMENDATION

Organizations looking to improve their competitive edge through the strategic use of insight of market and tailored AI might benefit from a number of recommendations based on the investigation's outcomes. First and foremost, companies must give top priority to building a strong data infrastructure that makes it easier to gather, examine, and understand market information. Advanced analytics tools and platforms that provide real-time data processing should be part of this infrastructure so that businesses can remain flexible and sensitive to changing customer patterns and behaviors. Managers should also fund training and improvement initiatives for staff members to improve their analytical and data literacy. Businesses may promote a culture of data-driven decision-making where insights are actively used in strategic planning and execution by giving teams the skills they need. This change in culture will make it easier to guarantee that insight of market are not only acquired but also successfully converted into workable plans. Also, businesses ought to aggressively pursue collaborations with digital companies that specialize in artificial intelligence solutions. Working together with these professionals may hasten the incorporation of personalized AI into current procedures, improving the capacity to customize goods and services to satisfy particular client requirements. Because businesses may use outside awareness to stay on the cutting edge of technology, this strategy can also encourage innovation. As a final point, companies are urged to implement an ongoing feedback system that assesses the performance of their AI applications and market intelligence methods on a regular basis. Businesses may improve their methods and better meet client expectations by methodically evaluating outcomes and modifying tactics as necessary. In conclusion, firms will be able to successfully use insight of market and tailored AI with a proactive focus on data infrastructure, staff training, strategic collaborations, and continuous review, creating long-lasting competitive edge in a changing environment.

FUTURE DIRECTIONS

The investigation's findings can guide future investigation in a number of substantial areas to further examine the associations among competitive edge, tailored AI, and insight of market. First, longitudinal investigation might be done to monitor how personalized AI influences insight of market over time. Deeper understanding of how the incorporation of AI technology influences competitive positioning and strategic decision-making in dynamic market situations may be possible with such investigation. It would also be advantageous to look at how industry-specific characteristics influence how successful insight of market and AI applications is. Diverse industries may provide distinct possibilities and problems, requiring personalized strategies to capitalize on these factors. Studies that compare different sectors might provide insightful information about best practices and manifest how contextual factors influence the association among competitive edge, tailored AI, and insight of market. Also, it is essential to investigate the difficulties and ethical ramifications of using tailored AI to extract insight of market. Understanding possible biases and privacy issues will be crucial for ethical deployment as businesses depend more and more on AI-driven solutions. Investigation in this field can help firms create frameworks that maximize AI's advantages while giving ethical issues first priority. As a final point, future studies should examine the ways in which organizational culture facilitates or impedes the influence use of market data and artificial intelligence. By understanding how internal dynamics, leadership styles, and employee engagement influence the adoption and usage of these technologies, organizations may create strategies to promote an environment that is conducive to innovation and data-driven decision-making.

REFERENCES

Adesoga, T. O., Olaiya, O. P., & Obani, O. Q. (2024). *Leveraging AI for transformative business improvement : Strategies for market analysis, customer insights, and competitive intelligence.*

Afriana, riza devi. (2017). No Title No Title No Title. *Angewandte Chemie International Edition, 6(11), 951–952., 6*(November), 5–24.

Ahsan, S., & Zaman, A. (2021). *The augmentation of Awareness Management through Industry 4 . 0 : A case of avia- tion sector of an emerging economy Miao Miao, Syed Imran Zaman, Arooba Zafar, Cristian Garcia Rodriguez and. 00.*

Alqurashi, D. R., Alkhaffaf, M., Daoud, M. K., & Ahmad, J. (2023). *Exploring the Influence of Artificial Intelligence in Personalized Content Marketing : A Contemporary Digital Marketing. 8*, 548–560.

Cadden, T., Weerawardena, J., Cao, G., Duan, Y., & Mcivor, R. (2023). Examining the function of big data and marketing analytics in SMEs innovation and competitive advantage : A awareness integration perspective ☆. *Journal of Business Investigation, 168*(June), 114225. DOI: 10.1016/j.jbusres.2023.114225

Choudhury, N., Meghwal, M., & Das, K. (2021). Microencapsulation: An overview on concepts, methods, properties and applications in foods. *Food Frontiers, 2*(4), 426–442. DOI: 10.1002/fft2.94

Govenance, J. O. F. (2021). EMPIRICAL ANALYSIS ON CORPORATE TRANSPARENCY, COMPETITIVE ADVANTAGE. *AND FIRM PERFORMANCE : AN INSIGHT OF MUSCAT SECURITIES MARKET, 4*(2), 96–102.

Ikbar, H., Rizky, A. M., Usman, O., & Bus, M. (2023). *The Influence Of Market Orientation, Product Innovation And Competitive Prices On Competitive Advantage And Marketing Performance Of Eco-Friendly Household Product Processing In The DKI Jakarta Area. 1*(12).

Khristianto, W., Suharyono, S., & Pangestuti, E. (2021).. . *The Influences of Market Sensing Capability and Information Technology Competency on Innovation and Competitive Advantage, 8*(3), 1009–1019. DOI: 10.13106/jafeb.2021.vol8.no3.1009

Madhani, P. (2010). Resource Based View (RBV) of Competitive Advantage: An Overview. ... *BASED VIEW: CONCEPTS AND PRACTICES, Pankaj ..., March*, 2–22. https://papers.ssrn.com/sol3/papers.cfm?abstract_id=1578704

Mauliddiyah, N. L. (2021). *No Title*. 6.

Wang, D. Y. (2018). Fashion Supply Chain and Logistics Management. *Fashion Supply Chain and Logistics Management*. https://doi.org/DOI: 10.4324/9781315466538

Weaver, J. (2024). *Strategic Insight of market : Harnessing AI-Driven Predictive Analytics for Strategic Insight of market : Harnessing AI-Driven Predictive Analytics for Competitive Advantage Date : December 13, 2022. December 2022*. https://doi.org/DOI: 10.13140/RG.2.2.21889.98407

KEY TERMS AND DEFINITIONS

Insight of Market: The understanding and interpretation of market data and trends that inform strategic business decisions. This includes consumer behavior, competitive landscape, and economic conditions.

Personalized AI: Artificial intelligence technologies that analyze data to tailor products, services, or communications to individual consumer preferences and behaviors, enhancing customer engagement and satisfaction.

Competitive Advantage: A condition or circumstance that puts a company in a favorable or superior business position relative to its competitors, often achieved through unique resources, capabilities, or strategies.

Chapter 17
Shaping Consumer Behaviour With AI:
Exploring the Impact of Personalization, Efficiency, and Trust

Balpreet Kaur
https://orcid.org/0000-0002-4396-0226
DAV University, India

Preeti Mehra
https://orcid.org/0000-0002-8979-9431
Campbell College, Canada

ABSTRACT

Artificial intelligence has emerged as a transformative force profoundly shaping consumers' intentions to adopt it for shopping. The study attempts to expand the scope of TAM by integrating the key dimensions of AI, including 'personalization', 'efficiency of AI-powered tools', and 'trust in AI'. The SEM technique was used to test the hypothesized model. The results revealed that personalization, through AI-driven recommendations, and the efficiency of chatbots significantly influence shoppers' intentions to adopt AI technology. Trust in AI also plays a critical role in shaping intentions to adopt AI-powered websites/apps for shopping. Moreover, a positive attitude towards adopting AI technology further enhances shoppers' behavioral intentions to use AI. The qualitative insights also indicated that consumers value AI-powered personalization, such as tailored recommendations and personalized offers, to enhance the shopping experience. However, data privacy has emerged as a primary concern when using AI for decision-making. Hence, the study provides valuable implications for marketers.

DOI: 10.4018/979-8-3693-9611-7.ch017

INTRODUCTION

Artificial intelligence (AI) has emerged as a disruptive force transforming entire sectors and business procedures. Numerous organizational functional areas have significantly benefited from the incorporation of AI, with marketing seeing the most significant gains. AI technologies have empowered marketers with advanced tools and insights, illuminating the path for future marketing innovations and strategies (Kumar, Ashraf, and Nadeem, 2024).

The escalating integration of AI into various sectors, be it retail, manufacturing, service providers, IT, and hospitality, has opened several doors to providing tailored and personalized customer experiences (Anderson et al., 2023; Pan et al., 2021; Thakur and Kushwaha, 2024)

Artificial Intelligence has rapidly become an imperative force in shaping consumer expectations. Understanding consumer behavior and redefining the way consumers interact with businesses has become a prime focus area of artificial intelligence. AI utilizes data and algorithms to analyze, predict, and influence consumer preferences, thus prompting businesses to stay competitive in today's dynamic era (Anderson et al., 2023). For these reasons, business houses have articulated much interest in using AI in marketing (Manoharan et al., 2024)

The role of AI in offering personalization has inculcated trust among consumers and has brought significant changes to consumer decision-making processes. By offering personalized experiences, AI ensures that consumers feel understood and valued. AI is expected to influence company strategies and consumer behaviours spectacularly (Davenport et al., 2020). In a survey, AI was predicted to be the technology that marketers would use optimally in the future (Columbus, 2019), thus pointing towards its growing popularity. Further, reliance on artificial intelligence is increasing day by day and has changed the way consumers do online shopping since COVID-19 (Sakaguchi and Aoki, 2022; Wang et al.,2023; Kaur and Mehra, 2023). Yeo et al. (2022) also emphasized the importance of AI-based digital technology experiences on instagrammers' purchase decisions. In line with that, Singh et al. (2024) specifically focused on the influence of AI in reshaping consumer recommendation models and consumer shopping decisions Several studies have been done on its role in influencing consumer purchase behaviour (Khan, 2022, Mogaji and Jain, 2024; Petrescu, 2024). Hence, AI transforms how consumers and brands communicate (Haleem et al., 2022).

Nevertheless, some challenges come with opportunities. There is a growing concern about investigating AI's most important ethical and legal issues in marketing (Kumar and Suthar, 2024). Consumers may have privacy concerns due to excessive personalization (Jain, 2023). However, the right mix between effective personalization and respecting consumer privacy is crucial for successful marketing campaigns.

Customers would avail of online services only if they were assured of the security and privacy of their financial data and the personal information they provided (Kaur and Sharma, 2022). Data privacy is a prime concern for customers while adopting information technology. Moreover, Davis (1989) opined that perceived usefulness and ease of use influence user acceptance of information technology. This technology acceptance model of Davis was further evaluated for Artificial Intelligence in E-Commerce (Wang et al., 2023).

Hence, Artificial intelligence (AI) has emerged as a revolutionary force in influencing the digital consumer experience, causing a seismic upheaval in the connection between technology and consumer behavior (Singh et al., 2024). This transformation is evident in how AI changes consumer interactions, streamlines procedures, and boosts engagement.

On the other hand, Peltier (2024) opined that though customers' experiences, as well as how businesses find, develop, nurture, and maintain interactive marketing interactions, are being revolutionized by artificial intelligence (AI), but on the other side, most marketers lack a thorough understanding of artificial intelligence (AI) and how it may benefit businesses and consumers. This knowledge gap presents a significant challenge as businesses struggle to leverage AI effectively to optimize consumer experiences and drive adoption.

As a result, understanding the factors that stimulate buyers to adopt AI technology for shopping has become a foremost concern for e-tailers. While prior research has explored the role of AI on consumer purchase decisions, there is a gap in understanding how AI-driven personalization, efficiency, and trust interact within the framework of consumer technology acceptance. The traditional Technology Acceptance Model (TAM) does not fully apprehend the complexities AI introduces in digital marketing and e-commerce. As AI continues to evolve, there is a requirement to expand this model by incorporating AI-specific factors that significantly influence consumer adoption.

So based on the studies of Davis (1989) and Wang et al. (2023), the present study proposes to expand the scope of the technology acceptance model (TAM) by integrating the dimensions of AI in marketing. TAM is somewhat outdated in the radical sphere of interactive digital technologies powered by AI and machine learning (Lim and Zhang, 2022). Therefore, we add personalization, efficiency, and trust to our model, which describes AI technologies' capabilities and effectiveness in shopping.

Hence, the study aims to bridge the gap by comprehensively understanding how AI-driven features such as personalization, efficiency, and trust influence shoppers' attitudes toward AI technology, consequently influencing their behavioral intentions to use AI-driven retail sites and apps for shopping. In addition, the study attempts to explore and extract insights from respondents regarding their likes and concerns about AI in online shopping.

Henceforth, we aim to address the following research questions:

1. How do AI-driven features such as personalization, efficiency, and trust influence online shoppers' attitudes toward AI technology?
2. How does consumer attitude toward AI technology impact their behavioral intention to use AI-driven retail sites and apps for shopping?
3. What aspects of AI-driven personalization do consumers find most appealing or helpful?
4. What are consumers' key concerns regarding using AI in online shopping?

CONCEPTUAL BACKGROUND AND MODEL FORMULATION

This section provides a conceptual basis for implementing AI-powered tools in e-business because the emergence of AI has opened up new paves for challenges that e-commerce organizations have long faced.

AI and Retail

AI offers brands an opportunity to deliver customized experiences to customers. Machine learning algorithms are sought to help determine customer preferences. Once the preferences have been outlined, targeted recommendations that increase customer engagement and loyalty will be adopted (Verma et al., 2021). Amazon's recommendation algorithm that AI powers leads to at least a 35% increase in sales. These experiences are further made delightful with the help of Amazon's 'Most Popular Products Recommendations', 'Review-based Products Recommendations', and 'Similar Products Recommendations, 'Customers are also Buying" products recommendation' (https://evdelo.com/amazons-recommendation-algorithm-drives-35-of-its-sales/).

AI enables retailers to estimate the market in real time. Amazon's pricing algorithm updates market conditions and product prices, contributing to the company's success.

Additionally, Netflix uses AI and machine learning to study user behavior, such as watch history, viewing time, and interactions. With this information, its recommendation engine offers personalized content, boosting user engagement and retention. This AI-based strategy allows Netflix to improve user satisfaction (Hong, 2024).

AI and Inventory Management

AI also facilitates inventory management by predicting demand patterns by analyzing historical data, estimating trends, and analyzing other situational factors like weather and holidays. AI helps companies avoid situations of overstocking and understocking. Walmart optimizes its stock by using AI. With a vast global network, it is an important tool that assists the giant retailer in optimizing its inventory.

Walmart is known for its stupendous technological applications of its inventory management. Through data-driven insights, Walmart has analyzed customer-driven insights, leading to optimizing its inventory and supply chain operations. Customer data is acquired through AI through diverse touch points. This covers online and offline purchases and customer interactions (Wairimu, 2023).

AI and Advertising

AI has simplified digital advertising through automatic advertisement placing and behavioural targeting. Advertising platforms like Google Ads use AI to predict user behaviour and place advertisements in real-time, thus ensuring that the marketers reach their targeted customers competently (Diamond, 2023). AI algorithms help marketers to line up their marketing strategies per customer preferences and likings (Tripathy et al., 2016). This also ensures the efficiency of the Return on Investment by managing the marketing campaign budgets.

Feng, Chen, and Xie (2024) also focused on the growing importance of artificial intelligence in advertising by unveiling the role of AI influencer-related attributes in shaping consumer attitudes and trust.

AI and Sentiment Analysis

AI-driven sentiment analysis tools monitor social media and review customer reviews and feedback to gauge customer perceptions about brands. Companies can reflect on their marketing strategies after an analysis of customer sentiments. Nike uses sentiment analysis to enhance its market position in its footwear segment. It has also been able to improve its customer retention and brand loyalty. Understanding customer repurchase intentions and re-patronage is essential for a sound business foundation (Zhou et al., 2019). A textual sentiment calculation can be done to understand customers' repurchase intentions by gathering online reviews, ratings, and emotional information.

AI and Efficiency

AI revolutionizes marketing by providing data-driven insights, automating processes, and personalising customer experiences. Across different industries, integrating AI into marketing strategies has enabled the delivery of excellent customer experiences. It offers companies a distinctive roadmap for leveraging AI effectively in marketing operations amidst the escalating dependence on digital platforms (Senyapar, 2024).

Key Dimensions of AI

The choice of personalization, efficiency, and trust as essential constructs primarily depends on their vital role in influencing consumer adoption of AI-based shopping platforms. Personalization supports user experience through customized suggestions, efficiency enhances convenience and decision-making, and trust reduces AI dependability and security anxiety. These constructs directly impact consumers' attitudes toward AI for shopping and are thus necessary additions to the classical TAM model.

AI and Personalisation

Personalization has become the most needed element of good customer experiences. AI plays a vital role in tailoring interactions to customer preferences. By collecting and analyzing different data patterns, AI can help predict behaviors and customize product and service offerings to enhance customer engagement and experiences. Personalization is a driving force for increasing loyalty, making it a remarkable strategy for building a firm place in the competitive markets. Companies showcase their recent AI, machine learning, and profound learning breakthroughs. Companies use AI to create customer personalization in almost all areas, ranging from CRM, e-commerce, customer recommendations, security, voice assistance, and Natural Language Processing for customer understanding (Pearson, 2020).

AI offers personalized and customized messages based on customers' preferences and profiles (Huang & Rust, 2020). This may include offering product recommendations, interacting on e-commerce platforms, providing targeted advertisements, and offering dynamic content to influence consumers. Machine Learning and Predictive Analytic tools stand as the pillars of AI enabling personalization in business.

Generative AI handles innovative marketing processes, allowing businesses to create tailored processes for a diverse audience (Cillo and Rubera, 2025). Davenport et al. (2020) opined that AI analyses consumer sentiments and creates emotionally reverberating advertisements, thus making the brand appear more relatable to consumers.

AI-driven Personalization uses data analytics and machine learning algorithms to design personalized content, recommendations, and ads based on the individual's preferences, demographics, and behaviour. AI-driven personalization helps organizations enhance overall marketing efficiency by increasing customer engagement and conversion rates (Broklyn et al., 2024; Sherly et al., 2024).

On the other hand, the intention to use AI technology for shopping means a consumer actively leverages AI-powered tools while shopping online to enjoy a more customized shopping experience facilitated by AI. Lim and Zhang (2022) also emphasized the usefulness of the technology acceptance model in foreseeing the users' adoption of AI-driven personalization in digital news platforms.

Briggs et al. (2004) opined that effective personalization strategies can boost the users' trust over time by consistently providing efficient experiences per their expectations, enhancing their platform experience. Hence, content personalization has emerged as a key driver of engagement and adoption of AI-driven platforms (Teepapal, 2025; Lim and Zhang, 2022).

Past studies have emphasized how AI may improve customization through data analytics, machine learning, and predictive algorithms, ultimately increasing customer trust and engagement. While the studies highlight the advantages of AI-driven personalization, there is a lack of detailed exploration of its direct impact on consumers' attitudes toward adopting AI-powered retail platforms. Furthermore, past studies primarily focused on AI's functionality rather than how it affects user acceptance psychologically. This gap in understanding the attitudinal shift driven by AI personalization necessitates the formulation of the following hypothesis:

H1: AI-driven personalization significantly influences online shoppers' attitudes toward using AI-driven retail sites/apps.

AI and Transforming Marketing Efficiency

Efficiency involves optimizing purchasing processes to enable customers to make decisions swiftly using automated systems (Chaffey, 2019). Modern consumer expectations rely heavily on the efficiency of the purchasing process. AI technologies play a role in improving operational efficiency in various ways. For example, human chat services are being replaced by chatbots and virtual assistants that are designed to communicate with human users using natural language based on artificial intelligence (Adam et al., 2021)

This system of AI makes it easier for customers to get instant service, helping them make well-informed buying choices without the usual delays of traditional customer support methods. Moreover, inventory management and supply chain logistics are enhanced by AI algorithms, guaranteeing that products are accessible whenever consumers want to purchase them (Gunasekaran and Ngai, 2014).

The study by Zhang et al. (2022) highlighted that consumers are more willing to pay for products designed by AI than professionally designed products. It is also emphasized that curiosity plays a significant role in this desire for AI-designed products. AI is also significantly assisting in boosting efficiency, resulting in shorter transaction times and increased customer satisfaction and loyalty. Customers are more inclined to revisit businesses that provide smooth and effective buying experiences, showing that consumer decision-making is significantly influenced by AI-powered operational efficiency.

Moreover, chatbots efficiently shape customers' attitudes regarding usefulness, usability, and trust when shopping online (Rana et al., 2024). Perceived ease of use and perceived usefulness significantly influence the consumer's attitude toward adopting AI chatbots, which consequently affects their intention to use AI chatbots for shopping (Myin and Watchravesringkan,2024). Along similar lines, Cheng and Jiang (2020) opined that brand managers need to understand users' motivations to improve satisfaction with chatbot services to cultivate the intentions of continued use and long-term loyalty among customers.

Furthermore, the service quality of artificial intelligence (AI) chatbots affects customer loyalty to an organization. AI chatbot service quality positively affects customer loyalty through affective trust, perceived value, and satisfaction. So, companies need to develop a way to improve customer loyalty in the development and post-development stages of AI chatbots (Chen et al., 2023).

Artificial Intelligence-driven customer segmentation assists in limitless possibilities, enabling companies to frame personalized marketing strategies that lead to the establishment of loyalty on behalf of the customer. Many companies are adopting AI-based models to market their products effectively to their customers. Segmentation is done by understanding behavioural patterns (Wang, 2022).

The merging of AI with marketing automation systems has impressively reduced the time spent on repetitive tasks, thus enabling marketers to focus on maintaining creativity in their endeavors. On the other hand, Li, Gan, and Zheng (2023) opined that even if chatbots are being used increasingly in customer service to lessen the workload of human workers and occasionally to replace human employees in online purchasing, it is still difficult to guarantee that customers will evaluate the service and purchase after using a chatbot.

Hence, the existing literature emphasizes using AI to improve efficiency with chatbots, supply chain improvement, and segmentation (Gunasekaran and Ngai, 2014; Rana et al., 2024). There is limited research on whether AI-driven efficiency directly impacts consumers' attitudes towards AI-based retail platforms. Most literature concentrates on how AI affects usability, trust, and loyalty (Chen et al.,

2023). However, it does not directly analyze the impact of perceived efficiency on consumer adoption behavior in online shopping.

So, based on past studies and considering the importance of the TAM model, the following hypothesis is proposed.

H2: The efficiency of AI-powered tools significantly influences online shoppers' attitudes toward using AI-driven retail sites/apps.

Trust in AI

Nowadays, the service industries are aggressively using automation tools such as chatbots, service robots, and virtual assistants to provide efficient services to customers online, and these tools frequently target of malicious applications that lead to substantial risks to consumer privacy. So, in the digital age, it is important to safeguard the users' personal information (Salih,2025) because the user's trust in Artificial Intelligence (AI) enabled systems has been considered a key to fostering adoption (Bach et al.,2024).

Further, trust is a significant component of good consumer experiences and is equally important in offline and online business. AI systems foster trust by building steadfast and unwavering interactions. A few instances can be the AI recommendation engines that deliver to-the-point and accurate responses, thus escalating customer faith and trust in a brand (Chen et al., 2022; Labib, 2024). Afroogh et al. (2024) emphasize that AI systems have diffused into several aspects of our lives, potentially affecting our thoughts and faith in different systems. Trust and distrust serve as regulators; where trust in AI can increase its adoption rate, distrust may lead to a fall in its adoption. The study identifies technical (safety, accuracy, and robustness) and non-technical (ethical, legal, and mixed) trustworthiness metrics as parameters that must be adopted to make AI trustworthy.

On one side, perceived utility and trust significantly foster positive interactions between users and technology (Teepapal, 2025). However, privacy concerns, challenges, and distrust hinder the effectiveness of AI-driven Personalization. So, organizations must commit to transparent and ethical AI practices, prioritizing data privacy and security and integrating human-like elements in AI interactions. Further, this approach is technically and strategically essential to develop a dependable and trustworthy AI user experience (Ahmed and Aziz, 2025)

While the current literature points out the importance of trust in AI systems in enabling adoption (Bach et al., 2024; Afroogh et al., 2024), the gap in understanding how trust, in particular, affects consumer attitudes toward AI-based retail platforms still exists. The majority of studies are centered on trust in general AI applications. However, they do not consider how trust in AI tools, especially in online shopping, affects consumer behavior and their intention to adopt such platforms.

The hypothesis is important since trust is a key motivator of AI adoption, and its particular influence on consumer sentiment towards AI-powered retail websites and applications is not adequately investigated. Privacy, accuracy, and ethics (Teepapal, 2025; Labib, 2024) are important drivers of consumer attitudes and willingness to use AI-powered systems, and thus it is important to investigate how these trust drivers directly influence online shopping behavior and decision-making.

Hence, the following hypothesis has been proposed based on the above-discussed studies.

H3: Trust in AI significantly influences online shoppers' attitudes toward using AI-driven retail sites/apps.

Further, the perceived usefulness, ease of use, and trust positively influence the users' attitude toward adopting AI technology. The positive attitude toward the adoption further leads to their behavioural intentions (Davis, 1989; Wang et al., 2023; Myin and Watchravesringkan, 2024 and Teepapal, 2025).

Though the Technology Acceptance Model (TAM) has been widely applied to examine variables like perceived usefulness, ease of use, and trust in the adoption of technology (Davis, 1989; Wang et al., 2023), but there is a research gap concerning how these variables influence consumers' behavioral intentions in AI-based retail platforms. This hypothesis is important since, although past studies have demonstrated that perceived usefulness, ease of use, and trust influence users' attitudes (Davis, 1989; Myin and Watchravesringkan, 2024), how these attitudes evolve into actual behavioral intentions is essential. As a positive attitude towards technology is a good predictor of behavioral intention (Teepapal, 2025), investigating this association in AI-based retail platforms will assist companies in maximizing user interaction, refining marketing efforts, and promoting the use of AI-based tools in e-commerce.

So, based on the framework, the following hypothesis is proposed.

H4: Attitude towards use significantly influences shoppers' behavioral intentions to use AI-driven retail sites/apps.

Henceforth, the intensive literature review provides an approach to propose the following model (Fig 1) to investigate the adoption of AI-driven features such as personalization, efficiency, and trust and their influence on behavioral intention to use AI-driven retail sites and apps for shopping.

Figure 1. Proposed Conceptual Model

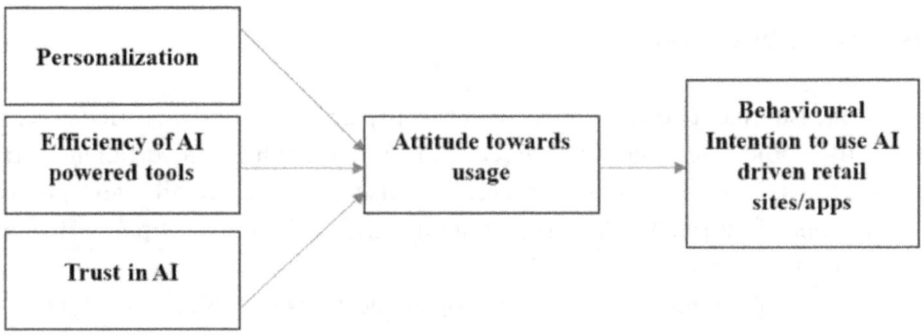

RESEARCH METHODOLOGY

This section covers the methodology, including the study's sample, the data collection procedure, the sample design, the development of the measurement scale, and the statistical techniques used for the data analysis.

Data Collection

An online survey was administrated to target a diverse sample of respondents residing in India who have engaged in online shopping for the past six months. The reason behind the selection of Indian respondents is the alteration in their shopping habits by the emergence of e-commerce, particularly in light of the nation's rapidly expanding internet and online infrastructure. A solid basis for the launch of e-commerce in the market was also established by the change in consumer purchasing habits following the pandemic and the growing presence of the organized sector in retail markets. With a population of over 1.4 billion and an economy that is expanding quickly, it is anticipated that in 2027, there will be 427 million online buyers (Statista, 2024).

Before distributing the questionnaire to the final respondents, a pilot survey was conducted to get the questionnaire filled out by 30 respondents. After that, the revised questionnaire was sent to 265 respondents, and the final 238 questionnaires were returned for data analysis. The virtual snowball sampling technique was used to assess the respondents. This method has been widely used because the respondents can share the survey form link with their social networks with similar backgrounds (Chen et al., 2022; Baltar and Brunet, 2012).

Measurement Scale

The measurement items were borrowed from past studies and modified to achieve the study's objective. The constructs such as personalization, efficiency, trust, attitude to use, and behavioural intention to use AI driven retail sites/apps were assessed on a five-point Likert-type scale (with 1 indicating "strongly disagree" and 5 "strongly agree").

Further, respondents were asked two open questions to explore what type of AI-driven personalization they found most helpful. Furthermore, what concerns them most about AI in online shopping?

Statistical Tools

A mixed research approach was used to achieve the objectives of the study. First, the quantitative analysis was performed. Structural Equation Modeling technique using AMOS was applied to test the proposed model's fitness and measure the degree and direction of relationship among the proposed constructs.

Further, the qualitative research approach was employed to analyze the answers given by respondents. For this purpose, word cloud analysis was performed using statistical software R.

ANALYSIS AND DISCUSSION

This section contains the data analysis results using different statistical techniques to achieve the objectives.

Table 1 shows the demographic-wise distribution of the respondents of the sample. The sample contained 52% males and 47% females. Age ranged from 18 to 55 and above, but 73% of respondents fall in the age group of 18-24. Most respondents (42.9%) held a Bachelor's Degree, followed by (32.8%) postgraduates. Further, (54.6%) of respondents are students, who are followed by (37.4%) of respondents who are employed.

Table 1. Demographic distribution of respondents

Characteristics		Percentage
Age	18-24 25-34 35-44 45-54 55 and above	73.5 16.4 6.7 2.5 .8
Gender	Male Female Other	52.2 47.0 .8
Education Level	Bachelor's Degree High School Master's Degree Ph.D. Other (Professional Degrees)	42.9 13.4 32.8 6.3 4.6
Employment Status	Employed Retired Self Employed Student Unemployed	37.4 .8 4.6 54.6 2.5

Validation of Measurement Scale

Before applying SEM, it is necessary to ensure the validity of the scale's content. The scale items were borrowed from past studies and then revised as per the requirements and objective of the study (Table 2).

Table 2. Content Validity

Constructs	Items	Adapted from
Personalization	• I often receive personalized product recommendations when shopping online. • Online advertisements seem tailored to my interests and preferences. • E-commerce platforms suggest products based on my past purchases or browsing history. • I frequently encounter personalized content or recommendations while using e-commerce websites.	Amil (2024)
Efficiency of AI-powered tools	• The chatbot service agent provides prompt feedback to customers' comments. • The chatbot service agent makes an adequate change based on customers' feedback. • The chatbot service agent addresses customers' complaints on time. • The chatbot service agent is sensitive to customers' needs at the moment. • The chatbot service agent addresses customers' complaints positively.	Jiang et al. (2022)
Trust in AI	• The AI recommendation system is honest about how it uses my personal information. • The AI recommendation system provides fair and unbiased recommendations. • I trust the AI recommendation system to protect my personal information.	Amil (2024)
Attitude toward usage	• Shopping in a webshop/shopping app powered by AI is a good idea. • Shopping in a webshop/shopping app that AI powers are a wise idea. • I am positive about the webshop/shopping app that AI powers.	Wang et al. (2023)
Behavioral Intention to use AI-driven retail sites/apps	• I intend to visit web shops and use shopping apps that are powered by AI more frequently. • I am willing to spend more on products offered by web shops and AI-powered apps.	Wang et al. (2023)

Fitness of the Measurement Model

Confirmatory factor analysis was employed to assess the data's fitness. The results demonstrated a good model fit (chi-square/degree of freedom (CMIN)=1.459, Comparative Fit

Index (CFI)=0.936, Tucker–Lewis Index (TLI)=0.918, Incremental Fit Index (IFI)=0.939, Root Mean Square Error of Approximation (RMSEA)=0.061 and Root Mean Square Residual (RMSR)=0.046. All the indices are in the acceptable range, as the range recommended by Hoyle (1995) and Fadlelmula (2011).

Further, the internal consistency of the measurement scale was assessed through reliability and validity.

Table 3. Assessment of Reliability and Validity of the Scale

Constructs	Composite Reliability	AVE	ASV	MSV
Personalization	**0.740**	**0.612**	**0.526**	**0.221**
Efficiency of AI-powered tools	**0.786**	**0.632**	**0.431**	**0.189**
Trust in AI	**0.726**	**0.628**	**0.510**	**0.228**
Attitude toward usage	**0.821**	**0.657**	**0.454**	**0.216**
Behavioral Intention to use AI-driven retail sites/apps	**0.762**	**0.642**	**0.432**	**0.168**

Table 3 shows the reliability and validity of the constructs. The composite reliability of each construct is above the value of 0.7, the minimum threshold value recommended by Malhotra and Dash (2010) to ensure reliability.

Further, to assess the convergent validity of the scale, two key indicators are used, i.e., Average Variance Extracted (AVE) and Composite Reliability (CR). In Table 3, each construct's AVE value exceeds the acceptable threshold of 0.5. Furthermore, the composite reliability of each construct is greater than its respective AVE value, which is a positive outcome (as stated by (Malhotra and Dash, 2010; Casalo et al., 2008).

However, two conditions must be met to ensure the discriminant validity, as Fornell and Larcker (1981) suggested. First, the maximum shared variance (MSV) should be less than the average shared variance (ASV), and second, ASV should be less than the average variance extracted (AVE). Both the conditions have been met satisfactorily.

Common Method Bias

Common method bias is a significant problem in primary surveys when data collection is done from the same respondents simultaneously. So, according to Harman's (1967), a single-factor test must be applied to find the possible presence of variance owing to the common method (Balaji et al.,2016). Hence, all the variables were loaded on a single factor to confirm the CFA model's fitness. The result indicated that a single factor accounted for 29% of the variance, less than the threshold limit of 50% recommended by Podsakoff et al. (2003), indicating that the measurement model is free from bias.

Path Analysis

After ensuring the reliability and validity of the scale, the next step is to develop a structural model. The AMOS maximum likelihood estimation method was used to test the degree and direction of the relationship between the constructs.

First, the fitness of the structural model was assessed through various indices. The results demonstrated a good model fit (chi-square/degree of freedom (CMIN)=1.259, Comparative Fit Index (CFI)=0.972, Tucker–Lewis Index (TLI)=0.963, Incremental Fit Index (IFI)=0.973, Root Mean Square Error of Approximation (RMSEA) =0.046 and Root Mean Square Residual (RMSR)=0.039. All the indices are in the acceptable range as recommended by Hoyle (1995) and Fadlelmula (2011).

Further, all the hypothesized relationships are significant, as depicted in Table 4

Table 4. Hypotheses Testing

Hypothesis	Standardized loadings	Sig	Decision
H1:Personalization→(+)attitude towards usage	0.689	***	Supported
H2: Efficiency of AI-powered tools →(+) attitude towards usage	0.668	***	Supported
H3: Trust in AI →(+) attitude towards usage	0.694	***	Supported
H4: Attitude towards usage →(+) behavioural intention to use AI-driven retail sites/apps.	0.704	***	Supported

Note: ***p<0.001

The results in Table 4 indicate that the constructs "personalization," "efficiency of AI-powered tools and "trust in AI" demonstrate significant positive influence on the "attitude toward the use of AI technology for shopping. So, H1, H2, and H3 were accepted at 0.001 significance level.

Further, the construct "attitude towards the use of AI for shopping" positively influences shoppers' "behavioral intention to use AI-driven retail sites/apps". Hypothesis 4 is also significant at 0.001 level.

After evaluating the quantitative data, the next step was initiated to evaluate the qualitative data using word cloud analysis

Word Cloud Analysis

Several steps have been followed to analyze the text data. The text mining process (as stated in the study of Stanca et al.,2023) was followed to extract the important words for analysis. R software package was used to analyze the qualitative data. Two open-ended questions were asked to respondents: What type of AI-driven personalization do you find most helpful.? What concerns you the most about AI in online shopping?

First, the data was cleaned by eliminating useless stop words (such as and, of, on, etc.) and punctuation marks. The seven keywords that were extracted are useful for further analysis. The keywords that have high frequency include “product”, “recommendations”, “personalized”, “discount”, “offers” and so on. Figure 2 indicates the frequency of keywords' appearance using the word cloud method.

Figure 2. Word Cloud highlighting the importance of AI-driven Personalization

Table 5. Frequency distribution of keywords

Keywords	Frequency
Product	77
Recommendations	77
Personalized	77
Discounts	77
Offers	77
Targeted	25
Ads	25

Figure 2 highlights the types of AI-driven personalization consumers found most beneficial when shopping online on AI-powered websites. The most helpful features are AI product recommendations to help with purchasing decisions and personalized discounts or offers. Further, Table 5 displays the frequency distribution of these keywords in numbers.

Figure 3. Word Cloud of Key Concerns About AI in Online Shopping

Figure 3 presents a word cloud illustrating consumers' primary concerns about AI in online shopping. The most significant concern is the privacy of data, as shoppers worry about how their personal information is collected and used. Concerns over a lack of transparency closely follow this. Because the consumers are unsure about how AI algorithms make decisions. This shows that employing AI in e-commerce requires more transparency and accountability. Table 6 displays the frequency distribution of these keywords in numbers.

Table 6. Frequency distribution of keywords

Keywords	Frequency
Data	71
Privacy	71
Lack	49
Transparency	49
Bias	29

continued on following page

Table 6. Continued

Keywords	Frequency
Recommendations	29
Unfair	28
Pricing	28
Over-reliance	28
Automation	28
Decreased	39
Human	39
Interaction	39

CONCLUSION

As the study concludes, artificial intelligence has become an evolutionary force in developing and redefining the digital consumer experience and establishing the consumer-technological behavioral relationship. This study primarily examined the drivers of the consumers' behavioral intention of AI-based retail platforms and apps by proposing an extended model combining personalization, efficiency, and trust into the Technology Acceptance Model (TAM).

Though TAM has served as a basis for prior work on technology adoption, the emergence of interactive, self-learning technologies such as AI revealed limitations in the model that warranted this augmentation. A mixed-method research design was used to meet the objectives of the study. Structural Equation Modeling technique was employed to perform quantitative analysis using AMOS. The aim was to assess how well the proposed model fit and to determine the relationships between important constructs.

The aim here was to examine the fit of the hypothesized model and test the hypotheses among the crucial constructs. This analysis demonstrated that "personalization" and "efficiency" significantly enhanced the shopping experience and facilitated the adoption of AI-driven websites and apps for shopping. "Trust in AI" emerged as another important construct, focusing on the AI system's fairness, security, and personal data privacy. Without trust, not even the latest AI technologies can achieve wide-scale adoption by the consumer.

These results offer insightful information about adopting AI for shopping and apply to various geographic areas across India and consumer demographics, especially young, tech-savvy consumers. The results provide a more comprehensive knowledge of AI-driven shopping behaviors across various educational and professional backgrounds because of the sample's diversified demographic representation.

In addition to the quantitative analysis, qualitative data was analyzed with R software and text-mining techniques. The remaining sections of the questionnaire comprised two open-ended questions to facilitate exploration and extracting insights from respondents regarding their likes and concerns about AI in online shopping. The findings revealed that while consumers value AI-powered personalization, like personalized recommendations and personalized offers, they still have concerns about data security and transparency around AI decision-making. The research highlights the importance of managing innovation with the safety and values of an innovative culture with ethical, transparent, and secure practices around the use of AI applications. This model presents a solution for e-tailers on how and where they need to go to alleviate the need for innovation while uncovering room for strategic technology adoption.

Further, at the societal level, policymakers need to take the initiative to enact strong data protection laws to secure customer privacy and reduce security threats related to artificial intelligence in e-commerce. Lastly, funding AI literacy initiatives can encourage ethical AI development and adoption, enabling customers to make knowledgeable decisions.

IMPLICATIONS OF THE STUDY

As AI technologies transform customer behavior and shopping experiences, the study's implications go beyond e-tailers and touch on broader societal impact. In a digital marketplace, e-tailers must prioritize personalization, efficiency, and trust to gain a competitive edge. E-tailers may significantly increase customer satisfaction, loyalty, and sales by emphasizing AI-driven customized recommendations and a seamless shopping experience. This will help them build lasting relationships with customers. Additionally, adhering to information security and maintaining transparency in data practices will foster trust, empowering customers to embrace AI-based purchasing solutions confidently.

Further, the growing use of AI in shopping has broadened the implications for consumer behavior and social norms. AI technology can potentially impact digital literacy, privacy concerns, and technology access as it transforms consumer interactions. In order to maintain a balance between innovation and ethical responsibility, society must adjust to these technological breakthroughs by ensuring that consumers are aware of their rights and data privacy. AI's increasing usage may impact employment in industries like retail, necessitating new training and upskilling initiatives as AI systems proliferate.

Further, the study significantly advances the literature by adding AI-driven components to the Technology Acceptance Model (TAM) and making it more applicable to the rapidly changing arena of interactive digital technology. The study offers a more thorough framework for comprehending customer acceptance of AI in e-commerce by combining personalization, efficiency, and trust. Furthermore, given AI's growing influence in shaping consumers' shopping experience, it provides insightful information on both present and future consumer behavior. The impact of digital AI technologies on consumer decision-making will only increase with their sophistication. This study lays the groundwork for future research, allowing academics and industry professionals to investigate how AI-driven advancements will continue to change customer behavior, purchasing patterns, and retail tactics in the years to come.

LIMITATIONS AND FUTURE SCOPE OF THE STUDY

Despite the contribution, the study has some limitations that open the door for further research. To begin, the generalizability of the results may be somewhat limited because of the sample size and demographic composition. A more precise examination of such demographic features as age, cultural background, and prior technology acceptance might provide deep insights into consumer behavior toward AI adoption in e-commerce. Apart from that, this research is about the influence of personalization, efficiency, and trust on customers; external factors like prior AI knowledge, shopping habits, and digital literacy can also play a role in determining the acceptance of the innovation. In light of forthcoming research, these factors could be examined as potential moderators to understand better consumers' decision-making process in the AI-driven shopping environment.

Further, the present study followed a mixed-method approach to provide a comprehensive understanding of consumer engagement and the adoption of AI-powered retail sites for shopping. However, certain limitations create a new pave for future research. First, the model fitness was tested using structural equation modeling (SEM). Although structural equation modeling (SEM) provided strong statistical validation for the model fitness test, other methods like longitudinal research or machine learning models could improve predictive accuracy and dynamic behavioral insights even more. Second, qualitative data was interpreted using word cloud analysis, which yielded insightful customer perspectives. In order to extract more profound emotional and attitudinal patterns from consumer reviews, feedback, and responses, future research could use advanced sentiment analysis or AI-driven text mining approaches.

Additionally, future research has a broad scope, especially in extending the knowledge of AI dimensions beyond the constructs taken under study. While the current research focused on personalization, efficiency, and trust within the e-commerce sector, there is significant potential to investigate how emotional intelligence and adaptive learning within AI affect consumer behavior across different sectors. Examining these aspects will unveil new patterns of behavior, particularly as AI technologies advance. In order to provide a more comprehensive picture of AI adoption and its revolutionary effects on consumer interactions, future research may focus on how these AI capabilities affect industries like healthcare, banking, and education. The study's findings align with broader AI adoption discussions while highlighting gaps for further exploration. The study recognizes the importance of conducting a more thorough analysis of AI-related risks, such as algorithmic bias and unjust pricing. It also emphasizes the need for comparative assessments with traditional shopping experiences for a more balanced perspective.

Furthermore, we recognize that while personalization, efficiency, and trust in AI are significant forces behind the adoption of AI in shopping, usability, accessibility, and ethical concerns all play a significant role in influencing customer behavior. Because these elements are essential to the evolving landscape of AI in e-commerce, the study focused on how AI-driven customization, efficiency, and trust directly affect customer adoption. Nonetheless, we acknowledge that accessibility and usability are crucial for making AI technologies inclusive and user-friendly, especially for users with different levels of digital literacy. Privacy and data security concerns are also becoming more important as AI technology is incorporated into purchasing experiences. Future studies could also examine the ethical and legal regulations of adopting AI, emphasizing how consumer protection laws, ethical standards, and AI regulations affect consumer behavior and trust. A more thorough grasp of how ethical and legal issues influence the broad use of AI in e-commerce might be possible by looking at these variables. In order to provide a more comprehensive view of the barriers and facilitators of AI adoption in retail, future studies might expand the scope to examine how these factors interact with personalization, efficiency, and trust.

REFERENCES

Adam, M., Wessel, M., & Benlian, A. (2021). AI-based chatbots in customer service and their effects on user compliance. *Electronic Markets*, *31*(2), 427–445.

Afroogh, S., Akbari, A., Malone, E., Kargar, M., & Alambeigi, H. (2024). Trust in AI: Progress, challenges, and future directions. *Humanities & Social Sciences Communications*, *11*(1), 1–30.

Ahmed, S., & Aziz, N. A. (2025). Impact of AI on customer experience in video streaming services: A focus on personalization and trust. *International Journal of Human-Computer Interaction*, *41*(12), 7726-7745.

Amil, Y. (2024). The Impact of AI-Driven Personalization Tools on Privacy Concerns and Consumer Trust in E-commerce. Master thesis of the HEC-Ecole de gestion de l'Université de Liège

Anderson, L., Kanneganti, D., Houk, M., Holm, R., & Smith, T. (2023). Generative AI as a tool for environmental health research translation, Advancing. *Earth and Space Science (Hoboken, N.J.)*, *7*(7). Advance online publication. DOI: 10.1029/2023GH000875 PMID: 37502196

Bach, T. A., Khan, A., Hallock, H., Beltrão, G., & Sousa, S. (2024). A systematic literature review of user trust in AI-enabled systems: An HCI perspective. *International Journal of Human-Computer Interaction*, *40*(5), 1251–1266.

Baltar, F., & Brunet, I. (2012). Social research 2.0: virtual snowball sampling method using Facebook. *Internet Research*, *22*(1), 57-74.

Briggs, P., Simpson, B., & De Angeli, A. (2004). Personalisation and trust: a reciprocal relationship?. *Designing Personalized user experiences in eCommerce*, 39-55.

Broklyn, P., Olukemi, A., & Bell, C. (2024). AI-driven Personalization in digital marketing: Effectiveness and ethical considerations. Available at SSRN 4906214.

Casalo, L. V., Flavian, C., & Guinaliu, M. (2008). The role of satisfaction and website usability in developing customer loyalty and positive word of mouth in the e-banking services. *International Journal of Bank Marketing*, *26*(6), 399–417.

Chaffey, D., & Ellis-Chadwick, F. (2019). *Digital Marketing: Strategy and Implementation* (6th ed.). Pearson.

Chen, Q., Lu, Y., Gong, Y., & Xiong, J. (2023). Can AI chatbots help retain customers? Impact of AI service quality on customer loyalty. *Internet Research*, *33*(6), 2205–2243.

Chen, Y., Prentice, C., Weaven, S., & Hisao, A. (2022). The influence of customer trust and artificial intelligence on customer engagement and loyalty–The case of the home-sharing industry. *Frontiers in Psychology*, *13*, 912339. PMID: 35992434

Cheng, Y., & Jiang, H. (2020). How do AI-driven chatbots impact user experience? Examining gratifications, perceived privacy risk, satisfaction, loyalty, and continued use. *Journal of Broadcasting & Electronic Media*, *64*(4), 592–614.

Cillo, P., & Rubera, G. (2025). Generative AI in innovation and marketing processes: A roadmap of research opportunities. *Journal of the Academy of Marketing Science*, *13*, 684–701.

Columbus, L. (2019). *10 charts that will change your perspective on artificial intelligence's growth*. Forbes. Retrieved from https://www.forbes.com

Davenport, T., Guha, A., Grewal, D., & Bressgott, T. (2020). How artificial intelligence will change the future of marketing. *Journal of the Academy of Marketing Science*, *48*, 24–42.

Davis, F. D. (1989). Perceived Usefulness, Perceived Ease of Use and User Acceptance of Information Technology. *Management Information Systems Quarterly*, *13*(3), 319–340.

Diamond, M. (2023). Book Review: Marketing Artificial Intelligence: AI, Marketing, and the Future of Business by Paul Roetzer and Mike Kaput. *Management and Business Review, 3*(1).

Fadlelmula, F. K. (2011). Assessing power of structural equation modeling studies: A meta-analysis. *Education Research Journal*, *1*(3), 37–42.

Feng, Y., Chen, H., & Xie, Q. (2024). AI Influencers in Advertising: The Role of AI Influencer-Related Attributes in Shaping Consumer Attitudes, Consumer Trust, and Perceived Influencer–Product Fit. *Journal of Interactive Advertising*, *24*(1), 26–47.

Fornell, C., & Larcker, D. F. (1981). Evaluating structural equation models with unobservable variables and measurement error. *JMR, Journal of Marketing Research*, *18*(1), 39–50.

Gunasekaran, A., & Ngai, E. W. T. (2014). Expert systems and artificial intelligence in the 21st century logistics and supply chain management. *Expert Systems with Applications*, *41*(1), 1–4. DOI: 10.1016/j.eswa.2013.09.006

Haleem, A., Javaid, M., Qadri, M. A., Singh, R. P., & Suman, R. (2022). Artificial intelligence (AI) applications for marketing: A literature-based study. *International Journal of Intelligent Networks*, *3*, 119–132.

Harman, D. (1967). A single factor test of common method variance. *The Journal of Psychology*, *35*, 359–378.

Hong, Z. (2024), Personalized recommendations: How Netflix and Amazon Use Deep Learning to enhance user experience, https://medium.com/@zhonghong9998/personalized-recommendations-how-netflix-and-amazon-use-deep-learning-to-enhance-user-experience-e7bd6fcd18ff, assessed on 19 January 2025

Hoyle, R. H. (1995). *Structural Equation Modeling: Concepts, Issues, and Application*. Sage Publications.

Huang, M. H., & Rust, R. T. (2020). A strategic framework for artificial intelligence in marketing. *Journal of the Academy of Marketing Science*, *49*, 1–21.

Jain, R. (2023). The Impact of Artificial Intelligence on Business: Opportunities and Challenges. *Available at SSRN* 4407114.

Jiang, H., Cheng, Y., Yang, J., & Gao, S. (2022). AI-powered chatbot communication with customers: Dialogic interactions, satisfaction, engagement, and customer behavior. *Computers in Human Behavior*, *134*, 107329.

Kaur, B., & Mehra, P. (2023). Impact of Pandemic on Behavioural Transition in Consumption Pattern, *Empirical Economics Letters*, 22 (Special Issue 1): (October 2023). *ISSN*, *1681*, 8997. DOI: 10.5281/zenodo.10207087

Kaur, B., & Sharma, R. R. (2022). Factors affecting behavioural intentions to use e-banking services: An extension of TAM in Indian context. *International Journal of Business and Globalisation*, *32*(4), 414–430.

Khan, S. I. (2022). Impact of artificial intelligence on consumer buying behaviors: Study about the online retail purchase. *International Journal of Health Sciences*, (II), 8121–8129.

Kumar, D., & Suthar, N. (2024). Ethical and legal challenges of AI in marketing: An exploration of solutions. *Journal of Information. Communication and Ethics in Society*, *22*(1), 124–144.

Kumar, V., Ashraf, A. R., & Nadeem, W. (2024). AI-powered marketing: What, where, and how? *International Journal of Information Management*, *77*, 102783.

Labib, E. (2024). Artificial intelligence in marketing: Exploring current and future trends. *Cogent Business & Management*, *11*(1), 2348728.

Li, Y., Gan, Z., & Zheng, B. (2023). How do Artificial Intelligence Chatbots Affect Customer Purchase? Uncovering the Dual Pathways of Anthropomorphism on Service Evaluation. *Information Systems Frontiers*, 1–18.

Lim, J. S., & Zhang, J. (2022). Adoption of AI-driven Personalization in digital news platforms: An integrative model of technology acceptance and perceived contingency. *Technology in Society*, *69*, 101965.

Malhotra, N. K., & Dash, S. (2010). *Marketing research: An applied orientation* (6th ed.). Pearson Education India.

Manoharan, G., Durai, S., Ashtikar, S. P., & Kumari, N. (2024). Artificial Intelligence in Marketing Applications. In *Artificial Intelligence for Business* (pp. 40–70). Productivity Press.

Mogaji, E., & Jain, V. (2024). How generative AI is (will) change consumer behaviour: Postulating the potential impact and implications for research, practice, and policy. *Journal of Consumer Behaviour*. *23*(5), 2379–2389. DOI: 10.1002/cb.2345

Myin, M. T., & Watchravesringkan, K. (2024). Investigating consumers' adoption of AI chatbots for apparel shopping. *Journal of Consumer Marketing*, *41*(3), 314–327.

Pan, C.-L., Bai, X., Li, F., Zhang, D., Chen, H., & Lai, Q. (2021). How Business Intelligence Enables E-commerce: Breaking the Traditional E-commerce Mode and Driving the Transformation of Digital Economy. Proceedings - 2nd International Conference on ECommerce and Internet Technology, ECIT 2021, 26–30. DOI: 10.1109/ECIT52743.2021.00013

Pearson, A. (2020). Personalisation the artificial intelligence way, available at http://dx.doi.org/.DOI: 10.69554/JJGR7331

Peltier, J. W., Dahl, A. J., & Schibrowsky, J. A. (2024). Artificial intelligence in interactive marketing: A conceptual framework and research agenda. *Journal of Research in Interactive Marketing*, *18*(1), 54–90.

Petrescu, M., Krishen, A. S., Gironda, J. T., & Fergurson, J. R. (2024). Exploring AI technology and consumer behavior in retail interactions. *Journal of Consumer Behaviour*, *23*(6), 3132–3151.

Podsakoff, P. M., MacKenzie, S. B., Lee, J. Y., & Podsakoff, N. P. (2003). Common method biases in behavioral research: A critical review of the literature and recommended remedies. *The Journal of Applied Psychology*, *88*(5), 879–903. PMID: 14516251

Rana, J., Jain, R., & Nehra, V. (2024). Utility and acceptability of AI-enabled Chatbots on the online customer journey. *International Journal of Computing and Digital Systems*, *15*(1), 323–335.

Sakaguchi, M., & Aoki, E. (2022, June). Study on the Comparison of Consumer Impression of E-commerce and Real Stores in the Fashion Tech Era, and the Effectiveness of VR Utilization. In *Computational Intelligence in Security for Information Systems Conference* (pp. 528-537). Cham: Springer International Publishing.

Salih, L., Tarhini, A., & Acikgoz, F. (2025). AI-Enabled Service Continuance: Roles of Trust and Privacy Risk. *Journal of Computer Information Systems*, •••, 1–16.

Şenyapar, H. N. D. (2024). The Future of Marketing: The Transformative Power of Artificial Intelligence. *International Journal of Management and Administration*, *8*(15), 1–19.

Sherly Steffi, L., Subha, B., Kuriakose, A., Singh, J., Arunkumar, B., & Rajalakshmi, V. (2024). The impact of AI-driven personalization on consumer behavior and brand engagement in online marketing. In Harnessing, A. I. (Ed.), *Machine Learning, and IoT for Intelligent Business* (Vol. 1, pp. 485–492). Springer Nature Switzerland.

Singh, B., Kaunert, C., & Vig, K. (2024). Reinventing Influence of Artificial Intelligence (AI) on Digital Consumer Lensing Transforming Consumer Recommendation Model: Exploring Stimulus Artificial Intelligence on Consumer Shopping Decisions. In *AI Impacts in Digital Consumer Behavior* (pp. 141-169). IGI Global.

Stanca, L., Dabija, D. C., & Câmpian, V. (2023). Qualitative analysis of customer behavior in the retail industry during the COVID-19 pandemic: A word-cloud and sentiment analysis approach. *Journal of Retailing and Consumer Services*, *75*, 103543.

Teepapal, T. (2025). AI-Driven Personalization: Unraveling Consumer Perceptions in Social Media Engagement. *Computers in Human Behavior*, *165*, 108549.

Thakur, J., & Kushwaha, B. P. (2024). Artificial intelligence in marketing research and future research directions: Science mapping and research clustering using bibliometric analysis. *Global Business and Organizational Excellence*, *43*(3), 139–155.

Tripathy, A., Agrawal, A., & Rath, S. K. (2016). Classification of sentiment reviews using n-gram machine learning approach. *Expert Systems with Applications*, *57*, 117–126.

Verma, S., Sharma, R., Deb, S., & Maitra, D. (2021). Artificial intelligence in marketing: Systematic review and future research direction. *International Journal of Information Management Data Insights*, *1*(1), 100002.

Wairimu, D. M. (2023). Relationship between dynamic supply chain capabilities and resilience of retail chain of stores in Kenya, Doctoral Dissertation, Jomo Kenyatta University of Agriculture and Technology.

Wang, C. (2022). Efficient customer segmentation in digital marketing using deep learning with swarm intelligence approach. *Information Processing & Management*, *59*(6). Advance online publication. DOI: 10.1016/j.ipm.2022.103085

Wang, C., Ahmad, S. F., Ayassrah, A. Y. B. A., Awwad, E. M., Irshad, M., Ali, Y. A., Al-Razgan, M., Khan, Y., & Han, H. (2023). An empirical evaluation of technology acceptance model for Artificial Intelligence in E-commerce. *Heliyon*, *9*(8), e18349. PMID: 37520947

Yeo, S. F., Tan, C. L., Kumar, A., Tan, K. H., & Wong, J. K. (2022). Investigating the impact of AI-powered technologies on Instagrammers' purchase decisions in digitalization era–A study of the fashion and apparel industry. *Technological Forecasting and Social Change*, *177*, 121551.

Zhang, H., Bai. X, & Ma. Zengguang. (2022). Consumer reactions to AI design: Exploring consumer willingness to pay for AI-designed products. *Psychology and Marketing*, *39*(11), 2171–2183. DOI: 10.1002/mar.21721

ADDITIONAL READING

https://evdelo.com/amazons-recommendation-algorithm-drives-35-of-its-sales/

E-Commerce In India: Statistics and facts, retrieved from https://www.statista.com/topics/2454/e-commerce-in-india/#topicOverview on August, 2024.

Chapter 18
Unlocking the Generative Artificial Intelligence in Small and Medium-Sized Enterprises (SMEs)

Wasswa Shafik
https://orcid.org/0000-0002-9320-3186
Dig Connectivity Research Laboratory (DCRLab), Kampala, Uganda & School of Digital Science, Universiti Brunei Darussalam, Brunei

ABSTRACT

This chapter explores the growing impact of Generative Artificial Intelligence (GAI) in driving innovation and supporting decision-making, particularly for small and medium-sized enterprises (SMEs) in the developing and developed countries. It provides an overview of GAI's mechanisms and its potential to empower enterprises with limited access to capital. The chapter presents practical insights from a two-and-a-half-year participatory action research study in academic and real-life contexts, examining how human-GAI interactions can enhance problem-solving and innovation. Finally, it addresses the benefits and risks of applying GAI-derived knowledge to create patent-worthy intellectual property, proposing a new hierarchical classification concept for knowledge transfer.

1. INTRODUCTION

The recent development of approaches to artificial intelligence[1] (AI) that go beyond tools that support knowledge-based and production processes and instead can generate knowledge-based processes creates opportunities to use generative

DOI: 10.4018/979-8-3693-9611-7.ch018

AI[2] (GAI) in small and medium-sized companies. However, most existing GAI tools are designed for large companies, and the rapid increase of data needed for generative GAI increases inequalities between them (Kanbach et al., 2024). Early adoption in large companies and their upstream partners of generative GAI reaps apparent economic benefits that dwarf the increase in inequality between intimate economic partners in digitization when compared to the effects of previous technological advancements. The recent development of generative GAI could change the balance between large companies and intimate economic partners. It could improve Small and medium-sized enterprises (SMEs) accessibility to a digitized superstructure that allows them to innovate with GAI, as had been suggested at the beginning of the internet (Soni, 2023). In this process, we "bring experts to data," using the pattern-finding capabilities of generative GAI to develop both predictive and generative models with an order of complexity that does not translate into slow deployment and dependency on specific experts. Increased adoption of scalable generative GAI generates the potential for investment to increase the quality and volume of data prepared by the efficient deployment of such models in SMEs (Chuma & De Oliveira, 2023).

Figure 1. Significant types of expert systems

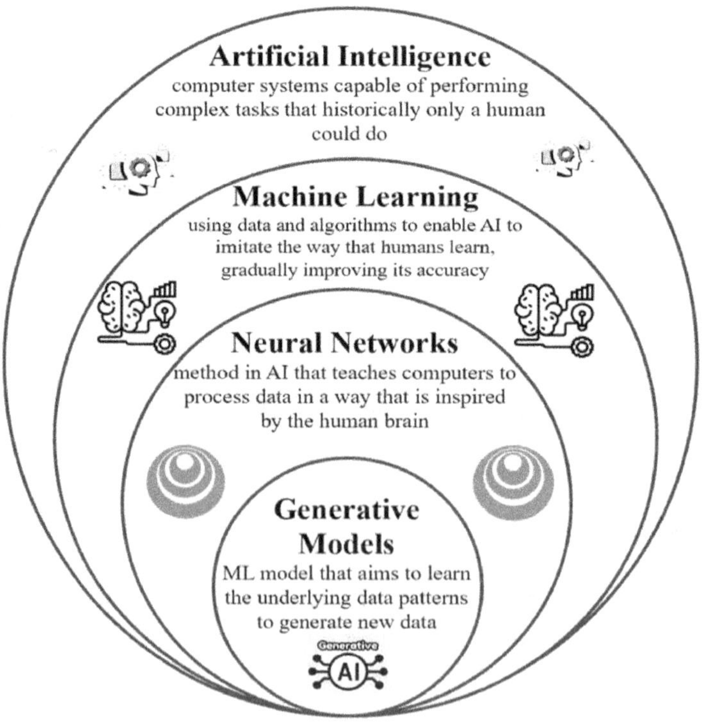

The size of the enterprise generally shapes the adoption of GAI in SMEs. This research is more focused on micro, small, and medium-sized enterprises, which are essentially in developing countries. The developed and developing countries have their own unique set of industries and formulas. While the developed countries focus on advanced and specialized industries, developing countries focus on traditional or labor-intensive and labor-absorbing industries. There also exist a variety of classifications, measurements, and statistics in this area. However, the results may vary according to the different terminology used by the industry; it has broad general implications (Korzynski et al., 2023). This study will focus on the GAI technology utilized in the automation of knowledge and data work, as well as other techniques and service functions. SMEs in the United Arab Emirates (UAE) will be chosen as a research object to evaluate and analyze the motives and barriers to adoption. The results and recommendations derived from the UAE case may also contribute to the decision support for managing the GAI adoption in other countries that have the same characteristics and features as the SMEs (Peruchini et al., 2024). Different significant aspects of expert systems as implemented in the SMEs are illustrated from artificial intelligence, machine learning, neural networks, and GAI models in Figure 1.

The critical success factors of GAI in smaller companies may have important implications. Reducing the lack of strategic initiative and IT dependencies would result in the surviving threshold decreasing. This research attempts to present the required supportive policies. On the other hand, the main contribution of this study would be from the side of the empirical research on the UAE-GAI in smaller companies, which mainly focuses on an under-researched area (Horak et al., 2023). The opportunities for machine learning in SMEs are great. The critical point is to populate the data set in medium-sized companies. Promoting data learning is essential to getting SMEs into the artificial intelligence game. The ideology of this industry's 4.0 is that all factories would be learning. The reason is that learning is the only way to conduct immediate environmental adjustments. SMEs are, by definition, much less bureaucratic than large companies (Wu, 2024). This will allow data to grow and will, no doubt, be helpful. I believe that rapid progress will be made to achieve this goal.

2. UNDERSTANDING GENERATIVE ARTIFICIAL INTELLIGENCE

It is artificial intelligence that can produce creative outputs such as images, music, or text. It is the latest evolution of GAI that uses machine learning principles to enable computers to learn from data and produce new and potentially limitless content unique to each user. There are three main types of generative GAI: style-based, language models, and chatbots. Style-based. Style-based GAI is best known for creating videos, but it can also generate images, text, and music that have never existed. It is recognized for creating iconic new art. We have to remember the need to develop our creative thinking to keep pace with GAI – this doesn't mean we can't use GAI to help us be more creative (Humphreys et al., 2024). Fresh and innovative ideas can leverage existing algorithms in new ways. Its key attributes are new content created from data, definite and direct representation of desired attributes, pulling disparate inputs together to create a cohesive main output, and the ability to work with multimodal input, such as combining sound and image with reading emotions better (Shafik, 2023; Wu, 2024).

Language models. An example of generative GAI uses a generative pretrained transformer. The model is composed of a complex set of algorithms that have been educated using both unsupervised and supervised learning. Unsupervised learning is when we use naturally occurring data that has not been labeled and points that have been sorted, and it is found to be the most effective in deep learning algorithms. Interactions with the model are natural language questions that could also include any combination of words and phrases, areas of interest, or specific criteria (PricewaterhouseCoopers, 2023). Its generosity is shown by the breadth of possible query scenarios – copywriters, data scientists, and financial analysts find it an indispensable tool. It can interpret the needs of a variety of niche businesses, and it generates as many different types of posts as there are potential queries. This model has almost endless potential application domains (Humphreys et al., 2024).

Generative technologies are different in that they directly manipulate objects or create new ones. They can create unique, creative, and profitable business opportunities. SMEs should understand the differences and where to apply such technologies in their organizations. Two types of generative GAI are tools that enhance creativity and tools that take over the entire creative process. This paper is about the latter and looks at what these capabilities are and how an enterprise can use them for profits (Yahaya et al., 2023). The paper reduces the technical issues of generative GAI to their conceptual framework and resolves the framework's issues by the design science methodology. Two case studies of generative GAI in use in typical small and medium-sized businesses, a specialist tooling maker and a cook in a leading restaurant, are described. The paper provides a comprehensive understanding of generative GAI and practical advice for deploying this essential tool in creative business enterprises (Li, 2022).

2.1. Definition and Concepts

To gain better insights and understanding of artificial intelligence, this study critically reviews and analyzes artificial intelligence and its concepts, which can help unlock generative artificial intelligence and thus detect new applications in

SMEs. The aim of the theoretical investigation and philosophical approach to artificial intelligence finds its roots and is presented as well as discussed from a more profound comprehension and understanding of the specifics of the interconnection of artificial intelligence and the development of generative artificial intelligence. This study's fundamental approach to developing generative artificial intelligence perceives and discovers knowledge that is known to us based on the flow and change of sensory and inducing information in the concept of generative learning (Sieja & Wach, 2023). Additionally, specific studies about transforming existing artificial intelligence platforms or systems into generative artificial intelligence platforms and systems represent the essence of artificial intelligence. In summary, the unique interconnection of intelligence exists in different cases of access and through various devices.

Figure 2. Generative artificial intelligence application in SMEs

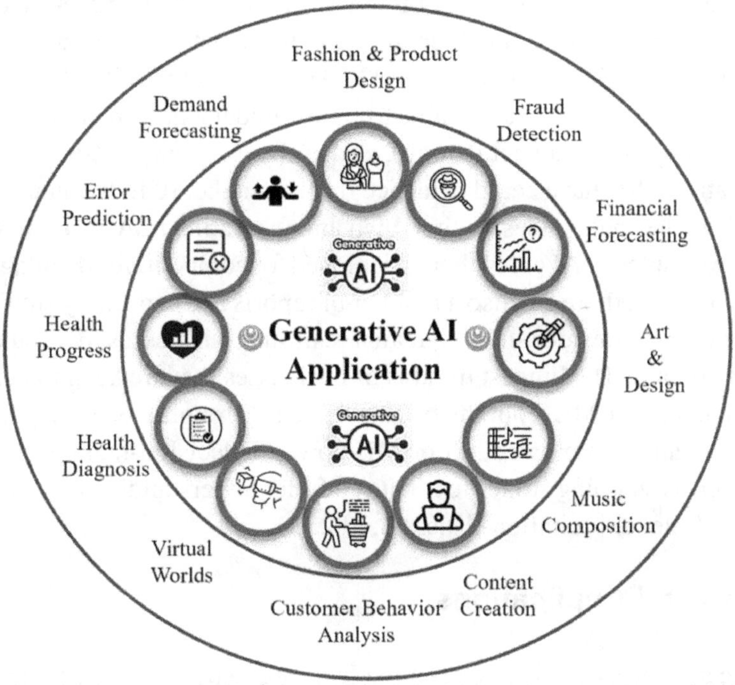

The development of artificial intelligence represents the problem of the artificial creation of intelligence that can assist in the creation of generative artificial intelligence. Introducing an approach that mimics how the mind retrieves information while ensuring continuous generation also provides essential information for professionals to gain main research insights (Rane et al., 2024). Furthermore, this research enhances the compatibility of these or similar derived systems, enabling a logical way to perform tasks. Issuing such unique concepts and innovative approaches to systematize the problems of generative artificial intelligence is of crucial importance because of the differences between natural and artificial objects themselves (Kim & Choi, 2024). These GAIs have a more comprehensive range of applying GAI in developing SMEs, specifically in developing nations, as illustrated in Figure 2.

2.2. Technological Significance in Finance Systems

There seems to be a growing consensus that the establishment of significant levels of AI in human society, particularly in the economy, is likely to be challenging for SMEs. This chapter outlines the people and organizational issues that need to be solved if the generative capability of AI is to be shared more widely. The adoption of AI is being observed through what is a natural community of interest point, where we have a vast crowd of 'observers' who are completely dependent upon this technology but a much smaller group of potential 'producers' or even 'programmers' of it (Korzynski et al., 2023). These are fully fledged AI or machine learning (ML) researchers who are able to create, understand, and innovate with the current technology and move it forward, such as by exploring, testing, and refining new applications. We have heard evidence from a number of individual studies that considered smaller businesses on their own and in relation to AI/ML, and there are significant examples of AI or ML being deployed for competitive advantage (Ratten, 2024). In summary, there are also a number of reports and especially studies that go out of their way to consider smaller, mainstream-use businesses, particularly those in the B2B domain. The biggest trend is of businesses that are keen to get involved and understand AI or ML from the bottom up. One grouping is more practical and focused on creating automated, AI or ML-powered decision-making tools, which might be seen as stepping stones to not just a fuller understanding of this capability but also to a fuller exploitation (Hussain, 2023).

2.3. Types and Applications

GAI creates forms of deeper machine learning, where new classifications can be called generative GAI. Such GAI organizes concepts into its learning process, helping it develop a human-like understanding of objects. By knowing the language and using senses like eyesight or touch, the GAI is able to generate new items after receiving knowledge by example. The generalization ability does not require human skills and, therefore, does not depend on the power of the computing hardware either (Beerbaum Dr., 2023a; Mondal et al., 2023). That level of GAI can quickly get involved in applications that require the synthesis of new items from inherited knowledge. Two significant autonomy gains about a complete generation part of automation are challenging:

1) verification, which questions both the social impact and the trust in the completeness of the generated item, and 2) adaptation, which matches the planned items online with the ad-hoc user's needs, leading to personalization and co-creation of new valuable items (Ratten, 2024). Generative GAI needs to learn through generative methods, like human learning using words and senses. Impressive examples are natural language processing, which learns to write and even say directly translated texts, and computer vision, which learns to draw verbally described objects just by name. Such a level of generalization is not present in today's formal systems-based GAI, and this is why this new class of GAI needs extra explanation for business management. To provide that explanation, it is also essential to separate generative ability models into unsupervised generative and supervised generative learning forms (Ooi et al., 2023). Unsupervised generative learning does not require individual input and, therefore, helps generate global representations of knowledge. In the meantime, supervised generative learning needs examples and helps generate private representations of knowledge. Both are necessary for GAI with generative ability that can be used by actual SMEs, raising digital literacy and reducing digital risk (Ahmed Ali Linkon et al., 2024). The GAI developers provide unique advantages. Because of this, another form of generative GAI is also presented in the next section. In SMEs, generative GAI can help technologies come up not only with networked digital books but also designs for engineering or coloured posters with messages. The t-boosting method for generative GAI is first used for learning from limited or incomplete proprietary databases. A plan with a growing generative GAI that has already achieved t-maturity with demonstrated autonomous generative business value implemented by volunteers worldwide gains benefits by using systems' GAI instead of such Small-to-Medium Enterprises' doer family members (Hussain, 2023). Because of a whole bunch of avoided gatekeeping or overcautiousness, the system exhibits a high-speed problem-solving cycle, making it quite valuable for small business implementation.

3. ADOPTION OF GAI IN SMES

Before discussing the approach to the adoption of GAI in SMEs and the specific cases, we will start with an analysis of the current status. The initial question is how GAI has been assimilated by SMEs or, in other words, to what extent GAI is part of their innovation DNA. For a first approximation, we will summarize the results from the surveys of GAI preference in SME support programs (Budhwar et al., 2023). The announcement of the initiative to provide world-class high-performance supercomputers with GAI capabilities for scientific, business, and industry use intends for the consortium specifically to grow the use of services provided to a significant number of European small and medium enterprises, accelerate the path of European SMEs to GAI, and stimulate the growth of some sectors through the application and development of GAI-based processing formulas (Peres et al., 2023). The analysis of GAI policies and initiatives has been enriched by recommendations to accelerate the progress of GAI systems in workplaces to support policymakers in ad hoc governance assessments. GAI is not just a concern of the economy's most dynamic sectors, the digital ecosystem, but also of the leading SME employers, commerce, and small industry. With the initiative of the Centre for Entrepreneurship, Education, and Research, there have been calls to facilitate research through established dialogues (Baxter & Schlesinger, 2023). With policymakers recognizing and respecting the role and implementation of the Guidelines, GAI workers can work safely, securely, and productively. Enterprises should be able to make independent decisions that meet the criteria and purposes and rely on elements, frameworks, and alliances used to develop the Guidelines and delve into the GAI landscape. However, the libraries and openness of the models, taxonomies, and methodologies that GAI produces will provide the best insurance at the lowest cost for the safety of firms, products, and services throughout their life cycle (Brown et al., 2024).

3.1. Current Landscape

Amidst the general buzz and growing investment in GAI, the reality is that current GAI applications represent path-dependent extrema on a scale that ranges from highly constrained, statistical, pattern-processing tools to general-purpose or human-equivalent intelligence. All systems that exist today, whether they are classified as narrow or AGI, can be placed somewhere within this landscape. Virtually all GAI research, development, and deployment efforts today are concentrated solely on enhancements to relatively simple, hand-engineered systems that lie at or near the statistical end of the GAI space, and this applies to both the private and public sectors (Beerbaum Dr., 2023b; Kanbach et al., 2024)So far, the other end of the spectrum holds the most significant promise for capability enhancement and disruption across almost all parts of the economy, across all sectors, and across all business models.

On the narrow[3] or artificial intelligence (ANI) side, the current boom in GAI is being driven exclusively by a single technology instantiated through a simple mathematical technique: the so-called neural network. Other technologies, statistical techniques, and general approaches to solving statistical problems hold little power and attraction to GAI researchers and practitioners. This general interest in and reliance on deep learning to the exclusion of everything else can be characterized as a bubble and is neither sustainable nor does it admit to essential and potentially disruptive new forms of innovation that forthcoming technologies will unleash (Ooi et al., 2023; Ratten, 2024). Despite significant progress in problems such as image or speech recognition, gaming performance, some forms of natural language understanding, and reinforcement-based problem-solving in virtual environments, driven much more by a continuing exponential increase in processing power using multiple graphics processing unit[4] (GPU) to significantly increased core counts than it does more conventional model-based aspects of learning or performance, deep learning[5] is allowing existing single-purpose, task-specific GAI to become better at doing the things it currently does (Brown et al., 2024; Rane, 2023). This does not and will not herald significant productivity improvements within firms or radical process transformation at the firm or industry level, which are statements that can be attributed to all other widely used narrow GAI technologies such as ChatGPT and its broader application, as illustrated in Figure 3.

Figure 3. ChatGPT application in developing SMEs

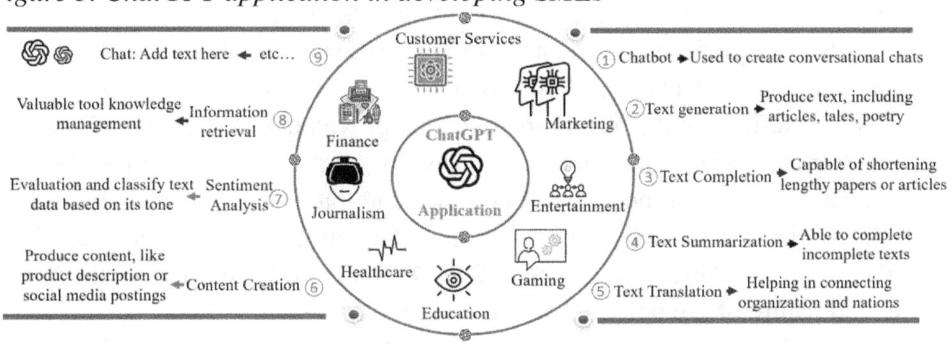

3.2. Barriers and Challenges

Barriers and Challenges. Despite the many potential benefits of small and medium-sized enterprises employing GAI, a number of possible barriers have been suggested. For the adoption of machine learning in a vast company, these include data and talent shortages, siloed data, and GAI pilots. There is a counter to all of these problems; however, if the number of people involved in this field can be increased at a sufficient pace, these problems will be considerably reduced or disappear (Abrokwah-Larbi, 2023). The rapid progress in computational capabilities, which continues to make the application of such technologies possible for institutions with fewer resources at their disposal, such as small and medium-sized enterprises, is also worthy of note. The first major obstacle is the technical complexity and the specific problems with the unrealistic expectations of SMEs. A range of other difficulties as a result of the efforts of this challenge will be recognized: the novelty of GAI, inadequate digital infrastructure, and the difficulty of the transformation process of the organization. A general concern is the economic impact of job loss, related labor force training issues, and public support for the priority of GAI research (Szilágyi & Tóth, 2024). Besides these, there are rumors, fake news, and wide-ranging social biases in GAI models. Compliance with new privacy regulations may be expected in addition. These include the right to explain and contest the use of the algorithm and the right not to be part of the decision-making process. It is argued that such moral and societal difficulties are relative and can, in fact, be exceeded. In particular, there is much discussion on how the improvement of skills can counteract job loss caused by GAI. Small and medium-sized businesses may be prototypes of agile learning businesses (Rajbhoj et al., 2024; Soni, 2023).

3.3. Opportunities and Benefits

From the results of the guided innovation discussion, it is clear that the participants can derive significant and relatively widespread benefits from the capabilities of GAI. The road test exercise found that twenty-one candidate activities could potentially benefit from the development and deployment of generative GAI. This high number of opportunities is positive. It suggests that SMEs may actually be very ready and able to exploit the new technologies and that if the actual penetration of the technologies is less than expected, then softer aspects of innovation are likely to be the obstacles (Abrokwah-Larbi, 2023). Drawing on the discussion, the mode, extent, and nature of the potential benefits are introduced.

The potential benefits that GAI technologies could bring to the activities are varied and include more competitive offerings, shorter development cycles, more effective processes, and broader markets. The answer to the challenge of how to ensure that the opportunities are exploited is not empirical; it cannot be answered with more or faster research to create new technologies (Brown et al., 2024; Kanbach et al., 2024). It requires the recognition, encouragement, and development of softer complementary innovation, mainly around organizational and sectoral factors. The road test showed that the full promise of GAI will not be realized just because it exists; implementation and use will only follow if SMEs are willing and able to innovate in less technical ways. The businesses will need to develop their capabilities and accommodate issues such as privacy, security, regulation, standards, and competition. As a first step, firms need a clear understanding of what is coming and how they could benefit from it (Peres et al., 2023).

3.3.1. Operational Efficiency

Operational efficiency is an important goal for SMEs, where efficient resources are essential for survival in the market. This can be achieved by introducing GAI to streamline processes at many levels, which include business planning, customer relationship management, supply chain management, market analysis, marketing, sales, distribution, finance, support, and staff administration. Some of the process streamlining solutions are mature and can be easily integrated into the routine work of an SME (Budhwar et al., 2023; Hussain, 2023). Such solutions can be found after defining problem statements or by working with vendors who can provide templates for further improvements. Data analysis, management, and synchronization enable GAI functions to discover new relationships among data inputs, present facts clearly, and uncover complex relationships that humans would overlook. People need these compelling infographics, especially management and stakeholders who are not close to the daily routine reports. After these tasks are automated, SMEs can focus on strategy, partnership, and growth (Ahmed Ali Linkon et al., 2024; Ratten, 2024). Furthermore, on-demand, specialized GAI solutions can quickly embrace more complicated problems by learning from the accumulated data and feedback aids through human supervision.

3.3.2. Innovation and Creativity

The Turing Test[6] results were directly associated with these personality aspects. It was a great accomplishment, and the winning team deserved the attention and recognition for the challenging work. But there are a few unique characteristics: it is a competitive TV show, it is a game with prizes, it was being played at specific frequencies and hours using specific hardware, and the questions were given a few days prior to the formal event. Subsequently, the competition had all the data required for matching the information with the answer during a typical competition. It becomes evident that the challenge, in this case, was to communicate knowledge between the QA system and the game show orchestration (Mondal et al., 2023). Creative? Absolutely! Curious? Perhaps, indeed. For a short period under artificially created specific conditions. It is the genius working on its specific guidelines. Parents, relatives, and friends around the world would often ask me about it. It was commonly related to creativity, curiosity, and some artistic traits. If the main goal was to generate a public relations machine, it must be admitted that the idea was great (Wu, 2024). The effect was instant and global. Not only was it mentioned, but it was positive press.

Most creative GAI results are related to music or pictures. It may seem odd, but when data are manipulated to deliver cloud pictures or abstract sound sequences, people are delighted. They seem to forget about logic and context. A few days ago, it was documented that a special team re-created sounds from a 3000-year-old mummified Egyptian singer. The news of the results was massive, and the possibility that the general public could listen to melodies produced by ancient Egyptians was even more compelling (Humphreys et al., 2024; ală et al., 2024). Some astonishing results for GAI were presented on a stand-up comedy stage. The results were subject to in-depth analysis, and it became apparent that researchers had ironed out the first and biased iterations. The goal was to generate the data so that a human performer could use them for entertainment. It is labor-intensive, and pure GAI solutions are yet to become apparent. Subsequently, in this subset of the entertainment business, specialists have a viable market. The piracy industry of award-winning scripts is there, and through a strange mix of manual, GAI, and computing capabilities, performances and films are sold to any customer (Li, 2022; Sieja & Wach, 2023). This, of course, is contrary to copyright laws; the world's great licensing organizations immediately burn it. The generation of a creative and marketable script by a GAI is undoubtedly seen as a futuristic task, something that will only be achieved in the not-too-distant future.

4. GENERATIVE GAI IMPLEMENTATION STRATEGIES FOR SMES

Generative GAI models provide new and vast opportunities that previously required a lot of domain-specific human intelligence[7]. GAI intra-domain implementation strategies are possible but have become increasingly more complex to implement inter-domain implementations. This means that companies have an accurate view of the implementation target and can provide a clear guiding objective. Alternatively, the GAI needs to be directed to learn these intents first, which may lead to various additional learning objectives. The communication sequence needs to be vivid; trying to recognize all possible intents or desires transformed from input language to the output type would result in GAI only learning what is the most likely intent out of a sea of all possible intents (Kim & Choi, 2024). The adapted use of case-driven generative GAI development methodology was determined through workshops and outside-in communication with SMEs. Formalization of the development aspect definition and a classification determining the development aspect relevance regarding necessary generative skill know-how was implemented afterward. The generative

GAI development requests need to categorize generative GAI development tools, categorize existing generative model development architectures, categorize related generative implementation circuits, categorize company-specific implementation obstructions, categorize the implementation judgment, domain and model validation preferences, and implementation resource know-how requirements (Ratten, 2024).

4.1. Planning and Preparation

Even though the SMEs developing the generative GAI-powered applications may not be conducting formal long-term strategic planning processes, these activities tend to be highly dynamic and iterative. This is also reflected in the nature of GAI technologies as a conflict between the need for detailed planning and the speed of iteration (Ahmed Ali Linkon et al., 2024). Despite the widespread realization of the potentially far-reaching impacts of the emerging generative GAI on the business operations of SMEs, various studies indicate that the majority of them are still at a low level of GAI readiness, often lacking the essential preconditions such as internal data analytics expertise, a continuous learning culture, and advanced information and communication technologies[8] (ICTs) infrastructure. Companies are aware of the increasing importance of digitalization and require further digital literacy (Budhwar et al., 2023).

To be successful in the digital transformation process, companies need to embrace new technological solutions, rethink business models, embrace new e-technologies, and allocate the right resources for the implementation itself. SMEs experience a particular set of challenges due to their size and complexity. Unfortunately, this leads to only half of SMEs having a notable digitalization maturity level, often caught up in the digital divide. The first step in generative GAI adoption requires comprehensive consideration regarding formal planning and preparation (Ooi et al., 2023). It is, therefore, evident that generative artificial intelligence readiness is grounded in three subsequent phases of the technology lifecycle: awareness, adoption, and learning. The awareness stage highlights the importance of a preparatory phase that brings business intelligence and business experts to the level where they become aware of the technology's potential, structure, and readiness. This preparatory phase may be divided into two stages: top-level management education and industry-specific awareness preparation (Hussain, 2023).

4.2. Technology Selection

The progress in generative GAI has made efficient large-scale pre-training methods beautiful for research and industry. We outline various generative pre-trained models, such as generative pre-trained transformers, that outperformed many other pre-trained models in the publicly available general language understanding evaluation and reading comprehension tasks (Li, 2022; Rane et al., 2024). This advancement in generative pretraining has not only enabled the technology to carry out many high-level human digital activities like language translation and develop a rich ecosystem of data and support tools but also elevated its accessibility by developers, scientists, and entrepreneurs operationalizing business activity - evident by the presence of marketplaces. While recent academic commercialization of GAI revolving around generative models has led to vast improvements in pre-training methodologies, including pre-training models for other modalities interacting with natural language processing, significant issues still exist concerning the scalability of domain-specific data and data distribution in deploying pre-trained models[9] for proprietary tasks (Peres et al., 2023). These domain-specific concerns can substantially affect how many instances would need to be collected to generate enough coherent tamable signals to train such a pre-trained model up to an acceptable threshold level of accuracy vertical to a specific subfield in a small company.

4.3. Data Acquisition and Preparation

Manual data collection has to be substituted by more automatic means to enable large-scale data-driven systems capable of learning from big data. When contemplating entering into the exciting world of generative GAI, the first step always revolves around acquiring large volumes of data, most often in the form of audio, images, or videos reflecting your industry's particular activities and operations. The challenge of incorporating data acquisition technology suggests partnerships with existing companies with generated assets (Baxter & Schlesinger, 2023). You can also employ predictive coding and analysis for assessing the type, scope, or potential adoption for your industry. Big tech and telecom companies are actively involved in GAI on the cutting edge, though data from concrete industrial application sites for start-ups and small companies are currently unavailable. Part of the sector is addressing this problem by utilizing solutions proposed by the ecosystem at large. Larger defense companies, general systems integrators, industrial technology developers, and professional digital security companies address other parts (Brown et al., 2024). Collaborative partnerships extend it with lessons learned and other parameters to benefit the system at large. Most small and medium enterprises do not collect a lot of raw data, frown over the existing quality, and do not generally participate in large industrial initiatives. The willingness to use data drives the data collection. A spontaneous collection representing their prior working activities and subsequent temporary logging is at the center of its efforts. All these data are later used in widely different research projects, such as reinforcing the shop floor operations from industrial wearables, seeking the essence of the operating procedure in process manufacturing, or tracking workers for adversarial task delegation in cloud robotics (Kanbach et al., 2024). Data should be acquired only when deemed really necessary, and the data owners can release only anonymized data or participate in joint research with partners.

4.4. Training and Testing

The legal issues linked with training and testing mainly arise from using or reusing works that are legally protected under copyright, such as books, recordings, and databases. In many jurisdictions, users may need a license from the right holders of the downloaded works to use them in training generative GAI. When the datasets are protected by copyright law, they can only be utilized when the user has permission from the copyright owner or a license agreement (Abrokwah-Larbi, 2023). As this is a global business, it would be beneficial to have a global pool of labeled data available. However, procurement of such data can be complex due to copyright law. Consequently, significant companies based in countries with lenient laws do not have to comply with rights and can benefit freely from the detailed and exhaustive rules in place in democratic countries. This legal discrepancy provides a competitive edge that law-abiding companies cannot match. The same goes for the use of copyrighted work used for testing. The same moral, and legal issue arises (Szilágyi & Tóth, 2024). How a business collects training data for GAI currently can be a much lengthier task than developing the GAI itself.

When it comes to testing, issues with privacy and human rights can arise when a GAI uses databases. The functionalities of such GAI draw on user data, as do many other studies connected with machine learning in particular. GAI must, therefore, be certified using accurate data, specifically personal data. This characteristic can, however, in some instances, pose ethical questions or even infringe rights, as the uses of the data will not necessarily conform to the authors' justified expectation of privacy. This is particularly the case for personal data from social networks, as the data is highly personal and detailed (Rajbhoj et al., 2024). The uses of personal data have been carefully considered in the case law and settings of the relevant authorities. In its jurisprudence, it has taken the view that any individual should be able to demand that personal data that they have uploaded be deleted or removed from the database of a publisher or service should they no longer want it available to the public. This sound jurisprudential basis allows individuals to ensure their data can be removed from databases in order to prevent possible harm (Rajbhoj et al., 2024).

5. IMPLEMENTATION STRATEGIES

Organizations have a wide variety of choices when it comes to implementing GAI. They also have broad autonomy on how to use GAI. In sharp contrast with previous generations of GAI, clients do not need to have specialized programming or GAI competence to benefit from GAI tools. Solutions are already available through application programming interfaces that can be implemented using the latest IT technology. Using these APIs, strategic solutions can be developed. The primary considerations should be how to connect different technologies with specific parts of business process improvements (Beerbaum Dr., 2023a). In many cases, both internal IT development and an externally provided service implementation are needed. We encourage business model innovation in collaboration with technology development and improved ways of using GAI. Short-term strategy should be directed towards internal recognition and providing an enabling internal organization to start exploring GAI opportunities. In view of dynamic algorithm performance, companies will start investigating important strategic positions that emerge in the data hierarchy (ală et al., 2024). Small companies capable of orchestrating a data hierarchy Guiding different informed sensors and actuators that are created and maintained by another party could offer valuable active and informed services themselves. Goal setting and performance metrics are essential. There are always many ill-structured questions that companies would like to see answered. Establish a small team intending to derive value from GAI. Possibly use assistance from a large company and work with strategic imperatives with specific design goals having a timeline. Note that senior managers in small companies indicated they feel obliged to answer more questions at the same time (Budhwar et al., 2023; Hussain, 2023). For these reasons, the struggle over the design needs to have high priority. Data project strategies are to be developed to sustain new data-driven activities.

5.1. Key Considerations

If SMEs can unlock the following vital considerations, then they have the opportunity to unleash enormous value. It is essential to be mindful of these factors and address them when considering creating enterprise GAI, as open questions are to be resolved. Data readiness and uniformity across these industries are not joint, and utilizing pre-existing platforms affords these industries access to the data needed directly out of the box. Custom data may be used to fine-tune these models, but there is no longer a requirement for large-scale data creation or commoditization (Brown et al., 2024; Kanbach et al., 2024). The most significant challenge, which is one to be solved at a higher level, may stem from different-sized organizations being able to trust that the model has adequately understood the training process, thus ensuring that it has the right ingredients to produce the correct outcomes. Data has unique intrinsic characteristics based on its origin, creation, refinement, and analysis. Several considerations will identify how the unification of data can be undertaken in the best possible way. SME responsiveness usually increases with the presence of faster feedback loops (Abrokwah-Larbi, 2023; Brown et al., 2024). Amidst the current race among GAI experts to create compos elegant, this is a great goal that will also serve the needs of addressing the practicalities and core challenges that GAI implementations simplify. Model degradation occurs when there are still several other optimization points in the GAI design space. This highlights the importance that available resources play when an ample solution space contains solutions operating at various efficiency levels (Hussain, 2023; Peres et al., 2023). Significant investments in infrastructure will result in placing expensive model operands that shift the operational point and model orchard creation complexity to a more optimal positioning.

5.2. Best Practices

Some crucial practices could be distilled from GAI vendors and SMEs who engage in the early stage of GAI generation. A generation service vendor needs to understand the fundamental nature of specific SMEs' business and then provide optimal GAI solutions to its specific operations. Vendors should simplify and clarify the technical performance without complex coding idioms used by engineers; they should make good use of non-specialist language, graphics, and many examples to make practical GAI easy to understand; allow detailed explanations and hands-on exercises for clients to understand how GAI functions and how performance is generated; and provide GAI services that offer SME employees real-time support together with personal knowledge acquisition services (Baxter & Schlesinger, 2023). With respect to SMEs, managers who operate SMEs must have a good understanding of their GAI vendors by acquiring concepts of business GAI systems without needing in-depth study. SME employees who participate in joint projects with GAI service vendors should actively discuss real-world operations with vendors for optimal GAI solution development in an active manner and not hold back. They should also request and commit to thorough GAI learning and practical training themselves whenever required. In this way, they may guide joint GAI projects, supporting the development of perfect GAI systems by themselves (Brown et al., 2024). This chapter has focused on the concept of innovation from the viewpoint of generation or production, which represents the first stage of the effects of artificial and general artificial intelligence. Furthermore, it stressed the critical requirement for business applications of GAI, which seems to lead to GAI generation by making humans and GAI work together. Finally, it articulates the practices required for the generation phase in SMEs, including the values and mindset of GAI personnel in innovation. However, it is too early to jump to the conclusion that SMEs can now safely approach GAI systems equipped with this mindset (Soni, 2023). It is essential to accompany the GAI generation mindset by continuing always to have high levels of education and the practical ability to use GAI.

6. ETHICAL AND LEGAL CONSIDERATIONS

GAI systems and computer algorithms, in general, are developed to act on the basis of applied computing functions like data processing. Therefore, they are exclusively covered by private law in the framework of the law governing applied computer science. With the emergence of GAI systems designed to act on an abstract basis, such as making decisions about individuals or conducting speech interactions, their actions must also be covered by public law (Ahmed Ali Linkon et al., 2024). These regulations are designed to ensure that the use of GAI systems is intended to avoid harm and facilitate the C3DR because they help explain what the actions of GAI systems are and what they are not. Control rights could be granted to GAI systems in the future if they were granted a legal status equal to that of natural persons, as is often suggested. GAI systems are software products that need data to realize their tasks. They process data that are mainly used to control software interfaces. Since GAI systems can hardly be considered entities with their specific aims, they do not process data with reference to their informative value but for purposes pre-set by the data controller to achieve a specific goal (Peres et al., 2023). We do not believe that the autonomous actions of GAI systems should be regulated separately from those of establishing and maintaining human-made hardware. They depend on the way the GAI systems have been designed, and this is already a required design principle according to the Product Liability Directive. Software developers must make sure that the product they design, intending it to act unsupervised, is able to act without harming third parties or performing illegal activities beyond everything that the application of safe technology can reasonably predict (Baxter & Schlesinger, 2023).

6.1. Privacy and Data Protection

SMEs have ongoing concerns like data security and data protection compliance. Providing a comprehensive privacy framework with clear accountability, transparency, and control metrics can help guide SMEs in managing risks when conducting business. In addition, handling privacy issues through innovative technologies and employee-based program management can ensure that privacy is incorporated into proprietary methodologies and business best practices. Explicit engagement with employees and respect for their personal information can bring significant benefits to employers who wish to unlock the potential of their workforce and establish the foundations of a high-trust environment (Rane et al., 2024). By striking a balance between business pragmatism and privacy and data protection law commitments made by resource-constrained SMEs, these small businesses can unlock the potential of data and generate an innovation culture with trust and privacy as its cornerstone. The use of generative GAI has the potential to test, verify employee knowledge, and identify any required corrective actions as it can direct the attention of the employee to better rules and best practices, track learning and adaptation, provide working examples and supporting materials, provide timely alerts and warnings, and provide a feedback loop to the employers where necessary (Kim & Choi, 2024; Ooi et al., 2023). GAI's interactive and real-time potential can result in the best combination of privacy upfront design and privacy integrated management. When applied in sectors that further their prudential aim, it has the potential to contribute to ensuring the policy objectives of job advancement, ensuring steadfast interaction and skill development with employees. Cloud, GAI, and internet-generated platforms with continual learning can not only provide interactive, real-time employer-employee mediation platforms but also open safer training and service environments for the employees (Budhwar et al., 2023; Peres et al., 2023).

6.2. Bias and Fairness

Product and its alignment with values play a crucial role in GAI model deployment in the real world. Bias in training data has a direct effect on the generated outputs and the decision-making processes. If training is performed on biased data, this bias can be inherited and enhanced by the ML model. It is important to note that the fairness requirement is not limited to any particular subset of the population; fairness is expected for everyone. However, model development carries the inherent risk of replicating existing biases and even potentially introducing unfair treatment (Baxter & Schlesinger, 2023). Additionally, a low willingness to provide sensitive information can further increase biases during model development. Therefore, a fair model includes a set of protected attributes in the training phase without a direct connection to the underlying protected classes. It should be noted that any GAI model needs to have forecasted or actual outcomes for evaluation. If the training data is biased, model outputs and decisions can be discriminatory or a proxy for discriminatory behavior. Sensitive biases can also affect the model's behavior in different ways, potentially putting people from different groups at disproportionate risks, holding people from different backgrounds to indifferent qualifications, or criminalizing acts (Abrokwah-Larbi, 2023). We define bias as a systematic error in the results of a model due to defective or distorted data. Personal attributes like race, sex, or religion, including proxies, should also be taken into account. They can also influence the model outcome distribution, often having negative consequences for affected groups. Influential bias can also exert control over decisions in terms of disfavoring a particular class of data (Soni, 2023).

6.3. Regulatory Compliance

With the increased use of GAI in areas traditionally managed by human expertise, the issue of regulatory compliance is a deep concern to many within SMEs, who are often caught between managing the commercial risks of compliance errors and increasing concern among regulatory authorities and customers that the right resources are used to manage their allocation of legal and other responsibilities in accordance with emerging expectations (Ahmed Ali Linkon et al., 2024; Beerbaum Dr., 2023a). This feeling of being 'caught in the middle' is deepening as regulatory authorities that are under-resourced from a technical expertise perspective are adapting surveillance, inspection, and other regimes to promote or force GAI upskilling in affected areas actively—all the while maintaining a sense of GAI that is often obsolete the moment regulations are issued. Our survey identified a more methodological approach taken by larger Canadian companies that regularly deploy GAI as part of their offering, that of wholesale legal consideration of GAI impacts from design to slight process changes less likely to invoke regulation (Budhwar et al., 2023). When SMEs are based close to the headquarters of these companies and employ C-level executives as officers of the larger companies, the generation of commercial outcomes that will promote advances that attitudes and behaviors suggest will be nervous.

7. ETHICAL AND REGULATORY CONSIDERATIONS

Within society, it is essential to establish trust in GAI that is generated by non-experts. There has not been a massive regulation of software development in SMEs, and now, the introduction of GAI into such companies will be impactful as well. Ethical considerations will influence the development of GAI and shall not be overlooked. In some scenarios, generative GAI will be used in smart transformation applications, and there will be a need for technology audits and impact assessments to be carried out on GAI-transformed industry processes (Baxter & Schlesinger, 2023; Budhwar et al., 2023). More concerning is the business ramifications associated with extended features, the combination of these, and the accountability of decisions that are made. Shaping modeling data, generating GAI while accounting for the human in the loop, and decision change consequences is more challenging than it may initially seem. Although much has been discussed in terms of bias in decision support systems, attention is also needed on how new small-scale generative GAI will affect recommendations that drive the output of the business. In applied fields of intelligent GAI process automation, tools can have far-reaching implications for society. Many SMEs have a broad customer base, and negative impacts that can occur in one space could have consequences in another, for example, a political or ecologically based scenario (Beerbaum Dr., 2023b). Comparatively, the SME context research is limited, but it is vital to address these issues in the early days for the ongoing collaboration of domain experts.

7.1. Privacy and Data Security

These are the cornerstone issues of any organization that deals with personal classified data, especially when GAI is part of the business model. So far, governments have recognized the importance of personal classified data and have adopted strict regulations. These regulations have not only generated the possibility of heavy sanctions for companies found to be non-compliant but also demanded changes in business models that have evolved to exploit this data. Despite the complexity and resource requirements to conform to these regulations, the main issues are covered by a global platform for reviews, and we have agreed on written cooperation (Rane et al., 2024; Shafik, 2024b, 2024a). This platform is used as a third party to request reviews of our company to enforce our open and honest privacy and data security policies. Until now, all our functionalities and applications have been developed with privacy and data protection as one of the primary concerns. To help decisions made on this topic, the company has experienced professionals with both a cybersecurity management background and a data science specialty (Kim & Choi, 2024). The resolution of withholding personal data is not only a legal issue but also a technologically advanced concern, which involves deep knowledge about how personal classified data is processed. Our systems were developed according to principles of data processing information, daily backups, and user data access transparency. The next improvement was to develop automatic introspection mechanisms to ensure personal data protection. These mechanisms would permit the initial audit of our domain, confidentiality, and data protection (Ahmed Ali Linkon et al., 2024).

7.2. Bias and Fairness

There has been a growing consciousness in the research community and society of the bias present and, importantly, fed into GAI and GAI technologies. Recently, it was noted that there had been an overinflation with the technology, and it was time to shift the focus to the legal, ethical, and social elements of GAI technologies. Many of the deployed GAI technologies are based on unsupervised or poorly supervised machine learning models. The effectiveness of these GAI technologies for SMEs is an open question and hence the necessity of the big data value argument to be carefully considered in SMEs. Most of the documented occurrences of GAI bias are on gender, race, nationality, and more visible biases which result in a contrary outcome to the logical and objective representations that the promise of GAI stipulated (Beerbaum Dr., 2023b). There is mention of existing benchmarks to assess the biases present in these GAI technologies. However, it is recommended that these benchmarks be augmented with more SME-centric characteristics, which are the lifeblood of larger organizations. Completing this is currently a difficult task since there is no line of research for working with the dynamic and complex SME landscapes with GAI technologies. When people talk, there is also implicit mention of fairness to accompany the biased discussion (Rane, 2023). The fairness of GAI systems is in relation to its impact and consequences thereof with respect to citizens. Discussions of fairness extend from source code quality to conforming to national and international law. Currently, the instruction in a GAI fairness framework comes primarily from humans and large corporations at a workable and understandable level with SMEs. Thus, we have to stretch to bring those SME idiosyncrasies to the forefront of the GAI and GAI fairness debate, no matter how unappealing (Abrokwah-Larbi, 2023).

8. IMPLICATIONS AND RECOMMENDATIONS

This chapter revisits the research's problem statement, which is oriented around knowledge-aware business processes that exploit both quantitative and qualitative data to predict and generate new business knowledge.

8.1. Key Findings

Through this chapter, a series of considered and deliberate steps introduce a new superintelligent automation model based on generative GAI to unlock the knowledge power of SMEs. The superintelligent automation model leverages the stores of real-world knowledge locked within an enterprise to improve, evolve, tailor, and teach GAI algorithms that can make sense of complex, non-linear, probabilistic, imprecise real-world data and offer advice to both non-GAI and GAI agents (Rane et al., 2024). In other words, the model characterizes the way forward with high-level guidance, with a particular focus on driving business improvement. To summarize, a new superintelligent automation model for business process improvement was developed that is built around the principle of generative GAI. This model avoids the tendency of other generative research streams in GAI that have squandered mainly the massive potential locked inside small and medium enterprises by perpetuating human GAI strategies like reinforcement learning and artificial evolution (Humphreys et al., 2024; Wu, 2024). These are bleak attempts that often mimic, exaggerate, and ultimately fail to free these businesses from the negative aspects of the intelligent technologies previously incorporated. However, applied generative GAI in the context of well-operating small and medium-sized enterprises has the potential to be a revenue multiplier in dealing with the so-called small data. Small data refers to complex and fuzzy data characterized by a small number of exceptions or outliers that are easily swamped by the vast technological deployment of alternative GAI, known as medium to big data (Sieja & Wach, 2023).

8.2. Implications and Recommendations for Future Research

As the discussion in this chapter highlights, progress in realizing the vision of artificial intelligence in SMEs to date has been somewhat limited. The challenges of capability development and organizational readiness for the era of generative models have been discussed. From the review, a number of ambitions have emerged that become recommendations to help develop the next generation of 'GAI-ready' SMEs. Each of these is an area rich in opportunity for further work (Rane et al., 2024). The first recommendation for future work is to increase the efforts demonstrated here to understand the actual barriers to developing GAI literacy in SMEs. Using large representative SME samples to explore the barriers – and enablers – present in this context is particularly important. Such future work could include the identification of the factors that have led to the successful implementation of GAI leveraging capabilities and the transferability of such capabilities between different types of GAI projects (Kim & Choi, 2024; Mondal et al., 2023). Accurate knowledge of the barriers to capability development then forms a crucial context for the structural, network, and design questions discussed at the end of the chapter – questions that are aimed at increasing SME awareness and understanding within the generative GAI context. Understanding and comprehension of generative GAI is then crucial for SME organizations to respond rapidly through the exploration of GAI opportunities and leverage evidence-based insights internally, prompting skills development and acquisition within functions (Ahmed Ali Linkon et al., 2024).

9. CONCLUSION

Upon thorough review of various design-science research products derived from building, testing, and fielding the Generative Research Literacy (GRL) framework in high-potential GAI contexts, this study develops an understanding framework. This framework guides potential future GRL utilization activities, especially in SMEs holding the potential to benefit from improved GRL software in their GAI-related efforts but who often fail to leverage it better. This section concludes the study by summarizing its contributions, suggesting potential topics of future research on GRL for the GAI domain, informing practitioners to leverage existing GRL better, and outlining its guidelines for action. This study contributes to the emerging body of design-science research on formulating understanding frameworks to support generative learning in high-potential GAI settings. It does so by providing a multi-faceted picture of potential challenges and mismatches in the practice of software-facilitated research across a number of cases. Subject to additional validation and refinements upfront, better use of this work's outputs may be at least in part impactful in helping design more usable and valuable GRL software. In addition, this work contributes additional knowledge about the opportunities, potential benefits and risks, and other iterative challenges involved in more active GRL use. In particular, the study enriches our understanding of the likely characteristics of various research models for individual and more collective GAI endeavors, the contributions provided by the nested GAI research activities, different modes for engaging with GRL-enabled service offerings, and which roles participants can and should play in more cyclically interactive research-learning efforts. Thereby, this study provides SME managers with further insight and guidance for making better-informed decisions on the initiation and execution of feasible and suitable research projects and so equips them to be more successful in unlocking the generative power of GAI.

REFERENCES

Abrokwah-Larbi, K. (2023). The role of generative artificial intelligence (GAI) in customer personalisation (CP) development in SMEs: A theoretical framework and research propositions. *Industrial Artificial Intelligence*, *1*(1). Advance online publication. DOI: 10.1007/s44244-023-00012-4

Baxter, K., & Schlesinger, Y. (2023). Managing the Risks of Generative AI. *Harvard Business Review*.

Brown, O., Davison, R. M., Decker, S., Ellis, D. A., Faulconbridge, J., Gore, J., Greenwood, M., Islam, G., Lubinski, C., MacKenzie, N. G., Meyer, R., Muzio, D., Quattrone, P., Ravishankar, M. N., Zilber, T., Ren, S., Sarala, R. M., & Hibbert, P. (2024). Theory-Driven Perspectives on Generative Artificial Intelligence in Business and Management. *British Journal of Management*, *35*(1). Advance online publication. DOI: 10.1111/1467-8551.12788

Budhwar, P., Chowdhury, S., Wood, G., Aguinis, H., Bamber, G. J., Beltran, J. R., Boselie, P., Lee Cooke, F., Decker, S., DeNisi, A., Dey, P. K., Guest, D., Knoblich, A. J., Malik, A., Paauwe, J., Papagiannidis, S., Patel, C., Pereira, V., Ren, S., . . . Varma, A. (2023). Human resource management in the age of generative artificial intelligence: Perspectives and research directions on ChatGPT. In *Human Resource Management Journal* (Vol. 33, Issue 3). https://doi.org/DOI: 10.1111/1748-8583.12524

Chuma, E. L., & De Oliveira, G. G. (2023). Generative AI for Business Decision-Making: A Case of ChatGPT. *Management Science and Business Decisions*, *3*(1). Advance online publication. DOI: 10.52812/msbd.63

Dr, B. D. O. (2023a). Generative Artificial Intelligence (GAI) Ethics Taxonomy-Applying Chat GPT for Robotic Process Automation (GAI-RPA) as Business Case. SSRN *Electronic Journal*. https://doi.org/DOI: 10.2139/ssrn.4385025

Dr, B. D. O. (2023b). Generative Artificial Intelligence (GAI) with Chat GPT for Accounting – a Business Case. SSRN *Electronic Journal*. https://doi.org/DOI: 10.2139/ssrn.4385651

Horak, J., Kolencik, J., Văduva, C., & Woodward, B. (2023). Generative Artificial Intelligence and 3D Virtual Simulation Technologies, Ambient Scene Detection and Automated Employment Decision Tools, and Visual Data Mining and Immersive Remote Collaboration Systems in Decentralized Autonomous Organizations. *Analysis and Metaphysics*, *22*. Advance online publication. DOI: 10.22381/am2220237

Humphreys, D., Koay, A., Desmond, D., & Mealy, E. (2024). AI hype as a cyber security risk: The moral responsibility of implementing generative AI in business. *AI and Ethics, 4*(3). Advance online publication. DOI: 10.1007/s43681-024-00443-4

Hussain, M. (2023). When, Where, and Which?: Navigating the Intersection of Computer Vision and Generative AI for Strategic Business Integration. *IEEE Access : Practical Innovations, Open Solutions, 11*. Advance online publication. DOI: 10.1109/ACCESS.2023.3332468

Kanbach, D. K., Heiduk, L., Blueher, G., Schreiter, M., & Lahmann, A. (2024). The GenAI is out of the bottle: generative artificial intelligence from a business model innovation perspective. In *Review of Managerial Science* (Vol. 18, Issue 4). https://doi.org/DOI: 10.1007/s11846-023-00696-z

Kim, J., & Choi, G. (2024). Assessing the Impact of Generative Artificial Intelligence on Customer Engagement in Business-to-Customer Scenarios. *Asia-Pacific Journal of Convergent Research Interchange, 10*(2). Advance online publication. DOI: 10.47116/apjcri.2024.02.09

Li, Z. (2022). Generative Logic of Digital Capitalism Based on Artificial Intelligence Technology. *Mobile Information Systems, 2022*. Advance online publication. DOI: 10.1155/2022/9068591

Linkon, A. A., Shaima, M., Md, S. U. S., Badruddowza, N. N., Md, N. U. R., Ghosh, S. K., Esa, H., & Chowdhury, F. R. (2024). Advancements and Applications of Generative Artificial Intelligence and Large Language Models on Business Management: A Comprehensive Review. *Journal of Computer Science and Technology Studies, 6*(1). Advance online publication. DOI: 10.32996/jcsts.2024.6.1.26

Mondal, S., Das, S., & Vrana, V. G. (2023). How to Bell the Cat? A Theoretical Review of Generative Artificial Intelligence towards Digital Disruption in All Walks of Life. In *Technologies* (Vol. 11, Issue 2). https://doi.org/DOI: 10.3390/technologies11020044

Ooi, K. B., Tan, G. W. H., Al-Emran, M., Al-Sharafi, M. A., Capatina, A., Chakraborty, A., Dwivedi, Y. K., Huang, T. L., Kar, A. K., Lee, V. H., Loh, X. M., Micu, A., Mikalef, P., Mogaji, E., Pandey, N., Raman, R., Rana, N. P., Sarker, P., Sharma, A., & Wong, L. W. (2023). The Potential of Generative Artificial Intelligence Across Disciplines: Perspectives and Future Directions. *Journal of Computer Information Systems*. Advance online publication. DOI: 10.1080/08874417.2023.2261010

Peres, R., Schreier, M., Schweidel, D., & Sorescu, A. (2023). Editorial: On ChatGPT and beyond: How generative artificial intelligence may affect research, teaching, and practice. *International Journal of Research in Marketing*, *40*(2). Advance online publication. DOI: 10.1016/j.ijresmar.2023.03.001

PricewaterhouseCoopers. (2023). 2024 AI Business Predictions. In *PwC*. https://www.pwc.com/us/en/tech-effect/ai-analytics/ai-predictions.html

Rajbhoj, A., Somase, A., Kulkarni, P., & Kulkarni, V. (2024). Accelerating Software Development Using Generative AI: ChatGPT Case Study. *ACM International Conference Proceeding Series*. https://doi.org/DOI: 10.1145/3641399.3641403

Rane, N. (2023). Role and Challenges of ChatGPT and Similar Generative Artificial Intelligence in Business Management. SSRN *Electronic Journal*. https://doi.org/DOI: 10.2139/ssrn.4603227

Rane, N., Choudhary, S., & Rane, J. (2024). Gemini or ChatGPT? Capability, Performance, and Selection of Cutting-Edge Generative Artificial Intelligence (AI) in Business Management. SSRN *Electronic Journal*. https://doi.org/DOI: 10.2139/ssrn.4731281

Ratten, V. (2024). Artificial Intelligence, Digital Trends and Globalization: Future Research Trends. *FIIB Business Review*, *13*(3). Advance online publication. DOI: 10.1177/23197145231222774

Shafik, W. (2023). Introduction to ChatGPT. In *Advanced Applications of Generative AI and Natural Language Processing Models*. https://doi.org/DOI: 10.4018/9798369305027.ch001

Shafik, W. (2024a). Artificial intelligence and Blockchain technology enabling cybersecurity in telehealth systems. In *Artificial Intelligence and Blockchain Technology in Modern Telehealth Systems*. https://doi.org/DOI: 10.1049/pbhe061e_ch11

Shafik, W. (2024b). Navigating emerging challenges in robotics and artificial intelligence in Africa. In *Examining the Rapid Advance of Digital Technology in Africa*. https://doi.org/DOI: 10.4018/978-1-6684-9962-7.ch007

Sieja, M., & Wach, K. (2023). Revolutionary artificial intelligence or rogue technology? The promises and pitfalls of ChatGPT. *International Entrepreneurship Review*, *9*(4). Advance online publication. DOI: 10.15678/ier.2023.0904.07

Soni, V. (2023). Impact of Generative AI on Small and Medium Enterprises' Revenue Growth: The Moderating Role of Human, Technological, and Market Factors. *Reviews of Contemporary Business Analytics*, *6*(1). https://researchberg.com/index.php/rcba/article/view/169

Szilágyi, R., & Tóth, M. (2024). Use of LLM for SMEs, opportunities and challenges. *Agrárinformatika Folyóirat, 14*(2). Advance online publication. DOI: 10.17700/jai.2023.14.2.703

ală, M. L., Müller, C. N., Năstase, I. A., State, O., & Gheorghe, G. (2024). Exploring university students' perceptions of generative artificial intelligence in education. *Amfiteatru Economic, 26*(65). Advance online publication. DOI: 10.24818/EA/2024/65/71

Wu, S. (2024). Artificial Intelligence-Enhanced Learning: A New Paradigm in the "Business Data Analysis and Application" Course. *Journal of Contemporary Educational Research, 8*(2). Advance online publication. DOI: 10.26689/jcer.v8i2.6081

Yahaya, M., Umagba, A., Obeta, S., & Maruyama, T. (2023). Critical Evaluation of the Future Role of Artificial Intelligence in Business and Society. *Journal of Artificial Intelligence. Machine Learning and Data Science, 1*(1). Advance online publication.

ENDNOTES

1 https://www.ibm.com/topics/artificial-intelligence

2 https://ai.google/discover/generativeai/

3 https://deepai.org/machine-learning-glossary-and-terms/narrow-ai

4 https://www.intel.com/content/www/us/en/products/docs/processors/what-is-a-gpu.html

5 https://aws.amazon.com/what-is/deep-learning/

6 https://www.techtarget.com/searchenterpriseai/definition/Turing-test

7 https://www.britannica.com/question/What-is-human-intelligence

8 https://aims.fao.org/information-and-communication-technologies-ict

9 https://www.kaggle.com/models

Compilation of References

Aaker, D. A. (2012). *Building strong brands*. Simon and Schuster.

Aayog, N. I. T. I. (2023). *National Strategy for Artificial Intelligence*. NITI Aayog.

Abadi, M., Agarwal, A., Barham, P., Brevdo, E., Chen, Z., Citro, C., . . . Zheng, X. (2016). TensorFlow: Large-scale machine learning on heterogeneous systems. *arXiv preprint arXiv:1603.04467.*

Abd Hair Awang, N. M. S., Hussain, M. Y., Ishak, S., & Yusof, R. M. (2014). Organizational learning and work environment: A formation of innovative work behavior at small medium enterprises (SMEs). In *ICICKM2014-Proceedings of the 11th International Conference on Intellectual Capital, Knowledge Management and Organisational Learning: ICICKM2014* (p. 30). Academic Conferences Limited.

Abdallah, M., Abu Talib, M., Feroz, S., Nasir, Q., Abdalla, H., & Mahfood, B. (2020). Artificial intelligence applications in solid waste management: A systematic research review. *Waste Management (New York, N.Y.)*, *109*, 231–246. DOI: 10.1016/j.wasman.2020.04.057 PMID: 32428727

Abid Haleem, M. J. (2022). Artificial intelligence (AI) applications for marketing: A literature-based study. *International Journal of Intelligent Networks*, 119-132.

Abid, M., Gheraia, Z., Abdelli, H., Sekrafi, H., & Diaw, A. (2022). COVID-19 pandemic and economic impacts in Arab countries: Challenges and policies. *Research in Globalization*, *5*, 100103. DOI: 10.1016/j.resglo.2022.100103

Abisuga-Oyekunle, O. A., Patra, S. K., & Muchie, M. (2020). SMEs in sustainable development: Their role in poverty reduction and employment generation in sub-Saharan Africa. *African Journal of Science, Technology, Innovation and Development*, *12*(4), 405–419. https://journals.co.za/doi/abs/10.1080/20421338.2019.1656428

Abitha, S. V. S. (2021, May 10). *ChatBots and Virtual Assistants*. https://doi.org/ DOI: 10.22541/au.162066507.77468411/v1

Abousaber, I., & Abdalla, H. (2023). Review of Using Technologies of Artificial Intelligence in Companies. *Nternational Journal of Communication Networks and Information Security, 15*(1), 217–228. DOI: 10.17762/ijcnis.v15i1.5743

Abrokwah-Larbi, K. (2023). The role of generative artificial intelligence (GAI) in customer personalisation (CP) development in SMEs: A theoretical framework and research propositions. *Industrial Artificial Intelligence, 1*(1). Advance online publication. DOI: 10.1007/s44244-023-00012-4

Acemoglu, D., & Restrepo, P. (2019). Automation and new tasks: How technology displaces and reinstates labour (Working Paper No. 25684). National Bureau of Economic Research. https://doi.org/DOI: 10.3386/w25684

Acemoglu, D., & Restrepo, P. (2020). Automation and new tasks: How technology displaces and reinstates labour.

Adam, M., Wessel, M., & Benlian, A. (2021). AI-based chatbots in customer service and their effects on user compliance. *Electronic Markets, 31*(2), 427–445.

Adesoga, T. O., Olaiya, O. P., & Obani, O. Q. (2024). *Leveraging AI for transformative business improvement : Strategies for market analysis, customer insights, and competitive intelligence.*

Adeyeri, T. B. (2024). Economic impacts of AI-driven automation in financial services. International Journal of Scientific Research and Management, ISSN: 2321-3418. https://ijsrm.net

Afeku-Amenyo, D. (2015). AI applications in financial risk management. *Journal of Financial Technology, 3*(2), 45–60.

Afeku-Amenyo, D. (2021). Dynamic pricing strategies using AI in retail. *International Journal of Business Analytics, 8*(4), 112–130.

Afeku-Amenyo, D. (2022). AI-driven personalization in e-commerce: The case of Stitch Fix. *Journal of Digital Marketing, 10*(1), 25–40.

Afriana, riza devi. (2017). No Title No Title No Title. *Angewandte Chemie International Edition, 6(11), 951–952., 6*(November), 5–24.

Afroogh, S., Akbari, A., Malone, E., Kargar, M., & Alambeigi, H. (2024). Trust in AI: Progress, challenges, and future directions. *Humanities & Social Sciences Communications, 11*(1), 1–30.

Aghabiglou, A., Chu, C. S., Dabbech, A., & Wiaux, Y. (2024). The R2D2 deep neural network series paradigm for fast precision imaging in radio astronomy. *arXiv preprint arXiv:2403.05452.*

Agrawal, S. (2022). Saurabh Agrawal of Lenskart reveals the key technologies for the company. (E. T. India, Interviewer) Retrieved from https://youtu.be/ZsgJAuQj6gs

Agupugo, C. P., Bassey, E. O., & Ibegbulam, C. (2022). Challenges of AI adoption in SME financial management. *African Journal of Business Technology*, *5*(1), 33–50.

Agupugo, C. P., Ezeh, C. I., & Ige, S. O. (2024). AI for financial accuracy and speed in SMEs. *Journal of Small Business Finance*, *12*(2), 78–95.

Agupugo, C. P., & Tochukwu, E. (2022). AI-driven financial advisory services for SMEs. *Journal of Financial Innovation*, *7*(3), 89–104.

Aheleroff, S., Mostashiri, N., Xu, X., & Zhong, R. Y. (2021). Mass Personalisation as a Service in Industry 4.0: A Resilient Response Case Study. *Advanced Engineering Informatics*. https://doi.org/https://doi.org/10.1016/j.aei.2021.101438

Ahmed, K., Tazi, N. E., & Hossny, A. H. (2015, October 1). *Sentiment Analysis over Social Networks: An Overview*. IEEE Xplore. https://doi.org/DOI: 10.1109/SMC.2015.380

Ahmed, S., & Aziz, N. A. (2025). Impact of AI on customer experience in video streaming services: A focus on personalization and trust. *International Journal of Human-Computer Interaction*, *41*(12), 7726-7745.

Ahsan, S., & Zaman, A. (2021). *The augmentation of Awareness Management through Industry 4 . 0 : A case of avia- tion sector of an emerging economy Miao Miao, Syed Imran Zaman, Arooba Zafar, Cristian Garcia Rodriguez and. 00.*

AIMS. (2020). African Institute for Mathematical Sciences. Retrieved from https://www.nexteinstein.org

AIMS. (2020). Institute for Mathematical Sciences. Retrieved from https://www.nexteinstein.org

Ajiga, O. P., Daramola, F. O., & Nwosu, C. E. (2024). AI-based accounting software for SMEs. *International Journal of Financial Technology*, *9*(1), 56–72.

Akoka, J., Comyn-Wattiau, I., & Laoufi, N. (2017). Research on Big Data–A systematic mapping study. *Computer Standards & Interfaces*, *54*, 105–115.

Aksoy, H. (2017). How do innovation culture, marketing innovation and product innovation affect the market performance of small and medium-sized enterprises (SMEs)? *Technology in Society*, *51*, 133–141. DOI: 10.1016/j.techsoc.2017.08.005

Al Ghunaimi, H., & Awashreh, R. (2025). Enhancing sustainability and competitiveness of self-funded SMEs: The hotel model. *International Journal of Innovative Research and Scientific Studies*, *8*(1), 1806–1817. DOI: 10.53894/ijirss.v8i1.4805

Alabi, A. T., Ubandawaki, A. T., & Issa, S. O. (2025). The Role of Digital Technology in the Sustainability Strategies of SMEs. In *The Future of Small Business in Industry 5.0* (pp. 347–378). IGI Global Scientific Publishing., DOI: 10.4018/979-8-3693-7362-0.ch014

Al-Busaidi, A., & Al-Harthy, A. (2017). Challenges facing small and medium-sized enterprises in Oman. [DOI: 10.1108/JSBED-02-2017-0040]. *Journal of Small Business and Enterprise Development*, *24*(4), 732–753.

Ali, H., & Hajjar, L. (2024). Empowering SMEs with AI and Digital Transformation: A Roadmap to Enhanced Competitiveness and Growth.

Aljarboa, S. (2024). Factors influencing the adoption of artificial intelligence in e-commerce by small and medium-sized enterprises. *International Journal of Information Management Data Insights*.

Allaymoun, M., & Shorman, S. (2024). AI-Powered Websites in e-commerce. *Health Care Education*, •••, 319–329. DOI: 10.1007/978-3-031-54379-1_28

Allen, T. D., Golden, T. D., & Shockley, K. M. (2013). How effective is telecommuting? Assessing the status of our scientific findings. *Psychological Science in the Public Interest*, *16*(2), 40–68. PMID: 26403188

Alqurashi, D. R., Alkhaffaf, M., Daoud, M. K., & Ahmad, J. (2023). *Exploring the Influence of Artificial Intelligence in Personalized Content Marketing : A Contemporary Digital Marketing*. *8*, 548–560.

Alvear, M. (2023). E-commerce strategies for SMEs in the digital age. *Journal of Digital Commerce*, *6*(2), 101–115.

Amil, Y. (2024). The Impact of AI-Driven Personalization Tools on Privacy Concerns and Consumer Trust in E-commerce. Master thesis of the HEC-Ecole de gestion de l'Université de Liège

Amoako-Adu, B., & Eshun, J. P. (2018). SME financing in Africa: Collateral lending vs cash flow lending. *International Journal of Economics and Finance*, *10*(6), 151–159. DOI: 10.5539/ijef.v10n6p151

Amorós, J. E., Cristi, O., & Minniti, M. (2011). Entrepreneurial volatility: A cross-country study. *Annual Proceedings of the Wealth and Well-Being of Nations*, *3*, 159–176.

Anderson, L., Kanneganti, D., Houk, M., Holm, R., & Smith, T. (2023). Generative AI as a tool for environmental health research translation, Advancing. *Earth and Space Science (Hoboken, N.J.)*, *7*(7). Advance online publication. DOI: 10.1029/2023GH000875 PMID: 37502196

Andreassen, H., & Gjerald, O. (2024). What drives consumer expectations for institutional food? Identifying antecedents of normative and predictive expectations in baby boomers. *Journal of Consumer Behaviour*, *23*(2), 769–795. DOI: 10.1002/cb.2238

Antikainen, R., & P. J. (2018). Circular economy: A new strategic approach for businesses. *Business Horizons*, *61*(3), 371–380.

Antonioli, D., Mazzanti, M., & Pini, P. (2010). Productivity, innovation strategies and industrial relations in SMEs: Empirical evidence for a local production system in northern Italy. *International Review of Applied Economics*, *24*(4), 453–482. DOI: 10.1080/02692170903426194

Appypie. (2025). *Appypie Homepage*. Retrieved from Appypie: https://www.appypie.com/

Ariffin, N. A., Yunus, A. M., & Kadir, I. K. (2021). The role of big data in the healthcare industry. *Journal of Islamic*, *6*(36), 235–245.

Arntz, M., Gregory, T., & Zierahn, U. (2017). Revisiting the risk of automation. *Economics Letters*, *159*, 157–160.

Atkins, K. E.. (2019). AI for optimizing water and energy use: Challenges and opportunities. *Environmental Research Letters*, *14*(1), 013003.

Autor, D. H. (2015). Why are there still so many jobs? The history and future of workplace automation. *The Journal of Economic Perspectives*, *29*(3), 3–30.

Autor, D. H., Katz, L. F., & Kearney, M. S. (2008). Trends in U.S. wage inequality: Revising the revisionists. *The Review of Economics and Statistics*, *90*(2), 300–323.

Autor, D. H., & Salomons, A. (2018). Does productivity growth threaten employment? In *Handbook of Labour Economics* (pp. 727–812). Elsevier.

Awashreh, R., & Hamid, A. (2024 a). A proposed framework for predicting the psychological determinants of youth entrepreneurship success: Gulf region perspective. In *Studies in Systems, Decision and Control* (Vol. 536, pp. 51–60). Springer. https://doi.org/DOI: 10.1007/978-3-031-63402-4_5

Awashreh, R. (2023). Enhancing Innovation among Business Colleges at Omani Universities: A Theoretical Framework. [https://seybold report.com]. *Seybold Report, 18*(02), 182–196.

Awashreh, R. (2025). Leadership strategies for managing change and fostering innovation over private higher education: Academic institutions in Oman. In *Evolving strategies for organizational management and performance evaluation* (pp. 399–422). IGI Global., DOI: 10.4018/979-8-3373-0149-5.ch018

Awashreh, R., & Hamid, A. (2024 b). *Understanding Wise Leadership: Employees' perspective in Oman's Government Sector*. South Africa Journal of Human Resources Management., DOI: 10.4102/sajhrm.v22i0.2747

Azevedo, N., Aquino, G., Nascimento, L., Camelo, L., Figueira, T., Oliveira, J., Figueiredo, I., Printes, A., Torné, I., & Figueiredo, C. (2023). A Novel Methodology for Developing Troubleshooting Chatbots Applied to ATM Technical Maintenance Support. *Applied Sciences (Basel, Switzerland), 13*(11), 6777. DOI: 10.3390/app13116777

Azfar, R. (n.d.). *Sephora wields AI for new wave shopping experiences, innovating in personalization*. Retrieved from Retail Drive: https://www.retaildive.com/ex/mobilecommercedaily/sephora-leverages-facebook-messenger-and-ai-to-help-consumers-navigate-ecommerce

Aziz, S., & Dowling, M. (2019). Machine learning and AI for risk management. In Gomber, P., & Dowling, M. (Eds.), *Disrupting finance: FinTech and strategy in the 21st century* (pp. 75–90). Palgrave Macmillan., DOI: 10.1007/978-3-030-02330-0_5

Baabdullah, A. M., Alalwan, A. A., Slade, E. L., Raman, R., & Khatatneh, K. F. (2021). SMEs and artificial intelligence (AI): Antecedents and consequences of AI-based B2B practices. *Industrial Marketing Management, 98*, 255–270. DOI: 10.1016/j.indmarman.2021.09.003

Babatunde, S. O., Odejide, O. A., Edunjobi, T. E., & Ogundipe, D. O. (2024). THE ROLE OF AI IN MARKETING PERSONALIZATION: A THEORETICAL EXPLORATION OF CONSUMER ENGAGEMENT STRATEGIES. *International Journal of Management & Entrepreneurship Research, 6*(3), 936–949. DOI: 10.51594/ijmer.v6i3.964

Bach, T. A., Khan, A., Hallock, H., Beltrão, G., & Sousa, S. (2024). A systematic literature review of user trust in AI-enabled systems: An HCI perspective. *International Journal of Human-Computer Interaction, 40*(5), 1251–1266.

Badghish, S., & Soomro, Y. A. (2024). Artificial Intelligence Adoption by SMEs to Achieve Sustainable Business Performance: Application of Technology–Organization–Environment Framework. *Sustainability, 16*(5), 1864. DOI: 10.3390/su16051864

Bagale, G. S., Vandadi, V. R., Singh, D., Sharma, D. K., Garlapati, D. V. K., Bommisetti, R. K., Gupta, R. K., Setsiawan, R., Subramaniyaswamy, V., & Sengan, S. (2023). Retracted article: Small and medium-sized enterprises' contribution in digital technology. *Annals of Operations Research, 326*(Suppl. 1), 3–4. DOI: 10.1007/s10479-023-05570-6

Bai, T., Goldfarb, A., & Tucker, C. E. (2021). Digital disintermediation and job quality: How AI and platforms are reshaping the labour market. *Strategic Management Journal, 42*(1), 105–128.

Baker, J. (2012). The technology–organization–environment framework. In Dwivedi, Y. K., Wade, M. R., & Schneberger, S. L. (Eds.), *Information systems theory: Explaining and predicting our digital society* (Vol. 1, pp. 231–245). Springer., DOI: 10.1007/978-1-4419-6108-2_12

Baker, R. S., & Siemens, G. (2014). Educational data mining and learning analytics. In Sawyer, R. K. (Ed.), *Cambridge handbook of the learning sciences* (2nd ed.). Cambridge University Press.

Baltar, F., & Brunet, I. (2012). Social research 2.0: virtual snowball sampling method using Facebook. *Internet Research, 22*(1), 57-74.

Bao, Y., Tang, Z., Li, H., & Zhang, Y. (2019). Computer vision and deep learning–based data anomaly detection method for structural health monitoring. *Structural Health Monitoring, 18*(2), 401–421.

Barbary, M. M. (2023). Global Competitiveness and Gross Domestic Product in MENA Countries. *Revue d'Economie Financiere, 21*, 116–1122. DOI: 10.55365/1923.x2023.21.124

Barney, J. B. (1991). Firm resources and sustained competitive advantage. *Journal of Management, 17*(1), 99–120. DOI: 10.1177/014920639101700108

Basavapattan, S. (2021). A study on talent management practices in small and medium enterprises. [Unpublished manuscript or specify source].

Bassey, E. O. (2022). AI-driven credit analysis for SMEs. *African Journal of Financial Management, 4*(3), 67–82.

Bassey, E. O. (2023). AI in financial decision-making for SMEs. *Journal of Business Technology*, *10*(4), 123–140.

Bassey, E. O., Ezeh, C. I., & Ige, S. O. (2024). AI for tax planning and compliance in SMEs. *Journal of Taxation and Business*, *8*(2), 90–107.

Bassey, E. O., & Ibegbulam, C. (2023). Technical expertise gaps in AI adoption for SMEs. *Journal of Small Business Innovation*, *11*(1), 44–59.

Bauer, J., & Jannach, D. (2018). Optimal pricing in e-commerce based on sparse and noisy data. *Decision Support Systems*, *106*, 53–63. DOI: 10.1016/j.dss.2017.12.002

Baxter, K., & Schlesinger, Y. (2023). Managing the Risks of Generative AI. *Harvard Business Review*.

Bayraktar, M., & Algan, N. (2019, June). The Importance of SMEs on World Economies. *International Conference on Eurasian Economies 2019*. https://doi.org/DOI: 10.36880/c11.02265

Behera, G., & Nain, N. (2019). A comparative study of Big Mart sales prediction. *International Journal of Research in Engineering. IT and Social Sciences*, *9*(5), 75–81.

Behura, A., Sahu, S., & Kabat, M. R. (2021). Advancement of Machine Learning and Cloud Computing in the Field of Smart Health Care. *Machine Learning Approach for Cloud Data Analytics in IoT*, 273-306.

Belk, R. (2021). Ethical issues in service robotics and artificial intelligence. *Service Industries Journal*, *41*(13–14), 860–876.

Bellamy, R. K. E., Dey, K., Hind, M., Hoffman, S. C., Houde, S., Kannan, K., & Zhang, Y. (2019). AI Fairness 360: An extensible toolkit for detecting, understanding, and mitigating unwanted algorithmic bias. *IBM Journal of Research and Development*, *63*(4/5), 4–1.

Ben Youssef, A., & Zeqiri, A. (2022). Hospitality industry 4.0 and climate change. *Circular Economy and Sustainability*, *2*(3), 1043–1063. PMID: 35098249

Berger, A. N., & Udell, G. F. (1998). The economics of small business finance: The roles of private equity and debt markets in the financial growth cycle. *Journal of Banking & Finance*, *22*(6–8), 613–673. DOI: 10.1016/S0378-4266(98)00038-7

Berisha, G., & Pula, J. S. (2015). Defining small and medium enterprises: A critical review. *Academic Journal of Business, Administration. Law and Social Sciences*, *1*(1), 17–27.

Besiri, D. (2024). AI-Driven Predictive Analytics: Transforming Decision-Making in Business. *Human-Computer Interaction*, *8*(1), 163–172. DOI: 10.62802/8ny1ww06

Bessen, J. E. (2019). AI and jobs: The role of demand. *AEA Papers and Proceedings. American Economic Association*, *109*, 1–7.

Bharadwaj, V. (2024). INTEGRATING ARTIFICIAL INTELLIGENCE IN HUMAN RESOURCE MANAGEMENT: A COMPREHENSIVE OVERVIEW. *Journal of Management*, *11*(3), 71–78. DOI: 10.34218/jom_11_03_006

Bhattacharya, P. (2018). *Artificial Intelligence in the Boardroom: Enabling "Machines" to "Learn" to Make Strategic Business Decisions. 2018 Fifth HCT Information Technology Trends*. ITT., DOI: 10.1109/ctit.2018.8649550

Bhoganadam, S. D., Rao, N. S., & Rao, D. S. (2017). A study on issues and challenges faced by SMEs: A literature review. Retrieved from https://www.researchgate.net/publication/316595283

Bhuiyan, M. R. I., Faraji, M. R., Rashid, M., Bhuyan, M. K., Hossain, R., & Ghose, P. (2024). Digital transformation in SMEs emerging technological tools and technologies for enhancing the SME's strategies and outcomes. *Journal of Ecohumanism*, *3*(4), 211–224. https://www.ceeol.com/search/article-detail?id=1271910

Biea, E. A., Dinu, E., Bunica, A., & Jerdea, L. (2024). Recruitment in SMEs: The role of managerial practices, technology and innovation. *European Business Review*, *36*(3). https://doi.org/https://doi.org/10.1108/EBR-05-2023-0162

Binh Thai Dang, N. X. (2019). Research on the Application of E-commerce to Small and Medium Enterprises (SMEs): the Case of India. *International Journal of Economics and Management*.

Binns, R. (2018). Fairness in machine learning: Lessons from political philosophy. *Proceedings of the 2018 Conference on Fairness, Accountability, and Transparency*, 149-159.

Bi, R., Davison, R. M., & Smyrnios, K. X. (2017). E-business and fast growth SMEs. *Small Business Economics*, *48*, 559–576. DOI: 10.1007/s11187-016-9788-8

Blink. (2023a). Enhancing team communication and collaboration. https://www.joinblink.com

Blink. (2023b). Flexible work and employee engagement. https://www.joinblink.com

Blink. (2023c). How Blink enhances team communication. https://www.joinblink.com

Blink. (2023d). How recognition improves team performance. https://www.joinblink.com

Block, S., & Galabuzi, G.-E. (2018). *Canada's colour coded labour market: The gap for racialized workers*. Canadian Centre for Policy Alternatives.

Bloom, N., Liang, J., Roberts, J., & Ying, Z. J. (2015). Does working from home work? Evidence from a Chinese experiment. *The Quarterly Journal of Economics*, *130*(1), 165–218.

Bocken, N. M. P., Short, S. W., Rana, P., & Evans, S. (2014). A literature and practice review to develop sustainable business model archetypes. *Journal of Cleaner Production*, *65*, 42–56.

Boehler, T. (2024, August 28). *Why AI Implementations Fail in SMEs: Examples of Common Pitfalls to Avoid*. Retrieved from LinkedIn: https://www.linkedin.com/pulse/why-ai-implementations-fail-smes-examples-common-pitfalls-boehler-pyawc/

Boons, F., & Lüdeke-Freund, F. (2013). Business models for sustainable innovation: State-of-the-art and steps towards a research agenda. *Journal of Cleaner Production*, *45*, 81–88.

Borgia, E. (2014). The Internet of Things: Calling for a New Ecology of Things. *IEEE Instrumentation & Measurement Magazine*, *17*(6), 17–22.

Borgia, E. (2014). *The Internet of Things: Calling for a New Ecology of Things*. IEEE.

Bostrom, N., & Sandberg, A. (2009). Cognitive enhancement: Methods, ethics, regulatory challenges. *Science and Engineering Ethics*, *15*(3), 311–341. DOI: 10.1007/s11948-009-9142-5 PMID: 19543814

Braunerhjelm, P., & Henrekson, M. (2024). Theories of growth, innovation, and entrepreneurship. In Unleashing society's innovative capacity (Vol. 55, International Studies in Entrepreneurship). Springer, Cham. https://doi.org/DOI: 10.1007/978-3-031-42756-5_2

Brennan, H. L., & Kirby, S. D. (2022). Barriers of artificial intelligence implementation in the diagnosis of obstructive sleep apnea. *Journal of Otolaryngology - Head & Neck Surgery*, *51*, 16. DOI: 10.1186/s40463-022-00554-4 PMID: 35468865

Breque, M., De Nul, L., & Petridis, A. (2021). *Industry 5.0: Towards a sustainable, human-centric and resilient European industry*. European Commission.

Briggs, P., Simpson, B., & De Angeli, A. (2004). Personalisation and trust: a reciprocal relationship?. *Designing Personalized user experiences in eCommerce*, 39-55.

Brock, J. K.-U., & von Wangenheim, F. (2019). Demystifying AI: What digital transformation leaders can teach you about realistic artificial intelligence. *California Management Review*, *61*(4), 110–134. DOI: 10.1177/0008125619863432

Broklyn, P., Olukemi, A., & Bell, C. (2024). AI-driven Personalization in digital marketing: Effectiveness and ethical considerations. Available at SSRN 4906214.

Brown, D. (1990). Global perspective perceptions of SME growth constraints in Nigeria. *Journal of Small Business Management*, *40*(1), 58–65.

Brown, O., Davison, R. M., Decker, S., Ellis, D. A., Faulconbridge, J., Gore, J., Greenwood, M., Islam, G., Lubinski, C., MacKenzie, N. G., Meyer, R., Muzio, D., Quattrone, P., Ravishankar, M. N., Zilber, T., Ren, S., Sarala, R. M., & Hibbert, P. (2024). Theory-Driven Perspectives on Generative Artificial Intelligence in Business and Management. *British Journal of Management*, *35*(1). Advance online publication. DOI: 10.1111/1467-8551.12788

Bruno, Z. (2024). The Impact of Artificial Intelligence on Business Operations. *Global Journal of Management and Business Research*, *24*(D1), 1–8. DOI: 10.34257/gjmbrdvol24is1pg1

Bryceson, D. F. (2002). The scramble in Africa: Reorienting rural livelihoods. *World Development*, *30*(5), 725–739. DOI: 10.1016/S0305-750X(02)00006-2

Brynjolfsson, E., & McAfee, A. (2014). *The second machine age: Work, progress, and prosperity in a time of brilliant technologies*. W. W. Norton & Company.

Brynjolfsson, E., & McAfee, A. (2017). *Machine, platform, crowd: Harnessing our digital future*. W. W. Norton & Company.

Brynjolfsson, E., & McElheran, K. (2016). The rapid adoption of data-driven decision-making. *The American Economic Review*, *106*(5), 133–139.

Brynjolfsson, E., Rock, D., & Syverson, C. (2018). Artificial intelligence and the modern productivity paradox: A clash of expectations and statistics. *NBER Macroeconomics Annual*, *33*(1), 97–142.

Budhwar, P., Chowdhury, S., Wood, G., Aguinis, H., Bamber, G. J., Beltran, J. R., Boselie, P., Lee Cooke, F., Decker, S., DeNisi, A., Dey, P. K., Guest, D., Knoblich, A. J., Malik, A., Paauwe, J., Papagiannidis, S., Patel, C., Pereira, V., Ren, S., . . . Varma, A. (2023). Human resource management in the age of generative artificial intelligence: Perspectives and research directions on ChatGPT. In *Human Resource Management Journal* (Vol. 33, Issue 3). https://doi.org/DOI: 10.1111/1748-8583.12524

Bulchand-Gidumal, J. (2022). Impact of artificial intelligence in travel, tourism, and hospitality. In *Handbook of e-Tourism* (pp. 1943–1962). Springer.

Burrell, J. (2016). How the machine 'thinks': Understanding opacity in machine learning algorithms. *Big Data & Society*, *3*(1), 1–12. 10.1177/2053951715622512

Business Today. (2024, June 24). *Here's how e-commerce unicorn Meesho is deploying AI for ease of business.* Retrieved from Business Today: https://www.businesstoday.in/technology/news/story/heres-how-e-commerce-unicorn-meesho-is-deploying-ai-for-ease-of-business-432051-2024-06-04

Business World. (2025, March 27). *MSMEs Can't Bear Rs 1.5 Lakh Annual Compliance Cost Amid IMS Rules.* (A. Sharma, Editor) Retrieved from Business World: https://www.businessworld.in/article/msmes-cant-bear-rs-15-lakh-annual-compliance-cost-amid-ims-rules-551894

Butt, J. S. (2024). The role of artificial intelligence (AI) in productivity & economic growth in Nordic welfare states. *Acta Universitatis Danubius. Œconomica, 20*(2), 50-72. https://www.ceeol.com/search/article-detail?id=1252928

Bwembya, J. (2022). *Addressing challenges in accessing finance by small and medium enterprises (SMES) in Zambia: a pragmatic approach* (Doctoral dissertation, The University of Zambia). https://dspace.unza.zm/handle/123456789/7880

Byder, J., Agudelo, D. A., & Arango, I. (2019). Gender matters most: The impact on short-term risk aversion following a financial crash. *Review of Financial Economics*, *37*(1), 106–117. DOI: 10.1016/j.rfe.2018.07.002

Cadden, T., Weerawardena, J., Cao, G., Duan, Y., & Mcivor, R. (2023). Examining the function of big data and marketing analytics in SMEs innovation and competitive advantage : A awareness integration perspective ☆. *Journal of Business Investigation, 168*(June), 114225. DOI: 10.1016/j.jbusres.2023.114225

Carayannis, E. G., Dumitrescu, R., & Falkowski, T. (2024). EMPOWERING SMES- "HARNESSING THE POTENTIAL OF GEN AI FOR RESILIENCE AND COMPETITIVENESS.". *IEEE Transactions on Engineering Management*, ●●●, 1–22. DOI: 10.1109/tem.2024.3456820

Carayannis, E. G., Dumitrescu, R., Falkowski, T., Papamichail, G., & Zota, N. R. (2025). Enhancing SME Resilience through Artificial Intelligence and Strategic Foresight: A Framework for Sustainable Competitiveness. *Technology in Society, 102835*. Advance online publication. DOI: 10.1016/j.techsoc.2025.102835

Carole, K. S., Theodore, T. P., & Kim, A. H. C. (2024). Enhanced Experiences: Benefits of AI-Powered Recommendation Systems. *2024 26th International Conference on Advanced Communications Technology*. https://doi.org/DOI: 10.23919/ICACT60172.2024.10471918

Car, T., Stifanich, L. P., & Šimunić, M. (2019). Internet of things (iot) in tourism and hospitality: Opportunities and challenges. *Tourism in South East Europe*, *5*, 163–175.

Casalo, L. V., Flavian, C., & Guinaliu, M. (2008). The role of satisfaction and website usability in developing customer loyalty and positive word of mouth in the e-banking services. *International Journal of Bank Marketing*, *26*(6), 399–417.

Cath, C., Wachter, S., Mittelstadt, B., Taddeo, M., & Floridi, L. (2018). Artificial intelligence and the "good society": The US, EU, and UK approach. *Science and Engineering Ethics*, *24*(2), 505–528. PMID: 28353045

CCI. (2023). *CCI Report*. CCI. Retrieved from https://www.cii.in/PublicationDetail.aspx?enc=zrcmdCxHMWEswep2zYcA3Vzk/ERmDwk1dkBmDlC6H0ag0JBIhqRVKXVTEH3sTmVfqI8AmPd0VkJkGjCk+92kKLipECaJcEJ+s2RLJUPd1QrOn1agl61sgNk75SVWZYW+PxVq6CGljo63XHLA5gLEyVUcGwsGLnqirsEYREThAyTRqd0NncccRRV3yHRr++9A

Chabalala, K., Boyana, S., Kolisi, L., Thango, B., & Lerato, M. (2024). Digital technologies and channels for competitive advantage in SMEs: A systematic review. *Available at SSRN* 4977280.

Chaffey, D., & Ellis-Chadwick, F. (2019). *Digital Marketing: Strategy and Implementation* (6th ed.). Pearson.

Chandraiah, M., & Vani, R. (2014). The prospects and problems of MSMEs sector in India: An analytical study. *International Journal of Business and Management Invention*, *3*(8), 27–40.

Chatterjee, S., Chaudhuri, R., Vrontis, D., & Thrassou, A. (2022). AI-driven customer engagement and SME competitiveness: A conceptual framework. *Journal of Business Research*, *140*, 308–319. DOI: 10.1016/j.jbusres.2021.11.042

Chatterjee, U., & Kanbur, R. (2015). Non-compliance with India's Factories Act: Magnitude and patterns. *International Labour Review*, *153*(3), 393–412. DOI: 10.1111/j.1564-913X.2015.00257.x

Chaturvedi, V. (2016). Talent analytics: The future of human capital management. *Journal of HR Management*, *4*(2), 88–102.

Chawla, M., Sahni, P., & Sadhwani, K. (2020). Can COVID-19 be the turning point for women entrepreneurs in India? *Economic and Political Weekly*, *55*(18), 11–14.

Chen, C. P., & Zhang, C. Y. (2024). Data-intensive applications, challenges, techniques and technologies: A survey on Big Data. *Information sciences, 275*, 314-347. Mayer-Schönberger, V., & Cukier, K. (2013). *Big data: A revolution that will transform how we live, work, and think*. Houghton Mifflin Harcourt.

Cheng, Y., & Jiang, H. (2020). How do AI-driven chatbots impact user experience? Examining gratifications, perceived privacy risk, satisfaction, loyalty, and continued use. *Journal of Broadcasting & Electronic Media*, *64*(4), 592–614.

Chenoy, D. (2012). Skill development in India: A transformation in the making. *India Infrastructure Report*, *2012*, 199–207.

Chen, Q., Lu, Y., Gong, Y., & Xiong, J. (2023). Can AI chatbots help retain customers? Impact of AI service quality on customer loyalty. *Internet Research*, *33*(6), 2205–2243.

Chen, Y., Liu, J., & Zhang, W. (2022). AI-enhanced disaster management: A systematic review. *Journal of Environmental Research*, *36*(5), 123–135.

Chen, Y., Prentice, C., Weaven, S., & Hisao, A. (2022). The influence of customer trust and artificial intelligence on customer engagement and loyalty–The case of the home-sharing industry. *Frontiers in Psychology*, *13*, 912339. PMID: 35992434

Choudhury, A., Singh, R., & Roy, R. (2021). Understanding consumer attitudes towards circular economy practices. *Business Strategy and the Environment*, *30*(3), 1315–1326.

Choudhury, N., Meghwal, M., & Das, K. (2021). Microencapsulation: An overview on concepts, methods, properties and applications in foods. *Food Frontiers*, *2*(4), 426–442. DOI: 10.1002/fft2.94

Chuma, E. L., & De Oliveira, G. G. (2023). Generative AI for Business Decision-Making: A Case of ChatGPT. *Management Science and Business Decisions*, *3*(1). Advance online publication. DOI: 10.52812/msbd.63

Cillo, P., & Rubera, G. (2025). Generative AI in innovation and marketing processes: A roadmap of research opportunities. *Journal of the Academy of Marketing Science*, *13*, 684–701.

Clampitt, P. G. (2012). *Communicating for managerial effectiveness*. SAGE Publications.

Clemente-Almendros, J. A., Nicoara-Popescu, D., & Pastor-Sanz, I. (2024). Digital transformation in SMEs: Understanding its determinants and size heterogeneity. *Technology in Society*, *77*, 102483. DOI: 10.1016/j.techsoc.2024.102483

cliMA. (n.d.). Climate Machine. GitHub repository. Retrieved December 9, 2024, from https://github.com/cliMA/ClimateMachine.jl

Cohen, M. A., & Kietzmann, J. (2014). Riding the IoT Wave: How the Internet of Things is Revolutionizing the Way We Do Business. *Business Horizons*, *57*(6), 707–716.

Coleman, S., Göb, R., Manco, G., Pievatolo, A., Tort-Martorell, X., & Reis, M. S. (2016). How Can SMEs Benefit from Big Data? Challenges and a Path Forward. *Quality and Reliability Engineering International*, *32*(6). https://doi.org/https://doi.org/10.1002/qre.2008

Columbus, L. (2019). *10 charts that will change your perspective on artificial intelligence's growth*. Forbes. Retrieved from https://www.forbes.com

Commons, A. I. (2021). About us. Retrieved from https://www.ai-commons.org

Cukier, K. (2021). Commentary: How AI Shapes Consumer Experiences and Expectations. *Journal of Marketing*, *85*(1), 152–155. DOI: 10.1177/0022242920972932

Daft, R. L., & Lengel, R. H. (1986). Organizational information requirements, media richness, and structural design. *Management Science*, *32*(5), 554–571.

Dalsaniya, A., & Patel, K. (2022). Enhancing process automation with AI: The role of intelligent automation in business efficiency. *International Journal of Science and Research Archive*, *5*(2), 322–337. DOI: 10.30574/ijsra.2022.5.2.0083

Daramola, F. O., Ezeh, C. I., & Ige, S. O. (2024). AI-powered expense tracking for SMEs. *Journal of Financial Optimization*, *7*(1), 34–49.

Darren, L., & Conrad, L. (2009). *Entrepreneurship: Opportunities and innovation*. [Publisher].

Darroch, G. (1983). Labour market change and industrialization in Canada. *The Canadian Historical Review*, *64*(3), 325–349.

Das, I. R., Talukder, M. B., & Kumar, S. (2024). Implication of Artificial Intelligence in Hospitality Marketing. In Kumar, S., Talukder, M. B., & Pego, A. (Eds.), *Advances in Hospitality, Tourism, and the Services Industry* (pp. 291–310). IGI Global., DOI: 10.4018/979-8-3693-1978-9.ch014

Das, S., Kundu, A., & Bhattacharya, A. (2020). Technology Adaptation and Survival of SMEs: A Longitudinal Study of Developing Countries. *Technology Innovation Management Review*, *10*(6), 64–72. DOI: 10.22215/timreview/1369

Dastin, J. (2018). *Amazon scraps secret AI recruiting tool that showed bias against women*. Reuters.

Davenport, T. H., & Kirby, J. (2016). *Only humans need apply: Winners and losers in the age of smart machines*. Harper Business.

Davenport, T., Guha, A., Grewal, D., & Bressgott, T. (2020). How artificial intelligence will change the future of marketing. *Journal of the Academy of Marketing Science*, *48*, 24–42.

David, G., & Sirmon, M. A. (2010). Resource Orchestration to Create Competitive Advantage: Breadth, Depth, and Life Cycle Effects. *Journal of Management*. Advance online publication. DOI: 10.1177/0149206310385695

Davis, F. D. (1989). Perceived Usefulness, Perceived Ease of Use and User Acceptance of Information Technology. *Management Information Systems Quarterly*, *13*(3), 319–340.

de Jesus, A. F., & Mendonça, S. (2018). Exploring the circular economy: A systematic literature review. *Journal of Cleaner Production*, *200*, 162–180.

Deci, E. L., & Ryan, R. M. (2000). The "what" and "why" of goal pursuits: Human needs and the self-determination of behavior. *Psychological Inquiry*, *11*(4), 227–268.

Deel, G., Cain, C., & Cain, L. (2023). Ethical considerations for the future of superhuman artificial intelligence: A viewpoint. *ROBONOMICS: The Journal of the Automated Economy*, *4*, 41–41.

DeepHealth. (n.d.). DeepHealth Project. GitHub repository. Retrieved December 9, 2024, from https://github.com/deephealthproject

Dehankar, P., Amudha, A., Jayasudha, S., Pallavi, R., Doda, D. K., & Mandela, N. (2023). Predictive Analytics Powered by Artificial Intelligence. *IEEE*, 1–595. https://doi.org/DOI: 10.1109/incoft60753.2023.10425117

Dekimpe, M. G. (2020). Retailing and retailing research in the age of big data analytics. *International Journal of Research in Marketing*, *37*(1), 3–14. DOI: 10.1016/j.ijresmar.2019.10.001

Deloitte. (2020a). *AI and the future of skills: How organizations can prepare for AI's impact on talent*. Deloitte Insights. https://www2.deloitte.com

Deloitte. (2020b). *AI and talent development: Embracing the transformation.* https://www2.deloitte.com

Demirgüç-Kunt, A., & Maksimovic, V. (2002). Small firms and environmental management. *International Small Business Journal, 20*(3), 235–251. DOI: 10.1177/0266242602203001

Demir, K. A., & Cicibas, H. (2022). Industry 5.0: Opportunities and challenges for SMEs. *Procedia Computer Science, 200,* 538–545. DOI: 10.1016/j.procs.2022.01.296

Despoudi, S., Sivarajah, U., Spanaki, K., Charles, V., & Durai, V. K. (2023). Industry 4.0 and circular economy for emerging markets: Evidence from small and medium-sized enterprises (SMEs) in the Indian food sector. Annals of Operations Research. https://link.springer.com/article/10.1007/s10479-023-05404-4

Dhiraj, A., Kumar, S., Rani, D., Grima, S., & Sood, K. (2023). Blockchain Payment Services in the Hospitality Sector: The Mediating Role of Data Security on Utilisation Efficiency of the Customer. *Data, 8*(8), 123.

Diabate, A., Allate, B., Wei, D., & Yu, L. (2019). Do firm and entrepreneur characteristics play a role in SMEs' sustainable growth in a middle-income economy like Côte d'Ivoire? *Sustainability, 11*(6), 1557. DOI: 10.3390/su11061557

Diamond, M. (2023). Book Review: Marketing Artificial Intelligence: AI, Marketing, and the Future of Business by Paul Roetzer and Mike Kaput. *Management and Business Review, 3*(1).

Digital Personal Data Protection Act. (2024). *Digital Personal Data Protection Act.* Government of India.

DiMaggio, W. W. (1983). The Iron Cage Revisited: Institutional Isomorphism and Collective Rationality in Organizational Fields. *American Sociological Association,* 147-160.

Dr, B. D. O. (2023a). Generative Artificial Intelligence (GAI) Ethics Taxonomy- Applying Chat GPT for Robotic Process Automation (GAI-RPA) as Business Case. SSRN *Electronic Journal.* https://doi.org/DOI: 10.2139/ssrn.4385025

Dr, B. D. O. (2023b). Generative Artificial Intelligence (GAI) with Chat GPT for Accounting – a Business Case. SSRN *Electronic Journal.* https://doi.org/DOI: 10.2139/ssrn.4385651

Duric, Z., & Potočnik Topler, J. (2021). The Role of Performance and Environmental Sustainability Indicators in Hotel Competitiveness. *Sustainability, 13*(12), 6574. DOI: 10.3390/su13126574

Dwivedi, Y. K., Hughes, L., Ismagilova, E., Aarts, G., Coombs, C., Crick, T., Duan, Y., Dwivedi, R., Edwards, J., Eirug, A., Galanos, V., Ilavarasan, P. V., Janssen, M., Jones, P., Kar, A. K., Kizgin, H., Kronemann, B., Lal, B., Lucini, B., & Williams, M. D. (2021). AI: Multidisciplinary perspectives on emerging challenges, opportunities, and agenda for research, practice and policy. *International Journal of Information Management, 57*, 101994. DOI: 10.1016/j.ijinfomgt.2019.08.002

Eberhardsteiner, L. (2024). Adopting AI in SMEs: development of a framework for adopting AI in SMEs with a focus on security and privacy concerns: Entwicklung eines Rahmenwerks für die Einführung von KI in KMU mit Schwerpunkt auf Sicherheits-und Datenschutzbedenken/Author Lukas Eberhardsteiner.

Economic Times Online. (2023, April 25). *AI and Privacy: The privacy concerns surrounding AI, its potential impact on personal data.* Retrieved from Economic Times: https://economictimes.indiatimes.com/news/how-to/ai-and-privacy-the-privacy-concerns-surrounding-ai-its-potential-impact-on-personal-data/articleshow/99738234.cms?from=mdr

EdTech Magazine. (2022). Adaptive learning's role in future-ready education. [URL if available]

Einav Peretz-Andersson, S. T. (2024). Artificial intelligence implementation in manufacturing SMEs: A resource orchestration approach. *International Journal of Information Management.*

Ekins, P., & Hughes, N., & R. P. (2020). The role of the circular economy in achieving the UK's net-zero target. *Environmental Science & Policy, 108*, 43–50.

Elkhwesky, Z., & Elkhwesky, E. F. Y. (2022). A systematic and critical review of Internet of Things in contemporary hospitality: A roadmap and avenues for future research. *International Journal of Contemporary Hospitality Management, ahead-of-print.*

Ellen MacArthur Foundation. (2013). *Towards the Circular Economy: Economic and business rationale for an accelerated transition* (Vol. 1). Ellen MacArthur Foundation.

Endeshaw, E., & Kassegn, A. (2022). The role of micro, small and medium enterprises (MSMEs) to the sustainable development of sub-Saharan Africa and its challenges: A systematic review of evidence from Ethiopia. *Journal of Innovation and Entrepreneurship, 11*(20). Advance online publication. PMID: 35223364

Ergas, H., & Orr, J. (2007). SMEs and innovation. [Specify publication details].

Esan, M. O. (2023). AI automation in accounting for small businesses. *Journal of Accounting Technology*, *5*(2), 56–70.

Esan, M. O., Ezeh, C. I., & Ige, S. O. (2024). AI in revenue optimization for SMEs. *Journal of Business Growth*, *13*(3), 101–118.

Esposito, A. (2021, July 16). *1822 Denim Quadruples Conversions with AI Fit Technology*. Retrieved from Retail Touch Points: https://www.retailtouchpoints.com/topics/digital-commerce/e-commerce-experience/1822-denim-quadruples-conversion-with-ai-fit-technology

Esteva, A.. (2017). Dermatologist-level classification of skin cancer with deep neural networks. *Nature*, *542*(7639), 115–118. PMID: 28117445

Esteva, A., Robicquet, A., Ramsundar, B., Kuleshov, V., DePristo, M., Chou, K., & Dean, J. (2019). A guide to deep learning in healthcare. *Nature Medicine*, *25*(1), 24–29. DOI: 10.1038/s41591-018-0316-z PMID: 30617335

European Commission. (2020). *Circular Economy Action Plan: For a Cleaner and More Competitive Europe*.

European Commission. (n.d.). What is an SME? https://single-market-economy.ec.europa.eu/smes/sme-definition_en

Evelynn, S., & Harlee, M. (2024). Digital Technology Adoption in SMEs: AI-Driven Strategies for Improving Competitiveness.

Ezeafulukwe, . (2024). AI for sustainable financial management in SMEs. *Journal of Sustainable Finance*, *22*(4), 45–62.

Ezeh, C. I.. (2024). AI-driven financial tools for SMEs. *Journal of Financial Innovation*, *10*(2).

Eziamaka, . (2024). Ethical issues in AI financial decision-making. *Journal of Business Ethics*, *35*(1), 78–92.

Faaique, M. (2024). Overview of Big Data Analytics in Modern Astronomy. *International Journal of Mathematics, Statistics, and Computer Science*, *2*, 96–113.

Fadlelmula, F. K. (2011). Assessing power of structural equation modeling studies: A meta-analysis. *Education Research Journal*, *1*(3), 37–42.

Fang, B., Yu, J., Chen, Z., Osman, A. I., Farghali, M., Ihara, I., Hamza, E. H., Rooney, D. W., & Yap, P.-S. (2023). Artificial intelligence for waste management in smart cities: A review. *Environmental Chemistry Letters*, *21*(21). Advance online publication. DOI: 10.1007/s10311-023-01604-3 PMID: 37362015

Farazi, S. (2014). Informal firms and financial inclusion: Status and determinants. *Journal of international commerce. Economic Policy, 5*(03), 1440011. DOI: 10.1142/S1793993314400110

Fargnoli, M., Costantino, F., Di Gravio, G., & Tronci, M. (2018). Product service-systems implementation: A customized framework to enhance sustainability and customer satisfaction. *Journal of Cleaner Production, 188*, 387–401. DOI: 10.1016/j.jclepro.2018.03.315

Farzaneh Shoushtari, E. G. (2021). Improving Performance of Supply Chain by Applying Artificial Intelligence. *International Journal of Industrial Engineering and Operational Research.*

Fayyaz, Z., Ebrahimian, M., Nawara, D., Ibrahim, A., & Kashef, R. (2020). Recommendation Systems: Algorithms, Challenges, Metrics, and Business Opportunities. *MDPI.* https://doi.org/https://doi.org/10.3390/app10217748

Felten, R., Raj, M., & Seamans, R. (2019). AI occupational exposure measure.

Felten, R., Raj, M., & Seamans, R. (2019). The variable impact of artificial intelligence on labour: The role of complementary skills and technologies. SSRN Electronic Journal.

Felten, R., Raj, M., & Seamans, R. (2023). How will language modellers like ChatGPT affect occupations and industries? SSRN Electronic Journal.

Feng, Y., Chen, H., & Xie, Q. (2024). AI Influencers in Advertising: The Role of AI Influencer-Related Attributes in Shaping Consumer Attitudes, Consumer Trust, and Perceived Influencer–Product Fit. *Journal of Interactive Advertising, 24*(1), 26–47.

Fernando, Y., Jabbour, C. J. C., & Wah, W. X. (2019). Pursuing green growth in technology firms through the connections between environmental innovation and sustainable business performance: Does service capability matter? *Resources, Conservation and Recycling, 141*, 8–20. DOI: 10.1016/j.resconrec.2018.09.031

Ferrazzi, K. (2015). Getting virtual teams right. *Harvard Business Review.*

FICCI. (2023, October). *FICCI Report on SMEs in India.* Retrieved from FICCI: https://www.ficci.in/study_details/23825

Fiseha, G. G., & Oyelana, A. A. (2015). An assessment of the roles of small and medium enterprises (SMEs) in the local economic development (LED). *The South African Journal of Economics, 6*(3), 280–290.

Fleisher, C. S., & Bensoussan, B. E. (2015). *Business and competitive analysis: effective application of new and classic methods*. FT press.

Flipkart. (2024, September 25). *Unleashing the Power of AI: Transforming E-commerce and Beyond – Insights from Mayur Datar, Flipkart's Chief Data Scientist*. Retrieved from Flipkart Stories: https://stories.flipkart.com/ai-qna-mayur-datar/

Flores, J.. (2020). AI tools for predictive analytics. *Journal of Educational Technology*, *8*(3), 67–81.

Floridi, L., & Cowls, J. (2019). A unified framework of five principles for AI ethics. *Harvard Data Science Review*, *1*(1). Advance online publication. 10.1162/99608f92.8cd550d1

Floridi, L., & Cowls, J. (2019). A unified framework of five principles for AI in society. *Harvard Data Science Review*, *1*(1). Advance online publication. DOI: 10.1162/99608f92.8cd550d1

Floridi, L., Cowls, J., & Beltrametti, M.. (2018). AI4People—An ethical framework for a good AI society: Opportunities, risks, principles, and recommendations. *Minds and Machines*, *28*(4), 689–707. DOI: 10.1007/s11023-018-9482-5 PMID: 30930541

Floridi, L., Cowls, J., King, T. C., & Taddeo, M. (2020). Designing AI for social good: Seven essential factors. *Science and Engineering Ethics*. Advance online publication. DOI: 10.1007/s11948-020-00213-5 PMID: 32246245

Fondue, S.. (2023). Machine learning in HR decision-making. *Journal of HR Analytics*, *5*(1), 33–49.

Forbes India. (2024, December 11). *How Nykaa is taking on intensifying competition in the beauty industry*. (N. Thakker, Editor) Retrieved from Forbes India: https://www.forbesindia.com/article/billionaires/how-nykaa-is-taking-on-intensifying-competition-in-the-beauty-industry/94824/1

Fornell, C., & Larcker, D. F. (1981). Evaluating structural equation models with unobservable variables and measurement error. *JMR, Journal of Marketing Research*, *18*(1), 39–50.

Foroudi, P., Gupta, S., Nazarian, A., & Duda, M. (2017). Digital technology and marketing management capability: Achieving growth in SMEs. *Qualitative Market Research*, *20*(2), 230–246. DOI: 10.1108/QMR-01-2017-0014

Frey, C. B., & Osborne, M. A. (2017). The future of employment: How susceptible are jobs to computerisation? *Technological Forecasting and Social Change*, *114*, 254–280.

Frobes India. (2021, Spetember 7). *Moglix: How Rahul Garg built an unexpected unicorn.* (M. Balachandran, Editor) Retrieved from Forbes India: https://www.forbesindia.com/article/startups/moglix-how-rahul-garg-built-an-unexpected-unicorn/68373/1

Gallup. (2022). Creating a culture of feedback. https://www.gallup.com

Gamage, S. N., Ekanayake, E. M. S., Abeyrathne, G. A. K. N. J., Prasanna, R. P. I. R., Jayasundara, J. M. S. B., & Rajapakshe, P. S. K. (2020). A review of global challenges and survival strategies of small and medium enterprises (SMEs). *Economies, 8*(4), 79. DOI: 10.3390/economies8040079

Garima, & Bansal, R. (2024). *Unveiling the Potential of ChatGPT for Enhancing Customer Engagement* (pp. 111–128). https://doi.org/DOI: 10.4018/979-8-3693-0815-8.ch007

Gartner. (2020). The future of learning analytics. [URL if available]

Gaurav, Khan, H., Pandey, S., Kumar, B. V., Akram, S. V., & Pal, P. (2024, March 13). Artificial Intelligence (AI) in the Field of Corporate Social Responsibility. *IEEE.* https://doi.org/DOI: 10.1109/icsadl61749.2024.00033

Geissdoerfer, M., Savaget, P., Bocken, N. M. P., & Hultink, E. J. (2017). The Circular Economy – A new sustainability paradigm? *Journal of Cleaner Production, 143,* 757–768. DOI: 10.1016/j.jclepro.2016.12.048

Geissdoerfer, M., Savaget, P., Bocken, N. M. P., & Hultink, E. J. (2018). The Circular Economy – A New Sustainability Paradigm? *Journal of Cleaner Production, 143*, 757–768.

Geng, Y., Sarkis, J., & Xue, J. (2019). Circular economy in China: Current practices and future challenges. *International Journal of Production Research, 57*(23), 7040–7056.

Georgieff, A., & Hyee, R. (2021). Artificial intelligence and employment: New cross-country evidence. OECD Social, Employment and Migration Working Papers, No. 265.

Georgieff, A., & Hyee, R. (2022). Artificial intelligence and employment: New cross-country evidence. *Frontiers in Artificial Intelligence, 5*, 832736. PMID: 35620279

Gihleb, R., Giuntella, O., Stella, L., & Wang, T. (2022). Industrial robots, workers' safety, and health. *Labour Economics, 78*, 102205. DOI: 10.1016/j.labeco.2022.102205

Gilmore, A., & Carson, D. (2018). SME marketing: Efficiency in practice. *Small Enterprise Research, 25*(3), 213–226. DOI: 10.1080/13215906.2018.1521740

Giousmpasoglou, C., & Hua, T. T. (2020). The use of self-service technologies in budget hotels: The case of Bournemouth. *European Journal of Tourism. Hospitality and Recreation*, *10*(3), 251–261.

Gkikas, D. C., & Theodoridis, P. K. (2022). *AI in Consumer Behavior.*, DOI: 10.1007/978-3-030-80571-5_10

Glassdoor for Employers. (2020). Recruiting statistics. [URL if available]

Gold, N. A. (2016). Adding fintech and blockchain to your curriculum. *Business Education Innovation Journal*, *8*(2), 6–12.

Gomez, A. L., & Lopez, S. J. (2024). Innovation and Transformation: Keys to the Success of SMEs in the Digital Age. *Deleted Journal*, *2*(3). Advance online publication. DOI: 10.59652/jeime.v2i3.253

Google, A. I. (2019). AI Impact Challenge. Retrieved from https://ai.google/social-good/impact-challenge/

Goos, M., & Manning, A. (2007). Lousy and lovely jobs: The rising polarization of work in Britain. *The Review of Economics and Statistics*, *89*(1), 118–133.

Govenance, J. O. F. (2021). EMPIRICAL ANALYSIS ON CORPORATE TRANSPARENCY, COMPETITIVE ADVANTAGE. *AND FIRM PERFORMANCE : AN INSIGHT OF MUSCAT SECURITIES MARKET*, *4*(2), 96–102.

Government of Canada. (2024). Chapter 4: Investing in the future. In Budget 2024. Retrieved from https://budget.canada.ca/2024/report-rapport/chap4-en.html 4-3.

Govori, A., & Sejdija, Q. (2023). Future prospects and challenges of integrating artificial intelligence within the business practices of small and medium enterprises. *Journal of Governance and Regulation*, *12*(2), 176–183. DOI: 10.22495/jgrv12i2art16

Gratton, L., & Erickson, T. J. (2007). Eight ways to build collaborative teams. *Harvard Business Review*, *85*(11), 100–109. PMID: 18159790

Gretzel, U., ... (2020). Tourism policy responses to COVID-19. *Journal of Tourism Futures*. https://doi.org/[DOI if available]

Grewal, D., Guha, A., Schweiger, E., Ludwig, S., & Wetzels, M. (2022). How communications by AI-enabled voice assistants impact the customer journey Dhruv Grewal, Abhijit Guha, Eli. *Journal of Service Management*. https://doi.org/https://doi.org/10.1108/JOSM-11-2021-0452

Guerrero, M., Liñán, F., & Cáceres-Carrasco, F. R. (2021). The influence of ecosystems on the entrepreneurship process: A comparison across developed and developing economies. *Small Business Economics*, *57*(4), 1733–1759. DOI: 10.1007/s11187-020-00367-3

Gunasekaran, A., & Ngai, E. W. T. (2014). Expert systems and artificial intelligence in the 21st century logistics and supply chain management. *Expert Systems with Applications*, *41*(1), 1–4. DOI: 10.1016/j.eswa.2013.09.006

Gungunawat, A., Khandelwal, N., & Gupta, N. (2024). AI-Powered Personalization in Digital Marketing: Transforming Consumer Engagement and Strategy. *RESEARCH REVIEW International Journal of Multidisciplinary*, *9*(11), 183–191. DOI: 10.31305/rrijm.2024.v09.n11.026

Gursoy, D., Li, Y., & Song, H. (2023). ChatGPT and the hospitality and tourism industry: An overview of current trends and future research directions. *Journal of Hospitality Marketing & Management*, *32*(5), 579–592. DOI: 10.1080/19368623.2023.2211993

Hackman, J. R. (2002). *Leading teams: Setting the stage for great performances*. Harvard Business Press.

Haggar, A., & Al-Khatib, I. A. (2021). Challenges and Opportunities in Implementing Circular Economy Practices in Organizations: A Literature Review. *Sustainability*, *13*(4), 1936.

Haleem, A., Javaid, M., Qadri, M. A., Singh, R. P., & Suman, R. (2022). Artificial intelligence (AI) applications for marketing: A literature-based study. *International Journal of Intelligent Networks*, *3*, 119–132. DOI: 10.1016/j.ijin.2022.08.005

Hampton, M., O'Hara, S., & Gearin, E. (2024). Assessing Restorative Community Development Frameworks—A Meso-Level and Micro-Level Integrated Approach. *Sustainability*, *16*(5), 2061. DOI: 10.3390/su16052061

Hansen, E. B., & Bøgh, S. (2021). Artificial intelligence and internet of things in small and medium-sized enterprises: A survey Author links open overlay panel. *Journal of Manufacturing Systems*. https://doi.org/https://doi.org/10.1016/j.jmsy.2020.08.009

Hanssen, S. B. (2022). General guidance principles for SMEs to meet the regulatory demands on safety and efficacy in the EU in order to reach the market [Master's thesis, Uppsala University]. https://www.diva-portal.org/smash/get/diva2:1674081/FULLTEXT01.pdf

Hard, A., Rao, K., Mathews, R., Beaufays, F., Augenstein, S., Eichner, H., . . . Kiddon, C. (2018). Federated learning for mobile keyboard prediction. *arXiv preprint arXiv:1811.03604.*

Häring, K., Pimentel, C., & Teixeira, L. (2023). Industry 4.0 Implementation in Small-and Medium-Sized Enterprises: Recommendations Extracted from a Systematic Literature Review with a Focus on Maturity Models. *Logistics (Basel)*, *7*(4), 99. DOI: 10.3390/logistics7040099

Harman, D. (1967). A single factor test of common method variance. *The Journal of Psychology*, *35*, 359–378.

Harvard Business Review (HBR). (2021). How mentorship programs boost employee engagement and team culture. https://hbr.org

Harvard Business Review. (2021). How AI is changing learning and development. [URL if available]

Haseeb, M., Hussain, H. I., Kot, S., & Androniceanu, A. (2019). Industry 4.0: A solution towards technology challenges of sustainable business performance. *Social Sciences*, *8*(5), 154. DOI: 10.3390/socsci8050154

Hayes, J. L., Brinson, N. H., Bott, G. J., & Moeller, C. M. (2021). The Influence of Consumer–Brand Relationship on the Personalized Advertising Privacy Calculus in Social Media. *Journal of Interactive Marketing*, *55*(1), 16–30. DOI: 10.1016/j.intmar.2021.01.001

Helfat, C. E., & Peteraf, M. A. (2003). The dynamic resource-based view: Capability lifecycles. *Strategic Management Journal*, *24*(10), 997–1010. DOI: 10.1002/smj.332

Hernandez, A. A., Caballero, A. R., Albina, E. M., Balmes, I. L., & Niguidula, J. D. (2023, May 1). *Artificial Intelligence for Sustainability: Evidence from select Small and Medium Enterprises in the Philippines*. IEEE Xplore. https://doi.org/ DOI: 10.1109/ICBIR57571.2023.10147579

Heron, C. (2012). *The Canadian labour movement: A short history* (3rd ed.). Lorimer.

High-Level Expert Group on AI. (2019). Ethics guidelines for trustworthy AI. Retrieved from https://ec.europa.eu

Hilbert, M. (2025). Big data for development: A review of promises and challenges. *Development Policy Review*, *34*(1), 135–174.

HireVue. (2020). AI and recruitment: Building fairness into hiring. [URL if available]

Hockerts, K., & Wüstenhagen, R. (2010). Greening goliaths versus emerging Davids: The role of incumbents and new entrants in sustainable entrepreneurship. *Journal of Business Venturing*, *25*(5), 481–492.

Holmes, W.. (2019). *Artificial intelligence in education: Promises and implications for teaching and learning*. UNESCO.

HolonIQ. (2021). Top trends in AI-powered education. [URL if available]

Hong, Z. (2024), Personalized recommendations: How Netflix and Amazon Use Deep Learning to enhance user experience, https://medium.com/@zhonghong9998/personalized-recommendations-how-netflix-and-amazon-use-deep-learning-to-enhance-user-experience-e7bd6fcd18ff, assessed on 19 January 2025

Hooi, L. W. (2006). Challenges faced by SMEs in developing economies. *Journal of Small Business Management, 10*(3), 123–135.

Horak, J., Kolencik, J., Văduva, C., & Woodward, B. (2023). Generative Artificial Intelligence and 3D Virtual Simulation Technologies, Ambient Scene Detection and Automated Employment Decision Tools, and Visual Data Mining and Immersive Remote Collaboration Systems in Decentralized Autonomous Organizations. *Analysis and Metaphysics*, *22*. Advance online publication. DOI: 10.22381/am2220237

Hossain, N., Alam, R. M. K., & Gavlovskaya, G. (2018). Effective microcredit banking for growth and development of small business and improvement of poverty conditions in Bangladesh. *Journal of Applied Economic Sciences*, *13*(2), 465–483.

Hoyer, W. D., Kroschke, M., Schmitt, B., Kraume, K., & Shankar, V. (2020). Transforming the Customer Experience through New Technologies. *Journal of Interactive Marketing*, *51*(1), 57–71. DOI: 10.1016/j.intmar.2020.04.001

Hoyle, R. H. (1995). *Structural Equation Modeling: Concepts, Issues, and Application.* Sage Publications.

Hsieh, Y. H., & Chou, Y. H. (2018). Modeling the impact of service innovation for small and medium enterprises: A system dynamics approach. *Simulation Modelling Practice and Theory*, *82*, 84–102. DOI: 10.1016/j.simpat.2017.12.004

Huang, M. H., & Rust, R. T. (2020). A strategic framework for artificial intelligence in marketing. *Journal of the Academy of Marketing Science*, *49*, 1–21.

Huang, M.-H., & Rust, R. T. (2017). Technology-driven service strategy. *Journal of the Academy of Marketing Science*, *45*(6), 906–924. DOI: 10.1007/s11747-017-0545-6

Huang, M.-H., & Rust, R. T. (2018). Artificial intelligence in service. *Journal of Service Research*, *21*(2), 155–172.

Huang, M.-H., & Rust, R. T. (2020). AI in place management for SMEs. *Journal of Marketing Technology*, *6*(1), 45–60.

Humphreys, D., Koay, A., Desmond, D., & Mealy, E. (2024). AI hype as a cyber security risk: The moral responsibility of implementing generative AI in business. *AI and Ethics*, *4*(3). Advance online publication. DOI: 10.1007/s43681-024-00443-4

Hussain, M. (2023). When, Where, and Which?: Navigating the Intersection of Computer Vision and Generative AI for Strategic Business Integration. *IEEE Access : Practical Innovations, Open Solutions*, *11*. Advance online publication. DOI: 10.1109/ACCESS.2023.3332468

IBM SkillsBuild. (2023). *Enterprise AI training roadmap*. https://skillsbuild.org

ICRIER. (2025). *AI Markets and Competition in India*. Center for Internet and Digital Economy. ICRIER. Retrieved from https://icrier.org/pdf/AI-Markets-and-Competition-in-India.pdf

IEBF. (2022, November 10). *The Open Network for Digital Commerce (ONDC) Initiative*. Retrieved from IBEF: https://www.ibef.org/blogs/the-open-network-for-digital-commerce-ondc-initiative

Ige, S. O.. (2024). Data quality challenges in AI financial decision-making. *Journal of Data Science in Business*, *9*(2), 88–103.

Ikbar, H., Rizky, A. M., Usman, O., & Bus, M. (2023). *The Influence Of Market Orientation, Product Innovation And Competitive Prices On Competitive Advantage And Marketing Performance Of Eco-Friendly Household Product Processing In The DKI Jakarta Area*. *1*(12).

Iloka, C. P. (2022). Effects of Climate Change on Medium, Small and Micro Enterprises's Financing in Nigeria: The Consequential Burden of Protecting the Right of the Less Privileged. *AJLHR*, *6*, 52.

Inc42. (2024, Feburary 11). *Nykaa Q3: Beauty Segment Powers Company To Yet Another Profitable Quarter*. (A. Pushkarna, Editor) Retrieved from Inc42: https://inc42.com/buzz/nykaa-q3-beauty-segment-powers-company-to-yet-another-profitable-quarter/#:~:text=Revenue%20from%20operations%20surged%2026.7,fared%20on%20the%20financial%20front

India, A. I. (2021a, November 19). *Bihar's strengthening AI footprint*. Retrieved from IndiaAI: https://indiaai.gov.in/article/bihar-s-strengthening-ai-footprint

India, A. I. (2021b, December 27). *How the adoption of AI led BigBasket to success*. Retrieved from IndaAI: https://indiaai.gov.in/article/how-the-adoption-of-ai-led-bigbasket-to-success

India, A. I. (2022a, Feburary 14). *How Liscious revolutionised the meat industry with AI*. Retrieved from IndiaAI: https://indiaai.gov.in/article/how-liscious-revolutionised-the-meat-industry-with-ai

India, A. I. (2022b, Feburary 03). *PharmEasy's AI and analytics advances online healthcare*. Retrieved from IndiaAI: https://indiaai.gov.in/article/pharmeasy-s-ai-and-analytics-advances-online-healthcare

Ingalagi, S. S., Mutkekar, R. R., & Kulkarni, P. M. (2021). Artificial intelligence (AI) adaptation: Analysis of determinants among small to medium-sized enterprises (SMEs).

Innovation, Science and Economic Development Canada. (2019). Key small business statistics. Small Business Branch, Research and Analysis Directorate.

Innovation, Science and Economic Development Canada. (2024). Artificial intelligence ecosystem. Retrieved from https://ised-isde.canada.ca/site/ised/en/artificial-intelligence-ecosystem

International Monetary Fund.(2024). Oman: Selected Issues. IMF Staff Country Reports, 2024, (32). https://doi.org/DOI: 10.5089/9798400266287.002

Irfan, M. (2021). AI and sustainable development goals: A review. *Journal of Sustainable Technology*, *3*(2), 56–72.

Irfan, M., Kassim, S., Shaikh, Z. H., Kumar, M., & Jhamnani, R. (2021). Do volatility and regime switching affect sustainable indices? Evidence from global stock markets based on inductive approach of GARCH family. *International Journal of Economics and Management*, *15*(2).

Irfan, M., Yadav, P., & Millán Tudela, L. A. (2023). Human-centered approaches in AI development and deployment. *Journal of AI and Ethics*, *1*(2), 45–60. 10.1007/s43681-023-00012-3

Islam, A., & Wahab, S. A. (2021). The intervention of strategic innovation practices in between regulations and sustainable business growth: A holistic perspective for Malaysian SMEs. *World Journal of Entrepreneurship, Management and Sustainable Development*, *17*(3), 396–421. DOI: 10.1108/WJEMSD-04-2020-0035

Islam, J. (2024). Leveraging Ai for Effective Human Resource Management: A Comprehensive Overview. *Social Science Research Network*. https://doi.org/DOI: 10.2139/ssrn.4833377

Ismail, I. J. (2022). The role of technological absorption capacity, enviropreneurial orientation, and green marketing in enhancing business sustainability: Evidence from fast-moving consumer goods in Tanzania. *Technological Sustainability*, *1*(2), 45–58.

Isson, J. P., & Harriott, J. (2016). *People analytics in the era of big data*. Wiley.

Ivanov, D. (2023). The Industry 5.0 framework: Viability-based integration of the resilience, sustainability, and human-centricity perspectives. *International Journal of Production Research*, *61*(5), 1683–1695.

Ivanov, S. H., & Umbrello, S. (2021). The ethics of artificial intelligence and robotisation in tourism and hospitality–a conceptual framework and research agenda. *Journal of Smart Tourism*, *1*(4), 9–18.

Iwuanyanwu, . (2024). AI for cash flow forecasting in SMEs. *Journal of Financial Planning*, *11*(1).

Iyelolu, T. V., Agu, E. E., Idemudia, C., & Ijomah, T. I. (2024). Driving SME innovation with AI solutions: overcoming adoption barriers and future growth opportunities. *International Journal of Science and Technology Research Archive, 7*(1), 036-054. DOI: https://doi.org/DOI: 10.53771/ijstra.2024.7.1.0055

Jabbour, C. J. C., Seuring, S., de Sousa Jabbour, A. B. L., Jugend, D., Fiorini, P. D. C., Latan, H., & Izeppi, W. C. (2020). Stakeholders, innovative business models for sustainability, and Industry 4.0: Impact on circular economy initiatives. *Journal of Business Research*, *122*, 488–498. DOI: 10.1016/j.jbusres.2020.09.033

Jacques Bughin, J. S. (2018). *Notes from the AI frontier: Modeling the impact of AI on the world economy*. McKinsey Global Institute.

Jadhav, D. S. (2021). *Understanding Artificial Intelligence Adoption, Implementation, and Use in Small and Medium Enterprises in India*. Walden Dissertations and Doctoral Studies.

Jain, A., Kakade, K. S., & Vispute, S. A. (2025). The Role of Artificial Intelligence (AI) in the Transformation of Small-and Medium-Sized Businesses: Challenges and Opportunities. *Artificial Intelligence-Enabled Businesses: How to Develop Strategies for Innovation*, 209-226. DOI: <ALIGNMENT.qj></ALIGNMENT>10.1002/9781394234028.ch12

Jain, L. (2023). Artificial Intelligence and Machine Learning for Healthcare.

Jain, A., Menon, M. N., & Chandra, S. (2015). Sales forecasting for retail chains. *International Journal of Scientific and Engineering Research*, *6*(7), 435–439.

Jain, R. (2023). The Impact of Artificial Intelligence on Business: Opportunities and Challenges. *Available at SSRN* 4407114.

Jain, R., Jayakumar, M., Christy, V., Singh, G., & Inamdar, A. M. (2023). The effect of organizational culture on employee engagement and job satisfaction: A HR perspective. *Journal of Survey in Fisheries Sciences*, *10*, 6212–6225.

Jamal, T., & Mandal, K. (2013). Skill development mission in India: An overview. *Economic and Political Weekly*, *48*(14), 34–41.

Jansen, M., & Lanz, R. (2013). *Skills and export competitiveness: An analysis of the World Input-Output Database*. WTO Staff Working Paper ERSD-2013-03. https://doi.org/DOI: 10.2139/ssrn.2227095

Javaid, M., Haleem, A., Rab, S., Singh, R. P., & Suman, R. (2022). Understanding the transition towards Industry 5.0: A review of features, challenges and applications. *Materials Today: Proceedings*, *51*, 1785–1792. DOI: 10.1016/j.matpr.2021.06.229

Jayakumar, M., Jenefa, L., Badrinarayanan, M. K., Sarah, K. S., Kumar, A., & Kumar, R. M. (2024, December). Exploring organizational adoption of innovative technologies in consumer online purchase. In *2024 International Conference on Emerging Research in Computational Science (ICERCS)* (pp. 1–6). IEEE.

Jayakumar, M., Jenefa, L., Mishra, N., Kumar, A., & Sumitha, S. (2024, December). Artificial intelligence in digital marketing platform: Impact on consumer buying behaviour. In *2024 International Conference on Emerging Research in Computational Science (ICERCS)* (pp. 1–6). IEEE.

Jean, N., Burke, M., Xie, M., Davis, W. M., & Lobell, D. B. (2016). Combining satellite imagery and machine learning to predict poverty. *Science*, *353*(6301), 790–794. DOI: 10.1126/science.aaf7894 PMID: 27540167

Jehn, K. A. (1995). A multimethod examination of the benefits and detriments of intragroup conflict. *Administrative Science Quarterly*, *40*(2), 256–282.

Jenefa, L., Kumar, A., Yiong, B. L. C., Jayakumar, M., & Sakthivel, M. (2024, November). The implementation of artificial intelligence tools in retail sector among consumers—A new evolution from traditional to modern. In *2024 International Conference on Electronic Systems and Intelligent Computing (ICESIC)* (pp. 220–223). IEEE.

Jenefa, L., Ramanathan, K., Mishra, N., Vishnu, V., Jayakumar, M., & Ashok, S. (2025). Future of the ready-made garments industry in real-time data: An application of AI. In Kumar, M., Mishra, S., & Chatterjee, A. (Eds.), *Real-time data decisions with AI and ChatGPT techniques* (pp. 127–148). IGI Global.

Jiang, H., Cheng, Y., Yang, J., & Gao, S. (2022). AI-powered chatbot communication with customers: Dialogic interactions, satisfaction, engagement, and customer behavior. *Computers in Human Behavior*, *134*, 107329.

Jindal, R., & Malaya, D. (2015). Predictive analytics in higher education. *Journal of Educational Data Science*, *3*(2), 45–60.

Johnson, K. B., Wei, W., Weeraratne, D., Frisse, M. E., Misulis, K., Rhee, K., Zhao, J., & Snowdon, J. L. (2021). Precision Medicine, AI, and the Future of Personalized Health Care. *Clinical and Translational Science*, *14*(1), 86–93. DOI: 10.1111/cts.12884 PMID: 32961010

Jones, P., & Patel, A. (2018). *Qualitative methods in marketing research.* SAGE Publications.

Jordan, M. I., & Mitchell, T. M. (2015). Machine learning: Trends, perspectives, and prospects. *Science*, *349*(6245), 255–260. DOI: 10.1126/science.aaa8415 PMID: 26185243

Kadirov, A., Shakirova, Y., Ismoilova, G., & Makhmudova, N. (2024). AI in Human Resource Management: Reimagining Talent Acquisition, Development, and Retention. *IEEE*, 1–8. https://doi.org/DOI: 10.1109/ickecs61492.2024.10617231

Kadyan, J. S., Jayakumar, M., Kumar, A., Jenefa, L., & Lakshmipathy, T. (2024, December). Enhancing customer delight—The implementation of artificial intelligence tools in sales and marketing in online platforms. In *2024 International Conference on Emerging Research in Computational Science (ICERCS)* (pp. 1–5). IEEE. https://doi.org/DOI: 10.1109/ICERCS56794.2024.1234568

Kahle, J. H., Marcon, E., Ghezzi, A., & Frank, A. G. (2020). Smart Products value creation in SMEs innovation ecosystems. *Technological Forecasting and Social Change*, *156*, 120024. DOI: 10.1016/j.techfore.2020.120024

Kalishina, D. (2023). Artificial Intelligence As An Enabler Of Growth: Advancing Business Analytics In Small And Medium Enterprises. *International Journal of Core Engineering & Management*, *7*(5), 289–300.

Kaliuta, K. (2023). Integration of AI for Routine Tasks Using Salesforce. *Asian Journal of Research in Computer Science*, *16*(3), 119–127. DOI: 10.9734/ajrcos/2023/v16i3350

Kamble, S. S., Gunasekaran, A., & Sharma, R. (2019). A Blockchain Technology Framework for Circular Economy in Manufacturing. *International Journal of Production Economics*, *211*, 108–120.

Kamilaris, A., & Prenafeta-Boldú, F. X. (2018). A review of the use of convolutional neural networks in agriculture. *Journal of Agricultural Science*, *156*(3), 312–322.

Kamilaris, A., & Prenafeta-Boldú, F. X. (2018). Deep learning in agriculture: A survey. *Computers and Electronics in Agriculture*, *147*, 70–90. DOI: 10.1016/j.compag.2018.02.016

Kanbach, D. K., Heiduk, L., Blueher, G., Schreiter, M., & Lahmann, A. (2024). The GenAI is out of the bottle: generative artificial intelligence from a business model innovation perspective. In *Review of Managerial Science* (Vol. 18, Issue 4). https://doi.org/DOI: 10.1007/s11846-023-00696-z

Kandukuri, V. (2023). Aligning talent and business: A key for sustainable HRM in SMEs. *Journal of Entrepreneurship and Innovation in Emerging Economies*, *9*(1). 80-91.

Kanellopoulou, D., Giannakopoulos, G., & Karkaletsis, V. (2025). Accelerating AI-powered digital innovation through "APSS": A novel methodology for sustainable business AI transformation. *Journal of Open Innovation*, *100495*. Advance online publication. DOI: 10.1016/j.joitmc.2025.100495

Kaplan, A. M., & Haenlein, M. (2019). Siri, Siri, in my hand: Who's the fairest in the land? On the interpretations, illustrations, and implications of artificial intelligence. *Business Horizons*, *62*(1), 15–25. .2018.08.004DOI: 10.1016/j.bushor

Kaplan, R. S., & Norton, D. P. (2004). *Strategy maps: Converting intangible assets into tangible outcomes*. Harvard Business School Press.

Karthikeyan, R., & Jothi Kumar, C. (2014). Improved reputation system for wireless sensor networks (WSNs). [IJISER]. *International Journal of Innovations in Scientific and Engineering Research*, *1*(3), 191–195.

Kashyap, H., Ahmed, H. A., Hoque, N., Roy, S., & Bhattacharyya, D. K. (2023). Big data analytics in bioinformatics: Architectures, techniques, tools and issues. *Network Modeling and Analysis in Health Informatics and Bioinformatics*, *5*, 1–28.

Kathuria, R. M. (2020). *Implications of AI on the Indian economy*. Indian Council for Research on International Economic Relations.

Katzenbach, J. R., & Smith, D. K. (2005). *The wisdom of teams: Creating the high-performance organization*. HarperBusiness.

Kaur, B., & Mehra, P. (2023). Impact of Pandemic on Behavioural Transition in Consumption Pattern, *Empirical Economics Letters*, 22 (Special Issue 1): (October 2023). *ISSN*, *1681*, 8997. DOI: 10.5281/zenodo.10207087

Kaur, B., & Sharma, R. R. (2022). Factors affecting behavioural intentions to use e-banking services: An extension of TAM in Indian context. *International Journal of Business and Globalisation*, *32*(4), 414–430.

Kaushal, N.. (2023). AI regression models for retail forecasting. *Journal of Business Analytics*, *6*(2), 78–93.

Kayser, D. (2013). Recent research in project finance – A commented bibliography. Procedia Computer Science, 17, 729-736. https://doi.org/ of FormDOI: 10.1016/j.procs.2013.05.094Top

Kealey, G. S. (1995). *Workers and Canadian history*. McGill-Queen's University Press.

Kedi, W. E., Ejimuda, C., Idemudia, C., & Ijomah, T. I. (2024). AI software for personalized marketing automation in SMEs: Enhancing customer experience and sales. *World Journal of Advanced Research and Reviews*, *23*(1), 1981–1990. DOI: 10.30574/wjarr.2024.23.1.2159

Keikhosrokiani, P. (Ed.). (2022). *Big data analytics for healthcare: datasets, techniques, life cycles, management, and applications*. Academic Press.

Kejriwal, M. (2023). AI in practice and implementation: Issues and costs. In *Artificial intelligence for industries of the future. Future of Business and Finance*. Springer., DOI: 10.1007/978-3-031-19039-1_2

Kelle, U. (2006). Combining qualitative and quantitative methods in research practice: Purposes and advantages. *Qualitative Research in Psychology*, *3*(4), 293–311. DOI: 10.1177/1478088706070839

Keskġn, H., Ġentürk, C., Sungur, O., & Kġrġġ, H. M. (2010, June). The importance of SMEs in developing economies. In *2nd international symposium on sustainable development* (Vol. 183). https://core.ac.uk/download/pdf/153446896.pdf

Khan, S., & Iqbal, M. (2020). AI-Powered Customer Service: Does it Optimize Customer Experience? *2020 8th International Conference on Reliability, Infocom Technologies and Optimization (Trends and Future Directions) (ICRITO)*, 590–594. https://doi.org/DOI: 10.1109/ICRITO48877.2020.9198004

Khan, S. I. (2022). Impact of artificial intelligence on consumer buying behaviors: Study about the online retail purchase. *International Journal of Health Sciences*, (II), 8121–8129.

KhataBook. (2025). *KhataBook Homepage.* Retrieved from KhataBook: https://khatabook.com/

Khristianto, W., Suharyono, S., & Pangestuti, E. (2021).. . *The Influences of Market Sensing Capability and Information Technology Competency on Innovation and Competitive Advantage*, *8*(3), 1009–1019. DOI: 10.13106/jafeb.2021.vol8.no3.1009

Kietzmann, J., Paschen, J., & Treen, E. (2018). Artificial intelligence in advertising: How marketers can leverage artificial intelligence along the consumer journey. *Journal of Advertising Research*, *58*(3), 263–267. DOI: 10.2501/JAR-2018-035

Kim, J., & Choi, G. (2024). Assessing the Impact of Generative Artificial Intelligence on Customer Engagement in Business-to-Customer Scenarios. *Asia-Pacific Journal of Convergent Research Interchange*, *10*(2). Advance online publication. DOI: 10.47116/apjcri.2024.02.09

Kirchgeorg, M., & S. G. (2020). Corporate responsibility and the circular economy: The importance of policy instruments. *Business Strategy and the Environment*, *29*(7), 3243–3257.

Kitchin, R. (2023). Big data and human geography: Opportunities, challenges and risks. *Dialogues in Human Geography*, *3*(3), 262–267.

Knezović, E., & Drkić, A. (2021). Innovative work behavior in SMEs: The role of transformational leadership. *Employee Relations: The International Journal*, *43*(2), 398–415. DOI: 10.1108/ER-03-2020-0124

Kong, H., Wang, K., Qiu, X., Cheung, C., & Bu, N. (2023). 30 years of artificial intelligence (AI) research relating to the hospitality and tourism industry. *International Journal of Contemporary Hospitality Management*, *35*(6), 2157–2177.

Kong, W., You, Z., Lyu, S., & Lv, X. (2024). Multi-dimensional stereo face reconstruction for psychological assistant diagnosis in medical meta-universe. *Information Sciences*, *654*, 119831.

KPMG. (2023, June). *2023 KPMG Generative AI Survey.* Retrieved from KPMG: https://kpmg.com/us/en/articles/2023/generative-artificial-intelligence-2023.html#:~:text=Prioritization%20of%20risk%20management%20has,their%20headcount%20will%20likely%20expand

Kshetri, N. (2018). 1 Blockchain's roles in meeting key supply chain management objectives. *International Journal of Information Management, 39*, 80–90.

Kumar, A., Syed, A. A., & Pandey, A. (2021). Adoption of online resources to improve the marketing performance of SMES. *Asia Pacific Journal of Health Management, 16*(3), 137-144. https://search.informit.org/doi/abs/10.3316/INFORMIT.081159555237037

Kumar, R. (2017). *Targeted SME financing and employment effects: What do we know and what can we do differently?* World Bank. https://documents1.worldbank.org/curated/pt/577091496733563036/pdf/115696-REVISED-PUBLIC-SMEs-and-Jobs-final.pdf

Kumar, D., & Suthar, N. (2024). Ethical and legal challenges of AI in marketing: An exploration of solutions. *Journal of Information. Communication and Ethics in Society, 22*(1), 124–144.

Kumar, L., & Kumar, N. (2025). Toward zero-waste cities: A comparative study of waste management strategies in Indore City and Surat City, India. In Varma, A., Chand Sharma, V., & Tarsi, E. (Eds.), *Proceedings of the 2nd International Conference on Trends in Architecture and Construction. ICTAC 2024. Lecture Notes in Civil Engineering* (Vol. 527). Springer, Singapore. https://doi.org/DOI: 10.1007/978-981-97-4988-1_30

Kumar, S., Dhiraj, A., Shah, M. A., & Rani, D. (2023). Application of Metaverse in the Hospitality Industry. In *Influencer Marketing Applications Within the Metaverse* (pp. 178–194). IGI Global.

Kumar, V., Ashraf, A. R., & Nadeem, W. (2024). AI-powered marketing: What, where, and how? *International Journal of Information Management, 77*, 102783.

Kumar, V., Rajan, B., Venkatesan, R., & Lecinski, J. (2019). Understanding the Role of Artificial Intelligence in Personalized Engagement Marketing. *California Management Review, 61*(4), 135–155. DOI: 10.1177/0008125619859317

Labib, E. (2024). Artificial intelligence in marketing: Exploring current and future trends. *Cogent Business & Management, 11*(1), 2348728.

Lane, M., Saint-Martin, A. (2021). The impact of AI on non-routine tasks.

Lane, M., Williams, M., & Broecke, S. (2023). *The impact of AI on the workplace: Main findings from the OECD AI surveys of employers and workers*. OECD Publishing., DOI: 10.1787/ea0a0fe1-

Lawton, R., Boswell, S., & Keeley Crockett SMIEE. (2023, December 5). The GM AI Foundry: A Model for Upskilling SME's in Responsible AI. *IEEE*. https://doi.org/DOI: 10.1109/ssci52147.2023.10371988

Leavitt, H. J. (1965). Applied organizational change in industry: Structural, technological and humanistic approaches. In March, J. G. (Ed.), *Handbook of organizations* (pp. 1144–1170). Rand McNally.

Lee, S. B. (2020). Chatbots and Communication: The Growing Role of Artificial Intelligence in Addressing and Shaping Customer Needs. *Business Communication Research and Practice*, *3*(2), 103–111. DOI: 10.22682/bcrp.2020.3.2.103

Lessem, R. (1982). Business and social expression: Understanding business growth and decline. *Omega*, *10*(1), 11–17. DOI: 10.1016/0305-0483(82)90031-6

Leung, P. H., Chui, K. T., Lo, K., & de Pablos, P. O. (2021). A support vector machine–based voice disorders detection using human voice signal. In *Artificial Intelligence and Big Data Analytics for Smart Healthcare* (pp. 197–208). Academic Press.

Levy, B. (1993). Obstacles to developing indigenous small and medium enterprises: An empirical assessment. *The World Bank Economic Review*, *7*(1), 65–83. DOI: 10.1093/wber/7.1.65

Li, D. (2024). Convergence and Innovation of Artificial Intelligence in Corporate Strategic Planning: Opportunities, Challenges and Future Research Directions. *Transactions on Economics. Business and Management Research*, *10*, 120–125. DOI: 10.62051/47zdfx74

Lightman, E., & Lightman, N. (2006). *Social policy in Canada*. Oxford University Press.

Lijauco, F., Gajendran, T., Brewer, G., & Rasoolimanesh, S. M. (2020). Impacts of culture on innovation propensity in small to medium enterprises in construction. *Journal of Construction Engineering and Management*, *146*(3), 04019116. DOI: 10.1061/(ASCE)CO.1943-7862.0001753

Lim, S. K. (2010). Dynamic resource-based view of entrepreneurial firm growth.

Lim, J. S., & Zhang, J. (2022). Adoption of AI-driven Personalization in digital news platforms: An integrative model of technology acceptance and perceived contingency. *Technology in Society*, *69*, 101965.

Lin, B., Lee, W., Wise, N., & Choi, H. C. (2023). Consumers' Ethical Perceptions of Autonomous Service Robots in Hotels. *Journal of Hospitality & Tourism Research (Washington, D.C.), 10963480231194693*. Advance online publication. DOI: 10.1177/10963480231194693

Lingxian, Y., Jiaqing, K., & Shihuai, W. (2019). Online retail sales prediction with integrated framework of K-means and neural network. In *Proceedings of the International Conference on Intelligent Computing* (pp. 115–118).

LinkedIn Learning. (2021). *2021 workplace learning report*. https://learning.linkedin.com/resources/workplace-learning-report

LinkedIn Learning. (2021). *Workplace learning report*. https://learning.linkedin.com

LinkedIn Talent Solutions. (2021). *Global talent trends*. [URL if available]

Linkon, A. A., Shaima, M., Md, S. U. S., Badruddowza, N. N., Md, N. U. R., Ghosh, S. K., Esa, H., & Chowdhury, F. R. (2024). Advancements and Applications of Generative Artificial Intelligence and Large Language Models on Business Management: A Comprehensive Review. *Journal of Computer Science and Technology Studies*, *6*(1). Advance online publication. DOI: 10.32996/jcsts.2024.6.1.26

Liu, B. (2012). Sentiment Analysis and Opinion Mining. *Synthesis Lectures on Human Language Technologies*, *5*(1), 1–167. DOI: 10.2200/s00416ed1v01y201204hlt016

Li, Y., Gan, Z., & Zheng, B. (2023). How do Artificial Intelligence Chatbots Affect Customer Purchase? Uncovering the Dual Pathways of Anthropomorphism on Service Evaluation. *Information Systems Frontiers*, 1–18.

Li, Z. (2022). Generative Logic of Digital Capitalism Based on Artificial Intelligence Technology. *Mobile Information Systems*, *2022*. Advance online publication. DOI: 10.1155/2022/9068591

Locke, E. A., & Latham, G. P. (2002). Building a practically useful theory of goal setting and task motivation: A 35-year odyssey. *The American Psychologist*, *57*(9), 705–717. PMID: 12237980

Locus. (2025). *About Us*. Retrieved from Locus: https://locus.sh/about/

Love, J. H., & Roper, S. (2015). SME innovation, exporting and growth: A review of existing evidence. *International Small Business Journal*, *33*(1), 28–48. DOI: 10.1177/0266242614550190

Luckin, R.. (2016). *Intelligence unleashed: An argument for AI in education*. Pearson Education.

Lukonga, I. (2020). Harnessing digital technologies to promote SMEs in the MENAP region. https://papers.ssrn.com/sol3/papers.cfm?abstract_id=3721177

Lund, S., & Manyika, J. (2019). *Global AI: Preparing for the future*. McKinsey Global Institute.

Lu, Y.. (2018). AI and healthcare: A review of technological advancements. *Health Informatics Journal, 24*(3), 381–393.

Lyytinen, K., & Damsgaard, J. (2001). What's wrong with the diffusion of innovation theory? In Ardis, M. A., & Marcolin, B. L. (Eds.), *Diffusing software product and process innovations* (pp. 173–190). Springer., DOI: 10.1007/978-0-387-35404-0_10

Macdonald, D. (2014). Industrial development and labour dynamics in Canada. *Canadian Journal of Economic History, 35*(2), 55–76.

Madan, N. (2020). A review of access to finance by micro, small and medium enterprises and digital financial services in selected Asia-Pacific least developed countries. https://repository.unescap.org/handle/20.500.12870/1190

Madhani, P. (2010). Resource Based View (RBV) of Competitive Advantage: An Overview. ... *BASED VIEW: CONCEPTS AND PRACTICES, Pankaj ..., March*, 2–22. https://papers.ssrn.com/sol3/papers.cfm?abstract_id=1578704

Madrid-Guijarro, A., García-Pérez-de-Lema, D., & Van Auken, H. (2013). An investigation of Spanish SME innovation during different economic conditions. *Journal of Small Business Management, 51*(4), 578–601. DOI: 10.1111/jsbm.12004

Magableh, I. K., Mahrouq, M. H., Ta'Amnha, M. A., & Riyadh, H. A. (2024). The Role of Marketing Artificial Intelligence in Enhancing Sustainable Financial Performance of Medium-Sized Enterprises Through Customer Engagement and Data-Driven Decision-Making. *Sustainability, 16*(24), 11279. DOI: 10.3390/su162411279

Maguire, S., Koh, S. C. L., & Magrys, A. (2007). The adoption of e-business and knowledge management in SMEs. *Benchmarking, 14*(1). https://doi.org/https://doi.org/10.1108/14635770710730928

Maksimov, V., Wang, S. L., & Luo, Y. (2017). Reducing poverty in the least developed countries: The role of small and medium enterprises. *Journal of World Business, 52*(2), 244–257. DOI: 10.1016/j.jwb.2016.12.007

Malhotra, N. K., & Dash, S. (2010). *Marketing research: An applied orientation* (6th ed.). Pearson Education India.

Manish, R., & Sharma, D. S. (2014). *Evolution of e-commerce in India: Creating the bricks behind the clicks*. PWC.

Manoharan, G., Durai, S., Ashtikar, S. P., & Kumari, N. (2024). Artificial Intelligence in Marketing Applications. In *Artificial Intelligence for Business* (pp. 40–70). Productivity Press.

Manyika, J., Chui, M., Brown, B., Bughin, J., Dobbs, R., Roxburgh, C., & Hung Byers, A. (2021). Big data: The next frontier for innovation, competition, and productivity.

Mao, H., Zhang, T., & Tang, Q. (2021). Research framework for determining how artificial intelligence enables information technology service management for business model resilience. Retrieved from https://www.researchgate.net/publication/367852652

Marchese, M., Lane, M., & Kirmizi, P. (2019). *Assessing and anticipating skills for the green transition: Emerging lessons from OECD countries* (OECD Green Growth Papers, 2019-03). OECD Publishing. https://doi.org/DOI: 10.1787/6ff6bdaf-en

Marchetti, R. (2025). Enhancing Organizational Ambidexterity in SMEs. The Critical Role of Digital Technologies. https://osuva.uwasa.fi/handle/10024/18609

Mariani, M., Baggio, R., Fuchs, M., & Höepken, W. (2018). Business intelligence and big data in hospitality and tourism: A systematic literature review. *International Journal of Contemporary Hospitality Management*, *30*(12), 3514–3554.

Mariotti, S., & Piscitello, L. (2001). Localized capabilities and the internationalization of manufacturing activities by SMEs. *Entrepreneurship and Regional Development*, *13*(1), 65–80. DOI: 10.1080/08985620150211234

Marjani, M., Nasaruddin, F., Gani, A., Karim, A., Hashem, I. A. T., Siddiqa, A., & Yaqoob, I. (2017). Big IoT data analytics: architecture, opportunities, and open research challenges. *ieee access, 5*, 5247-5261.

Martinez-Martin, E., Costa, A., & Cazorla, M. (2019). PHAROS 2.0—A physical assistant robot system improved. *Sensors (Basel)*, *19*(4531). Advance online publication. DOI: 10.3390/s19204531 PMID: 31635278

Martinsuo, M., & Luomaranta, T. (2018). Adopting additive manufacturing in SMEs: Exploring the challenges and solutions. *Journal of Manufacturing Technology Management*, *29*(6). https://doi.org/https://doi.org/10.1108/JMTM-02-2018-0030

Mauliddiyah, N. L. (2021). *No Title*. 6.

Maznevski, M. L., & Chudoba, K. M. (2000). Bridging space over time: Global virtual team dynamics and effectiveness. *Organization Science*, *11*(5), 473–492.

McCartney, G., & McCartney, A. (2020). Rise of the machines: Towards a conceptual service-robot research framework for the hospitality and tourism industry. *International Journal of Contemporary Hospitality Management, 32*(12), 3835–3851.

McKinsey & Company. (2021). The future of work after. *COVID, 19*, •••. https://www.mckinsey.com/featured-insights/future-of-work

Mckinsey Global Institute. (2017). *Artifical Intelligence: The Next Digital Frontier. Mckinsey Global Institute: Discussion paper*. Mckinsey & Company.

McKinsey Global Institute. (2021). Reskilling and The future of work after. *COVID, 19*, •••. https://www.mckinsey.com/featured-insights/future-of-work

McMahan, H. B., Moore, E., Ramage, D., Hampson, S., & Arcas, B. A. y. (2017). Communication-efficient learning of deep networks from decentralized data. *arXiv preprint arXiv:1602.05629.*

Megersa, K. (2020). Improving SMEs' access to finance through capital markets and innovative financing instruments: some evidence from developing countries. *Nairobi Securities Exchange website:* https://www. nse. co. *ke*. https://core.ac.uk/download/pdf/287772261.pdf

Mehrabi, N., Morstatter, F., Saxena, N., Lerman, K., & Galstyan, A. (2021). A survey on bias and fairness in machine learning. *ACM Computing Surveys, 54*(6), 1–35. DOI: 10.1145/3457607

Mehrotra, S., Gandhi, A., & Sahoo, B. K. (2013). Estimating India's skill gap: Projections for 2022. *Economic and Political Weekly, 48*(38), 45–52.

Melinda, V., Williams, T., Anderson, J., Davies, J. G., & Davis, C. (2024). Enhancing Waste-to-Energy Conversion Efficiency and Sustainability Through Advanced Artificial Intelligence Integration. [ITEE]. *International Transactions on Education Technology, 2*(2), 183–192. DOI: 10.33050/itee.v2i2.597

Mensah, J., & Casadevall, S. (2019). Sustainable development: Meaning, history, principles, pillars, and implications for human action: Literature review. *Cogent Social Sciences, 5*(1). Advance online publication. DOI: 10.1080/23311886.2019.1653531

Mercan, S., Akkaya, K., Cain, L., & Thomas, J. (2020). *Security, privacy and ethical concerns of IoT implementations in hospitality domain*. 198–203.

Mercan, S., Cain, L., Akkaya, K., Cebe, M., Uluagac, S., Alonso, M., & Cobanoglu, C. (2021). Improving the service industry with hyper-connectivity: IoT in hospitality. *International Journal of Contemporary Hospitality Management, 33*(1), 243–262.

Meressa, H. A. (2020). Growth of micro and small scale enterprises and its driving factors: Empirical evidence from entrepreneurs in emerging region of Ethiopia. *Journal of Innovation and Entrepreneurship*, *9*, 11. DOI: 10.1186/s13731-020-00121-9

Meta. (2024, June). New insights to help India's MSMEs use AI to drive growth. https://about.fb.com/news/2024/06/new-insights-to-help-indias-msmes-use-ai-to-drive-growth/

Meyer, C., & Schwager, A. (2007). Understanding customer experience [14]. *Harvard Business Review*, *85*(6), 137. PMID: 17345685

MGI. (2018). Big data: The next frontier for innovation, competition, and productivity. https://www.mckinsey.com/~/media/mckinsey/business

Michael, O. (2025). Maximising the Potentials of Small and Medium Scale Business Enterprises in Developing Nations Through the Use of Artificial Intelligence: AI Adoption by SMEs in the Developing Nations. In *The Future of Small Business in Industry 5.0* (pp. 215-246). IGI Global Scientific Publishing. DOI: DOI: 10.4018/979-8-3693-7362-0.ch009

Microsoft. (n.d.). Microsoft AI for Earth. GitHub repository. Retrieved December 9, 2024, from https://github.com/Microsoft/AIforEarth

Milanez, A. (2023). The impact of AI on the workplace: Evidence from OECD case studies of AI implementation. OECD Social, Employment and Migration Working Papers, No. 289.

Milwood, P. A., Hartman-Caverly, S., & Roehl, W. S. (2023). *A scoping study of ethics in artificial intelligence research in tourism and hospitality*. 243–254.

Ming, L. W., Anderson, J., Hidayat, F., Yulian, F. D., & Septiani, N. (2024). AI as a Driver of Efficiency in Waste Management and Resource Recovery. [ITALIC]. *International Transactions on Artificial Intelligence*, *2*(2), 128–134. DOI: 10.33050/italic.v2i2.547

Ministry of Industrialization, Trade and Enterprise Development. (2020). *Kenya Micro and Small Enterprises Policy for Promoting Micro and Small Enterprises (MSEs) for Wealth and Employment Creation*. State Department for Industrialization.

Ministry of Micro, Small and Medium Enterprises. (2015). *Annual report 2014–15*. Government of India. https://msme.gov.in/.../2015_02_MSME_Committee_report_Feb_2015

Ministry of Micro. Small & Medium Enterprises. (2023). *Annual Report 2023-2024*. Government of India.

Ministry of MSME. (2006). *MSME Development Act*. Government of India, District Industry Centers (DIC). https://msme.gov.in *(verify and provide direct link if possible)*

Misra, K., Schwartz, E. M., & Abernethy, J. (2019). Dynamic online pricing with incomplete information using multiarmed bandit experiments. *Marketing Science*, *38*(2), 226–252. DOI: 10.1287/mksc.2018.1129

Mogaji, E., & Jain, V. (2024). How generative AI is (will) change consumer behaviour: Postulating the potential impact and implications for research, practice, and policy. *Journal of Consumer Behaviour*. *23*(5), 2379–2389. DOI: 10.1002/cb.2345

Mohamed, Z. O., & Al Mqbali, N. S. (2015). Challenges and constraints faced by small and medium enterprises (SMEs) in Al Batinah governorate of Oman. *World Journal of Entrepreneurship, Management and Sustainable Development*, *11*(2), 120–130. DOI: 10.1108/WJEMSD-05-2014-0012

Mohammadi, M., Al-Fuqaha, A., Guizani, M., & Mohammadi, M. (2018). Internet of Things: A survey on enabling technologies, protocols, and applications. *IEEE Communications Surveys and Tutorials*, *20*(3), 1863–1887.

Mondal, S., Das, S., & Vrana, V. G. (2023). How to Bell the Cat? A Theoretical Review of Generative Artificial Intelligence towards Digital Disruption in All Walks of Life. In *Technologies* (Vol. 11, Issue 2). https://doi.org/DOI: 10.3390/technologies11020044

Monteiro, A. C. B., França, R. P., Arthur, R., & Iano, Y. (2021). An overview of medical Internet of Things, artificial intelligence, and cloud computing employed in health care from a modern panorama. *The Fusion of Internet of Things, Artificial Intelligence, and Cloud Computing in Health Care*, 3-23.

Moones, . (2024). AI in financial process optimization for SMEs. *Journal of Financial Technology*, *13*(1).

Moore, G. C., & Benbasat, I. (1991). Development of an instrument to measure the perceptions of adopting an information technology innovation. *Information Systems Research*, *2*(3), 192–222. DOI: 10.1287/isre.2.3.192

Morea, D., & Gebennini, E. (2021). New project financing and eco-efficiency models for investment sustainability. *Sustainability*, *13*(2), 786. DOI: 10.3390/su13020786

Moreno-Munoz, A., Bellido-Outeirino, F. J., Siano, P., & Gomez-Nieto, M. A. (2016). Mobile social media for smart grids customer engagement: Emerging trends and challenges. *Renewable & Sustainable Energy Reviews*, *53*, 1611–1616. DOI: 10.1016/j.rser.2015.09.077

Morgan Stanley. (2017, October). *India's e-commerce market to grow 30% to $200 billion by 2026: Morgan Stanley*. Retrieved from India Brand Equity Foundation (IBEF): https://www.ibef.org/research/case-study/india-s-e-commerce-market-to-grow-30-to-200-billion-by-2026-morgan-stanley

Moriguchi, C. (2020). The rise of the gig economy and the transformation of work. *The Journal of Economic Perspectives*, *34*(4), 105–120.

Mubeen, S. A., Ravikumar, A., Ravikumar, A., & Nazneen, Q. (2017). Economic diversification in Sultanate of Oman amidst oil crises. IOSR Journal of Business and Management, 19(06), 09-12. https://doi.org/DOI: 10.9790/487X-1906030912

Muhika, D. W. (2019). *Influence of credit access requirements on formalization decision of small and medium enterprises in Nairobi* (Doctoral dissertation, JKUAT-COHRED). http://ir.jkuat.ac.ke/handle/123456789/5014

Müller, J. M., Buliga, O., & Voigt, K. I. (2021). The role of absorptive capacity and innovation strategy in the design of Industry 4.0 business models. *Technological Forecasting and Social Change*, *132*, 119–131. DOI: 10.1016/j.techfore.2018.12.019

Mumford, E. (2006). The story of socio-technical design: Reflections on its successes, failures and potential. *Information Systems Journal*, *16*(4), 317–342. DOI: 10.1111/j.1365-2575.2006.00221.x

Murphy, C. B. (2024, June 06). *Fixed-Income Security Definition, Types, and Examples*. (M. R. Julius Mansa, Editor) Retrieved December 18, 2024, from Investopedia: https://www.investopedia.com/terms/f/fixed-incomesecurity.asp

Murray, A., Skene, K., & Haynes, K. (2017). The Circular Economy: An Interdisciplinary Exploration of the Concept and Its Applications. *Journal of Business Ethics*, *140*(3), 369–380.

Musa, I.. (2021). AI for targeting poverty alleviation programs: Case studies from sub-Saharan Africa. *World Development*, *146*, 105575.

Muthuraman, D. S., Al Haziazi, D. M., Veerasamy, D. R., & Al Yahyaei, M. N. (2020). Economic development through small & medium enterprise – A conceptual framework. In *Proceedings of the 3rd International Conference on Business, Management & Economics*

Muthuraman, S., Haziazi, M. A., Veerasamy, R., & Yahyaei, N. A. (2020). Economic development through small & medium enterprises. In *3rd International Conference on Business*.

Mwangi, P. C. N. (2014). *Factors influencing tax compliance among small and medium enterprises in Nairobi's industrial area, Kenya* (Doctoral dissertation, University of Nairobi,). https://erepository.uonbi.ac.ke/handle/11295/73605

Myin, M. T., & Watchravesringkan, K. (2024). Investigating consumers' adoption of AI chatbots for apparel shopping. *Journal of Consumer Marketing*, *41*(3), 314–327.

Nadkarni, S., Kriechbaumer, F., Rothenberger, M., & Christodoulidou, N. (2020). The path to the Hotel of Things: Internet of Things and Big Data converging in hospitality. *Journal of Hospitality and Tourism Technology*, *11*(1), 93–107.

Naeem, R., Kohtamäki, M., & Parida, V. (2024). Artificial intelligence enabled product–service innovation: Past achievements and future directions [PDF]. Retrieved from file:///C:/Users/dasha/Downloads/Artificial_intelligence_enabled_product-service_in.pdf

Nam, K., Dutt, C. S., Chathoth, P., Daghfous, A., & Khan, M. S. (2021). The adoption of artificial intelligence and robotics in the hotel industry: Prospects and challenges. *Electronic Markets*, *31*, 553–574.

Nasscom. (2025). *Transforming India's Technology SMEs for a Digital Future: Navigating the AI Frontier.* Nasscom.

National Stock Exchange of India. (2024). *Report on Corporate Bond Markets.* NSE. Retrieved from https://nsearchives.nseindia.com/web/sites/default/files/inline-files/NSE_Assocham_Corporate_Bond_Report_2024.pdf

Ndiaye, N., Razak, L. A., Nagayev, R., & Ng, A. (2018). Demystifying small and medium enterprises' (SMEs) performance in emerging and developing economies. *Borsa Istanbul Review, 18*(4), 269-281.

Ndung'u, N., & Signé, L. (2020). The Fourth Industrial Revolution and digitization will transform Africa into a global powerhouse. Brookings Institution. Retrieved from https://www.brookings.edu

Negroponte, N. (1995). *Being Digital.* Knopf Doubleday Publishing Group, 1995.

Newbert, S. L. (2007). Empirical research on the resource-based view of the firm: An assessment and suggestions for future research. *Strategic Management Journal*, *28*(2), 121–146. DOI: 10.1002/smj.573

NewsRoom. (2024, November 12). *The Hidden Costs of AI Implementation in Small Businesses.* Retrieved from Mordern Diplomacy: https://moderndiplomacy.eu/2024/11/12/the-hidden-costs-of-ai-implementation-in-small-businesses/

Ng, H. S., & Kee, D. M. H. (2012). The issues and development of critical success factors for the SME success in a developing country. *International Business Management*, *6*(6), 680–691.

Niekerk, A. J. (2020). Inclusive Economic Sustainability: SDGs and Global Inequality. *Sustainability*, *12*(13), 5427. DOI: 10.3390/su12135427

Nielsen. (2015). The Sustainability Imperative: New Insights on Consumer Expectations.

Nishanth, P., & Zakkariya, K. A. (2014, May). Barriers faced by micro, small and medium enterprises in raising finance. *Abhinav International Monthly Refereed Journal of Research in Management & Technology*, *3*(5), 40–43. http://abhinavjournal.com/journal/index.php

Nishchint Tiku, Jindal, S. K., & Lokeshwari, M. (2024). Artificial Intelligence in Corporate Social Responsibility and Environment Sustainability. *IEEE*, 1–6. https://doi.org/DOI: 10.1109/csitss64042.2024.10816872

Nwaimo, . (2024). NLP applications in SME financial management. *Journal of Business Technology*, *10*(2).

Nwankwo, . (2024). Future trends in AI for SME financial decision-making. *Journal of Financial Innovation*, *12*(1).

Nwosu, C. E.. (2024). AI tools for financial efficiency in SMEs. *Journal of Small Business Technology*, *8*(1).

Nylén, D., & Holmström, J. (2015). Digital innovation strategy: A framework for diagnosing and improving digital product and service innovation. *Business Horizons*, *58*(1), 57–67. DOI: 10.1016/j.bushor.2014.09.001

Oanh, V. T. (2024). Evolving Landscape Of E-Commerce, Marketing, and Customer Service: The Impact of Ai Integration. *Journal of Electrical Systems*, *20*(3), 1125–1137.

Obokoh, L. O., & Goldman, G. (2016). Infrastructure deficiency and the performance of small-and medium-sized enterprises in Nigeria's Liberalised Economy. *Acta Commercii*, *16*(1), 1–10.

Ocran, G., Omokhafe, S., Owusu, N. P., Enis, N., & Obeng, S., & None Adedamola Hadassah Paul-Adeleye. (2024). AI-driven business analytics for SMES: Unlocking value through predictive and prescriptive analytic. *International Journal of Science and Research Archive*, *13*(1), 3009–3022. DOI: 10.30574/ijsra.2024.13.1.2001

Odukoya, O. (2024). The Transformative Impact of Cloud Computing on Small and Medium-sized Enterprises (SMEs): A Comprehensive Analysis. In *2024 International Conference on Smart Applications, Communications and Networking (SmartNets)* (pp. 1-5). IEEE. DOI: DOI: 10.1109/SmartNets61466.2024.10577703

OECD. (2004). *Promoting entrepreneurship and innovative SMEs in a global economy: Towards a more responsible and inclusive globalization*. OECD Publishing.

OECD. (2005). *SME and Entrepreneurship Outlook*. OECD Publishing.

OECD. (2019). *OECD Skills Outlook 2019: Thriving in a digital world*. OECD Publishing. https://doi.org/ Ministry of Tourism, Government of India. (2023). *Tourism statistics report*.DOI: 10.1787/df80bc12-en

OECD. (2019). *OECD skills outlook 2019: Thriving in a digital world*. OECD Publishing., DOI: 10.1787/df80bc12-

OECD. (2019). *OECD SME and entrepreneurship outlook 2019*. OECD Publishing., DOI: 10.1787/34907e9c-

OECD. (2020). *AI in the tourism sector: Opportunities and challenges*.

OECD. (2022). *OECD SME and Entrepreneurship Outlook 2022*. OECD Publishing., DOI: 10.1787/69a88f50-

OECD. (2023). *OECD employment outlook 2023*. OECD Publishing., DOI: 10.1787/bb17314a-

OECD. (2023). *OECD employment outlook 2023: Artificial intelligence and jobs*. OECD Publishing.

Office for National Statistics. (2009). [Publisher]. *Labour Market Trends*.

Ogedengbe, . (2024). Data availability issues in AI for SMEs. *Journal of Database Management*, *7*(2).

Ogujiuba, K. K., Olamide, E., Boshoff, E., Agholor, I., & Ogujiuba, C. (2023). SMEs, success, and capital startups: Evidence from the service sector in South Africa. *Administrative Sciences*, *13*(5), 127. DOI: 10.3390/admsci13050127

Ogunleye, . (2024). AI for strategic financial planning in SMEs. *The Journal of Business Strategy*, *15*(1).

Okatta, . (2024). Real-time AI decision-making for SMEs. *Journal of Financial Technology*, *11*(2).

Okeke, N. I., Alabi, O. A., Igwe, A. N., Ofodile, O. C., & Ewim, C. P. M. (2024). AI-driven personalization framework for SMES: Revolutionizing customer engagement and retention. *World Journal of Advanced Research and Reviews, 24*(1), 2019–2035. DOI: 10.30574/wjarr.2024.24.1.3208

Oldemeyer, L., Jede, A., & Teuteberg, F. (2024). *Investigation of artificial intelligence in SMEs: a systematic review of the state of the art and the main implementation challenges*. Management Review Quarterly., DOI: 10.1007/s11301-024-00405-4

Olshannikova, E., Ometov, A., Koucheryavy, Y., & Olsson, T. (2025). Visualizing Big Data with augmented and virtual reality: Challenges and research agenda. *Journal of Big Data*, *2*(1), 1–27.

Olusanya, Emmanuel. (2021). Job rotation as training and development. .DOI: 10.60392/eoe-16-01-21-01

Oluwatamilore, . (2023). AI-driven talent analytics in U.S. organizations. *Journal of HR Technology*, *5*(2).

Oman Ministry of Commerce and Industry. (2019). *Annual Statistical Report*. Retrieved from. [insert URL]

Ooi, K. B., Tan, G. W. H., Al-Emran, M., Al-Sharafi, M. A., Capatina, A., Chakraborty, A., Dwivedi, Y. K., Huang, T. L., Kar, A. K., Lee, V. H., Loh, X. M., Micu, A., Mikalef, P., Mogaji, E., Pandey, N., Raman, R., Rana, N. P., Sarker, P., Sharma, A., & Wong, L. W. (2023). The Potential of Generative Artificial Intelligence Across Disciplines: Perspectives and Future Directions. *Journal of Computer Information Systems*. Advance online publication. DOI: 10.1080/08874417.2023.2261010

OpenAg Initiative. (n.d.). OpenAgToolkit. GitHub repository. Retrieved December 9, 2024, from https://github.com/OpenAgInitiative/OpenAgToolkit

Organisation for Economic Co-operation and Development, & International Labour Organization. (2011). *OECD-ILO strategies for local job creation, skills development and social protection*. OECD Publishing.

Osundare, O., & Ige, S. O. (2024). Dynamic pricing for SMEs using AI. *Journal of Pricing Strategy*, *6*(1).

Ou, C. (2006). Bank lending to small businesses in the United States. [Publication details].

Oyindamola, O., & Esan, M. O. (2023). Model interpretability in AI financial decision-making. *Journal of Business Analytics*, *8*(1).

Ozdemir, O., Dogru, T., Kizildag, M., & Erkmen, E. (2023). A critical reflection on digitalization for the hospitality and tourism industry: Value implications for stakeholders. *International Journal of Contemporary Hospitality Management.*

Pack8. (2023). *Live now! The Great Indian Plastic Packaging Dump*. Retrieved from Pack8: https://www.pack8.in/blogs/3?title=Live+now%21+The+Great+Indian+Plastic+Packaging+Dump&id=3

Pack8. (2024). *But is the packaging sustainable? Consumers want to know.* Retrieved from Pack8: https://www.pack8.in/blogs/4?title=But+is+the+packaging+sustainable%3F+Consumers+want+to+know.&id=4

Pan, C.-L., Bai, X., Li, F., Zhang, D., Chen, H., & Lai, Q. (2021). How Business Intelligence Enables E-commerce: Breaking the Traditional E-commerce Mode and Driving the Transformation of Digital Economy. Proceedings - 2nd International Conference on ECommerce and Internet Technology, ECIT 2021, 26–30. DOI: 10.1109/ECIT52743.2021.00013

Panigrahi, R. R., Shrivastava, A. K., & Nudurupati, S. S. (2024). Impact of inventory management on SME performance: A systematic review. *International Journal of Productivity and Performance Management.* Advance online publication. DOI: 10.1108/IJPPM-08-2023-0428

Panigrahi, R. R., Shrivastava, A. K., Qureshi, K. M., Mewada, B. G., Alghamdi, S. Y., Almakayeel, N., Almuflih, A. S., & Qureshi, M. R. N. (2023). AI Chatbot Adoption in SMEs for Sustainable Manufacturing Supply Chain Performance: A Mediational Research in an Emerging Country. *Sustainability*, *15*(18), 13743. DOI: 10.3390/su151813743

Pantano, E., & Pizzi, G. (2020). Forecasting artificial intelligence on online customer assistance: Evidence from chatbot patents analysis. *Journal of Retailing and Consumer Services*, *55*, 102096. DOI: 10.1016/j.jretconser.2020.102096

Pappas, N., Caputo, A., Pellegrini, M. M., Marzi, G., & Michopoulou, E. (2021). The complexity of decision-making processes and IoT adoption in accommodation SMEs. *Journal of Business Research*, *131*, 573–583. DOI: 10.1016/j.jbusres.2021.01.010

Parsani, P. (2024, Feburary 23). *Beauty and the Bot: How Sephora Reimagined Customer Experience with AI.* Retrieved from Cut The SAAS: https://www.cut-the-saas.com/ai/beauty-and-the-bot-how-sephora-reimagined-customer-experience-with-ai

Partala, T., & Fakhreldin, H. (2015). Evaluating the effect of government policies on small and medium enterprise (SME) development: Cases from nine different countries. In *Proceedings of SMHB 2015* (Vol. 3). Zurich, Switzerland. https://doi.org/DOI: 10.15224/978-1-63248-067-5-108

Pavlou, P. A., & El Sawy, O. A. (2011). Understanding the elusive black box of dynamic capabilities. *Decision Sciences*, *42*(1), 239–273. DOI: 10.1111/j.1540-5915.2010.00287.x

Pearson, A. (2020). Personalisation the artificial intelligence way, available at http://dx.doi.org/.DOI: 10.69554/JJGR7331

Pedersen, P. O. (1998). *The role of small enterprises and small towns in the developing countries*. Center for Development Research.

Pedraza, J. M. (2021). The micro, small, and medium-sized enterprises and its role in the economic development of a country. *Business and Management Research*, *10*(1), 33–44. DOI: 10.5430/bmr.v10n1p33

Peltier, J. W., Dahl, A. J., & Schibrowsky, J. A. (2024). Artificial intelligence in interactive marketing: A conceptual framework and research agenda. *Journal of Research in Interactive Marketing*, *18*(1), 54–90.

Peres, R., Schreier, M., Schweidel, D., & Sorescu, A. (2023). Editorial: On ChatGPT and beyond: How generative artificial intelligence may affect research, teaching, and practice. *International Journal of Research in Marketing*, *40*(2). Advance online publication. DOI: 10.1016/j.ijresmar.2023.03.001

Petrescu, M., Krishen, A. S., Gironda, J. T., & Fergurson, J. R. (2024). Exploring AI technology and consumer behavior in retail interactions. *Journal of Consumer Behaviour*, *23*(6), 3132–3151.

Petrunenko, I., Khmarska, I., & Tkachenko, T. (2021). *The importance of small and medium enterprises in the economic development of Eastern Europe*. Economic Journal of Lesya Ukrainka Volyn National University.

Philbin, S., Viswanathan, R., & Telukdarie, A. (2022). Understanding how digital transformation can enable SMEs to achieve sustainable development: A systematic literature review. *Small Business International Review*, *6*(1), e473. DOI: 10.26784/sbir.v6i1.473

Piccialli, F.. (2021). AI in healthcare predictive analytics. *Journal of Medical Technology*, *9*(2).

Podile, V., Reddy, K. P., Sai, N., Babu, M. S., & Phani, A. K. (2024). Artificial Intelligence and Corporate Social Responsibility: Synergies, Challenges, and Future Directions. *International Journal of Advanced Multidisciplinary Research and Studies*, *4*(6), 95–99. DOI: 10.62225/2583049x.2024.4.6.3399

Podsakoff, P. M., MacKenzie, S. B., Lee, J. Y., & Podsakoff, N. P. (2003). Common method biases in behavioral research: A critical review of the literature and recommended remedies. *The Journal of Applied Psychology*, *88*(5), 879–903. PMID: 14516251

Porlles, . (2024). AI-driven insights for SME financial planning. *Journal of Small Business Strategy*, *10*(1).

Pradhan, T., Nimkar, P., & Jhajharia, K. (2024). Machine Learning and Deep Learning for Big Data Analysis. In *Big Data Analytics Techniques for Market Intelligence* (pp. 209–240). IGI Global.

Prakash, B., Kumar, I., & Verma, J. K. (2021). Barriers and potential solutions for MSMEs in developing economies: Evidence from India. *Problems and Perspectives in Management*, *19*(4), 325–337. DOI: 10.21511/ppm.19(4).2021.27

Prasanna, R., Jayasundara, J., Gamage, S. K. N., Ekanayake, E., Rajapakshe, P., & Abeyrathne, G. (2019). Sustainability of SMEs in the Competition: A Systemic Review on Technological Challenges and SME Performance. *MDPI*. https://doi.org/ttps://doi.org/10.3390/joitmc5040100

Prentice, C., Weaven, S., & Wong, I. A. (2020). Linking AI quality performance and consumer interaction: The moderating effect of AI preference. *International Journal of Hospitality Management*, *90*, 102629. DOI: 10.1016/j.ijhm.2020.102629

PricewaterhouseCoopers. (2023). 2024 AI Business Predictions. In *PwC*. https://www.pwc.com/us/en/tech-effect/ai-analytics/ai-predictions.html

Priem, R. L., & Butler, J. E. (2001). Is the resource-based "view" a useful perspective for strategic management research? *Academy of Management Review*, *26*(1), 22–40. DOI: 10.5465/amr.2001.4011928

Prismetric. (2024, December 6). *How AI is Transforming Ecommerce Business in 2025*. Retrieved from Prismetric: https://www.prismetric.com/ai-in-ecommerce/

Proenca, J. C. (2024). Business Innovation Self-Assessment With Artificial Intelligence Support For Small And Medium-Sized Enterprises. *Бизнес управление*, (4), 5-17. https://www.ceeol.com/search/article-detail?id=1293603

Przegalinska, A., Triantoro, T., Kovbasiuk, A., Ciechanowski, L., Freeman, R. B., & Sowa, K. (2025). Collaborative AI in the workplace: Enhancing organizational performance through resource-based and task-technology fit perspectives. *International Journal of Information Management, 81*, 102853. DOI: 10.1016/j.ijinfomgt.2024.102853

Public, A. W. S. (2018, June 18). *AWS EdStart Launches in India to Bring Tech to Classrooms.* Retrieved from AWS: https://aws.amazon.com/blogs/publicsector/aws-edstart-launches-in-india-to-bring-tech-to-classrooms/

PWC & FICCI. (2022). *AI in Indian financial services.* Feburary. Retrieved from https://www.pwc.in/assets/pdfs/research-insights/2022/ai-adoption-in-indian-financial-services-and-related-challenges.pdf

PwC. (2020). *AI and training: The next competitive edge.*

Qureshi, R., Irfan, M., Ali, H., Khan, A., Nittala, A. S., Ali, S., & Alam, T. (2023). Artificial Intelligence and Biosensors in Healthcare and its Clinical Relevance: A Review. *IEEE Access : Practical Innovations, Open Solutions.*

Ra'ed Almashawreh, M. T. (2024). AI Adoption in Jordanian SMEs: The Influence of Technological and Organizational Orientations. *Global Business Review.*

Rahman, M., Khan, A., & Hossain, S. (2022). Precision agriculture: The role of AI in achieving SDG 2. *Agricultural Advances, 18*(4), 56–72.

Rajbhoj, A., Somase, A., Kulkarni, P., & Kulkarni, V. (2024). Accelerating Software Development Using Generative AI: ChatGPT Case Study. *ACM International Conference Proceeding Series.* https://doi.org/DOI: 10.1145/3641399.3641403

Raman, R., Bhattacharya, S., & Pramod, D. (2019). Predict employee attrition by using forecasting tools. *Benchmarking, 26*(1), 2–18. DOI: 10.1108/BIJ-03-2018-0083

Ramirez, J. G. C. (2024). The power of planning: how business plans drive effective management strategies. *Integrated Journal of Science and Technology, 1*(3).

Rana, J., Jain, R., & Nehra, V. (2024). Utility and acceptability of AI-enabled Chatbots on the online customer journey. *International Journal of Computing and Digital Systems, 15*(1), 323–335.

Rane, N. (2023). Role and Challenges of ChatGPT and Similar Generative Artificial Intelligence in Business Management. SSRN *Electronic Journal.* https://doi.org/DOI: 10.2139/ssrn.4603227

Rane, N., Choudhary, S., & Rane, J. (2024). Gemini or ChatGPT? Capability, Performance, and Selection of Cutting-Edge Generative Artificial Intelligence (AI) in Business Management. SSRN *Electronic Journal*. https://doi.org/DOI: 10.2139/ssrn.4731281

Rane, N. L., Paramesha, M., Choudhary, S. P., & Rane, J. (2024). Artificial intelligence, machine learning, and deep learning for advanced business strategies: A review. *Partners Universal International Innovation Journal*, *2*(3), 147–171. DOI: 10.5281/zenodo.12208298

Rane, N., Choudhary, S. P., & Rane, J. (2024). Acceptance of artificial intelligence technologies in business management, finance, and e-commerce: Factors, challenges, and strategies. *Studies in Economics and Business Relations*, *5*(2), 23–44. DOI: 10.48185/sebr.v5i2.1333

Rantalaiho, H. (2017). Challenges in implementing value-based pricing strategy. https://lutpub.lut.fi/handle/10024/135205

Ranta, V., Aarikka-Stenroos, L., & Peltola, S. (2018). The Role of Circular Economy in Sustainable Business Models. *Sustainability*, *10*(7), 2483.

Ratten, V. (2024). Artificial Intelligence, Digital Trends and Globalization: Future Research Trends. *FIIB Business Review*, *13*(3). Advance online publication. DOI: 10.1177/23197145231222774

Rauch, E., Dallasega, P., & Unterhofer, M. (2019). Requirements and barriers for introducing smart manufacturing in small and medium-sized enterprises. *IEEE Engineering Management Review*, *47*(3), 87–94. DOI: 10.1109/EMR.2019.2927321

Rebecca, D., & Benjamin, M. (2009). *Understanding small business dynamics: Innovation and shared leadership*. [Publisher].

Reddy, B. M. (2023). Amalgamation of Internet of Things and Machine Learning for Smart Healthcare Applications–A Review. *Int. J Comp. Eng. Sci. Res, 5*, 08-36.

Rescon Partners. (2025). *Omnichannel: Bringing the World to Rural Doorsteps*. Retrieved from Rescon Partners: https://www.resconpartners.com/fb-2933/#:~:text=Vernacular%20language%20support:%20Meesho%20added,from%20non%2DEnglish%20speaking%20regions

Ribeiro, M. T., Singh, S., & Guestrin, C. (2016). "Why should I trust you?" Explaining the predictions of any classifier. Proceedings of the 22nd ACM SIGKDD International Conference on Knowledge Discovery and Data Mining, 1135-1144.

Richardson, C. L. (2023). *Successful Strategies for Obtaining Financial Funding by Minority-Owned Small Businesses* (Doctoral dissertation, Walden University). https://www.proquest.com/openview/654aa3103f0814c6d69287411a977ed7/1?pq-origsite=gscholar&cbl=18750&diss=y

Righetti, F., Vallati, C., & Anastasi, G. (2018). *IoT applications in smart cities: A perspective into social and ethical issues*. 387–392.

Robinson, S., & Hullinger, H. (2008). New benchmarks in higher education: Student engagement in online learning. *Journal of Education for Business*, *84*(2), 101–109.

Rogers, E. M. (1962). *Diffusion of innovations*. Free Press.

Rolnick, D., ... (2019). Tackling climate change with machine learning. *arXiv preprint arXiv:1906.05433*.

Rolnick, D., Donti, P. L., Kaack, L. H., Kochanski, K., Lacoste, A., Sankaran, K., . . . Bengio, Y. (2019). Tackling climate change with machine learning. *arXiv preprint arXiv:1906.05433*.

Rönnberg, H., & Areback, J. (2020). Initiating transformation towards AI in SMEs. In Mittal, S., Khan, M., Romero, D., & Wuest, T. (2020). A smart manufacturing adoption framework for SMEs. *International Journal of Production Research*, *58*(5), 1555–1573. DOI: 10.1080/00207543.2019.1656830

Roy, R. (2021). AI in workforce management in India. *Journal of HR Management*, *7*(1).

Rudin, C. (2019). Stop explaining black box machine learning models for high stakes decisions and use interpretable models instead. *Nature Machine Intelligence*, *1*(5), 206–215. PMID: 35603010

Russell, B. (2018). Canada's labour market: Past, present, and future. *Labour (Halifax)*, *81*, 45–68.

Saadat, M. N., & Shuaib, M. (2020). Advancements in deep learning theory and applications: Perspective in 2020 and beyond. *Advances and Applications in Deep Learning, 3*.

Sadiku, M. N. O., Fagbohungbe, OmobayodeI., & Musa, S. M. (2020). Artificial Intelligence in Business. *International Journal of Engineering Research and Advanced Technology*, *06*(07), 62–70. DOI: 10.31695/ijerat.2020.3625

Safarishahrbijari, A. (2018). Workforce forecasting models: A systematic review. *Journal of Forecasting*, *37*(6).

Sagar, S. (2024). Entrepreneurship: Catalyst for Innovation and Economic Growth. Entrepreneurship. *Catalyst for Innovation and Economic Growth*, *9*(1), 81–92. DOI: 10.5281/zenodo.10494931

Sakaguchi, M., & Aoki, E. (2022, June). Study on the Comparison of Consumer Impression of E-commerce and Real Stores in the Fashion Tech Era, and the Effectiveness of VR Utilization. In *Computational Intelligence in Security for Information Systems Conference* (pp. 528-537). Cham: Springer International Publishing.

Sakshi, , Shashi, , Cerchione, R., & Bansal, H. (2020). Measuring the impact of sustainability policy and practices in tourism and hospitality industry. *Business Strategy and the Environment*, *29*(3), 1109–1126. DOI: 10.1002/bse.2420

Salami, C. G. E., Ekakitie, S. E., & Ebinim, L. O. (2023). Impact of government policy on entrepreneurship growth and development of small-scale business. Journal of Global Social Sciences, 4(14), 73-102. Print ISSN: 2735-9328, Online ISSN: 2735-9336.

Salih, L., Tarhini, A., & Acikgoz, F. (2025). AI-Enabled Service Continuance: Roles of Trust and Privacy Risk. *Journal of Computer Information Systems*, •••, 1–16.

Samuel Fosso Wamba, S. A. (2015). How 'big data' can make big impact: Findings from a systematic review and a longitudinal case study. *International Journal of Production Economics*, •••, 234–246.

Sangster, J. (2016). *Transforming labour: Women and work in post-war Canada*. University of Toronto Press.

Sanjeev, S., & Ingalagi, R. R. (2021). Artificial Intelligence (AI) adaptation: Analysis of determinants among Small to Medium-sized Enterprises (SME's). *IOP Conference Series: Materials Science and Engineering*. Montreal, Canada: IOP.

Santamaría, K. M., & Arias, E. R. (2023). AI in digital advertising campaigns. *Journal of Marketing Technology*, *8*(1).

Santoro, G., Bertoldi, B., Giachino, C., & Candelo, E. (2023). Digital transformation and business model innovation: A systematic literature review. *Journal of Business Research*, *148*, 181–197. DOI: 10.1016/j.jbusres.2022.04.051

Santos, J. R., Silva, R. S., & Camilo, J. M. (2019). Internet of Things in manufacturing: A literature review. *Advances in Manufacturing*, *6*(1), 41–58.

Saraswat, P., Bhardwaj, B., Naresh, P., Ashok, A., Kumar, R., & Kumar, M. (2021). Voice Assistants and Chatbots Hands on Essentials of UI and Feature Design Development and Testing. *Chapman and Hall/CRC EBooks*, 217–240. https://doi.org/ DOI: 10.1201/9781003121466-11

Saridakis, G., Lai, Y., Mohammed, A. M., & Hansen, J. M. (2018). Industry characteristics, stages of E-commerce communications, and entrepreneurs and SMEs revenue growth. *Technological Forecasting and Social Change*, *128*, 56–66. DOI: 10.1016/j.techfore.2017.10.017

Saunders, M., Lewis, P., & Thornhill, A. (2019). *Research methods for business students* (8th ed.). Pearson Education.

Saunila, M. (2016). Performance measurement approach for innovation capability in SMEs. *International Journal of Productivity and Performance Management*, *65*(2), 162–176. DOI: 10.1108/IJPPM-08-2014-0123

Schaltegger, S., & Wagner, M. (2011). Sustainable entrepreneurship: A conceptual framework. *Business Strategy and the Environment*, *20*(3), 222–237.

Schmitt, B. (1999). Experiential Marketing. *Journal of Marketing Management*, *15*(1–3), 53–67. DOI: 10.1362/026725799784870496

SCHÖNBERGER, M. (2023). ARTIFICIAL INTELLIGENCE FOR SMALL AND MEDIUM-SIZED ENTERPRISES: IDENTIFYING KEY APPLICATIONS AND CHALLENGES. *Journal of Business and Management*, *21*, 89–112. DOI: 10.32025/JBM23004

Schwab, K. (2016). *The Fourth Industrial Revolution*. Crown Business.

Schwaeke, J., Peters, A., Kanbach, D. K., Kraus, S., & Jones, P. (2024). The new normal: The status quo of AI adoption in SMEs. *Journal of Small Business Management*, •••, 1–35.

Scoones, I. (2009). Livelihoods perspectives and rural development. *The Journal of Peasant Studies*, *36*(1), 171–196. DOI: 10.1080/03066150902820503

Selamat, M. A., & Windasari, N. A. (2021). Chatbot for SMEs: Integrating customer and business owner perspectives. *Technology in Society*. https://doi.org/https://doi.org/10.1016/j.techsoc.2021.101685

Semiawan, C. R. (2010). *Metode penelitian kualitatif*. Grasindo.

Senarathna, I., Yeoh, W., Warren, M., & Salzman, S. (2016). Security and Privacy Concerns for Australian SMEs Cloud Adoption: Empirical Study of Metropolitan Vs Regional SMEs. *AJIS. Australasian Journal of Information Systems, 20*, •••. https://doi.org/https://doi.org/10.3127/ajis.v20i0.1193

Şenyapar, H. N. D. (2024). The Future of Marketing: The Transformative Power of Artificial Intelligence. *International Journal of Management and Administration, 8*(15), 1–19.

Seraphin, H. (2020). Big Data and Analytics in Tourism and Hospitality: Opportunities and Risks. *Journal of Tourism Futures.*

Shafik, W. (2023). Introduction to ChatGPT. In *Advanced Applications of Generative AI and Natural Language Processing Models.* https://doi.org/DOI: 10.4018/9798369305027.ch001

Shafik, W. (2024a). Artificial intelligence and Blockchain technology enabling cybersecurity in telehealth systems. In *Artificial Intelligence and Blockchain Technology in Modern Telehealth Systems.* https://doi.org/DOI: 10.1049/pbhe061e_ch11

Shafik, W. (2024b). Navigating emerging challenges in robotics and artificial intelligence in Africa. In *Examining the Rapid Advance of Digital Technology in Africa.* https://doi.org/DOI: 10.4018/978-1-6684-9962-7.ch007

Shah, F., Li, J., Shah, Y., & Shah, F. (2017, November). Broad big data domain via medical big data. In *2017 4th International Conference on Systems and Informatics (ICSAI)* (pp. 732-737). IEEE.

Shahid, Z. (2021). Distributed Machine Learning for Anomalous Human Activity Recognition using IoT Systems.

Shaikh, A., Kumar, A., Jani, K., Mitra, S., García-Tadeo, D. A., & Devarajan, A. (2022). The role of machine learning and artificial intelligence for making a digital classroom and its sustainable impact on education during COVID-19. *Materials Today: Proceedings, 56*, 3211–3216. DOI: 10.1016/j.matpr.2021.11.310 PMID: 35464152

Shane, S. A. (2003). A general theory of entrepreneurship: The individual-opportunity nexus. https://doi.org/DOI: 10.4337/9781781007990.00001

Shapira, P., Youtie, J., Kay, L., & Liu, J. (2015). Proximity and the use of public science by innovative small firms in the United States. *Science & Public Policy, 42*(5), 688–701. DOI: 10.1093/scipol/scu088

Sherly Steffi, L., Subha, B., Kuriakose, A., Singh, J., Arunkumar, B., & Rajalakshmi, V. (2024). The impact of AI-driven personalization on consumer behavior and brand engagement in online marketing. In Harnessing, A. I. (Ed.), *Machine Learning, and IoT for Intelligent Business* (Vol. 1, pp. 485–492). Springer Nature Switzerland.

Shinta, A. (2011). *Manajemen pemasaran.* Universitas Brawijaya Press.

Shouran, Z., & Ali, D. A. (2024). The Implementation of Artificial Intelligence in Human Resources Management. *Journal of International Conference Proceedings*, *7*(1), 244–258. DOI: 10.32535/jicp.v7i1.2993

SHRM. (2020). Hiring for culture fit. Society for Human Resource Management. https://www.shrm.org

SHRM. (2022). *HR tech trends: The role of AI in hiring*. https://www.shrm.org

Sieja, M., & Wach, K. (2023). Revolutionary artificial intelligence or rogue technology? The promises and pitfalls of ChatGPT. *International Entrepreneurship Review*, *9*(4). Advance online publication. DOI: 10.15678/ier.2023.0904.07

Siemens, G. (2013). Learning analytics: The emergence of a discipline. *The American Behavioral Scientist.*

Simonson, I. (2005). Determinants of Customers' Responses to Customized Offers: Conceptual Framework and Research Propositions. *Journal of Marketing*, *69*(1), 32–45. DOI: 10.1509/jmkg.69.1.32.55512

Singh, B. (2024). Evolutionary Global Neuroscience for Cognition and Brain Health: Strengthening Innovation in Brain Science. In *Biomedical Research Developments for Improved Healthcare* (pp. 246-272). IGI Global.

Singh, B., Kaunert, C., & Vig, K. (2024). Reinventing Influence of Artificial Intelligence (AI) on Digital Consumer Lensing Transforming Consumer Recommendation Model: Exploring Stimulus Artificial Intelligence on Consumer Shopping Decisions. In *AI Impacts in Digital Consumer Behavior* (pp. 141-169). IGI Global.

Singh, R., & Kaur, R. (2015). Sentiment Analysis on Social Media and Online Review. *International Journal of Computer Applications*, *121*(20), 44–48. DOI: 10.5120/21660-5072

Siswanto, J., Wahyuni, S., & Rizki, M. (2021). Talent management and skill gap analysis for SMEs. [Publication details].

Siswanto, J., Cahyono, E., Monang, J., Aisha, A. N., & Mulyadi, D. (2021). Identifying talent: Public organisation with skewed performance scores. *Journal of Management Development*, *40*(4), 293–312. DOI: 10.1108/JMD-06-2020-0272

Sloan, P., Legrand, W., Tooman, H., & Fendt, J. (2009). Best practices in sustainability: German and Estonian hotels. In Chen, J. S. (Ed.), *Advances in Hospitality and Leisure* (Vol. 5, pp. 89–107). Emerald Group Publishing Limited., DOI: 10.1108/S1745-3542(2009)0000005009

Smiee, K. C., Brophy, S., Attwood, S., Monks, P. L., & Webb, D. J. (2022, July 18). From Ethical Artificial Intelligence Principles to Practice: A Case Study of University-Industry Collaboration. *2022 International Joint Conference on Neural Networks (IJCNN)*. https://doi.org/DOI: 10.1109/ijcnn55064.2022.9892760

Smith, J. (2020). *Quantitative Methods in Economics*. Oxford University Press.

Smith, L., Brown, T., & Patel, A. (2023). Wildlife conservation with machine learning: Innovations and challenges. *Conservation Letters*, *14*(3), 34–50.

Sobaih, A. E. E., & Elshaer, I. A. (2022). University incubator support and entrepreneurial intention among tourism graduates: Mediating role of personal attitude. *Sustainability*, *14*(1), 111. DOI: 10.3390/su14010111

Sonia, & Rajeev, K. (2009). Globalization and its impact on small scale industries in India. *PCMA Journal of Business, 1*(2), 135–146.

Soni, V. (2023). Impact of Generative AI on Small and Medium Enterprises' Revenue Growth: The Moderating Role of Human, Technological, and Market Factors. *Reviews of Contemporary Business Analytics*, *6*(1). https://researchberg.com/index.php/rcba/article/view/169

Spangler, W. E. (1991). The role of artificial intelligence in understanding the strategic decision-making process. *IEEE Transactions on Knowledge and Data Engineering*, *3*(2), 149–159. DOI: 10.1109/69.87995

Spittlehouse, R. (2024, June 27). *Public Crowd Group*. Retrieved from Exploring the Business Benefits of Generative AI: https://pcg.io/insights/exploring-business-benefits-generative-ai/

Srinivasan, S., & Vallipriya, R. (2025). Entrepreneurial Success and Decision-Making Power With the Support of Assistive Technology. In *Improving Entrepreneurial Processes Through Advanced AI* (pp. 181–216). IGI Global., DOI: 10.4018/979-8-3693-1495-1.ch009

Staff, E. T. (2024, May 9). Empowering decision-making: The transformative role of data analytics. The Economic Times. https://economictimes.indiatimes.com/jobs/mid-career/empowering-decision-making-the-transformative-role-of-data-analytics/articleshow/109589355.cms

Stagliano, A. (2021, October 04). *Technology Is The Future of Fashion, Here's Why*. Retrieved from 1822denim: https://1822denim.com/blogs/the-denim-diary/technology-is-the-future-of-fashion-heres-why

Stanca, L., Dabija, D. C., & Câmpian, V. (2023). Qualitative analysis of customer behavior in the retail industry during the COVID-19 pandemic: A word-cloud and sentiment analysis approach. *Journal of Retailing and Consumer Services*, *75*, 103543.

Statistics Canada. (2020a). Canadian survey on business conditions: Impact of COVID-19 on businesses in Canada, March 2020. The Daily, 1-4. Statistics Canada Catalogue No. 11-001-X.

Statistics Canada. (2020b). Canadian survey on business conditions: Impact of COVID-19 on businesses in Canada, May 2020. The Daily, 1-4. Statistics Canada Catalogue No. 11-001-X.

Statistics Canada. (2022, June 27). Small and medium businesses: Driving a large-sized economy.

Storey, D. J. (2016). *Understanding the small business sector*. Routledge.

Strang, K. D. (2007). E-strategy first, e-technology free: Building an online university with open source software (case study). In *Innovation, Education, Technology, and You: Online Conference for Teaching & Learning*. University of Illinois.

Strielkowski, W., Vlasov, A., Selivanov, K., Muraviev, K., & Shakhnov, V. (2023). Prospects and Challenges of the Machine Learning and Data-Driven Methods for the Predictive Analysis of Power Systems: A Review. *MDPI*. https://doi.org/https://doi.org/10.3390/en16104025

Sumukadas, N., & Sawhney, R. (2004). Workforce agility through employee involvement. *IIE Transactions*, *36*(10), 1011–1021. DOI: 10.1080/07408170490500997

Sustainable Development Solutions Network. (2019). *AI for good: Leveraging artificial intelligence to achieve the SDGs*. Retrieved from https://www.unsdsn.org

Szilágyi, R., & Tóth, M. (2024). Use of LLM for SMEs, opportunities and challenges. *Agrárinformatika Folyóirat*, *14*(2). Advance online publication. DOI: 10.17700/jai.2023.14.2.703

Taherdoost, H., & Madanchian, M. (2023). Artificial Intelligence and Sentiment Analysis: A Review in Competitive Research. *MDPI, 12*(2). https://doi.org/https://doi.org/10.3390/computers12020037

Tahi Hamonangan Tambunan, T. (2011). Development of small and medium enterprises in a developing country: The Indonesian case. *Journal of Enterprising Communities: People and Places in the Global Economy*, *5*(1), 68–82. DOI: 10.1108/17506201111119626

ală, M. L., Müller, C. N., Năstase, I. A., State, O., & Gheorghe, G. (2024). Exploring university students' perceptions of generative artificial intelligence in education. *Amfiteatru Economic*, *26*(65). Advance online publication. DOI: 10.24818/EA/2024/65/71

Taneja, B. (2021). *The Digital Edge for M-Commerce to Replace E-Commerce.*, DOI: 10.4018/978-1-7998-8587-0.ch016

Tapscott, D., & Tapscott, A. (2017). *Blockchain Revolution: How the Technology Behind Bitcoin Is Changing Money, Business, and the World*. Penguin.

TechCrunch. (2024, November 24). *AI helps India's Meesho cut some customer call costs by 75%.* (M. Singh, Editor) Retrieved from TechCrunch: https://techcrunch.com/2024/11/26/ai-helps-indias-meesho-cut-customer-call-costs-by-75/

Teece, D. J., Pisano, G., & Shuen, A. (1997). Dynamic capabilities and strategic management. *Strategic Management Journal*, *18*(7), 509–533. DOI: 10.1002/(SICI)1097-0266(199708)18:7<509:AID-SMJ882>3.0.CO;2-Z

Teepapal, T. (2025). AI-Driven Personalization: Unraveling Consumer Perceptions in Social Media Engagement. *Computers in Human Behavior*, *165*, 108549.

Temel, S., & Durst, S. (2021). Knowledge risk prevention strategies for handling new technological innovations in small businesses. *VINE Journal of Information and Knowledge Management Systems*, *51*(4), 655–673. DOI: 10.1108/VJIKMS-10-2019-0155

Thakur, J., & Kushwaha, B. P. (2024). Artificial intelligence in marketing research and future research directions: Science mapping and research clustering using bibliometric analysis. *Global Business and Organizational Excellence*, *43*(3), 139–155.

Thapa, C., & Camtepe, S. (2021). Precision health data: Requirements, challenges and existing techniques for data security and privacy. *Computers in Biology and Medicine*, *129*, 104130. PMID: 33271399

The Clearing Corporation of India Ltd. (n.d.). *CCIL Broad and Liquid Index for Indian Bond Markets*. Retrieved from https://www.ccilindia.com/documents/43866/1293307/CCIL%20Bond%20Index%20Methodology_1716298351593.pdf

The Global AI Index. (2021). *AI's impact on sustainable development*. Retrieved from https://www.tortoisemedia.com

The Hindu. (2024, July 12). *Kerala offering incentives to AI-driven MSMEs and companies, says CM*. Retrieved from The Hindu: https://www.thehindu.com/news/national/kerala/kerala-offering-incentives-to-ai-driven-msmes-and-companies-says-cm/article68392149.ece

Tigmasa, C. M. (2011). Marketing strategies for SMEs: A case study. *Journal of Small Business Marketing*, *3*(2), 56–70.

Tiwari, V., & Thakur, S. (2021). Environment sustainability through sustainability innovations. *Environment, Development and Sustainability*, *23*(5), 6941–6965. DOI: 10.1007/s10668-020-00899-4

Toluwalase Vanessa Iyelolu, E. E. (2024). Driving SME innovation with AI solutions: overcoming adoption barriers and future growth opportunities . *International Journal of Science and Technology Research Archive*, 036–054.

Tong, L., Yan, W., & Manta, O. (2022). Artificial Intelligence Influences Intelligent Automation in Tourism: A Mediating Role of Internet of Things and Environmental, Social, and Governance Investment. *Frontiers in Environmental Science*, *10*, 853302. DOI: 10.3389/fenvs.2022.853302

Topol, E. (2019). *Deep medicine: How artificial intelligence can make healthcare human again*. Basic Books.

Tornatzky, L. G., & Fleischer, M. (1990). *The processes of technological innovation*. Lexington Books.

Tripathy, A., Agrawal, A., & Rath, S. K. (2016). Classification of sentiment reviews using n-gram machine learning approach. *Expert Systems with Applications*, *57*, 117–126.

Trist, E. L., & Bamforth, K. W. (1951). Some social and psychological consequences of the longwall method of coal-getting. *Human Relations*, *4*(1), 3–38. DOI: 10.1177/001872675100400101

Truby, J. (n.d.). Governing artificial intelligence to benefit the UN Sustainable Development Goals. Retrieved from https://scholar.google.com/citations?view_op=view_citation&hl=en&user=9oFnEiEAAAAJ&citation_for_view=9oFnEiEAAAAJ:w1MjKQ0l0TYC

Tsiu, S. V., Mathabela, L., & Ngobeni, M. (2024). Applications and competitive advantages of data mining and business intelligence in SMEs performance: A systematic review. *SSRN*, *4958874*, •••. https://papers.ssrn.com/sol3/papers.cfm?abstract_id=4958874

Tukker, A. (2015). Product Services for a Resource-Efficient and Circular Economy. *Product-Service Systems and Sustainability: 1st International Conference on Product-Service Systems for a Sustainable Society.*

Tyrväinen, O., Karjaluoto, H., & Saarijärvi, H. (2020). Personalization and hedonic motivation in creating customer experiences and loyalty in omnichannel retail. *Journal of Retailing and Consumer Services*, *57*, 102233. DOI: 10.1016/j.jretconser.2020.102233

Udaan. (2025). *About Us - Udaan*. Retrieved from Udaan: https://udaan.com/about-us

Ulas, D. (2019). Digital Transformation Process and SMEs. *Procedia Computer Science*, *158*, •••. https://doi.org/https://doi.org/10.1016/j.procs.2019.09.101

Ulas, D. (2019). Digital transformation process and SMEs. *Procedia Computer Science*, *158*, 662–671. DOI: 10.1016/j.procs.2019.09.101

Umbrello, S., Capasso, M., Balistreri, M., Pirni, A., & Merenda, F. (2021). Value sensitive design to achieve the UN SDGs with AI: A case of elderly care robots. *Minds and Machines*, *31*(3), 395–419. DOI: 10.1007/s11023-021-09561-y PMID: 34092922

UNCTAD. (2024). *Digital economy report 2024 - Shaping an environmentally sustainable and inclusive digital future*. UNCTAD.

UNESCO. (2012). *EFA global monitoring report 2012: Youth and skills—Putting education to work*. UNESCO Publishing.

Unicommerce. (2022, feburary 14). *Why an Inventory Management Software is a Must-have for an E-commerce Business*. Retrieved from Unicommerce: https://unicommerce.com/blog/why-ecommerce-businesses-needs-inventory-management-software/

United Nations. (2018). The sustainable development goals report. https://www.un.org/en/sustainabledevelopment/

United Nations. Department of Economics & Social Affairs. (2018). Micro, Small, and Medium-Sized Enterprises and Their Roles in Achieving the Sustainable Development Goals. Retrieved from https://sustainabledevelopment.un.org

University of Texas at San Antonio (UTSA). (2021). *UTSA Small Business Development Center International Trade Center Annual Report*. https://txsbdc.org

UNWTO. (2022). *International tourism and COVID-19: Recovery trends*.

Urme, U. N. (2023). The impact of talent management strategies on employee retention. *International Journal of Science and Business*, *28*(1), 127–146. DOI: 10.58970/IJSB.2209

Vander Schee, B. A., Peltier, J., & Dahl, A. J. (2020). Antecedent consumer factors, consequential branding outcomes and measures of online consumer engagement: Current research and future directions. *Journal of Research in Interactive Marketing*, *14*(2), 239–268. DOI: 10.1108/JRIM-01-2020-0010

Varga, J. W., & Szántó, R. (2021). Defining the economic role and benefits of micro, small and medium-sized enterprises in the 21st century with a systematic review of the literature. *Acta Polytechnica Hungarica*, *18*(11), 209–228. DOI: 10.12700/APH.18.11.2021.11.12

Varshney, K. R.. (2014). Analytics-driven expertise management at IBM. *Journal of Business Analytics*, *2*(1).

Vásquez, O. A. (2022). Professional research for SME business planning. *The Journal of Entrepreneurship*, *5*(1).

Venkatesh, V., Morris, M. G., Davis, G. B., & Davis, F. D. (2003). User acceptance of information technology: Toward a unified view. *Management Information Systems Quarterly*, *27*(3), 425–478. DOI: 10.2307/30036540

Vermanen, M., Rantanen, M. M., & Harkke, V. (2022). Ethical framework for IoT deployment in SMEs: Individual perspective. *Internet Research*, *32*(7), 185–201. https://doi.org/https://doi.org/10.1108/INTR-08-2019-0361

Verma, S., Sharma, R., Deb, S., & Maitra, D. (2021). Artificial intelligence in marketing: Systematic review and future research direction. *International Journal of Information Management Data Insights*, *1*(1), 100002.

Vinuesa, R., Azizpour, H., Leite, I., Balaam, M., Dignum, V., Domisch, S., & Fuso Nerini, F. (2020). The role of artificial intelligence in achieving the Sustainable Development Goals. *Nature Communications*, *11*(1), 233. DOI: 10.1038/s41467-019-14108-y PMID: 31932590

Viscarra, D. A., Ninabanda, J. P., & Garcia, J. M. (2019). E-commerce opportunities for SMEs. *Journal of Digital Business*, *4*(2).

Viswanath Venkatesh, M. G. (2003). User Acceptance of Information Technology: Toward a Unified View. *Management Information Systems Research Center, University of Minnesota*, 425-478.

Vuong, T. D. N., & Nguyen, L. T. (2022). The key strategies for measuring employee performance in companies: A systematic review. *Sustainability, 14*(21), 14017. DOI: 10.3390/su142114017

Wachter, S., Mittelstadt, B., & Russell, C. (2020). Why fairness cannot be automated: Bridging the gap between EU non-discrimination law and AI. *Computer Law & Security Review, 34*(2), 271–289.

Wairimu, D. M. (2023). Relationship between dynamic supply chain capabilities and resilience of retail chain of stores in Kenya, Doctoral Dissertation, Jomo Kenyatta University of Agriculture and Technology.

Walia, P. (2024). Role and Application of Artificial Intelligence in Business. *Shodh Sari, 03*(02), 244–252. DOI: 10.59231/sari7700

Wamba, S. F., Akter, S., Edwards, A., Chopin, G., & Gnanzou, D. (2021). How 'big data' can make big impact: Findings from a systematic review and a research agenda. *International Journal of Production Economics, 165*, 234–246. DOI: 10.1016/j.ijpe.2014.12.031

Wang, D. Y. (2018). Fashion Supply Chain and Logistics Management. *Fashion Supply Chain and Logistics Management*. https://doi.org/DOI: 10.4324/9781315466538

Wang, G., Tang, I. L., Chan, E., & Chan, W. H. (2021). The coverage of AIOT based functional service: Case study of Asian futuristic hotel. *University of South Florida M3 Center Publishing, 5*(2021), 99.

Wang, C. (2022). Efficient customer segmentation in digital marketing using deep learning with swarm intelligence approach. *Information Processing & Management, 59*(6). Advance online publication. DOI: 10.1016/j.ipm.2022.103085

Wang, C., Ahmad, S. F., Ayassrah, A. Y. B. A., Awwad, E. M., Irshad, M., Ali, Y. A., Al-Razgan, M., Khan, Y., & Han, H. (2023). An empirical evaluation of technology acceptance model for Artificial Intelligence in E-commerce. *Heliyon, 9*(8), e18349. PMID: 37520947

Wang, L., Lin, Z. Q., & Wong, A. (2020). COVID-Net: A tailored deep convolutional neural network design for detection of COVID-19 cases from chest X-ray images. *Scientific Reports, 10*(5), 12345. DOI: 10.1038/s41598-020-71194-4 PMID: 33177550

Wang, W. (2024). Artificial Intelligence in Strategic Business Decisions: Enhancing Market Competitiveness. *Advances in Economics Management and Political Sciences, 117*(1), 87–93. DOI: 10.54254/2754-1169/117/20241987

Wang, Y. (2016). What are the biggest obstacles to growth of SMEs in developing countries? An empirical evidence from an enterprise survey. *Borsa Istanbul Review, 16*(3), 167–176. DOI: 10.1016/j.bir.2016.06.001

Wang, Y., Gunasekaran, A., & Ngai, E. W. T. (2021). The Role of Artificial Intelligence in Sustainable Manufacturing: A Review and Research Agenda. *Journal of Cleaner Production, 283*, 124697.

Wang, Z., Wang, Y., & Wang, L. (2018). Artificial intelligence and the future of marketing: An empirical study. *Journal of Business Research, 96*, 269–276.

Wardati, N. K., & ER, M. (2019). The Impact of Social Media Usage on the Sales Process in Small and Medium Enterprises (SMEs): A Systematic Literature Review. *Procedia Computer Science, 161*, 976–983. DOI: 10.1016/j.procs.2019.11.207

Warner, K. S. R., & Wäger, M. (2019). Building dynamic capabilities for digital transformation: An ongoing process of strategic renewal. *Long Range Planning, 52*(3), 326–349. DOI: 10.1016/j.lrp.2018.12.001

Weaver, J. (2024). *Strategic Insight of market : Harnessing AI-Driven Predictive Analytics for Strategic Insight of market : Harnessing AI-Driven Predictive Analytics for Competitive Advantage Date : December 13, 2022. December 2022*. https://doi .org/DOI: 10.13140/RG.2.2.21889.98407

Wei, R., & Pardo, C. (2022). Artificial intelligence and SMEs: How can B2B SMEs leverage AI platforms to integrate AI technologies? *Industrial Marketing Management, 107*, 466–483. DOI: 10.1016/j.indmarman.2022.10.008

Whig, P., Bhatia, A. B., & Yathiraju, N. (2024). AI-Driven innovations in service marketing transforming customer engagement and experience. In *AI Innovations in Service and Tourism Marketing* (pp. 17–34). IGI Global., DOI: 10.4018/979-8-3693-7909-7.ch002

Wickramansinghe, N., & Sharma, S. K. (2005). Key factors that hinder SMEs in succeeding in today's knowledge-based economy. *International Journal of Management and Enterprise Development, 2*(2).

Wirtz, J., Patterson, P. G., Kunz, W. H., Gruber, T., Lu, V. N., Paluch, S., & Martins, A. (2018). Brave new world: Service robots in the frontline. *Journal of Service Management, 29*(5), 907–931. DOI: 10.1108/JOSM-04-2018-0119

World Bank. (2013). *World development report 2013: Jobs*. World Bank Publications.

World Bank. (n.d.). How do economies define micro, small and medium enterprises (MSMEs)? International Finance Corporation. https://www.ifc.org/wps/w

World Bank. (n.d.). *Small and Medium Enterprises (SMEs)*. Finance. [URL if available]

World Economic Forum. (2020). *The future of jobs report 2020*. http://www.weforum .org

World Economic Forum. (2020). *Upskilling for shared prosperity*.

Woschke, T., Haase, H., & Kratzer, J. (2017). Resource scarcity in SMEs: Effects on incremental and radical innovations. *Management Research Review*, *40*(2). https:// doi.org/https://doi.org/10.1108/MRR-10-2015-0239

Wu, F., Lu, C., Zhu, M., Chen, H., Zhu, J., Yu, K., Li, L., Li, M., Chen, Q., & Li, X. (2020). Towards a new generation of artificial intelligence in China. *Nature Machine Intelligence*, *2*(6), 312–316.

Wu, S. (2024). Artificial Intelligence-Enhanced Learning: A New Paradigm in the "Business Data Analysis and Application" Course. *Journal of Contemporary Educational Research*, *8*(2). Advance online publication. DOI: 10.26689/jcer.v8i2.6081

Wu, X., Zhu, X., Wu, G. Q., & Ding, W. (2023). Data mining with big data. *IEEE Transactions on Knowledge and Data Engineering*, *26*(1), 97–107.

Xu, H.. (2019). Deep sequence prediction for talent flow analysis. *Journal of HR Analytics*, *3*(1), 1.

Yadav, J. (2023). *Sentiment Analysis on Social Media*. Qeios., DOI: 10.32388/yf9x04

Yadav, P. (2023). The role of AI in assessing and achieving the Sustainable Development Goals (SDGs). In *The Role of AI in Assessing and Achieving the Sustainable Development Goals (SDGs)* (pp. 1–18). IGI Global., DOI: 10.4018/979-8-3693-3282-5.ch001

Yahaya, M., Umagba, A., Obeta, S., & Maruyama, T. (2023). Critical Evaluation of the Future Role of Artificial Intelligence in Business and Society. *Journal of Artificial Intelligence. Machine Learning and Data Science*, *1*(1). Advance online publication.

Yanamala, K. K. R. (2024). Strategic implications of AI integration in workforce planning and talent forecasting. https://www.researchgate.net/publication/385031502

Yaqoob, I., & M. I. (2021). Internet of Things: Applications, opportunities, and challenges in healthcare. *Future Generation Computer Systems, 114*, 172–180.

Yeo, S. F., Tan, C. L., Kumar, A., Tan, K. H., & Wong, J. K. (2022). Investigating the impact of AI-powered technologies on Instagrammers' purchase decisions in digitalization era–A study of the fashion and apparel industry. *Technological Forecasting and Social Change, 177*, 121551.

Yu, G. J., Lee, J., & Kim, B. (2024). Enhancing innovation performance through business process innovation: The strategic role of external collaboration. [GBFR]. *Global Business & Finance Review, 29*(5), 33–44. DOI: 10.17549/gbfr.2024.29.5.33

Yuniati, N. (2021). Green Hotel Concept and Practices in Indonesia. *E-Journal of Tourism, 184*. Advance online publication. DOI: 10.24922/eot.v8i2.76346

Yusuf, S. O., Durodola, R. L., Ocran, G., Abubakar, J. E., Echere, A. Z., & Paul-Adeleye, A. H. (2024). Challenges and opportunities in AI and digital transformation for SMEs: A cross-continental perspective. *World Journal of Advanced Research and Reviews, 23*(3), 668-678.I doi:DOI: 10.30574/wjarr.2024.23.3.2511

Zafar, A., & Mustafa, S. (2017). SMEs and its role in economic and socio-economic development of Pakistan. *International Journal of Academic Research in Accounting, Finance and Management Sciences, 6*(4). https://papers.ssrn.com/sol3/papers.cfm?abstract_id=3085425

Zapata, G., Murga, J., Raymundo, C., Dominguez, F., Moguerza, J. M., & Alvarez, J. M. (2019). Business information architecture for successful project implementation based on sentiment analysis in the tourist sector. *Journal of Intelligent Information Systems, 53*, 563–585. https://doi.org/https://doi.org/10.1007/s10844-019-00564-x

Zaridis, A., Vlachos, I., & Bourlakis, M. (2021). SMEs strategy and scale constraints impact on agri-food supply chain collaboration and firm performance. *Production Planning and Control, 32*(14), 1165–1178. DOI: 10.1080/09537287.2020.1796136

Zhang, H., Bai. X, & Ma. Zengguang. (2022). Consumer reactions to AI design: Exploring consumer willingness to pay for AI-designed products. *Psychology and Marketing, 39*(11), 2171–2183. DOI: 10.1002/mar.21721

Zhou, S., Zhang, R., Chen, D., & Zhu, X. (2021). A novel framework for bringing smart big data to proactive decision making in healthcare. *Health Informatics Journal, 27*(2), 14604582211024698. PMID: 34159834

Zhu, K., Kraemer, K. L., & Xu, S. (2006). The process of innovation assimilation by firms in different countries: A technology diffusion perspective on e-business. *Management Science, 52*(10), 1557–1576. DOI: 10.1287/mnsc.1060.0487

Zoho Analytics. (2023, November 6). *The 15% difference: How data analytics boosts small business sales*. (Sanjay, Editor) Retrieved from Zoho: https://www.zoho.com/blog/analytics/the-15-difference-how-data-analytics-boosts-small-business-sales.html

Zou, J., & Schiebinger, L. (2018). AI can be sexist and racist—It's time to make it fair. *Nature*, *559*(7714), 324–326. PMID: 30018439

Zuboff, S. (2019). *The Age of Surveillance Capitalism: The Fight for a Human Future at the New Frontier of Power*. Profile Books.

About the Contributors

Pawan Kumar is working as a Professor in the Marketing Domain at Mittal School of Business, Lovely Professional University, Punjab, India. He has 17 years of experience in academics and research. His areas of interest in research include entrepreneurship, marketing, e-commerce, consumer behaviour, marketing research, etc. He is active in Ph.D. research supervision and has good number of publications in Q1 and Q2 Journals to his credit in various research papers published Scopus indexed journals namely: The TQM Journal from Emerald, Visions: Journal of Business Perspectives from Sage, International Journal of Business and Globalization, International Journal of Business Information Systems from Inderscience and other national/international journals of repute. He has edited book on Opportunities and challenges in Business5.0 and drivers of SME Growth and Sustainability in Emerging Markets from IGI global. He is actively serving Editorial Board Member in Inderscience journal.

Preeti Mehra is a Business Faculty with Campbell College working in collaboration with Portage College Continuing Education, a public board-governed college based in Alberta, Canada and is focussed on providing the definitive educational experience for international learners. Additionally, she is a Sessional Instructor (Marketing) with Keyano College, Alberta and is teaching students pursuing business programs. She is a doctorate from Guru Nanak Dev University, Amritsar, India and her specialisation is marketing. She has an experience of 15 years in Corporate and Academics and was a professor in marketing with a leading private university in India. She is dedicated to imparting knowledge and is passionate about research and e-content development. She has an expertise in public speaking, academic instruction, and research management. She offers an history of delivering marketing advancements and developing substantial university curricula and is devoted to creating future field leaders through education and mentoring. She specialises in Micro Branding, Sachet Marketing, Gesture Recognition, Rural

Marketing Strategy, Services Marketing and Brand Management. Her research work focusses on expressively enriching organizational reach and market share through the application of robust strategies, effective pricing and excellent client relationship management. She has contributed towards distinguished journals of national and international repute like Emerald, Sage and has participated and presented in many national and international conferences. She has acted as editor of several books and has contributed towards many book chapters in the field of marketing. She has acted as an external trainer in many workshops and Faculty Development Programmes related to marketing and research methodology. She has several copyrights and patents to her credit and has supervised several doctorate students.

Oye Abioye is a seasoned educator at different post-secondary institutions Canada and have taught a good blend of business courses. He is an astute academician and a business expert with cognitive professional experience in finance and accounting with specialty in corporate management efficiency and performance management. Well vast and highly experienced in performance management techniques, management planning tools and control of business operations as well as corporate efficiency key performance indicators in service-oriented businesses. He is a researcher with special interest in railway system key performance indicators and transport modal services. He is a chartered accountant, business professional, mentor and a coach, thesis supervisor, and an examiner. Dr. Abioye is a management consultant with focus of professional practice in corporate governance, audit and assurance, personal finance, development infrastructure finance, and corporate finance in public service.

***

Adenike Adesanmi is a distinguished academic with a robust career spanning over a decade. She began her journey in the United Kingdom as a Lecturer, where she has made significant contributions to the field of business education. With over 10 years of experience, Adenike has taught a wide range of business subjects and is currently specializing in Business Analytics at Seneca Polytechnic in Canada, North America. Her academic interests are diverse and interdisciplinary, encompassing behavioural sciences, humanities, and beyond. Adenike's research often explores the intersection of these fields, providing valuable insights into the complexities of human behaviour and organizational dynamics. Her dedication to education and research has earned her recognition and respect among her peers and students alike.

Pinky Agarwal is a Chartered Accountant with a Doctoral degree in Commerce. She is a recipient of Impactful Finance Leader, Global faculty and Most Influential

Professor Award. She was also felicitated as the "Pride of CA" and contributor to the Guiness World Record Book for promoting accounting profession. She has post qualification experience of 25 years with profound knowledge in financial reporting, accounting and taxation. Her area of expertise is Financial Accounting Corporate Finance, Cost Accounting, Direct Taxation, Indirect Taxation, Business Simulation, Financial Planning, Alternative Finance & Sustainability Reporting. She has co-authored books in International Financial Management and Accounting for Management

Raed Awashreh is an Assistant Professor of Management at A'Sharqiyah University in Ibra, Oman. He brings over 20 years of combined academic and industry experience, teaching undergraduate and postgraduate courses. Dr. Awashreh has authored 70 articles, several chapters, and 3 books spanning topics such as, human resources, governance, public policy, strategy, leadership, and management. In addition to his academic role, Dr. Awashreh serves as a consultant in business, management, governance, HR, and organizational development, working closely with government, private, and non-governmental sectors. He earned his degrees in Public Administration and Management from Flinders University, Australia, and Monterey, USA.

Saurabh Chandra is an accomplished legal scholar and currently serves as an Associate Professor & Assistant Dean at the School of Law, Bennett University, India. With a robust academic foundation, he earned his Bachelor of Arts and Bachelor of Laws (B.A. LL.B.) from the prestigious Aligarh Muslim University (A.M.U.). He further specialized in Business Laws, completing his Master of Laws (LL.M.) at the renowned National Law School of India University (NLSIU), Bangalore. Dr. Chandra's academic journey culminated in a Doctorate in Law (Ph.D.) from the esteemed National Law University (NLU) Delhi. In addition to his impressive legal education from some of India's most prestigious institutions, Dr. Saurabh Chandra also holds a master's degree in Management with specialization in Human Resources in Management and another in Journalism and Mass Communication. With 16 years of teaching experience, he has established himself as an expert in Business and Corporate Laws, with numerous publications to his credit. Dr. Saurabh Chandra is a distinguished expert in Business and Corporate Laws, with a profound understanding of the intricate legal frameworks that govern the business world. His expertise is complemented by a robust portfolio of scholarly publications, which underscores his commitment to advancing knowledge in his field. Throughout his career, Dr. Chandra has consistently produced high-impact research that addresses critical issues in Business and Corporate Law. His publications are widely recognized for their depth of analysis, innovative perspectives, and practical relevance. He has contributed extensively to leading journals, where his work has often set new standards for legal scholarship. His publications not only reflect his scholarly rigor but also his dedication to addressing contemporary challenges faced by businesses and policymakers. By bridging the gap between theoretical insights and real-world applications, Dr. Chandra's work serves as a valuable resource for academics, legal practitioners, and industry professionals alike. Dr. Chandra brings a wealth of experience in Academic Administration, having successfully held various key administrative positions. His diverse qualifications and extensive experience make him a distinguished figure in the academic and legal communities.

Puja Chopra, Ph.D., MBA, is an accomplished academician and Assistant Professor at Christ University, with over 15 years of teaching experience in renowned private and government universities. She holds a Ph.D. in Applied Economics, along with double M.A. degrees in Economics and English, showcasing her strong interdisciplinary foundation. Dr. Chopra specializes in the intersection of Economics and Finance and has an impressive record of publications in prestigious journals, including those indexed in Scopus, ABDC, and UGC CARE. Her passion for academic excellence and innovative teaching has shaped countless future leaders, and she remains committed to fostering intellectual growth in higher education.

Pratham Gupta is a dedicated student at Christ University, Delhi NCR, pursuing a Bachelor of Business Administration with a specialization in finance. Simultaneously preparing for his Chartered Accountancy qualifications, Pratham has demonstrated a strong commitment to academic excellence and professional growth. During his tenure as an intern at Zillion Space, he successfully led teams to collect and manage comprehensive financial data for over 250 properties, showcasing his aptitude for data-driven decision-making and client advisory services. His role as an Operations Executive at the Centre for Academic and Professional Support highlighted his leadership skills, where he orchestrated events and managed a large team with efficiency. Pratham's academic achievements include distinctions in the CA Foundation and certifications in data analytics from NPTEL and IIT Bombay, underscoring his technical expertise in financial analysis and data visualization. With proficiency in tools like Tableau, SPSS, R Studio, and Tally Prime, he brings a robust technical skill set to the table. An multiple time state level football player and gold medalist in athletics, Pratham balances his academic pursuits with a passion for teamwork and resilience. His dedication to blending practical experience with theoretical learning positions him as a promising contributor to the fields of finance and business management.

Neeraj Gupta is a faculty in the area of finance. He has more than 20 years of experience in corporate, academics, and research. His special interests lie in Derivatives, Security Analysis, Business Laws, Ethics and Governance. He has been associated as a faculty with ICFAI, AMITY University, Kanpur University and Jaipuria Institute of Management. As a researcher, he has to his credit various 'A' and 'B' category research publications in international journals of repute.

Leena Jenefa, working as an Associate Professor in Hindustan Institute of Technology and Science, Chennai India, Prior that she worked in Vel Tech Rangarajan Dr Sagunthala R&D Institute of Science and Technology, Avadi, Chennai. She is having 19 years of experience in the teaching field. Prior to joining to Vel Tech -Chennai, she worked in Tecnia Institute of Advanced Studies-Delhi, DMI- St. Eugene University-Zambia, Linton University affiliated to University of East London-Malaysia

Rishikaysh Kaakandikar boasts an exceptional academic journey, spanning over 12 years of dedicated teaching and a year of valuable industrial experience, and currently holds the esteemed position of Associate Professor at SaiBalaji Education Society's SaiBalaji International Institute of Management Sciences in Pune. His scholarly contributions shine brightly, encompassing a remarkable portfolio of over 40 research papers in prestigious journals. A sought-after intellectual resource, He has contributed substantially to academia through guest lectures, seminars, workshops, and conferences at esteemed institutions across India. His insights have enriched the academic community and stimulated engaging discussions on various facets of his field. He is a prominent finance columnist for leading newspapers in Maharashtra, including Sakal, Lokmat, Punyannagari, and Prabhat.

Christian Kaunert is Professor of International Security at Dublin City University, Ireland. He is also Professor of Policing and Security, as well as Director of the International Centre for Policing and Security at the University of South Wales. In addition, he is Jean Monnet Chair, Director of the Jean Monnet Centre of Excellence and Director of the Jean Monnet Network on EU Counter-Terrorism.

Balpreet Kaur is an Assistant Professor in the Department of Commerce and Business Management, DAV University, Jalandhar. She did her Ph.D. from Guru Nanak Dev University, Amritsar, Punjab, India. Her area of research is Viral Marketing, and has expertise in Scale Development, Model Building, and Structural Equation Modeling using AMOS. She has teaching and research experience for more than twelve years. She is a lifetime member of the Indian Commerce Association. She has been selected as the reviewer of many journals listed in the Australian Business Dean Council Journal Quality List. She has presented papers in various international and national conferences, including the International Conference on Marketing, Technology, and Society, the Indian Institute of Management, Kozhikode, The 6th IIMA International Conference on Marketing in Emerging Economies, Indian Institute of Management, Ahemdabad, etc. She was the paper's co-author, awarded Gold Medal and Prof. Manubhai M. Shah Memorial Research Award for the Best Empirical Research paper presented at the annual 66th All India Commerce Conference. Her research papers have also been selected as 'Best Research Paper' at the International and National Conferences organized by UBS, Panjab University, Chandigarh, Mittal School of Business, Lovely Professional University, and All Indian Commerce Association. She has several research papers in her credit published in ABDC and Scopus indexed, UGC-listed journals. Also, she is co-editor of the book entitled "Revive to Survive: Initiatives and Innovations" by Bharti Publications, New Delhi. In addition, she has delivered lectures as a resource person in various colleges and institutions.

Sanjeev Kumar is an accomplished expert in Food and Beverage. He currently holds the positions of Professor in Lovely Professional University, Punjab, India. With over a decade of experience in the field, food Service Industry, his research focuses on Alcoholic beverages, Event management and Sustainable Management Practices, Metaverse, AI Machine Learning and Artificial Intelligence. He has published more than 60 research papers, articles and chapters in Scopus Indexed, UGC Approved and peer reviewed Journals and books. Dr. Sanjeev Kumar participated and acted as resource person in various National and International conferences, seminars, session chair, research workshops and industry talks and his work has been widely cited.

M. Jayakumar started his career at the Year 2006 at Vel Tech Institutions and promoted as Assistant Registrar at the Year 2014 in Vel Tech Rangarajan Dr.Sagunthala R&D Institute of Science and Technology (Deemed University). He is also working as Assistant Professor in the Department of Management studies He has done his B.Com. Degree from Bishop Heber College, Tiruchirapalli (Affiliated to Bharathidasan University) and MBA (HR & Marketing) Degree from Sathyabama University (Deemed University) and done his Ph.D in Management from Vel Tech Rangarajan Dr. Sagunthala R&D Institute of Science and Technology.

Dheeraj Nim is a seasoned educator and industry veteran boasting over 16 years of immersive training experience for students and academics alike, coupled with an additional 6 years in the corporate sphere. With a rich background encompassing Business Analytics, Marketing Analytics, and Data Analysis, Dr. Nim is passionate about the latest advancements and trends shaping research and analysis. Currently serving as Professor and Dean Student Welfare at Oriental University, Indore,. Beyond academia, Dr. Nim's commitment to excellence shines through his extensive certification portfolio in Data Analytics from esteemed institutions like the University of Virginia, University of Michigan, and IITs, among others. His academic contributions are equally impressive, with six book chapters, 30 research publications, and five awarded Ph.D. scholars under his mentorship. Noteworthy are his publications in renowned journals, including Scopus Indexed, Web of Science, and ABDC Journals. His dedication to academic excellence extends to his role as a reviewer for numerous Scopus and Web of Science indexed journals. Notably, he has chaired technical sessions in prestigious international conferences.

P. Thirumoorthi, currently working as Professor in Management Studies. Having specialized in Operations and Systems Management. Current research works are related to Technology Management and Supply Chain Economics. He has authored more than 50 journal articles and 5 books. He has also produced 15 Ph.D scholars and 21 M.Phil scholars. He has completed 3 funded projects sponsored by various funding agencies.

Supriya Pathak is an accomplished academic and researcher with extensive contributions to the fields of technology, sustainable development, and artificial intelligence (AI). She is renowned for her work in leveraging AI to advance global initiatives, including the United Nations' Sustainable Development Goals (SDGs). Dr. Pathak's academic journey reflects her dedication to excellence and innovation. She holds a Ph.D. in [Field/Discipline, if available] from [University/Institution, if available], where her groundbreaking research focused on [specific area of research, if known]. With a keen interest in the transformative potential of emerging technologies, Dr. Pathak has authored numerous scholarly articles and book chapters that explore the intersection of technology and societal development. A thought leader in her domain, Dr. Pathak has been instrumental in projects aimed at promoting ethical AI governance, inclusivity, and sustainable development. Her work emphasizes the importance of transparency, accountability, and fairness in AI systems, ensuring they benefit diverse communities worldwide. Dr. Pathak is also an active participant in global conferences and workshops, where she shares insights on how AI and technology can be responsibly harnessed to address pressing challenges such as poverty, climate change, and healthcare disparities. Her collaborative approach has made her a sought-after speaker and advisor in academic and professional circles. In addition to her academic achievements, Dr. Pathak has played a vital role in mentoring young researchers and fostering interdisciplinary collaboration. Her leadership and vision continue to inspire advancements in technology for social good, underscoring her commitment to creating a sustainable and equitable future.

Wasswa Shafik (Member, IEEE) received a Bachelor of Science degree in information technology from Ndejje University, Uganda, a Master of Engineering degree in Information Technology (Computer and Communication Networks) from Yazd University, Iran, and a PhD in Computer Science with the School of Digital Science, Universiti Brunei Darussalam, Brunei Darussalam. He is also the Founder and Research Director of the Dig Connectivity Research Laboratory (DCRLab) after serving as a Research Associate at the Network Interconnectivity Research Laboratory at Yazd University. Prior to this, he worked as a Community Data Analyst at Population Services International (PSI-Uganda), a Community Data Officer at the Programme for Accessible Health Communication (PACE-Uganda), a Research Assistant at the Socio-Economic Data Centre (SEDC-Uganda), Uganda, an Assistant Data Officer at TechnoServe, Kampala, IT Support at Thurayya Islam Media, Uganda, and Asmaah Charity Organization. He has hundreds of publications with renowned publishers. His research interests include Computer Vision, Explainable AI, Smart Agriculture, Health and ecological informatics, Security and Privacy.

Ajay K. Singh is working as an Associate Professor (Research) in the Department of Humanities and Social Science, Graphic Era (Deemed to be University) Dehradun. He has worked as Assistant Professor (Economics) in the School of Liberal Arts & Management, DIT University Dehradun for 6 years. He did Post-Doctorate Research with EDI of India, Ahmedabad, Gujarat (India). He received MPhil (Economics) from DAVV Indore (India), and PhD (Economics) from IIT Indore (India. He has published several research papers in the diversified area such as climate change, agricultural productivity, assessment of food security; estimation of GFSI, development of environmental sustainability index (ESI) and its association with socio-economic indicators; measurement and determinants of entrepreneurship ecosystem, and dimension of sustainable development and its interlinkages with economic development.

Bhupinder Singh working as Professor at Sharda University, India. Also, Honorary Professor in University of South Wales UK and Santo Tomas University Tunja, Colombia. His areas of publications as Smart Healthcare, Medicines, fuzzy logics, artificial intelligence, robotics, machine learning, deep learning, federated learning, IoT, PV Glasses, metaverse and many more. He has 3 books, 139 paper publications, 163 paper presentations in international/national conferences and seminars, participated in more than 40 workshops/FDP's/QIP's, 25 courses from international universities of repute, organized more than 59 events with international and national academicians and industry people's, editor-in-chief and co-editor in journals, developed new courses. He has given talks at international universities, resource person in international conferences such as in Nanyang Technological University Singapore, Tashkent State University of Law Uzbekistan; KIMEP University Kazakhstan, All'ah meh Tabatabi University Iran, the Iranian Association of International Criminal law, Iran and Hague Center for International Law and Investment, The Netherlands, Northumbria University Newcastle UK,

R. Vallipriya has been working in the Department of Physical Sciences at the Institute of Education (Affiliated to Tamilnadu Teacher Education University) as an Assistant Professor. With a wealth of experience, Mrs. R.Vallipriya has accumulated 12 years of extensive teaching. Her scholarly contributions include publishing 7 papers, with 1 peer review in various UGC-CARE, SCOPUS, and peer-reviewed journals.

Srinivasan Vasan is an Assistant Professor in the Department of Humanities and Social Sciences at Graphic Era (Deemed to be University), with 14 years of teaching and field expertise. He has served in the Ministry of Health and Family Welfare, as a Guest Faculty, and as a Mobilization Training Specialist with the State Government. Recently, he contributed to a tuberculosis project funded by GFATM and USAID. He has published 60 papers, with 20 more under peer review in UGC-CARE and SCOPUS journals.

Kittisak Wongmahesak is a lecturer at the Faculty of Political Science, North Bangkok University, and the Director of the Association of Legal & Political Studies in Thailand. He also holds the position of Research Fellow at Shinawatra University, Thailand, and Universiti Sultan Zainal Abidin, Malaysia. His influence extends to Indonesia, where he is an Adjunct Professor at Sekolah Tinggi Ilmu Administrasi Abdul Haris and an Adjunct Research Professor at several Indonesian universities, including Universitas Muhammadiyah Sinjai, Universitas Muhammadiyah Makassar, and Universitas Muhammadiyah Sidenreng Rappang. With a wealth of academic experience and a robust set of qualifications, Kittisak WONGMAHESAK has held the position of Full Professor of Public Administration at Huanghe Business School, Henan University of Economics and Law in China, and the University of City Island in Cyprus. He has also contributed as an Adjunct Researcher at Ton Duc Thang University and Duy Tan University in Vietnam. His academic qualifications include a Ph.D. in Social Sciences, an M.A., and a B.A. in Political Science, all from Kasetsart University. Additionally, he earned an M.B.A. and an M.P.A. from Ramkhamhaeng University and a B.Pol.Sc. in International Relations and Comparative Government and Politics from Sukhothai

Thammathirat Open University. Kittisak WONGMAHESAK's expertise spans Political Science, Public and Private Management, International Political Economy, and Social Research. He is the editor of numerous prestigious journals worldwide, including Sustainability, Frontiers in Psychology, PLOS One, World Food Policy, Asian Academy of Management Journal, International Journal of Public Policy and Administration Research, International Journal of Innovative Research and Scientific Studies, and Recent Advances in Computer Science and Communications. His global recognition as one of the world's top 2% of scientists by Stanford University since 2020 is a testament to his influence. His extensive publication record, with over 450 indexed Scopus/Web of Science documents and an h-index of 56 with more than 10,000 citations, is a wealth of knowledge that informs his significant scholarly contributions.

Index

A

B

C

D

E

G

H

I

L

M

N

O

T

V

W

www.ingramcontent.com/pod-product-compliance
Lightning Source LLC
LaVergne TN
LVHW080354011026
849161LV00009B/2296